JOURNEY OF HOPE
NAMES AND GAMES REMEMBERED

HOPE COLLEGE ATHLETICS
1955-1970

Gordon M. Brewer
Hope '48

Published by Hope College
Holland, Michigan

ON THE FRONT COVER

Clockwise from the left:

The 1962 Hope Tennis Team — only MIAA team to win over Kalamazoo since 1935. L. to R.: (front) Stan Vugteveen, Norm Hess, Dave Nykerk, (rear) Dave Zwart, Arlyn Lanting, Bud Hoffman, Coach Larry Green

Ray Ritsema (31) hauls down one of 28 rebounds against Albion — 1960. Jim Vander Hill in background. Albion Player is Garth Richey.

Cliff Haverdink takes a fourth gold medal in the mile relay — MIAA meet At Western Michigan's Waldo Stadium - 1970.

Right-handed Floyd Brady scores his 2,000th point with a left-hand hook against Olivet — 1968.

Guard Chuck Truby leads the way for halfback John Vandenburg on the famous "Heidelberg" reverse. Rowland Van Es (82) blocks, Sharky Vander Woude on the ground. — 1959.

Joey Bosworth fogs one in against Kalamazoo College — 1964.

ON THE BACK COVER

Steve Piersma '68 played games in sunshine and shadows — sometimes the gloom was even deeper.

Second Volume — First Edition

Copyright 2002 by Hope College

International Standard Book Number (ISBN): 0-9634061-3-2

All rights reserved. No part of this book may be reproduced in any manner without the written permission of the publisher — Hope College, PO Box 9000, Holland MI 49422-9000.

Design and text preparation by Hope College Public Relations Office, Holland, Michigan.

Typesetting by Foremost Graphics, Walker, Michigan

Cover design by Holland Litho, Inc., Holland, Michigan

Printing by Thomson-Shore, Inc., Dexter, Michigan

For Susan, Dan, Larry, and Bob

JOURNEY OF HOPE
NAMES AND GAMES REMEMBERED

Hope College Athletics - 1955-1970

CONTENTS

1. Native's Return 34

2. Joining Up 56

3. An Era Underway 76

4. Excellence Assembled — Hope and Glory 104

5. Farewells 126

6. Coaching Plus 140

7. Struggles and Comebacks 156

8. Sports and "*Camelot*" 188

9. Ups and Downs and New Sports 204

10. Big Time Springtime 220

11. The Best of Brady 252

12. When Pride Still Mattered 284

Epilogue — Moving On 285

Appendices
   MIAA Championship Teams (1933-34 to 2001-02) 286
   Coaches of MIAA Championship Teams 288
   All-time All-MIAA MVPs (thru 2001-02) 289
   All-time All-MIAA Honorees (thru 2001-02) 290

References 295

Index 296

THE AUTHOR

Although retired from the college's faculty, Gordon Brewer is the dean of Hope athletic history. He has been a participant in or observer of the Hope College sports scene since his enrollment as a freshman in the fall of 1941. This latest volume complements an earlier history, *. . . But How You Played the Game! A History of Intercollegiate Athletics at Hope College*, published in 1992 and covering through 1955. Both books are the result of exhaustive research of archival sources, and together chronicle more than a century's worth of Hope sports history.

The second son of Robert and Helen Brewer, Gordon was born in Kalamazoo, Mich., in 1923. When he was six months old, his family moved to the small town of Martin, some 18 miles north of Kalamazoo. Educated in the Martin Public Schools, he was influenced to attend Hope College by high school principal Herman Laug (Hope '29) and the Reverend Albert Mansen.

The Japanese attack on Pearl Harbor in December of Brewer's freshman year served notice that his education would be interrupted. He was called to active duty on March 29, 1943, in his sophomore year. After 31 months of service with the 8th Air Force in England, he was discharged at Fort Sheridan, Ill., in November of 1945. He then served as interim basketball coach at Martin High School until his re-enrollment at Hope in February of 1946. His graduating classmates in June of 1948 included his sister Margery and Lorraine Virginia Bult; the latter became Mrs. Brewer later that summer.

The Brewers were first employed by the Byron Center Public Schools, where Lorraine taught elementary grades and Gordon initiated a football program and also coached basketball and baseball. Moving to Kelloggsville High School in 1950, Brewer taught history and literature while his coaching responsibilities included football, basketball, and track.

Following eight years in the high school ranks, Brewer was invited to return to Hope in 1956 as head track coach and an assistant coach in football. He also coached jayvee basketball for four years. His tenure as track coach spanned 32 seasons. In 1960, Brewer was named director of athletics, succeeding Al Vanderbush, who now devoted full time to his responsibilities in the Department of Political Science. During this period, Brewer was active as Hope's delegate to the NCAA, serving on various committees, including the Division III Steering Committee and the Post-Graduate Scholarship Committee.

After 20 years in the athletic directorship, Brewer was appointed chairman of the Department of Physical Education, Recreation, and Athletics. He served five years in this capacity before retiring in 1988. His previous writings include sport essays titled, "In Pursuit of True Sport," and "When the Cheering Stops." He also authored a short history of Hope's years in the MIAA as part of the 1988 Michigan Intercollegiate Athletic Association publication, *Celebrating a Century of the Student Athlete*.

On April 27, 1991, the newly refurbished Hope track was named in his honor. In May of 1996, the Hope College Alumni Association presented him with a "Meritorious Service" Award. During Homecoming in October of 2001, the alumni H-Club, which consists of Hope alumni who were athletic letter winners and other honorary letter winners, presented him with the group's 11th annual "Hope for Humanity" Award. The H-Club had also honored him and long-time colleague Russ DeVette '45 with a luncheon during Homecoming in October of 1987.

The Brewers' children are Robert James, Lawrence Gordon, Daniel Richard, and Susan Marie (Hayes).

FOREWARD

If you love Hope College and you like intercollegiate sport, you will find this book most enjoyable. No one is better able to make the Hope sports stories of the 1950s and 60s come alive than Gordon Brewer, longtime Hope professor, coach, athletic director, and mentor. Gord's professional education as an historian and his integral involvement with Hope sport during this time lend a special credibility to this account of Hope's athletic history.

Those of you familiar with Gord's previous book *. . . But How You Played the Game!* and his numerous pre-season essays on Hope sport like *When the Cheering Stops* and *In Pursuit of True Sport*, will recognize again the eloquence of his writing. He has more ability than anyone I know to choose just the right words for any occasion and to articulate them with conviction. Gord can capture the poignancy of the moment, often with a reference to history or literature.

There is considerable factual information about every sport at Hope during the 1950s and 60s. This was a time when Milton (Bud) Hinga, Russ DeVette, Gord Brewer, Ken Weller, Al Vanderbush, Lawrence (Doc) Green, Daryl Siedentop, and Joan Pyle Vander Kolk were making their marks as Hope coaches. It was also an era when very talented athletes still chose loyalty to Hope over the lure of university scholarships. In typical Brewer humility, which we have all grown to admire, he understates the significance of himself and his colleagues in influencing the lives of hundreds of Hope student-athletes. These were professionals of conviction, uncommon decency, and unwavering dedication to family, church, community, and Hope College. Each was especially committed to those entrusted to their care. They did not disappoint!

The men and women who fashioned sport at Hope during the 1950s and 60s were very special. Both in victory and defeat, they never wavered from principles and ethics which guided both individual and team behavior. Hope College gave true, legitimate meaning to the term "scholar/athlete." Sport was a big part of campus life, but it was not bigger than life itself. Coaches and athletes did not compromise the integrity of intercollegiate sport by allowing it to grow out of perspective. Winning with this noble philosophy made Hope then and now the envy of like-minded opponents nationwide.

Gord summarizes many important contests which occurred during this particular era of Hope sport. Yet, this account is so much more! He captures both the ecstasy and agony of sport that inevitably occur in competitive situations. Fortunately for Hope there have been many more of the former than the latter through the years. Still more, however, Gord is able to share many "behind the scenes" insights that captivate both participant and spectator alike.

Intercollegiate sport for women is in its infancy during this time period. Title IX had not yet ushered in the necessity of equal opportunities for men and women. Yet, I am confident that even without Title IX, Hope would have been a leader in providing opportunities for women. This confidence is based on nothing more than knowing the personnel in the physical education department and their propensity for doing what was right and good and just.

Gordon Brewer allows us to look at intercollegiate sport at Hope with a reflective review. And, when we do, we realize that a foundation in sport at Hope was built that would transcend won-loss records. Guided by an overarching and wholesome philosophy of sport which kept it in perspective at the small college level, Hope developed a model that would become in succeeding decades the cornerstone of NCAA Division III athletics. The author has captured all of this in a subtle but compelling way!

It is my hope that you will enjoy reading about intercollegiate sport at its finest—sport at a level where disciplined effort is recognized, skillful play is applauded, sportsmanship is integral to competition, defeat is buoyed by hope, and victory is graced by humility. May it ever be so at Hope College.

Permit me to share this personal note. My fondest recollection of sport at Hope did not occur on the playing field. There were no fans, no scoreboards, no media. There were only two people who experienced it; I've rarely told another. It was in the spring of my last year at Hope. My heart was heavy at the thought of leaving the people and place I loved so much for the presidency at sister college Northwestern in Iowa. Coach Brewer had earlier that afternoon wrapped up another MIAA championship in track at Buys Field. On an adjacent field, I had stolen fleeting glances at the meet amidst my own practice leading up to the MIAA championships in baseball. I knew for me, and soon for Gord, the cheering would be over. As I raked the diamond for one last time, I was alone with my own thoughts. Twilight had settled in around me, and there remained the silhouette of just one other figure—Brewer—it was Brewer. In the impulse of the moment, I dropped my rake and trotted toward him, slowly at first but then in almost a dead run. I hollered, "High five, Brew!" Not certain he heard me, I saw him turn and move toward me. We met midway on the track and there, in mid-air, we hit a resounding "high five." I doubt it was graceful; no one cheered. Two grown men—one about to become a college president, the other near retirement—were acting like a couple of teenage kids. But, in that instant, it symbolized for me the true meaning of sport—the thrill of competition shared with a special friend. No other justification was necessary—we played the game just because it was fun!

James E. Bultman

Jim Bultman presently serves as the eleventh president of Hope College. He has also held the positions of professor, coach, and dean at Hope.

*After the tedious hours of studying and
strenuous hours of final exams, it is over; it is the
end of one more year. For some, it is the end of four
years, the end of a career, but also the end
of a beginning, a large step forward
into a new and different life.*

*We watch them leave, some with tears,
some with joy. We know that the summer of freedom
will pass all too quickly; we know that in the
fall it will become one more component in the
cycle, a cycle that must end— and is never ending.*

From the 1968 *MILESTONE*
– Author unknown

PREFACE

Journey of Hope is essentially a continuation of an earlier work, *. . . But How You Played the Game!*, published in 1992. One difference would be my presence "on the scene" for all but one of the years covered in this later account. For those who played, every contest was important. With that in mind, I have endeavored to cover results in reasonable detail. By adding behind the scenes incidents and appropriate photos it is hoped that the narrative will become more readable for fan and player alike.

Athletics for women were yet to come of age in the time period covered, but with the advent of Title IX in the early '70's women's sports would proliferate and their skills would soon rival those of the men. A much deserved volume on their achievements will be authored by another.

One cannot escape a certain sameness of succeeding seasons, yet each game, meet, or match is unique in its own right. Many human interest "asides" never reach the headlines but serve to flesh out the bare bones of sport statistics and should be part of the record.

During the later '50s and through the '60s, a parade of very special student-athletes graced the scene at Hope College. With sport in proper perspective, they played for the right reasons. Because of this and their subsequent contribution to society, I felt strongly that their experience in formative years should be shared. That is my *raison d'etere* for some eight years of research and this book.

Now of course, they have scattered to the four winds, but interviews, letters, and late night phone calls have brought them back, challenging their powers of recall. The results have made me a happy and grateful beneficiary. An attempt has been made to include full names of players on both sides. Opposing teams make contests possible and deserve at least this courtesy. If I have a regret, it would be that inadequate recognition is given to non-starters, bench warmers, and others who fill out the squad and expend great effort. All this without accolades. Team achievement does not occur without them.

In checking a variety of sources I was painfully aware that memory plays strange tricks on us. Striving for accuracy, I surely did not always succeed. My hope is that readers may derive a measure of enjoyment from these pages. If so, the effort will have been worthwhile.

Gordon M. Brewer
July, 2002

ACKNOWLEDGMENTS

The history of sports at Hope could not have been written without help from some of those who made that history. I am indebted to them for their interest in this project, not to mention their patience and forbearance. Others, who were not directly involved in the games, provided invaluable assistance. I must single out Randy Vande Water, former Sports Editor of *The Holland Evening Sentinel,* whose write-ups during this 15-year period were not only comprehensive, but done with great sensitivity. Larry Wagenaar, Geoffrey Reynolds, and Lori Tretheway at the Joint Archives of Holland went out of their way to accommodate my every request. Hope Sports Information Director Tom Renner was at his usual best in ferreting out needed facts and compiling the appendices with the able assistance of Karen Bos, Greg Olgers, Melissa Pikaart and Lynne Powe.

As I list these names and others, it is of grave concern to me that I have probably forgotten some who made a valuable contribution by answering my many queries. Rest assured that no slight was intended. My heartfelt thanks then, to the following and any others who took time to help me fill out these pages: Darrell Beernink, Gordon Beld, John Blom, Karen Bos, Bob Brewer, Jim Bultman, Russ De Vette, Bob DeYoung, Bruce Geelhoed, Norm Japinga, George Kraft, Don Mitchell, Harold Molenaar, Greg Olgers, Stuart Post, Tom Renner, Geoffrey Reynolds, Bill Rink, Bob Ritsema, Harry Rumohr, Harvey Scholten, Craig Schrotenboer, Daryl Siedentop, Dwayne Teusink, Lori Tretheway, Randy Vande Water, Bill Vanderbilt Sr., Warren Vander Hill, Glenn Van Wieren, Larry Wagenaar, Ken Weller, and Dave Zwart.

CHAPTER I

NATIVE'S RETURN

Twelve hundred miles in an overloaded station wagon can be a long and wearisome journey, especially with two small children. For the De Vettes in the summer of 1955 it was not. Their year at the University of Maine in Orono had been a positive one. Russ had first enjoyed his role as assistant to longtime friend and head football coach Harold Westerman, and then, as head coach, had known the satisfaction of guiding the Black Bears to a successful season in basketball. Along the way the family had reveled in Maine's storied autumn colors and the beauty of a New England winter. Thoughts of change were hardly in the air when an unexpected opportunity presented itself.

Some measure of an institution's worth may be found in the hold it maintains on those who have departed for a season. People come back to Hope College. Reasons and circumstances may vary but come back they do, and to a welcome that rivals that of the most closely knit families. Russ De Vette's third return to Hope did not come at the conclusion of a war, as had the other two, but was, in some respects a summons. It may be recalled from Volume I . . . *But How You Played the Game* of this work that the magnanimous offer was tendered by head football coach Al Vanderbush with the blessing of President Irwin J. Lubbers. Vanderbush's conviction that De Vette would play a vital role in Hope's athletic future was so strong that he offered his own position as an enticement. A faithful following would question the head mentor's move in light of his impressive nine-year tenure, but 34 subsequent years would prove the wisdom of this unselfish step. The decision of Russ and Doris was never in doubt, and a disappointed Harold Westerman could only wish them well. Now, as the miles melted away, an air of expectancy filled the light green Ford. The De Vettes indeed were coming home.

In the late summer the De Vettes settled in at 34 East 14th Street, a venerable dwelling just two blocks south of the campus. If there was a sameness about the town they had left a short year ago, there was also change. As might be expected, the general mood in the Holland of 1955 was shaped by events both at home and abroad. A giant passed from the political scene when Prime Minister Winston Churchill stepped down for the last time. His friend Dwight Eisenhower would continue in office for another five years despite a September heart attack, its serious nature withheld from the public. Also that September, Juan Peron, the last of the big-name dictators, fled in exile to Paraguay.

For the younger set, the "must" movie was *Rebel Without a Cause* starring James Dean and Natalie Wood. Dean's meteoric career would end in tragedy on September 30 when his Porsche Spider careened off a road between L.A. and Salinas.

On the sport scene, baseball was alive and well as strikes were as yet unknown. Local pitcher George Zuverink was sold by the Tigers to the Baltimore Orioles, Stan Musial won the All-Star game for the National League with a 12th inning homer, and Leo "The Lip" Durocher quit as manager of the New York Giants. Closer to home, the Holland American Legion All-Stars under manager Clairie Van Liere took on their counterpart from Grand Rapids. "Little" Jim Kaat pitched a three-hitter for the locals and won 4-3 after helping his own cause with a game-tying homer. One year later he would enroll as a freshman at Hope before moving on to fame in the majors.

In the fall of '55 Hope College boasted an enrollment of more than 900, plus some new faces on the faculty. Besides

De Vette, these included Phil Crook, Gene Jekel, Tom Van Dahm, and John Van Ingen. Vice President John Hollenbach, on leave of absence, was serving as dean of the faculty of arts and sciences at the University of Cairo, Egypt. With wife Ruth dutifully typing his dissertation, Larry Green was granted his PhD. by the University of Iowa. Jay Folkert and Morrette Rider also received doctorates.

Men's housing received a boost on Oct. 2, when ground was broken for the 150-room, 300-person dormitory to be known as Kollen Hall, after Hope's third president, Gerrit J. Kollen. To make room for the structure, the historic Beach House at 12th and Columbia was razed. It had been the birthplace of Jack Schouten, Hope's first full-time coach and director of athletics. The three-story home had later served as the Emersonian fraternity house, and during the war years as a dormitory for women.

* * *

ROLES REVERSED

Russ DeVette (left) became the head football coach at Hope College in 1955. Al Vanderbush (right), who had urged him to take the position, volunteered to be his assistant.

The business at hand was football. Since his high school days, Russ DeVette had been a "first cousin" to basketball. He had played the game at several levels and had served as head coach at a college and a university. Now it would be 11 men instead of five. Aided by a solid base, he welcomed the new challenge, and a challenge it would be. On the down side was the fact that the appointment made no provision for assistants. To fill the gap Al Vanderbush volunteered his services in whatever capacity De Vette deemmed wise. There may have been concern in some quarters with this reversal of roles. While the move from lieutenant to general was a natural one, there was speculation that the reverse might be fraught with problems. De Vette, however, saw no difficulty in this arrangement and both coaches proceeded to plan for the season. At this writing, nearly 50 years later, the two correspond regularly, often recalling an era when small college football was left to its own devices. Meanwhile, some early-season help came from Ken Weller, a longtime assistant to Vanderbush. Weller had been awarded a prestigious Danforth grant to pursue doctoral studies in business administration at the University of Michigan, but was available for the first game or two.

* * *

Construction of a new music building (later named Nykerk Hall of Music) on the field adjacent to Carnegie-Schouten Gym forced a move to new practice facilities. College officials found an answer to the problem at the Van Raalte homestead located two blocks east of the campus. The property had been donated to the college in 1947 by William B. Eerdmans of Grand Rapids. A practice field was now fashioned on the east side of Fairbanks Avenue, almost in the shadow of the founder's rapidly deteriorating home.

On Sept. 1 De Vette met his charges for the first time. The squad included a number of holdovers from the 1953 championship team, Hope's first undisputed MIAA champion. The team would be led by co-captains Lynn Post and Johnny Adams. Post, a local product, had played the end position at both Holland High and Hope. Adams hailed from Saginaw, and was a two-time All-MIAA halfback and also a standout in basketball. Both men would become ordained ministers.

The new coach's first test came on Sept. 17 at Ypsilanti against a strong Eastern Michigan squad. The Hurons were coached by Fred Trosko, a former teammate of Tom Harmon at Michigan. His team had compiled an impresive 8-1 record in 1954. Hope's starting offensive line included Post and Paul Wiegerink at ends, John Hollander and Donald "Doc" Van Hoeven at tackles, Dick Gantos and Ken "Mick" Faber at guards, and Ron De Graw at center. In the backfield it was Adams and Tom Carey at halfbacks, Dave Kuyers at fullback, and strong-armed John Holmlund at quarterback. It was a group with considerable experience, but the practice period had been short and after a scoreless first quarter, Hope's fortunes turned sour. Huron halfback Doug Wilkins broke off-tackle and rambled 42 yards for the game's first score. Bob McCullough's kick hit the crossbar, but bounced over to give Eastern an early 7-0 lead. Three minutes later a bad lateral resulted in Adams being tackled in the end zone for a safety and the Hurons' halftime lead stood at 9-0. In the third quarter an Adams punt was blocked by tackle Jim Allen and Jim Haywood recovered on the two. Quarterback Leroy Mawby then sneaked in to make it 15-0. The count was increased a short time later when Huron halfback Kerry Keating plunged off-guard for the touchdown. A low kick left the Huron lead at 21-0. Also in the third quarter, as Hope attempted to play catch-up, halfback Mike Warner

NEW PRACTICE FIELD

In 1955 the Hope team moved to a new practice field on Fairbanks Avenue. Here players loosen up with the historic home of Albertus C. Van Raalte in the background. Van Raalte was Holland's founder.

picked off a Holmlund pass on the Huron 28 and ran 72 yards for the game's final score. The kick was not good, but Eastern's victory was convincing at 27-0. Hope's only real threat came in the fourth quarter, when the Dutchmen penetrated to the 21. When the drive bogged down there was little choice but to lick wounds and prepare for the home opener against the Student Princes of Heidelberg College.

De Vette had enlisted the aid of Ron Schipper and Dutch Van Engen to scout Hope's next opponent. At the time the two were coaching at Northville High School and their report offered little encouragement. Coach Paul Hoerneman's nine-year record at Heidelberg was an impressive 65-10-4. His '54 squad had gone 7-1-1 and he had been named Ohio Coach of the Year. His big gun was a speedy, shifty halfback named Walt Livingston, who many thought was good enough for the big time.

A rash of injuries plagued the Dutchmen following the opener. Most healed somewhat, but Gantos and Kuyers would be forced to sit out the next contest with knee and ankle sprains. The good news was that halfback Ron Wetherbee seemed fully recovered from a broken foot suffered in a summer softball game. De Vette's adjustments included moving Holmlund to fullback and inserting Harry Voss at quarterback. Five minutes into the contest Livingston showed his stuff with a sweep-cutback for a five-yard TD run to cap a 73-yard drive. Matt Rock converted to make it 7-0, and many feared the beginning of a blowout. But the Dutch dug in and there was no more scoring in the half. With five minutes remaining in the third quarter, Bill Demidovich scored from the two to make it 14-0. Long runs by Livingston in the fourth quarter set up scores for the Student Princes. Roy King went off tackle from the seven, increasing the lead to 21-0. Hope finally scored its first touchdown of the season when freshman halfback Jack Faber took a pass from fullback Holmlund on the seven and went the distance to make it 21-6. Livingston setup the game's final score on a long reverse play. He was pulled down on the 25 by De Graw. Roy King later scored from the 16. Final score: Heidelberg 28, Hope 6.

On Oct. 1 Coach Mickey Mc Cormick brought his Carroll Pioneers to Riverview Park for a night game. The teams were evenly matched, but the Wisconsin squad held the edge in the early going. With 4:25 remaining in the half, quarterback Jack Fendt scored on a keeper play. The conversion was good and the visitors' halftime lead was 7-0. A hard-fought third period was scoreless, but with one minute gone in the fourth quarter the Pioneers padded their lead. Reserve quarterback Ken Grabic passed to end Glenn Braunschweig, who took the ball on Hope's 20 and went the distance. The kick was wide, but the score stood 13-0 and Hope had posed little threat in three quarters of play. At this point Dave Woodcock, substituting for the injured Kuyers, broke loose on an impressive 37-yard touchdown jaunt. A successful point-after cut the margin to 13-7. Hope's second TD came with 6:54 remaining. Holmlund hit Adams with a scoring pass to tie the game at 13. Then, in the closing moments, the same combination produced the deciding tally. For a second time Adams managed to outmaneuver safety man Jack Fendt and go all the way. The kick was not good, but the team's impressive comeback had given Coach De Vette a 19-13 victory, his first as Hope's new varsity coach.

The ice had been broken, but guard Blaine Timmer had

17

been added to a long list of injured players. Hope now faced its first league opponent, when Coach Rolla Anderson brought his Kalamazoo team to Riverview on Oct. 8. The Hornets had suffered a 15-6 setback at the hands of Alma the previous week but Anderson had uncovered a find in freshman quarterback Bob Urshalitz. At 5' 7", diminutive Bob had led his Jackson St. Mary's high school team to two perfect seasons. He would be heard from in MIAA circles.

Following a scoreless first quarter, Kazoo got on the board first with two minutes gone in the second period. Urshalitz passed 10 yards to Vic Landeryou for the score and 235-pound tackle Rudy Wolchina kicked the point. The Kalamazoo lead was extended to 14-0 with just 1:50 remaining in the half. Defensive back Jim Smith intercepted a Holmlund pass on Hope's 35. Picking up two good blocks, he rambled down the north sideline and into the end zone. Wolchina again converted and the Hornets went to the locker room with a two-touchdown lead.

Neither team scored in the third period as defenses stiffened. In the final stanza Hope attempted to move through the air, but a Holmlund pass bounced off Adams' shoulder pad and Jim Smith was again on hand to intercept. Hope's stubborn defense eventually forced The K-men to setup for a field goal, but the wiley Anderson called for a fake. Joe Fowler took a direct pass from center and passed quickly to end Vic Landeryou who stepped into the end zone. The point try by Ron Low was not good, but Kazoo's 20-0 lead loomed large.

In the late stages of the game Holmlund connected with freshman end Jerry Hendrickson, who took the 21-yard pass to the four, where he was pushed out of bounds. Halfback Mert Vander Lind then went off-tackle for the score. The conversion was good but time ran out, leaving the final score at 20-7. Rolla Anderson had drawn first blood in what would be a long series of contests between the two coaches. De Vette would win his share.

Hope continued in conference play at Adrian on Saturday, Oct. 15. The long bus trip, always a concern for Hope coaches, did not prevent a strong first-quarter effort by the Dutchmen, especially on defense. Neither team managed a score in the first period, but with 9:07 gone in the second quarter, Hope capped an 80-yard drive with a Holmlund to Lynn Post touchdown pass. The TD was a career first for the Hope captain, and Doc Van Hoeven's point-after gave De Vette's squad the early lead. Paul Wiegerink, Hope's other end, was not as fortunate, being forced to the sidelines with a leg injury. With 3:47 left in the half, Adrian quarterback Fred Hobart hit Tom Hodge with a screen pass good for 40 yards and the Bulldogs' first score, but De Graw broke through to block John Zupko's point attempt and preserve Hope's halftime lead at 7-6.

The narrow margin was erased in the third quarter when Adrian halfback Brian Graffa got behind Hope safety Jim Stout and went all the way with a pass from quarterback Norm Carlson. This time John Zupko's kick was good and the Bulldogs' lead was 13-7. In the fourth period Adrian added two more points when big Leon Harper, of basketball fame, tackled a Hope back in his own end zone. With the score at 15-7 Coach De Vette inserted Del Grissen at quarterback. In the "catch up" attempt Grissen's pass was incercepted on the Adrian 42. A subsequent 48-yard scamper by Tom Hodge led the home team to a 26-yard field goal by John Zupko, stretching the lead to 18-7. With 1:39 remaining in the game, Holmlund connected with Adams for a 37-yard scoring pass. The point try was not good, leaving the final tally at 18-13. The Hope offense racked up 16 first downs to six for Adrian and led in total yards 264 to 210, but Hope miscues, including three lost fumbles, had made the difference. The quiet trip home was a time for analysis and planning for the week ahead.

Student life in the '50s centered around a variety of campus activities. Television, still in its infancy, was not a major distraction and students welcomed each chance to interact. One of the best opportunities came on Homecoming Weekend. In 1955 the event would climax with the Hope-Hillsdale football game, but lead-up activities began on Friday. A signal event was the groundbreaking ceremony for the aforementioned men's dormitory to be known as Kollen Hall. Appropriately, Dean Milton "Bud" Hinga turned the first spadeful of dirt and declared the occasion "a red letter day in my life." Halfback Adams, as Student Council President, also participated. By late afternoon the sophomores made sure that freshmen would remain in their place by winning the annual Pull (tug-of-war) across the Black River. In the evening students milled about the athletic field adjacent to Carnegie-Schouten Gym awaiting the traditional bonfire and pep rally. Co-captain Lynn Post crowned the Homecoming Queen, a Muskegon beauty named Isla Van Eenanaam, who was also presented a necklace bearing a miniature gold football. Queen Isla then completed the formalities by lighting the bonfire. On today's campus such simple pageantry would evoke little more than a titter, but at mid-century it was woven into the fabric of student life and remains memorable.

Hillsdale's football team came to Riverview Park with justifiable confidence. The defending MIAA champions were riding the crest of a 12-game winning streak and a dynasty was in the making. Coach Frank "Muddy" Waters had produced a champion in his first year at the helm and his "pipeline" to Michigan State University was already paying big dividends. *

---

* As mentioned in volume one of this work, Waters, an MSU graduate, enjoyed a close relationship with Athletics Director Clarence "Biggie" Munn and football coach Hugh "Duffy" Daugherty. Quality players at MSU, not quite good enough for the big time, were encouraged to transfer to Hillsdale. The incentives were athletic scholarships (albeit somewhat smaller) and the then current eligibility rule which enabled transfers to compete the following fall.

Despite a series of injuries and a 1-4 record, the Dutchmen were not overawed. Coach De Vette had seen enough to know that his roster included quality players confident in their abilities. Patience and persistence were needed to turn the corner. The four veteran officials who made their way to the 50-yard line for the coin toss had all made, or would make, their own storied contributions to sport and education. John C. Hoekje would one day serve as MIAA Commissioner. Wendell Emery was recreation director for the city of Grand Rapids. His booming voice could be heard clearly, even in the top row of Riverview's covered grandstand. Dan Nameth had introduced zone press basketball to western Michigan while coaching at Grand Rapids Central, and Jay Formsma would become a much-respected principal at Holland High School.

The partisan Homecoming crowd feared the worst when the Bearcats took the opening kickoff and marched to paydirt in 11 plays. Most of the work was done by a splendid halfback from Benton Harbor named Nate Clark, who finally bulled into the end zone from the one-yard line. A failed try for the point left the score at 6-0 with 6:30 remaining in the quarter. Hope's defense stiffened in the second period, forcing a Hillsdale punt. Taking the ball on their own 35, the Dutchmen began their own drive. In 11 plays they had moved to the visitors' 13. At this point Adams broke free on an end sweep, was hit on the two, but squirmed away and into the end zone. Van Hoeven's kick was true and the scoreboard showed Hope leading Hillsdale 7 to 6. Few teams in the latter half of the '50s would enjoy this enviable position, even temporarily.

In the second quarter the aroused Bearcats engineered another impressive drive built around a 41-yard pass play from Bill Allinder to Ken Borgne. Allinder and Hope's Jim Stout had been teammates in Coach Dick Smith's fine program at Greenville High School. Allinder's efforts almost netted another score, but he was pulled down by Post and Van Hoeven on the three-yard line as time ran out. Halftime: Hope 7, Hillsdale 6.

In the third quarter Hope was forced to punt after two pass plays failed, but Nate Clark and John Moffat managed to botch a handoff attempt on the return and Post recovered on the Dales' 25. Two running plays put Hope on the 20, but the threat ended as two Harry Voss passes fell incomplete in the end zone. Hope's failure to capitalize on the Dale turnover proved a turning point in the game. In nine plays Coach Waters' team marched all the way to the one and Clark went in for the score. A missed kick left the score at 12-7. Still in the game, an overanxious Dutchman fumbled the ensuing kickoff, allowing end Andy Kincannon to recover on the Hope 30. Clark's 13-yard gain was nullified by a holding penalty and it appeared that the Dutchmen might survive their miscue. But Ken Borgne gained six and sub quarterback Jack Rosetti hit end Lee Jones with a pass good to the four. Borgne gained two more and Clark went over for his third TD of the afternoon. This time Wayne O'Shaughnessy's kick was good, making it 19-7.

The game appeared to be over and some made their way to the exits, but there were a few bombs left in the Hope arsenal. In the closing moments quarterback Holmlund completed a pass to Woodcock, whose shifty running style took him through the Dale defense to the one. The play covered 62 yards. Freshman halfback Paul "Pete" Watt went the final yard to paydirt. Van Hoeven's point try was not good, leaving Hillsdale's victory margin at 19-13. Muddy Waters' team would repeat as MIAA champions and post a perfect 9-0 record, but they would remember their six-point victory in Holland as their stiffest challenge of the season.

In yet another defeat, the Dutchmen had decidedly "turned the corner." Hope's stellar performance had been achieved without the services of Kuyers, Wiegerink, Hilmert, and Del Grissen, all on the injury list. Such talent was sorely missed, but others stepped forward. Returning from an injury, halfback Bob De Young carried eight times for 26 yards and made several solid tackles on defense. Linebacker Mick Faber intercepted an Allinder pass in the end zone to end one threat, and Woodcock had 50 yards in 11 carries. Ken Weller, now immersed in graduate studies at the University of Michigan, had managed to find time to scout the Alma-Hillsdale game and his report had played a key role in Coach De Vette's preparations.

Olivet, a charter member of the MIAA in 1888, had struggled in recent years. Hard times continued for the Comets in the 1955 football season, but as they viewed Hope's 1-5 record there appeared to be light at the end of the tunnel. A home-field advantage was in the mix as they played host to the Dutchmen in a night game on Oct. 29. The Olivet coaching staff could hardly anticipate the Hope resurgence which was further fueled during the week by the return of nearly all of the injured squad members. Across the "T" in the backfield De Vette could now field Woodcock, Kuyers, and Adams, with several above-average subs anxious to take their place. Voss, Holmlund, and Grissen were available at quarterback, and the Dutchman line was at full strength.

As Hope's camouflaged juggernaut pulled into tiny Olivet, the temperature hovered at 30 degrees. About 250 fans, most of them in parked cars, turned out to see the teams do battle. Hope received the opening kickoff and scored in three plays. Woodcock, now at left halfback, went 30 yards off-tackle for the score and Van Hoeven converted for the 7-0 lead. One minute of playing time had elapsed. Also in the first period, Adams went off-tackle for 28 yards and Hope's second TD. Van Hoeven's kick was wide and the score stood at 13-0.

On the first play of the second quarter, De Young took the ball on a reverse and went 18 yards for Hope's third score. The point try failed again, but the Dutchman lead was now 19-0. Olivet's woes continued with a fumble on a subsequent possession. An alert Gantos recovered for Hope, and De Young repeated the reverse play with the same result. This time Greenville's Jim Stout was called upon for the point-after. His kick was good, making it 26-0. Coach De Vette, sensing a mismatch, had already substituted freely. The Dutchmen's next drive totaled 68 yards and included a 40-yard sweep by freshman halfback Pete Watt. Wetherbee went off-tackle for five yards and Hope's fifth touchdown. Stout's second kick was also good and the halftime scoreboard showed the Hope lead at 33-0.

Six plays into the second half, Hope received a punt and moved to their own 49. Fullback Kuyers was stopped at midfield, but on the following play halfback Vander Lind had good interference around right end and ran 50 yards for the touchdown. Van Hoeven's kick was blocked, leaving the score at 39-0. As the Comets attempted an air attack things again went sour. Quarterback Roland Wahl's sideline pass was intercepted by Adams, who took it all the way to paydirt. Since the Hope performance on extra points had been erratic at best, Adams himself was now given the opportunity. His kick was true and at the end of the quarter the score had ballooned to 46-0. Adams would appear but briefly in the fourth period.

Clean Hope jerseys dotted the field in the final quarter and Coach Swede Thomas' crew salvaged some satisfaction. Roland Wahl hit Bill Shade with a 26-yard scoring pass and Comets were on the board. A missed kick left the count at 46-6. Later in the period Wahl connected with end Joe Iauch, who raced 52 yards for the TD. Wahl then passed to Frank Troesch for the point to make it 46-13. Joe Iauch would one day coach at West Ottawa High School in Holland.

Olivet appeared to be on a roll, but a short kickoff was returned to the Hope 42 and on the first play from scrimmage Adams sidestepped weary tacklers and went 58 yards for the game's final score. Jim Stout's kick was not good and the game ended at 52-13. Somewhat lost in the offensive display was an outstanding defensive performance by Wiegerink.

Coach De Vette's first MIAA victory had come at the expense of Warren "Swede" Thomas, who would suffer through a 1-8 season. The likeable Thomas had paid his dues at Olivet and had enjoyed a 20-6 victory over Hope in 1954, but lack of funds and staff had left him holding the bag. Included in his various activities were the laundry and custodial duty. Following the '55-56 year Thomas would move to Kalamazoo College and enjoy a successful tenure as coach of track and cross country.

A Mom and Dad's Day crowd of 1,900 made their way to Riverview Park on Nov. 5 to see if the "new" Dutchmen were for real. The Olivet victory, welcome as it was, had not changed the minds of early-season sceptics. Albion would be different. Coach Morley Fraser, now in his second season, had posted victories over Adrian, Olivet, Beloit, and Alma. Losses were to Wabash and Hillsdale, but in each case, only by the margin of one touchdown. The Britons had finished second to Hillsdale in the '54 campaign.

Hope's starting backfield now included two Saginaw products, sophomore Woodcock at left half and senior co-captain Adams at right half. Woodcock had prepped at Saginaw St. Mary's, while Adams hailed from Arthur Hill. With Kuyers at fullback and Harry Voss at quarterback, the Dutchmen could not be taken lightly.

Midway in the first quarter Hope began a drive from their own 41. A 35-yard scamper by Woodcock advanced the ball to the Briton 13. On the next play the 205-pound Kuyers went the remaining distance for the game's first score. Van Hoeven's conversion made it 7-0. Albion retaliated with their own drive. Quarterback Bob Gamble's 25-yard pass to Waterman was the key play placing the ball on the Hope one-yard line. Freshman fullback Jim Hurd plunged in for the score, but Erv Ritt's kick was not good and Hope maintained the lead at 7-6. The only other score came with 1:05 left in the half, when Kuyers broke through on a five-yard trap play. An errant kick by Van Hoeven made it 13-6 at the intermission.

As the second half got underway the game appeared to be a toss-up between two evenly matched teams, but after an Albion possession Wiegerink and De Graw combined to block the fourth down punt. The ball was chased down and recovered by Voss on the Albion 10. Kuyers moved up the middle to the three and Dave Woodcock went off right tackle for the score. After Van Hoeven's successful kick, Hope led 20-6. Still in the third quarter, the Dutchmen took possession on their own 47 and again moved to paydirt, this time in 11 plays. Notable in the series was a 25-yard Voss to Faber pass that placed the ball on the Briton seven. Holmlund, now at fullback, was called upon for two successive carries. His first attempt netted five yards and second produced Hope's fourth TD of the afternoon. Adams' conversion widened the gap to 27-6.

Albion's frustration mounted with a fumble on the first play of the fourth quarter. Big Jim Hilmert recovered for Hope on the Albion 15 and three plays later Holmlund scored a second time, moving in from the four. Center De Graw was given the chance to convert and made good - Hope 34, Albion 6.

Coach Morley Fraser would have his share of good days against Hope, but this had not been one of them. With three minutes remaining, Wetherbee intercepted a long Albion pass on the Hope 24. Holmlund, now at quarterback, passed to Adams for 32 yards. Two running plays plus an Albion penalty placed the ball on the Britons' 30. Adams, in his final appearance at Riverview, was given the ball for a last carry. He was slowed slightly at the 10, but picked up speed and crossed into the end zone. Hope continued to play "musical chairs" with conversion attempts. Tackle Hollander, tallest and heaviest man on the squad, was now given

RUSS DE VETTE'S FIRST HOPE FOOTBALL TEAM - 1955

Front Row L. to R.: Manager David Markusse, Dick Gantos, Dave Woodcock, Earl De Witt, John Hollander, Co-Captain John Adams, Co-Captain Lynn Post, Ron De Graw, Don "Doc" Van Hoeven, Dick Schulz, Dave Kuyers, Manager Bob Hoffman. **2nd Row:** Assistant Coach Al Vanderbush, Manager Carlton Failor, Jim Stout, Jack Faber, Larry Ter Molen, Ron Wetherbee, Mert Vander Lind, Del Grissen, Tom Harris, Fred Leaske, Bill Brookstra, Harry Voss, Blaine Timmer, Paul "Pete" Watt, Carl Coates, Ray Beckering, Trainer Larry Green, Ken "Mick" Faber, Head Coach Russ De Vette. **Top Row:** Bob De Young, Bill Waggoner, Dave Boerigter, Jim Hilmert, Paul Wiegerink, Ron Beuker, Curt Menning, Don Lautenbach, Jerry Hendrickson, Dale Schoon, Jim "Tiger" De Witt, Matt Peelen. Missing from picture – John Holmlund.

Picture taken at southwest corner of refurbished Carnegie-Schouten Gym.

the opportunity. When his kick fell far short of the crossbar he received some good-natured ribbing by the bench, but Hope's offensive linemen had earned their spurs. Tackles Hollander and Van Hoeven, guards Gantos and Faber, ends Post, Wiegerink, and Hilmert, along with center De Graw, had paved the way for 313 rushing yards. A total of 41 Hope players saw action in the 40-6 victory, which could only be described as convincing. The Dutchmen's margin in first downs was 22 to 12. John Leppi, Albion's all-round athlete, led his team with 42 yards.

With the Albion win, Hope's late-season resurgence was deemed genuine. As momentum continued to build, no one wanted the season to end, least of all the seniors: co-captains Adams and Post, tackles Van Hoeven and Hollander, center De Graw, and guard Dick Schulz. The finale came in a night game at Alma on Nov. 12. Coach Lloyd Eaton's charges carried a 5-3 record into the contest and needed a win to garner a share of second place. Leading the Scots was halfback "Marvelous Marv" Raab. He would have to be contained if the Dutchmen were to continue their impressive comeback.

After a scoreless first quarter, fullback Kuyers exploded up the middle on the winged T trap play. With knees high and deceptive speed the 205-pounder streaked 80 yards to the end zone. Van Hoeven made it 7-0 with his successful conversion. Hope's second score followed a fumble recovery by Jim Hilmert on the Hope 37. The score came on a swing pass from Voss to Woodcock, who maneuvered past all defenders. The Hope lead stood at 13-0 after the failed conversion. In the final minute of the first half, the Scots' speedy "Marvelous Marv" broke loose for a 45-yard touchdown run and quarterback Dick Ayling converted to narrow the gap to 13-7.

Coach Eaton welcomed the momentum swing at halftime, but the charged-up Dutchmen quickly regained the advantage. Early in the third period Kuyers scored again and

21

the Hope lead lengthened to 19-7. The Scots were forced to punt and Hope began yet another drive, this time from their own 19. On the first play, behind a perfect trap block, Kuyers streaked 60 yards up the middle to the Alma 21. His next try netted nine more to the 11, where Adams took over. He was given the ball on three successive plays, finally going over from the one. A failed point attempt made it 25-7.

On the ensuing kickoff MIAA hurdle champion Wiegerink was in the first wave. When the Scots' receiver mishandled the kick he pounced on the ball and Hope had possession on the Alma 33. Subsequent carries by Holmlund and Faber moved the ball to the six and on the first play of the fourth period, quarterback Grissen passed to Faber in the end zone. Another missed conversion left the score at 31-7.

Midway in the fourth quarter Holmlund intercepted a Dick Ayling pass on the Alma 40 to set up Hope's final score. Dave Kuyers broke free to the seven and John Adams went off-tackle for the last touchdown in his brilliant career. With the score at 37-7 the Dutchmen were thankful that on this day victory would not be determined by extra points. They had missed on five in-a-row.

With 1:30 remaining, Alma moved into Hope territory and punched in a touchdown as Dick Ayling went in from the one. Raab's conversion made it 37-14 and rang down the curtain for the season. Kuyers had an outstanding game with 204 yards in 13 carries, while Raab had 110 yards in 17 attempts. Adams and Raab were named to the All-MIAA team, but Kuyers would have to wait another year for that honor. The deserving Raab was voted the league's most valuable player.

Coach De Vette's first season had ended on a positive note with an overall record of 4 and 5. After a sluggish start the team had found itself and performed with increasing confidence. Its 3-3 MIAA record produced a third-place tie with Albion and Alma, both of whom had been soundly beaten by the Dutchmen. At season's end many followers felt that Hope was the strongest team in the conference. Muddy Waters and Rolla Anderson, of course, were not about to make such a concession.

*   *   *

Hope's other fall sport was cross country. Lacking the drama of football, it none-the-less called for equal dedication and considerable discipline. In 1955 Hope's coach for its "loneliest sport" was Dr. Larry Green, who also served as trainer for all sports. In an unusual move, sophomore Jim Cooper was named captain, a tribute to his leadership potential. Other squad members included Carroll Bennink, Dick Brockmeier, Ron Den Uyl, Ev Nienhouse, John Soeter, Doug Vander Hey, Jack Ver Steeg, Jack Walchenbach, Herb Widmer, and Glenn Williams.

The Dutchmen dropped their first two meets, losing to Grand Rapids Junior College 22-32 and to Kalamazoo 16-47. Hope's top finisher in the Kazoo meet was Herb Widmer in fifth place, but at Adrian on Oct. 15 he moved up to first place with a time of 22:54 for the four-mile course. Hope's 21-38 victory was followed by a 22-35 loss to Calvin on the 19th. Hope hosted Hillsdale on Oct. 22 and prevailed 26-29 in the season's most exciting matchup. Inspired by the hard-earned victory, Hope's harriers journeyed to Detroit to take on a strong contingent from Wayne State University. The Dutchmen suffered a 15-50 shutout at the hands of the Tarters but meeting a superior team on a non-league basis was not all bad. Doc Green's crew took the loss in stride and were themselves dominant at Olivet on Oct. 29, downing the Comets 16-41.

The up-and-down season continued with a 15-48 loss to Albion in Holland on Nov. 4, and a 27-32 victory at Alma in the final dual meet on Nov. 12. Hope's fourth place finish in the league meet at Albion closed out the season on Nov. 16.

*   *   *

Peter Pleune organized Hope's first basketball team in 1901 and the sport had been king of the campus ever since. Enthusiasm and fan support had not diminished in the fall of 1955. Coach John Visser had produced MIAA champions in 1951-52 and '52-53, but the '53-54 team's league 8-6 record dropped the Dutchmen to fourth place. Joining returnees Hal Molenaar, Dwight Riemersma, and John Adams was 6' 10" freshman Paul Benes, giving Visser hope to once again claim the top spot.

Practice sessions began on Nov. 1 in refurbished Carnegie-Schouten Gym. By arrangement with the Holland Recreation Department, some sessions were conducted in the recently opened Civic Center. Through the years Hope teams had known four different home courts, but in 1955-56 all home games would be played in the 2,500-seat Civic Center arena at Eighth Street and Pine Avenue. Co-captains Molenaar and Riemersma were on hand for the opening turnout along with Benes, Bob Ritsema, Dwayne "Tiger" Teusink, Bob Thomson, Albert "Jun" Buursma, and John Jeltes. No fewer than seven members of De Vette's football squad would join the group on Nov. 14. In addition to Adams this group included Bob De Young, Jerry Hendrickson, Jim Hilmert, Dale Schoon, Mert Vander Lind, and Dave Woodcock. Benes at 6' 10", Hilmert at 6' 7", and Ritsema at 6' 4" appeared to provide the board power necessary for a successful campaign. Ritsema, a junior, was out for the first time, having played fraternity and city league ball during his first two years.

Hope opened the season by joining an eight-team tournament hosted by Earlham College in Richmond, Ind. An 11-man squad made the initial trip. It consisted of Adams, Riemersma, Molenaar, Ritsema, Vander Lind, Jeltes, Teusink, Benes, Buursma, Thomson, and Schoon. It was hoped that some of the fabled Hoosier tradition would rub off, but the Dutchmen drew Mc Neese State of Lake Charles, La., on opening night, Thursday, Nov. 24. Hope led for the first 15 minutes but was hampered when Benes picked up his third foul in the first half. Ritsema, in his first collegiate contest, was effective on the boards and overall did an admirable job of filling in for tall Paul, but included in the Mc Neese line up was one Bill Riegel, a transfer from Duke University, who seemed to be able to score at will. Mc Neese forged ahead in the second half and went on to a 94-65 rout. Riegel led the Cowboys with 40 and was followed by Bud Carver with 20. With limited playing time, Benes led Hope with 18. Co-captains Molenaar and Riemersma each had 12.

Hope's second-round opponent was Manchester of Indiana and the Dutchmen fared somewhat better, leading most of the first half. The Spartans pulled ahead 34-32 at the intermission, but with 10 minutes left in the game the score was knotted at 54. With four minutes remaining Coach Visser elected to employ a press. The strategy backfired as the Dutchmen had not had sufficient time to perfect this device. The result was a 79-65 Manchester victory, but Hope had played well for the most part. Benes was again the scoring leader, this time with 32, mostly on tip-ins. Paul Butts led Manchester with 33.

On Saturday, Nov. 26, the Dutchmen tangled with Centre College of Danville, Ky. The high-scoring affair was tied 37-37 at the intermission after Hope had led by as many as 12 during the first half. The Hope five maintained the pace for the first six minutes of the second half, then lost the touch, allowing Centre to move on to a 106-90 victory. The Dutch downfall came with its inability to contain the Colonels' Burt Dechko, who rang up a total of 44 points. Hope's leader was again Benes with 27 and Adams was back in form with 19.

While no coach can be pleased with an 0-3 record to begin the season, Visser now had more immediate concerns. The MIAA opener was scheduled for Saturday, Dec. 3, with Hillsdale furnishing the opposition. Hillsdale's prowess on the gridiron tended to obscure a solid basketball program. Visser hoped his charges would not take the Dales lightly.

The Dutchmen were off to a sizzling start in the friendly confines of the Holland Civic Center. Molenaar hit on five straight outcourt shots and Benes scored three times with his patented hook shot. With his back to the basket, long arms and a 6' 10" frame, the shot was virtually unstoppable. In addition, he was fouled repeatedly and cashed in on seven free throws. The visitors meanwhile, were having trouble with unfamiliar surroundings, a large crowd, and Hope's 2-3 zone defense. The Dutchmen shot 50 percent for the half and found themselves with a comfortable 44-30 lead.

Teams with a sizeable lead and confidence in their ability sometimes tend to coast, albeit subconsciously. This malady now hit the Dutchmen as their shooting cooled off and the opponents found the range. The Dales' point total in the second half ballooned to 50, compared to 30 in the first half. Benes fouled out with 5:44 remaining and the Dales narrowed the margin to two. Molenaar and Adams managed to score in the closing moments to insure the 84-80 victory. John Wood led the Hillsdale comeback with 18 points. Earlier, in the preliminary game, the Hope jayvees hosted the Western Michigan College freshmen. Coach Lynn Post was subjected to a humbling experience as the young Broncos crushed Hope 100 to 30. Wayland's Phil Regan had 15 for Western. He would later be heard from in major league baseball circles as a pitcher, coach, and manager.

Hope's narrow victory over Hillsdale prompted a serious practice session on Monday before the team departed for Olivet on Tuesday, Dec. 6. The Comets competed in Mac Kay Gymnasium which had been built in 1927. A fine facility in its day, the structure had come to be known as "the Pit" due to placement of the floor several feet below the bleacher space on either side. This night the Dutchmen were not bothered by the court and again were off to a flying start. Benes sank five straight on his way to 21 points in the first half and Hope's 47 percent shooting produced a 46-31 halftime lead. In light of recent performances, there was some doubt about the team's ability to maintain the advantage. The question was answered when board work by Hilmert and Benes got the fast break into high gear. Adams was on the receiving end and scored five straight layups as Hope built a 20-point lead. Twelve Dutchmen saw action in the 72-57 win. Benes led his team with 25, while Adams had 14 and Riemersma 13. Norm Schultz was high for Olivet with 14.

On Dec. 7 the sports world paused to honor the passing of Honus Wagner, baseball's greatest shortstop and Hall of Fame member. Wagner died at age 81 in Pittsburgh, scene of so many great performances by the "Flying Dutchman." Hope's Jack Schouten coached baseball for many years and, stationed in the third base coaching box in baggy pants, bore a striking resemblance to that other Dutchman from Pittsburgh.

On Friday, Dec. 9, Hope made the long trip to Ypsilanti for a game with Michigan Normal. Coach Jim Skala's team was now playing in the new Bowen Arena and they were more than ready for the visiting squad. If the weather was cold, the Dutchmen were even colder. Shooting a paltry 23 percent in the first half, Visser's crew was literally snowed under by the red hot Hurons, whose first half average was 56 percent. The Hope five played better in the second half, but the 56-27 margin was too much to overcome and Normal went on to post a 91-73 win. The Hurons got balanced scoring from Nick Pappadikis and Bill Stephans with 18 each and from Dave Parks with 15. Benes was high for Hope with 17. He was followed by substitute Vander Lind with 13. Riemersma and freshman Hendrickson each had 10.

Stung by a dismal performance against Normal, the

THE 1955-56 HOPE VARSITY - JOHN VISSER'S LAST LOOK AT COACHING

Back row L. to R.: Manager Fred Leaske, Albert "Jun" Buursma, Co-Captain Dwight "Whitey" Riemersma, Paul Benes, Bob Ritsema, Coach John E. Visser.
Front Row: Mert Vander Lind, Co-Captain Hal Molenaar, Dwayne "Tiger" Teusink, Dave Woodcock, Bob Thomson.

Dutchmen rebounded against Albion in the Civic Center on Thursday, Dec. 15. Coach Visser's starters were Adams, Riemersma, Benes, Hilmert, and Molenaar. Everything seemed to click and by halftime Hope held commanding 39-24 lead. The lead was increased to as many as 28 in the second half and subs played most of the period. John Hannett, the league's leading scorer, was superb with 25, but no other Briton scored more than six. Benes racked up 28 for Hope, and Riemersma followed with 17. Hilmert, on the defensive board, was responsible for numerous fast-break baskets. Adams and freshman Thomson each contributed eight points. It was Hope's best performance to date and provided needed momentum at the Christmas break.

Four days after Christmas, Hope hosted Lawrence Tech of Detroit in the Civic. Visser seemed to have found the right combination as the Dutchmen were again impressive. Hope scored 52 points in the first half to 39 by the Blue Devils, and the margin widened in the second period. As the game neared its conclusion the score stood at 98-67 and a chant from the Hope crowd asked for more, but Tech gained control and stalled out the last 45 seconds to prevent Hope from reaching the century mark. The value of Benes was evident as he again led his team with 28 points. Riemersma was close behind with 24, while Molenaar collected 16 and Adams 12. Stan Sylvester took honors for the Blue Devils with 14.

On Saturday, Dec. 31, Coach Visser was able to schedule a scrimmage with the Western Michigan College varsity in the Civic Center. The Hope mentor was anxious to have his team maintain the edge they had displayed in recent games and knew that extra effort would be required to contain the Western players, if only in a practice setting.

Hope resumed MIAA play at Alma on Wednesday, Jan. 4. The Scots had abandoned their dark and narrow gym of yesteryear and were now playing all home games in the new Alma High School gym. Knowing that the teams were evenly matched, Visser had anticipated the close game that followed. In the second half Hope built a 10-point lead, then saw it slip away as guard George Carter engineered the Scot comeback. Hope trailed by four with one minute left and prospects were grim at best, but a determined Hope effort would cause the contest to end in dramatic fashion. With 37 seconds showing on the clock, Riemersma was fouled and made good on both attempts to pull the Dutchmen within two. The Scots moved to their end of the floor and drove for a seemingly sure layup, but Ritsema moved in, blocked the shot, secured the rebound, and got a long pass to Molenaar, whose pressure jump shot tied the game at 69 with 20 seconds remaining. Alma's hope for a game-winning shot missed the mark and big Jim Hilmert took the rebound. His quick pass found freshman Buursma with 12 seconds left. Buursma was farther out-court than his accustomed spot, but took aim and saw his bomb part the netting: final score, Hope 71 - Alma 69. Hope's scoring was evenly divided with Riemersma getting 19, Adams 18, Molenaar 14, and Benes 10. Alma's George Carter led all scorers with an outstanding effort that produced 34 points. He was followed by erstwhile quarterback Dick Ayling, who had 10.

On the night of Jan. 12, 1956, 5,900 fans jammed into the Grand Rapids Civic Auditorium (now known as Welsh Auditorium) to witness yet another Hope-Calvin tussle. Auditorium manager Fred Barr declared the figure a new record attendance for the Civic, and it may well have been the largest crowd to witness a small college game in the nation. The smaller schools were not well organized and attendance records were not kept systematically.

Both teams were undefeated in the young MIAA season, and no one was surprised to see the opening half closely contested. Calvin claimed a 32-31 advantage at the intermission, but Hope scored the first two baskets of the second half. From that point on it was a night for the Knights. While centers Tom Newhof and Benes seemed to neutralize each other, Calvin forwards Tony Diekema and 6' 6" Jim Kok went on a scoring spree. Each scored 18 and Newhof added 16. Ed Start came off the bench to score 12, and captain Don Vroon controlled play from his guard spot while contributing 14. Overall in the second half, the Knights hit on 21 of 36 field goal attempts. Now in his third season at Calvin, Coach Barney Steen had done a masterful job with two MIAA titles to his credit and a third one pending. Benes had done a reasonable job on Tom Newhof, outscoring his former teammate at Grand Rapids Christian by one point. Following Benes' 17 points was Molenaar with 13. All in all, the 85-57 defeat was one the Dutchmen would rather forget.

It was back to basics as the Dutch prepared for a second meeting with Michigan Normal. Coach Jim Skala brought the Hurons to the Civic Center on Tuesday, Jan. 17, hoping to repeat the Dec. 9 victory. For a time it appeared that the Hurons would do just that. Hope trailed most of the first half, but a late-period surge led by Tiger Teusink and Buursma brought the Dutchmen into striking distance. Four buckets by Benes then gave Hope a 42-38 lead. However, the determined Normal team soon caught up and led 56-50.

But down the stretch it was Paul Benes at his best. For a change the freshman did not foul out and ended with a game-high 34 points. Riemersma, Molenaar, and Buursma each scored 14 in the 82-76 Hope victory. Co-captain Riemersma had four clutch points in the final minute and Ritsema sank two free throws to lock up the win. Leading the Hurons was 6' 5" center Dave Parks, who had prepped at Highland Park. Parks's 32 counters kept his team in the game while Nick Pappadikas added 16. The victory was especially sweet after the discouraging Calvin defeat.

But just as conditions appeared on the upswing, Coach Visser received some bad news. Jim Hilmert, a chemistry major, decided to drop from the team and concentrate on studies before going out for track in the spring. Hope's next MIAA test would come as they hosted Kalamazoo on Saturday, Jan. 21. Dave Woodcock, who had not tried out for the team following football, was now invited to join the squad and was pleased to help fill the breach.

Coach Ray Steffen had played for Pete Newell at Michigan State and was in his first year at the helm in Kalamazoo. His strategy for the Hope game was to play a physical (to say the least) game against the slender, high-scoring Benes. To do the job he had 6' 7" center Doug Steward, who looked and played like a pro football tight end. It was soon evident that the tactic was working. In retaliation Benes picked up three fouls in the first 10 minutes and ended up sitting out half of the game. Hope enjoyed an early 10-2 lead, but the Hornets came on strong and led 41-34 at halftime. In the second half Steffen's crew was firmly in control, and at one point pushed the lead to 17. Steward ended the game with 18 counters and was followed closely by guard Gary Morrison with 17. Riemersma and Molenaar had 15 and 13 for Hope, and Benes, with limited playing time, had 11. The 76-63 defeat at home was a serious blow to any hopes for a title.

On Tuesday, Jan. 24, the team traveled to Manchester, Ind., hoping to reverse the earlier six-point tournament loss. Benes was again plagued by early foul trouble. With the tall one on the bench, Hope switched to a scrappy man-to-man but Manchester still led at halftime, 47-33. Benes had registered but one field goal in the first half but brought his team back within six in the second half. Hope controlled the boards and pulled within three at 79-76 with four minutes remaining, but Riemersma had fouled out with six minutes left and the Dutchmen lost much of their scoring punch. Despite an early departure, Riemersma led his team with a fine 23-point performance. Molenaar and Benes each had 14 while Paul Butts led Manchester to its 91-83 victory with 18.

Hope was scheduled to close out the first round of MIAA play at Adrian on Saturday, Jan. 28, but at a time when things weren't going well even nature intervened. An overnight sleet storm made roads impassable and the game had to be postponed. This quirk of fate was especially unfortunate for the Dutchmen as Adrian had two of its players about to re-establish their eligibility in the second semester. The most notable of these was Henry Hughes, the league's most valuable player in 1954-55.

Bad tidings continued for John Visser on Feb. 2, when Adams announced that he would not continue during the second semester. Adams had been accepted at Union Theological Seminary in New York and hoped to enhance his academic record before graduation. He was also serving as Student Council president. Additional attrition, in various forms, now left Visser with a squad of nine men and practice scrimmages became a problem.

Adjustments were made as Hope prepared to host Olivet on Saturday, Feb. 4. Buursma, who had started the Manchester game, remained at the forward position while Riemersma and Ritsema exchanged positions. Riemersma now teamed up at guard, with Molenaar and Benes continued at center. After a slow start the Dutchmen managed a 30-24 halftime lead. In the second half, as players became accustomed to their new roles, the offense shifted into high gear and Hope moved on to a satisfying 96-53 victory. Benes was again effective as high-point man with 22 and new guard Riemersma had 15. Visser's bench strength was in evidence as Vander Lind came through with 11 and freshman Thomson followed with 10. Thomson's quickness and savvy helped in overcoming the disadvantage of being totally deaf. Olivet, despite a 17-point performance from Maynard Stafford, continued in a discouraging season.

Hope's next test was a nail-biter at Albion on Tuesday, Feb. 7. As expected, the game in Kresge Gym was close all the way. The Britons eked out a 45-44 halftime advantage, but the score was knotted at 73 as time ran out in regulation play. Hope's extra effort in the overtime paid off as Benes sank two hook shots plus a free throw. Riemersma contributed a jumper and free throw, and Ritsema's tip-in with 10 seconds remaining sealed the hard-fought 80-77 win. Benes' 26 points led the Hope contingent in a team effort that saw Molenaar collect 17, Riemersma 15, and Ritsema 12. MIAA scoring leader John Hannett had 34, Bill Collison 17, and George Vivlamore 12 in the tough Albion loss.

A small but vocal crowd of 1,200 made their way to the Civic Center on Saturday, February 11 to witness the Hope-Alma contest. The Dutchmen were lodged in second place with a 7-2 record and were battling to stay in contention. Play was ragged at times, but the Hope five got it together and built a 48-35 halftime lead. Benes was again in foul trouble, but the Scots were not having a good night and the other Dutchmen pushed the score to 70-44 for the biggest margin of the evening. Riemersma was high man for Hope with 19, matching Ron Lude of Alma. Benes was limited to 13, but Buursma chipped in with 12 and Ritsema had 10. Coach Visser was impressed with the all-around play of Woodcock, who scored 12. George Carter, who had nearly beaten the Dutchmen in the first game, had an off night with 11. The final count was Hope 86, Alma 69.

Barney Steen brought the 10-0 Calvin Knights to the Civic Center on Valentine's Day and 2,700 fans squeezed into the place anticipating a classic between the first-and second-place teams. Calvin's starting five of Don Vroon, Arnie Rotman, Tom Newhof, Tony Diekema, and Jim Kok had been impressive against all comers, including the earlier 85-57 handling of Hope. But Hope-Calvin contests are hard to explain. At the half it was Hope on top 35-32. Many waited for the Dutchmen to cave in as in the first contest, but Buursma scored seven and Benes five in the first three minutes, and the home team was off and running. Midway in the period a basket by Riemersma made it 59-37 for the game's biggest margin. At this point Calvin's Newhof took over, scoring 14 in the final 10 minutes, but Vroon fouled out with four minutes left and Kok with three, and the Knights could get no closer than 10. Woodcock, at 6' 0" and 200 pounds, did an outstanding defensive job on the 6' 6" Kok, who had helped destroy the Dutch in the first game. At the last tick the scoreboard showed Hope with an 89-73 upset win. Riemersma, in his last Calvin game, was the scoring leader with 26. Benes totaled 18, Molenaar 15, Ritsema 14, and Buursma nine. Newhof's late surge produced 26 points to lead the Knights. Ed Start, as first reserve, had 11 and Diekema 10. It was Hope's high-water mark for the '55-56 season and Visser's last coaching victory, though that was unknown to all at the time.

Three days later in Kalamazoo's Treadway Gym, the dreaded let-down came. The Dutchmen went completely flat and scored only 14 points in the first half while the Hornets chalked up 36. Guard Gary Morrison was out with an injury, but Holland native Dave Moran moved to Morrison's spot and sparked his team to the eventual 16-point victory. Hope finally got it together in the second half and actually outscored Kazoo 43-37, but the damage had been done and the Dutch never got closer than 10. Dave Moran, son of Holland's Joe Moran, was superb with 23 points to lead his team to the 73-57 win. Doug Steward was not far behind with 19. Chuck Tucker added 14 and Walt Maser 10. Buursma was high for Hope for the first time with 18. Benes collected 14 and Riemersma 11.

A meager crowd of 1,000 turned out at the Civic Center as Hope hosted Adrian on Wednesday, Feb. 22. The Bulldogs were sporting a new look with the second semester addition of MVP Henry Hughes and Bob Ohrman. The Dutchmen kept pace for the first 20 minutes and trailed only 41-40 at the intermission, but Hughes, Leon Harper, and Bob Ohrman controlled the boards and Dutchman efforts seemed to produce only fouls. Eight of Adrian's last 10 points came at the free throw line. As many had feared, Henry Hughes made the difference. His stellar board work was matched by a 30-point scoring performance that impressed all, including the partisan Hope crowd. Bruce Stephans was also effective with 24 and Ohrman had 14 as the visitors went home with a hard-fought 89-82 victory. Benes had a tough night against Hughes, but led Hope with 16. Buursma had 14, Molenaar 12, and Ritsema and Riemersma 10 each.

When the Hope squad traveled to Hillsdale on Saturday, Feb. 25, they found that Coach Dick Wickens now had the services of 6' 10" Jerry Hilton to cope with Benes. The teams traded baskets for most of the first half, with Hope finally leaving the floor with a 41-40 lead. Hope's tendency to foul proved their undoing. The Dutchmen led in field goals 31 to 24 but the Dales cashed in on 34-of-43 free throws, including six straight in the last two minutes after Hope's comeback brought them within two points. There was some irony in Hillsdale's 84-80 victory. In the first-round contest they had lost to the Dutchmen by the identical score. John Woods scored 22 in the winning effort and Frank Wesner added 16. Hope's evenly divided scoring included 14 by Riemersma and Buursma, 13 by Molenaar, 12 by Benes, including five tip-ins, and 11 by Thomson. After "climbing the mountain" against Calvin, the Dutchmen had now dropped three straight, and the misery was not over.

Hope's make-up game with Adrian had to be squeezed in on Monday, Feb. 27, just two days after the exhausting Hillsdale encounter. At Adrian the shoe was on the other foot as far as free throws were concerned, and the Dutch cashed in on 14 straight enroute to gain 38-33 halftime lead. Henry Hughes was held to three field goals in the first half, but broke loose with eight more in the second stanza. His 26 points, combined with 21 from Harper and 11 from Bob Brown, were too much for the game Dutchmen, now playing mainly for pride and their coach. In their last game for the orange and blue, co-captains Molenaar and Riemersma acquitted themselves well. "Mo" had 18 and "Whitey" 12. Benes was in between with 16, but the curtain came down with a deserving Adrian team on top 84-70.

With an 8-6 MIAA record Hope slipped into a fourth-place tie with Hillsdale. The overall season mark of 10-11 was the product of meeting tough teams, bad breaks, and some inconsistency, but Coach Visser had remained upbeat. The wrap-up included a team meeting in which Riemersma was named the team's most valuable player and Ritsema was voted captain-elect for the '56-57 season. The All-MIAA team included Tom Newhof, Jim Kok, and Don Vroon from champion Calvin, Leon Harper from Adrian, and scoring leader John Hannett from Albion. Vroon was named the league's most valuable player and, as such, recipient of the Randall C. Bosch Award.

In 1956 there was no accommodation for small colleges in the National Collegiate Athletic Association (NCAA), but many of the smaller schools had banded together to form the National Association of Intercollegiate Athletics (NAIA). Each season in March the NAIA sponsored a basketball tournament in Kansas City. John Visser would give a lifetime of support to the organization and now helped facilitate the selection of Michigan's representative. State playoffs determined the participants. Calvin took itself out of the running, citing an institutional rule prohibiting post-season play. This left second-place finishers Adrian and Kalamazoo to hold a playoff for the right to play Lawrence Tech. The Hornets prevailed 83-62, then downed the Detroiters 65-60 before being eliminated at Kansas City.

John Visser could be justly proud of his four-year tenure as Hope's coach. Three of the four had been winning seasons and two had produced MIAA champions. Highly respected around the league, he had built lasting relationships with players and coaches alike. Visser's leadership qualities would face a new challenge as he now contemplated a career in college administration.

*   *   *

In the spring of 1956 Hope president Irwin J. Lubbers announced several changes as the college sought to restructure its administrative set-up. One of the changes involved the creation of the new post of Dean of Students. The appointment of Milton L. Hinga to this position came as no surprise and was welcomed by the entire college community. As teacher, coach, and administrator, his rapport with students was legendary. The now-vacated position of Dean of Men was a natural for one with John Visser's talent, interest, and sterling reputation. President Lubbers lost little time in moving Visser to this new post, the first step in a varied journey that would culminate in a college presidency.

Spring sports and Michigan weather have always been at odds. As the last piles of dirty snow melt away, athletes eagerly venture onto their various practice areas, but the few balmy days of late March and early April are always deceiving. In Holland, Michigan northwest winds sweep in from Lake Michigan, down Eighth Street and across diamonds, running tracks, courts, and courses. Batted balls sting batter and fielder alike, and the specter of pulled muscles haunts coaches and overzealous players trying to speed up their conditioning. But despite postponements, cancellations and general frustration, the show goes on and somehow schedules are completed.

Of all our sports, baseball is the most nostalgic, the most conscious of tradition. So speaks A. Bartlett Giamatti, late commissioner of baseball and former president of Yale University. Hope College reaches back into the 19th century for its baseball roots, and has worked its way through low budgets, bad fields, rainstorms, mini blizzards, and uncertain transportation. Patient and devoted coaches have known that the grass would turn green, and it always has.

The MIAA's new format in 1956 would consist of seven-inning double-headers with each league opponent to shorten somewhat the long afternoon of baseball. Single non-league contests would continue to go nine innings. Russ De Vette was back at the helm following his one-year hiatus at Maine. Second baseman Dick Ortquist was captain of a squad that included some holdovers from De Vette's '54 team, seven lettermen, and several members of last fall's football squad. Home games were played at venerable Riverview Park, located at Columbia Avenue and Fifth Street. The city-owned facility faced northeast with a small, covered grandstand behind home plate. Most of the outfield was made up of the east-west football field where the covered grandstand ran from left field to left center. The latter was an inviting target for would-be home run hitters.

Hope's opener was played at Ferris Institute in Big Rapids on Friday, April 13. Any superstitions the players may have had were quashed with the opening pitch, and an interesting game ensued. Ferris pitcher Mike Troup put down 13 Dutchmen in-a-row before Arnie Boeve singled in the fifth. Wayne Westenbroek also singled and both men eventually scored. Meanwhile, Hope starter Jack Kempker pitched shutout ball for his three-inning stint. Freshman lefty Wayne Westenbroek pitched the next three and gave up one run. He would be the winning pitcher as coach De Vette elected to use four hurlers. Mert Vander Lind pitched innings seven and eight, while Jim Stout was called upon to close out the ninth. The Dutchmen erupted for four runs in the seventh, including a two-run triple by Kempker, who had moved to the outfield after his pitching chores. Jack Faber also had a double in Hope's 6-3 victory.

Continuing in non-league competition, Hope journeyed to Richmond Park in Grand Rapids on Wednesday, April 18. The opponent was Grand Rapids Junior College and the game was marked by ragged play. Along the way each team committed eight errors. Such could be chalked up to meager practice time, cold weather, and general field conditions. Hope held a 5-1 lead in the third inning, but JC countered with three in the seventh to take a 7-6 lead. In the eighth a Dave Woodcock fly was dropped in the outfield and Woody was safe at second base. He advanced to third on Mert Vander Lind's infield out. At this point JC pitcher Bob Andree uncorked a wild pitch which allowed Woodcock to tie the score at 7-7. There was some irony in this as Andree would become a top-line pitcher for Hope for the next two seasons. His battery mate would be catcher Woodcock. Jack Kempker's diving catch in left field in the ninth inning preserved the tie, which was allowed to stand due to a Park rule which made the field available to other teams after 6 p.m.

MIAA action began at Riverview Park on Saturday, April 21, as the Dutchmen hosted Adrian. Reportedly, the Bulldogs by virtue of a spring trip had already played 16 games. Starter Kempker had sore arm problems and was removed after one and two thirds innings in favor of Vander Lind. Adrian had built an 11-2 lead before Hope came to life in the seventh inning. The bases were loaded when first baseman John Adams stepped to the plate. In a long-ago speech FDR had intoned the words, "Unto whom much is given, much is expected." Whether a long touchdown run, or the winning basket against Calvin, Hope fans and players had come to expect a great deal from Johnny Adams. Now his grand slam home run added an exclamation point to his varied and brilliant career. The seven-run seventh could not overcome six errors, eight free passes, and 15 Adrian hits. The Bulldogs prevailed by a score of 11 to 9, but Adams' dramatic delivery was the main topic of conversation as the second game got under way.

Ortquist opened the second game with a home run but Adrian knotted the count in the second. Hope made it 2-1 in their half of the second and the pitchers were in charge until the sixth, when Hope scored five as 11 men went to the plate. Woodcock had a triple, Westenbroek a double, and outfielder Jerry Boeve had the distinction of stroking two singles in the same inning. Lefty Westenbroek was effective until the seventh, when control problems allowed the Bulldogs to score four times, but the Dutchmen garnered 13 hits, made no errors, and emerged with a 7-5 victory.

Rain forced postponement of the Hillsdale doubleheader on April 28, but Hope gained another split at Kalamazoo on Tuesday, May 1. In the first game Westenbroek pitched a strong game through six innings, giving up only two hits. The Hornets picked up a run in the third but Hope answered with two in the sixth. The contest was decided in the seventh, when Kazoo combined three bunt singles, two walks, and another single to score five runs and take the game 6-2.

In the nightcap Kempker set down the Hornets with two hits, a bunt single in the first and a single to deep short in the fourth. Ron Low of Kalamazoo also gave up but two hits in the pitchers' battle. In the seventh Kempker led off with a double, but was tagged out as he overran second. Bobby Thomson was later safe on a fielder's choice and scored when Ortquist's fly ball was dropped in the outfield. Adams drew a walk. Woodcock then came through with Hope's second hit, a single scoring Ortquist and Adams. Kempker held off the Hornets in the final frame to post the 3-0 shutout.

The Calvin Knights played host to the Dutchmen in Grand Rapids on Saturday, May 5. In the opener Hope was off to a good start with two runs in the first inning, then enjoyed a big fifth inning, which featured a bases loaded-triple by Arthur "Swede" Olson. Westenbroek, with relief from Stout, was the starting and winning pitcher in the eventual 10-2 victory. Rain washed out the second game which, for reasons unknown, was never made up.

Tuesday, May 8, was not a good day for Hope at Albion. The Britons' Elvin Ritt started things off with a homer in the first and ended the game with five RBI's. He was joined by freshman right fielder Howard De Witt, whose homer and two singles produced Albion's other four runs. The Hope attack was led by Dick Ortquist with two singles and a triple, but Albion had little trouble in posting the 9-6 win. In the second game Coach Morley Fraser called on his ace hurler, John Baty. This spelled more trouble for the Dutchmen as Baty was in top form and limited Hope to just two hits. Woodcock and Thomson had singles, but no one else seemed able to solve the Baty slants in the 10-1 Hope defeat.

The Hope slump continued on Saturday, May 12, at Riverview Park. Alma's Charlie Skinner, chemistry professor turned baseball coach, had his team in the MIAA driver's seat. The Scots showed little mercy on Hope's Westenbroek and Stout as they collected 19 hits. Meanwhile, Alma's Loren Cook limited the Dutchmen to just three safeties. Hope's hits belonged to Ortquist, Olson, and Arnie Boeve. The 13-0 whitewashing would be Hope's worst defeat of the season.

The second game was a different story, but with a similar outcome. The Scots scored twice in the fourth when Hope committed two errors. The Dutch responded with one in the sixth on singles by Ortquist and Adams, but Alma added one more, also in the sixth, to make it 3-1. In the top of the seventh, Carl De Vree was on with a single. Kempker then powered a long home run onto the roof of the center field bleachers, tying the score at 3-3. But Alma, in championship style, pushed across a run in the seventh to notch the win 4-3. In relief Vander Lind absorbed the tough loss.

Hope was now out of the championship race but some good baseball remained to be played. On Monday, May 14, the rainout with Hillsdale was played at Riverview. Hope appeared to be back on track as they scored three in the first inning, but Hillsdale catcher Don Eugenio hit a two-run homer onto the roof of the left field stands in the second and outfielder Bob Duncan followed with a solo blast that cleared the center field grandstand to tie the score at 3. Kempker, though somewhat shaken, was still in charge. Hope took a 4-3 lead in the fifth but the Dales tied it in the sixth. In the final frame catcher Woodcock made the difference with a 350' home run over the center field fence. Kempker had survived the early onslaught and was the winning pitcher in the 5-4 victory.

Westenbroek took the mound for Hope in the second game and was effective all the way. A ground rule double plus a single gave Hillsdale a 1-0 lead in the second, but Hope answered with two in the third. Adams singled and Arnie Boeve was safe on an error. De Vree then drove both runners home with a single. This ended the scoring for the day. Westenbroek was tough in the late innings, holding the Dales to a total of four hits in the 2-1 victory, his third of the season. All in all, it was a satisfying sweep for the Dutchmen, who had bounced back from hard times.

Two days later Hope wound up the season by hosting Olivet. A Tulip Time band review was scheduled for Riverview Park, forcing a move to the Zeeland High School field. Coach De Vette decided that all squad members had earned the right to some playing time in this last twin bill. Seventeen would see action before the afternoon was over. Vander Lind started on the mound and gave up two runs in the first inning, but Hope got one in the third and another in the fourth to tie it up at 2-2. Olivet scored one more in the sixth, but in the same inning Vander Lind doubled home a run to aid his own cause. With the score tied 3-3 in the bottom of the ninth, Ortquist and Adams were both safe on errors. Ron Wetherbee then delivered a bunt single to load the bases. Arthur "Swede" Olson then took his place in the batter's box and was equal to the task. His sharp single drove in the winning run and made Vander Lind the winning pitcher.

As the second game got under way both teams were suffering from overworked pitchers. The combination of regularly scheduled games and make-up doubleheaders accounted for the dilemma. Arnie Boeve started for Hope and held his own, but at some point in the game he moved to his more familiar spot in right field. He was replaced by Stout, who went the rest of the way. Stout also collected two singles in Hope's seven-hit attack. In his last contest as a Hope College athlete, Adams scored three of the Dutchmen's 10 runs. The final tally of Hope 10, Olivet 2, closed the season on a positive note. The overall record of 8-6-1 afforded yet another winning season, and Hope's 7-6 MIAA record was good enough for a third place finish behind champion Alma and Albion. In a team meeting Ortquist was voted most valuable player and Woodcock was named captain-elect for 1957. The team of 1956 had done its part in maintaining a noble tradition.

* * *

MIAA golf had been initiated in 1934 with Hope winning the first championship under the direction of Milton "Bud" Hinga.

There followed a 13-year drought before Coach Albert Timmer brought home another title in 1947. More lean years followed but now, in 1956, Coach Timmer was again in charge, hoping to find the right combination. There were numerous candidates in early try-outs, but when the dust had cleared, Timmer's team included Ray De Does, Bill Kramer, Bill Holt, Bob Burwitz, and Joe Martin, with Bill Sandahl as alternate. Hope opened the season by hosting Grand Rapids Junior College at the Saugatuck course. Kramer took medalist honors with a 76, thereby defeating JC's Frank Skestone 2½-½. De Does defeated Jim Kudiack (JC) 3-0, Slack (JC) defeated Bob Burwitz 3-0, Holt defeated Arnie Junewjck (JC) 2½-½, and Martin defeated Marvin Jacoby (JC) 2-1. In an extra match Carole Lee Evertse, JC's first female golfer, was paired with Hope's Sandahl. Each team was given 1½ points for the exhibition, making the final score, Hope 10, GRJC 5.

Hope traveled to Kalamazoo on Tuesday, April 17, with an understandable lack of enthusiasm. Temperatures hovered around the freezing mark and high winds dusted the Milham Park course with occasional snow. But once on the course, players on both sides made the best of the unwelcome conditions. De Does and Kalamazoo's Skip Marx had decent rounds with 79's and tied for medalist honors. In the overall scoring De Does defeated Hornet quarterback Bob Urshalitz 3-0. Skip Marks (K) defeated Kramer 2½-½. Holt (H) defeated Schram 2½-½. Basketball guard Bob Fletcher (K) defeated Martin 2-1, and Burwitz was beaten 3-0 to give Kalamazoo the narrow 8-7 victory.

Hope's next MIAA encounter took place on Friday, April 27, against a talented Hillsdale team at the Saugatuck course. Kramer had his best day of the season carding a 73 to take medalist honors, but his efforts were not enough to prevent the Dales from taking the match 10½ to 4½. Low man for Hillsdale was Jim Sennet with a 76 to defeat Holt 3-0. Several matches were decided on the last one or two holes. Kramer (H) defeated Wimer 2-1, King (HI) defeated De Does 2-1, Grossfuss (HI) defeated Burwitz 2-1, and Schlander (HI) defeated Martin 2½-½.

The Dutchmen played well again on Tuesday, May 1, at the Duck Lake course, but they were up against defending champion Albion. Four of five Britons shot in the low 70's and the fifth came in with an 80. Nienhaus (A) defeated De Does 3-0, Kramer (H) defeated Bell 3-0, Tom Ochsner (A) defeated Holt 2½-½, Fox (A) defeated Burwitz 3-0, and Wilson (A) defeated Martin 3-0, making the final score Albion 11½, Hope 3½.

Back home at Saugatuck on Friday, May 4, the Dutchmen took out their frustrations on hapless Adrian. The Bulldogs faced a season with a dearth of polished golfers on campus but, in keeping with the best MIAA tradition, fielded a team anyway. All of Coach Timmer's charges played well and this added to the Adrian woes. De Does and Kramer tied for medalist honors with 75's, Holt followed with a 76, Burwitz had an 88, and diminutive Sandahl, in his first official match, also shot an 88. Don Hoffman was low man for Adrian at 104. In the overall scoring Kramer defeated Hartung 3-0, De Does defeated Don Hoffman 3-0, Holt defeated Streib 3-0, Burwitz defeated Kieler 3-0, and Sandahl defeated Evans 3-0 to give Hope the 15-0 shutout.

The good news continued on Monday, May 7, at the Blythefield Country Club in Grand Rapids. In a tri-match Hope defeated Calvin 12-3 and Grand Rapids Junior College 8½-6½. In the Calvin match Kramer (H) defeated Wiedenaur 2-1, De Does (H) defeated Brusser 3-0, Holt (H) defeated Brasser 3-0, Swoot (C) defeated Martin 2-1, and Burwitz (H) defeated Schneider 3-0. The JC match-up was a different story. JC's Frank Skestone was medalist with a 77 and the outcome hung in the balance until Hope's Burwitz sank a 12' putt on the final hole. Skestone (JC) defeated Kramer 2-1, De Does (H) tied Salik 1½-1½, Holt (H) defeated Hudiak 3-0, Jurewick (JC) defeated Martin 2-1 and Burwitz (H) defeated Schneider 3-0.

An hour-long rain on Friday, May 11, left Alma's Pine River Club course soggy at best, but the match was played as scheduled. De Does took medalist honors with a 75 and thereby defeated Bob Rudisell 3-0. Bill Kramer (80) and Joe Martin (86), also had shutout victories, but Bill Holt had to settle for an 89 and Bob Burwitz ballooned to 100. Under the conditions the Dutchmen were happy to travel home with a 9-6 victory.

Hope notched its second shutout of the season on Tuesday, May 15, at the Saugatuck course against Olivet. The Comets' two top men played well. Byrel Triggs and Burton Columbus each had 78's, but Hope's De Does was medalist with a 75 and Kramer followed with a 76. In addition, Burwitz recorded an 86, Holt an 89, and Sandahl a 95. In the overall match-ups De Does (H) defeated Triggs 3-0, Kramer (H) defeated Columbus 3-0, Burwitz (H) defeated King 3-0, Holt (H) defeated Tyll 3-0, and Sandahl (H) defeated Pomeroy 3-0 to complete the 15-0 team sweep.

The Dutchmen appeared to be ready for the MIAA tournament at the Kalamazoo Country Club on the weekend of May 18-19, but the competition proved to be tougher than in recent outings. Albion, as anticipated, captured its seventh straight title with Hillsdale in second, Alma third, Hope fourth, Kalamazoo fifth, Adrian sixth, Calvin seventh, and Olivet eighth. Kalamazoo's Dan Winterhalter took medalist honors with a two-day total of 154 (76-78).

* * *

Professor John Van Ingen, interim replacement for Ken Weller in business administration, also agreed to assume Weller's tennis coaching responsibilities in the spring of 1956. Weller's '55 team had made a fine showing in finishing second to perennial champion Kalamazoo, but many stalwarts had graduated and John Jeltes remained as the only experienced squad member. Undaunted, Van Ingen managed to put together a team that was off to a flying start. Included, in addition to Jeltes, were Phil Boersma, Dwayne "Tiger" Teusink of the basketball team, Jim Remmelts, Bob Saunders, and Harry Voss, who had performed at quarterback the previous fall.

Hope met Calvin at the 13th Street courts on Friday, April 20. Six of the 10 players involved were either from Holland High or Holland Christian. Playing at number one singles, John Jeltes (H) defeated Rich Sharda 6-2, 6-0. Phil Boersma (H) defeated Paul Dykema 6-1, 6-2, Duane Teusink (H) defeated Jim Kok (basketball forward) 6-2, 6-4, Jim Remmelts (H) defeated Roger Boer 2-6, 8-6, 6-3, and William Kooistra (C) defeated Harry Voss 8-6, 6-4. In doubles Jeltes-Boersma (H) defeated Sharda-Dykema 6-0, 6-3, and Teusink-Remmelts (H) defeated Kok-Boer 6-8, 6-4, 6-2, giving the new coach a 6-1 victory in the season opener.

On the following Tuesday, Hope took on the Raiders from Grand Rapids Junior College in another home match. The going proved tougher this time around, but the Dutchmen again prevailed. John Jeltes (H) downed Dave Berles (7-5, 6-1, Phil Boersma (H) defeated Bill Grieg 6-1, 6-2,

Juris Sliede (JC) defeated Tiger Teusink 3-6, 6-2, 6-3, Jim Remmelts (H) defeated Dick Irwin 6-0, 6-0, Ron Spaeth (JC) defeated Bob Saunders 6-4, 8-6, and Harry Voss (H) defeated Gordon Tolodziecki 6-1, 6-0. In doubles Berles-Grieg (JC) defeated Jeltes-Boersma 2-6, 6-3, 6-4, Teusink-Remmelts (H) defeated Sliede-Irwin 3-6, 6-3, 7-5, and Saunders-Voss (H) defeated Spaeth-Tolodziecki 6-0, 6-1. The teams had been evenly matched with three three-setters and the Dutchmen were understandably pleased with the hard-earned 6-3 win.

Rain on April 27 forced postponement of the Saturday match, but the courts dried up by Monday as Hope hosted Alma. The Dutch continued to roll as Jeltes (H) defeated Bob Darbee 6-2, 6-4, Boersma (H) defeated Bob Danforth 7-5, 1-6, 9-7, Teusink (H) defeated Harry Andreason (A) 6-3, 10-8, Remmelts (H) defeated Dick Wallace 6-1, 6-3, and Bob Saunders (H) defeated Jerry Schubel 6-2, 6-3. In doubles Jeltes-Boersma (H) got the best of Darbee-Andreason 6-2, 4-6, 6-3, and Teusink-Remmelts (H) defeated Danforth-Jim Ford 6-3, 6-1 for the 7-0 team victory.

The Hope College women's tennis team took the spotlight briefly on Wednesday, May 2, when they traveled to Kalamazoo to take on the team from Western Michigan College (later Western Michigan University). Coach Mary Louise Breid was a tennis enthusiast and was effective in passing along her knowledge of the game. As a result, the Hope women were well prepared for the "Lady Broncos." In number one singles Alice Warren (H) defeated Holtz 6-3, 6-3, Janice Evert (H) defeated Noorman 6-3, 0-6, 6-2, Donna Hardenberg (H) defeated Thomson 8-6, 6-3, Fauch (W) defeated Joyce Leighley 6-2, 7-5, and Kerr of Western defeated Mary Kay Diephuis (H) 6-1, 8-6. In doubles Hardenberrg-Leighley (H) defeated Thomas-Berry 3-6, 6-4, 8-6, and Van Valkenburg-Wienke (W) defeated Betty Burnett-Mary Kay Diephuis 6-1, 8-6. The 4-3 Hope victory furnished proof that a tennis match could be won in the city of Kalamazoo-but not very often!

The men's scheduled matches with Adrian, Olivet, Wayne State, and Hillsdale were all postponed and eventually canceled due to rain. The Dutchmen might have hoped for rain on Thursday, May 3, when the Kalamazo Hornets came to town, but the weather was fair and Hope suffered a 7-0 shutout at the hands of Les Dodson and company.

Saturday, May 12, was also a clear day in Holland with Albion as Hope's opponent. Things began on a high note as John Jeltes (H) defeated Dale Brubaker 6-1, 6-0, and Phil Boersma (H) downed Bill Johnson 6-1, 6-0. It was Albion's turn next as Don Hines (A) defeated Tiger Teusink 4-6, 6-3, 6-0, and Gary Riley (A) downed Jim Remmelts in another three-setter, 2-6, 6-1, 6-3, but Hope's fortunes soared when Harry Voss (H) got the best of Don Malton 6-3, 6-2. In a hard-fought number one doubles match Brubaker-Hines (A) defeated Jeltes-Boersma 6-4, 5-7, 7-5. Johnson-Riley (A) then took Teusink-Remmelts 6-1, 6-0 to give the Britons the 4-3 team victory.

The weekend of May 18-19 was designated MIAA Field Day in Kalamazoo and the tennis tournament extended over both days. Saturday, May 19, was a red-letter day for Kalamazoo's coach, Dr. Allen B. Stowe. As expected, the Hornets captured their 21st MIAA Championship, the last 17 coming in-a-row. The fabled coach chose 1956 as the year to step down. An annual sportsmanship award is named in his honor, and Kalamazoo's state-of-the-art tennis stadium also bears his name. Hope's John Jeltes played well in the tourney, but was eliminated in the quarterfinals, 6-2, 6-1 by Dean Pinechaff of Kalamazoo. Hope managed a fourth-place finish behind Kalamazoo, Hillsdale, and Albion. Kalamazoo's Les Dodson won the singles title.

* * *

As coach Larry Green began the 1956 track season, he was well aware that depth would be a problem if the Dutchmen were to move up from their '55 second-place finish. Green had little choice but to rely on his "big four" as the main point getters: captain John De Vries in the pole vault and broad jump, Paul Wiegerink in the hurdles and dashes, Jim Hilmert in the hurdles, discus, high jump, and javelin, and Dave Spaan in the 440, 220, and mile relay. The temptation was ever present to spread such talent over too many events. Herb Widmer and Carroll Bennink showed promise in the distance runs as did Larry Ter Molen in the shot. Others would contribute, depending on specific match-ups with the opposition.

Hope's only home meet of the season took place on Tuesday, April 24, at Holland High's cinder track on 22nd Street. Coach Dave Tuuk was building a track program at Calvin College and was somewhat accustomed to limited facilities. The Knights were strong in the field events and swept the discus and javelin, but Hope took 11 of 15 firsts enroute to a 75-55 opening win. An injury to captain De Vries kept the junior from competing, but Wiegerink took up the slack by taking firsts in the high hurdles, low hurdles, and 100 yard dash, as well as a tie for first in the broad jump. In addition to Wiegerink's 19 point performance, Spaan won both the 440 and 220, and Hilmert won the high jump, tied Wiegerink for first in the broad jump, and took second in the high hurdles. Other firsts for Hope included Widmer in the mile, Bennink in the two-mile, and Ter Molen in the shot put. Calvin had no entries in the pole vault. Dave Kuyers and Dick De Freese of Hope then made the opening height of 8' 6" (!), thereby claiming a tie for first place. Curt Menning placed second in the 880, and third in the high jump, while Widmer had a second in the two-mile behind Bennink. Vander Griend of Calvin won the discus and Van Hofwegen took first in the javelin. Calvin also won the 880 and the mile relay. Performances generally were not good, but this could be attributed to the early season and the unsettled condition of the track. Doc Green however, was more than satisfied with the final score.

Hope's next "home" meet was conducted at the Allegan High School track. Allegan football coach Dick Higgs (Hope '48) and later Clair De Mull (Hope '50) acted as facilitators. The Albion Britons of coach Elkin Isaac came to Allegan on Tuesday, May 1, and were grateful not only for the shortened trip, but also for the solid cinder track. In the '50s many tracks were laid out with a 220 straightaway in front of the home team stands. Allegan's fine facility followed this pattern. In such cases the 440-yard dash was usually run around one turn with the finish at the end of the backstretch.

After winning titles in '54 and '55 Ike Isaac's team was again loaded with fine performers and plenty of depth. Competition was keen as the Britons had eight firsts to seven for Hope, but depth made the difference in the 82-49 Albion victory. Albion's John Leppi edged Wiegerink in the high hurdles, but the defeat only spurred Wiegerink to a greater effort in capturing the 220 lows with a new Hope College record of 24.0. The old record by Don Martin had been in place since 1937. Wiegerink was also first in the 100-yard dash. Hilmert was first in the discus, tied for first in the high jump with Menning, and managed a third in the high hurdles, broad jump, and shot put. De Vries, recovering from a foot injury, took second in the broad jump and pole vault, while Widmer came in second in the mile run. Albion's splendid Jim Taup, ahead of his time in distance running, won both, the mile and two-mile. The Britons closed out their victory by winning the mile relay.

Hope's meet at Hillsdale on Saturday, May 5, was a back and forth affair that proved to be the most exciting of the season. The Dales dominated the field events, scoring 42½ to Hope's 11½. Prospects were grim until Wiegerink took over in his specialties. Timers in the high hurdles were astounded when their watches showed his winning time to be 14.1! A hurried review revealed that the course was 10 yards short of the required 120, but the victory stood and Paul moved on to a very legitimate 10.1 win in the 100. He also won the low hurdle race and tied for second in the broad jump. Spaan took the 440 in 51.9 and the 220 in 23.4, but it was Hope's distance crew that made the difference on this day. Widmer and Bennink went 1-2 in both the mile and two-mile, while Menning, Fred Leaske, and Ron Den Uyl combined for a sweep of the 880. Hilmert took first in the high jump and second in the high hurdles, Ter Molen was second in the shot and Blaine Timmer chipped in with a third in the pole vault. But as the meet came down to its final event, the score stood at 65½ for Hope, 60½ for Hillsdale. Hope would need a victory in the mile relay to prevent a 65½-65½ tie. Based on the day's performances, Coach Green chose Menning, Widmer, Spaan, and Wiegerink to do the job. Hillsdale's track was somewhat short of the standard 440 yards and the race was actually a 4/5 mile relay. Hope's winning time of 2:45.6 was of course meaningless, but the victory gave Hope the meet by a score of 70½ to 60½.

Hope and Kalamazoo each came halfway for a dual meet at Allegan on Tuesday, May 8. Never was the value of Hope's "Big Four" more in evidence. Versatile Hilmert led the way with 21 points as he took first in the discus, tied for first in the high jump, and took seconds in the high hurdles, broad jump, shot put, and javelin. Wiegerink was close behind with firsts in the high hurdles, low hurdles, and 100-yard dash, and third in the broad jump for 16 points. His high hurdle time of 15.5 was equal to the standing MIAA record. De Vries, now recovered from a foot injury, placed first in the broad jump and javelin, and second in the pole vault, for 13 points. Spaan had good times in winning the 440 in 51.0 and the 220 in 22.9. He also ran a leg on the winning relay team for a total of 11½ points. Hope's other first place came with Ter Molen's 41' 2" shot put. In addition, Widmer had seconds in both the mile and two-mile. Hope's team effort included valuable third-place points from Pete Bylenga in the 100 and 220, Den Uyl in the 880, and Carl Coates in the low hurdles. The winning Dutch mile relay team was composed of Jack Walchenbach, Menning, Den Uyl, and Spaan. Their time of 3:40.8 was good enough to put the finishing touch on the 86-44 victory. Kalamazoo's Dick Ehrle won the mile and two-mile.

For a change of pace, Doc Green entered a few of his outstanding performers in the prestigious Elmhurst Relays on Saturday, May 12. Elmhurst College, on Chicago's west side, had hosted the meet for several years and entries were not limited to small schools. Most of the spectators had never heard of Hope College, but before the afternoon was over they were interested. Wiegerink was the center of attention as he breezed to a first-place win in the high hurdles in 15.2, his best time of the year. He also won the 220 low hurdles in 24.2 and took fourth in the 100-yard dash with the fine time of 10.0. During the course of the afternoon he ran six races including preliminaries, and was the winner of five. Dave Spaan won the 440 and placed fifth in the 220, while Hilmert was third in the high hurdles at 15.4 and tied for third in the high jump at 5' 10". Hope placed fourth in the team standings with 23 points. The meet winner was the University of Dubuque, Iowa.

Hope's last dual meet of the season took place on Tuesday, May 15, at the Allegan track. Alma furnished the opposition, but the Dutchmen were in charge all the way in posting a 93-38 victory. Wiegerink again led the way with firsts in his specialities, the high hurdles, low hurdles, and 100-yard dash. Hope's 880 men swept the event with Den Uyl, Menning, and Fred Leaske, in that order. Another sweep occurred in the high jump with Hilmert, Menning, and Spence Weersing. De Vries won the javelin with a throw of 149' 10", then shared first place in the pole vault with teammate Timmer, and did the same in the broad jump with Gray of Alma. Widmer won the mile and, by design, tied for first

HOPE'S BIG FOUR IN 1956

Paul Wiegerink

Jim Hilmert

Captain John De Vries

Dave Spaan

in the two-mile with teammate Bennink. Spaan, suffering a let-down after the Elmhurst meet, finished second in the 440 and third in the 220. Ter Molen took second in the shot put and Bylenga beat out Spaan for second in the 220. Hope's winning mile relay team included Menning, Den Uyl, Leaske, and Spaan. Coach Green now felt that his team was as prepared as it could be for the upcoming conference meet.

On Saturday, May 19, the Dutchmen headed for Kalamazoo and the MIAA championship meet. All were aware that Albion was in the driver's seat, but good performances, upsets, and records were always possible. The Dutchmen however, experienced a disappointing morning. DeVries was not in top form and Hope was able to score but two points in the field events. Things picked up in the afternoon with the running events. Many would agree that the race of the day took place with the running of the finals in the 120-yard high hurdles. As a freshman Wiegerink had been the winner in a one-two-three finish for Hope, but in their dual meet on May 1 Albion's Leppi had edged Wiegerink. Now, in the blocks, all eyes were on this duo. But Hilmert, before a hometown crowd, was especially inspired, and in the race of his career edged teammate Wiegerink at the tape. Leppi finished third. Hilmert's time of 15.4 was a new MIAA record, the only one of the day. The mark broke a 19-year-old record set by Hope's Don Martin in 1937 and tied in 1950 by Mel Reed of Kalamazoo. Wiegerink followed his second-place finish with a 10.3 for first in the 100-yard dash. Later, his winning time in the 220 lows was 24.3, a new Angell Field record. Spaan won the 440 dash in 51.1 and placed third in the 220. Herb Widmer placed second in the mile with a time of 4:33.2, his best of the year, and was fifth in the two-mile. Hilmert had ended up in an unusual five-way tie for first place in the high jump, and Hope's relay team ended the day with silver medals. The final team tally showed powerful Albion again the champion with 92$\frac{1}{7}$ points. Hope was nearly 50 points behind with 42$\frac{9}{14}$ but managed to hang on to second place. It would be the highest finish of any Hope sports team during the '55-'56 school year.

In a post script to the season, coach Green took nine of his squad to the third annual John Bos Relays. The meet was held on the evening of Saturday, May 26 at Houseman Field in Grand Rapids. I watched from the stands with a special interest as Paul Wiegerink pleased a hometown crowd with a double victory, 15.3 in the high hurdles and 10.2 in the 100-yard dash. Throughout the season "Wigs" had taken on this difficult double without complaint. The two races were back-to-back in the order of events with but 10 minutes between for recovery time. It was also a homecoming of sorts for Dave Spaan (Grand Rapids Ottawa Hills), Larry Ter Molen (Grand Rapids Central), and Curt Menning (Grand Rapids Lee). Spaan captured first in the 440, Menning tied for first in the high jump and took fourth in the 880, and Ter Molen was second in the shot put.

* * *

Albion won the 1955-56 race for the MIAA All-Sports Trophy with 75 points, Kalamazoo had 67, Hillsdale 62, Hope 55, Alma 51, Calvin 46, Adrian 25, and Olivet 11. Russ De Vette had come back to a solid program at Hope College. His presence would make it even stronger. The "return of the native" had produced no championships, but able performers and exciting contests were harbingers of things to come.

The 1956-57 school year would offer a new challenge with De Vette taking over as head man in three sports: football, basketball, and baseball.

CHAPTER 2

JOINING UP

Most of us can point to a chain of circumstances which, more than others, shaped our future. In the spring of 1956 I was not fully aware of the events at my *alma mater* as just described. Employed by the Kelloggsville Public Schools in Grand Rapids, Mich., I was enjoying my eighth year as a high school teacher and coach. It was in the midst of the track season that I received a call from Athletics Director Al Vanderbush informing me of an opening in the Department of Physical Education at Hope College. The position to be filled was that of assistant professor and head track coach. Also included would be duty as an assistant football coach and J.V. basketball coach. Vanderbush said he was offering me the post with the approval of President Irwin J. Lubbers and, asked that I give it serious consideration.

Perhaps the dream of most young educators is to one day return to their educational roots, to that place where a life's vocation was hammered out by able and caring mentors. To say that I was humbled and flattered by the offer would be an understatement, yet decisions involving family livelihood are not entered into lightly. The Kelloggsville school system was well administered by a responsible Board of Education, and especially by Superintendent Russell "Rud" Formsma. The latter had assembled a faculty of young men and women in their late 20's or early 30's who had done their undergraduate work at a variety of schools, Michigan, Michigan State, Hope, Calvin, Western Michigan, Eastern Michigan, and Central Michigan. It had proven to be a harmonious mix, and with the quiet but firm leadership of Formsma morale was extremely high. My coordinated classes in U.S. history and American literature were rewarding, with coaching football or track at day's end a welcome change. High school principal Bob Fry was also a positive influence, as was his junior high counterpart, Frank Hunnes. Salaries were moderate for the time, but increases were automatic and always fully explained.

As wife Lorraine and I pondered pros and cons, my high school track season was in progress. On a late afternoon following practice I was replacing equipment when a familiar figure approached from across the field. I soon recognized Mr. Ekdal J. Buys, Sr., Hope Class of '37. Ek Buys was by this time a successful and well-known investment broker in the area. He was also a leading churchman and booster of Hope College. He would become president of the college's Board of Trustees in 1961. Respected in all quarters, he was a most effective ambassador for the school. His mission this day was to encourage my acceptance of the Hope position. His counsel at this juncture was a strong factor in our eventual decision to return to Hope.

The school year was closed out with mixed emotions. Goodbyes are seldom easy. To this day I return to Kelloggsville for retired faculty reunions twice each year. My final act as a high school coach occurred on the night of May 26, 1956, at Houseman Field. My track team was entered in the John Bos Relays. As my charges warmed up in the backstretch, they were garbed in navy and orange sweatsuits. Ironically, alongside them were several young men, larger in stature, with almost identical warm-ups, the orange and blue of Hope College. This would be my first look at Wiegerink, Hilmert, Spaan, Ter Molen, and company, and what lay ahead.

In the final days of the school calender we attended a Hope College faculty picnic at the invitation of Russ and Doris De Vette. The picnic, scheduled for Kollen Park, was forced inside by rain. We met the YMCA-YWCA room in the basement of the Hope Chapel to a welcome both warm and genuine. Several of my former professors were now colleagues and I experienced the awkwardness of using first names with those much revered. In due time we would feel at ease in this new setting. House hunting in Holland was considerably eased by the efforts of Arie Weller, father of Ken Weller. In retirement Mr. Weller dabbled somewhat in real estate and soon found us a brown and cream ranch home on Holland's undeveloped but growing north side. During the summer months our Grand Rapids home was sold and moving day arrived. Members of my Kelloggsville football squad volunteered to do the heavy work and loaded my Hertz rental truck. As I drove away their young faces receded in the rear view mirror. With a huge lump in my throat I realized that a chapter had closed.

* * *

Our new address was, for some months, quite a novelty. We moved in at 465 Rifle Range Road. Two blocks west of our home could be found the abandoned site of a rifle range formerly used by the Holland Company of the Michigan National Guard. For several months our two small boys had a picnic collecting empty shell casings and other military paraphernalia, but developers, fearing a "war zone" perception, soon changed the street name to the more sedate "Rose Park Drive." It would be our place of residence for the next 22 years.

On Hope's campus, the newly renovated Carnegie-Schouten Gymnasium was home to the Department of Physical Education. On the main floor at the west end of the building, a classroom had been fashioned. It was bright and cheery, but ventilation was not the best. The four-person department found office space in various corners of the venerable structure. Mary Breid was sole tenant of the upper floor, with a bathroom and some storage space adjacent to her office. Male members were relegated to the basement. Chairman Larry Green had an office in the building's southwest corner, while Russ De Vette made room for me in his adjacent office. The rust-colored tile floor gave way to cinder block walls painted light green in combination with sections of glass brick.

In this somewhat spartan setting I received indoctrination in the secrets of the "Winged-T" system of offensive football. I was soon to become fascinated with the strong points of this formation and its wide range of possibilities. This is not a football textbook and too many details will certainly send the reader scurrying for lighter fare, but a brief summary of this pattern of offense will perhaps add meaning to various maneuvers in game descriptions yet to come.

The Winged-T formation was the brain child of Dave Nelson, longtime coach and athletics director at the University of Delaware. It was an outgrowth of his playing days at the University of Michigan under Coach Fritz Crisler, who

THE BEGINNING
The author in the fall of 1956 – Enthused and ready to go

enjoyed great success with the single wing formation. Nelson's objective was to combine the best features of the single wing with the now more popular "T" formation. A strength of the Michigan system had been the use of double-team and trap blocking in the line. In "laymanese" this meant simply that two offensive linemen blocked against one defensive lineman at the point where the team meant to run the ball. At the same time, an offensive teammate, usually a guard, would pull out from his position, run parallel behind the line, and block out on the next defensive man as he attempted to penetrate. Nelson retained this as a basic part of his procedure. The quarterback was positioned under center in conventional "T" formation style while one halfback usually lined up behind and just outside the end thus becoming the "wing" of the winged T. The fullback was directly behind the quarterback and the remaining halfback behind the tackle. The quarterback, of course, was the key person in the attack, in contrast to the "triple threat" tailback of the single wing system. I would soon learn that variations of this basic set were almost limitless. The large number of plays thus generated was not as confusing as one might expect. For the most part, linemen needed to be concerned only with the runner's point of attack along the line and the fact of pass or punt. As line coach I was grateful for any

1956 KICKOFF DINNER - JULIANA ROOM, DURFEE HALL
Top Row L. to R.: Sophomore tackle Larry Ter Molen, Junior end Paul Wiegerink, and senior Captain and fullback Dave Kuyers. **Seated L. to R.:** Assistant coaches Gordon Brewer, Al Vanderbush, Ken Waller, and head coach Russ De Vette.

simplification that would allow more time for the teaching of fundamentals.

I had a great deal to learn about football defense. High school coaches generally are overwhelmed with teaching an offense and with time limitations. The result is that defense is short-changed. Basics are taught, but real strategy and finesse go begging. Such an approach would not be adequate in college coaching, even at the small college level. Coach De Vette's grasp of what opposing teams were trying to do was extraordinary. His ability to see the "big picture," and the analysis of same, made it possible to effectively marshall his own defensive forces. Carrying out such strategies is, of course, another matter, but to teach the required skills, now at a new level, was an exciting challenge. My enthusiasm mounted in those last days of August as the season approached.

During the week preceding the first practice, the coaching staff was busy in the lower level of Carnegie-Schouten Gymnasium. Lockers were assigned and equipment placed in each. A fulltime equipment manager was as yet unknown, but the usual student managers would arrive with the team. By mid-afternoon on Friday, Aug. 31, squad members began to filter in. This coming together of young men in their prime is always a time of exhilaration for coaches. Past failures and disapointments are blotted out by the great promise of this team in the season just ahead. An undefeated season, why not!

The group of returnees included 19 letterwinners led by senior fullback Dave Kuyers, a unanimous choice for captain. The picture was further brightened by 18 freshmen and transfer Don Paarlberg from the University of Illinois. Al Vanderbush again agreed to assist with the coaching and Ken Weller would be available for some of the early sessions. Weller's main function would be to scout Hope's various opponents. Such trips could be made from his post in Ann Arbor as he continued graduate studies at the University of Michigan. At 6:30 p.m. on the 31st, players and coaches assembled in the Juliana Room of Durfee Hall for the opening dinner. Amidst the usual instructions, Hope's strong finish in 1955 was recalled and unbridled optimism was the order of the day. There was some concern when it was learned that strong-armed John Holmlund had elected not to come out for the team and that guard Blaine Timmer had received an appointment to the U.S. Naval Academy, but newcomers vowed to take up the slack.

Two-a-day practices began at 9 a.m. on Saturday, Sept. 1, and continued until classes began after Labor Day. A few days into the sessions Dave Woodcock complained of severe leg pains. A thorough examination revealed a spinal condition, congenital in nature. Paralysis could result from overextension or a severe blow. With great reluctance, Woodcock accepted the doctor's advice to give up football. His departure was felt keenly by the coaches who had been deeply impressed with his '55 performance.

Hope's opening game would be played on Saturday, Sept. 23, in Tiffin, Ohio, against Heidelberg College. The Student Princes had handed the Dutchmen a 28-7 defeat in 1955 enroute to a 9-0 season and the championship of the Ohio Athletic Conference. Coach Paul Hoerneman's 10-year record now stood at 74-10-4. De Vette put his charges through a workout under the lights at Riverview Park on Thursday night, then tapered off somewhat on Friday. Budget considerations dictated that the 29-man traveling squad leave at 7:30 a.m. on Saturday for the 8 p.m. game. The Heidelberg team was "riding the crest" and 3,500 fans turned out for the evening contest. There was consensus among long-time Hope followers that this would be the toughest opener in the history of Hope College football. Accepting the challenge, the Dutchmen kept the crowd quiet throughout a scoreless first period. On the final play of the quarter, Kuyers broke loose on a patented 45-yard run that ended on the Heidelberg two. The defense stiffened, but on the third play Kuyers bulled into the end zone. His kick attempt failed, but Hope held an unexpected 6-0 lead. The Dutchmen continued to do good things on defense as Jack Faber intercepted a pass on the Heidelberg 21. Unable to move the ball late in the second quarter, Hope was forced to punt. Things began to unravel when the snap from center was fumbled and the Student Princes recovered. Eight plays later fullback Jim Previte plunged in from the one. Dave Dow converted to give Heidelberg a narrow 7-6 halftime lead.

Coach Hoerneman's charges wasted little time in taking over the game in the second half. All-American Walt Livingston received Hope's kickoff and returned it to his own 48. On the next play the speedy back got behind Hope defenders and took a pass from quarterback Bryan Powers that covered 52 yards. The scoring play gave the home team momentum that was never really surrendered. Dow added the conversion to make it 14-6. Next it was Bill Groman, who returned a Dutch punt to the Hope 18. After moving his team to the six, Bryan Powers scored on a bootleg. Faber broke through to block Dow's kick, leaving the score at 20-6. There was more bad luck for the Dutchmen when Cal Dilworth intercepted a pass on the Hope 40 and returned it to the 23. Running plays advanced he ball to the 10, where sub quarterback Jim Grunden scored on the second bootleg of the night. Dow's kick made it 27-6 at the end of the third quarter. Hope's offense sputtered, forcing surrender of the ball and enabling Grunden to once again move his team to the Hope 10. Chuck Scheid eventually scored from the two, and Dow's kick increased the margin to 34-6.

Hope's kickoff return to the 39 finally ignited the Dutch offense, The resulting 61-yard drive was climaxed when Pete Watt went one yard off-tackle for the score. Watt's try for the point was wide of the mark, leaving the score at 34-12. An exchange of punts favored the home team and the weary Dutchmen were unable to prevent yet another score. From the Hope 23, Grunden, on a keeper play, was dragged down at the three. Walt Livingston scored on the next play and Frey's conversion left the final score at 41-12.

As the Hope staff looked ahead to the next encounter, prospects were grim. The Dutchmen had not only suffered a resounding defeat, but had taken a physical beating as well. Kuyers had suffered a badly sprained ankle while his back-up, Gene Van Dongen, had sustained a mild concussion and would be out for a week. Halfback Mert Vander Lind had a badly bruised hip, and Faber was also hobbling. Hope's home opener would be with Wabash College of Crawfordsville, Ind. It would be the first meeting in a long series between the two schools. Coach Garland Frazier, now in his sixth season, had posted a 5-3-1 record in 1955, but his 1956 aggregation appeared to be on a par with Heidelberg. In the previous week's contest the Little Giants had downed Albion 26-7.

More than 3,000 Hope faithfuls turned out for the night game at Riverview Park on Sept. 29. Coach De Vette was forced to make a number of changes due to the rash of injuries. Earl Welling, a hometown product, would start at fullback. Welling had never played high school ball, but had some experience while in the service. Faber had recovered sufficiently to fill in at left half, while Pete Watt would start at right half. None of the three had ever started a game. Harry Voss, at quarterback, was the only regular. Freshman Ron Siebling of Kohler, Wis., was now the first line replacement at fullback. De Vette also decided to shift Jerry Hendrickson from end to right halfback, a move that would pay off during the remainder of the season.

Wabash College, with an official enrollment of 600 men, had channeled the most talented onto the football squad. This night they would attempt only eight passes, but three would be for long touchdowns. Midway in the first quarter, Vic Lodovisi returned a Welling punt to the Hope 40. Eleven plays later the Little Giants reached paydirt for the game's first score. Tom Hankinson, attempting a halfback pass, fumbled the ball, chased the bouncing ball, picked it up and fired a completion to Bill Gabbert on the Hope three. Hankinson scored on the next play. Vic Lodovisi passed to end Bob Allen for the point-after to give Wabash a 7-0 lead at the end of the first quarter. Hope would attempt 29 passes in the contest, with 18 failing to reach their mark. In the second period Lodovisi picked off a Voss pass on his own 15 and returned it to the Hope 43. The Wabash drive included a 21-yard dash off tackle by Hankinson and a four-yard touchdown sweep by Gabbert. Mike Monchan's kick was low, leaving the count at 13-0.

Hope's most glaring weakness seemed to be in secondary coverage. With seven minutes remaining in the half, Hankinson sped past Hope defenders to gather in a well-thrown ball from Lodovisi. The scoring play covered 51 yards. This time Mike Monchan's kick was good and the

Wabash lead was increased to 20-0. Still in the first half, Hope's woes continued. Center Dick Davoob recovered a Watt fumble on the Hope 34 and the visitors were on the march again. End Bob Allen took Lodovisi's pass to the two, where sub halfback Ron Bean went in for the score. Lodovisi's kick was not good, but the Little Giants were clearly in charge with a 26-0 lead at halftime.

In the third quarter tackle Matt Peelen recovered a Wabash fumble on their 23. Eight plays later Faber scored on an off-tackle play from the three and Watt converted to make it 26-7. Quarterback Voss suffered a knee injury during this series and was forced to leave the game. In the fourth quarter Lodovisi lofted a pass to Hankinson, who once again got behind Hope defenders and scored on the 53-yard play. Lodovisi's kick increased the margin to 33-7. The Little Giants would strike one more time. With 2:43 left in the game reserve quarterback Harold Travola passed to Gabbert in the end zone. Mort Grayam kicked the final point, and the visitors returned to Crawfordsville with a decisive 40-7 victory.

On Saturday, Oct. 6, the Dutchmen traveled to Kalamazoo's Angell Field for the Hornets' Homecoming. The injury to Voss proved to be a torn ligament, and he would see little action for the remainder of the season. After being mauled by two non-league opponents, Hope looked forward to its first league encounter. An estimated 2,500 fans, many from Holland, turned out for this traditional battle for a pair of wooden shoes. Some of Hope's wounded were returning to the lineup, but Del Grissen would start at quarterback and Siebling at fullback. Despite a week of hard practice, the Dutchmen were off to a discouraging start. Jim Hilmert received the opening kick-off on the 30 and moved to the 35, but on the second play Hope lost possession on a fumble. Kazoo's Jim Smith then scored on an end sweep with the game but three minutes old. Tackle Rudy Wolchina made good on the extra point to give Rolla Anderson's men the early 7-0 lead. Hope proceeded to turn the ball over again a short time later as Bob Urshalitz intercepted a Grissen pass on the Hope 30. The Hornets moved into scoring position and fullback Bob Steward broke through from the 12 for the score. Alvira's kick was not good, but the Hornets were in good shape with a 13-0 lead. Still in the first quarter, Hope gained possession on its own 30. Vander Lind was now in the ball game at halfback, apparently recovered from an earlier hip injury. On a routine off-tackle play, he broke free, picked up an escort from end Paul Wiegerink, and streaked 70 yards for the touchdown. Watt's point-try failed, but Hope was on the board with the score at 13-6. Unfortunately, the momentum shift could not be sustained. In the second period a strong defensive effort by Kalamazoo forced the Dutchmen into a punting situation deep in their own territory. At this point tackle Jim Preston broke through to block Vander Lind's punt on the two-yard line. The Hornets' Ken Mossier fell on the ball in the end zone for his team's third score of the half. Rudy Wolchina's second conversion made it 20-6 at the intermission.

Hope mounted a threat in the third period by moving to the "K" 30, but loss of possession via a fumble squelched the drive. An aroused Hope defense now rose to the occasion and forced the Kazoo offense back to their own 25. Inspired by the defense, the Hope offense responded with a 65-yard drive led by Vander Lind. With a minute left in the quarter, Grissen's short pass was good to Watt, who made it to the end zone. The play covered 18 yards, but the all-important kick was again missed, this time by Vander Lind. With the score at 20-12 and a quarter remaining, the game was clearly up for grabs.

Following Hope's kickoff, the defense again did its job. On fourth down Dick Gantos and Gene Van Dongen combined to block the Kalamazoo punt with Gantos recovering on the 10. Watt then circled left end for his second TD of the afternoon. His second try for the extra point was like his first and the score was now 20-18. The Hornets now took over and marched the length of the field, but a fourth down pass from Urshalitz to Vic Landeryou was caught just outside the end zone. With one last chance late in the game Hope put together a 59-yard drive. Ends Hilmert and Wiegerink forced a "K" fumble and recovered on the Hope 35. Vander Lind went off-tackle for nine yards, then repeated the play for 28 more to the Kalamazoo 28.

Six plays later Hope was knocking at the door. With one minute to play, Coach De Vette was faced with fourth and one on the Kalamazoo six-yard line. Common sense dictated that the ball be given to the league's leading rusher, fullback Dave Kuyers. But Rolla Anderson surmised as much and his forward wall was equal to the task. Kuyers was stopped at the line of scrimmage and the Hornets had little to do but run out the clock. A great goal line stand and the educated toe of Rudy Wolchina had given the K men the 20-18 victory. The wooden shoes would remain in Kalamazoo for one more year.

After the two debilitating losses to outstate foes, Hope appeared to be on the way back, yet victory remained elusive. Monday-morning quarterbacks were busy as usual, but attention was diverted from Hope's woes on Oct. 8, when the New York Yankees' Don Larsen pitched the first perfect game in World Series history against the Brooklyn Dodgers. The picture of catcher Yogi Berra leaping into the arms of Larsen would become a classic in the lore of baseball aficionados. Meanwhile, the Dutchmen went back to work in preparation for homecoming on Saturday, Oct. 13. The homecoming opponent would be Adrian under first-year coach Bob Gillis. The Bulldogs were coming off a 9-6 squeaker over Alma and could see the 0-3 Dutchmen as their next victim. Hope coaches were pleasantly surprised when more than 4,000 fans filed into Riverview Park to witness the contest. Coach Gillis' offense was bolstered by two of the best ends in the conference. Big Leon Harper and Bob

DOWN TO DEFEAT

Jerry Hendrickson (84) scored both of Hope's touchdowns in the 1956 34-14 defeat at Hillsdale. With no set rule, Hillsdale elected to wear white at home. Hope wore orange jerseys with navy blue pants and helmets.

Orhman were both basketball players with good hands, Quarterback Ed Sadler wasted little time in going to Harper with a 30-yard scoring strike early in the first quarter. John Zupko's kick was good and Adrian seemed to be in charge at 7-0. But the Hope defense came up strong and the Bulldogs would not again enter Dutchmen territory for the remainder of the game! Hendrickson received the Adrian kickoff on the nine and returned it to the 47. Eleven plays later, Ron Wetherbee, playing his first game in two weeks, went off tackle for Hope's first TD. Watt's kick was not good and the Adrian lead was 7-6 at the end of the first quarter. With 2:20 gone in the second period, linebacker Van Dongen intercepted an Adrian pass on their 47 and advanced it to the 36. The Dutchmen were on the march again, and this time halfback Vander Lind went off-tackle for the score. Harper broke through to block the point attempt, but Hope held a halftime lead of 12-7.

The teams played on even terms for most of the third quarter, but with 2:10 remaining Paarlberg blocked Ohrman's punt. Tom Harris recovered for Hope on the Adrian two and Vander Lind went in for his second TD of the afternoon. Van Dongen's point try was wide of the mark and the Hope lead was now 18-7. With 2:10 gone in the final period, Van Dongen came up with his second interception of the day, this time on the Hope 47. Hope retained possession for 11 plays before Wetherbee scored from the two. Wetherbee closed out the scoring for the game with a running pass to end Wiegerink for the point-after. Hope's 25-7 victory pleased the large Homecoming crowd and gave the Dutch coaches reason to believe that they were now headed in the right direction.

The glow of victory faded somewhat during the following week with the realization that Hope's next opponent would be defending champion Hillsdale, now 5-0 on the season. Saturday, Oct. 20, was homecoming for the Dales, and a crowd of 4,500 was on hand. Coach Muddy Waters' powerhouse wasted little time in getting on the scoreboard. With six minutes gone, quarterback Bill Allinder hit halfback Walt Poe with a touchdown pass and John Moffat's kick made it 7-0. Three minutes later halfback Nate Clark reeled off a 64-yard TD scamper and Bill Dilbone converted to up the lead to 14-0. The Dutchmen countered by grinding out a 73-yard scoring drive of their own. In the 22-play march, no running play netted more than five yards. Four pass plays were interspersed for a total of 30 yards. Finally, with two minutes gone in the second quarter, Hendrickson crossed the goal line from the two. Watt's conversion was good, and with the score at 14-7 Hope was back in the ball game. Later in the period Hope's punt coverage broke down, allowing Howard Rogers to return the ball all the way to the Hope 10. The Dutchmen were tough up front, but on fourth down Allinder passed seven yards to end Andy Kincannon for the Dales' third score. John Moffat's point try was not good, but the Dales' halftime margin was a comfortable 20 to 7.

Midway in the third quarter Hope's punter fumbled the snap from center and the Dales recovered on the Dutch 27. The Dales quickly moved to the one, where Clark went in for his second score of the day. Moffat's kick was true, widening the lead to 27-7. During the course of the game, Coach Waters' defense was able to force the Dutchmen into a punting situation 10 times. This proved to be their undoing. With four minuutes remaining in the game, tackle Warren Spragg and end Lee Jones broke through to block a Hope punt on the 18. The force of the block drove the ball into Hope's end zone, where Andy Kincannon, Hillsdale's other end, recovered just before the ball reached the end line. The resulting TD, along with Moffat's kick, put the game out of reach at 34-7. The Dutchmen, however, were game to the end. With two minutes left, Faber, now installed at quarterback, lofted a 52-yard pass to Hendrickson, who got behind the defenders on the Dale's 15 and pulled away for the touchdown. The score and Watt's successful conversion made it 34-14, but it was too little too late. However, the Dutchmen had moved the ball, scored twice, and led in first downs 9-6 against the league's best team. Frank Waters' team was strong at every position, well coached, and deserving of its eventual championship and undefeated season.

The Hillsdale game proved costly. Freshman center and linebacker Gene Van Dongen suffered a knee injury which at first appeared to be a simple strain, but by Monday the team doctor had prescribed a cast and crutches. Van Dongen's season was over, just as he was making his greatest contribution.

Coach De Vette, reviewing the situation, decided that what the team needed at this juncture was a day off. Accordingly, practice was resumed on Tuesday in preparation for Olivet, who would invade Riverview Park for a night contest on Saturday, Oct. 27. Henry Paul was the Comets' new coach, but the team he inherited from Swede Thomas continued to struggle and Hope substitutes knew they would probably see considerable playing time. Approximately 1,500 faithful fans braved the cold to huddle in the covered grandstand as the teams took the field. Vander Lind opened the scoring with eight minutes gone in the first quarter with a 16-yard end sweep. Watt's kick gave Hope an early 7-0 lead and the Dutchmen were on the march. After an impressive showing against Hillsdale, Faber was installed at quarterback and proceeded to pass successfully to Wiegerink, who took the ball on the 11 and raced into the endzone. Watt's second kick made it 14-0. Early in the second quarter halfback Hendrickson reeled off a 56-yard run to set up a TD by Wetherbee, who was in the game at fullback for Kuyers. Watt's third conversion raised the count to 21-0. Third-string halfback Jim Menzer was the next to break away, this time on a 23-yard scoring sprint. Faber passed to Hendrickson for the extra point to close out Hope's first half scoring. With substitutes now dotting the field, Olivet's veteran quarterback, Roland Wahl, engineered a Comet scoring drive of 56 yards. Wahl carried the ball in himself from the one. The point try failed and the score stood 28-6 at halftime. Unfortunately, the Comets' star running back, Bill McNally, was injured early in the game, thereby limiting their offensive punch. McNally would later be named to the All-MIAA team.

Hope scored four more times in the third quarter, but failed to convert after any of the touchdowns. Watt was the first to cross the goal line. Faber then passed to Hendrickson, who took the ball over his head in the end zone to widen the margin to 40-6. Kuyers added six more as he broke through up the middle for 29 yards and the score. De Vette now cleared the bench and limited play selection in the obvious mismatch, but Menzer got through off-tackle and sprinted 66 yards for yet another score to make it 52-6.

The fourth quarter had to be endured by the hapless Comets and was really not much fun for anyone except the Hope substitutes. Tyrone Rupp, a freshman from Wauseon, Ohio, was now the Hope quarterback. Sometime in the final minutes, probably without the coach's permission, he threw a short pass to Wetherbee, who rambled 16 yards to paydirt. The conversion ended Olivet's nightmare at 59-6. The Dutchmen had amassed 662 yards in total offense. As the game progressed DeVette had limited the passing game to just four throws, but three had gone for touchdowns.

On Thursday, Nov. 1, Russ De Vette began double duty as head coach for both football and basketball. The two seasons would overlap by about 10 days, making evening basketball practice sessions necessary. De Vette had a precious hour and 15 minutes between practices to shift gears, but his love for both sports made it not like work at all. Two football games remained and the Dutchmen would be sorely tested in each one.

Saturday, Nov. 3, was Mom and Dads' Day at Albion. A crowd of 1,000 turned out on a belated Indian Summer day. Mild temperatures and sunny skies set the stage for a tough MIAA contest. Officials for the afternoon included Max Johnson, Ken Schuman, Ken Otis, and Jay Formsma, with Lee Kleis as official timer. Voss had been nursing a knee injury since the second game of the season, but now appeared recovered and started at quarterback for the Dutchmen. The fates were not kind to Voss this day as the knee was re-injured in Hope's first offensive series. He was replaced by Faber. With the ball on Hope's 44, Faber lofted a 30-yard pass to Vander Lind, who gathered the ball in along the sideline at the 16 and went in for the score. The score remained at 6-0 as Watt's kick sailed wide of the mark.

Defense ruled for most of the second quarter, but shortly before halftime Kuyers, on a trap play, took the hand-off on his 32 and broke away for 37 yards before being dragged down at the Albion 31. Faber's pass to Wiegerink was incomplete, but interference was called on the two-yard line. Vander Lind went off-tackle for his second TD of the half, but the Britons broke through to block Watt's point attempt. Hope's 12-0 lead at the intermission would be challenged by Morley Fraser's crew in the second half.

In the third period Vander Lind's punt was partially blocked and Albion recovered on the Hope 35. Quarterback Gamble wasted little time in passing to end Tom Taylor for the touchdown. Gene Bohn's kick was good and the Hope lead was quickly narrowed to 12-7. As the momentum continued to swing, Kuyers was injured in a pile-up. Hope's coaches rushed onto the dusty field fearing the worst. An ankle sprain removed Kuyers from the game just when he was needed most.

Early in the fourth quarter Albion's Jim Gilder intercepted a Faber pass on the Hope 40 and returned it all the way to the seven. Hope's bad luck continued as Faber twisted an ankle on the play and joined Kuyers on the bench. Two plays later fullback Jim Hurd plunged in from the two. Bohn's coversion attempt failed, but the Britons had taken the lead, 13-12 with 11:29 remaining in the game.

The ensuing kickoff was taken by Watt on the Hope five. With some good running he advanced to the 35, but Vander Lind failed to break away on two straight plays. Hope was now operating with its third quarterback of the afternoon in the person of Del Grissen. On third down he took the snap, danced away from tacklers, and passed 20 yards to Watt, who took the ball on the Albion 40, got past a defender, and raced down the sideline for the go-ahead touchdown. Once again Watt's point try was blocked, but Hope's 18-13 lead held up for the remainder of the contest. Tackle Larry Ter Molen had suffered a concussion on the opening kick-off when his ill-fitting helmet was dislodged. He was unable to return to the game. This, along with the injuries to Voss, Kuyers, and Faber, left the Dutchmen in somewhat battered condition, but all save Voss would be back in action the next week. Victory is a great healer.

On Saturday, Nov. 10, Hope entertained the Alma Scots under second-year coach Art Smith. A Mom and Dads' Day crowd of 1,200 braved the cold, hoping to see the Dutchmen extend their winning streak to three. On the Scots' first play from scrimmage the ball came loose and Bill Brookstra recovered for Hope. On Hope's third play the Hope guards did the job with the quick trap, and Kuyers was away up the middle for a 42-yard romp and the game's first score. Hope's extra point troubles continued as Watt's kick was wide of the mark. The Dutchmen's 6-0 lead was increased midway in the first quarter when the Scots gambled on fourth down and failed to convert. The Dutchmen took over at midfield and marched to paydirt in eight plays. The big play in the drive was a 21-yard run by Vander Lind. Watt went off left tackle for the TD to make it 12-0. This time Watt could not be blamed for the botched extra point as an errant snap from center foiled his attempt.

With time running out in the first period, Hendrickson intercepted a Scot pass on the Alma 26. On the first play of the second quarter, Faber passed to Hendrickson who took the ball on the Hope 20, wrestled for possession with Tom Johnson, won the battle, and ended on the one-yard line. Hendrickson was given the ball on the next play and went in for Hope's third score. Hope's third failure to garner an extra point could again be chalked up to a bad snap from center. Staring at an 18-0 deficit, the Scots got their offense rolling, but Wetherbee stopped the drive with an interception on the Hope 11. The determined Scots got even closer on their next drive, only to fumble on the seven, where Dyke Rottschafer recovered for Hope. Persistence finally paid off for the visitors on a third drive as Tom Johnson passed seven yards to Bob Hill for the touchdown. Hill's point try was not good, and the half ended with the score at 18-6.

Early in the second half Kuyers brought the crowd to its feet with a 47-yard dash, but Watt fumbled on the four-yard line. Alma failed to gain a first down and punted to their 42. Eight plays later the Dutchmen were again knocking at the door with the ball on the five. Grissen, adept at the short pass, was now at quarterback. His quick pass to Watt was good for Hope's fourth and final TD of the afternoon. The Hope coaches, conceding that the kicking combination was worse than rusty, had Grissen pass successfully to end Curt Menning for the point and up the lead to 25-6. Alma was not through. On the final play of the third period, Frank Lawrence scored on an end-sweep and Bill Klenk converted

RUSHING CHAMPION
Fullback Dave Kuyers (with the ball) was the MIAA rushing champion in 1956 with 508 yards. Mert Vander Lind (40) was also a rushing leader and captain-elect for 1957. Referee John C. Hoekje is in the background. Face masks were in the experimental stage in 1956.

to make it 25-13. Still later in the quarter, the Scots took over on the Hope 40, and in seven plays moved to the 10. Fullback Pat Brady then broke through a tired Hope defense for Alma's third touchdown. Klenk again made good on the point-after, and at 25-20, Hope's victory was in jeopardy. But the Hope offense was back on track and, taking the kickoff on their own 10, the Dutchmen moved systematically down the field, ending finally on the five-yard line as time ran out.

In several ways the '56 season resembled the '55 campaign, but this time the mid-season surge netted a 4-2 MIAA record, an improvement over the 3-3 mark of 1955. Again the Dutchmen were forced to share third place, this time with Albion despite the 18-13 victory over the Britons.

Overall, De Vette's charges stood at 4-4 in the eight-game schedule. Dave Kuyers notched the MIAA rushing title with 508 yards and was named to the All-MIAA team. Guard Dick Gantos was also a first-team selection. From a personal standpoint, my first experience as a college coach had been rewarding beyond anything I might have anticipated. The caliber of young men and their response to our coaching was more than gratifying.

* * *

ON TO VICTORY
Captain Herb Widmer led the Flying Dutchmen to a third place finish in the 1956 MIAA cross country season.

In his second year at the helm, cross country coach Larry Green was forced to go with a seven-man squad, but despite this handicap managed to finish the season in third place. Captain Herb Widmer, of Edgewater, N.J., was top man for Doc Green's crew, but able assistance came from Ron Den Uyl, Carroll Bennink, John Needham, Harry Wristers, Andre Felix and Jack Hoogendoorn. Hope was off to a good start with a 24-31 victory over Grand Rapids Junior College, but dropped a 17-39 decision to Kalamazoo. The Dutchmen bounced back with a close 26-30 win over Calvin, and a second victory over GRJC, this time by the score of 19-38. Against Olivet it was Widmer, Den Uyl, Bennink, and Wristers taking the first four places in the 21-35 win. It was a different story at Wayne State, where the Dutchmen absorbed an 18-37 defeat at the hands of the Tartars. As expected, Albion was equally tough as the Britons posted a 19-42 win at the expense of Doc Green's squad. Most would agree that the high point of the season occurred on Nov. 10, when Hope hosted the Scots of Alma. Widmer was at his best as he led his team to a 19-38 victory while setting a course record of 20:57 for the four-mile run. There is no record of a dual meet with Hillsdale, though the Dales' squad was alive and well. Adrian, however, failed to field a team.

The MIAA conference meet was held at Alma on Wednesday, Nov. 14, and proved exciting for the top contenders. Kalamazoo managed to edge Albion 31-32 on the strength of Jim Wallace's first place finish. Hope was a distant third with 100 points. Widmer finished fifth, Bennink was 14th, Den Uyl 16th, and Wristers 27th. Jack Hoogendoorn and Andy Felix also participated. Hillsdale followed Hope closely with 104 points, Calvin was fifth with 136, Alma sixth with 138, and Olivet seventh with 145.

* * *

Russ De Vette had coached Hope's basketball team for three seasons prior to his recall to the U.S. Marine Corps in 1951. In the interim he had served as head coach of the Quantico Marines and the Black Bears of the University of Maine. Now, as John Visser moved to the administrative post of Dean of Men, De Vette was once again asked to assume the reins. As mentioned earlier, the first practice had been called on Nov. 1 resulting in double duty for the coach until the football season concluded on Nov. 10. With pads and helmets packed away, athletes moved inside and the round ball reigned supreme.

The departing Visser had not left the cupboard bare. Though for the most part a young group, the candidates possessed considerable talent. Three starters returned from the 1955-56 team. Captain Bob Ritsema was the only senior. He was joined by sophomores Paul Benes and Albert "Jun" Buursma. Juniors included Dwayne "Tiger" Teusink, footballer Mert Vander Lind, baseball pitcher Jack Kempker, and Dave Woodcock, who had been given the green light for basketball after being forced to withdraw from football due to a back condition. Sophomores Bobby Thomson, John Hood and Jerry Hendrickson added depth. Four freshmen with unusual talents completed the picture. Ray Ritsema, of St. Anne, Ill., had been heavily recruited by the big schools, but in the end decided to follow brother Bob to Hope. Warren Vander Hill, an all-New York City selection, had accepted an athletic scholarship to the University of Maryland, but was not pleased with the arrangement there and transferred to Hope in February of 1956. Vander Hill's father, the Reverend Laverne, had served as captain of the 1928-29 Hope basketball team and his influence was a factor in Warren's transfer. Roland "Pooch" Schut had been an All-State selection at Class C Hudsonville High. Daryl Siedentop, of Downers Grove, Ill., was forced to undergo an appendectomy as the season began, but would recover to make an important contribution as the season progressed.

One month after the first practice session, Hope opened its season in Richmond, Ind., against Earlham College. De Vette's starting five included Vander Lind and Vander Hill at the guards and 6' 10" Benes at center. Jun Buursma and Ray Ritsema held down the forwad spots. Ray Ritsema began his first college game with mixed emotions, having relegated brother Bob to the role of first substitute. Bob, meanwhile, always a "team man," did not appear to be upset by this turn of events. The Quakers of Earlham featured balanced scoring and accuracy from the free throw line, but Hope was able to post an early lead of 14-8. However, as the half progressed, Benes picked up three fouls and had to be sidelined. Taking advantage of tall Paul's absence, the home team moved to a 50-45 lead at the intermission. The final tally showed Hope with 36 field goals to 31 for Earlham, but the latter had swished 29 free throws while the Dutchmen could manage only nine. The hard-to-take result was a 91-81 Earlham victory. Buursma led the Dutchmen attack with 20. Ray Ritsema followed with 17, Benes had 14 in spite of foul trouble, and Vander Hill chipped in with 11. Earlham had five men in double figures. Despite his team's somewhat ragged play, Coach De Vette had seen enough to envision a bright future. The teams would meet again during the Christmas break.

Tuesday, Dec. 4, found the Dutchmen on the road again. This time the destination was Ypsilanti, with Jim Skala's Eastern Michigan team furnishing the opposition. In a low-scoring contest, Hope's defense was especially effective. Bob Ritsema's work on the defensive board in the half initiated numerous fast break opportunities, with Vander Hill scoring 10 and Benes 11. Hope led 30-16 at halftime and kept up the pressure for the eventual 54-34 victory. Benes stayed out of foul trouble and led his team with 21 points. Vander Hill was next with 10. Harold Rainey was high for Eastern with 10. Coaches will testify that in any season, the first victory carries special significance. Until it happens,

teams are haunted by the specter of a hard-to-break losing streak. The Dutchmen now returned to Holland confident that a little polish could make the season one of real promise.

Coach Henry Paul brought his Olivet Comets to the Civic Center on Saturday, Dec. 8. Like De Vette, Paul was serving as head coach in both football and basketball. The Comets had struggled in football in Paul's initial year, and hoped for better things in the winter sport. The turn-around would not happen this night. Hope was off and running with substitutes seeing early action. Kempker scored eight points as the Dutchmen moved to a 41-22 halftime lead. Following the intermission, Buursma hit on seven of eight field goal attempts and the margin was pushed to 26. Olivet rallied in the late stages, but the final count was Hope 75, Olivet 60. Benes and Buursma had 14 each for the winners and Ray Ritsema followed with 11. Guard Norm Schultz had a game high-16 for Olivet. Neither team showed much accuracy from the field; Hope shot 39 percent, still better than the visitor's 30 percent.

The Hope community was pleased on Dec. 11 when it was announced that Bill Hinga had been appointed head football coach at Holland High School. Bill was the son of legendary Hope coach Milton "Bud" Hinga, who had held the Holland position prior to his long and distinguished career at Hope. Bill would eventually move to Central College in Pella, Iowa, where he would serve in several capacities.

Hope's second MIAA encounter was played in Albion's Kresge Gym on Wednesday, Dec. 12. Coach Elkin Isaac had assembled a team that was loaded with talent and the game turned out to be a classic, as had so many in the long series between the schools. The first half belonged to the Dutchmen as Benes and Vander Hill took charge with 14 and 11 points. Hope's 38-27 halftime advantage would soon disappear. The Britons, regrouping, pumped in eight of their next 10 shots and were back in the game. Included were four straight from outcourt by Virgil Hall. Meanwhile, Hope kept pace on the strength of 14 points by Ray Ritsema. The contest was tied five times in the last 12 minutes before Warren Vander Hill put the Dutchmen back in the lead by one. The Hope lead was 72-71 with but seconds remaining, but the Britons had possession. With the clock showing two seconds, George Vivlamore fired a jump shot from beyond the circle. The pressure shot parted the net, giving Albion the 73-72 victory. Bedlam reigned in Kresge Gym as the largely student crowd went wild. In perhaps the finest performance of his career, Vivlamore pumped in 34 points. He was followed by league leader John Hannett with 19 and Hall with 12. Vivlamore's final shot would loom large when the books were closed on the 1956-57 MIAA season. Those who have known Coach Isaac well remember it as a great game for a deserving coach. Hope had also played very well. Benes was high with 24, while Ray Ritsema and Vander Hill contributed 15 each. Buursma had a solid game with eight points.

In a Saturday night game on Dec. 15, Hope entertained the Alma Scots at the Civic Center. Even with Christmas shopping in full swing, a crowd of 1,600 was on hand. Scots coach Gary Stauffer relied heavily guard George Carter, a seasoned, take-charge person who got the most out of his team mates. A back-and-forth first half ended in a deadlock at 33. The pressure-packed action continued in the second half, with six points the largest margin. In the final four minutes, the Scots gained the lead with seven successful free throws. The Dutchmen fought back, and with 14 seconds remaining Ray Ritsema's lay-up brought them within one at 77-76, but Alma ran out the clock and saddled the Dutch with their second straight one-point MIAA loss. Vander Hill and Ray Ritsema led the De Vette men with 20 and 18. Benes was held to 13, while Vander Lind was good for eight. Hope again suffered at the free throw line, cashing in on only 12 of 27 tries. George Carter carried the winners with a game-high 24. Bob Postma had 19 to aid the Scot cause.

As the Christmas break approached, De Vette and his squad concentrated on shooting skills as well as the art of defense with a minimum of fouling. Both had been weaknesses in the season thus far. Athletics Director Al Vanderbush had scheduled a Holiday Classic tourney for the Civic Center to be played on December 28 and 29. Two of the teams, Earlham and Eastern Michigan, were familiar names, but the third, Central State of Wilberforce, Ohio, had never been a Hope opponent. In the Friday opener, Coach E. C. "Gibby" Gibbs and his Ohio team proved to be crowd pleasers. The Marauders controlled the boards with great leaping ability and were in charge all the way enroute to an impressive 81-65 victory over Jim Skala's Hurons.

In the second game Hope met Earlham, very much aware of the season-opening loss to the Quakers. This time the homecourt advantage was enough. The Dutchmen led all the way, though the visitors narrowed the gap to two on several occasions. Benes was at his very best with 30 points, including hook shots, tip-ins, and a lion's share of the rebounds. Vander Hill was also on target with 26, as was Ray Ritsema with 23. Vander Lind added eight to make the final, Hope 94, Earlham 85. Marv Arnold led the losers with 28. Earlham Coach Merle Ramsey was not happy with the score or the officiating.

Saturday's consolation game turned out to be a rough-and-tumble affair with a total of 61 fouls called. A game was a game to the Hurons, and they had come to play. A disgruntled Coach Ramsey badgered the officials and registered his final protest as the game wound down. When the Quakers gained possession they held the ball. By this time Earlham trailed by a considerable margin and the maneuver made little sense except to register the coach's protest. An otherwise impartial crowd now rallied to the support of Jim Skala's Hurons, who walked away with a 107-90 victory.

In the championship game Hope was off to a surprising start with an early 32-8 lead over Central State. The halftime margin was still impressive at 37-16, but things would change after the intermission. Coach Gibbs brought the Marauders back with a pressing defense that caused major problems, but the Dutchmen hung on and finally prevailed by a score of 66-61. Benes was high for Hope with 21, and Vander Hill was right behind with 20. Buursma netted 10, while Phil Payne was high for the losers with 22. The championship trophy consisted of an oversized pair of wooden shoes with shiny paint and a proper inscription. Benes and Vander Hill were named to the all-tourney team, and all-in-all the "Dutch Classic" was deemed a success.

Hope returned to MIAA competition on Thursday, Jan. 3, at Hillsdale. The Dales, under Coach John Williams, had good balance and a fine array of talent. The Dutchmen were off to a good start with an 26-18 lead, but it was wiped out by a Hillsdale press and the home team forged ahead 38-33. At this point Vander Hill took over with a hot streak and brought the Dutch back to a 45-44 halftime lead. The second half continued to be a nail-biter as the lead see-sawed. Hope trailed in the final minutes, but Vander Hill's lay-up tied the count at 75-75. The Dales scored next and led 77-75 with less than two minutes remaining. A Benes tip-in tied it once more before the Dutchmen took over the game with a seven-point burst. Hope got fast-break lay-ups from Vander Hill and Woodcock, Benes got a final tip-in and Ray Ritsema added a free throw. The 84-77 victory had been hard earned, but it seemed that the Dutchmen had arrived. Warren Vander Hill had his best performance to date with 27 points to lead his team. A 1-2 punch was completed with Benes' 25 markers. Ray Ritsema contributed 11 and Buursma added eight. Teusink, in a substitute's role, caught the coach's eye with seven points and several impressive assists. For Hillsdale it was Tom Tate leading the way with 20 and Jim "Jellybean" Reynolds with 17. Lee Jones and Bob Duncan also helped in keeping the Dales in the game.

The Spartans of Manchester, Ind. came to Holland on Saturday, Jan. 5, for a non-league encounter. The team from the Hoosier state was hungry for a win, having dropped eight straight, but De Vette saw a team that was better than its record. Using a tough man-for-man defense, the Dutchmen managed a 30-22 lead at halftime and increased the margin in the final period. At one point the visitors enjoyed a 10-point run, but the Dutchmen still led 59-52 and were not threatened thereafter. Vander Hill again led Hope, this time with 24, while Benes had 18 and Ray Ritsema 11. Bob Ritsema and Teusink had solid games with six each. Ron Stork led Manchester with 14 and Dan Anglin had 13.

Everyone knew it would be different when Barney Steen brought his MIAA champions to the Civic Center on Wednesday, Jan. 9. De Vette and Steen would enjoy fiercely contested games over the years, but in the end, forge a life-long friendship. At this writing, 41 years later, they replay the games during the winter months in the warm rays of Sun City, Ariz. The Jan. 9 contest was in keeping with the Hope-

Calvin tradition. Warren Vander Hill found himself pitted against his cousin, Dave Vander Hill of Calvin. The latter, a product of Holland Christian High School, had a hot hand in the first half with four straight buckets, and the Knights pushed to a 35-28 halftime lead. Hope trailed 50-45 with 10 minutes remaining, then tied the score at 52 and went into the lead on two free throws by Woodcock, who had seven-for-nine overall. Hope maintained its lead into the final minute of play, but with 44 seconds remaining Calvin center Tom Newhof connected with a graceful hook shot, making it 62-61 Calvin. The Knights added two more for the emotional 64-61 victory. Newhof led the winners with 14, and was followed closely by Dave Vander Hill and Ed Start with 12 each. Warren Vander Hill was high for Hope with 18, Benes had 12, and Ray Ritsema nine. Teusink, who found himself in a starting role for the first time, played a fine floor game and scored 11.

Hope's title aspirations had been dealt a severe blow by its third MIAA loss, but the team remained confident, and with good reason. At week's end, on Jan. 12, De Vette took his charges to Big Rapids to take on Chuck Smith's Ferris Bulldogs. The Dutchmen struggled with the unfamiliar fan-shaped backboards and had to settle for a 33-33 tie at halftime. Hope had taken 15 more shots than the home team, but had missed numerous lay-ups. Early in the second half Coach Smith elected to go with a press, which was largely ineffective. The Dutch broke through repeatedly and the score soon ballooned to 68-46. At this point subs came in and maintained the margin for a final score of 78-56. Scorers for Hope included Buursma with 18, Benes 16, Ray Ritsema 12, Vander Hill 10, and Hendrickson six. Jim Tetzlaff led the Bulldogs with 23.

On Tuesday, Jan. 15 the Hope entourage made its way to Kalamazoo for a crucial MIAA game. Coach Ray Steffen's Hornets stood at 9-1 overall and 6-0 in conference play. Hope's strong following in Kalamazoo made for a full house as 1,000 crowded into the aging Treadway Gym. Play was intense on both sides in the first half, with the Dutchmen pulling ahead 43-38 at the intermission. The Hornets fought back in the second half, largely on the outcourt shooting of Gary Morrison. They moved ahead 69-68 with five minutes remaining, but Tiger Teusink countered with two free throws and Hope was ahead to stay. Morrison fouled out with three minutes left and was sorely missed by his team. In the closing minutes it was Benes with two jump shots, Vander Hill with a lay-up plus a long, two-handed set shot, and Ray Ritsema with two free throws for the final 10-point margin of 83-73. Vander Hill and Benes led the winners with 22 and 20 while Jun Buursma had a strong game with 17. Morrison led Ray Steffen's crew with a game-high 25. He was followed by Bob Fletcher with 15 and Bob Ellis with 10. Hope was still in the hunt, and the victory over league-leading Kazoo was a confidence builder, to say the least.

Basketball teams have their ups and downs and individual players their mood swings, but on Saturday, Jan. 19, the Hope team was ready to play. Adrian coach Stan Albeck was aware that Hope was a team on the move. The personable Albeck was a true student of the game. He would later coach at Bradley University and finally move on to coach four different teams in the NBA. In this, his first coaching assignment, he would depend upon the all-round play of big Leon Harper. Some 1,800 fans made their way to the Civic Center to see if the Dutch could extend their two-game win streak. They did not have long to wait. Benes had four tip-ins in the first 10 minutes, and Buursma had his shooting eye as he connected on seven jump shots. Hope's lead at halftime was 48-35. The pace continued in the second half until the point spread reached 35. With 10 minutes remaining De Vette turned the game over to deserving substitutes. The final count was Hope 99, Adrian 73. Ray Ritsema was the Hope leader with 24. Benes was next with 18, Buursma and Vander Hill each had 16, and Hendrickson had seven. As expected, Harper led the Bulldogs with 21. Guard Jerry Gilbert scored 19 and Bob Ohrman had 13.

Semester examinations now occupied the Dutchmen and no games were scheduled for a period of two weeks. There were periodic practices, but Coach De Vette was concerned lest the layoff produce a loss of the momentum seen in recent games. His answer came on Saturday, Feb. 2, when Ferris Institute came to the Civic Center for a return encounter. He was much relieved when his charges picked up where they had left off two weeks earlier. Hope's 40-29 halftime lead, while not overwhelming, was an indication of things to come. The Dutch regulars broke the game open early in the second half and De Vette substituted freely. Hope reached the century mark on Kempker's two free throws, giving Hope its 100-64 non-league victory. Benes had scored 30 in limited playing time, Vander Hill followed with 21, Buursma had 12, Jack Kempker 10, and Schut eight. Roger Vander Laan led Ferris with 19 and Jim Tetzlaff had 17.

Coach Isaac brought the Albion Britons to the Civic Center on Wednesday, Feb. 6. Interest was now kindled in Hope's fortunes, and 2,000 fans all but filled the Civic. Coach Isaac hoped for a repeat of the Briton's dramatic December 12 victory. He decided to employ a press in the early going to offset Hope's height advantage. Teusink, however, had come of age as a floor general and successfully maneuvered through the maze to supply his big men with numerous scoring opportunities. Meanwhile, Buursma was limiting high-scoring John Hannett to seven points in the first half. Hope's halftime advantage stood at 49-32 and the pressure continued. In the end it was Hope's big three that made the difference, Benes with 25, Vander Hill with 22, and Ray Ritsema with 20. Teusink had seven in addition to his many assists en route to the surprising 92-63 victory. For Albion it was John Hannett leading the way with 19. Virgil Hall had 17 and George Vivlamore 16.

**THE 1956-57 HOPE BASKETBALL SQUAD
MIAA CO-CHAMPIONS WITH ALBION**

Front Row L. to R.: Jack Kempker, Albert "Jun" Buursma, Dwayne "Tiger" Teusink, Captain Bob Ritsema, Warren Vander Hill, Dave Woodcock, Mert Vander Lind. **Back Row:** Coach Russ De Vette, Roland "Pooch" Schut, John Hood, Paul Benes, Ray Ritsema, Daryl Siedentop, Manager Charlie Pettingill.

The Dutchmen appeared to be on a roll, but with three MIAA losses every contest was now in the "crucial" category. On Saturday, Feb. 9, a serious Hope team headed north to meet the Alma Scots of Coach Gary Stauffer. Alma had prevailed in the Dec. 15 meeting on the strength of seven late-game free throws, and the Dutchmen hoped to stay out of foul trouble. In spite of best efforts however, Benes picked up two quick ones in the first half and his defensive play was compromised. Bob Ritsema was now called upon to fill the breach and responded in stellar fashion. Buursma attempted to contain George Carter with help from Woodcock. Teusink and Siedentop did their best to put the clamps on Stan Stolz as the game see-sawed to a half-time tie of 44-all. The second half began as the first, with Benes called for two more fouls. Once again it was Captain Bob to the rescue. In perhaps the finest performance of his career, the Hope senior was tough on defense, rebounded effectively, and scored a season-high 15 points. De Vette's halftime adjustments, plus a true team effort, enabled the team to pull away for the eventual 92-75 win. Vander Hill led Hope with 24, Ray Ritsema had 16, Bob Ritsema 15, Buursma 10, and Teusink nine. Carter was again impressive for the Scots with 24 and Stolz's out-court shooting produced 20, but on this night the Dutchman roll continued.

With both Hope and Calvin in championship contention, interest in the Feb. 13 game reached a fever pitch. An estimated 6,000 fans were on hand in the Grand Rapids Civic Auditorium fully expecting another close one. An early 10-10 tie seemed to bear this out. The Calvin lineup now included a flashy transfer student from Baldwin Wallace College named Bill Morgan. Morgan made his presence known by scoring 10 of Calvin's first 14 points. In uncharacteristic fashion, Buursma found himself with three quick fouls and unwanted time on the bench. Woodcock and Siedentop filled in effectively as Hope built a surprising 47-30 half-time lead. Spurred on by the huge crowd, the Dutchmen increased the

47

margin in the second half. Tom Newhof and Dave Vander Hill fouled out with some two minutes remaining and another Hope-Calvin tussle was history.

The final score read Hope 89, Calvin 62. Benes was at his best in leading his team with 22. Ray Ritsema scored 20, Vanderhill 15, and Bob Ritsema nine. Bill Morgan was high for the Knights with 21, while Newhof collected 13 and Ed Start 11.

A footnote to the evening involved the JV contest. My junior varsity charges played a limited schedule but did meet the JV's from Calvin and Kalamazoo. This night bordered on the bizarre as everything worked, for a half that is. Fast breaks produced quick scores from high percentage shots and the score ballooned to 62-46 at the half. Holland Christian coach Art Tuls, arriving at halftime, thought the scoreboard displayed the final score. In the second half reality returned and Hope could muster only 23 points but hung on for the 85-78 win. Al Kober led my crew with 20, Dave White (later "Admiral" White) had 18, and Jim Kaat, of future baseball fame, had 17 in Hope's evening sweep.

By the time Coach Ray Steffen brought his Kalamazoo team to the Civic Center on Feb. 16, earlier skeptics had decided to jump on the bandwagon. A crowd of 2,700 jammed into the auditorium creating a standing-room-only situation that worried the fire marshal. Steffen employed a deliberate "control" game in a attempt to blunt the high-flying Hope offense. Another Steffen strategem was to encourage his big men to play very aggressively, lots of elbows and hips plus a little "within the rules" pushing. A steady diet of same sooner or later prompted retaliation. With seven minutes remaining in the first half, both Benes and Ray Ritsema had been charged with three fouls. Bob Ritsema was able to spell both men, and at halftime it was Hope 33, Kazoo 26. During the intermission De Vette reminded his charges that getting ahead was more important than getting even, and the fouling tapered off. An added plus was perfect execution of the Benes hook shot. Ray Ritsema fouled out just prior to the final horn, but Benes and Vander Hill survived with four fouls each. Benes led Hope to the 69-57 win with 21 points. Buursma was second in line with 16 and Vander Hill tallied 15. Morrison was high for the Steffen crew with 15 and Doug Steward had 14.

Henry Hughes had been in and out of school at Adrian but he was back for the Hope game at Adrian on Wednesday, Feb. 20. Now with an eight-game winning streak, it was a confident Hope team that suited up in Ridge Gymnasium. But the Dutchmen would suffer a devastating blow before a single point was scored. With the game but 37 seconds old in a rebound tangle with Henry Hughes, Ray Ritsema came down hard in an awkward position. As he writhed in agony on the floor it was evident to all that this was more than a simple sprain. The grotesque angle of Ray's right foot told trainer Doc Green that a painful dislocation had occurred. An ambulance was summoned and Ray was taken to the Adrian hospital. It was obvious that his season was over. Bob Ritsema's concern for his brother did not make his replacement duty any easier, but he played a steady game and the Dutch managed a 36-36 tie at the half. The Bulldogs took the lead early in the second half, but Warren Vander Hill brought his team back to a 60-58 score with four jumpers. At this point splendid Henry Hughes took over and pushed the Adrian lead to nine. The Hope team was relieved when Ray Ritsema hobbled in on crutches and took a seat on the bench. The inspired subs made one more run. "Pooch" Schut came off the bench to score eight points including two tip-ins, but Bob Ohrman sank four straight free throws to put the game out of reach. In Adrian's 80-71 victory, Hughes scored 28, Ohrman 26, and Harper 14. For Hope it was Benes with 22, Buursma 17, Vander Hill 14, and Schut with eight. The question now was, could a team with four MIAA defeats still be in the running for the title? Two games remained and additional help would have to come from another quarter.

On Saturday, Feb. 23, 2,300 fans filled the Civic Center hoping to see the Dutchmen rebound from their disappointment at Adrian. Hillsdale coach John Williams now had the services of tall Frank Wesner and hoped to slow down the Benes scoring machine. It was soon apparent, however, that there were simply too many Dutch guns, even without Ray Ritsema. De Vette's first-half zone defense proved to be very effective and the boards were dominated by Benes, Bob Ritsema, and Schut. Hope's 22-point (46-24) lead at halftime was insurmountable, as there would be no let-up after the intermission. With five minutes remaining, Jack Kempker sank two free throws to make it 83-52, the game's largest margin. The final was Hope 92, Hillsdale 63. Vander Hill led his team with 24 points on 12 field goals. Benes enjoyed a fine, all-round game with 19 counters, Teusink had 12 and Buursma 11. Lee Jones, Hillsdale's top man, could muster only 11, while Jellybean Reynolds and Frank Wesner each had nine. Hope's defensive effort was obviously a key factor in the decisive win. There was more good news. Following the game it was learned that Calvin had defeated Albion 68-65 on the Knights' floor. Hope was now back in a first-place tie with the Britons. As the Dutchmen departed Hillsdale, they found highway M-99 a glare of ice. Despite best efforts, Coach De Vette's Ford station wagon soon careened into a ditch. Fortunately, there were no injuries and after some delays in the late-night cold, the team made its way back to Holland. The incident was enough to trigger a change in Hope's transportation policies. Treasurer Henry Steffens was finally convinced that winter roads called for team transportation by bus. Henceforth the Dutchmen would profit from the increased safety of a chartered Greyhound.

Wednesday, Feb. 27, marked the season finales for the league leaders. Hope traveled to Olivet, while Albion enjoyed home-court advantage in hosting Alma. The Dutchmen were taking nothing for granted, knowing that strange things could happen in "the Pit" at Olivet. Vander Hill scored six field goals in the first half to help his team to a 42-33 lead at the end of the first 20 minutes. "The V" added five more in the second half for a total of 22 as Hope breezed to a 78-56 victory and a 10-4 record in the MIAA. Paul Benes had 16 and Captain Bob Ritsema, playing his final college game, scored 11. Joe Iauch, with 14, was the leader for the Comets. Maynard Stafford and Mike Troesch each had 12.

Restaurateur Win Schuler, an Albion graduate, catered to MIAA teams and the high point of any trip south was a post-game meal at Schuler's Marshall establishment. As the team was seated in the "Michigan Room" there was a phone call for Coach De Vette. On the other end was Elkin Isaac in nearby Albion. His team had taken the measure of Alma, 84-77, and the Hope-Albion tie remained. There was precedent for a playoff, but as the coaches discussed the pros and cons of this procedure it was decided that both teams were deserving of a championship. John Hannett and George Vivlamore were closing out impressive careers and would not have another chance. The same was true of Bob Ritsema, and brother Ray was out of action. The co-championship decision of the coaches was referred to Athletic Directors Al Vanderbush and Dale Sprankle, who in turn polled the league. With but one dissenting vote, the co-championship would stand.

Paul Benes and Warren Vander Hill were named to the All-MIAA team along with John Hannett and George Vivlamore of Albion, Gary Morrison of Kalamazoo, and Henry Hughes of Adrian.

Through the efforts and influence of John Visser, Hope College held membership in the National Association of Intercollegiate Athletics. The membership would eventually be dropped in favor of the College Division of the National Collegiate Athletic Association (NCAA), but as this season concluded Russ De Vette was named NAIA Coach of the Year for the State of Michigan. All of these honors were duly observed by the campus community on Monday, March 4, when a "Glory Day" was declared. Student Council President Dave Van Eenenaam presided at a morning celebration in Carnegie-Schouten Gym after classes had been canceled for the day. A huge cake was presented to the team and the remainder of the day was spent in a variety of leisure pursuits.

Senior Bob Ritsema did not make the All-MIAA team, but he seemed an ideal example of the liberal arts student-athlete. An accomplished cellist with late-afternoon rehearsals, he was resigned to bypassing intercollegiate basketball when Coach John Visser recruited him from city league play at the end of his sophomore year. An agreement was worked out with Dr. Morrette Rider of the music department whereby certain rehearsals could be missed or rescheduled. Visser also allowed Bob to miss an occasional practice without penalty. The result was an enriching experience for Bob, for two coaches, and for numerous team members.

* * *

The March lull between basketball and spring sports weighed heavily on eager athletes and impatient young coaches. I was included in the latter category. After coaching high school track and field for six years, I found the challenge of a college team an exciting new experience. I welcomed the assignment with great anticipation in that spring of 1957. Larry Green, my predecessor, now moved to men's tennis, where he would enjoy a long and successful career. Doc Green's track teams had taken the MIAA championship in 1953, then finished second in '54, '55, and '56. Returnees from the '56 squad included the "big four" alluded to earlier, namely Paul Wiegerink, Jim Hilmert, Dave Spaan, and John De Vries. To inherit performers of this caliber was indeed a windfall. I looked forward to working with them and the remainder of the 20-man turnout.

Early-season conditioning was a difficult undertaking. Late afternoon gym time was divided between the track and baseball squads. Carnegie-Schouten Gymnasium, though recently renovated, was largely inadequate for spring training. Pitchers and catchers got in some work and sprinters

GREAT COMBINATION

Mary Alice (Ferguson) Ritsema '57 and Robert Ritsema '57 were typical of student leaders who graced Hope's campus in the late '50's. Bob was able to successfully combine athletics and the arts (music). On campus and in subsequent years they enriched the college and community. — Van Raalte Hall and the venerable Beech (background) have passed from the scene.

THE 1957 HOPE COLLEGE TRACK TEAM
2nd PLACE – MIAA

Top Row L. to R.: Ron Bronson, Dave White, Harold Gazan, John Hood, Jan Robbert, Roland Schut, Harvey Van Farowe. **Middle Row:** Harry Wristers, Charlie Smits, Bill Huibregtse, Jim Menzer, John Needham, Manager John Van Dam. **Front Row:** Coach Gordon Brewer, Jim Hilmert, Paul Wiegerink, Captain John De Vries, Jim Mohr, Carroll Bennink. **Missing from the picture:** Ray Ritsema, Dave Spaan, Larry Ter Molen, Bill Elzinga.

practiced starts, but weight training had not yet come of age and the absence of such a room reduced workouts to jogging and the monotony of calisthenics. The latter tended to dampen enthusiasm as wind and snow swirled about outside. When winter finally relented, workouts were conducted at the Holland High School track on 22nd Street and at the football practice field on Fairbanks Avenue. The long-awaited first meet was scheduled for Saturday, April 13, with Hope hosting Olivet, but when the day arrived impossible weather conditions forced a postponement. The meet was never rescheduled. A week later the season finally got underway when Hope traveled to Houseman Field in Grand Rapids to meet Grand Rapids Junior College. As might be expected, performances were nothing to write home about, but Hope's first-year coach was pleased with the 88-42 victory, which included 10 first-place finishes out of 15. Captain John De Vries led the way with firsts in the pole vault, long jump, and javelin. Jim Hilmert took the high hurdles and Paul Wiegerink the lows. Dave Spaan won his specialty, the 440, and Bill Huibregtse captured the shot. Larry Ter Molen and Hilmert made it a sweep in the latter event. Ron Bronson was first in the 880 and Ray Ritsema, now recovered from his basketball injury, took the discus. Hope's mile relay team of Jim Mohr, Jim Menzer, Roland Schut, and Dave Spaan rounded out the day's scoring by winning this final event.

One week later, on April 27, the Hope team returned to Houseman Field for a triangular meet with Calvin and Alma. Houseman was not really the home track of any of the three schools. The City of Grand Rapids maintained the facility for use by the city's high schools and Grand Rapids Junior College. This day the maintenance men were substitutes and not overly conscientious in preparing the site. The issue caused a serious incident in the 120-yard high hurdle race. At the third hurdle both Hilmert and Wiegerink struck the timbers broadside and went crashing to the cinders. I immediately had visions of fractured legs and a season going up in smoke. Fortunately, the two were not seriously hurt, only irate. As accomplished hurdlers, both realized at once that something was radically wrong. A check of the hurdle placement revealed that they had been placed opposite the wrong marks on the cement curbing. Meanwhile, the other two entrants had gingerly "five-stepped" their way to the finish line and were claiming first and second place. My hurdlers, with the support of their coach, demanded that the race be re-run. After some argument with the starter and opposing coaches, our position prevailed. In the second run Wiegerink and Hilmert proved their point by finishing 1-2 as the others trailed by 20 yards. In other events Wiegerink captured firsts in the 100-yard dash and the 220-yard low hurdles to lead his team with a total of 15 points. De Vries and Hilmert followed closely with 12 and 11 while Spaan tallied 8¾. Overall, Hope had 7½ firsts, Calvin five, and Alma 2½. Larry Essenmacher won the shotput and J. Acton the javelin for Alma. Orville Vande Griend won the discus for Calvin, Pete Steen took the mile run, Alkema the 880, Rich Hertel the 220. Calvin's mile relay team of Stonehouse, Tanis, Bert De Vries, and R. Kingma took first place in a time of 3:39.1.

The final tally of the triangular showed Hope the victor with 79⅘ points, Calvin second with 60⅕, and Alma third with 22.

Hope's winning ways ground to a halt at Albion on Tuesday, April 30. The MIAA champions showed their stuff by dominating the meet with 11 first-place finishes. The race of the day featured Wiegerink nipping teammate Jim Hilmert at the finish line in the high hurdles. Albion's John Leppi was a close third. Wiegerink's time of 15.0 was a new Hope College record. Leppi, a fierce competitor, also finished third in the 100-yard dash behind Wiegerink and teammate Mohr. But the determined Leppi came back to win the 220 in the excellent time of 22.7. Wiegerink was also in top form in the 220-yard low hurdles, winning in the fine time of 24.5. For the third meet in a row, Spaan won the 440-yard dash, this day lowering his time to 50.7, but the Britons of Coach Elkin Isaac walked away with the victory by a score of 83⅓ to 47⅔.

On Saturday, May 4, Coach Dan Goldsmith brought his Hillsdale team to Holland for a dual meet at the 22nd Street track. The Dales took the shot, discus, and javelin, but the Dutchmen captured the remaining 12 events. Wiegerink was a three-time winner with victories in the 100, the high hurdles, and the low hurdles. Spaan won the 440 and the 220, and anchored the winning mile relay team which also included Menzer, Jan Robbert, and Ron Bronson. Harold Gazan took the mile, John Needham the 880, and Harvey Van Farowe the two-mile, while De Vries was again successful in taking his specialties, the pole vault and broad jump. Hilmert won the high jump and was second in discus and high hurdles. In the high hurdle race Wiegerink and Hilmert had to contend with Jim "Jellybean" Reynolds, a talented, three-sport athlete mentioned earlier. Reynolds was a quick starter, but his hurdling form left something to be desired. In the center lane, with clenched fists, his arms would flail high and wide to either side. In the early stages of the race both Wiegerink and Hilmert were on the receiving end of unintentional blows from the Jellybean. It proved a great incentive to get ahead, which they proceeded to do in a 1-2 finish. The final score of Hope 88⅖, Hillsdale 42⅗ put the Dutchmen back on track after the Albion defeat.

On Tuesday, May 7, Hope hosted Adrian on the Allegan High School track. The fabled Henry Hughes was in the Bulldog entourage, but the team was otherwise undermanned. Hughes won the high jump, but Hope dominated the remainder of the meet with sweeps in the pole vault, shot put, 100, high hurdles, 880, 220, two-mile, and low hurdles. De Vries and Wiegerink were again triple winners, with the former taking the vault, the javelin, and the broad jump while Wiegerink copped the 100 and both hurdle races. Spaan was also first three times, taking the 440 and the 220, and running the anchor leg on the winning mile relay team. Hilmert won the discus and placed second in the high jump and both hurdle races. The 117-14 victory was not one to gloat over, but several of Hope's usual "down the line" finishers had their day in the sun.

Hope departed from league competition on Saturday, May 11, to participate in the well-established Elmhurst Relays. Four of Hope's stalwarts made the trip to Chicago in the coach's '55 Buick Special. In addition to host Elmhurst and Hope, 12 other colleges participated. It proved to be a red-letter day for Wiegerink, who rose to the occasion with first-place finishes in the 100-yard dash, the 120-yard high hurdles, and the 220-yard low hurdles. De Vries tied for first in the pole vault and took third in the broad jump. Hilmert was third in the high hurdles, and Spaan managed a fourth-place finish in a fast field of 440 men. Beloit College of Wisconsin was the overall winner with 52 points, followed by the University of Dubuque with 46, Carroll College with 38⅓, and Hope with 27. The Dutchmen were able to edge North Central by 1/2 point. The latter would become an NCAA Division III track power in years to come. Other finishers in order were, Lakeland, Illinois Wesleyan, Milliken, Elmhurst, St. Josephs, Lake Forest, Lyons Jr. College, Concordia of River Forest, and Morton Jr. College.

Hope's final contest prior to the league meet was a triangular at Kalamazoo's Angell Field on Tuesday, May 14. Participants were Kalamazoo, Hillsdale, and Hope. On the strength of eight first-place finishes, the Dutchmen took the meet with 62 1/12 points to 53⅚ for Kalamazoo, and 45½ for Hillsdale. Spaan led the way with a season's-best 50.6 to win the 440, then followed it up with a 23.6 to take the 220. His anchor leg in the mile relay helped his teammates, Menzer, Robbert, and Bronson, win the event in a time of 3:34.2. De Vries won the pole vault and broad jump, and Hilmert won both hurdle races. Wiegerink won the 100 in a time of 10.4. The Dutchmen were rounding into shape and performances were improving, but lack of depth would be a problem, especially in the distance runs.

The MIAA conference track meet was held in Kalamazoo on Friday and Saturday, May 17 aud 18. The weekend of competition was officially termed MIAA Field Day as the tennis and golf tournaments were also conducted in the same city. Track preliminaries began at 1:30 p.m. on the Angell Field track with the final at 8:20 p.m. under the lights. Hope had five of 15 first-place finishes, as did Albion, but the Britons, with nine seconds, four thirds and seven fourths ran away with the eight-team meet. The final tally showed Albion with 88¾ points, Hope a distant second with 46, and host Kalamazoo third with 34¾. Others, in order, were Calvin 21, Hillsdale 13, Olivet 12, Alma 7, and Adrian 2. A knee injury prevented Wiegerink from participating in the high hurdles, but his duel with Albion's John Leppi continued. Leppi drew first blood in the 100, edging Wiegerink in a time of 10.4, but a charged-up Wiegerink came back to reverse the finish in the 220 with a time of 23.0. Hilmert was a double winner with victories, in the discus (125' 3"), and in the 120-yard highs (16.0), where his victim was again the persistent Leppi. Hilmert was also part of a four-way tie for fifth place in the high jump, as was Ray Ritsema.

JIM KAAT
All-MIAA in 1957

His major league career would span 4 decades.

The 440-yard dash in 1957 was run from a one-turn stagger down a 220-yard straightaway, with the finish at the end of the backstretch and well out of the view of the spectators. This practice was discontinued a few years later. Spaan won the event in 52.2, then anchored Hope's winning mile relay team for the Dutchmen's final gold medals of the night. Other relay members were Menzer, Bronson and Robert. The winning time was 3:39.5.

The two-day Field Day had included coaches meetings and a dinner for athletics directors and coaches with plenty of camaraderie. The closeness thus engendered would gradually dissipate in years to come.

*   *   *

The strength of Russ De Vette's 1957 baseball squad would be pitching. Mert Vander Lind, a three-sport man, led the returnees. He was joined by Bob Andree, who had transferred to Hope from Grand Rapids Junior College after pitching well against the Dutchmen in 1956. Freshmen with a reputation included Al Kober of Herkimer, N.Y., and Jim Kaat from nearby Zeeland. Kaat had been impressive in the local area, but no one could predict that he would go on to fame in the major leagues in four decades. Also on hand, though primarily an outfielder, was Jack Kempker, who had considerable experience on the mound.

The season opened on Saturday, April 13, amidst cold and occasional snow flurries. A few brave spectators had their choice of seats at Riverview Park as Ferris Institute furnished the opposition. In the first game Mert Vander Lind gave up four hits and two unearned runs over four innings while striking out four. Al Kober took over in the fifth, allowing no hits, no runs, and striking out one. Hope scored in the first when Jack Faber doubled and Captain Dave Woodcock singled, then scored on a shortstop error to make it 2-0. Ferris tied the game in the fourth on a single and three Hope errors, but Art Olson led off the fifth with a double and scored on Tim Vander Mel's double with what proved to be the winning run in Hope's 3-2 victory.

Kaat pitched the first four innings of the second game. The left-hander gave up a single in the first inning, but quickly got out of trouble by striking out the side. In his abbreviated first outing he allowed one hit while striking out five. Bob Andree was equally effective in the final three innings, striking out three, and allowing one hit and no runs to preserve the eventual 4-0 shutout. Hope scored in the third inning on a walk to Faber, a wild pitch, and a Woodcock single. In the fifth Kaat and Faber walked, then scored on Kempker's long single to make it 3-0. Hope's final run came in the sixth, when Jerry Boeve walked and reached third when pitcher Hal Stulberg threw over the first baseman's head trying to retire Daryl Siedentop. Boeve scored on Andree's long fly to center, completing the 4-0 shutout and giving Kaat his first win as a Dutchman.

In a third non-league game on Tuesday, April 16, Hope hosted Grand Rapids Junior College at Riverview Park. It was a ragged, early season game with each side committing five errors. Pitching duties were shared equally by Vander Lind, Kober, and Kaat in the nine-inning contest. Hope scored three times in the first inning, largely due to three errors by third baseman Leroy Davis. A fourth tally came in the second on singles by Vander Lind and Olson. In the fifth Hope added two more on another Olson single which drove

DAVE WOODCOCK
All-MIAA — 1957
Captain, catcher, and Hope's most valuable player.

in Woodcock, who had singled, and Kempker, who drew a walk. Three more crossed the plate in the sixth. Woodcock and Kempker were safe on JC errors. Olson's third single scored Woody, and Kempker came home on Arn Boeve's long fly to center. Olson scored on Vern Zuverink's grounder to short, giving the Dutchmen their ninth run. But the game was hardly one-sided. In the top of the third, two hits, three walks, and two Hope errors produced seven JC runs. The visitors added two more to tie the score. In the seventh with the score at 9-9, Kempker walked, was sacrificed to second, went to third on a balk, and scored on Art Olson's bloop single behind first base. Jim Kaat pitched the final three innings, striking out five. Hope's 10-9 victory was a shaky one, but welcome none-the-less, especially since numerous squad members were able to see some action.

Hope's MIAA opener was played at Hillsdale on Saturday, April 20. Andree went the distance in a close ball game. Hope took an early 4-0 lead, but the Dales fought back. In the third Dick Gliha tripled and scored on a Hope error. In the fifth, the home team bunched two hits, a walk, and a stolen base to score two more and make it 4-3. In the bottom of the seventh, the Dales' Dick Gliha followed up his earlier triple with a two-run homer over the right field fence to give his team the 5-4 victory.

The second game was begun under overcast skies. After two innings Kaat had struck out five of the six men he faced, but a downpour ensued, canceling further play. It was agreed that the game would be replayed only if it would appear to affect the final standings. In the end, the game was not replayed and Kaat's fine effort went by the boards.

On Tuesday, April 23, Hope traveled to Richmond Park in Grand Rapids for another single game with Grand Rapids Junior College. Kaat pitched the first three innings and gave up no runs. He also contributed two singles and two RBI's. Vander Lind relieved in the fourth, and from that point on the game became somewhat of a laugher. Both teams had a lot of fun as Hope emerged on the long end of a 21-14 count. Newspaper accounts rightfully labeled it "the battle of the bats." Kober led Hope with two doubles and five RBI's, and Ron Bekius was close behind with a home run and three RBI's. Woodcock also had two RBI's.

Saturday's scheduled doubleheader with Kalamazoo College was rained out, and the games at Riverview Park were moved to Monday, April 29. Kaat continued in top form with a two-hit, 6-0 shutout in the first game. Bekius and Jerry Boeve each had a single and a double. Hope's final run came on a bases-empty home run by Carl De Vree in the sixth inning.

Andree was effective in the second game, giving up single runs in the third and fifth innings while Hope was cashing in with a total of 10. The Hornets were unable to recover from Hope's three-run first inning. A big blow for Hope was Bekius' home run with Kober on board.

Calvin invaded Riverview Park on Wednesday, May 1, and the Knights proved troublesome. On the mound for the Dutchmen in game one was Vander Lind. The Hope pitcher aided his own cause in the second inning by initiating that rarest of all baseball feats, a triple play. With no outs and first and second occupied, Vander Lind was in trouble. However, the next batter blooped one toward the mound. The runners were off seeing a possible sacrifice, but Vander Lind dove for the ball, caught it, and, while on the ground, threw to Dick Morgan at first. Morgan quickly fired to Faber at second to complete the play and end the inning. Things had gone well for Hope in the early going. In the first inning, Bekius reached first on a walk and came home when Woodcock stroked a home run to make it 2-0. In the third, Faber walked and scored on Woodcock's second hit, a single making it 3-0. Calvin scored one run in the fifth, but Hope came back in their half of the inning when Bekius tripled and came home on a wild pitch, 4-1. The Knights tied the game in the sixth with three runs as Vander Lind weakened somewhat. In the bottom of the seventh Woodcock walked, stole second and third, and came home on a wild pitch to give Hope the 5-4 victory.

Kober was on the hill for the Dutchmen in the nightcap as Hope assumed the role of visitor. With the score tied 5-5 in the seventh inning, Tim Vander Mel singled over the shortstop's head to score Bekius and Woodcock with what proved to be the winning runs. Siedentop relieved Al Kober in the bottom of the seventh. Successive singles loaded the bases, but with two out, the left-hander bore down and

53

struck out Calvin's pinch hitter to end the game with Hope on top 7-5. John De Mey did his part for Calvin, striking out 12 Dutchmen in the first game and slamming a homer into the leftfield grandstand in the second inning of game two.

On Saturday, May 4, it was Albion's turn to battle the Dutchmen on their home turf. In game one Jim Kaat was in command all the way as he gave up but two hits while striking out 12. Hope scored its first run in the third on a walk to Kaat and singles by Woodcock and Kempker. The Dutchmen padded their lead in the fifth with five more including Kempker's triple. Hope's seventh run came in the sixth inning on a double by Kempker and Olson's third single of the game. Kaat held the Britons in check in the seventh for the 7-1 victory. Albion's two hits and one run were registered in the fourth inning. Jack Kempker was the batting leader for Hope with a single, double, and triple.

In game two, Andree gave up a Briton run in the second, but Hope tied it in the third and added another in the fourth. In the fifth, Vander Mel singled home one run and Olson two to ice the game. Andree's four-hit 5-1 victory set up a showdown with league-leading Alma.

On Tuesday, May 7, Coach De Vette's squad traveled north to meet the undefeated Scots. Coach Charlie Skinner sent his ace Albie Roman to the mound to meet Hope's red-hot Jim Kaat. The expected pitchers' duel ensued. Roman's three-hit performance should have been enough to win, but Hope bunched them in the fourth inning. Bekius broke the ice with a single and Woodcock was safe on a shortstop error. With two outs, Tim Vander Mel singled scoring Bekius to make it 1-1. Morgan then produced the game's big blow, a long single to center scoring Woodcock and Vander Mel. Kaat scattered four hits and continued unbeaten with the 3-1 win.

In the nightcap, Alma scored one run in the first, another in the third, and three more in the fifth. Hope collected eight hits, all singles, but failed to push across a run until the seventh, when Siedentop, batting for Morgan, singled. Ron Wetherbee, batting for Jerry Boeve, was safe on an error. The runners advanced on Kober's ground out. Faber then hit a smash to the pitcher which was deflected to the shortstop, who threw wide to first base, allowing both runs to score. But the rally fell short and Alma gained the needed split with the 5-2 victory.

On May 11 word was received on the Hope campus that Hudsonville High School had hired a new football coach in the person of Dave Kempker. Dave (Hope '54) was the older brother of Jack and had been employed at Lowell High School. Hope coaches welcomed the appointment, knowing that the former three-sport athlete would encourage his charges to enroll at his alma mater.

As the spring semester drew to a close it was necessary to crowd in two more doubleheaders. On Monday, May 13, Hope met Adrian at Riverview Park with Jim Kaat on the mound. In the second inning, Jack Kempker singled and Art Olson beat out a bunt. Kaat then singled both runners home. In the third, Kempker's home run into the left field grandstand made it 3-0. Hope added single runs in the fourth and fifth, the former as a result of Kaat's third RBI of the afternoon. The fifth inning score came when Woodcock doubled and scored on Olson's sacrifice fly. Jim Kaat's final appearance as a Hope pitcher was memorable. Tension mounted as he moved through 6⅔ innings without giving up a hit. Finally, with two gone in the seventh, Adrian's Jim Saddler stroked a double to center, breaking up the no-hit bid. Kaat retired the next batter to complete the 5-0 shutout.

Vander Lind was on the hill for the Dutchmen in the second game, which was forced into extra innings. With the score tied at 4-4 in the eighth, Siedentop, Wetherbee, and Vander Lind all bunted successfully. Siedentop was then forced at the plate, but Ron Bekius lifted a long fly to left which scored Wetherbee and gave Vander Lind the 5-4 victory.

The next day, May 14, the Dutchmen traveled to Olivet to close out the season. In the opener, the Comets played hardball against Hope starter Bob Andree, collecting three runs in the first, one in the second, and two more in the fourth. Hope countered with two in the first and one in the third on singles by Olson and Faber but came up short. The 6-5 defeat ended any thoughts of a championship tie, but a game remained to be played.

In game two, Kober took the mound and received excellent support from his teammates. Hope scored three in the first, three in the second, and one in the third. Hope put the game away in the fifth inning with seven big runs, but the effort was costly. Olson, going all out for a base hit, collided at first base with Olivet second baseman Bud Dean. Olson suffered a broken jaw on this last day of the season, while Dean received a gash in the head. Coach De Vette used 16 players in the 14-2 victory. The Dutchmen collected 11 hits, all singles, but also capitalized on nine Olivet errors. Kober's four-hitter left coach and players feeling good about their season. Hope's 10-3 MIAA record was good for a solid second place and the overall record included 14 wins, the most ever by a Hope baseball team. In a post-season meeting, Woodcock was named the Dutchmen's most valuable player by his teammates, and Olson, with his jaw wired shut, was elected captain for 1958. Kaat and Woodcock were named to the All-MIAA team. Kaat would shortly sign with the Washington Senators in a prelude to a brilliant major league career.

*   *   *

Prospects were bright for Coach Al Timmer as he began his final stint at the helm of Hope's golfers. Junior captain Ray De Does had proven himself dependable in nearly every meet. He would be joined by veterans Bob Burwitz and Joe Martin. Filling out the team were freshmen George Bitner and Bob Holt. The latter was a brother of Bill Holt from Hope's '56 team. In the early stages Dave Ousterling and Peter Cupery were also squad members, as was Ray Beckering.

Coach Timmer knew that he had some quality golfers, but considerable patience would be necessary during the initial weeks. In the season opener with Grand Rapids Junior College, De Does took medallist honors with an 80 and also won 3-0. Burwitz, a sophomore, was also a 3-0 winner, but the remainder of Timmer's troops were not so fortunate. Martin, Beckering, and Bitner were all shut out and the Grand Rapids team emerged with a 9-6 victory.

The Dutchmen would experience more disappointment on Friday, April 19, at the Baw Bise Country Club in Hillsdale. The Dales' Bob King was in mid-season form to take medalist honors with a 74. De Does and Bob Holt were not far behind with 76's, but both lost 2½-½. Burwitz shot an 82 but was beaten 3-0. Martin had an 86 and Dave Ousterling a 94 to end up on the short end of 3-0 scores. The 14-1 drubbing called for additional practice in the week ahead.

On Thursday, April 25 Hope entertained the Albion Britons at the American Legion Country Club. Recent rains had left puddles and considerable mud in spots throughout the course, but such conditions did not deter Burwitz. His 73 made him medalist for the day and gave him a 2-1 victory over Albion's Bob Bell, who shot 74. De Does had a 76 to defeat B. Fox 2-1, but Holt, with an 81, lost to Peter Young 2-1. Bitner lost to Barry Johns 2½-½, and Martin lost to Bob Hamilton 3-0. The Dutch had shown some improvement, but the 10½-5½ defeat left them somewhat in the doldrums.

The worm finally turned on Tuesday, April 30, at the Lenawees Country Club in Adrian. De Does, with a 79, defeated Adrian's Don Gatsden 3-0. He was also medalist for the day. Holt (80) was a winner over Bill Watts, 3-0, and Bitner, with the same score, defeated John Henderson 3-0. Martin (89) closed out the day with a 2½-½ win over Charles Bomer (92). The Dutchmen were finally able to savor an 11½-½ team victory and gain some much needed confidence.

The good news continued on Friday, May 3, at home as Hope met Calvin at the Legion Country Club. Burwitz was medalist with a 77 while getting the best of J. Bielema (89) 3-0. De Does, with a 78, defeated Calvin's Weidenaar (88) 3-0. Holt also carded a 78 in winning over Eskes, Martin (82) beat out Schneider (102), and Bitner (82) defeated Vander Ark (98). All scores were 3-0 to complete the 15-0 shutout.

When the Alma Scots came to Holland on Monday, May 6, the score was not quite as lopsided, but Hope still dominated the match. De Does again took charge as medalist with a 73 as he defeated Bob Postma (79) 3-0. Burwitz, not quite on top of his game (84), lost to Gord Snyder (79) 2½-½. But Holt (79) got the best of quarterback Dick Ayling (84) 3-0 and Bitner (82) defeated Tom Jackson (87) 3-0.

Alma's Bill Jones (84) edged Martin (85) 2-1 to complete the Scots' scoring. Hope's 11½-4½ victory evened their season at 3-3, with Olivet and Kalamazoo yet to play in the dual meet section of the season.

The Dutchmen continued to be impressive on Thursday, May 9, when they made the trip to Olivet. De Does was medalist yet again with a 76, but had strong competition from the Comets' Bob Burton (79) before winning 2-1. Burwitz (79) was back in form defeating Olivet's Verhoh (90) 3-0. Holt, with a 77, took Ritchit (86) 3-0 while Martin, enjoying his best performance of the year, with a 77, defeated Hackon (92) 3-0. Bitner (81) closed out Hope's scoring with a 3-0 win over Winter (103). Hope's 14-1 victory put them on the plus side of the ledger at 4-3.

The Dutchmen streak ended on Wednesday, May 15, at the Saugatuck course with the Kalamazoo Hornets doing the damage. Kazoo's Don Winterhalter (78) took medalist honors in defeating Bitner (88) 3-0. Skip Marx (81) caught De Does (86) on an off day and beat him 2-1. In the day's closest match, Kazoo's De Kreek (80) defeated Holt (81) 2½-½, but Martin (81) returned the favor by besting Bill Western (84) 2½-½. K's football quarterback, Bob Urshalitz (81), proved his versatility by winning over Burwitz (88) 3-0. The 11-4 Kalamazoo victory put them in the driver's seat for the coming league meet.

The MIAA conference meet was held on Friday, May 17, at the Kalamazoo Country Club. The hometown Hornets stayed true to form in taking first place with 811 strokes. Their ace, Don Winterhalter, captured medalist honors for the second straight year with rounds of 77 and 75 for a 152 total. De Does was not far behind with 74 and 80 for a total of 154. Hope, in second place, was 17 strokes behind the winner with 828. In somewhat of a surprise, Hope finished three strokes ahead of Hillsdale. Other team scores were Hillsdale 831, Albion 856, Alma 883, Adrian 952, Calvin 958, and Olivet 965. Hope's overall third-place finish was due to the earlier dual meet losses, but it had been a good season. Coming through at the Field Day meet was a fitting sendoff for retiring Coach Al Timmer.

*   *   *

Athletics Director Al Vanderbush, who had coached football, cross country, and track at Hope, took over the tennis team in 1957. John Jeltes, Phil Boersma, and Tiger Teusink were the returning veterans. They were joined by Jim Kamp, Ron Hughes, Jim Engbers, and Rowland Van Es. Details of Hope's opening match at Alma on Friday, April 12, are sketchy, but the Dutchmen managed to squeeze out a 5-4 win that would be significant down the line. In Grand Rapids on Saturday, April 20, the team had a similar experience, this time against Grand Rapids Junior College. Dave Berles, at number-one singles for JC, was able to down Jeltes 6-3, 3-6, 6-2, but Boersma (H) defeated Walt Jolley 6-0, 6-1, and Teusink (H) won over Ron Betten 6-1, 6-2.

Kamp (H) defeated Clyde Walker 6-0, 6-2, and Jim Engbers (H) downed Pat Rosenboom in a three-setter, 6-4, 5-7, 6-3, but Jim Lind (JC) took Hughes 4-6, 6-1, 6-1, leaving the matter up to the doubles players. Momentum was with JC as Berles-Betten defeated Jeltes-Teusink 6-4, 6-4, and Jolley-Walker got Boersma- Van Es 8-6, 8-6. With the match on the line, Hope's two Jims, Kamp and Engbers, defeated Jim Lind-Pat Rosenboom 6-1, 6-3. The Dutchmen had been extended, but enjoyed their second 5-4 victory.

Hope won its third match in a row one week later in Holland against Olivet but details of that contest are not available. On Tuesday, April 30, the Hope team traveled to Kalamazoo with the usual result. The only Dutchman victory came as Kamp defeated Bob Yuell 6-2, 7-5. In the other match-ups, Jerry Schram (K) took Jeltes 8-6, 6-4, Bill Japinga (K) defeated Phil Boersma 6-1, 6-0, Bob Brice (K) won over Teusink 6-1, 6-0, and Charles Nisbet (K) defeated Engbers 8-10, 6-4, 6-1. In doubles Schram-Japinga (K) downed Jeltes-Engbers 6-0, 6-3. and Brice-Yuell (K) defeated Boersma-Teusink 6-4, 6-3 making the final, Kalamazoo 6, Hope 1. The Dutchmen had played well in spots, but the Hornets continued to be too strong for anyone in the league.

The Hope team bounced back on Friday, May 3, against Hillsdale on the Holland courts. Jeltes won over Jerome 6-4, 6-2, and Boersma followed with a victory over Tanallali 6-4, 6-0. Mac Intosh (HI) defeated Teusink 6-4, 6-2, but Kamp (H) downed Briggs 8-6, 6-1, and Van Es (H) was a winner over Zukerberg 6-3, 8-6. In doubles Jerome-Mac Intosh (HI) defeated Jeltes-Kamp 6-0, 6-4, and Boersma-Teusink (H) won over Tanallali-Zukerberg 6-4, 6-1 to complete the 5-2 team victory.

The Dutchmen were off to a good start at Albion on Tuesday, May 7. Jeltes (H) defeated Dale Brubaker 6-2, 8-6, and Boersma (H) got the best of Don Hines 2-6, 6-3, 6-0. But Albion's Bill John downed Tiger Teusink 8-6, 6-4, and Gary Riley (A) defeated Jim Kamp 6-1, 6-0. In the crucial number five singles match, John Kraft (A) outlasted Rowland Van Es 4-6, 6-4, 6-0. The doubles were divided, with Brubaker-Hines (A) winning over Jeltes-Kamp 6-3, 6-1, and Boersma-Teusink (H) defeating Riley-Johnson 6-3, 6-0. The 4-3 team loss was hard to take. It would eventually give Albion second place.

On Monday, May 13, Hope was back on track with a 7-0 shutout of Adrian on the Holland courts. It was Jeltes (H) over Craft 6-2, 6-3, Boersma (H) over Engwall 6-0, 6-2, Teusink (H) winning from Moore 6-0, 6-0, Kamp (H) defeating Pavelko 6-3, 7-5, and Van Es downing Boudreau 6-2, 6-0. In doubles, the team of Jeltes-Kamp defeated Craft-Engwall (A) 6-0, 4-6, 6-2, and Jim Engbers-Ron Hughes (H) were winners against Moore-Pavelko (A) 6-0, 6-1.

The next day the Dutchmen traveled to Grand Rapids to close out the dual season against traditional rival Calvin. In singles, John Jeltes (H) was victorious over Ken Zandee 6-1, 6-1, and Phil Boersma defeated Bill Dozeman (C) 6-0, 6-0.

Teusink (H) won from Rich Sharda 4-6, 6-2, 6-3, and Kamp (H) was the winner over Ed Meyering 6-3, 7-5. Warren Borr (C) defeated Van Es 8-6, 6-4, and Dirk Jellema (C) downed Ron Hughes 2-6, 6-1, 6-3. The extra singles match was by mutual agreement of the coaches. In doubles it was Sharda-Dozeman (C) over Jeltes-Kamp 6-1, 7-5, and Boersma-Teusink (H) over Boer-Zandee 6-0, 6-2 to give Hope the 5-3 team win.

The conference meet was scheduled for Friday and Saturday, May 17-18, but cold and continuing rain made the courts unplayable. Not even Kalamazoo had an indoor facility in 1957 and the only alternative was to cancel the meet. This meant that the championship would be determined by the schools' dual-meet records. Kalamazoo at 7-0 was again the champion. Following were Albion, 6-1; Hope, 5-2; Hillsdale, Alma, and Calvin, tied with 3-4 records; Adrian at 1-6; and Olivet 0-7.

Women's tennis was alive and well at Hope in the spring of '57 with Coach Mary Breid in charge. The team included senior Jan Evert, juniors Joyce Leighley and Alice Warren, sophomores Donna Hardenberg and Carolyn Scholten, and freshmen Jan Owen and Mary Kay Diephuis. Scores were as follows: Calvin 4 - Hope 3, Hope 4 - Calvin 3, Hope 6 - Aquinas 1, Hope 4 - Western Michigan 3, Western Michigan 5 - Hope 2. Details are lacking, but in the Aquinas match singles winners were Evert, Owen, Scholten, and Dephuis. The doubles winners were Warren- Owen, and Leighley- Hardenberg. Kalamazoo's women captured the WMIAA meet, with Albion second and Hope third.

In the race for the MIAA All-Sports Trophy, it was Kalamazoo winning for the first time since 1937-38 with 80 points. Hope was a close second with 77 and Albion third with 71. Following in order were Hillsdale 53, Alma 40, Calvin 38, Adrian 21, and Olivet 12.

* * *

Thus ended my first full year as a member of the Hope College faculty and coaching staff. It had been rewarding in a great many ways, most notably the association with high-caliber colleagues and students. There was much to look forward to. My summer would be spent representing the college at various Reformed Church youth camps and eagerly anticipating the first days of football practice in the fall of '57.

CHAPTER 3

AN ERA UNDERWAY

Every school with athletic program has known it, a special stretch of time when things fall into place and strong teams result. In the fall of 1957 Hope's coaches could envision the onset of such a period. A corps of talented athletes, mostly "homegrown" underclassmen, dotted the ranks. They had been joined by some outstanding transfers, several from larger schools, and the resulting depth was beginning to pay off. In '55 Warren Vander Hill had come from the University of Maryland and Don Paarlberg from the University of Illinois. Bill Huibregtse and Duane Voskuil also moved from the Big Ten to the MIAA, both from the University of Wisconsin. End George Van Verst made the move from Williams College, and fullback Ron Berkius transferred from Western State College of Colorado. Four junior college transfers would be heard from during the next two years. Linebacker-guard Tom Miller from Grand Rapids Junior College would bolster the grid picture, and Bob Andree, also from GRJC, had already made his mark in baseball. Wayne Vriesman from Muskegon Community College, and Darrell Beernink from Northwestern Junior College in Iowa, were known quantities and brightened the basketball picture.

In addition, one sensed an unusual degree of compatibility. On field or court the mix was good. It extended to and included the banter of dormitory life. When books and sports were put aside, players might be found in the confines of "Charlie's Fine Foods," a small restaurant of stellar reputation on the corner of 18th Street and Columbia Avenue (the building remains at this writing). Owner Charlie Telgenhof welcomed athletes with open arms and reveled in his role as *maitre d'*. The sessions at Charlie's included an appraisal of sport at all levels, not to mention a careful classification of current campus co-eds.

CHARLIE'S FINE FOODS

"Charlie's Fine Foods" at 18th and Columbia in Holland was a haven for Hope College athletes. In this photo, owner Charlie Telgenhof greets Jerry Boeve. Others, L. to R. are Bob Hilbelink, Bill Vanderbilt, Wayne Vriesman, Paul Benes, Stuart Post, (unidentified), Warren Vander Hill, and Lawrence "Doc" Green.

As the '57 football season approached, the mood was upbeat, to say the least, but there were sobering moments. A top prospect on the 1956 squad had been tackle Tom Zwemer, a freshman from Norfolk, Va. Tom was the son of Jim ('33) and Marian ('35) Zwemer. He had been trained well as a football player, and more importantly, as a gentleman. His quiet manner and controlled intensity made him popular with players and coaches alike. The Hope staff placed him in the tradition of his father, and also teammate Larry Ter

Molen. Such was praise of the highest order.

Near the end of the first semester, illness forced Tom to withdraw from school and on March 11, 1957, word arrived that he had succumbed to cancer. His sudden and untimely passing jolted the campus and prompted serious reflection by all young athletes.

On Monday, Sept. 2, Coach De Vette greeted a turnout of 50 prospects, the largest since 1949. Experience would be provided by 22 returning lettermen. De Vette's early assessment was that backfield depth and defense would be the team's strength. In early sessions coaches worked to perfect a 4-3 defensive alignment popularly known as the "Eagle" after the system used by Earl "Greasy" Neale of the Philadelphia Eagles. De Vette's placement of various members of the defensive front gave it an unorthodox appearance which was confusing to opposing linemen. Movement of players at the snap added further to the offense's dilemma. De Vette tagged it "55" to distinguish it from Hope's other basic set, "54" (later 52).

The '57 opener was a night game at Riverview Park with Eastern Michigan College providing the opposition. Hope's faith in its strong defense suffered an early blow when Eastern halfback Dale Nichols broke free on his own 45, reversed his field, and raced 55 yards for the game's first touchdown. The now-aroused Dutchmen blocked the point try by Jerry Wedge, but the Hurons enjoyed a 6-0 lead with but 4:45 gone in the first quarter. Four minutes later, with the ball on the Hope 35, quarterback Jack Faber unloaded a long pass which Jerry Hendrickson gathered in on the Eastern 35 and ran untouched for Hope's first score. Bill Huibregtse's kick was not good and the score stood 6-6 at halftime. A hard-fought third quarter was scoreless, but early in the final period the Dutchmen put together a 43-yard drive that featured runs by Hendrickson, Jim Hoeksema, and a 16-yarder by Mert Vander Lind. Hoeksema finally pushed to the two-yard line and Faber went in on a quarterback sneak. This time Huibregtse's kick was good and Hope moved ahead 13-6. The TD came with 2:30 gone in the fourth quarter. Midway in the period, linebacker Tom Miller intercepted an Eastern pass on the Hope 47 and, on a fine return, took the ball all the way to the Eastern 30. The Hurons dug in and the going got tougher, but in seven plays Hoeksema, Voskuil, and Ron Bekius moved Hope to the five-yard line. The hard-earned score came on a left end sweep by Voskuil. Huibregtse's kick was blocked, but Hope's 19-6 victory had the Dutchmen off on the right foot.

De Vette's squad sought its first MIAA win on Saturday, Sept. 28, when they journeyed to Alma for a night game. Ends Wiegerink and Jim Hilmert would miss the contest due to nagging knee injuries and would be replaced by Ron Bronson and Curt Menning. The Scots of Coach Art Smith were led by fullback Pat Brady, quarterback Dick Ayling and speedy receiver Len Fase. The Dutchmen drew first blood in the opening quarter when Huibregtse recovered a Brady fumble on the Alma 27. The Dutch converted the miscue into a score when Hendrickson went off-tackle from the four. Huibregtse's conversion made it 7-0, and the score held until halftime.

Turnabout seemed fair play in the third quarter, when Alma recovered a Hope fumble which led to a Brady touchdown. Murray's kick made it 7-7. Late in the quarter, Mick Faber broke through to block an Alma punt and then downed the ball on the Alma two. Jack Faber sneaked in for the TD for a 13-7 Dutchmen lead, but the all-important point try by Huibregtse sailed wide. The Hope lead held up until the final two minutes of the game. At this point the Scots mounted a drive that was climaxed by a 20-yard pass from Ayling to Fase for the tying score with 1:40 remaining. Alma took the lead for the first time on Murray's perfect conversion. In the time remaining, Jack Faber threw four desperation passes. Three fell incomplete and the fourth was intercepted. The 14-13 come-from-behind victory was sweet music for Scottish ears, but a devastating blow to Hope's title hopes.

Hope's next contest, though non-league, was one of those not-to-be-forgotten experiences. On Saturday, Oct. 5, the Dutchmen met the Wildcats of Northern Michigan College for the first time in the history of the schools. The 450-mile trip to Marquette in Michigan's Upper Peninsula necessitated an 11 a.m. departure on Friday. While professors grumbled at lost class time, players were elated to be off on such a long jaunt. At Mackinaw City, Hope's chartered Greyhound was driven aboard a car ferry for the trip across the Straits to St. Ignace, where motel accommodations had been made by Athletics Director Al Vanderbush. Enroute, the Mackinac Bridge could be seen as it neared completion. On Saturday afternoon as the team journeyed westward, the glory of a Michigan autumn was everywhere apparent. As we descended a hill outside Munising, the brilliance of the panorama before us was awe-inspiring. The combination of colors and late-afternoon sun caused the bus to become very quiet. For a few moments football was not important.

Kickoff was at 8 p.m., and Coach Frosty Ferzaca's Wildcats were ready. In the early going Hope fumbled a snap from center and the Northerners recovered on their own 35. A 65-yard drive followed with quarterback Tom Schwalback going in on a sneak. He then converted to make it 7-0 with but three minutes gone. It was an inauspicious start for the Dutchmen, and the coaches were not happy. The remainder of the half was a series of missed chances by both teams. At one point Hope drove to the five-yard line only to fumble the ball away. Northern had a similar drive, but Hoeksema intercepted a Schwalback pass in the end zone and returned it to the 22 to end the threat.

The Hope coaches felt strongly that the 7-0 halftime deficit was not a true measure of the team's capability. During the intermission, team members were urged (perhaps not too gently!) to produce an effort consistent with their potential. The team's spirited response was a 65-yard third quarter drive that featured long runs by fullback Ron Wetherbee and Jim Hoeksema. It was Hoeksema off-tackle for the final eight yards to paydirt. Huibregtse's kick evened the score at 7-7.

In the fourth quarter the Wildcats pushed the tired Dutchmen toward their own goal. As the drive concluded, Schwalback passed successfully to fullback Bill Brodeur near the Hope goal line. A crushing tackle by linebacker Gene Van Dongen jarred the ball loose and into the end zone, where it was recovered by end George Knecht for the go-ahead score. But this time, the reliable Schwalback missed the conversion and Northern's lead remained at 13-7. With but three minutes remaining in the game it was Van Dongen again. This time he intercepted an ill-advised pass on the Northern 30 and returned it to the eight-yard line. The defense stiffened knowing that the game, was on the line. Three Dutch running plays failed to move the ball, but on fourth-and-eight, Jack Faber found end Bronson in the end zone and the score was tied. Huibregtse then split the uprights in what would be the second-most important kick of his career. In the closing minutes the air was filled with passes, but Hope end George Van Verst intercepted one with a minute to go and the game was over. The 14-13 Hope victory was almost an exact reversal of the previous week's tussle at Alma. In the team effort, the defensive performance by Van Dongen was outstanding. When victory or defeat hangs on the accuracy of one kick, the loss is a bitter pill. The Hope coaches could empathize with Frosty Ferzacca, but their own elation was in no way diminished.

The trip home on the following day was long only in miles. The game's high points were reviewed and retold in varying versions as team members savored a significant accomplishment. At one stop, center Bill Brookstra and manager Stu Post secured a sizeable supply of apples and set up a concession aboard the bus. Their margin of profit remains a secret, but camaraderie was enhanced and the overall experience remains vivid to this day.

With the non-league interlude complete, it was time to concentrate once more on MIAA opponents. During the practice week, Coach De Vette moved Vander Lind from halfback to quarterback. De Vette hoped to capitalize on Vander Lind's running ability, especially in the roll out run-pass option. Jack Faber, in addition to his defensive post, would continue to be available in long-pass situations.

Kalamazoo's Hornets came to Holland for a night game on Saturday, Oct. 12, and 2,500 fans turned out for the contest at Riverview. For the first quarter and most of the second, defense prevailed, but, with 56 seconds left in the half, Hope moved to the Kalamazoo 15. Vander Lind then rolled out to the right, hugged the sideline, faked out two defenders at the two and went in for the score. The conversion by Huibregtse gave Hope a 7-0 halftime advantage. The Dutch had fumbled away two other scoring opportunities, one on

PRESSURE DEFENSE

Hillsdale's Jim "Jellybean" Reynolds, an excellent athlete, was always a thorn in the side of Hope athletes. Here, in the 1957 game he harasses quarterback Mert Vander Lind.

the 15 and another on the nine. In the second half Vander Lind intercepted a Bob Urshalitz pass on the Hornet 35 and returned it to the 20. Six plays later Voskuil went over on an off-tackle play and Huibregtse's conversion made it 14-0. There would be no more scoring in the game. Hope's defense put on its best performance of the season in stifling the Hornets. Urshalitz, who had given the Dutchmen trouble in '56, was nailed often and ended with negative 37-yards. Tackles Ter Molen and George Peelen were effective in freeing middle linebacker Huibregtse to roam and tackle at will. End Paul Wiegerink made his first appearance of the season, and Dick Gantos, coming off an injury, played briefly. The Hornets were held to 24 yards rushing while the Dutchmen were piling up 245. Hope was plagued by numerous fumbles to prevent the score from reaching a higher figure than the 14-0 final. The "Wooden Shoes" were back in Holland and Coach De Vette had recorded his first win over friend Rolla Anderson.

On Oct. 19 it was once again the long journey to Adrian for the Bulldogs' homecoming. An estimated 3,000 fans turned out to support coach Bob Gillis' team, which featured the Fred Hobart-to-Leon Harper combination, plus a strong defense. Twice in the early going, Hope drove to the three-

COOL UNDER PRESSURE

Bill Huibregtse notches a first quarter extra point from the hold of Jack Faber. In the 1957 contest Hope capitalized on Albion turnovers to gain a 47-7 victory.

yard line only to be turned back, once due to a fumble. The Dutchman defense was again in evidence later in the quarter, when Mick Faber and Huibregtse blocked an Adrian punt. The Hope ground attack then took over with Hendrickson going in for the score. Huibregtse's kick gave the Dutchman an early 7-0 lead.

In the second quarter Jack Faber intercepted a Hobart pass on the Adrian 48 and returned it to the 25. A Vander Lind pass to Wiegerink put the ball on the nine. At this point De Vette called on Jerry Herp, a 145-pound halfback from tiny Hopkins High School. Herp responded by going off-tackle through five defenders for the touchdown. Huibregtse's second conversion made it 14-0 at halftime.

The determined Bulldogs made a bid in the third quarter when they moved to the Hope 19 on a 22-yard pass play, again from Hobart to Harper, but the Dutchmen defense held to end the threat. Early in the fourth period, Huibregtse intercepted a Hobart pass and Hope was on the move. A long pass from Jack Faber to Hendrickson put the ball on the Adrian six, but it was the Bulldogs' turn to play tough and the Dutchmen failed to score. The Hope defense, led by Ter Molen and Mick Faber, was effective against the run, as Adrian was held to 98 yards rushing. The home team had 157 yards in the air with Harper getting 74. Gantos, Bronson, and Voskuil missed the contest due to injuries, but the De Vette men had notched their second straight 14-0 shutout and looked forward to their Homecoming showdown with Hillsdale on Oct. 26.

The Dales of Frank "Muddy" Waters moved into Riverview Park with the usual strong contingent that was well-coached, confident, and undefeated. Two days of heavy rains had forced Hope practice into the narrow confines of Carnegie-Schouten Gym and everyone knew that victory would be a tall order. Hope's defense showed well in the early going, but, with 1:50 remaining in the first quarter, halfback Walt Poe got behind the Dutchman defenders to gather in a Doug Maison pass on the 17. The scoring play covered 47 yards, and with Wayne O'Shaughnessy's conversion the Dales seemed on their way with a 7-0 lead. But in the closing minutes of the half, Huibregtse intercepted a Maison pass on the Hope 35 and returned it to the 47. A Jack Faber-to-Vander Lind pass was complete on the Dales' 20. Vander Lind made it to the 13 before being forced out-of-bounds. Faber then passed to the end zone to freshman Mike Blough, who dropped the ball! With confidence in Blough, De Vette sent in the word to repeat the play. With 12 seconds remaining in the half, Blough caught the ball for the touchdown. Huibregtse's conversion attempt sailed wide by one foot, but with the score at 7-6 the Dutchmen knew that they could play with their esteemed opponent.

The second half proved to be an exhibition of classic defense by both teams. Hope, after ringing up 104 yards through the air in the first half, was held to zero in the second. To make matters worse, Hillsdale's big defensive linemen were hard to move and Hope's ground game had trouble making first downs. This resulted in the Dutchman defense being on the field a great deal while staving off one drive after another. In the third period, two Maison passes to Jellybean Reynolds put the ball on the Hope nine, but Hope forced a fumble by halfback Don Eugenio and the Dutchmen recovered. In the fourth quarter, Maison passes got the ball to the Hope 11 with first down. Four plays later, Hope had held once again, this time on the three. In the closing two minutes, the persistent Dales were stopped on the one-yard line. The Dutchmen were unable to make a first down and punted the ball away to end the game. The Dales had had the best of it with 281 total yards to 169 for Hope and deserved the hard-fought 7-6 victory, but Hope's stellar defense would stand them in good stead the rest of the way.

Hope traveled to Olivet on Nov. 2 minus the services of Voskuil, Tom Miller, and Gantos, all out with injuries sustained in the Hillsdale encounter. After a scoreless first quarter, the Dutchmen got their offense in gear. From the Olivet 36, Vander Lind picked up 18 yards on a rollout. This was followed by a 17-yard scamper up the middle by substitute fullback Tyrone Rupp. Vander Lind's sneak from the one opened the scoring. A Huibregtse conversion made it 7-0. Olivet fumbled the ensuing kickoff and Curt Menning recovered on the six-yard line. Fullback Bekius went the distance on the first play and Huibregtse's kick made it 14-0 at the half. The Comet defense stiffened in the third quarter, but with five minutes left in the period, Bekius intercepted a pass on the Olivet 40 and rambled all the way to the five. Two plays later he went up the middle from the three for Hope's third TD. "Hubie's" conversion upped the count to 21-0. Near the end of the quarter, Hope's Jerry Herp intercepted another Comet pass, this one on the Hope 40. Subs now dotted the Hope lineup and quarterback Jim Fox connected on a pass to halfback John Vandenburg on a scoring play that covered 44 yards. Once again Huibregtse converted, moving the score to 28-0.

Coach De Vette cleared the bench for the entire fourth quarter and the Comets were able to mount a 40-yard scoring drive. A long pass from quarterback Joe Diaz to end Joe Iauch put the ball on the Hope 11. Bob Jones eventually scored from the one and the conversion was good to make the final score 28-7. The Comets of Coach Henry Paul were obviously experiencing a tough year, as the touchdown against Hope was their first of the season.

Saturday, Nov. 9, had been designated "Mom and Dad's Day" at Hope with Albion furnishing the opposition. During the night the mercury plunged to 20 degrees. Cold northwest winds swept in from Lake Michigan and coated Riverview Park with four inches of snow. Holland City maintenance crews scrambled to plow off the snow and at least make the yard lines visible. A partisan crowd, mostly parents, bundled up and were thankful for the covered grandstand on the north side of the field. Athletics Director Al Vanderbush and the Hope coaches decided that it would only be fair to Albion to have the bench areas for both teams on the north side of the field, thus affording some protection from the strong winds. Straw was scattered in the bench areas to cover the snow and a kerosene heater was provided for each team. Albion was positioned at the west end of the field while Hope moved its team to the east, which was slightly more protected. (There was a limit to charity!)

Coach Morley Fraser came to town with a solid Albion team. Lodged in second place, the Britons had lost only to powerful Hillsdale, and that by the respectable score of 20-14. Quarterback Bob Gamble teamed with premier receiver Tom Taylor, who would one day coach the Britons to an MIAA Championship. Garth Richey, another talented athlete, played the other end. A Hope victory would mean a second place tie in the MIAA.

From the beginning, things went wrong for the visitors. The Dutchmen won the toss and elected to defend the west goal with a strong wind at their backs. On their first possession, they had success running the ball up the middle and off-tackle. Hendrickson broke free for a 35-yard run to the Albion five, then scored on the next play. Huibregtse's kick with the wind behind it, threatened a window in the house across Columbia Avenue and the Dutchmen were ahead 7-0 with but four minutes into the contest. Two plays after the kickoff, Menning recovered a Gamble fumble on the Briton 10-yard line. On Hope's second play from scrimmage, Rupp went up the middle for the touchdown. With Huibregtse's second conversion, Hope led 14-0 with 5:44 gone in the first quarter.

Hope continued to have success with interior line plays, but a third score was set up when Vander Lind reeled off a 34-yard run behind good blocks from Wiegerink and Bekius to move the ball to the Albion 10. Three plays later Rupp went up the middle for his second TD of the quarter, and again the Huibregtse kick was good. The early 21-0 lead seemed unbelievable, but Albion's woes continued. Two plays after the kickoff, Huibregtse recovered a Briton fumble on the Albion 31. On the first play from scrimmage, Bekius, on a trap play, went the distance for Hope's fourth touchdown of the quarter. Huibregtse's fourth conversion made it 28-0. On defense, Ter Molen, Huibregtse, and Don "Punch" Paarlberg were outstanding as the Britons were held to 12 yards rushing in the quarter and were unable to advance beyond their own 31.

The pace slowed somewhat during the rest of the game, but Hope scored in each of the remaining periods. Four minutes into the second quarter, Hendrickson intercepted a Gamble pass on the Albion 36. Rupp was free up the middle for 19 yards, and Bekius followed with another gainer to the five. Bekius tried the middle again and slipped through for the fifth Dutchmen TD. Huibregtse's kick attempt against the wind did not reach the goal post, but the Dutchmen enjoyed a 34-0 halftime lead.

With 6:54 remaining in the third period, Hope sustained a 55-yard, eight-play drive. Hoeksema was tough off tackle with 20 yards in two plays, and Hendrickson followed with a 15-yard left end sweep for the score. Running against the wind had proven more successful than kicking. Hoeksema ran his favorite play for the point, and Hope was ahead 41-0. At this point the Britons bounced back and demonstrated their true colors. Gamble, now with the wind, led a 62-yard, six-play drive that was climaxed by a 12-yard pass to Taylor for the lone Albion score. Dick Larson converted to make it 41-7.

As Albion continued to play catch-up in the fourth period, Gene Van Dongen intercepted a Gamble pass on the Hope 20 and lateraled to Hendrickson, who moved down the sideline to the Albion 28. Four plays later the lateral was again employed, this time with Hendrickson tossing back to Vander Lind, who went the remaining 10 yards for Hope's final score. Bekius' kick attempt was not good and the wild contest ended at 47-7. Statistics alone would belie the score. Hope had 354 yards in total offense, but went 0-for-5 in the passing department. Albion had a respectable 236 in total offense with 103 in the air and made 12 first downs to 11 for the Dutchmen, but turning the ball over on eight fumbles proved the Britons' undoing.

During the contest coach Fraser had sighted a large container of analgesic balm in the Hope bench area. He became convinced that the Dutchman secret to good footing in the snow and mud was a painting of shoe soles with said balm. He voiced the opinion that the advantage thus gained was a factor in the Hope victory. Hope coaches and players were bewildered by such an interpretation, but took it in stride. The Hope team managers have assured me that their only adjustment was to substitute 3/4" mud cleats for the conventional ones.

The season finale was anti-climactic at best, but 1,800 loyal followers turned out at Riverview Park on Nov. 16.

**THE 1957 HOPE FOOTBALL TEAM — 7-2 OVERALL
2nd PLACE TIE WITH ALBION IN MIAA**

Front Row L. to R.: Ken "Mick" Faber, Curt Menning, Jim Hilmert, John De Fouw, Head Coach Russ De Vette, Captain Mert Vander Lind, Paul Wiegerink, George Van Verst, Ron Wetherbee, Dick Gantos. **2nd Row:** End Coach Al Vanderbush, Jerry Herp, Tom Stoel, Rich Leonard, Jim Mohr, Ty Rupp, Jim Menzer, Keith White, Jim Hoeksema, Larry Ter Molen, Jack Faber, Assistant Trainer Stu Post, Trainer Lawrence "Doc" Green. **3rd Row:** Manager Carl Ver Beek, Tom Miller, John Vandenburg, Jim "Tiger" De Witt, Gene Van Dongen, Ron Bekius, Bill Huibregtse, Jim Fox, Charlie Smits, Ron Bronson, Manager Cal Rynbrandt, Manager Hank Doele. **4th Row:** Line Coach Gord Brewer, George Peelen, Chuck Coulson, Ted Van Zanden, Stu Dorn, Jerry Hendrickson, Don Lautenbach, Bill Brookstra, Don "Punch" Paarlberg, Art "Swede" Olson, Don De Young, Mike Blough.

The MIAA scheduling practice of placing a non-league game at the end of the season was ill-advised and would be changed in years to come. Beloit College of the Midwest Conference adhered to a league rule which prevented freshman participation. To offset this loss of personnel the league permitted free substitution when other conferences did not. Hope officials agreed to this rule change, but the beleaguered Buccaneers were beset with other problems. Two of their games had been canceled due to an outbreak of flu. Prior to departure for Holland, the Wisconsin team suffered another blow when Head Coach Carl "Pill" Nelson was called to Colorado due to the death of his brother. Assistant coaches Clare Eddy and Bob Nichols were determined to put up a good fight and this became evident with a scoreless first period. But Hope was near the end of a 40-yard, nine-play drive that featured a 15-yard run by Hendrickson and a 14-yard pass play from Vander Lind to Rupp. The scoring play came on a three-yard pass from Vander Lind to Bekius. A Huibregtse conversion gave Hope the early 7-0 lead.

Later in the period a personal foul penalty gave Hope the ball on the Beloit 25. Eight plays later, with 4:40 gone in the quarter, Jim Hoeksema broke off-tackle for the touchdown. The snap from center on the point try was fumbled, but an alert Huibregtse picked up the ball and ran it in to make the score 14-0. The Dutchmen would score once more before closing the book on 1957. With just 40 seconds gone in the final period, Hendrickson went over on a nine-yard left end sweep. Bill Huibregtse made good on his last kick of the season and Hope led 21-0. In the closing minutes Mert Vander Lind got loose on a 17-yard touchdown romp, but the play was called back because of a holding penalty. The Beloit team had put forth a noble effort, but had too much to overcome. Hope's overall 7-2 record had netted a second-place tie with Albion in the MIAA. Just two points had kept the Dutchmen from an undefeated season and things looked good for '58. Guard Mick Faber was selected as Hope's most valuable player, and Ter Molen was named captain for 1958. Vander Lind, Ter Molen, and Mick Faber were named to the All-MIAA team. Quarterback Doug Maison of Hillsdale was the league's MVP, and his team was selected to play Pittsburg State of Kansas in the small-college Holiday Bowl in St. Petersburg, Fla., on Dec. 21. The undefeated Dales lost by the narrow margin of 27-26, but Maison was chosen as the game's outstanding player.

* * *

Carroll Bennink was captain of Doc Green's 1957 cross country aggregation. Other team members were Bill Elzinga, John Ten Pas, John Needham, Cal Bruins, Gerald Kirchoff, Jim Rozeboom, and Roland Schut. It proved to be an unspectacular season, with the Dutchmen finishing fifth in the league meet and fifth overall in the MIAA. There were, however, some bright moments. Rozeboom, a freshman, emerged as the team's number-one performer and led the group to dual meet wins over Alma, GRJC, and Ferris Institute. Schut did his part for the team, but his primary purpose was basic conditioning for the upcoming basketball season.

* * *

Dwayne "Tiger" Teusink, a hometown product, was captain of Coach Russ De Vette's 1957-58 basketball squad. Hope was the pre-season favorite to win the MIAA title, and with good reason. The 1956-57 co-champs returned the entire starting five, plus perhaps the strongest bench in Hope history. With so many quality returnees, John Kleinheksel was the only player to move up from the previous year's jayvee team. Meanwhile, co-champion Albion had lost the services of stalwarts John Hannett and George Vivlamore via graduation.

The season opener for Hope on Wednesday, Dec. 4, was noteworthy in two respects. For the first time in several years, the first contest was with a league team. Secondly, it involved the two teams that had battled down to the wire for the co-championship in 1956-57, Hope and Albion. As a result, 2,100 fans crowded into the Civic Center, many playing hooky from mid-week church meetings. They would not be disappointed. As expected, 6' 11" Paul Benes and 6' 5" Ray Ritsema dominated the boards while Warren Vander Hill was hot from outside as the Dutchmen took a 35-24 lead into the locker room at the half. It was more of the same in the second half until the scoreboard showed a spread of 71-54 with four minutes remaining. At this point substitutes entered and played the rest of the way. The final count was Hope 77, Albion 66. Vander Hill led the Dutchmen with a game-high 21 points, while Benes had 16, Ray Ritsema 13, and Wayne Vriesman 10. Whitey Beernink added seven and Teusink six. Conrad Stover was high for the Britons with 20 and Virgil Hall and Jim Wilson each had 11.

With an important victory under their belt, the Dutchmen traveled to Alma on Saturday, Dec. 7. The Scots had a new coach in the person of Wayne Hintz, who had formerly served at Whitworth College in Spokane, Wash. Coach Hintz's team centered around high-scoring George Carter, and Hope's Jun Buursma was singled out by De Vette to hold the veteran in check. Buursma took the assignment seriously and held Carter scoreless until the Dutchmen had built a 20-point lead. Ray Ritsema had another of his great games on the boards, helping Hope to a 44-29 halftime lead. Early in the second half, the Dutchman lead increased to 25 and substitutes got their chance. Benes was high for Hope with 24, Ritsema tallied 15, and Vander Hill 12, while Buursma and Beernink each had 10. Carter led the Scots with 21, most of which came in the closing minutes. George Arrick followed with 11.

A late-night return from Alma always presented problems in terms of a post-game meal for the team. Restaurants were few and far between along the roads between Alma and Grand Rapids, and all were closed long before the weary and hungry players boarded their bus. But Hope's resourceful Athletics Director Al Vanderbush had convinced the proprietor of a small establishment in Cedar Springs to remain open after hours to accommodate the Dutchmen. The warm glow of the restaurant's windows was indeed a welcome sight on the deserted streets of the Red Flannel town. Aside from the owner, all employees had been sent home. This, however, was no problem as Benes and Ritsema were soon behind the counter dispensing milk shakes and speeding up the serving in other ways. As the team bus resumed its trek, all were grateful for such an oasis, one that would be remembered perhaps, when game details were no longer clear.

Two days later, the Dutchmen entertained Eastern Michigan College at the Civic Center. With two solid MIAA victories, the Hope squad continued to roll in the Dec. 9 non-league encounter. The teams played on even terms for about 12 minutes. Eastern enjoyed a 20-19 advantage with 13:11 remaining in the half, but at this point the Hope fast break shifted into gear and the team exploded. Benes scored 27 points enroute to an amazing 65-42 halftime lead, but with 1:57 remaining he suffered a mild sprain to the right ankle and would be through for the evening. But the rest of the talented squad soon picked up the slack and the pace continued. With 18:07 remaining, Ritsema was called for his fourth personal foul and made his way to the bench having scored but seven points. He would not return. Now, with both big guns out of action, the crowd looked for a slowdown. Such did not occur. With 11 minutes left, the subs took over. All of them scored, and with Daryl Siedentop's two free throws the Dutchman count reached 100. The final score stood at 112 to 80, with the winner's mark being the most scored by a Hope team in the Civic to that date. Playing less than a half, Benes led his team with 27. Vander Hill and Vriesman followed with 17 each, Buursma scored 12 and Bob Thomson eight. Fred Ireland led Eastern with 15. Next on the schedule was archrival Calvin.

Excitement intensified and by the end of the week reached a fever pitch. More than 5,000 fans crowded into the Grand Rapids Civic Auditorium to witness the battle between the league's two strongest teams. Ritsema kept the team loose with a few remarks about Hope's dressing room, which was located on the third floor adjacent to the stage. But both teams were tense as the game got underway. Buursma gave Hope an early lead with five first-half field goals but, with seven minutes remaining, Benes picked up his third foul and was forced to sit down. Coach Barney Steen's Knights then battled back to overcome an eight-point Hope lead and go to the locker room on the long end of a 43-41 score.

Six minutes into the second half, Teusink's two free throws put the Dutchmen up 58-56 and they would not again surrender the lead. Ritsema was strong on the defensive board during this period and numerous fast breaks resulted. At the 10-minute mark, Hope had widened its margin to 71-61. Vriesman was instrumental in this drive. His free throw with two minutes remaining made it 89-69, the largest spread of the game. The Knights kept up the pressure and narrowed the margin somewhat, but at the final buzzer it was Hope 92, Calvin 77. Ritsema and Vander Hill were high for the Dutchmen with 20 and 19. Buursma had 15, Benes 12, and Vriesman 11. Ed Start was most productive for Calvin with 18. Bill Morgan followed with 16, Don Koopman notched 13, and Tom Newhof scored 10.

As the Christmas season approached, the Dutchmen played two nonleague games on an out-of-state junket. On Thursday, Dec. 19, the team made its way to Wilberforce, Ohio, to take on the Marauders of Central State. Ritsema continued his outstanding play with strong work on the boards and a game-high 28 points. But leaping ability was the trademark of "Gibby" Gibbs's Marauders and Ritsema's efforts were matched by Eugene Beard and Sam Wagner. Central enjoyed a 44-41 lead at the intermission and hung on for a hard-earned 77-74 victory. Beard led the winners with 27, Bill Fox had 14 and Sam Wagner added 13. Following Ritsema was Benes with 15, Vriesman 12, and Vander Hill eight. Hope's first defeat of the season was disappointing, but all knew that they had been beaten by a worthy opponent.

The following day the team moved on to Illinois, where half of the contingent spent the night at the home of Ray Ritsema in Momence while the remainder journeyed on to Downers Grove, where they were guests at the home of Daryl Siedentop. In the late afternoon of Saturday, Dec. 21, the team reassembled for a contest at the University of Chicago. Located on the city's south side, the campus was impressive with gothic spires and a lofty reputation in the world of academe. Former Chancellor Robert Hutchins had taken a dim view of physical activity, but such could not erase the memory of Coach Amos Alonzo Stagg, the grand old man of football, or Jay Berwanger, first winner of the Heisman Trophy. The Hope squad was understandably impressed and looked forward to participating in such an atmosphere, but a let-down was in store. Joe Stampf, the Maroons' coach, had witnessed the second half of Hope's tussle with Calvin and decided that his five could not compete under ordinary circumstances. His only chance, he felt, was to prevent the high-powered Hope offense from getting into gear. His strategy would be to get ahead and then hold the ball.

Chicago scored first, but the Dutchmen responded with a field goal and two free throws to take the lead. Undaunted, the Maroons decided to stall anyway. Their tactic was to dribble to the end line, pass back out court, and then repeat the maneuver. Fourteen minutes of game time were consumed in this manner. Hope's lead at halftime was 17-12.

The Dutchmen scored first in the second half, and then went into a zone. It should be remembered that rules at that time did not include a 35-second clock. The dull display of slowdown basketball continued for another 16 minutes. Finally, with four minutes remaining, Coach Stampf gave his players the signal to try and score. They managed to score their only field goal of the second half with 2:30 remaining. In the time left, Hope scored on a tip-in by Ritsema, a lay-up by Vander Hill, and a free throw by Teusink. The final score stood at 24-14. Benes was high for the winners with eight and Chicago's center Woods led his team with a like number. Amos Stagg had played in Dr. James Naismith's very first basketball game at Springfield College. One wonders how he might have reacted to such a display.

With the holidays behind them, the Dutchmen did their best to forget the Chicago fiasco and prepared for a return engagement with Central State of Ohio, the only team to best Hope in the young season. An estimated 2,400 fans turned out at the Civic Center to see if stall tactics would again be employed. But "slowdown" basketball was hardly the style of Coach Gibbs, and the Marauders were at top speed throughout. It was soon apparent that the Chicago experience and the holiday layoff had taken a toll. The game was "loosely played" according to one source, with Hope in a 2-3 zone much of the time. Cold shooting (29 percent) kept the Dutchmen scrambling for more shots, but they managed to stay in front from the start. Central State pulled to within three twice, but could get no closer. Saturday, Jan. 4, 1958, was not exactly a red-letter day in Hope basketball, but it did produce a 68-56 victory and got the De Vette squad back on track. For Hope it was Benes with 21, Ritsema 16, and Vander Hill 14. Vriesman, in a starting role for the first time, scored eight. Jack Conyers led Central with nine field goals for 18 and Eugene Beard followed with 10.

MIAA play resumed on Tuesday, Jan. 7, when Coach Ray Steffen brought his Kalamazoo Hornets to the Civic. The Kalamazoo squad was strong at every position and very well coached. Atis Grinbergs and Walt Maser were effective on both boards and this, coupled with Hope again shooting but 29 percent, caused the lead to change hands 11 times before halftime. At the intermission the Dutchmen could manage but a 32-31 lead. In the second half Maser was on fire, scoring 13 of his game high 18 points, but Buursma had five of five from the free throw line and other players were tough when it counted. At the final buzzer Hope had inched ahead 67-62 and remained undefeated in league play. Ritsema led his team with 16, Benes had 13, Buursma scored 11, and Vriesman eight. Following Maser's outstanding performance, Kazoo's scoring was evenly divided. Atis Grinbergs had 13, Bob Brice 11, and guards John Thompson and Bob Fletcher 10 each. Down the road this was a team to be reckoned with, but for the time being the Dutchmen would need to concentrate on other foes.

On Saturday, Jan. 11, the team made a long, wintertime trip to Adrian to meet the Bulldogs under new coach Gregg Arbaugh. It was a tough go for the Dutchmen from the start. Hope was in a zone defense for much of the first half hoping to neutralize under the basket work by Leon Harper, but the big man showed his versatility by hitting five field goals from out-court to build a 39-33 halftime lead for the home team. In the second half Coach De Vette switched to a man-to-man and Benes was able to limit Harper to just three field goals, but at this point a fine young freshman named Vince Giles took over to keep his team in the game. The Dutchmen eventually gained the lead, but Adrian narrowed the margin to one at 66-65 and again at 68-67, both on steals by Giles. Hope had the benefit of unselfish teamwork from Teusink, Vander Hill, and Buursma, who concentrated on feeding their big men, Benes and Ritsema. Both sides were unhappy with the officiating. A questionable call finally put Ritsema out of the game, but it was near the end of the contest and the Dutchmen were able to hang on for the hard-fought 70-67 victory. Benes led the winners with 26 and Ritsema was close behind with 23. Vander Hill collected 11. Giles demonstrated quickness and agility in leading Adrian with 24, while Harper was next with 13.

Two days later the Dutchmen were back on the road at Olivet. The Comets would not be an easy touch. In recent days they had defeated Ferris Institute, then lost to Calvin by two points. Hope got off to a bad start in "the pit" by missing its first five shots. Olivet enjoyed a 7-0 lead, and then, with the score at 7-5, the Comets went into an eight-minute stall. Word of the Chicago tactic had reached tiny Olivet and Coach Henry Paul decided to give it a shot. Hope, however, managed to tie the count at eight and then, thanks to a spurt by Ray Ritsema, moved to a halftime lead of 22-18. The Dutchmen changed the tempo in the second half with interceptions, rebounds, and resulting fast breaks. To further aid the cause, Benes blocked a goodly number of Olivet shots. Beernink was a starter for the first time and worked well from out court with Teusink. Ritsema led the Dutchmen to the eventual 65-42 victory with 20 points. Benes had 14, Beernink nine, and Vander Hill eight. Ben Bernoudy was high for the Comets with 12. Joe Iauch followed with 11, and sophomore Owen Whitkoph added 10.

Veteran officials Al Krachunas and Lee Telfer worked the Hope-Hillsdale contest at the Civic Center on Saturday, Jan. 18. Benes was in for a hot night and led his team to a 42-32 halftime lead, mostly on tip-ins. The Dutchmen also cashed in on nine of 10 free throws. But the contest was far from over. With seven minutes gone in the second half, Don Bohannon and Jellybean Reynolds had brought their team to within one, 53-52. Coach De Vette halted the run by switching to a 2-3 zone. This maneuver got the fast break in motion. Teusink scored three lay-ups and the 10-point spread was reestablished at 68-58. The Dales made one more run, and with 7:04 remaining were within four, but Beernink got three fast-break lay-ups to make it 91-71 with

3:30 left. Meanwhile, Paul Benes, who was on the bench for six minutes of the first half, was making Hope College history. His game-high 39 points was a new Hope scoring record, breaking the old mark of 36 set by Ron Bos in 1952-53. Hope's 96-77 win also included 16 points from Ritsema, 15 from Beernink, and 11 from Tiger Teusink. Coach John Williams' club had given the Dutchmen all they wanted. Reynolds led the Dales with 22 and Bohannon had a stellar performance with 21.

The semester break for exams put Hope out of action for two weeks, but on Saturday, Feb. 1, they resumed play at home against Earlham of Richmond, Ind. Coach Merle Ramsey would uphold the Hoosier tradition with a strong team, but Warren Vander Hill opened the scoring for Hope with four straight field goals and the Dutch were ahead to stay. The halftime margin favored the home team 36-25, but there was concern when the Quakers scored the first seven points of the second half. With 10 minutes remaining Earlham went to a press with Benes on the bench, but Ritsema was having one of his better nights and, with 32 points, led his team to the eventual 75-60 victory. Warren Vander Hill was back in form with 17, while Buursma and Beernink each scored seven. For Earlham it was Murray Vincent with 12, Bill Himelink 11, and Milo Bean 10.

One week later, the Dutchmen tackled the second round of MIAA play when the Alma Scots came to the Civic amidst the shouts of a highly partisan crowd of 2,250. The Scots of Coach Wayne Hintz were racked by injury and ineligibility. Most notable was the absence of George Carter, who would see no action due to injury, but talent remained and Hintz expected spirited play from his charges. Officials for the evening were Chuck Bult and Marv Bylsma, two of the league's finest. They were soon greeted by a deep-voiced Hope fan who had become an institution. Three rows up behind the far end of the Hope bench sat Harm Van Ark. In periods of relative quiet, Harm would issue greetings to coaches, players, and officials. He would persist until acknowledged. Knowing this, Bult and Bylsma, with broad grins, gave a wave or nod and were free to work the game. Harm's other device for securing attention was a high pitched "peep-peep" which amused the crowd and added to the color of the game.

Hope was soon in charge of the undermanned visitors, and moved to a 50-26 halftime advantage. Benes played slightly more than half of the game, but scored 26 points to lead the team. Ritsema followed with 19, Vriesman had 14, and Beernink eight. Hope's substitutes played the last 12 minutes of the game. George Arrick led the Scots with 15, York contributed 11, and Jim Northrup, of future baseball fame, had 10. In the end the scoreboard read Hope 95, Alma 62.

The second Hope-Calvin game of the season was played at the Civic Center on Wednesday, Feb. 12. Veteran officials John Clevenger and Ray Crocker were in charge as 2,700 fans stood in the corners and spilled over into the aisles. In the stifling atmosphere, fans from both sides had much to cheer about. The Knights had prepared well and were red-hot in the first half with 17 of 34 field goals for a 50 percent average. Coach Barney Steen employed a 1-3-1 zone which proved troublesome for the Dutchmen, and in the battle of centers Tom Newhof was on fire with 17 points while Benes was limited to just three. Vander Hill kept Hope in the game with five field goals and a free throw, but the Knights went to the locker room with a 36-30 lead.

In the second half, Benes suddenly came alive with four baskets and five of six free throws. Vander Hill continued on target and delighted the crowd with a long, two-hand set shot. Longtime Hope fans saw it as a throwback to the "Whiz Kids" of '43 and Captain "Ets" Kleinjans, who made that shot his specialty. Meanwhile, Newhof's great effort was producing fouls. With 13:47 remaining he picked up number four and took a seat by his coach. With 12:31 on the clock, Benes connected to tie the count at 45. At the 10-minute mark the Knights came back to take a 52-50 lead on Ed Start's basket, but Whitey Beernink's layup made it 52-all and a hook shot by Benes with 7:57 left put Hope ahead to stay. Tom Newhof came back to score two more times before fouling out with 3:29 remaining. Coach Steen called it Newhof's finest performance ever. Hope's largest margin was 70-56. Another Calvin comeback fell short, and at the buzzer it was Hope 70, Calvin 62. Vander Hill led Hope with 17, Benes' second-half comeback gave him a total of 16, Beernink had 12, and Vriesman eight. For the Knights it was Newhof leading all scorers with 23, Ed Start with 15, and Ed Meyering with nine. As the Civic Center emptied into the the winter night, players, coaches, and fans were emotionally drained. Once again sport had been honored by the maximum effort of both teams.

Amidst the "Calvin hangover," Hope had two days to prepare for their Jan. 15 meeting with Kalamazoo in aging Treadway Gym. Ray Steffen, now in his third year as head coach, had dropped but one home game in that time period. The one loss had been to Hope during the previous season. A capacity crowd of 1,500 seemed to be about equally divided between Hope and Kazoo followers. A large contingent of Hope fans made the 50-mile trip from Holland and were joined by a goodly number of Hope alumni who resided in Kalamazoo. This night they would be disappointed. The Hornets were more than ready and never trailed in the contest, shooting 41 percent to a cold 24 percent for the Dutchmen. Kazoo's halftime lead was 39-30. In the early stages of the second half De Vette's squad narrowed the gap to 45-43 but got no closer. In the next eight minutes the K-men made 10 of 12 shots while Hope could do no better than four of 15. With 1:20 remaining the score stood at 68-51 and subs for both teams filled the floor. Atis Grinbergs scored a final basket for the home team and Jack Kempker got one for Hope making it 70-53, an impressive

HOPE COLLEGE BASKETBALL TEAM — 1957-1958
MIAA CHAMPIONS — 19-3 OVERALL 13-1 MIAA

Front Row L. to R.: Jack Kempker, Darrell Beernink, John Kleinheksel, Warren Vander Hill, Albert "Jun" Buursma, Captain Dwayne "Tiger" Teusink, Daryl Siedentop, Bob Thomson. **Back Row:** Manager Dave Clark, Roland "Pooch" Schut, Ray Ritsema, Paul Benes, John Hood, Wayne Vriesman, Coach Russ De Vette.

win for Ray Steffen's crew and Hope's first loss in MIAA play. Kalamazoo's team effort showed Walt Maser leading with 21, Bob Brice close behind with 20, guard John Thompson had 14 and Bob Fletcher eight. Benes tallied 20 for Hope, but Ritsema was hobbled with an ankle sprain and played only periodically, scoring eight. Buursma and Vander Hill each had seven and Vriesman six, clear evidence of the fine defensive effort by Kalamazoo.

Life continued of course, following the "Treadway Trauma." On Wednesday, Feb. 19, Adrian had the misfortune to catch Hope on the rebound in the Civic Center. The determined Dutchmen were hot on the home court, shooting 44 percent overall while the Bulldogs could only muster 23 percent. Benes and Ritsema combined to put the clamps on big Leon Harper. Harper scored five points in the first half and none in the second. Hope's halftime lead was 45-21 and, with 9:25 remaining, Benes and Ritsema were on the bench and through for the evening after collecting 12 and nine rebounds respectively. Hope's substi-

tutes were equally effective. Roland Schut dropped in four field goals, belying his teammates' good natured handle of "the four o'clock shooter." Kleinheksel also scored three times before the final buzzer. Hope's 88-47 win bore special significance in assuring the Dutchmen of at least a share of the MIAA title. Despite limited playing time, Hope's big three did most of the scoring. Benes was high with 20, while Ritsema and Vander Hill each scored 13. Vriesman and Schut each added eight. Guard Bruce Stephens led Gregg Arbaugh's team with 16.

If doubts lingered about Hope's comeback, they would be dispelled at Hillsdale on Feb. 22. Ray Ritsema was assigned to stop Hillsdale's big gun, Jim Reynolds. Ritsema accepted the challenge and proceeded to hold the "Jellybean" to three points. Reynolds did score twice off substitutes, but it was a Hope night and the Dutchmen were ahead 55-32 at the half. During the intermission, Holland industrialist Randall Bosch took the floor to present a diamond-studded gold football to Hillsdale quarterback Doug Maison, the league's most valuable football player. Bosch's glowing, if somewhat bumbled tribute, relieved tension and was well received.

Hope's defense plus a 30-point performance by Benes decided the issue early. In the first game Jerry Schaffer had scored 18, but this time around he was held scoreless thanks to the defense of Buursma. Vander Hill scored 15 points before going to the sidelines with a bruised knee. Referring to Warren's effectiveness in feeding Benes, Coach De Vette called it his best performance in two years. Ritsema had another good night with 17 and Buursma had 11. Daryl Siedentop scored three points as the game ended to give Hope the impressive 94-54 victory and lock up an undisputed MIAA championship. Bob Duncan was high for Hillsdale with 12, and Ken Sippel added 10.

Three games remained on the regular schedule. With the title in hand, the incentive now would be to look and play like a champion. This would not always be easy. On Tuesday, Feb. 25, the team traveled across the state to meet Eastern Michigan in Ypsilanti. Coach Mike Skala's Hurons led most of the first half, but Hope caught up with a surge to go ahead 52-37 at the intermission. The Dutchmen led by as many as 26, but the Hurons went into a zone press against Hope's subs and the lead slipped to six points at 86-80. At this point the regulars returned and stretched the lead to 12. Eastern scored a basket at the buzzer, but Hope took the non-league contest 94 to 84. Hope's post men, Benes and Ritsema, were impressive with 24 points each, and Vriesman was on fire with 14 second half tallies for a total of 18. Vander Hill was also on target with 16. Eastern's Chuck Crickmore led all scorers with 26, and Manley was next with 15.

Hope College had joined the newly created College Division of the NCAA in 1957 and for a time held membership in both the NAIA and the NCAA. As the 1957-58 season neared its conclusion, Hope received an invitation to represent Michigan in the Great Lakes Regional Tournament of the NCAA College Division. Harvey Chrouser, Wheaton College director of athletics and chairman of the selection committee, informed Hope officials of the other participants. They would be Wheaton, as champion of the College Conference of Ill., and two at-large selections, Northern Illinois University of De Kalb, Illinois, and St. Norbert College of De Pere, Wis. Hope was also invited to participate in the NAIA Tournament beginning on March 3. In choosing the NCAA tourney, Hope, in effect, severed its membership in the NAIA.

On Saturday, March 1, the Dutchmen traveled to Albion for the return match with the Britons. Coach De Vette chose to go with a man-for-man defense the entire game and the choice proved effective. Hope enjoyed a comfortable half-time lead of 52-33 and continued to dominate in the second half. Benes was the Hope leader with 28, Ritsema had 20 and Vander Hill 16. Teusink had his best game of the season with 10 points, numerous feeds, and a fine floor game. Albion's 6' 6" Con Stover was limited to four points, but Virgil Hall dropped in 22 for Coach Elkin Isaac. The final score stood at 91-66.

The final game of the regular season was played on Monday night, March 3, at the Civic Center. A crowd of 1,700 turned out hoping to see the high-scoring Dutchmen continue their winning ways. The Olivet Comets continued to struggle, but Coach Henry Paul did not resort to a stall as he had done in the earlier game. The Comets simply did not have a match for Hope's center. Benes scored 20 points in just 21 minutes of play, then watched the remainder of the game from the bench. The halftime spread was 53-28 and Hope substitutes played well the rest of the way. Ritsema followed Benes with 18 points, and Vander Hill put on a superb passing demonstration before retiring to the bench with Ritsema. Vander Hill and Teusink ended with 11 each and Kempker, playing his last home game, came through with nine, including a pair of two-hand sets. The Vander Hill influence seemed to be spreading. Ben Bernoudy led the Comets with 13 and Norm Schultz had 12. At game's end it was Hope 91, Olivet 54.

For the first time in the history of the school, Hope College would participate in a post-season basketball tournament. The experience would be "frosting on the cake" for the MIAA champions. The Holland community was soon caught up in the excitement of the week of March 3-8. Wheaton College's new gymnasium was not yet complete and the contests were to be played at the Aurora East High gym, which boasted a seating capacity of 4,000. The team left Holland on Thursday, March 6, and set up headquarters in the Leland Hotel. Hope would meet Northern Illinois University in the opening game the following night.

Much of Hope's information on the Huskies came from sophomore Daryl Siedentop. One of Siedentop's teammates at Downers Grove High School had been Larry Wyllie, now the leading scorer at Northern. The Dutch were warned that Wyllie was good. They would soon find out just how good. There was some concern regarding the fan-shaped backboards then in vogue, but fair for one would be fair for all. As the game got under way the Dutchmen held their own and Hope fans were relieved that their favorites could compete against the much larger school. Larry Wyllie poured in 21 first-half points, but Hope went to the locker room with a 52-47 first-half lead.

The torrid pace of the game continued in the second half. Hope's 14-point lead at 11:25 diminished to three at 83-80 with 4:48 remaining. Hope clung to a 97-91 lead with 1:25 to go when Wyllie dropped in two more field goals, the last one with 35 seconds showing on the clock. Ten seconds later Paul Benes put in a lay-up to make it 99-95. Hope got possession one more time and, with nine ticks left, Ritsema scored the game's final basket making it Hope 101, Northern Illinois 95. Benes was again the Hope leader with 38, Ritsema had 23, and Vander Hill 20. Buursma had a strong game with 11. Northern's Wyllie lived up to his reputation with 48 counters. Earlier in the season he had scored 52 in a contest with Eastern Michigan. Capers, May, and Gentry each had 10 for the Huskies. A crowd of 3,900 viewed the game.

In the tournament's second game, defending national champion Wheaton College defeated St. Norbert 68-66 and would meet Hope for the regional championship in the 9 p.m. contest on Saturday, March 8. The Crusaders were coached by able and colorful Lee Pfund. Pfund, a man of deep religious convictions, had earlier drawn attention when, as a pitcher for the Brooklyn Dodgers, he refused to play ball on Sunday. This ended his major league career and moved him into the coaching ranks, where he enjoyed great success. As mentioned above, his 1957 Wheaton team captured the first NCAA College Division basketball championship. The brightest light for the talented Wheaton team was forward Mel Peterson. I recalled watching him in action as a high school senior in Michigan State's Jenison Field House. Almost single-handedly, Peterson led tiny Stephenson, in Michigan's Upper Peninsula, to the State Class "B" championship. Now at Wheaton, Mel was a main cog in the high-powered Crusader offense.

After five minutes of play, the score was knotted at 16. This was followed by a Wheaton spurt that pushed the count to 31-18. Bill Gehrig shot eight of 10, while Mel Peterson and Don Anderson each had six of nine. Hope's only field goal in this stretch was scored by Benes. With five minutes left in the half, Wheaton's lead was 50-32. Hope staged a mini-comeback, but the Crusaders, shooting a torid 60 percent, enjoyed a 61-45 halftime lead.

In the first five minutes of the second half, the Dutchmen served notice that the game was not over as they outscored their opponents 13-5. At the 10-minute mark it was 77-68, and shortly thereafter Hope whittled the lead to 86-81. But at this point Peterson stepped up with six straight field goals as Ritsema watched from the bench with four fouls.

Ray had left the game with 13:49 remaining. He returned with four minutes left and picked up foul number five just 45 seconds later. At the buzzer it was Wheaton 104, Hope 93. The 4,300 fans who witnessed the game were treated to stellar performances on both sides. True to form, Mel Peterson led his team with 35 points, including seven of seven from the free throw line. He was followed by Bill Gehrig with 26, Don Anderson with 17, and Bob Whitehead with 16. The only Wheaton player who did not fare well was freshman center John Dobbert. He was simply no match for 6' 11" Paul Benes, who led Hope with 33 points and an incredible 25 rebounds. Vander Hill was next with 24; Ritsema, with limited playing time, had 14; Beernink scored nine; and Buursma eight.

Hope's longest and most successful season was now over. When the league coaches met to select the All-MIAA, team they named Benes and Ritsema of Hope, Newhof of Calvin, Harper of Adrian, and Hall of Albion. Vander Hill made the second team. Hope fans of course, felt he deserved a better fate and Kalamazoo's Walt Maser was also hard to ignore. Ritsema, Hope's splendid sophomore, was selected as the league's most valuable player. The Hope squad elected Benes to captain the 1958-59 team.

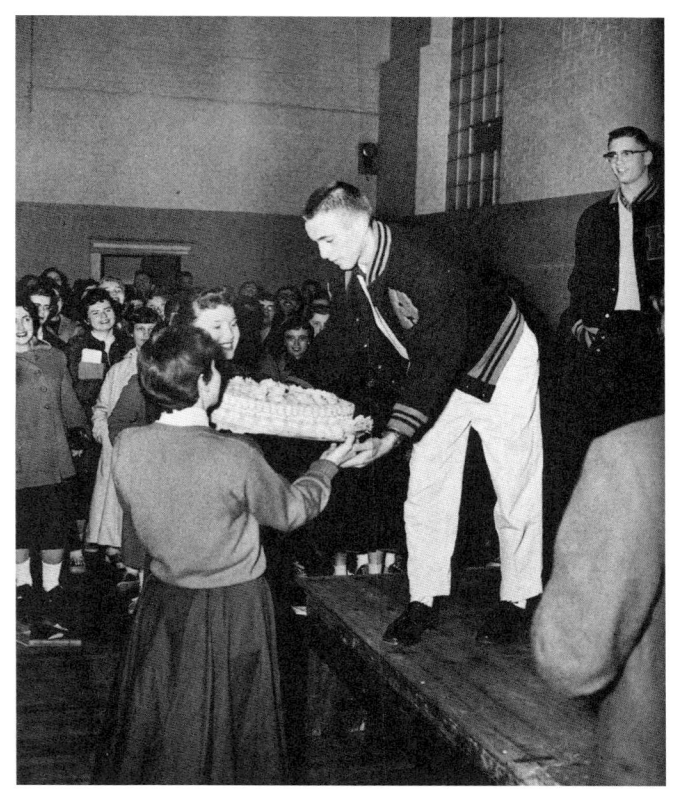

"GLORY DAY" IN CARNEGIE-SCHOUTEN GYM — 1958

Coed Marilyn Hendrickson (facing) and cheerleader Joy Philip present a Championship cake to Captain Dwayne "Tiger" Teusink. John Hood stands in the background. Miss Hendrickson would become Mrs. Paul Benes while Joy Philip would be the bride of Warren Vander Hill.

*   *   *

The afterglow of Hope's successful season was short lived. A "Glory Day" celebration took place in Carnegie-Schouten Gym with kudos all around Then it was time to move on. As winter waned in the long month of March, players experienced the usual let-down. Some time off sounded good, but boredom was soon rampant and most were more than ready for the spring sports meetings called by the coaches. For Whitey Beernink, Daryl Siedentop, Jack Kempker, and Bob Thomson it would be baseball. Roland Schut, Ray Ritsema, and John Kleinheksel opted for track, and Tiger Teusink continued his career in tennis.

With a first in basketball, a second-place tie in football, and a fifth in cross country, Hope was well positioned to make a run for the coveted MIAA All-Sports Trophy. All knew that the issue would be decided by performance in the four spring sports.

Hope's new coach on the block would be William Hilmert. The Reverend Hilmert was the newly appointed Dean of Men. His love for golf had prompted him to volunteer to succeed Albert Timmer, who stepped down at the close of the '57 season. Coach Hilmert was pleased with the talent at his disposal. Veterans Ray De Does and Bob Holt returned and, when playoffs were completed, the other team members were Tom Klaasen, Dennis Camp, and John Van Dyke.

Weather in the spring of '58 was cooperative. Postponements were rare and very few games or matches had to be canceled. Hope opened its 1958 golf season at home at the American Legion Course on Friday, April 18, against Kalamazoo. Holt (H) with a 73 was medalist for the day as he defeated Ben Schram 90 by a 3-0 score. De Does (H) was close behind with a 74 to defeat Bob Pixley 82, also by a 3-0 count. Tom Klaasen (H) 79, defeated Tom Kreilick 85, 3-0. Kalamazoo's Bob Fletcher 79, defeated Dennis Camp 86, 3-0, and Wally Preston (K) 82, defeated John Van Dyke 89, 3-0. Hope was awarded one point for low team score, making the final count Hope 10, Kalamazoo six.

On Tuesday, April 22, Hope traveled to Grand Rapids for a non-league match with Grand Rapids Junior College. The two-year institution benefited from several large high schools in the city and was loaded with fine athletes, as Hope would realize as the spring progressed. In this match JC's Herb Miller emerged as medalist (79) as he defeated De Does 2½-½. Holt evened things out by defeating JC's Jay Roseley 2½-½, and Klaasen split with Jay Wagner 1½-1½, but Mike Coddington (JC) got the best of Camp (H) 3-0, and Norm Roger (JC) shaded Van Dyke 2-1, giving the Grand Rapids team the match 9½ to 5½.

On Thursday, April 24, Hope traveled to Alma for a triangular played in heavy winds. Dick Ayling, the Scots' football quarterback, was medalist with an 81, but the Hope team downed the Scots 10½-5½. The Dutchmen also had the best of it with Calvin, besting the Knights 12-3.

Hope continued its winning ways in a close match at Albion on Tuesday, April 29. Records of the match are sketchy, but De Does was medalist with a 72 to lead his team to the 8½-6½ victory. De Does won over Bell 3-0, and Holt defeated Johns 2½-½. Camp defeated Krsul 3-0, but Carpenter of Albion bested Klaasen 3-0, and Young (A) defeated Van Dyke, also by a score of 3-0. The Dutch win would be especially significant at the season's end. In the same meet, Hope also prevailed over Olivet. De Does won over Davis 3-0, Holt took Metnessner 2-1, Blood (O) defeated Van Dyke 3-0, Camp was the winner over Winter 2½-½, and Klaasen defeated Brown 3-0 to give Coach Hilmert's team the 11½-4½ victory.

The Hope team, now on a roll, entertained an undermanned Adrian team at the American Legion course on Thursday, May 8. The result was a 15-0 shutout. De Does defeated Bill Gardner 3-0, Holt took Gene Melin 3-0, Camp defeated Cline 3-0, Klaasen won from J. Smith 3-0, and Bill Kuyper, playing in place of Van Dyke, defeated Ron Dilbone 3-0.

It now appeared that this would be the best Hope team since Al Timmer's championship in 1947. But the bubble would burst on Monday, May 12. The Dutchmen traveled to Marshall for a triangular with Hillsdale and nearby Olivet. Hillsdale Coach Dick Cain had assembled an outstanding group of golfers. Led by medalist Del Carnes (72), the Dales dominated the Hope team 13-2. They also defeated Olivet 14-1. Hope's 13-2 victory over Olivet was a non-league contest.

The MIAA league meet was held at the Kalamazoo Country Club on Friday, May 16. Hillsdale proved that its dual meet record was no fluke as it carried the day including medalist honors. The Dales' Ed Swanson posted a 36-hole total of 156. He was followed closely by Hope's De Does and Kalamazoo's Bob Fletcher, each with 157. The remainder of Hope's team faltered somewhat and the Dutchmen were forced to settle for fourth place. The final team tally showed Hillsdale winning its first undisputed title with a team score of 819. Others in order of finish were: Albion 838, Kalamazoo 846, Hope 868, Alma 873, Calvin 963, Olivet 970, and Adrian 1,029. Due to its fine 6-1 dual meet record, Hope was able to finish in a second place tie with Albion overall.

* * *

I looked forward to my second season as Hope's track coach with great anticipation. Our chances, however, were dealt a severe blow when it was learned that knee injuries sustained in football would prevent Paul Wiegerink and Jim Hilmert from participating in the high hurdles. Arguably the league's two best hurdlers, their absence from this event would be keenly felt. Wiegerink, however, would still be able to compete in the 100-yard dash and the low hurdles, and Hilmert would be active in several field events.

Hope opened the season by hosting Grand Rapids Junior College on Saturday, April 19. As mentioned earlier, the Raiders enjoyed top talent from the city's several Class "A" high schools. This day it was Jerry Priebe who took first place in the shot put, discus, and javelin as his team jumped out to an early lead by capturing five of the six field events. Overall, Hope had eight firsts to seven for JC, but depth spelled the difference as the visitors led throughout in posting a 70-61 victory. Dave Spaan was the winner in the 440 and 880, a difficult double, and Wiegerink took first in the 100 and the 220 low hurdles. Roland Schut was Hope's only

PERFECT FORM
Bob Holt (left) and Ray De Does led the 1958 Hope golf team to a second place tie with Albion in MIAA play.

winner in the field events, winning the pole vault with a height of 11' 6". Jim Rozeboom won the mile and Harold Gazan the two-mile. The Dutchmen ended the meet on a positive note by taking the mile relay in a time of 3:44.5. The team included Jim Vander Lind, Ron Bronson, Bob Hilbelink, and Rozeboom.

Hope met Hillsdale on a windy, chilly day at the Allegan High School track. The Dales of Coach Dan Goldsmith were victorious in the javelin, long jump, 880, and two-mile, but Hope took firsts in the remaining 10 events to wrap up the meet 87-44. The shot put belonged to football players as Hope's Larry Ter Molen took the event. He was followed by teammate Bill Huibregtse in second, and Hillsdale's Jim "Jellybean" Reynolds in third. Wiegerink was first again in the 100-yard dash and the 220 low hurdles. The Dutchmen managed a sweep in the 440 with Spaan, Vander Lind, and Bronson doing the honors. Hope's Rich Bakker, participating in track for the first time, won the high jump, and Schut took his speciality, the pole vault. Hilmert won the discus, Rozeboom the mile, and Jim Mohr the 220. Hope also won the mile relay in notching its first win of the season.

Any contest between Hope and Calvin produces excitement. The track meet in Holland on Tuesday, April 29, was no exception. Coach Dave Tuuk had a well-balanced squad and the teams were evenly matched. In the early going, it was Calvin's Stan Koster who stood out with a first in the javelin and a tie for first in the pole vault. He was also part of a four-way tie for first in the high jump which also included Hope roommates Bill Vanderbilt and Rich Bakker as well as Bergsma of Calvin. In years to come Koster would return to Holland as the much-revered superintendent of the Holland Christian School System.

Hope went one-two in the long jump, with Duane Voskuil winning the event and John Kleinheksel close behind. Ter Molen took the shot put for the Dutchmen, but Calvin swept the discus with Altena, Vande Grind, and De Young to take a three-point lead at the end of the field events. At this point team members moved from the Van Raalte estate on Fairbanks Avenue to the Holland High School track on 22nd Street. The first running event was the mile run. The Knights boasted two fine distance men in Barry Koops and Jim De Bie. They would be pitted against Hope's only entry, freshman Jim Rozeboom. I would realize later that Jim was better suited for the 880, but this day we decided to try to capitalize on his strong finishing kick. The strategy was to follow as closely as possible to the final turn, then employ the kick against the more two-mile-oriented veterans. The plan worked and Hope inched closer to the lead. As the meet progressed, Hope was strong in the dashes while Calvin took the high hurdles and swept the 880. The Dutchmen maintained a narrow lead most of the way, but in the two-mile run Koops and De Bie were back with Barry setting a new Calvin record in 10:20.4 and De Bie finishing second. This gave the Knights a 59-58 lead with but two events remaining.

RECORD LEAP
There were no photographs on hand in 1958 to capture John Kleinheksel's record long jump of 23' 6½". This 1959 photo shows the form that brought him repeat championships in both 1959 and 1960.

Roland Schut volunteered to try the low hurdles for the first time in an attempt to pick up a much-needed point. His surprising second behind Paul Wiegerink put his team up by six and sealed the victory for Hope. In the final event, the Dutchmen mile relay team of Mohr, Vander Lind, Bronson,

THE 1958 HOPE COLLEGE TRACK TEAM
2nd PLACE — MIAA

Front Row L. to R.: Jim Combs, Jim Rozeboom, Bill Drake, Bob Hilbelink, Gale Damhof. **Second Row:** Carl Vermeulen, John Pleune, Dave Spaan, Larry Ter Molen, Jim Mohr, Hal Whipple. **Third Row:** Coach Gordon Brewer, Norm Peddie, Cal Bruins, Roland Schut, Harold Gazan, Jerry Wondra, Duane Voskuil, Don Gallo. **Top Row:** Manager Jay Nyhuis, Alan Beede, Bill Vanderbilt, Rich Bakker, Charlie Smits, Ron Bronson. **Missing from the picture:** Jim Hilmert, Bill Huibregtse, John Kleinheksel, Ray Ritsema, Paul Wiegerink.

and Spaan was also victorious, making the final score Hope 71, Calvin 60. Mohr, a sophomore, led the Dutchmen with a first in the 220, second in the 100, and third in the pole vault, plus a leg on the winning relay team for a total of 10¼ points.

The Dutchmen did not have long to savor victory. On Tuesday, May 6, they hosted the Albion Britons of Coach Elkin Isaac at the Allegan track. The Britons were coming off four straight MIAA championships and were loaded again. Hope was never ahead in the meet as Albion racked up 11 firsts, including five of the six field events. Kleinheksel took the long jump for Hope with a leap of 20' 6¾", his best to date, and Mohr won the 100 in 10.3. The Albion runners pushed Spaan to a new Hope record of 50.3 in the 440 (around one turn), and Hope's three Jims, Mohr, Vander Lind, and Rozeboom, joined Spaan as the Dutchmen took the mile relay in 3:31.9, also a new Hope record. Keith Lepard was a double winner for Albion in the shot and discus, as was distance ace Jim Taup in the mile and two-mile. The final score of Albion 83⅔, Hope 47⅓ left little doubt as to who would prevail in the league meet.

Two days later the Dutchmen rebounded at Kalamazoo's Angell Field as they downed the Hornets 77-54. Kleinheksel was unable to make the trip due to illness, but Wiegerink was back in top form. With a tailwind helping some, he breezed to victory in the 100 in 10.0, the 220 (straightaway) in 22.0, and the 220 low hurdles in 25.4. Hope registered seven additional firsts. Included were Schut in the pole vault, Ter Molen in the shot put, Ray Ritsema in the discus, Rozeboom in the mile, Dave Spaan with a new Hope record (50.1) in the 440, Jerry Hill in the high hurdles, and the mile relay team of Mohr, Vander Lind, Rozeboom, and Spaan. Casey Clark, Kalamazoo's ace high jumper, took that event with with a height of 6'-even and tennis star Les Dodson placed second.

On Saturday, May 10, seven Hope team members, with their coach, made their way to Chicago for the Elmhurst College Invitational. The meet was a favorite of Wiegerink and he again performed well. His first-place time in the 220 low hurdles was 24.7, best of the season. He also placed second in both dashes with a 10.0 in the 100, and 21.6 in the 220. Hope placed third in four events, namely Schut in the pole vault, Spaan in the 440, Rozeboom in the mile, and the mile relay team of Mohr, Vander Lind, Rozeboom, and Spaan, who did the event in 3:29.2, their fastest of the season. Mohr finished fourth in both dashes to give Hope a team total of 29 points, good enough for fourth place in the 18-team field. The University of Dubuque won the meet with 41⅗ points.

Ferris Institute and Hope College had competed in a number of sports for several years, but the schools had never met in track and field. The first meeting would take place in Big Rapids on Tuesday, May 13. The undefeated Bulldogs matched up well with the seven firsts. Every point counted as the lead changed hands several times throughout the afternoon. At the conclusion of the 880-yard run, Ferris led by a score of 49⅗ to 49⅖, but going into the final relay Hope had regained the lead by the narrow margin of four-fifths of a point. Rozeboom, a regular member of Hope's mile relay team, was not available, having already participated in the difficult double of the mile run and the 880. He was a winner in both, greatly aiding the Hope cause. Sprinter Bob Hilbelink took Rozeboom's place knowing that the meet was on the line. Bob, along with Mohr, Vander Lind, and Spaan, came through with a winning time of 3:31, making the final score Hope 68⅖, Ferris 62⅗. First-place winners for Hope were Schut in the pole vault (tie), Ter Molen in the shot, Kleinheksel in the long jump, Rozeboom in the mile and 880, Mohr in the 220, and the relay as mentioned.

The MIAA track teams gathered at Kalamazoo's Angell Field on Saturday, May 17, a gray day plagued by intermittent rain. The 1958 league meet would produce five MIAA records. Albion, the overwhelming favorite, had trouble in the early going. Surprisingly, Hope was the leader 25⅖ to Albion's 19⅕ as the field events concluded. Albion took first in the shot put, pole vault, and discus. Meanwhile the Dutchmen just seemed to hang around, picking up points in all six of the events. Ter Molen took second in the shot. Kalamazoo's Casey Clark set a new record in winning the high jump with a leap of 6' 3⅛", but Ritsema tied for second while Bill Vanderbilt and Rich Bakker ended in a five-way tie for fifth. Hope's Jack Kempker was on loan from the baseball team. With a strong right arm he managed to take third place in the javelin. The event was won by Calvin's Stan Koster. Keith Lepard won the discus for Albion, but Hilmert was a strong second with a throw of 122' 6" and Ritsema finished fifth. The Britons' Bruce Foulke set a new record in the pole vault with a jump of 13' 3/4". The mark was impressive considering the equipment available at the time. Again, Hope's Schut was close behind in second.

Midway in the morning a shout went up from the long jump pit. Rushing to that area I was informed that John Kleinheksel had just gotten off a jump of 23' 6½"! The feat was remarkable in that John's longest jump to that point was 20' 8". His new mark would remain an MIAA record for 34 years and is still a Hope College record at this writing.

Hope's lead in the meet continued through the first three running events as Rozeboom was third in the mile, Spaan captured the 440 in 50.5, and Mohr and Wiegerink went 1-2 in the 100-yard dash. But with Hilmert and Wiegerink unable to compete in the high hurdles, Albion forged into the lead by taking the first three places while Hope was shut out. The inspired Britons also took firsts in the 880, the 220, the two-mile, and the low hurdles. The Dutchmen closed out the meet by winning the mile relay with a new Hope record of 3:30.8. Team members were Mohr, Vander Lind, Hilbelink, and Spaan, who could show two gold medals in his final appearance in Hope uniform. Wiegerink and Hilmert had to settle for silver this day, but all three had contributed greatly to the program over a four-year period. They would be sorely missed by coach and team alike.

Albion's fifth straight MIAA Championship was won in impressive fashion with a total of 87⅕ points. Hope was a solid but distant second with 61⅖ points. Others in order of finish were Calvin 29½, Kalamazoo 25½, Alma 16⅕, Hillsdale 11, Olivet 4⅕, and Adrian 2.

* * *

Baseball, America's pasttime and Hope's oldest sport, had its ups and downs in 1958. The departed battery of Jim Kaat and Dave Woodcock would be hard to replace. On-hand in the pitching department were veterans Bob Andree and Mert Vander Lind, also reliever Daryl Siedentop. A freshman find was left-hander Bruce Hoffman, who showed considerable talent. As the season got underway, it was Dick Morgan at first, Whitey Beernink at second, Bob Thomson at short, and captain Art Olson at third. The outfield appeared solid with Jack Kempker, Jerry Boeve, Jack Faber, and Gary Bylsma. Catching chores would be handled by Vern Essenberg and Talmage Hayes.

The home opener for the Dutchmen was played at Riverview Park on Friday, April 11, with Grand Rapids Junior College furnishing the opposition. Bob Van Slyke, another of JC's fine athletes, proved Hope's undoing. The right-hander scattered eight Hope hits and registered 10 strike-outs. In the fifth, Van Slyke aided his own cause with a line drive homer over the right field fence with two on base. Hope scored first with two runs in the second inning. Faber singled and scored when Bylsma was safe on an error. Bylsma came home on Essenberg's double, but the Dutchmen failed to score again as Van Slyke was tough in the clutch. Meanwhile, the Raiders were having a field day with Hope pitchers, scoring one in the third, five in the fourth on four hits, three in the fifth, two in the eighth, and one more in the ninth. Mert Vander Lind started for Hope. He was relieved in the fourth by Andree, who had four strikeouts before giving way to Siedentop in the eighth (three strikeouts). Coach De Vette used numerous players in the 12-2 rout. second baseman Ed Bredeweg led Hope with two singles, while Bylsma, Doug Japinga, Darrell Beernink, Morgan, and Faber each had a single. Essenberg's double was the only extra base blow.

Things got better as the Dutchmen opened the MIAA season at Adrian on Saturday, April 19. In the opener Hope's Andree was in charge all the way. His two-hit 6-0 shutout included eight strikeouts and was a pleasant surprise for so early in the season. Hope scored four runs in the first, then added two more in the fifth to give Andree more than enough. Hoffman took the mound in the nightcap. The lefthander gave up four hits, three walks, and one hit batsman, but he whiffed 10 enroute to a 4-3 victory. Adrian got one in the first, then added two more with two out in the seventh. Hope's runs came in the third, fourth, and fifth, and were aided by a couple of wild pitches. Jack Kempker's fifth-inning triple was the big blow of the game.

Back in Riverview Park on April 23, De Vette's squad hoped to continue its winning ways against Hillsdale. It would not be easy. Hope could manage only three hits against the slants of pitcher Wayne Schurr, who struck out eight and walked none. Two of Hope's hits were doubles by Beernink. The lone Hope run came in the first on a Beernink double and a long fly to center by Kempker. Essenberg had Hope's other hit. Hillsdale tied the game in the fourth, then went ahead in the fifth on a two-run homer by catcher Ed Tallman. Andree gave up eight hits, four runs, and three walks in the 4-1 loss. He struck out five.

Hoffman was effective in the second game, allowing but five hits while striking out 11. With the Dutchmen on top 4-1 in the seventh, the young pitcher ran into trouble. Two hit batsmen were followed by a single and two walks. Two runs scored. But with the bases loaded Hoffman bore down and struck out two to preserve the 4-3 victory. Beernink had three singles to make it five-for-five in the two games.

On Saturday, April 26, Hope traveled to Kalamazoo to meet the Hornets at Woodworth Field. Coach De Vette sent Kempker to the mound in an attempt to give Andree and Hoffman some rest. Kempker was effective through four innings, but tired in the fifth. He was relieved by Don Andree, younger brother of Bob. Hope out-hit Kalamazoo seven to four, but the Hornets pushed across five runs and took the contest 5-3.

With Bob Andree not in uniform due to illness and Hoffman nursing a sore arm, the second game was up for grabs. De Vette turned to veteran Vander Lind, and the senior did not disappoint. The contest remained scoreless for three innings, but in the fourth Hope got on the board. Olson, who was safe on a shortstop error, advanced to second on Kempker's single. A missed pick-off play put Olson on third, and when the center fielder bobbled the ball, Olson crossed the plate. The Hornets tied it up in the fifth on a single by Ligget and a long single to right by Yohdes. The deadlock remained and the teams went into extra innings. In the last of the eighth, Vander Lind determined his own fate as he hit a grounder to third. When the third baseman threw wildly to first, Mert took second. With two out, Olson singled to center and Vander Lind raced home sliding under the catcher's attempted tag. The 2-1 victory kept Hope in the MIAA race.

MIAA competition continued on Tuesday, April 29, as Hope met Calvin at Franklin Field in Grand Rapids. Bob Andree returned for mound duty and went all the way for the Dutchmen in the first game. Bylsma was the big gun for Hope with three hits and four RBI's. Hope was off to a good start in the first inning when Beernink walked, stole second, and scored on a Bylsma single. In the second, Bredeweg tripled and scored on a passed ball. Four more runs were added in the third, and the final two in the sixth as Thomson and Beernink singled. Both came home on Bylsma's single. Calvin threatened with a homer by Mulder in the second and a two-run shot by relief pitcher Schultz in the fourth, but despite the long ball the Knights came up short and the Dutch notched the victory, 8-4.

Hoffman was off to a shaky start in the second game as he hit the first two Calvin batters, then gave up two singles resulting in two runs, but he settled down and struck out the side in both the first and second innings. In the third frame, Thomson singled and Beernink was safe on a fielder's choice. Both came home on Olson's long home run to deep center. Calvin tied the score in the fifth on a well-executed squeeze play, but the Dutchmen went ahead to stay with three runs in their half of the inning. Beernink's double was the big blow. Two insurance runs in the sixth wrapped up the 8-3 Dutch win. Singles by Morgan, Boeve, and Essenberg scored one run, and Boeve crossed the plate on a double steal when the ball was thrown into center field. The double victory kept the Dutchmen in contention at the mid-point of the MIAA season.

Hope's next four games were played in a three-day span and the fates would not be kind to the Dutchmen. At Albion on Monday, May 5, the Britons of Coach Morley Fraser racked up two decisive wins over the De Vette men. In the opener it was Jerry Masteller setting the Dutch down with four hits as Vander Lind took the loss. Albion scored one run each in the second, third, and fourth, then added two more in both the fifth and sixth for a total of seven. The big blow was Don Van Gilder's home run in the fifth. Hope's lone run came in the sixth. Thomson was safe on an error and scored on successive singles by Beernink and Olson.

The Dutchmen hoped for better things in the second game, but the Britons were enjoying a big day and the game ended in a 17-3 blowout. Hoffman started for Hope and was relieved by Don Andree in the fifth. The sixth was a big inning for Albion with seven runs, and the seventh produced six more. Don Van Gilder stroked two more home runs and Chuck Boyle also had a round tripper. Thomson homered for Hope with Hoffman on base. The other Hope run was scored by Beernink.

The somewhat shell-shocked Dutchmen returned to Riverview Park to host Alma on Wednesday, May 8. Coach Charlie Skinner, who had garnered four straight MIAA titles, now turned over the reigns to Bill Carr. It made little difference. Jim Northrup, a future Detroit Tiger, scattered eight Hope hits in the opener enroute to a 6-2 victory. Hope starter Bob Andree was tagged for four hits and three runs in the third. Vander Lind, in relief, gave up the other three in the fourth. Beernink led Hope with a triple and double. Faber also had a triple.

The Scots added insult to injury in the second game as Bud Jacobson hurled a no-hit 7-0 shutout. Four walks plus Alma errors gave Hope base runners in the second, third, fourth, and seventh, but no runs resulted. Kempker pitched well, giving up eight hits, but was hurt by several Hope errors. Now 6-6 in MIAA play, the Dutchmen hoped to close out the season on a positive note. The Olivet Comets met Hope at Riverview in the league windup for both teams. In the first game the visitors collected 10 hits from the offerings of Hoffman and Vander Lind, who relieved in the seventh. The net result was nine runs while the Dutchmen could muster only five. Hope made a bid in the seventh when Beernink hit a three-run homer, but it was too little, too late. Kempker had a double and single, Thomson two singles, and Essenberg two singles in the losing effort.

In the final game of the season, Hope was off to a good start. Thomson opened the game with a home run in the left field stands, and before the inning was over the Dutchmen had crossed the plate four times. Two more were added in the third and another pair in the fourth. In addition to his homer, Thomson had a double. Bylsma banged out a triple and single, while Andree and Bredeweg each had two singles. Meanwhile, senior Bob Andree wound up his collegiate career by limiting the Comets to five hits as Hope chalked up an 8-5 victory.

The up-and-down season left Hope with a 7-7 mark in league play and fifth place in the MIAA. The 7-8 record overall was less than the team had hoped for, but the season had its moments and some good baseball had been played. Shortstop Bob Thomson was named to the All-MIAA Team, and Whitey Beernink was voted Hope's most valuable player. Beernink was also captain-elect for 1959.

* * *

Athletics Director Al Vanderbush continued as Hope's tennis coach in the spring of '58, but as his responsibilities increased in the department of history and political science, he turned to seniors John Jeltes and Dwayne "Tiger" Teusink to help with instruction of the new team members. Hope opened the season on a positive note with a 5-2 MIAA victory over the visiting Alma Scots. The match was played on Thursday, April 17, at the 22nd Street courts. In singles, Jeltes defeated George De Vries 6-0, 6-1, Teusink defeated Richard Johnson 6-2, 6-2, and Hope's Marshall Elzinga was the winner over Dalton Cantrell 6-2, 7-5. The four and five singles were both three-set matches. Bill York (A) defeated Rowland Van Es 4-6, 6-0, 6-3, and Jim Engbers bested Larry Woodcock (A) 3-6, 6-3, 6-4. In doubles George De Vries and Dalton Cantrell (A) defeated Jeltes-Teusink 5-7, 7-5, 6-4, and Elzinga-Engbers downed Richard Johnson-Bill York 6-0, 6-1.

On Saturday, April 19, Hope met Grand Rapids Junior College at the Franklin Park Courts in Grand Rapids. Both coaches needed to pare their squads and it was agreed to play extra matches to give team candidates a chance to show their stuff in intercollegiate competition. In singles, Jeltes defeated Bob Driscoll 6-3, 6-0, Bill Dozema (JC) won in three sets over Teusink 4-6, 6-2, 6-2, Elzinga defeated Herb Westover 7-5, 6-2, Ron Betten (JC) got the best of Engbers 8-6, 7-5, Bob Top (JC) defeated Van Es 6-4, 2-6, 6-4, John Tanja (JC) was the winner over Dennis Wiersma 6-4, 6-2, Ron Wiegerink (H) defeated Jim Lind 6-4, 6-4, and Tom Hoekstra (JC) took Ross Boersma 6-2, 6-3.

In doubles, Jeltes-Teusink defeated Bob Driscoll-Herb Westover 6-3, 6-0, Elzinga-Engbers won from Bill Dozema-Ron Betten 8-6, 2-6, 6-4, and John Tanja-Jim Lind (JC) defeated Wiersma-Wiegerink 13-11, 6-3. It had been an interesting day, but the team score showed JC with six to five for Hope. The Raiders had now managed to sweep Hope in all four spring sports. The Dutchmen would hope that some of JC's fine athletes would make their way to Hope for their final two years.

Hope's second league encounter took place on Tuesday, April 22, in Marshall against Olivet. Much like the baseball team, the Dutchmen were in the midst of an up-and-down season, but this day they were on target. Without the services of Teusink, Hope still managed to shut out the Comets. Jeltes defeated Don Barton 6-1, 6-0, Elzinga defeated Dave Graham 6-3, 6-0, Engbers won from Bob Waddell 6-1, 6-2, Van Es took Dick De Ryke 6-0, 6-1, and Wiegerink defeated Cliff Dean 6-2, 6-3. In doubles it was Elzinga-Engbers over Barton-Graham 6-1, 6-2, and Van Es-Wiegerrink over De Ryke-Waddell 6-2, 6-3 to give Hope the 7-0 team victory.

In Holland three days later, the Hope squad could better appreciate Olivet's frustration. On Friday, April 25, the Kalamazoo team came to town and did the Dutchmen in. In number-one singles it was Kalamazoo's Les Dodson over Jeltes 6-3, 6-2, Holland native Bill Japinga defeated Teusink 6-1, 6-0, Bob Yuel won from Elzinga 6-2, 6-2, Les Overway defeated Engbers 2-6, 6-2, 6-2, and Roger Miracle took Van Es 6-4, 6-1. In doubles it was Dodson-Yuel over Jeltes-Teusink 6-0, 6-3, and former Holland High teammates Japinga and Overway over Elzinga-Engbers (H) 6-0, 3-6, 6-1 to complete the 7-0 team shutout.

Hope's performance at Hillsdale on Thursday, May 1, was somewhat better but short of victory as the Dales prevailed by a 5-2 score. Jeltes defeated Howard Johnson 6-3,

6-3, Larry Jerome (HI) defeated Teusink (H) 6-1, 6-0, Tom Purdy (HI) won from Elzinga 6-0, 6-1, Dick Scripter (HI) defeated Engbers (H) 6-3, 6-2, and Wiegerink defeated Rick Bazany 6-4, 6-4. In doubles it was Johnson-Jerome (HI) over Jeltes-Teusink 6-4, 6-4, and Purdy-Scripter (HI) over Elzinga-Engbers 6-2, 6-1.

The Dutchmen met another strong team on Wednesday, May 7. At the 22nd Street courts it was the Albion Britons winning 6-1. At number-one singles Jeltes won a hard-fought three-setter from Dale Brubaker, 3-6, 6-1, 6-4, but it was down hill the rest of the way. Don Hines defeated Teusink 6-2, 6-2, Ron Johnson won from Elzinga (H) 6-4, 6-2, Brad Iverson defeated Engbers 6-4, 6-0, and Larry Elkins downed Van Es 6-4, 6-3. In doubles it was Brubaker-Hines over Jeltes-Teusink 6-1, 6-3, and Johnson-Iverson getting the best of Elzinga-Engbers 6-2, 8-6.

A season begun with some promise had faltered in the final weeks. A hoped-for comeback in the league meet at Kalamazoo on May 16 did not materialize, and the Dutchmen had to settle for fifth place overall. Seniors Jeltes and Teusink, however, had contributed much in keeping the program intact. In years to come, Teusink would succeed his mentor, Joe Moran, as "Mr. Tennis" in Holland.

* * *

Women's sports were hardly front page news in 1958, but on March 26 Hope's Mary Breid met with the other MIAA coaches to make arrangements for the league tennis and archery tournament. The event would be held at Hillsdale in early May. The tennis team included Joyce Leighley, Donna Hardenberg, Mary Kay Diephuis, Carolyn Scholten, Alice Warren, Winona Keizer, and Janet Owen. In home matches, Hope posted a 7-2 victory over Aquinas on April 18, but lost to Calvin 5-4 the next day. On April 26 the three schools met again at Calvin, and Hope emerged a double victor, downing Calvin 6-3 and Aquinas by the same score. At Kalamazoo on May 3 it was the lady Hornets winning, again by the score of 6-3. Hope placed third in the league tennis tourney, but captured first in archery. Lois Bonnema finished first, Paula Nykamp second, and Diane Faulkenberg fourth in a field of 20 archers.

* * *

The 1957-58 MIAA All-Sports Trophy was won by Albion College with 76 points. Kalamazoo followed with 68, edging Hillsdale (67) by one and Hope (66) by two. Alma finished fifth with 53, Calvin sixth with 43, Adrian seventh with 10, and Olivet eighth with seven.

Hope had not won the All-Sports Trophy, but there remained a feeling among the Hope coaches that something good was afoot. It was obvious that returning athletes had enjoyed themselves and were eager for the next season to begin. Talent was not lacking, especially in football and basketball, and coaches found it necessary to bridle their enthusiasm. September was a long way off and much could transpire in the interim.

CHAPTER 4

EXCELLENCE ASSEMBLED — HOPE AND GLORY

Coaches' wives look forward to the summer months when there are no games, no late nights, no long weekends to keep spouses from sharing family responsibility. Coaches also have prized this time of relieved pressure and family "reacquaintance." But in an era of stay-at-home moms and sole bread-winners, income had to be augmented. President Lubbers was aware of the situation and, as usual, found a solution. Coaches De Vette, Green, and Brewer were dispatched to various Reformed Church youth camps in the East and Midwest. College Night programs were conducted, and numerous students were thus recruited. Included were some fine athletes. But once again, fathers were absent for week-long periods and long-suffering wives were holding the fort. An otherwise average summer became momentous for the Brewers when third son Daniel Richard was born on Aug. 4, 1958.

Three weeks later, on Aug. 26, the Hope staff conducted a football clinic on campus. Forty-four area coaches were in attendance and once again the grid game took center stage. Presenters included Hope alumni coaches Dick Higgs, Abe Moerland, and Gene Rothi. Meanwhile, Lee Kleis, Hope '28, had organized a campaign to install a new scoreboard at Riverview Park. Contributions were received from Holland High, Hope College, local industries, and service clubs. Kleis served as official scorer at Riverview and his job would now be much easier.

Football was in the air well before Hope's first practice on Monday, Sept. 1. On this much-anticipated day, Captain Larry Ter Molen led a group of 17 returning lettermen plus 18 eager freshmen. All told, the squad would number 43. Quality rather than quantity characterized the '58 squad. The team could boast of unusual maturity. Six members of the group were married, some with infants at home. Included in this group were Ron Bekius, Ron Boeve, Bill Huibregtse, Paul Mack, Tom Miller, and Paul "Pete" Watt. Watt had seen action on the '55 and '56 Hope teams, then dropped out of school for a year. Paul Mack had played halfback at Holland High School, but had not played football for four years. It was soon obvious that Mack was an able athlete, and Coach De Vete was not long in converting him to a winged-T quarterback. Ron Boeve had been a member of the 1953 Hope championship team and also an All-MIAA baseball catcher in '54. After a stint with Uncle Sam in the Army he had returned to Hope with no real intention of playing football. However, following the Eastern Michigan game, Coach Ken Weller used his persuasive powers to convince Boeve to come out. This gave De Vette "3 B's", Bronson, Blough, and Boeve, at the end position. All were experienced and could catch the ball. Rangy Charley Coulson could spell them on defense. The entire offensive line returned with Larry Ter Molen and George Peelen at tackles, Don Paarlberg and Tom Miller at guards, and Gene Van Dongen at center. With Mack, Jack Faber, and Jim Fox at quarterback the Dutch were in good shape, while Duane Voskuil, Watt, and Jerry Herp were effective runners at halfback. Bekius had found his niche at the crucial fullback position in the winged-T offense, had performed effectively in '57, and was destined for even greater things in '58.

The defense was designed to free the agile Huibregtse at middle linebacker to plug holes from tackle to tackle and beyond. Bekius, Mack, Faber, and the speedy Jim Mohr roamed in the secondary. Talented back-ups at every position further brightened the picture, but the Hope coaches were well aware that games are not played on paper.

The first scrimmage was held on Thursday, Sept. 4, then followed a week later with a full-scale scrimmage against Grand Rapids Junior College. The drudgery of pre-season practice finally came to an end, and the team prepared for the opener at Eastern Michigan. On Friday, Sept. 19, at 1:30 p.m. the team left for Ypsilanti. The game was a night contest to be played at Briggs Field. A crowd of 5,000 turned out hoping to see Eastern off on the right foot. Fred Trosko's Hurons dominated the statistics with 110 yards rushing and another 109 in the air while holding the Dutchmen to 83 yards of offense, all on the ground. Hope attempted six passes, completing none, but the Dutch defense was tough at crunch time and converted three Huron turnovers into scores.

Midway in the first quarter, Mack intercepted a pass and returned it to the Eastern 37. Alternating runs by Voskuil and Jerry Herp put the ball on the one and it was Bekius up the middle for the score. Huibregtse converted for the early 7-0 lead. With about six minutes remaining in the first quarter, Van Dongen recovered a Sam Holloway fumble on the Eastern 15. A penalty placed the ball on the two-yard line. Faber then rolled around right end and into the end zone. Huibregtse's kick was not good, leaving the score at 13-0.

In the second quarter a handoff to Voskuil was botched and Dan Matthews recovered for Eastern on the Hope 11. Brian Dunn carried to the one, and quarterback John Kubiak sneaked in for the TD. Chuck Shonta kicked the point to make it 13-7 at halftime.

A strained right knee kept Van Dongen out of action in the second half, but versatile Bill Huibregtse was active at guard, fullback, and linebacker. In the latter capacity he intercepted a pass on the Eastern 40 and returned it to the 18, but Hope lost the ball on downs. The Hope defense held, and on fourth down Paarlberg broke through to block Eastern's punt. This gave Hope possession on the five. Two plays later Ron Bekius moved up the middle from the four for the third Hope touchdown. The kick was again wide of the mark, but there would be no more scoring and the opportunistic Dutchmen journeyed home with a 19-7 win.

A victory on opening day is always welcome, but the Hope staff was clearly concerned about the lack of offense. Alma, Hope's next opponent, was coming off an impressive 26-0 win over Indiana Central. It was also remembered that the Scots of Coach Art Smith had administered one of but two defeats suffered by the Dutchmen during the '57 season. The '58 league opener for both teams was a night game played at Riverview Park on Saturday, Sept. 27, with the drama unfolding early. Van Dongen, with a strained right knee, turned over the kickoff duty to Huibregtse. Hubie's opening kick from the field's east end was a good one, high and far, and rolling into the end zone. Hope's first-wave coverage included MIAA dash champion Jim Mohr. Mohr's assignment, to go all out for the ball, was carried out to perfection. As the confused Scot safety man let the ball roll, Mohr pounced on it short of the end line-touchdown! Huibregtse added the point, and Hope led 7-0 with no time having elapsed on the scoreboard.

The Dutch secondary continued to shine as Bekius intercepted a Bill Klenk pass on the Hope 40 and returned it to the Alma 34. Three running plays put the ball on the 10. On a trap play up the middle, Bekius was into the end zone with 9:43 remaining in the quarter. The point try was not good and the Hope lead moved to 13-0. Following an Alma punt Voskuil was off on a 17-yard run, then, quite uncharacticly, Hope went to the air. Mack and Faber completed passes to Ron Bronson, Voskuil, and Blough for a total of 33 yards. This placed the ball on the six and Pete Watt covered the remaining distance on an off-tackle power play. The kick was not good, but Hope's 19-0 lead looked good as the quarter ended.

The Scots came on strong in the second quarter with a 51-yard drive of their own. Harold Vandenberg went the final yard to score. The conversion failed, leaving the Dutchmen lead at 19-6. Hope returned Alma's kickoff to the 36 and seven plays later it was Bekius up the middle on a 25-yard sprint to the end zone. Hope's lack of success at conversions continued, and the score stood 25-6 at halftime.

Late in the third period, Hope mounted another seven-play drive, this one for 43 yards. Again it was Bekius following a guard trap for the score. This time Huibregtse split the uprights and the Dutch lead increased to 32-6. Hope substitutes were now in the game.

Midway in the final stanza, Alma's Bill Klenk intercepted a Fox pass and, with 7:14 remaining, a Klenk-to-end Tom Taber TD pass made the final score 32-12. Statistics showed Hope with 312 yards rushing plus 69, in the air compared to 100-27 for Alma. The offense was back.

Hope's two-year contract with Northern Michigan would be concluded at Riverview Park on Saturday night, Oct. 4. An estimated 3,800 fans turned out for the non-league game. Coach Frosty Ferzaca had lost a tough one to the Dutchmen in 1957, and he hoped for a reversal after the long trip from the Upper Penninsula. His cause would be hampered by a back injury to quarterback Tom Schwalback, a standout in the '57 game. He would be replaced by Jack Hero.

The Alma game proved a confidence builder and the Dutchmen were off to a fast start. A 70-yard drive in 14 plays produced the first score. Included were Mack passes of 12 and 15 yards to Mike Blough and Watt, plus 28 yards in five carries by Bekius. The score came on an eight-yard pass in the flat from Mack to Bekius. A successful conversion by Huibregtse put the Dutchmen ahead 7-0 on the new scoreboard.

The Wildcats were not long in responding. In the second quarter, a nine-play drive was completed when Roy Langsford went 10 yards off tackle to score. Bud Tomkins kicked the point to even the score at 7-7, and fans realized that they were in for a game between evenly matched teams.

HOPE'S BALL

Tackle Larry Ter Molen (71) pounces on a fumble in the 1958 Adrian game at Riverview Park. Ter Molen was named the MIAA's most valuable player along with end Tom Taylor of Albion.

As the action see-sawed it was Hope's turn again. A 16-play, 65-yard drive was climaxed when Voskuil went four yards over left guard for the TD. With 5:16 remaining in the half, Huibregtse added the point to make it 14-7. A Bekius interception on the Hope 35 gave the Dutchmen one more shot in the period, but the Wildcat defense rose to the occasion, stopping Bekius on the one as the half ended.

Defense prevailed in the third quarter and there was no scoring. Midway in the fourth, however, Northern tackle Gus Krantz recovered a Hope fumble on the Dutchman 18. Four plays later, Paul D'Arres went over from four yards out. Bud Tomkins' kick was centered correctly but hit the crossbar and bounced back onto the field! For the second year in a row the Dutchmen would chalk up a 14-13 victory over a strong Northern team. The teams would not meet again due to size variation, the distance factor, and different NCAA classifications.

Hope's first string players, who had played most of the Northern game, were given the day off on Monday while the remainder of the squad worked out in preparation for the next encounter. The Oct. 11 game would be played at Kalamazoo's Angell Field and would be the Hornets' Homecoming. During the week, Jim Menzer informed the Hope coaches that he would drop football in an attempt to boost his grade point average. Faber was nursing a sprained thumb and Sherwood "Sharkey" Vander Woude was moved up to spell Mack.

A crowd of 1,700 witnessed the traditional battle for a pair of wooden shoes. Three minutes into the game, the Hornets found themselves in a punting situation deep in their own territory. Somehow, blocker Doug Perry backed into his kicker, Bill Liggett, causing the ball to scoot toward the Kalamazoo goal, where Mike Blough recovered on the one-yard line. Two plays later Voskuil scored on an off-tackle play and Huibregtse converted. The score remained at 7-0 into the second quarter. At this point, Watt returned a Kazoo punt 17 yards to the Hornet 46. Two carries by freshman fullback Steve Slagh netted 22 yards. A further push put the ball on the six. On fourth down Mack passed six yards to Watt for Hope's second TD. A Huibregtse kick sailed wide, leaving the score at 13-0 with 8:10 remaining in the period.

Near the end of the quarter, Hope safety Jim Mohr intercepted a pass on the Kalamazoo 47 and returned it to the 41. This time it would take the Dutchmen 12 plays to reach paydirt. A 15-yard pass from Mack to Ron Bronson helped in the drive. Watt finally pushed over from the one with just 1:55 remaining. Huibregtse's kick made it a satisfying 20-0 at halftime.

The defensive teams showed their stuff in the third period, and there was no scoring. In the final quarter, Kalamazoo suffered another turnover as Huibregtse intercepted on the K 47 and reeled off 19 yards before being stopped on the 28. In six plays, including a 16-yard Mack to Watt completion, Hope was again knocking at the door. Bekius was given the ball on his patented play up the middle, and Hope had its fourth TD of the afternoon with 19:10 left in the game. Huibregtse's toe found the mark and

79

the Hope lead lengthened to 27-0.

In the closing minutes it appeared that Rolla Anderson's team would get on the board, but play deteriorated somewhat as a comedy of errant passes ensued. Faber intercepted a Kazoo pass on the Hornet's 34 and was pulled down on the 16 in what today is known as the "red zone." But two plays later the Hope threat was stymied when Lou Vild picked off a Fox pass. On the next play Fox, now on defense, returned the favor by intercepting on the 44 and cruising back to the 22. The game ended at 27-0 with Hope in possession once more on the 16.

Hope's Oct. 18 game with Adrian brought an estimated 5,000 fans to Riverview Park. It was the largest Homecoming crowd ever. Many had to see if Bekius could continue his torrid touchdown pace. The 25-year-old senior had graduated from Holland High in 1951, spent time in the Army, did a stint at Western Colorado College in Gunnison, and then transferred to Hope in 1956. A two-way player, he was extremely effective in the defensive secondary. Coach De Vette found it necessary to give him a breather at some point and such breaks usually came on offense. One can only speculate on what his TD total might have been in platoon football. His performance would be a tough act to follow for son Greg in 1977-80.

Adrian chose to receive, but the Dutchman defense held and a Bulldog punt gave Hope possession on the Adrian 47. In five plays the Dutchmen reached the 11, where the ball was jarred loose from Watt. However, Watt was able to recover his own fumble, and on the next play Bekius went over guard for the game's first score. Less than five minutes had elapsed as Huibregtse kicked the point to make it 7-0. Adrian's troubles continued later in the quarter as Peelen recovered a fumble on the Bulldog 34. Hope's four-play drive featured a 14-yard gain by Voskuil and a touchdown leap over right tackle by Bekius. Hubie's second conversion made it 14-0.

In the second quarter, Adrian's first scoring threat bogged down and Hope took over on its own 28. Eleven plays later, Bekius dashed 20 yards up the middle for his third touchdown of the half. The kick was not good and Hope's lead expanded to 20-0. Minutes later, an Adrian punt was partially blocked by Vander Woude. Mack fielded the ball on the 21 and moved to the 17, but Hope did not score and the 20-0 margin remained at the half.

Adrian's kickoff opened the second half. Hope's subsequent drive featured the longest run of the season, a 54-yard right end sweep by Watt to the 26. On the next play fullback Bekius broke through, picked up an offside blocker, and went the remaining distance for his fourth touchdown. The Huibregtse conversion pushed the lead to 27-0 with but 1:02 gone in the third period. Bekius reluctantly took a seat on the bench as substitutes took over.

Six plays later, Peelen, who was having a great day on defense, recovered his second fumble of the afternoon. Hope moved in from the Adrian 42 in seven plays, with Watt ripping away from tacklers for the final 18 yards. Huibregtse's kick upped the count to 34-0 and all regulars departed.

Sub halfback Bob Bonnette made his presence known by intercepting an Adrian pass on the Hope 47 and running it back to the Bulldog 35. Eight plays later, Bonnette, now on offense, went one-yard off-tackle to score. Huibregtse's fifth conversion lengthened the lead to 41-0 with 3:04 remaining in the third period.

Coach Bob Gillis' crew got on the board early in the fourth quarter, when Larry Bowser passed to Bill Hamilton for the TD and thereby averted the shutout. Gene Melin's conversion made the final score 41-7. Few in the partisan crowd could recall a more satisfying Homecoming performance.

SATURDAY, OCTOBER 25, 1958. In the annals of Hope football, no game shines brighter than the one played at Hillsdale in 1958. In succeeding eras, rules, techniques, and equipment have changed, making comparisons difficult. However, for excitement, tension, and sheer drama, this encounter stands alone. The game, "replayed" and embellished for 41 years, is now fraught with innocent fabrications. Ironically, as one examines the action as it occurred, there is little need to embellish.

Circumstances preceding the match-up undoubtedly increased the interest and attention it received. Hype was rampant in Holland and increased daily with the countdown. Frank "Muddy" Waters had taken over at Hillsdale in 1954 and promptly won the MIAA title with a perfect 6-0 record. In stunning fashion he had repeated the feat in 1955, 1956, and 1957. Now in 1958 the Dales had posted three more MIAA wins to extend their streak to 27. But the Dutchmen had challenged in 1957 before falling by the narrow margin of 7-6. Hope's last victory in the series had been by a 28-7 count in the 1953 championship year. The stage was set for a small-college classic, and fans would not be disappointed.

The game was played on Saturday, Oct. 25, at Hillsdale College's Recreation Field with kickoff at 8 p.m. A clear majority of the 2,200 in attendance had made the trip from Holland and took their place in the stands, all of which were on the home team's side of the field. Press box facilities were adequate for the time, but no field phones were available for the visitors' bench. Anticipating this, coaches Russ DeVette and Ken Weller could be seen prior to game time stringing wire around the field and up to the press box, where Weller would later take his perch.

Hope won the toss and chose to kick off for a variety of reasons. De Vette had great faith in a defensive front made up of ends Bronson and Blough along with linebackers Paarlberg, Van Dongen, and Huibregtse. Rounding out the unit were tackles Peelen and Ter Molen. Van Dongen, Hope's kickoff man, could put the ball in or near the end zone, while leading the first wave of tacklers was MIAA dash champion Mohr. De Vette also felt that early game jit-

'58 HILLSDALE GAME — HOPE 16, HILLSDALE 13

Dashman Jim Mohr set up Hope's first touchdown.

Linebacker-guard Don "Punch" Paarlberg played 60 minutes and drew the plaudits of Hillsdale Coach Muddy Waters.

Paul "Pete" Watt scored Hope's second touchdown on a "Heidelberg" reverse — 42 yards.

In later years Bill Huibregtse shortened his name to Hubregs.

ters could be handled best on defense. So much for strategy. As the opening whistle sounded, Van Dongen lofted a boomer. The ball was fumbled by the Dales' Don Eugenio on the two-yard line and promptly recovered by the streaking Mohr. It was almost a repeat of Mohr's earlier feat against Alma. On the first play, quarterback Paul Mack sneaked into the end zone and Huibregtse added the extra point. Only 15 seconds had elapsed. Hope's 7-0 lead was a nightmare start for Coach Waters, while De Vette's decision had paid big dividends.

As the contest settled into a defensive struggle, each team had its chances and each made its mistakes. Van Dongen blocked a Hillsdale punt on the eight-yard line, but as Hope took over a mishandled snap from center was recovered by big Jim Larkin to end the threat. Late in the second quarter, the home team worked its way to the Hope 10, but Huibregtse intercepted a Chuck Redding pass and the half ended with the score still at 7-0.

There was no scoring in the third period, but in the final stanza the Dales marched 90 yards in 10 plays to tie the score. The drive featured a 30-yard run by All-MIAA halfback Walt Poe. The score came on a 13-yard pass from freshman quarterback Chuck Redding to end Jim "Jellybean" Reynolds in the corner of the end zone. Jim Dilbone's conversion made it 7-7 with 9:50 remaining in the game.

Every team has in its repertoire a few plays known as "game breakers." In 1956 Hope had been beaten 40-6 by Heidelberg College of Tiffin, Ohio. A play that did considerable damage to the Dutchman cause was a deep reverse which employed remarkable deception. De Vette was impressed enough to incorporate the play into his own system. Now, with six minutes remaining and Hope on the Dales' 42, De Vette called for the "Heidelberg." Right wingback Pete Watt would be the eventual ball carrier. Opposite Watt on defense was end "Jellybean" Reynolds, an outstanding athlete who had already scored the Dales' only touchdown. The play began as a right end sweep with the flow of backs in that direction. As Watt started back across the formation, Reynolds perceived the trickery and came hard across the line. The Hope coaches held their collective breath as Jellybean's long arm reached out for the diminutive halfback. He missed by the narrowest of margins, and from that point the play proceeded as diagrammed in the play book. Watt was untouched around left end in a 42-yard touchdown romp. There was concern when Huibregtse's kick sailed wide of the mark, but the Dutchmen now led 13-7.

As time became more of a factor, young Redding showed his stuff. In a 75-yard, 11-play drive he completed nine of 10 passes. A 23-yarder to Walt Poe was a big gainer. The same combination produced the score. Poe gathered in the ball in front of the defenders three yards into the end zone. Jim Dilbone's go-ahead kick was good, but the Dales were charged with illegal procedure. Given a second chance, several desperate Dutchmen combined to block the kick. Included were Bronson, Blough, Faber, and Bekius. With 3:50 remaining: Hope 13 - Hillsdale 13!

The ensuing kickoff was taken by halfback Jerry Herp from tiny Hopkins High School. His return to the 31 gave Hope reasonable field position. With the game in the balance, it was once again decision time for Coach De Vette. For Hope's "last chance" he now employed a semispread formation with Bronson split wide to the left and various halfbacks in the position of wide flanker to the right. The two set backs were Voskuil and Watt. Hope was not really a passing team, but Coach Waters could not take a chance. His response was a loose 5-3 "prevent" defense. This opened the door for Hope's preferred running game. On trap plays, Voskuil and Watt had runs of 16 and 13 yards while quarterback Mack mixed in just enough short passes to keep the Dales in their prevent alignment. Such procedures, however, tended to eat up the clock. As the final seconds ticked away, Hope found itself with first down on the Hillsdale 21.

Timeouts had been expended and bedlam reigned in the Hope bench area. Seemingly, De Vette alone retained his composure and concentration. The ball was placed by the referee and the Hope players rushed to get into their offensive set. What actually happened in those fading seconds is subject to some conjecture, but the following is gleaned from those on-hand and subsequent newspaper accounts. On the sideline DeVette decided on a field goal and nodded to Huibregtse, who raced onto the field with the kicking tee (1958 rules permitted a tee). Rotund Dick Buckley, who usually centered for kicks, started onto the field. About eight yards in he was called back by the coaches, who realized that he could not negotiate the distance in time. Mack and Faber got the picture as Huibregtse ran in. Mack moved away from his position under center and Faber took his place as the holder on the 29. Van Dongen, realizing that Mack was not in position, looked back between his legs to see the kneeling Faber. He snapped the ball on Faber's signal. A *Holland Sentinel* account reported that Bronson went out for a pass. As Faber placed the ball, the clock took its final tick. Huibregtse's splendid 39-yard kick sailed through the uprights and into Hope football folklore. Hope 16 - Hillsdale 13!

Several instances in the game's aftermath seem worthy of mention. As might be expected, Hope fans and players stormed onto the field in wild celebration. Huibregtse was hoisted on shoulders and general euphoria prevailed. Line coach Gordon Brewer cast dignity to the winds and danced a jig with guard Swede Olson. Faber remembers that the field lights were turned out shortly after the game ended, perhaps symbolic of Hillsdale feelings at the moment. The lights were back on in a few minutes and the revelry continued. In a show of class after a tough loss, Coach Waters made his way to the Hope locker room to offer congratulations. He was especially impressed with the performance of Paarlberg, who had played the entire 60 minutes.

The trip home included a stop at Win Schuler's Restau-

Savoring the victory 37 years later were Bill Hubregs and Coach Brewer. The occasion was a 50's reunion of Hope athletes during the 1995 Homecoming.

Jack Faber (above) is now a prominent area dentist.

In the posed shot above, Gene Van Dongen holds for Bill Huibregtse. For the game-winning kick Van Dongen snapped the ball to holder Jack Faber.

83

rant in Marshall, where the team enjoyed a post-game steak dinner. The drama and overall import of the victory were now beginning to sink in. When the bus arrived in Holland at 3 a.m., the campus was alive with running students, who escorted the Greyhound up the winding road to Carnegie Gym. The silence of an early Holland Sabbath was shattered by a new round of celebration. An apprehensive coaching staff waited for complaints, but none were received.

Muddy Waters would salvage a tri-championship and would be more than ready in 1959, but this night belonged to Coach De Vette and his team. To this day Waters maintains that Hope had more than the allotted 11 men on the field during the final play. He may have been right. He also may have been the only one counting. Did Dick Buckley make it to the sideline before the snap? We may never know. The Hillsdale game photographer ran out of film just before the final plays and thus the needed verification disappeared. Hope filmed only its home games in 1958, depending on duplicates for away contests.

Hope's final home game was a Parents Day encounter with Olivet on Saturday, Nov. 1. Beleaguered Olivet, now with an enrollment of 350, held the distinction of being the smallest school in the nation sponsoring intercollegiate football. In marked contrast to Hillsdale, the Comets of Coach Henry Paul were attempting to end a 28-game losing streak. It would not happen this day. More than 2,000 fans turned out to see Ter Molen, Bekius, Paarlberg, Tom Miller, Jim De Witt, and Bill Brookstra in their final home appearance. Dr. Morrette Rider managed to produce a 50-piece band to entertain on the field at halftime. Early in the first quarter, Hope forced an Olivet punt, which was taken by Watt on the Hope 48 and returned to the Olivet 36. Three first downs in three plays took the ball to the 11, where Voskuil broke off-tackle for the touchdown with but four minutes gone. Huibregtse's kick made it 7-0. The Olivet offense was not clicking, and another punt gave the Dutchmen possession on the Comets' 36. Included in Hope's seven-play drive was a 29-yard off-tackle run by Voskuil. The scoring play was a 14-yard counter play by Herp. A second conversion by Huibregtse increased the count to 14-0 as the quarter ended.

In the second quarter, the Comets moved the ball somewhat better, but ended up punting into the Hope end zone. The touchback was placed on the 20-yard line where, on the first play, Herp, with fine blocking from Bekius, raced 80 yards for Hope's third TD. The point-try by Bekius was wide of the mark, leaving the score at 20-0. Hope substitutes now began to dot the field. Freshman linebacker Dave Simala broke through to block Olivet's next punt attempt, and freshman tackle Bob Vandenberg recovered on the Comet 14. Two plays later, freshman fullback Steve Slagh went 13 yards up the middle to score. A Huibregtse kick increased the margin to 27-0.

Olivet now produced its first scoring threat of the afternoon. The drive included a 31-yard pass from quarterback Lu Diaz to Walt Green, which placed the ball on the Hope nine. But the Dutch defense held for four downs and took over. A series of running plays moved the ball to the Comets' 40, where Voskuil once again broke free off-tackle for a long run. He was hit on the 20, but bounced away and into the end zone. Bekius begged for another try for the point, and Coach De Vette relented. This time the fullback made good and the score stood at 34-0. The Comets had little choice but to fill the air with passes, and Faber soon picked one off. Fox now passed to end Jerry Nieusma for 19 yards, but Hope lost nine on the next play. On third down Fox passed to Faber, who was open in the end zone. Another Bekius kick made it 41-0 at the half.

The obvious mismatch placed Coach De Vette in a tough position. Coaches know that what goes around, comes around. De Vette had no desire to humiliate Coach Paul and his team when they were down. Substitutes had been used liberally in the first half and the score had mounted anyway. The Hope coaches felt that regulars needed to see some action to stay sharp for the championship game with Albion, now just a week away. It was finally decided that subs would continue to carry most of the load and the offense would be limited to selected basic plays.

Ten plays into the second half, Bekius, who had seen very little action, went 11 yards over guard for another score and Huibregtse added the point. It was the only score of the third quarter, but the count now stood at 48-0. In the fourth period, Simala blocked his second punt of the afternoon and Dick Buckley recovered for Hope on the Olivet 36. Faber had replaced Mack at quarterback. He now passed 35 yards to Watt for yet another TD. Watt's kick was good, making it 55-0. Fox replaced Faber and, with four minutes remaining, passed to Bonnette for Hope's final score. In his last home appearance, Captain Larry Ter Molen was given a chance to score a point. His great ability as a blocker and tackler did not necessarily transfer to kicking, and the game ended at 61-0. Olivet's day would come.

Coach Morley Fraser, now in his fifth season at Albion, was ready for Hope on Saturday, Nov. 8. The day dawned dark and cold with intermittent rain. A big crowd of 4,000 fans gathered at the Britons' Alumni Field with the MIAA championship on the line. Hillsdale was scheduled to meet Adrian, but it was a night game and Muddy Waters was on-hand this afternoon and took his place with the Albion coaches in the press box. His interest in a Hope defeat was understandable, as it would give the Dales a share of the MIAA championship, assuming a Hillsdale win over Adrian.

As the game got underway, the Hope coaches were puzzled as to the whereabouts of Albion's end and co-captain Tom Taylor. Eventually he was spotted in a slot-back position wearing a different number. He was a key figure in the Briton offense, and the Dutchmen would make a special effort to keep him covered.

Midway in the first quarter, Albion's Jim Kreider inter-

HOPE AT ALBION — 1958

Hope led 7-6 in the second quarter, but Albion won 18-13 to force a three-way tie for the MIAA Championship. The tackle above is vintage Don Paarlberg. Also in the picture for Hope are Larry Ter Molen (71), Jack Faber (42), Bill Huibregtse (64), and safety Jim Mohr (46).

cepted a Mack pass on the Hope 46 to set up the game's first score. A nine-play drive featured an 18-yard pass play from quarterback Tom Dewey to Taylor. The Dutchmen defense stiffened, but with fourth and six on the 12, halfback Don Van Gilder threw a running pass to end Garth Richey in the endzone. The kick attempt by Bill Friberg was not good, but the Britons had drawn first blood at 6-0.

Hope took the ensuing kickoff, kept possession, and drove 64 yards in 17 plays. A key play in the drive was a fourth down pass from Mack to Bekius which moved the ball to the 12. On the second play of the second quarter, Mack sneaked in from the one. A Huibregtse conversion made it 7-6 and gave Hope its first and only lead of the game.

Later in the quarter, guard and co-captain Lanny Leak sacked Mack and recovered the resulting fumble on the Albion 45. Two plays put the ball on the Hope 46. At this point, halfback Mike Stone broke away off-tackle and raced all the way to the four, where he was pulled down by Mohr. The Dutchmen held for three plays, but on fourth down Van Gilder went over guard for the TD. The point-try by Jim Bowser was wide of the mark, but the Britons had regained the lead at 12-7 and led by that margin at the half.

Field conditions deteriorated as the slow rain continued. There would be no scoring in the third period, but Van Gilder brought the Dads' Day crowd to its feet with a 74-yard run which ended on the Hope two. Jim Mohr trailed Van Gilder by 10 yards, but caught up and jumped on his back to bring him down. With its back to the wall, the Dutchman defense displayed its mettle by holding the Britons for four downs. On fourth down it was Miller and Faber who downed Van Gilder on the four.

Late in the fourth quarter, Albion punted to the Hope 15. The Dutchmen gained six yards on a Faber-to-Blough pass. With fourth and four the decision was to go for it. In one of the game's biggest plays, Lanny Leak broke through to smother Pete Watt on the 16. Three plays later, Don Van Gilder scored on a pitchout. An attempted pass for the point failed, but Albion's lead increased to 18-7 with 2:10 remaining in the game. Hope took the kickoff and moved to midfield. Faber then lofted a 30-yard pass to Bronson, who got behind the defenders and ran the remaining 20 yards for the score. Huibregtse's kick was not good and Albion's hard-fought 18-13 victory ended Dutchman hopes for an undisputed championship and the school's first undefeated season. Coach Fraser's game plan had worked well, with Van Gilder being especially effective. On at least one occasion the Dutchman defense had been caught in the wrong alignment and the Britons had capitalized, but nothing could detract from Albion's much-deserved victory. Sharing in the jubilation was Albion line coach Fritz Shurmur who, 39 years later, would gain fame as defensive coordinator of the Super Bowl champion Green Bay Packers.

Hope's disappointment was hidden in a last week of hard practice. One game remained, albeit an anticlimactic one. At 1 p.m. on Friday, Nov. 14, the team left for the season finale, to be played the next day at Beloit College. Following an overnight stay in Rockford, Ill., the bus moved into Wisconsin and on to Beloit's Strong Stadium. About 50 die-hard Hope fans followed the Dutchmen around the lake for this final encounter on a chilly November afternoon. Included in this group were President and Mrs. Irwin Lubbers. Beloit followers had, to some degree, lost interest in the Buccaneers' 2-5 season, and the 3,000-seat stadium was largely empty. In fairness to Coach Carl "Pill" Nelson, his team had suffered a rash of injuries to key personnel. But football is football, and with the opening kickoff there was no lack of incentive by either team.

For the first time all season, Hope chose to receive. Beloit's kick with the wind carried to the goal line, was gathered in by Herp and returned to the 24. Hope's first touchdown drive included long runs by Bekius and Herp, and was climaxed when Watt, on a counter criss-cross play, went 25 yards for the score. Huibregtse kicked the point, and the Dutchmen led 7-0 with 10:45 remaining in the quarter. Taking advantage of the wind, Beloit responded with a passing attack that carried them to the Hope 11, where Ter Molen and Bekius teamed up to stop the drive.

With six minutes to go in the second quarter, Huibregtse recovered a Buccaneer fumble on Beloit's 21. Voskuil then drove off-tackle, broke free at the 10 and went in for the TD. The kick was not good, leaving the halftime score at 13-0. As in several of Hope's games, there was no scoring in the third period, but with 7:45 left in the final stanza Bekius scored again on his special play up the middle. The conversion by Huibregtse extended the lead to 20-0.

85

Coach Russ De Vette
1958

LASTING MEMORY

Players and coaches of the 1958 Hope team received minature gold footballs (left), lasting reminders of "That Championship Season."

HOPE COLLEGE FOOTBALL SQUAD — 1958
MIAA TRI-CHAMPIONS (WITH ALBION AND HILLSDALE)

Front Row L. to R.: Ron Bronson, Ron Bekius, Bill Brookstra, Jim De Witt, Captain Larry Ter Molen, Tom Miller, Jack Faber, Bill Huibregtse, George Peelen. **2nd Row:** Manager Jim Peterman, Manager Tom Bos, Bob Vandenberg, Sherwood "Sharky" Vander Woude, Dyke Rottschafer, Rich Bakker, Chuck Coulson, Steve Slagh, Mike Blough, Phil Annis, Dave Meyer, Howard Jansen, Ron Boeve, Manager Cal Rynbrandt. **3rd Row:** Assistant Coach Gordon Brewer, Assistant Trainer Stu Post, Duane Voskuil, John Vandenburg, Dave Den Ouden, Jim Fox, Jerry Nieusma, Rowland Van Es, Rich Machiele, Tom Klomparens, John Hubbard, Jim Vande Wege, Head Coach Russ De Vette. **4th Row:** Trainer Dr. Lawrence Green, Paul "Pete" Watt, Bruce Van Leuwen, Paul Mack, Dave Simala, Jim Mohr, Elmer Phail, Bob Bonnette, Keith White, Jerry Herp, Dick Buckley, Assistant Coach Ken Weller. **Missing from the picture:** Don Paarlberg, Gene Van Dongen.

Beloit had its moment after returning Hope's kickoff to the 27. Halfback Rich Kirtley broke free and raced 73 yards for the touchdown. The kick was not good, but the home team was on the board at 20-6. Following the kickoff, Hope began what would be its last drive of the season. Long runs by Bekius and Vander Woude, plus a 14-yard pass from Faber to Van Es, were highlights of the 12-play drive that put the ball on the one-yard line. Bekius plunged over guard for the final touchdown of a brilliant career. Hubie's kick missed the mark, but this time it really didn't matter. The Dutchmen would go home with a 26-6 victory to cap the best record in the school's football history to that point. The MIAA tri-championship was Hope's first since 1953.

In the season's aftermath there seemed to be accolades for all. Paarlberg, Bekius, and Ter Molen were named to the All-MIAA team, and Ter Molen was selected as the league's most valuable player along with Tom Taylor of Albion. Hope players and coaches were presented with appropriately engraved miniature gold footballs at a season-ending banquet. The plaudits for Ter Molen were not quite finished. After being named "Little All-American" by one of the news services, he was selected to play in the Optimists Bowl at the University of Arizona Stadium on Jan. 3. Tom Taylor of Albion was also selected to the 23-man squad made up of small-college stars. Their opponents were a similar number of stars from large universities. Included in this group were Bronco Nagurski Jr. of Notre Dame and Boyd Dowler of Colorado. The latter would later team up with Bart Starr to win the first Super Bowls for the Green Bay Packers of Vince Lombardi. The university stars prevailed by the narrow margin of 14-12, but Ter Molen and Taylor saw considerable action. At the game's conclusion, they were presented with an engraved watch, a football signed by all team members as well as their respective game jerseys. A never-to-be-forgotten season could not have ended on a finer note.

*   *   *

Al Vanderbush and Larry Green decided to swap coaching responsibilities for the 1958-59 school year. Vanderbush would assume the cross country post, and Green would take over men's tennis in the spring. The move benefited both men. Doc Green, as athletic trainer, needed more time to attend to the numerous football injuries in the fall. Vanderbush felt the time pinch more as his history and political science classes wound down in the spring.

Coach Al's 1958 cross country squad was led by Captain Carroll Bennink. Also included were Roland Schut, Alan Teusink, Carl De Jonge, Jerry Wondra, Harvey Feenstra, Dave Needham, and Bob Hoogendoorn. John Needham, a former runner, assisted as manager. Bennink was consistent throughout the year, and the much-improved Schut finished first three times for the Dutchmen.

In the dual meet season, Hope recorded victories over Alma, Hillsdale, and Olivet while dropping decisions to eventual champion Calvin, Albion, Kalamazoo, and Grand Rapids Junior College. At the conference meet, held at Hillsdale on Nov. 12, Hope finished in fifth place with Alma in fourth. This meant an overall tie for fourth for Hope. The tie would loom large when All-Sports points were tabulated in the spring.

*   *   *

Basketball practice for the 1958-59 season got underway with two football games yet to be played. Coach De Vette met the squad on Monday, Nov. 3, for two weeks of evening workouts before moving to afternoons on Nov. 17. Few would deny that prospects were brighter than at any time in recent history. Tiger Teusink and Jack Kempker had been lost to graduation, but all others returned save senior John Hood. The 6' 7" Hood had not seen much playing time, but had contributed immeasurably in practice sessions. As the squad's second-tallest man, he had furnished the main opposition in the dramatic development of captain-elect Paul Benes. After much soul searching, Hood decided to forego sports during his final year in deference to his pre-seminary studies.

Benes was also a pre-seminary student. His father, the Rev. Dr. Louis Benes, was editor of *The Church Herald*, official publication of the Reformed Church in America. He was pleased that his sons had chosen Hope College, but perhaps hard-pressed financially to see them through. Hope did not award athletic scholarships. To make ends meet, Benes could often be found in a white apron behind the meat counter in the A & P grocery store at 10th Street and River Avenue. As a means of conveyance, Paul drove an ancient Dodge sedan which teammates dubbed "The Pre-semobile." He would lead the Dutchmen in their quest for a third straight MIAA championship.

Joining Benes were Ray Ritsema, Warren Vander Hill, Wayne Vriesman, Darrell Beernink, and Albert "Jun" Buursma. All had been starters in 1957-1958, with Ritsema named the league's most valuable. The strong supporting cast included Daryl Siedentop, Roland Schut, John Kleinheksel, Bill Vanderbilt, Don Boyink, and Norm Schut. Freshman Bob Reid would be brought up from the junior varsity squad following the Christmas break.

Hope opened the season on Monday, Dec. 1, at Valparaiso University, where Dr. Paul Meadows was in his first year as Crusader coach. Basketball was given greater emphasis than other sports at the Indiana school. School officials pressed for a big-time association by including Notre Dame and a few other large institutions on the schedule, but Hope felt prepared for the challenge. From the start, the game was a rough one, with officials calling 52 fouls overall. Hope managed a 38-35 halftime lead, but Vander Hill had been whistled three times and picked up his fourth

TWO FROM OUTSIDE

Warren Vander Hill unloads a jumper in the closing minutes of the 1959 game against ball State. Referee Marv Bylsma is in the background. — At this writing Dr. Vander Hill serves as Provost and Vice President for Academic Affairs at Ball State University.

minutes into the second half. Valpo gained the lead when Benes and Ritsema both fouled out, but Vriesman scored to tie the count at 80 as time ran out. Vander Hill fouled out in the overtime, but Vriesman again picked up the slack, scoring all six of Hope's points. It was not quite enough, as the Crusaders finally prevailed 90 to 86. The winners were led by 6' 8" center Lou Keller with 25. Topper Woelfer followed with 18, and senior guard Dick Schroer had 15. For Hope it was Vander Hill with 25, Vriesman 16, Ritsema 13, Benes 12, Beernink 10, and Buursma eight.

On Wednesday, Dec. 3, Hope entertained Alma in the MIAA opener for both schools. Hope took the floor in new warm-ups. The spun nylon sweat pants were navy and white with orange trim to match the jackets purchased the previous season. Hope's play in the early going was so-so, but halftime showed them leading 48-40. The team jelled quickly after the intermission and led by 14 with but 1:30 gone in the second half. With 6:15 remaining, the lead had grown to 26, 86-60, and substitutes took the floor. Both teams shot 43 percent overall in the 94-73 Hope win, but the Dutchmen were 20 for 40 in the second half. Benes was high for the victors with 26, Vander Hill had 24, Ritsema 15, and Beernink 11 plus numerous assists. For the Scots of Coach Wayne Hintz, it was the multi-talented Jim Northrup leading with 26, followed by Ferris Saxton with 11, and Bill Klenk with nine.

Hope's third game in six days was played at Adrian's Ridge Gymnasium on Saturday, Dec. 6. The long bus trip on a winter afternoon always made Coach De Vette wary of what might take place on the Bulldogs' court. This night, however, the Dutchmen dominated from the start. Hope had built a 20-point lead (30-10) at the 10-minute mark and Coach Gregg Arbaugh's squad never quite recovered. The Bulldogs rallied somewhat in the second quarter, but Hope led at halftime, 47-30. It was 54-40 with 12 minutes remaining, when Vander Hill hit six straight points to build the lead back to 20. Paul Benes controlled the offensive boards with numerous put-backs for scores. The Dutchman defense was especially strong leading to the eventual 77-56 win. Benes tallied 27 before retiring to the bench. He was followed closely by Ritsema with 24, and Vander Hill added 18. Ray Rolley was the leader for Adrian, and Bruce Stephens had 10.

As might be expected, it was a different story when the Knights of Calvin invaded the Civic Center on Wednesday, Dec. 10. A full-house crowd of 2,500 watched the Dutchmen scratch their way to a 40-37 lead over the determined Calvin five at the half. A spurt by the home team in the first five minutes of the second half made it 56-43, and was a key factor as the game progressed. Calvin had enjoyed leads of one to four points before Hope took charge. Coach Barney Steen elected to employ a press in the second half, but Whitey Beerink consistently worked through it and drew the plaudits of Coach Steen after the game. Without the benefit of today's three-point shot, Ritsema scored seven points in one minute to push the margin to 89-70 with 2:17 remaining. He was especially effective with a sweeping left-hand hook. A Knight rally narrowed the margin to 11, but time ran out and the Dutchmen notched their third victory of the young season, 92-81. Ritsema led Hope with 27, Vander Hill had 22, Benes 18, and Beernink 16. Don Koopman was high for Calvin with 20, future coach Ralph Honderd had 16, Ed Meyering 12, and Hank De Mots nine.

With but two days of rest, the Dutchmen made their way to Kalamazoo's Treadway Gym for a match-up with the Hornets. The contest resembled Hope's Valpo game in terms of rough play. A total of 50 fouls were called, 31 on Kazoo to 19 for Hope. Ray Steffen's crew took an early 12-9 lead, but the Dutch enjoyed an 18-2 run before a K comeback narrowed Hope's lead to 33-25 at the half. Hope's defense was effective throughout, with Benes holding Walt Maser without a field goal while Bob Brice was limited to just one. The score stood 56-43 at the 10-minute mark of the second half, and the Dutch maintained that margin to the end for the 70-57 victory. Vander Hill was in foul trouble early and Siedentop played about three-fourths of the game as his substitute. Kalamazoo outdid the Dutchmen in field goals 13-9 in the second half, but rough play caught up to them as Hope cashed in on 26-of-41 free throws. Benes was again high for Hope with 22, while Beernink, with a superb all-round game, scored 18. Ritsema was next with 17. For the home team it was guard Bob Fletcher with 20, and Atis Grinbergs with 15.

Two non-league games remained to be played before the squad would depart for the holidays. During the practice week, Kleinheksel suffered a dislocated shoulder and would be sidelined for some time. An 11-man squad made the trip to Indiana Central for a game on Wednesday, Dec. 17. The first half was evenly contested, with the host team holding a 41-40 edge at the intermission. In the second half Hope controlled the boards, moving to a 56-43 lead while limiting Central to just two free throws. Benes scored five field goals in the first half and 10 more in the second to lead his team with 35. The lead was 82-62 with two minutes left, with the final at 85-69. Ritsemsa followed Benes with 25, and Vander Hill had eight. Guard Jerry Lewis was tops for the losers with 15, Harold Boyd had 13, and Mickey Shercliff 12.

The following night found the Dutchmen in Wilberforce, Ohio, for a game with the Central State Marauders. Hope was again in form and had built a 28-20 lead at the 10-minute mark. The contest was reasonably close at halftime, with Hope leading 47-36. In the second half, the combination of Vander Hill outside plus Benes and Ritsema inside was too much and the result was soon a 20-point Hope lead. But Benes picked up his fourth personal, and while he was on the bench Central notched six quick ones. Benes returned to the lineup, but fouled out with three minutes remaining. With Buursma and Beernink concentrating on assists the die was cast, and the De Vette men went on to an 83-72 win. Vander Hill was back in form to lead Hope with 24, Ritsema scored 21, and Benes 18. Tony Blaine was high for Coach "Gibby" Gibbs' team with 19, and Russell added 16. Hope's 6-1 record was satisfying as squad members now scattered for the holidays. Unwritten term papers were put aside for another day as each player savored the 15-day break.

The squad reassembled on Saturday, Jan. 3, for a game at the Civic Center with Ball State Teachers College of Muncie, Ind. The two-year agreement with the larger Indiana school had been worked out through the efforts of Athletics Director Al Vanderbush and Cardinal Coach Jim Hinga, who was a cousin of Milton "Bud" Hinga, Hope's dean of students. An estimated 2,500 fans crowded into the Civic hoping to see the Dutchmen extend their home winning streak to 18. Coach Hinga's team, made up largely of seniors, was off to an early 11-4 lead, but with 13:29 remaining in the half Ritsema's basket gave Hope a 16-15 lead which the Dutchmen never surrendered. With 7:50 left, Ball State managed to tie the count at 28, but could not push ahead. Three straight field goals by Benes gave Hope a 45-35 lead at the half. The Dutch continued with hot hands in the second half and moved the score to 69-47 at the 10-minute mark. With 3:55 left in the game, a Vanderbilt basket made it 89-61 for the biggest spread of the game. Hope's scoring in the 94-69 victory was evenly divided: Benes had 24, Vander Hill 22, and Ritsema 21. Freshman Reid, heir apparent to Whitey Beernink, saw action for the first time and scored seven points. For Ball State it was 6' 6", 215 lb. Wilbur Davis with 17 and Jim Sullivan with 16.

All the world loves a winner, and followers were now adopting the Dutchmen as their own. An empty seat at the Civic Center was a rarity, even at weeknight games. The diversity in team talent allowed fans to select their special favorites. One with a special flair was Vander Hill. His sheer enjoyment of the game was obvious to all. His variety of shots supplemented the stellar work of big men Benes, Ritsema, and Vriesman, and sometimes bordered on "show biz" to the great delight of the packed-in patrons. For the older set, Vander Hill offered the "two-hand set," taking them back to 1943 and Ets Kleinjans of the "Blitz Kids." For others it was his off-the-wrong-foot layup, a New York trademark. But mostly it was his consistent jump shot. One version appeared to me to be his "foregone conclusion" shot. After releasing the ball "the V" would turn quickly and retreat to a defensive position amidst the crowd's roar of approval. He was careful to exercise a certain amount of restraint in all of this, knowing that Coach De Vette took a dim view of "hot dogs." On one occasion the temptation was simply too great. Leading the fast break from the center position, it appeared that he would go "coast to coast." At the last moment however, he flicked a behind-the-back, over-the-shoulder pass to a startled Beernink on the left wing. Only the quickest of reactions allowed Beernink to lay it in for two points. As they ran back up the floor, Beernink was shaking his head while Vander Hill stole a hurried glance at the bench. Hot dog or not, Coach De Vette was having a hard time suppressing a grin.

It was another full house at the Civic Center as Hope returned to MIAA play on Saturday, Jan. 10. The Albion Britons were unfortunate enough to catch the Dutchmen in what Coach De Vette termed their "best game this season." Shooting percentages were not impressive by either team, but the Hope defense was outstanding. The Dutch lead at halftime was 43-26, and Benes deserved much of the credit. The big center collected 19 rebounds before retiring to the bench with 12 minutes left in the game. The other regulars were taken out three minutes later. With 10 minutes remaining it was 72-42, and the Dutchmen were completely in charge. Ray Ritsema led his team with 21 points and many blocked shots. Vander Hill had 16, Benes 14, and Jun Buursma 11 as Hope made the final score 84-55. For the Britons it was Bill Losey with 14 and Garth Richey with 13.

Hope's game at Hillsdale College on Jan. 14 was played in Stock Fieldhouse. Coach John Williams had his team ready, and after 15 minutes of play they held a slim lead of

28-27. Their success was due to some fine shooting plus a pressure defense, but the Dutchmen were on-track by halftime and owned a 42-33 lead. Siedentop was effective against the press, and scored two field goals and five of six from the free throw line. It was 66-52 at the 10-minute mark, but Ritsema fouled out with six minutes left and the Dales were able to narrow the margin to 79-69. A final Hope spurt built the lead to 20 at 89-69. Benes was again at his best with 32; Vander Hill had 22; Ritsema had 13 including seven-of-seven from the line; Beernink had 10, and Siedentop had nine in the 94-77 victory. Don Bohannon had an outstanding game for the Dales with 26 points, and Fernen Badgley added 13. The outcome might have been different had not Jim Reynolds been slowed by a toe injury. The Jellybean scored but a single point.

Hope closed out the first round of MIAA play by hosting Olivet on Saturday, Jan. 17. Anticipating a mismatch, a meager crowd of 1,700 made its way to the Civic Center. It was essentially a game for Hope substitutes to display their wares. After four minutes and 40 seconds of play and the score at 19-3, all regulars save Benes were replaced. Benes would join them on the bench after another five minutes. Hope built a 53-29 halftime lead, which prompted De Vette to start five subs in the second half. It made little difference. It was simply a hot-shooting night for all Hope squad members, with 49 percent the final figure. Boyink and Schut scored 12 each to lead the Dutchmen, while Vander Hill, Buursma, and Siedentop had 11 apiece in the 100-54 win. Dick Groch had a game-high 21 to lead the Comets, but no one else could manage more than six.

Two non-league contests would close out the month of January. Both were played at the Civic Center. On Saturday, Jan. 24, it was Central State of Ohio. The Marauders were great leapers, played hard, and displayed good sportsmanship. The combination brought 2,500 to the Civic, and they were not disappointed. Throughout the first half, Sam Wagner battled mightily with Benes and Ritsema for control of the boards, but Hope led 43-29 at the intermission. The Dutchmen began the second half with four fast-break field goals and continued to build. With four minutes remaining and the score at 83-51, substitutes took over. Marauder tenacity was then in evidence as Coach Gibbs's charges scored the final 10 points of the game. Hope's 83-61 win was the 11th in 12 starts. For the first time, Beernink with 18 points, was high man for Hope. He was followed by Benes with 17, Ritsema with 14, and Vriesman with 12. Turner Russell dropped in 19 for the losers, John Harris had 13, and Sam Wagner 12.

Hope met Lawrence Tech on Wednesday, Jan. 28, before a crowd of 1,800. The Detroit school, affiliated with the NAIA, did not match up well with the Dutchmen, who were out to an early lead. Vriesman left the game in the first half with a sprained ankle and would miss the next contest, but teammates pushed the score to 59-28 by halftime. De

**NEW LOOK DUTCHMEN
1958-59**

Paul Benes, Whitey Beernink, John Kleinheksel, and Bill Vanderbilt (partially hidden) show off Hope's first set of sweat pants. They matched the warm-up jackets purchased the previous season.

Vette substituted freely in the first half and throughout the game. At the end, the scorebook showed Paul Benes with 30 points, Ritsema with 17, Beernink 13, Vander Hill 10, Buursma and Vriesman eight each, and Siedentop seven. Henry Pollard scored 23 for the Blue Devils in a losing cause and Clayton Pethers had 17. Pethers had played football for Hope's Ron Schipper at Northville High School. Bradley added another 17, but the visitors were short on defense as Hope prevailed 108-82.

There would be no games for the next 10 days as Hope geared up for semester exams. The term "student-athlete" has been used loosely, but the Hope players knew why they were in school and were enrolled in demanding disciplines. Basketball was great, but it was extra-curricular. When grades came out, the team could boast of several on or near the dean's list. Practice time was limited during test week, but to keep the team sharp De Vette scheduled a scrimmage with the Zeeland Texaco Oilers. The semi-pro team included former college stars like Michigan State's Bob Armstrong. Also on-hand was Jim Kaat, who had just finished his third semester at Hope and was playing on the Zeeland team while awaiting his baseball assignment to Charlotte, N.C., in the Washington Senators' organization. Kaat had played jayvee basketball at Hope and would have been varsity material had he not chosen the major league route.

The second round of MIAA play got underway at Alma on Saturday, Feb. 7. Hope was again hot in the first period, and led 49-30 at the half. This would prove to be the largest margin of the game. Ferris Saxton was hot throughout the contest, but rough play was costly to the Scots as they were whistled for 25 fouls to 12 for the Dutchmen. Saxton, Jim Northrup, and Dalton Cantrell all fouled out near the end of the game. Hope led 79-63 with 2:24 remaining. Alma scored three field goals in the last minute, but Hope went home with an 83-76 victory. Benes led the winners with 27, Vander Hill had 18, Ritsema 17, and Buursma 13. Ferris Saxton was high for the Scots with 23, Hussey had 18, and York 10.

Coach Barney Steen and a determined Calvin squad hosted the Dutchmen in the Grand Rapids Civic Auditorium on Wednesday, Feb. 11. A crowd of 5,300 filled the arena for another chapter in West Michigan's best-known rivalry. Calvin had the best of it in the first period and battled to a 41-35 lead at halftime. Hope managed to hold Ralph Honderd to a basket and two free throws, but center Bill Wolterstorff had nine and freshman guard Carl De Kuiper put on a fine performance with 11. The game was tied eight times, but Hope inched ahead 62-58 with less than two minutes remaining. At this point Beernink missed on a one-and-one attempt and Warren Otte quickly scored for the Knights. The Hope lead was now 62-60 with 1:12 left. A Benes shot failed to connect and Calvin, taking the rebound, found Wolterstorff for a lay-up to tie the score at 62 with just 29 seconds left. As the roar of the crowd increased, an errant Hope pass was intercepted and the ball went again to Wolterstorff with eight seconds on the clock. His layup gave the Knights a lead they would not surrender. As the game slipped away, Hope called timeout. It turned out to be one over the limit, resulting in a technical foul. Wolterstorff missed the free throw, but Calvin had possession and inbounded to Wolterstorff, who was immediately fouled by Ritsema. Big Bill sank both shots to give Coach Steen and his charges the dramatic 66-62 victory. Wolterstorff was clearly the man of the hour as the Knights prevailed under great pressure during the final minute. In the winners' column it was Wolterstorff with 17, Carl DeKuiper 13, and Artie Kraai 11. For Hope it was Warren Vander Hill leading with 19, Benes 17, Ritsema nine and Beernink eight. Hope's 13-game winning streak had ended in the hands of a worthy opponent.

There was little time for the Dutchmen to bemoan the tough loss. On Saturday, Feb. 14, it was Kalamazoo at the Civic Center. Warren Vander Hill scored the game's first field goal, but thereafter it became apparent that Coach Ray Steffen would adopt the Chicago-Olivet strategy of slow-down basketball. Before 2,500 jeering fans, the Hornets employed their stall tactics. At the 10-minute mark the score stood at 5-2 and Hope's halftime lead was 12-9. Kazoo had

TOPS ON COURT AND IN CLASSROOM—These four Hope College basketball players have made the dean's list with a B or better average for the fall semester. Pictured left to right are: Wayne Vriesman, Muskegon senior; Rolland Schut, Hudsonville junior; Warren Vander Hill, Queens Village, N.Y., junior and Jun Buursma, Holland senior. Vriesman, Schut and Vander Hill made the dean's list last year while Buursma just missed. Vander Hill and Vriesman are regulars and Buursma is the first replacement on the Hope team which has won 12 straight games after losing the opener in an overtime to Valparaiso University. (Sentinel photo)

Four Hope Cagers Honored on Dean's List

Besides excelling on the basketball court with a United Press International rating of 20th among small-college teams in the nation, Hope College's basketball team also knows its way around the classroom.

The Hope dean's list, which includes the names of students who have all A's and B's and are carrying higher than a three-point average, lists four basketball players.

Seniors Wayne Vriesman and Jun Buursma and juniors Warren Vander Hill and Rolland Schut have each made the coveted list for grades compiled during the just completed first semester.

This marked the second straight year that Vriesman, Vander Hill and Schut were honored while Buursma, who just missed the list last winter, was named for the first time.

Vriesman and Vander Hill are regulars on Hope's basketball team which has won 12 straight games since dropping an overtime decision to Valparaiso University in the opener. Buursma is the first substitute and Schut sees frequent action.

Three players just missed the dean's list, including two, Darrell Beernink and John Kleinheksel, who were on last year. Beernink, a senior, is a regular and Kleinheksel is a junior. The other player just missing the list is junior Daryl Siedentop.

The rest of the team all improved their marks from last basketball season and all are well above a C average. The overall team scholastic record is better this year than last season when Hope put six on the dean's list, Coach Russ De Vette said.

Sophomores, juniors and seniors must maintain a two-point (C) average while freshmen must have a 1.7 average. Bob Reid of Buffalo, N. Y., is the lone freshman on the club and he has a 2.3 average.

Other team members are senior Paul Benes, junior Ray Ritsema and sophomores Rich Bakker, Don Boyink, Norm Schut and Bill Vander Bilt.

Hope's players were "student athletes" in the very best sense of that term.

stayed close, and for a time it appeared that the unpopular pattern might work. Steffen now shifted gears, and play assumed a near-normal pace. With 10:57 left, Hope led by a single basket, 28-26, but the Dutchmen moved ahead from that point and with less than two minutes to go the lead was 47-32. The Hornets scored the last five points to make the final Hope 47, Kalamazoo 37. Ritsema led the winners with 15, while Benes and Vander Hill followed closely with 14 each. John Thompson was the leader for Kazoo with 11 and Bob Fletcher had 10.

The following Wednesday, Feb. 18, Coach Gregg Arbaugh was in town with the Adrian Bulldogs. Hope enjoyed a decided advantage on the boards with Benes and Ritsema, resulting in a sizeable lead of 46-26 at the half. Adrian had a 10-2 run to start the second half, but the Dutchmen recovered and at the 10-minute mark the lead was 62-44. Substitutes played most of the remainder in the eventual 81-66 win. Benes led Hope with 19 points and 10 rebounds. Ray Ritsema scored 17 and had 12 rebounds. Wayne Vriesman had 12 and Vander Hill 11. Two of Vander Hill's points came on a long two-hand set to the delight of the crowd. Vanderbilt and Reid each scored two buckets in the final minutes. Both would be starters in 1959-1960. For Adrian it was Bob Howard with 16 and Ray Rolley with 13.

There was good news for the Dutchmen on Feb. 17. For the second year in a row, Hope was invited to participate in the NCAA College Division Great Lakes Regional Tournament. Athletics Director Al Vanderbush received the word from Harvey Chrouser of Wheaton College, the tournament director. The games would be played on March 6 and 7 in the new Biester Gymnasium at Glenbard High School in Glen Ellyn, Ill. Hope's 1958 experience had been positive, and acceptance of the invitation was almost immediate. More good news around the MIAA was the appointment of Elkin Isaac as director of athletics at Albion College. Isaac would replace longtime AD Dale Sprankle, who was giving up the post for health reasons.

Three games remained on the regular schedule. On Saturday, Feb. 21, an overflow crowd of 2,600 fans jammed into the Civic Center to witness the final home appearance of Benes, Beernink, Buursma, and Vriesman. John Williams and Hillsdale had the misfortune to catch the Dutchmen in an inspired moment which led to a 47-26 halftime advantage, Hope's best all-round half of the season. The huge crowd was further entertained during the intermission, when Randall Bosch, Holland industrialist, presented the MIAA most valuable player award to Hope football captain Larry Ter Molen.

Hillsdale made a run in the second half when substitute guard Jack Fowster reeled off four straight field goals, but Benes and Ritsema took control of the boards and the margin at the 10-minute mark was 70-47. The spread reached 76-51, and subs played much of the half. With 1:47 remaining, the seniors came back for a token appearance. With 33 seconds left, they were taken out to a standing ovation. The 81-66 final score pleased everyone except, understandably, the visiting Dales. Benes and Vander Hill were co-leaders for Hope, each with 21 points. Ritsema had 17, Beernink 11, and Vriesman eight. Don Bohannon led Hillsdale with 13, eight coming in the final 10 minutes. J. Agar had nine.

Hope's game at Olivet on Thursday, Feb. 26, was an example of how not to play basketball. Comet coach Henry Paul once again chose to hold the ball. Olivet made little or no attempt to score, choosing instead to execute a weave at midcourt. Hoots and whistles echoed from the Mc Kay Gymnasium crowd of 150 as they watched Hope manage a lead of 12-3 at halftime. After the intermission, the Dutchmen went into what amounted to a "standing" zone defense. At one point Comet guard Dick Groch dribbled the ball for three solid minutes. When the misery was over, the Comets had controlled the ball for 32 of the game's 40 minutes. The Dutchmen had not broken a sweat, but won the contest 22-6. A frustrated Coach De Vette decided to hold a post-game intra-squad scrimmage, shirts against skins. Coach Paul put an end to this by turning out the gym lights and the Dutchmen decided it was time to get out of town. Each coach had a post-game comment. "We knew we were going to get beat, but we were determined it wouldn't be by 100 points," said Henry Paul. De Vette expressed dismay at the existing rules, "Basketball is the only game where you can hold the ball and play by not playing."

The game on Saturday, Feb. 28, closed out the regular season. The contest was played at Albion's Kresge Gym, where the Britons played tough in the early going. Bill Losey kept his team in the game and Hope led by a single point, 20-19, with eight minutes gone. But this was as close as Coach Isaac's team would get. The Dutchmen soon had things their own way, and moved to a 46-26 lead at the half. Randall Bosch had made the trip to Albion with the Hope team, and at halftime presented a gold football to end Tom Taylor, the MIAA's co-most valuable player.

Hope scored the first 13 points of the second half with the fast break working to near perfection. Meanwhile, Albion's half-court offense, somewhat involved, made catch-up ball difficult. The scrappy Britons played well in the second half, outscoring the Dutchmen 39-34, but the damage had been done and at the buzzer it was Hope 80-65. Vander Hill was the Hope leader with 20, Benes and Ritsema had 14 each, Buursma and Vriesman had eight apiece, and Beernink added seven. Albion's Bill Losey led all scorers with 28, and Garth Richey, with a strong second half, had 13. Hope's journey home included a stop at Schuler's Restaurant in Marshall to celebrate the team's third MIAA championship in-a-row.

On Feb. 26 the Dutchmen had learned that they would play the first game in the NCAA Great Lakes Regional Tournament. Their opponent would be Loras College of Dubuque, Iowa, a Catholic, all-male instituion with an enrollment of 1,200. After three days of intense practice, the team left on Thursday, March 5, for Chicago and the Oak Park Arms Hotel. Following room assignments and a brief settling in, the team journeyed to Downers Grove High School for a short practice session. Downers Grove was home to team member Daryl Siedentop. Few players ever have the opportunity to come home with their college team. I will not soon forget the picture of Daryl leading his teammates around his home gym enroute to the lockers. High school students gaped at the likes of Benes, Ritsema, et. al., and all of us could appreciate Daryl's private pride.

The Loras Duhawks were coached by Vince Dowd, now in his seventh year as head mentor. The team sported a 17-5 record and relied heavily on forward Jack Frasco, who claimed a 20.5 scoring average over 22 games. Center Bill Rhomberg was also a key figure in Coach Dowd's offense. It seemed a natural to assign Ray Ritsema to guard Frasco. The strategy would pay big dividends. The new gymnasium at Glenbard High School was equipped with fan-shaped backboards and had a seating capacity of 3,500. Hope made a statement early, when Benes and Ritsema took control of the boards while Beernink and Vander Hill made great feeds to their big men. The fan boards, a pre-game concern, proved a non-factor as the Dutchmen moved to a commanding 52-32 lead by halftime. It was more of the same in the second half. In their concern for the scoring of Ritsema, Benes, and Vander Hill, the Duhawks forgot about Wayne Vriesman, who poured in 16 points. With 1:45 remaining, he scored Hope's 100th point, then dropped in a bucket at the buzzer to make the final 102-73. Ray Ritsema led his team with 21 points, but didn't neglect his defensive responsibility. Jack Frasco was held scoreless. Hope had six men in double figures. Benes followed Ritsema with 19, Vriesman had 18, Vander Hill and Beernink 13 each, and Jun Buursma 10. Bob Naughton was high for the Iowa team with 20, and center Bill Rhomberg contributed 11. Hope remained for part of the second game to get a look at the next night's opponent. In a game similar to Hope's, the Wheaton Crusaders defeated Wabash 102-83 in spite of a spectacular out-court performance by Little Giants guard Charley Bowerman. An estimated 500 Hope fans had made the journey to the Windy City. They would be joined by 500 more for Saturday's championship faceoff. A happy but reflective group of Dutchmen returned to the Oak Park Arms Hotel. All knew that their toughest game of the season would be played in less than 24 hours.

Wheaton College, with a 22-3 record was rated sixth in the nation by the UPI. Hope was rated 19th by the same agency. Coach Lee Pfund returned the entire starting five from his 1958 team, which had beaten Hope 104-93. Leading the entourage was junior forward Mel Peterson. As a freshman he had been a regular on Wheaton's national championship team. Joining him as starters were Captain Bill Gerig, Bob Whitehead, John Dobbert, and Don Anderson. The Crusaders were quickly into a 9-2 lead, and seven of the nine belonged to Peterson. The Dutchmen fought back as the score was tied seven times before Peterson's

FINEST HOUR
SATURDAY, MARCH 7, 1959

Dr. V. Raymond Edman, President of Wheaton College, presents the trophy. Hope defeated Wheaton College 81-76 to win the NCAA College Division Great Lakes Regional Tournament. **L. to R.:** Roland Schut, Don Boyink, Bob Reid, Albert "Jun" Buursma, Norm Schut, Daryl Siedentop, Bill Vanderbilt, Whitey Beernink, Coach Russ De Vette, Captain Paul Benes, Wayne Vriesman, Dr. Edman, Ray Ritsema, Warren Vander Hill.

TUESDAY, MARCH 10, 1959
In topcoats and porkpie hats — on to Evansville!
L. to R.: Ray Ritsema, Wayne Vriesman, Paul Benes, Warren Vander Hill, Al Buursma, Darrell Beernink, Coach Russ De Vette.

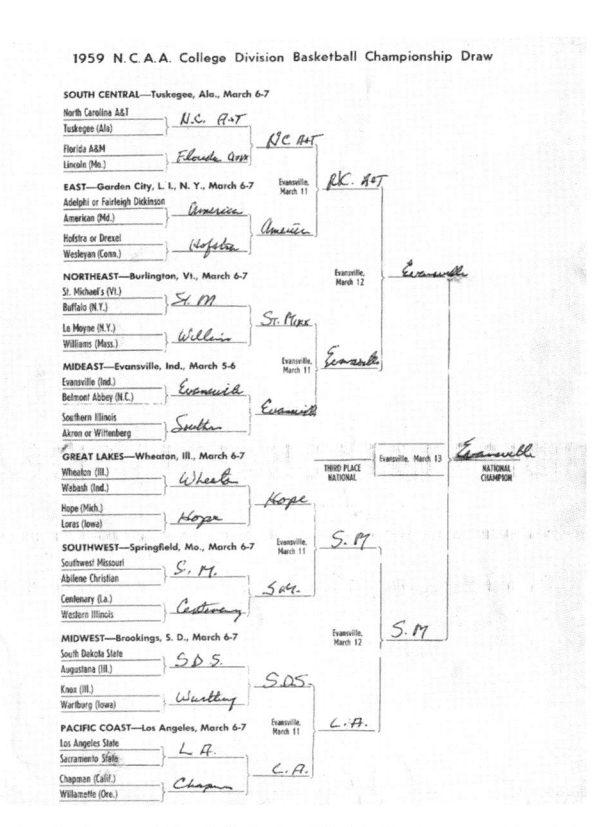

Game programs in 1959 served the purpose but were neither sophisticated nor expensive. Junior guard Daryl Siedentop filled in the tournament brackets.

94

THE 1958-59 HOPE BASKETBALL TEAM - 20-3
MIAA AND NCAA GREAT LAKES REGIONAL CHAMPIONS

Back Row L. to R.: Trainer Dr. Larry Green, manager Jay Nyhuis, Darrell "Whitey" Beernink, Wayne Vriesman, Captain Paul Benes, Ray Ritsema, Warren Vander Hill, Albert "Jun" Buursma, Coach Russ De Vette. **Front Row:** Bob Reid, John Kleinheksel, Bill Vanderbilt, Don Boyink, Rich Bakker, Roland "Pooch" Schut, Daryl Siedentop, Norm Schut. It would be 25 years before another Hope team would win 20 ball games.

tip-in at the halftime buzzer gave Wheaton a 39-37 lead. Coach Pfund's flashy forward had a point total of 21 by halftime, and any doubters now knew that Mel Peterson was for real. Vanderbilt and Buursma took turns spelling Benes in the first half as he experienced some foul trouble.

Hope scored first in the second half to tie the score on a Ritsema field goal, but Peterson and Gerig continued with hot hands and Wheaton built a 61-52 lead, the largest margin of the game. Coach Pfund tried a press in an attempt to break the game open, but Beernink and teammates were equal to the task. At the 10-minute mark it was Wheaton 61-57. Ritsema seemed to accept the Peterson challenge, and his basket with 6:45 remaining gave Hope the lead at 65-64. A Peterson free throw with 3:43 left made it 71-71, but Ritsema's three-point play 10 seconds later made it 74-71. The crowd of 3,200 felt the intensity and realized that they were witnessing a small-college classic. Two free throws by Peterson brought the Crusaders within one, but Ritsema countered with two of his own and it was 76-73.

Then, with 2:04 remaining, the unthinkable happened. Marvelous Mel Peterson fouled out of the game. As time ticked away the Crusaders were forced to foul. Vander Hill dropped in a free throw with 57 seconds left, then two more with 23 seconds showing. Ritsema put in two more free throws as time expired, a fitting climax to perhaps his greatest game ever. Hope 81, Wheaton 76! Hope's starting five had played the entire second half - Benes with three, then four fouls. Ritsema's 29-point performance had lifted his team, but all had contributed. Benes scored 16, Vander Hill 14, Vriesman 12, and Beernink 10. For Wheaton it was Peterson leading all scorers with 35, Gerig had 20, and Dobbert eight.

Tournament post-game ceremonies, unavoidably, are fraught with conflicting emotions. At one end of the spectrum are exuberant victors, wreathed in smiles, cutting down nets, waiting eagerly for the all-tourney selections. In marked contrast, the losers stand fatigued and devastated. Their gallant fight now seems empty, and one could care

SEASON ENDING BANQUET — MARCH, 1959

L. to R.: Bill Vanderbilt, Roland Schut, Norm Schut, Rich Bakker, Al Buursma, Warren Vander Hill, Coach Russ De Vette, Paul Benes, Ray Ritsema, Wayne Vriesman, Whitey Beernink, Don Boyink, Bob Reid, John Kleinheksel. **Missing from the picture:** Daryl Siedentop.

OCTOBER, 1978
20th REUNION — STILL IN GOOD SHAPE

Back Row L to R: Bob Reid, Coach De Vette, Wayne Vriesman, Al Buursma, Dr. Daryl Siedentop, Dr. Warren Vander Hill, Dr. Bill Vanderbilt, Rev. John Kleinheksel, Norm Schut. **Kneeling:** Don Boyink, Ray Ritsema, Rev. Paul Benes, Rev. Rich Bakker, Darrell Beernink. All present save Roland Schut of Carmel, California.

less about all-tourney honors. However, the laws of sportsmanship demand they endure the ordeal. The haven of a quiet locker room must wait. The Wheaton team, composed of high-caliber people, accepted its role, putting its best foot forward. Dr. V. Raymond Edman, president of Wheaton College, graciously presented the trophy to Hope captain Paul Benes. The all-tournament team included Ritsema and Benes of Hope, Peterson and Gerig of Wheaton, and Bowerman of Wabash. Ritsema was named the tournament's most valuable player to complete the finest hour in Hope basketball history to that point. The trip back to Holland was not unlike the return from Hillsdale five months earlier.

By virtue of their victory, the Dutchmen now qualified for the College Division quarterfinals to be held at the University of Evansville in the southwest corner of the Hoosier state. Others advancing were North Carolina A & T (Agricultural & Technical) State University, American University of Washington, D.C., Saint Michael's College of Vermont, Southwest Missouri State University, South Dakota State University, Los Angeles State University, and host Evansville. Hope's draw was Southwest Missouri, a school located in Springfield and boasting an enrollment of 2,500 compared to Hope's 1,126. The Bears were coached by Eddie Matthews and had compiled a 21-2 record.

Hope's game would be played on Wednesday, March 11. The semis would follow on the 12th, with the final on Friday, March 13. In short, most of the week would be taken up with basketball. At this point there were rumblings amongst some disgruntled faculty that the athletic tail was beginning to wag the academic dog. To allow for Tuesday class attendance, it was decided that the team should fly to Evansville. At 5:45 p.m. in Grand Rapids, coach and players boarded a Lake Central Airlines DC 3 to become Hope's first airborne athletic team. Headquarters for the tournament was the McCurdy Hotel in Evansville, where the Dutchmen would soon meet players from across the country.

The games would be played in Roberts Memorial Stadium, an imposing structure in downtown Evansville with a seating capacity of 12,300. It served as the home court for the Evansville Purple Aces and their legendary coach, Arad Mc Cutchan. An upper gallery included photos of each member of the Aces' team. The pictures, in color, were full-length and larger than life. Coach McCutchan had his team arrayed in quarter-sleeve jerseys, a novelty at the time, and one that Hope would copy in subsequent years.

Seventy-five of Holland's faithful had abandoned jobs, classes, and other mid-week responsibilities to be part of the overall crowd of 5,000 to witness the contest. Opening ceremonies included introduction of "Miss Indiana," 19-year-old Anita Marie Hursh, a De Pauw sophomore who sat in a special royal box. The Dutchmen, while impressed by the scope and glitter, were not distracted from the business at hand. As the game got underway, both teams performed well. Hope enjoyed early leads of 10-4 and 22-14, but neither team would lead by more than six. Hope led at halftime 40-39. The lead changed hands 13 times and was tied 13 times. At the 10-minute mark of the second half, it was Missouri leading 58-53. Vander Hill picked up his fourth foul early in the second half. After agonizing minutes on the bench he returned and with 7:50 remaining, sank a jumper to tie the count at 60-60. Hope led 72-68 with 2:39 left when Jay Kinsey put in a field goal and followed with two free throws to knot the game at 72-72. Vander Hill cashed in on two free throws with 58 seconds remaining, but the Bears moved down the floor and Jack Israel scored his 11th field goal to even the count at 74. With 28 seconds remaining, Hope took a timeout to set up a final shot. Following the inbound pass, Missouri's Dale Russell, with tough defense, stole the ball and dribbled downcourt. The ball went to Jack Israel in the corner, who lofted a 20-foot jumper with four seconds showing on the clock. The shot parted the net for the 76-74 victory for Southwest Missouri. Hope's season was over, 20-3.

In the closest game of the quarterfinals, Hope had done itself proud. Paul Benes, with 30 points and 27 rebounds, was the talk of the tournament. Bill Mokray of the Boston Celtics was in the crowd and afterward spoke with Coach De Vette about the possibility of Benes turning pro. Vander Hill, despite foul trouble, scored 16, and Ray Ritsema had 15 plus 11 rebounds. Whitey Beernnk added nine. For the winners it was Israel with 29, including five-for-five from the free throw line. Dale Russell had 14, and Robinson 13. The Missouri team disposed of Los Angeles State the following night but lost in the championship game to favored Evansville, 83-67. The all-tournament team included Hugh Ahlering of Evansville, Jack Israel of Southwest Missouri, Paul Benes of Hope, Leo Hill of Los Angeles State, and Joe Cotton of North Carolina A & T.

Back in Michigan the All-MIAA team was announced: Benes, Ritsema, and Vander Hill of Hope, Honderd of Calvin, and Saxton of Alma. Benes was a popular choice as the league's most valuable player. In basketball, it's a long way from December to March but the end had finally come. A season-ending banquet was held in the Juliana Room of Durfee Hall. To no one's surprise, Ritsema and Vander Hill were named co-captains for 1959-60. Together for the last time, players savored the season and reflected on a special relationship that could not be easily explained to outsiders. The bond would remain: a 20-year reunion was held at Homecoming, 1978. All returned save Roland Schut, who was unable to make it from his home in Carmel, Calif.

* * *

With the celebrations over, it was time to move on to spring sports. Whitey Beernink made the transition to baseball as captain and second baseman of the Hope nine. Russ De Vette, now coaching his third sport, enjoyed the luxury of a veteran baseball squad plus a bonus. Junior Gene Van Dongen had not participated at Hope due to a severe arm fracture sustained in high school play. Now recovered, he joined the squad and soon nailed down the third base position. All-MIAA shortstop Bob Thomson returned at that position, and Tim Vander Mel took over at first. The outfield found Gary Bylsma in right, Jerry Boeve in left, and freshman Bob Reid in center. Other than Van Dongen, rifle-armed Reid was the only newcomer. Lefty Bruce Hoffman returned for mound duty and was joined by senior Wayne Westenbroek, also a lefty, who had been a squad member as a freshman. Righthander Don Andre also returned. Two promising freshmen, Sherwood "Sharkey" Vander Woude and Larry Dykstra, rounded out the staff. Behind the plate it was Ron Boeve, All-MIAA catcher in 1955, now back after a stint in the Army. Vern Essenberg would be the back-up.

Hope opened the season at Riverview Park on Friday, April 10, against Grand Rapids J.C. The weather was typical for season openers, flurries and temperatures hovering around 32 degrees. The Dutchmen got two in the fourth when Van Dongen singled and Bylsma walked. Van Dongen scored when Vander Mel was safe on an error. Vander Mel advanced to third on an error and scored on Reid's infield out. With two out in the fifth, Boeve singled, advanced to second on a Van Dongen walk, then scored on Bylsma's single. Van Dongen and Bylslma both scored on Reid's single. The Raiders scored two in the fifth on two singles, a fielder's choice, and an error. Hoffman gave up but one hit over four innings. Vander Woude finished allowing four hits. Hope's 5-2 victory included a double by Vander Mel and two singles by Reid.

Hope's game at Muskegon Community College on Wednesday, April 15, allowed Coach De Vette to get a look at all of his squad members in action. The Muskegon team had not had time to prepare adequately, and Hope coasted to a 15-0 win on 15 hits. Starter Westenbroek gave up but one hit, a single, over three innings while striking out four. Dykstra followed with three innings of no-hit ball, and Andree finished up, also allowing no hits. Ten errors contributed to the Muskegon demise while Hope had only one miscue.

The Dutchmen traveled to Olivet on Saturday, April 18, to open the MIAA season and came away with a double victory. In the first game, Hoffman pitched a masterful two-hit shutout while striking out 14. Gene Van Dongen led the Hope attack, driving in three of Hope's four runs with a triple and double. In the nightcap it was Vander Woude pitching no-hit ball until the sixth inning and allowing just three safeties overall. He also recorded six strikeouts. In the first inning, Beernink and Van Dongen both singled. Whitey then stole home as Hope was successful with a double steal. In the second, Thomson doubled, went to third on an error, then scored on Vander Woude's single. In the fourth, Jerry Boeve walked, then scored when Thomson delivered his second double. Hope's fourth and final run came in the fifth inning when Van Dongen was safe on a fielder's choice, then scored on a Jerry Boeve single. The final count was Hope, 4-1. The Comets' lone run came in the sixth inning.

On Wednesday, April 22, the Dutchmen took on the Adrian Bulldogs at Riverview. Westenbroek pitched five strong innings in the opener, giving up three hits and one run, and striking out four. Larry Dykstra went the rest of the way, allowing but one hit while striking out two. Van Dongen had two hits, Ron Boeve a triple, and Jerry Boeve a home run enroute to the 13-1 victory. In the nightcap, Andree was touched for one run in the first and three in the third. Vander Woude took over in the fourth and closed the door. He allowed no hits and no runs the rest of the way. Meanwhile, Hope was obliged to play catch-up. The Dutchmen got three in the fourth, when Beernink walked, Ron Boeve doubled, and Van Dongen walked. Thomson's single drove in Beernink and Boeve and another single by Tim Vander Mel scored Van Dongen. In the sixth, Boeve drew a walk and went to third on Gene Van Dongen's double. Bobby Thomson then delivered the game-winner, a single scoring Boeve and Van Dongen. Each team had seven hits, but the Dutchmen bunched theirs to edge Adrian pitcher Larry Ostermeyer, 5-4.

Hope split a pair at Hillsdale on Saturday, April 25. Hoffman went the distance in the first game, giving up five hits and striking out eight. The Dales scored one in the second on two hits, and got two more in the sixth on two hits, a walk, and a fielder's choice. Hope got four in the first inning on four hits, including doubles by Thomson and Jerry Boeve. Two more crossed the plate in the third on three hits, including a double by Vander Mel. Hope's other run came on a home run by Van Dongen in the fourth. Van Dongen had three hits while Reid, Thomson, and Jerry Boeve had two each in the 7-3 win. It was a different story in the second game as the home team collected eight hits off Vander Woude. The Dales got two runs in the second and one in the fifth. They added two in the seventh after Vander Woude had fanned two. He then struck out the third man, but the damage had been done. Hope's only run came in the second on a double by Jerry Boeve and a single by Gary Bylsma. The 5-1 setback was Hope's first in MIAA play.

The Calvin Knights came to Riverview Park on Saturday, May 2. Dykstra was the starter for Hope in the first game and was effective through five innings. He gave up one run in the first and two in the fifth while striking out five. Westenbroek came on in the sixth, allowing but one hit and no runs. Hope scored in the first on a single by Beernink and a double by Jerry Boeve. The Dutchmen pushed across four more in the third on singles by Ron Boeve, Beernink, and Jerry Boeve plus a double by Tim Vander Mel. A walk, an error, and a wild pitch were also involved in the rally. One more came in the fifth on singles by Dykstra and Beernink, with Dykstra scoring on Thomson's sacrifice fly. In the sixth, Ron Boeve doubled, then moved to third as Vander

The luxury of two "lefties" Bruce Hoffman (L) and Wayne Westenbroek.

RON BOEVE
Two-Time All-MIAA Catcher; Hope College most valuable – 1959

BRUCE HOFFMAN
All-MIAA Pitcher

GENE VAN DONGEN
All-MIAA 3rd Baseman
MIAA Batting Champion – 1959

BOBBY THOMSON
Two-Time All-MIAA Shortstop

Mel and Reid both walked filling the bases. Beernink then stepped to the plate and delivered a grand slam home run! The 10-3 victory would be a memorable one for the Hope captain, who went five-for-five. Ron Boeve contributed three hits.

In the second game, the Dutchmen were stymied by the slants of Calvin pitcher Artie Kraai, who shut them out with four scattered hits. Hoffman pitched well, striking out five in three innings, but the Knights scored two in the second on walks to Kraai and Kingma, followed by a double by Schultze. They added two more in the fifth off Vander Woude, who also whiffed five. The 4-0 loss was a tough one for the Hope pitchers, who allowed a total of just three hits while striking out 10.

Hope entertained first-place Albion in a crucial doubleheader on Wednesday, May 6. The Britons stood 7-1 in MIAA play, while the Dutchmen were 6-2. Hoffman went the distance for Hope in the first game, giving up seven hits while striking out eight. Albion hurler Jerry Masteller held the Dutch to just five hits, but in the first Beernink singled, went to second on an error, and scored on Van Dongen's single. In the second, Reid walked, took third on Hoffman's single, and scored on an error by the Briton shortstop. It was, however, Hope's fifth inning that made the difference. Ron Boeve singled and Van Dongen drew a walk. Rightfielder Bylsma then stroked a three-run homer to win the game 5-4.

The second game was also a nail-biter. Westenbroek pitched a five-hitter and struck out six, but gave up a two-run homer to Bob Mc Conkie in the first after Hope had taken a 1-0 lead. Albion got two more in the second, just enough for the eventual 4-3 victory. The Dutchmen got one back in the fourth, when Reid doubled, went to third on a wild pitch, and scored on Westenbroek's single. Hope's comeback attempt continued in the fifth, when Thomson singled and Van Dongen was hit by the pitcher. Ron Boeve's sacrifice moved the runners along and a sacrifice fly by Vander Mel scored Thomson, but the rally fell short and the Britons maintained their league lead with the split.

Hope remained in the title chase at Alma on Saturday, May 9. Hoffman tossed a four-hitter in the opener as he struck out five. The Scots got one in second and two in the third to lead 3-0, but Hoffman bore down and the Dutchmen responded with a four-run fourth inning. Two runs came on a single by Van Dongen and a home run by Ron Boeve. Tim Vander Mel doubled and came home when the shortstop mishandled Bylsma's drive. Bylsma later scored on an error by the leftfielder. Hope had five hits in the important 4-3 win.

In the second game, Sharkey Vander Woude scattered eight Alma hits while Hope was held to six by Alma pitcher Jim Northrup. Alma scored one in the fourth and another in the sixth, but along the way Vander Woude was aided by some fielding gems. Gary Bylsma made the catch of the season in deep right field when he hauled in Denny Stolz's long fly. With the help of a good relay, he was able to double a Scot runner off first base. Hope got two in the fourth on successive singles by Van Dongen, Ron Boeve, and Vander Mel. A stolen base and a wild pitch also contributed. Jim Northrup then struck out the side. The Dutchmen were forced to scratch for their final two runs. In the fifth, Beernink singled. He was sacrificed to second by Jerry Boeve, then to third on Thomson's sacrifice. He came home on Van Dongen's sacrifice fly. In the sixth, Ron Boeve singled and went to second on Vander Mel's sacrifice. He advanced to third when the second baseman was handcuffed by Reid's grounder. Vander Woude then aided his own cause by driving in Boeve with a single. Jim Northrup fanned seven Dutchmen, but Hope completed a rare sweep at Alma with the 4-2 victory.

On Monday, May 12, Hope was forced to practice at the 19th Street diamond due to Tulip Time activity at Riverview Park. While warming up with Reid, Beernink was distracted by someone. Reid had already released one of his fireball pitches. It struck Beernink full in the face, breaking his nose and putting him out of action for the final doubleheader at Kalamazoo the next day. The games were played at the Hornets' Woodworth Field. Wayne Westenbroek was off to a shaky start. The K men scored four runs on four hits and a walk in the first inning, but Westenbroek weathered the storm and settled down while the Dutchmen got their own offense in gear. Hope got two in the first, three in the second, two more in the third, and one in the sixth. Ron Boeve's final performance for Hope would be his best. In the second, Schut, in for the injured Beernink, singled and Westenbroek walked. Boeve then drove the ball over the left field fence to put Hope up 5-4. The Hornets' final run came in the fourth on a home run by outfielder Jerry Aftowski. Westenbroek survived to notch the 8-5 victory.

Bruce Hoffman was in command from the start in the second game. He allowed but five hits while striking out nine enroute to a 6-0 shutout. Hope was off and running when Thomson beat out a bunt. Ron Boeve followed with a triple, scoring Thomson, then crossed the plate himself when the throw back in got away. In the sixth, Boeve was safe on an error and Van Dongen singled. They advanced when a pick-off attempt failed. Both scored on Reid's single. Hope's final runs came in the seventh. Jerry Boeve singled and Ron Boeve wound up a great day with his second home run of the afternoon, a drive over the center field fence. He had been on base six of eight times. Van Dongen had four hits and Norm Schut three. Beernink, with a battered face and a black eye, made the trip and dressed for the games. In the final inning, Coach De Vette inserted his captain as a pinch hitter. It was a last chance to reach the .300 mark in batting, and much deserved. His pop out to second base ended a rewarding season at 13-3. Hope's 11-3 MIAA mark needed an assist from Olivet in order to win or share the title. This was not to be, as the Britons swept the Comets and captured the championship at 12-2.

Van Dongen won the MIAA batting title with a mark of .442 and Ron Boeve was second at .422. Both were named to the All-MIAA team, along with Thomson and Hoffman. Teammates selected Ron Boeve as Hope's most valuable player. The league did not begin naming an MVP until 1965, but had the honor existed in '59 Coach De Vette believed it would have gone to Boeve. At this writing Boeve continues as a long-time assistant baseball coach at Hope.

* * *

Second-year golf coach Bill Hilmert had four returning lettermen in 1959. Bob Holt, Bob Burwitz, Dennis Camp, and Tom Klaasen were joined by freshman Wes Nykamp to make up the team. Some of the scheduled matches did not materialize due to weather or other conditions, but on Saturday, April 25, a triangular was held at Albion involving Alma, Hope, and host Albion. The Dutchmen were off to a good start as they edged Albion 8-7 and took Alma 10-5. Bob Holt was medalist for the day with a 75, while freshman Wes Nykamp surprised his coach with a 78. Bob Burwitz shot an 82, Tom Klaasen 86, and Dennis Camp 89.

The first year for golf as an official MIAA sport was 1934 and Hope, under Coach Bud Hinga, had won the championship in a close contest with Kalamazoo. The team of Ben Timmer, Russ Paalman, Harvey Scholten, and Marv Kruisenga was still around and available. Coach Hilmert thought it would be a novel idea to have his team meet the very first MIAA champs, and was able to schedule a match on Saturday, May 9, at the American Legion course. There is no record of the outcome, but Harvey Scholten confirmed that the match did in fact take place. At this writing Scholten, a resident of Freedom Village in Holland, is nearing his 87th birthday. His only recollection was that his opponent was accompanied by his girlfriend on the first nine and did not perform very well. It went better on the second nine. One is left to speculate on which of Hope's players this might have been.

Another triangular took place at Adrian on Monday, May 11. The Dutchmen continued their winning ways with a 9½-5½ victory over the host school, but a talented Kalamazoo team was too tough and embarrassed the Hope team with a 15-0 shutout. Holt led Hope with an 83, Nykamp carded an 85, Burwitz had an 88, Camp 91, and Klaasen 96. Hope's final match before the league meet was played at the Legion course on Tuesday, May 12, against Grand Rapids Junior College. The Dutchmen improved their scores, but succumbed to JC by a score of 9½ to 5½. Holt had a 73, Camp 78, Nykamp 79, Burwitz 79, and Klaasen 89.

At the MIAA meet in Kalamazoo on Friday, May 16, it was the Hornets and Hillsdale tying for first place. Kalamazoo's Bill Western took medalist honors with a 36-hole total of 156. Alma had struggled in the dual meet competition, but finished a surprising third this day with a team total of 861, Hope followed with 869, Albion 878, Olivet 917, Calvin 922, and Adrian 934. The Dutchmen managed to beat out Albion and Alma for third place overall in the league. Nykamp continued his improvement by leading his team with a 36-hole total of 164, Holt shot 167, Camp 171, Burwitz 175, and Klaasen 192.

* * *

I was aware in the spring of 1959 that a Hope track team without Hilmert, Wiegerink, and Spaan would present a real challenge. With an eye on the All-Sports Trophy, the team hoped to do its part. We opened at home on Tuesday, April 21, against Hillsdale. Coach Dan Goldsmith's squad lacked numbers, but we would be introduced to a new phenom in the person of Jim Drake. Before the afternoon was over, he would win the high jump and both dashes, and take second in the broad jump and third in the pole vault. But Hope would put together eight firsts, 11 seconds, and seven thirds to win the meet 81 to 49. Jim Rozeboom was a double winner for the Dutchmen in the difficult double of the mile and 880-yard run. Rich Bakker won the high hurdle race, took second in the high jump, and third in the low hurdles. Ray Ritsema contributed a first in the discus and a second in the javelin.

On Saturday, April 25, the Hope thinclads made their way to Houseman Field in Grand Rapids to meet Calvin. The meet, close and exciting all the way, went down to the final event. As it turned out, it would be Hope's best performance of the season. Calvin took six firsts and tied for first in a seventh. The latter was an unusual tie in the discus, when Ritsema and Calvin's Dave Altena each threw 122' 11". Distance ace Jim De Bie was a double winner for the Knights, taking first in both the mile and two-mile. Calvin swept both events, while the Dutchmen managed a sweep in the pole vault with Roland Schut, Tom Tornga, and Bill Elzinga. With stiff metal poles, all three bettered 12', a real accomplishment at the time. Schut's mark of 12' 4½" was a Hope record. The Dutchmen had eight firsts and a tie for a ninth. In winning the low hurdles, Schut became a double winner along with fellow Hudsonville product Jim Mohr, who won both dashes. Rozeboom ran to victory in the 880 in a time of 2:03.1, also a Hope record.

Late in the meet, Calvin's sweep of the two-mile run put them ahead 61½ to 55½, but Hope came back to take first and third in the low hurdles to narrow the margin to 64½ to 61½. The Dutch mile relay team of Mohr, John Vandenburg, Gale Damhof, and Rozeboom then ran to victory to give Hope the meet by a two-point margin, 66½ to 64½.

Hope's victory string of two ended in Kalamazoo on Wednesday, April 29. The Dutchmen received some bad news following the Kazoo meet, when it was learned that

Rozeboom had suffered a heart strain during the meet's mile run and, per doctor's orders, would be lost for the remainder of the season. Swede Thomas, the genial Kalamazoo coach, was not above a little good-natured gamesmanship. His tactic was to delay as long as possible in committing his team members to various events. Once he knew where the competition would be placed, he would assign his men to best advantage. I would deal with this at a future time, but this day his team was strong enough to win under any circumstances. The Hornets collected 11 of 15 firsts enroute to the 76½-54½ victory. Hope's blue-ribbon winners were Bakker in the high hurdles, Mohr in the 100, Chuck Truby in the javelin, and Damhof in the 220, and a tie in the pole vault between Schut and Tornga.

The Dutchmen could do no better the next day, when Coach Norm Bennett brought his Ferris Institute team to Holland. The Bulldogs were led by all-round athlete Willie Prewitt, who had firsts in the broad jump and the 100-yard dash, and a tie for first in the high jump. Larry Ter Molen won the shot put for Hope with a toss of 42' 4½", and Ritsema's throw of 122' 9½" was good enough for victory in the discus. Schut was Hope's double victor for the day, with firsts in the pole vault and low hurdles. Bakker and Jerry Hill finished 1-2 for the Dutchmen in the high hurdles, but the mile relay without Rozeboom went down to defeat. The Bulldogs' 88-43 win was decisive and dropped Hope to 2-2 on the season.

Hope returned to Houseman Field on Saturday, May 2. The Dutchmen did not match up well with the Grand Rapids JC team, which dominated the meet. The Raiders captured 11 firsts and tied for a 12th. Schut had his best vault to date at 12' 8", but JC's Rodney Den Hart, a Comstock Park product, went 13' to take the event. Ter Molen in the shot and Ritsema in the discus were again victorious, and the team of Bakker and Hill repeated with first and second in the highs, but it was a Raider day as they outscored the Dutchmen 72-59.

In a final dual meet at Albion on Tuesday, May 5, the Dutchmen were beaten by the champion Britons, 95½ to 35½. It was not a fun afternoon for the Hope team. Albion's overall strength was in evidence as they swept the mile, two-mile, 880, 440, high hurdles and low hurdles. An unexpected bright spot for Hope was the 10.2 victory in the 100 by John Kleinheksel. He was Hope's only double winner, also taking the broad jump. Schut was first in the pole vault, TerMolen won the shot put, and Ritsema took the discus to round out Hope's five first place finishes. Garth Richey stood out for the Britons with firsts in both hurdle races plus a tie for first in the high jump.

Four squad members took part in the annual Elmhurst Relays in Chicago on Saturday, May 9. The Dutchmen gave a good account of themselves in finishing sixth in a field of 18 schools. Schut tied for first in the pole vault, Kleinheksel was second in the broad jump, Ritsema took second in the discus, and Tornga tied for third in the pole vault.

The MIAA conference track meet was held on Saturday, May 16, at Kalamazoo's Angell Field. Albion, the overwhelming favorite, repeated as champion with 78½ points. Calvin and Hope battled for second, with the Knights winning out with 42½ points to 31½ for Hope. Kalamazoo was fourth with 27½, Hillsdale fifth with 26, Alma sixth with 16, Olivet seventh with three, and Adrian failed to score. Hillsdale's Jim Drake set records in the 100 and 220-yard dashes with outstanding times of 9.8 and 21.5. (The 220 was run on a straightaway.) Albion's Garth Richey had a record in the high hurdles with 15.1, as did Jim Kreider in the 880 with 1:59.7.

Kleinheksel was again outstanding in the broad jump, winning the event with a leap of 23' 3". Schut was the pole vault champion with a height of 12' 4¾", and Bill Vanderbilt tied for first in the high jump with Casey Clark of Kalamazoo at 5' 11½". The latter was an unexpected but welcome bonus, as Vanderbilt had spent the entire season as a member of the baseball squad. Kleinheksel had a third in the 100, as did Ter Molen in the shot. Bakker tied for third in the high jump, Don Gallo got fifth in the shot, and Mohr tied for fifth in in the broad jump. Hope's mile relay team of Jack Hoogendoorn, John Bloemendaal, Vandenburg, and Sharky Vander Woude placed fifth.

* * *

Coach Larry Green's 1959 tennis squad was composed of Paul Mack, Norm Hess, Marshall Elzinga, Bruce Laverman, Rowland Van Es, Doug Johnson, Ron Wiegerink, and Stan Vugteveen. Paul Mack was not available for the first three matches, and Coach Green found himself experimenting as to the placement of his players. The season opened at Alma on Thursday, April 16, with the Scots of Coach George Gazmararian squeezing out a 4-3 win. In singles, George De Vries (A) defeated Elzinga 6-2, 6-4. Dalton Cantrell (A) shut out Van Es 6-0, 6-0, but Hess, a freshman, got the best of Dick Johnson 6-1, 8-6. Laverman defeated Dave Turner (A) 6-2, 4-6, 6-2, and Jim Delavan (A) won over Wiegerink 6-0, 6-3. In doubles, it was De Vries-Cantrell (A) over Elzinga-Van Es 6-4, 6-2, and Hess-Laverman defeating Johnson-Turner 6-0, 6-2.

Two days later, on Saturday, April 18, the Dutchmen hosted Grand Rapids Junior College at the 22nd Street courts. Coach Green used the non-league encounter to give all who had tried out for the team a chance at competition. In singles, Westover (JC) defeated Elzinga (H) 8-6, 6-8, 7-5. Hess defeated Malmberg (JC) 2-6, 6-2, 6-3, and Laverman took Driscil (JC) 9-7, 6-2. Lischner (JC) defeated Johnson 6-4, 1-6, 6-3. Hoogstra (JC) won from Van Es 6-1, 6-3, and Higley (JC) defeated Nykerk 6-2, 6-4. Vugteveen (H) took Betten (JC) 5-7, 6-2, 6-3, and Wiegerink (H) defeated Nielson 6-4, 7-5. In the final singles match, Tanja (JC) defeated

Ron Van Eenenaam 6-2, 6-3. In doubles, Westover-Driscil (JC) were victors over Hess-Laverman 7-5, 3-6, 6-1, Malmberg-Higley (JC) defeated Elzinga-Vugteveen 6-0, 4-6, 8-6, and Kirchner-Betten (JC) won from Nykerk-Johnson 6-4, 4-6, 6-0. The totals amounted to an 8-4 Junior College team victory.

The Dutchmen hosted Olivet on Tuesday, April 21, and, with a revised line-up, shut out the Comets 7-0. In singles, Hess defeated B. Pratt (0) 6-3, 6-0, Elzinga bested B. Waddell 6-2, 6-0, Laverman took Rod Robinson 6-2, 6-2, Vugteveen won from D. Mc Kale 6-1, 6-1, and Johnson defeated Paul Mc Grath 6-1, 6-0. In doubles, it was Hess-Elzinga over Pratt-Robinson 6-0, 6-1, and Laverman-Vugteveen over Waddell-McKale 6-2, 6-1.

Paul Mack made his first appearance for Hope at Kalamazoo on Thursday, April 23. Doc Green placed him at number one singles, but he was hardly ready for Kazoo's Bill Japinga and lost 6-0, 6-0. Bob Brice (K) defeated Elzinga 6-3, 6-3, but Hess surprised Les Overway (K) 9-7, 6-1. Jim Van Zandt (K) took Laverman 6-2, 6-2, and Bob Hader (K) defeated Johnson 6-4, 6-0. In doubles, Japinga-Brice defeated Hess-Elzinga 6-4, 6-0, and Van landt-John Brenneman won from Van Es-Vugteveen 6-2, 6-1, to give the Hornets the 6-1 team victory.

There was more bad news for the Dutchmen at Albion on Tuesday, May 5. Dale Brubaker (A) beat Mack 6-3, 6-1, Hess won from Don Hines (A) 8-6, 6-0, Larry Elkins (A) defeated Elzinga 6-2, 6-0, Laverman defeated John Krafft (A) 3-6, 6-2, 6-2, and Spencer Holmes (A) took Van Es 6-3, 6-3. In doubles, it was Brubaker-Hines (A) over Elzinga-Hess 3-6, 6-3, 6-4, and Elkins-Krafft (A) over Laverman-Mack 7-5, 3-6, 6-1, making the final, Albion 5, Hope 2.

Hope had better luck on Thursday, May 7, when the Dutchmen played host to the Hillsdale team coached by Harry Brand. In a three-set singles match, the Dales' Tom Purdy outlasted Mack 3-6, 6-4, 7-5. Norm Hess defeated Dick Scripter (HI) 6-2, 6-1, Elzinga defeated Jon Hering (HI) 7-5, 2-6, 6-3, Dave Bahlman (HI) took Laverman 6-3, 6-3, and Johnson defeated Phil Pixley (HI) 6-1, 6-4. In doubles, it was Mack-Hess over Purdy-Scripter 2-6, 6-4, 6-3, and Elzinga-Vugteveen over Hering-Bohlman 4-6, 8-6, 6-4 for the 5-2 Hope win.

On Saturday, May 9, Hope hosted the Adrian team coached by basketball mentor Gregg Arbaugh. The hard-fought match would play a key role in Hope's overall finish. In singles, Hess defeated Lavon Wolfe (A) 6-2, 6-2, but Fred Woodby (A) got the best of Mack in a three-setter, 3-6, 6-4, 6-2. Elzinga defeated Harold Craft (A) 3-6, 6-4, 7-5, Johnson won over Bruce Wolfe (A) 6-0, 6-0, and Dick Venus (A) took Laverman 6-0, 6-0. In first doubles, Wolfe-Woodby (A) defeated Hess-Mack 8-6, 10-8, and in the crucial second doubles it was Craft-Venus (A) prevailing over Elzinga-Johnson 5-7, 6-4, 6-1. The 4-3 Adrian win was an example of sport at its best but, of course, a bitter disappointment for Coach Green and his team.

Undaunted, the Dutchmen met the Calvin Knights at the Franklin Street courts in Grand Rapids on Monday, May 11. In singles, Hess defeated Phil Dommisse (C) 6-3, 6-1, Ed Meyering (C) edged Mack 5-7, 6-3, 8-6, Elzinga won over Ron Vanden Berg (C) 6-8, 6-4, 6-2, Johnson defeated Dave Flietstra (C) 6-4, 6-4, and John Munisch (C) took Laverman 6-4, 6-3. In doubles, Hess-Elzinga defeated Dommisse-Flietstra (C) 6-4, 6-4, and it was Johnson-Mack over Vanden Berg-Munisch (C) 4-6, 6-4, 6-3. Hope's 5-2 win completed the team's dual meet league competition at 3-4. Following the the league meet in Kalamazoo on May 15-16, Hope's overall finish was a fourth-place tie. Albion meanwhile, ended in second place behind perennial champion Kalamazoo.

* * *

As the All-Sports points were tabulated, it was evident that Albion's spring sports surge had paid off. The final count showed the Britons, winning the coveted trophy by the narrowest of margins. It was Albion with 74 points to 73 for Hope. Kalamazoo was third with 66, Hillsdale fourth with 49, Alma fifth with 48, Calvin sixth with 38, Adrian seventh with 26, and Olivet eighth with 12.

Failure to bring home the All-Sports Trophy prompted all sorts of theories as to what might have been. Perhaps most telling was the football loss to the Britons, which deprived the Dutchmen of an undisputed championship, but, despite the disappointment, it had been a memorable year in Hope sports.

On Monday, June 1, at 10 a.m., Hope College convened its 94th Commencement. As usual, a solemn parade of students in caps and gowns marched across the stage to receive diplomas. But this time it included the likes of Beernink, Bekius, Benes, Buursma, Faber, Miller, Paarlberg, Ter Molen, and Vriesman, now on to bigger things. Seated in the faculty section, Hope's coaches sensed their loss. Could there ever be another year like 1958-1959?

CHAPTER 5

FAREWELLS

Summer responsibilities in 1959 took me to Camp Hope in New Jersey in June, to Camp Geneva on the shores of Lake Michigan in July, and to Camp Manitoqua in Illinois in August. New friendships were formed with camp counselors, Reformed Church clergymen, and a host of vibrant young students. Many of the latter would find their way to Hope College in succeeding years. Upon my return I learned that Jim Kaat, former Hope pitcher, had been called up from the Chattanooga Lookouts by the Washington Senators. He would make the most of the opportunity.

On Monday, Aug. 24, as the summer of '59 slipped away, Hope College held its 11th annual football clinic. The one-day affair, initiated by Al Vanderbush in 1948, had become increasingly popular with West Michigan coaches. Forty would attend this session, which featured Ron Schipper (Hope '52), coming off a 9-0 season at Northville High School, and Jarold Groters (Hope '51) who had enjoyed considerable success at nearby Zeeland. Utilization of the Iowa Winged-T formation was the general theme, and Hope staff members spoke to Hope's version of this offense. A good deal of general football scuttlebutt circulated throughout the day, but also news of coaches and their new positions. One such was Ernie Post (Hope '48), who had been hired as line coach at Juniata College in Huntingdon, Pa.

On Wednesday, Sept. 2, a squad of 52, the largest in Hope history, reported to head coach Russ De Vette. Included were 25 freshmen, several showing great promise. Almost unnoticed was number 43, a freshman defensive back from Fremont, Mich. In three years he would be captain of the team. In 40 years he would be named president of the institution he was now entering.

De Vette's main concern was the loss via graduation of linemen Miller, Larry Ter Molen, and Paarlberg, not to mention high-scoring Ron Bekius and versatile Jack Faber. On paper, however, prospects were still pretty good. Co-captains Gene Van Dongen at center and Bill Huibregtse at guard were proven quantities, as was George Peelen at tackle. Chuck Truby had been a regular guard on the Northwestern University freshman team in 1957 and had practiced with the Dutchmen in '58. To further shore-up the depleted line, De Vette shifted Mike Blough from end to tackle. Veterans Ron Boeve, Ron Bronson, and Charlie Coulson were available at the end positions.

But as practice began, a series of bizarre happenings served to dampen the coaches' early optimism. Pete Watt, star running back in '58, was involved in a summer traffic accident while driving a UPS truck. He suffered two badly sprained ankles and slashed thumb. He made valiant attempts to return to form, but a knee injury added to his woes and he was lost for the season. Tackle Howard Jansen broke an arm during the summer and never quite recovered. Halfback John Vandenburg sent word from Bellflower, Calif., that a summer job would keep him from early workouts. Halfback Duane Voskuil, who had spent the summer in Germany, had difficulty booking passage home and did not show up until after Sept. 12. It was also soon learned that three promising sophomore linemen had fallen short academically. On the plus side, halfback Jerry Hendrickson returned, and Ty Rupp, who had transferred to Ohio State, also returned. Just as things began to shape up, however, quarterback Paul Mack suffered a hairline fracture of his right thumb, his throwing hand.

The Dutchmen welcomed the Grand Rapids Junior College team to Riverview Park for an afternoon scrimmage on

Wednesday, Sept. 8. The Raiders were coached by Gordon Hunsberger. He was assisted by Tom Van Wingen, former Hope fullback and MIAA most valuable player. The workout proved beneficial to both clubs. De Vette had earlier scheduled practices at 8 a.m. and 5:45 p.m. in an attempt to beat the extreme heat.

The MIAA decision to allow free substitution in 1959 was welcomed around the league, but the NCAA continued its rule of limited substitution, which permitted a player to return to the lineup only once during a quarter. Needless to say, game officials were hard pressed to prevent violations in this practice. Tommy Mont, former head man at Maryland, was the new coach at De Pauw and insisted on NCAA rules for Hope's opener at Greencastle. A rule to widen the goal posts from 18' 6" to 24' was accepted across the country and was good news for Hope's Bill Huibregtse. A 31-man Hope squad left Holland by bus at 1:30 p.m. on Friday, Sept. 18, enroute to Lafayette, Ind. Al Vanderbush had made arrangements for the team to stay at the Purdue University Student Union. The short trip to Greencastle would be made the next morning.

Hope's starting backfield was not exactly a familiar one. Defensive specialist Jim Mohr would start at one halfback, with Jerry Hendrickson at the other. Ty Rupp and sophomore Steve Slagh would share the fullback slot. Jim Fox, third string in '58, would be the starting quarterback. The Dutchmen were off to a bad start. De Pauw held on the first series and Hendrickson, attempting to punt, received a bad snap. The Tigers recovered on the eight-yard line, and three plays later Dick Mace scored from the five. Les Dillman kicked the point for the early 7-0 lead. Hope drives to the 28 and 39 were halted by fumbles. De Pauw drove to the Hope 11, but the quarterback mishandled a snap and the Dutchmen recovered on their 23. Fox then showed his stuff by completing a 13-yard pass to freshman end Jon Schoon and following it with a 29-yarder to Hendrickson, who ran 30 more yards to score. A Huibregtse kick tied the count at 7-7. With three minutes left in the half, De Pauw attempted a hook pass, but an alert Huibregtse stepped in front of the receiver, grabbed the pass and raced 30 yards down the sideline for Hope's second TD. A bad pass on the extra point try left the halftime score at 13-7.

The Dutchmen defense was especially strong in the second half, as the Tigers were held to a single first down and not allowed to penetrate beyond the Hope 45. Late in the third quarter, Hope attempted a 23-yard field goal, but the Huibregtse kick fell short. With 5:30 left in the game, Hope took over on its own 32. A 68-yard drive included quarterback sneaks of six and eight yards by Fox behind effective blocking by center Van Dongen. The drive was climaxed by Vandenburg, who went 20 yards on the Heidelberg reverse. From his guard position, Truby led the way to the end zone. A successful conversion by Huibregtse completed the scoring and gave Hope the 20-7 victory. Fox, in his first start, completed five of eight passes for 120 yards and played an all-around fine game. Mohr sprained an ankle early in the contest and did not return. The injury was not believed to be serious.

Watt returned for Monday practice, but was still hobbled by his summer injuries. Also, Mack was back expecting to play at least on defense. An estimated 4,500 fans turned out for Hope's MIAA opener with Albion at Riverview Park on Sept. 26. Coach Morley Fraser's crew had spoiled Hope's bid for an undisputed championship in '58, and the Dutchmen were eager to reverse things in the 8 p.m. contest. Roy Shaberg of Hope's music department had assembled a 50-piece marching band with Bill Kuyper as drum major. By game time, however, the field was inundated with a windswept rainstorm and band members were forced to retreat to the covered grandstand. There was no scoring in the first period, but in the second quarter with 12:21 to go, Albion's Dick Larson got off a punt to the Hope 22. Vander Woude fielded the kick from his safety position, was hit by end Rex Harkness, broke away and raced 78 yards up the sideline for what would be the game's only touchdown. Bill Huibregtse added the point to make it 7-0. Late in the quarter, Hope tackle Tom Moore recovered a fumble by Briton quarterback Bill Friberg to put the Dutchmen in scoring position, but Gordie Blakeman intercepted a Dutchmen pass on the goal line to end the threat. Bad weather had plagued the game at Albion in '58, and conditions were even worse this night in Holland. At times during the first half, fans in the north grandstand could not see across the field due to the driving rainstorm.

Game statistics reflect the deplorable weather conditions. In the fourth quarter, Albion's Bill Friberg completed an 11-yard pass to Monte Clute on the Albion 46. It was the Britons' only first down of the game. Hope had nine. The visitors could manage only 44 yards rushing, while Hope had 126. Albion was one of 12 in passing for 11 yards; Hope was one of 10 for three yards. Hope would take the 7-0 victory, maintaining that it rained on both sides of the line of scrimmage. Bad news was an injury to Fox, who suffered a severed nerve in his leg. The injury did not respond to repeated treatments and seemed to end Jim's career just as he was coming into his own.

Hope traveled to Alma on Oct. 3 for another night contest. Approximately 2,700 fans filled Bahlke Stadium to watch the Scots do battle with the Dutchmen. Coach Art Smith, now in his third season, relied heavily on Jim Northrup, who had been switched from end to quarterback. Late in the first quarter, Jerry Hendrickson intercepted a Northrup pass on the Alma 44 and returned it to the eight-yard line. On the next play, Vander Woude, now at right half, went off-tackle to score. Huibregtse's kick was true, and the Dutchmen enjoyed an early 7-0 lead which held up until halftime.

In the third quarter, Hope got off a very short punt. In

Hope 19 - Wabash 13 — October 10, 1959

Hope's Jerry Hendrickson (41) runs the "Heidelberg" reverse 56 yards to paydirt. Paul Mack (37) leads the interference.

six rushing plays, the Scots moved 31 yards to score. Tom Thorpe went in from the two, and Dave Peters converted to make it 7-7. Midway in the fourth period, Huibregtse intercepted a Northrup pass and Hope moved to the Alma 13. When Hendrickson was nailed back on the 19, De Vette chose to go for the field goal. Van Dongen's attempt fell short, and Alma took over on the 20. The Scots failed to move in three plays, and Lyndon Salathiel dropped back to punt. Van Dongen then came up with the play of the game as he broke through to block Salathiel's kick. The ball rolled into the end zone, where it was recovered by Bronson for the deciding touchdown. Huibregtse's kick was wide, leaving the final at 13-7. Three freshmen were singled out by De Vette as making a significant contribution to the victory. They were Jim Van Dam and Jim Bultman on defense, and Bob Teall on offense.

Approximately 2,500 fans witnessed Hope's second meeting with Wabash College at 2 p.m. on Oct. 10. The Little Giants had humbled the Dutchmen in 1956, and Coach Garland Frazier brought another strong team to Riverview. Mohr was back in the Hope line-up, but a recovering Vander Woude saw action on only one play. Freshman halfbacks Jim Shuck and Bob Teall started for the Dutchmen. Following a scoreless first quarter, Wabash attemped a fake kick but mishandled the ball. End Chuck Coulson recovered the fumble on the Wabash 41 and in five plays, all on end runs, the Dutchmen notched the game's first score. Teall went the final distance around right end after Jim Shuck had reeled off a 13-yard sweep. The conversion attempt was not good, and Hope went to the lockerroom with a hard-earned 6-0 lead.

In the third quarter, Hope received a punt on the Wabash 43 and reached paydirt in nine plays, all on the ground. Jim Shuck picked up 19 yards on a pitchout and 11 more on two other plays. Slagh hit the middle twice from his fullback spot for 11 yards and Voskuil carried to the one, where the ball slipped from his grasp. Fortunately, an alert Peelen recovered the fumble and Mack went in for the score. Hubie's kick again missed the mark, but Hope now led 12-0.

Late in the third quarter, Hope moved its offensive set to the left with Hendrickson in the left wing position. The flow of the play was to the left with even the linemen starting in that direction, only to peel back to the right and cut down the defenders as Hendrickson once again executed the "Heidelberg" reverse. Mack enjoyed this play, as it allowed him to become a bona fide blocker. With the way cleared, Hendrickson made his way around right end and rambled 56 yards for Hope's third touchdown. Hendrickson eluded several tacklers by cutting back to the middle for the final 15 yards. This time the Huibregtse kick was true, and Hope's lead was 19-0.

Hope substitutes flooded the field in the fourth quarter, and the Little Giants were not long in taking advantage of this situation. Van Dongen's long kick was taken on the two, but in 15 plays Wabash was knocking at the door. Dick White went in from the one and then kicked the point to make it 19-7 with 9:51 remaining in the game. Following the kickoff, Hope quarterback Howie Glupker lost the snap and Wabash recovered. It was Dick White again, first reeling off a 14-yard run, then taking a pass from Scott Polizotto to the four-yard line. Sub quarterback Jack Mc Henry then went in from the one with seconds remaining. Dick White's kick failed, and the score stood at 19-13 with just time for a kickoff. The drama was not quite over. Wabash, of course, tried an on-side kick. The ball bounced into the hands of Peelen on the Wabash 48, and his moment of glory seemed at hand. Somehow he broke free and headed goalward. The sight of a lumbering tackle carrying the ball like a loaf of bread, streaking down the sideline, brought a huge roar from the crowd. The Little Giants, however, were not about to suffer such humiliation and dragged George down finally on the one foot line! Peelen, who had played an outstanding game, was in for some good-natured razzing by teammates for not making that final foot. He took it all in stride and was satisfied that his team now stood at 4-0 on the season.

Hope resumed MIAA action at Kalamazoo on Oct. 17 with a 2 p.m. homecoming game. News on the previous day had been sobering. First it was learned that Fox and Jansen would be lost for the season, then the entire college community was saddened by news of the death of five-star General George C. Marshall, Chief of Staff during World War II, Secretary of Defense, Secretary of State, and author of the Marshall Plan, a giant in American history.

Rolla Anderson's young team put up stubborn resistance in the first quarter and the period remained scoreless. Late in the quarter, Van Dongen recovered a Kazoo fumble on the K 43. Eight running plays later, Slagh went five yards on a trap play over guard for the game's first score. A Huibregtse conversion made it 7-0 with 35 seconds gone in the second quarter. On the first play after the kickoff, linebacker Gene Van Dongen stole the ball from freshman halfback Ray Comeau, then flipped it to Ty Rupp who dropped it but recovered on the Kalamazoo 19. Voskuil moved to the 16 before Jim Shuck circled left end for the score. Hope led 13-0 after a Huibregtse kick sailed wide. Van Dongen's kickoff to the five was advanced to the 26, where Al Altenbernt fumbled and the ever-present Van Dongen recovered. Mack's 21-yard pass to Ron Bronson put the ball on the five, but an offside penalty pushed it back to the 10. A Mack rollout was good to the five, again, and Hendrickson concluded the drive with a right end sweep for the touchdown. A successful conversion by Huibregtse made it 20-0. With 57 seconds remaining in the half, it was Hendrickson again with his favorite play, the Heidelberg reverse. This time he was forced to hurdle two tacklers as he made his way 53 yards for the score. A third conversion by Huibregtse left the halftime score at 27-0.

There was no scoring in the third period, but with 13:08 left in the game the Hornets got on the board with a 54-yard, nine-play drive. The touchdown came on a 13-yard pass from quarterback Jim Smith to end George Mc Leod. The kick attempt was not good, and Hope's lead was now 27-6. An on-side kick attempt was recovered by Hope's Truby on the Dutchmen's 47. Voskuil was back in form with a 35-yard end sweep to the Kalamazoo 18. With 11:06 remaining, Mack connected with Bronson in the end zone. Huibregtse's kick upped the Dutchman lead to 34-6. The scoring appeared to be over as Hope punted to Kazoo's Norm Young, but the kick was fumbled and sub end Jerry Nieusma recovered. Quarterback Glupker followed with a touchdown pass to Vander Woude. Bill Huibregtse's fifth conversion of the afternoon made the final score 41-6. Voskuil led Hope with 81 yards in nine tries, while Ray Comeau totaled 60 for the Hornets.

Hope's game at Adrian on Oct. 24 was played at 7:30 p.m. and followed a two-day drizzle. As a result, only 400 spectators were on-hand. The new Adrian coach was Les Leggett, formerly of Portland State College in Oregon. Bob Gillis was now devoting full time to teaching and the post of director of athletics. On their first possession, the Dutchmen drove 51 yards in 10 plays to score. Included were effective runs of 35 yards by Voskuil, 10 by Shuck, and five by Slagh, and a 20-yard pass from Mack to end Ron Boeve. Mack went in from the one on a sneak, and the conversion by Huibregtse gave Hope the early 7-0 lead. The Dutchmen threatened twice in the second quarter, once reaching the one-half-yard line, but the Bulldogs held and the half ended at 7-0.

Late in the third quarter, Rupp, who had just entered the game, intercepted an Adrian pass on the Bulldog 15. Voskuil moved to the 12, but a penalty put the Dutchmen back on the 17. Mack then threw a sideline pass to Hendrickson, who went in for the touchdown. The conversion failed, and Hope led 13-0 with 1:22 left in the period. There was no further scoring until the closing seconds of the game, when Mohr intercepted a George Almasy pass. He ran seven yards and then lateraled to Hendrickson, who made it to the seven. Following a timeout, Teall went off-tackle to the three. During another quick time out, De Vette decided to send Teall on the identical play. The decision paid off. This time the freshman went in for the score as time expired. The kick by Huibregtse made the final 20-0. In posting their sixth straight win the Dutchmen had dominated in all categories. Hope had 20 first downs to three for Adrian, 235 yards rushing and 70 passing to 35 and 35 for the Bulldogs, who failed to advance beyond their own 31 in the second half.

Considerable hype surrounded the Hope-Hillsdale game at Riverview on Oct. 31. Both teams sported 6-0 records, the only undefeated teams in the state. Coaches, players, fans, and the media recalled the '58 classic in anticipation of the 2 p.m. contest. Coach Muddy Waters believed his team to be his best ever and predicted a victory over Hope. Such an unusual statement was based in large part on the Hillsdale line, which boasted Jim "Jellybean" Reynolds and Jerry Taylor at ends. At tackle it would be 230-pound Jim Larkin and Jerry Snyder at 260. Jim Richendollar, a 240-pounder was a defensive sub for Larkin, while Duke Davis did double duty at center and linebacker. A host of able running backs featured Howard Rogers and was directed by sophomore quarterback Chuck Redding, who had been outstanding in the '58 game. We, as a Hope coaching staff, knew we were in for trouble when the Dales downed a strong Albion team 34-7, but the general public looked for another close game. A record crowd was anticipated for the showdown, and city employees moved extra bleachers into the northwest corner of Riverview Park. Athletics director Al Vanderbush faced a nightmare in deciding who should or should not occupy the tiny press box. To complicate matters, television station WOOD requested space to do part of the game for a later Hope College feature.

An overused, muddy field did not deter spectators and, as predicted, Riverview was jammed. A standing-room crowd watched the Dutchmen advance to the Dales' 21, but Mack, dropping back to pass, was hit hard and Neil Thomas recovered his fumble on the Hillsdale 38. Coach Waters's multiple offense now took charge. From the single wing, freshman fullback Gary Everling broke off-tackle for 46 yards and the game's first score. Bart Misyiak's conversion made it 7-0 with only 4:55 gone. Hope managed only one more penetration into Dale territory during the half, reaching the 47. The 7-0 halftime score was somewhat deceiving as the Dales had rushed for 140 yards to Hope's 17. The Dutchmen had thwarted one drive on the seven.

In the third quarter, Hillsdale drove to the Hope 14 but was stopped again. Hope took over and moved to the 24, but Mack was sacked again and the forced fumble was recovered by the Dales. Eight plays later, a two-yard pass from Redding to end Taylor produced the game's second score. Bart Misyiak's second conversion made it 14-0 with 1:35 left in the quarter. Despite the dominance by the Dales, it was still a ball game. Less than a minute into the fourth quarter, Mack attempted a flat pass to the right. The rangy Reynolds rushed across the line, reached out with a big hand and intercepted. His touchdown scamper broke the game open. A Misyiak conversion made it 21-0. Mack was having a tough day. On the first play after the kickoff, his pass attempt was intercepted by sophomore linebacker Bruce Anderson, who was downed on the Hope 43.

Two running plays advanced the ball to the 36, where Redding, on a rollout, passed to end Bob Hankinson for the touchdown. Misyiak converted again to make it 28-0. Later in the period, a Hope punt plus a penalty put the ball on the Dales' 41. Muddy Waters's substitutes appeared to be as talented as his starters. Freshman tailback Torn Ridley now broke loose around right end and streaked 59 yards to score.

Hillsdale 35 - Hope 7, October 31, 1959
Duane Voskuil finds the going tough as Hillsdale end Jerry Taylor (86) moves in for the tackle. Paul Mack (37) is in the background.

Automatic Misyiak's fifth conversion raised the count to 35-0 with 9:21 remaining in the game.

The issue was no longer in doubt, but the battered Dutchmen were able to make a final statement. Teall returned the kickoff to the Hope 25, where the offense at last put things together. In eight plays Hope moved 75 yards to score. Included was a 21-yard completion from Mack to Bronson. Hillsdale had scouted Hope thoroughly and certainly knew about the "Heidelberg." It didn't seem to make any difference. Hendrickson was untouched going the final 22 yards to put Hope on the board. Huibregtse converted to make the final score 35-7. Muddy Waters had made good on his prediction. His well-coached team had 354 total yards to 185 for Hope. The Dutchmen had been decisively beaten by a superior team before the largest crowd ever to witness a game at Riverview Park.

Two games remained. Hope's goals now were to preserve second place and equal the 8-1 record of 1958. The Dutchmen closed out the MIAA season with a night game at Olivet on Nov. 7. Approximately 500 fans braved the cold to see if the Dutchmen could recover from the Hillsdale drubbing. Stu Parsell, the new Olivet coach was the former coach at Dimondale High School and a gentleman of the first order. In due time he would take over the Comet program and make Olivet competitive in all sports. It would, however, not begin on this particular evening. Hope took the opening kickoff all the way to the Olivet 17, where the Comets' Dave Masters intercepted a Mack pass. The home team failed to gain a first down in three plays, and Chuck Cilibraise dropped back to punt. When the snap was mishandled, Hope took over once more on the 17 and moved to the one. Hendrickson went off-

THE 1959 HOPE FOOTBALL SQUAD
8-1 overall, 2nd place MIAA (5-1)

Row 1 L. to R.: Pete Watt, Duane Voskuil, Jim Mohr, Ron Boeve, Rowland Van Es, George Peelen, Co-Captain Bill Huibregtse, Co-Captain Gene Van Dongen, Charlie Coulson, Tom Moore, Ron Bronson, Jerry Hendrickson, Ty Rupp, John Gilmore. **Row 2:** Manager Tom Bos, Sherwood "Sharkey" Vander Woude, Jerry Nieusma, Bob Bonnette, Chuck Truby, John Vandenburg, Rich Bakker, Jim Fox, John Hubbard, Mike Blough, Paul Mack, Ken Simpson, Steve Slaugh, Manager Allen Ruiter. **Row 3:** End Coach Ken Weller, Bill Vandenberg, Tom Bishop, Elmer Phail, Kurt Van Genderen, Gordon Nederveld, Jim Bultman, Jim Shuck, Bob Teall, Paul Hyink, Jim Van Dam, Bruce Van Leuwen, Dick Buckley, Manager Rod McLeod. **Row 4:** Line Coach Gord Brewer, Student Trainer Vern Essenberg, Ralph Jackson, Don Mitchell, Bill Byrne, Dave Zwart, Doug Hoffman, Jim Vander Wege, Dave Delisle, Tim De Jong, Jan Nienhuis, Jon Schoon, Howard Glupker, Bob Polen, Head Coach Russ De Vette. **Missing from the picture:** Trainer Dr. Larry Green.

tackle for the TD and the Huibregtse kick gave Hope a 7-0 lead with 3:56 left in the quarter. The Dutchmen mounted a 61-yard drive in the second quarter, with Vanden Burg going three yards off tackle to score. The Huibregtse kick split the uprights, and the Hope lead was 14-0. Late in the quarter, end Rowland Van Es recovered an Olivet fumble on the Hope 20. Eight running plays, mostly off-tackle, took the ball to the Comet 35, where Hendrickson took a quick pitch from Vander Woude and went the remaining distance. A third conversion made it 21-0 at the half.

During the third quarter, Hope had drives to the eight and to the 13, but failed to score. In the fourth period, the Comets attempted a pass from their own 17. It was picked off by Hendrickson, who returned it to the seven. Two plays later, Vandenburg went in for his second TD. Huibregtse's fourth conversion increased the lead to 28-0 with 13:36 left in the game. Yet another Hope drive was good for 51 yards in nine plays. This time Teall went the final 10 yards to paydirt. Huibregtse's toe continued to be accurate, making it 35-0. Vanden Burg was sent in to receive the next Olivet punt. He took the ball on the Hope 45 and made it all the way to the Comet 28. At this point Glupker, Hope's third quarterback, passed to Schoon for the sixth Hope touchdown. Huibregtse's perfect night ended the Dutch scoring at 42. Late in the game, Olivet, with the aid of an interference call, drove to the Hope eight. But a defensive hit forced a fumble which was recovered by Van Es, his second of the night. Time ran out and the Dutchmen were sure that second place was better than third.

Saturday, Nov. 14, marked the end of the line for 13 Hope seniors. The MIAA race had been settled, but pride remained an incentive. A Mom and Dads Day crowd of 2,500 made it to Riverview Park for the 1:30 p.m. contest with Ohio Northern University of Ada, Ohio. It would be the first meeting between the two schools. Roy Shaberg's 50-piece Hope band was on hand to make the occasion festive despite huge piles of snow that had been plowed from the muddy field. The Polar Bears, aptly named for this day, were coached by John Nettleton and his assistant, Bob Gobin.

On its first possession, Hope pleased the fans with a 73-yard drive which was climaxed by an 11-yard plunge over guard by fullback Rupp. With 5:46 remaining in the quarter, Huibregtse's kicking streak came to an end and Hope led 6-0. The next time the Dutchmen gained possession, the Polar Bears were introduced to a special Hope play that had its origins in Ohio. Boeve and Bill Huibregtse played their roles perfectly as Hendrickson romped 66 yards for a touchdown on the "Heidelberg." The kick was not good, and the score stood at 12-0. In the second quarter, Ohio Northern drove to the Hope 18, but quarterback Herb Strayer let the wet ball slip away and Boeve was there to recover. In spite of, or perhaps because of, bad field conditions, Hope now took to the air. Mack completed a pass for 39 yards to Hendrickson and another of 22 yards to Boeve. Three plays later, Voskuil drove seven yards off-tackle for the third TD. This time Hubie was back on track, and the Dutchmen lead at halftime was 19-0.

The Polar Bears came alive in the third period, moving from their own 34 in 10 plays to score. Strayer went the final nine yards on a keeper with 4:17 left in the quarter. The kick attempt by Doyle Foultz was not good, leaving the score at 19-6. In the fourth quarter, Vander Woude and Van Es combined to recover a Northern fumble on the Polar Bear 21. On the next play, Shuck circled right end for Hope's fourth TD. A pass attempt by Mack for the point was not good, but the Hope lead increased to 25-6. Still later, quarterback Glupker hit Hendrickson with a 30-yard pass play that put the ball on the five. Hope drove to the one, but the Northern defense held. The Hope defense, now made up of subs, also held and Northern got off a short punt to the 28. Two plays later, the freshman combination of Glupker to Schoon put the ball in the end zone. In his final act as a Hope football player, co-captain Van Dongen kicked the extra point to cap the 32-6 victory. De Vette's team could now boast of 16 wins over the past two seasons against but two defeats.

Huibregtse, Van Dongen, Peelen, and Mohr were named to the All-MIAA team. Alma's Jim Northrup was selected as the league's most valuable player and would receive the Randall Bosch Award. On Friday, Nov. 20, Hope athletes met in the Juliana Room of Durfee Hall for the annual Fall Sports Banquet. "H" Club President Gene Rothi presided and Ekdal Buys Sr. was the speaker. Blough and Mack were elected co-captains for the 1960 season. Of note was the fact that Dean of Students Bud Hinga was unable to attend due to illness.

As Hope wound up its season with Ohio Northern, Hillsdale stepped out of its class to meet Northern Illinois University at De Kalb. After a hard-fought game, the Dales tasted defeat for the first time, 33-27. Despite the loss, the team was invited to a Dec. 5 NAIA playoff game in Kingsville, Texas against Texas, A & I. The Dales found the going tough in the Lone Star State, losing 20-0. Thus ended their bid for a spot in the Florida Holiday Bowl.

* * *

Cross country at Hope College in the fall of 1959 was anything but spectacular, but Coach Al Vanderbush had 13 dedicated runners and he deeply appreciated athletes who try. With senior Roland Schut as captain, the team was off to a slow start, suffering a 15-50 shutout at the hands of powerful Calvin. In addition to Schut, the team consisted of Harry Wristers, Fred Overkamp, Dave White, Dave Maris, Dave Needham, John Murdoch, Bruce Roe, Sam Tomlinson, Randy Menken, Dave Waanders, Dave Viel, and Fred Colvin. The discouraging start continued with losses of 17-44 to Kalamazoo and 15-49 to Albion. The bright spot was freshman Fred Colvin, who finished first for Hope in all of its meets. His example seemed to inspire the team to greater effort.

After three devastating losses, the Dutchmen turned the corner with a 21-37 win against Adrian on Oct. 24. This was followed by victories over Alma (21-40), Olivet (16-45), and Hillsdale (18-43). The four-meet win streak came to an end when a strong Grand Rapids Junior College team downed the Dutchmen 17-43. Readers are reminded that the lower score wins in cross country.

It was Hope's turn to host the MIAA meet, which took place at the American Legion Memorial course on Wednesday, Nov. 11. Calvin's Coach Dave Tuuk had assembled an impressive group of runners who were not seriously challenged in the meet, which included 49 runners. Barry Koops, Jim De Bie, and Nelson Miedema finished one, two, three, to help the Knights finish with a low score of 20. Kalamazoo was a distant second with 50. Albion followed with 67, Hope had 119, Adrian 171, Alma 176, Hillsdale 186, and Olivet 200. After a disastrous start, Dutchman dedication had brought the team back to a solid overall fourth place finish.

* * *

With the loss of Benes, Beernink, Vriesman, and Buursma, Hope was not favored to repeat as MIAA basketball champion. The Calvin Knights were the 1959-60 favorites, and justly so. Coach Barney Steen had lost only Don Koopman from a team that had gone 18-2 on the season, finished second in the league, and handed the Dutchmen their only conference defeat. Hope's only returning starters were co-captains Ray Ritsema and Warren Vander Hill. Bill Vanderbilt would replace Wayne Vriesman, and Bob Reid would take over the guard spot vacated by Whitey Beernink. The remaining guard position was up for grabs in the early going. Top prospects among the newcomers were freshmen Jim Vander Hill, brother of Warren, and John Oosterbaan, a Class C all-stater from Kalamazoo Christian. Jim Hulst had been a standout at Holland Christian, while Ek Buys Jr. and Jerry Hesslink were up from my junior varsity team. Illness prevented Roland Schut from participating until after the Christmas break.

On the local high school scene, Coach Bill Noyd had a fine team that featured guard Ron Maat and a forward named Glenn Van Wieren. The latter would find his way to Hope, where he would make history as player and coach. The new West Ottawa High School would field its very first basketball team under the guidance of Coach Herb Maatman (Hope '50).

The Dutchmen opened the season with a tough assignment. On Wednesday, Dec. 2, Hope hosted Northern Michigan at the Civic Center. The Wildcats were coached by Stan Albeck, the former Adrian coach. His 1958-59 team had gone 16-8 on the season, including an impressive 78-61 win over Wheaton. The Wildcats were also the NAIA champions of Michigan. Hope's 25 home-game winning streak was clearly in jeopardy.

A crowd of 2,000 turned out to see De Vette's new lineup in action. The opening half was close all the way, with Ritsema's rebounding a key factor. A spurt by Hope in the closing minutes gave the Dutchmen a 35-29 lead as the half ended. The Wildcats came on strong in the second half with 6' 1" Wayne Monson of Green Bay leading the way. The Dutchmen were tough on the defensive boards, as Ray Ritsema pulled down 17 rebounds and Bill Vanderbilt 10. The score was tied at 53 with 9:21 remaining, but Northern kept up the pressure and came out the winner, 74-71. Monson led both teams with 34, while Kaiser and Ghiardi each dropped in 11 for the Wildcats. For Hope it was Warren Vander Hill picking up where he left off to lead his team with 28. Ritsema followed with 18 and Reid had seven.

Hope's second non-league encounter took the Dutchmen to Wisconsin to meet Lakeland College. A large contingent of Hope alumni helped make up a crowd of 1,500. The game was played on Saturday, Dec. 5, in the Sheboygan Armory, with Hope in charge all the way. The entire Hope squad of 13 saw action, with the regulars playing about half of the game. With the halftime score at 42-21, it was evident that Lakeland was simply outmanned. Ritsema led the Dutchmen to a 98-57 win with 18. Warren Vander Hill chipped in with 14. Brother Jim showed his stuff with 12, and Don Boyink had 10. Jonas led the Muskies with 10.

It was feared in some quarters that the easy win over Lakeland might not be the best preparation for Hope's next contest. The game would be played against archrival Calvin on Wednesday, Dec. 9. A partisan crowd of 5,500 in the Grand Rapids Civic Auditorium did not help matters any. Coach De Vette decided to open with a zone against the favored Knights, who now had won 17 straight. Tough defense by both teams left the halftime score at 36-32 in favor of Calvin. With nine minutes left in the game it was Calvin 57, Hope 50, but the Dutchmen used a zone press and at 5:33 the score was tied at 64. A spurt by Calvin pushed it to 69-64, but the Dutchmen did not fold. Vanderbilt came up with three crucial interceptions. On the first he was fouled and converted both free throws. The second steal was passed to Warren Vander Hill for a lay-up. Calvin's last lead was 72-71 on two free throws. Reid put on a fine display of ball control in the final minutes and was fouled repeatedly. In addition to a driving layup, he made eight-of-eight free throws to put the game away. He dropped in the final two after time had expired, and Hope had an unexpected upset victory, 80-71. Warren Vander Hill enjoyed a great night with 14 field goals and two of two free throws for 30 points. Ritsema scored 24 points and was dominant on the boards. Reid had his best game to date with 10 points plus a superb floor game. Hope's combination of defenses held Ralph Honderd to seven points and Bill Wolterstorff to six, but Hank De Mots, who would always give Hope trouble, scored 21. Guard Carl De Kuiper followed with 17 and Warren Otte had eight.

Ray Steffen brought his Kalamazoo Hornets to the Civic Center on Saturday, Dec. 12. Some 2,100 fans turned out to see whether or not the Dutchmen would have a letdown after the big win at Calvin. Ritsema and Bill Vanderbilt took charge of the boards early, and Hope cruised to a 40-26 halftime lead. Ritsema blocked numerous Kazoo shots and the Hornets responded with a parade of fouls. Hope cashed in on 27 of 34 attempts. The Dutchmen increased their lead to 18, 67-49, on a layup by Ek Buys, the biggest spread of the game. In the eventual 81-66 win, Vander Hill and Ritsema continued to be the big guns. Warren was again tops with 22 while Ray added 16. Freshmen Jim Vander Hill and John Oosterbaan were impressive with 10 apiece, and Bill Vanderbilt had eight. For Kalamazoo it was Atis Grinbergs with 25.

Hope's game at Adrian on Wednesday, Dec. 16, was played before a disappointing crowd of 200 in Ridge Gymnasium. Frequently now, the Dutchmen were resorting to a pressing defense to prevent the opposition from slowing down the game. The Bulldogs were not prepared for this tactic which, combined with Ritsema rebounding, produced many fastbreak opportunities. The halftime score ballooned to 55-28. Jim Vander Hill was in the starting lineup for the first time and would remain there for the remainder of the season. With nine minutes left, the score stood at 83-48, and by game's end it was Hope 99, Adrian 83. Warren Vander Hill led the way with 28 and Ritsema followed with 22. Reid had another fine game with 15, and Jim Vander Hill added nine. Siedentop scored six quick points in the first half to help put the contest out of reach. Bob Howard and Ron Schult did most of the work for Adrian, each scoring 22. Jim Neff was strong on the boards and scored 13.

The team continued on from Adrian to Wilberforce, Ohio, for a Thursday night game with Central State. The Marauders were ready for Hope's pressing defense, solved it, and moved to a 40-32 halftime advantage. The rebounding of Sam Wagner and James May was a factor. Reid was hobbled by a pulled thigh muscle and did not score. Vander Hill and Ritsema scored all of Hope's first-half points save one field goal by Don Boyink. The Dutchmen did manage a 54-52 lead at one point in the second half, but Central State pulled away for a well-deserved 79-71 win. Coach Gibby Gibbs had balanced scoring from his team. Sam Wagner led with 15, James May had 14, and Tony Blaine 12. For Hope it was Vander Hill with 33, Ritsema 24, and Daryl Siedentop with six. Team members now left for their various homes and a much-needed Christmas break.

The squad reassembled in Holland on Thursday, Dec. 30, in preparation for an important non-league home game on Sat., Jan. 2. The two-year tournament relationship with Wheaton College had generated nearly as much interest as the Calvin series. The teams were similar in many respects. Wheaton had lost starters Gerig, Anderson, and Whitehead, but they still had marvelous Mel Peterson and big John Dobbert. Hope had lost Benes, Vriesman, Beernink, and Buursma, but still had Ritsema and Warren Vander Hill. The Crusaders' record in 1958-59 was 23-4, while Coach Lee Pfund's nine-year record showed 112 wins against but 13 losses. This night an overflow crowd of 2,600 jammed the Civic Center expecting another exciting game in this new rivalry. The fans would not be disappointed. Vanderbilt was assigned the thankless job of trying to contain superstar Mel Peterson. In a recent conversation, Vanderbilt jokingly said it was because he was expendable and Ritsema was not. In reality, Coach De Vette felt that Vanderbilt was the best man for the job and was pleased with his performance.

Visiting coaches will tell one that playing in the Civic Center is an experience neither to be desired nor forgotten. It was a first time for Wheaton, and at the 10-minute mark they trailed Hope 25-20. In the next 10 minutes, Warren Vander Hill and Siedentop each scored four field goals and the margin moved unbelievably to 50-33 with 1:18 remaining. Peterson then came through with two baskets to make it 51-37 at the half.

Hope's prosperity was simply too good to last. Coach Pfund applied an effective press in the first six minutes of the second half, and the seemingly comfortable lead quickly evaporated. With 14:42 remaining Hope's lead was 58-56. During this stretch, Wheaton took 20 shots and made nine while Hope hit on only two of six. The Dutchmen rallied to make it 62-56, but a Crusader comeback closed the gap and guard Rog Johnson tied it at 63 with 9:03 on the clock. The score was tied three times in the next two minutes, but Hope pushed ahead 85-81 on field goals by Jim Vander Hill and Reid, plus a free throw by Warren Vander Hill. With 45 seconds remaining, Rog Johnson broke through for a layup to cut the Hope lead to 85-83 and clutch player Peterson tied it again at 85 all with just 13 seconds showing on the clock. Amidst the bedlam, De Vette succeeded in calling a timeout to set up a play. The ball came in to Warren on the right side, he passed back to Reid at the point. From the left side, Jim Vander Hill moved to a spot near the left lane line, where he was joined by Ritsema coming across to form the

MILESTONE VICTORY

A cake with 100 candles marked on MIAA coaching milestone for Russ DeVette who was recognized by Athletic Director Al Vanderbush and fans during a game.

double screen. Warren, meanwhile, circled under the basket, came out close behind the double screen, took a pass from Reid, faced the basket and lofted his specialty. It was a foregone conclusion! The ball parted the net with two seconds left - Hope 87, Wheaton 85. The game lives on as one of the most dramatic in Hope history. Warren Vander Hill led all scorers with 27. Ray Ritsema was in the thick of the fight and had part of a tooth knocked out in the early going. His total was 20 points. Freshman Jim Vander Hill played like an upperclassman and scored 12. Reid and Siedentop followed with 10 apiece. For the Crusaders it was Mel Peterson again with 24, Rog Johnson 17, Dick Cole 15, and John Dobbert 10. As the still keyed-up crowd moved out into the January night, all were aware that they had witnessed small-college basketball at its very best.

Ritsema had a temporary cap put on his broken tooth on Friday and Jim Vander Hill missed two days of practice due to illness, but "Pooch" Schut returned to the team after a long illness. On Saturday, Jan. 9, the Dutchmen were back at the Civic Center to host John Williams's Hillsdale team. Fans thrilled at the Wheaton outcome came back for more. This time the crowd numbered 2,400. The Dales had a solid team, but this year, at least, they were not a Wheaton or Calvin. Hope was quickly ahead 13-6 and led 51-33 at halftime. Each member of the Hope squad played at least five minutes in the 99-69 victory. To no one's surprise, Warren Vander Hill led his team with 29 and Ray Ritsema had 23. Jim Vander Hill collected 10, and Ek Buys, who played the final eight minutes, also had 10. Don Bohannon was high for the Dales with 25 but no one else reached double figures.

On the following Monday, Jan. 11, the Olivet Comets of Coach Henry Paul came to Holland with the unlikely prospect of halting their losing streak. The Dutchmen were prepared for slowdown tactics with a pressing defense, but such would not be necessary. Forward Dick Groch was one of the leading scorers in the MIAA and, in deference to his star, Coach Paul decided on conventional play. Groch would be the evening's only bright spot for the Comets. Anticipating a meager crowd, Athletics Director Vanderbush invited all area Boy Scouts to attend as guests with their Scoutmaster. A decent crowd of 1,800 resulted. De Vette's regulars played less than half the game, but by halftime Hope had built a 35-point lead, 59-24. Groch, who had scored only six points in the first half, took advantage of Dutchman subs in the second half, putting on a fine performance with 25 more. While Groch was doing his thing, the Dutchmen continued on a scoring rampage that resulted in a final score of 124-64. Warren Vander Hill watched much of the game from the bench, but still led his team with 26. Ritsema followed with 16 and all the rest of DeVette's 14-man squad got into the act. Reid scored 11, Siedentop and Hesslink 10 each, Vanderbilt nine, and Oosterbaan eight. Groch, with 31, was the only Comet in double figures. The Dutch total of 124 points was a new Hope record, breaking the old mark of 114 set in the 1953-54 season against Albion.

Hope's fourth straight home game brought the Albion Britons to the Civic Center. Elkin Isaac had surrendered the coaching reigns to one of his favorite former players, Cedric Dempsey. Isaac would now concentrate on his duties as director of athletics. Warren Vander Hill began the game in uncharacteristic fashion by missing his first four shots. He then proceeded to can the next four enroute to a 31-point evening. Ritsema was matched against Garth Richey, a fine athlete in his own right, but Ritsema would haul down an astonishing 28 rebounds and score 30 points. After leading by a modest nine points at halftime (44-35), the Dutchmen broke it open in the second half with 66 more. Oosterbaan scored Hope's 100th point with 3:20 left to play. The home team's 49 percent shooting average aided the cause. Most of Ritsema's points came on left-hand hook shots and tip-ins. In addition to the point production by Hope's big guns, Siedentop scored 10 and Oosterbaan eight. Jim Vander Hill made his contribution by snaring 17 rebounds. Don Barich led Albion with 17, and teammates Garth Richey and Bill Losey each had 10. Dempsey was philosophical about the lopsided 110-68 loss. One of Albion's all-time great athletes, the affable Dempsey was confident in his own ability. He would serve as director of athletics at three major universities before being selected to head the nation's athletic program as executive director of the NCAA, surely a credit to Albion College and his mentor, Elkin Isaac.

Hope completed its two-year contract with Ball State in Muncie, Ind., on Tuesday, Jan. 19. There was some confusion with travel time and time zones, with the result that the Dutchmen arrived one hour late for the game. An anxious coach Jim Hinga breathed a sigh of relief when the De Vette men finally arrived. The Cardinals had had a longer warmup than they needed. As the Hope team marched across the floor toward their locker room, the Ball State band broke into a chorus of "Hail, Hail, the Gang's All Here." That fact was emphasized as Hope led throughout the half. Ball State narrowed the margin to two with four minutes remaining, but five field goals got the Dutchmen back on track and the score at the half was Hope 45, Ball State 35. Warren Vander Hill had scored 21 of the 45. The Dutch were outscored in the second half, but managed to hang on for the 86-81 victory. Hope scoring was pretty much a two-man show. It was a memorable night for Vander Hill. The "V" scored 37 points, including 18 field goals, the latter a Hope record. The previous mark of 16 had been set by Paul Benes against Northern Illinois in 1958. Ray Ritsema racked up 14 field goals and four free throws for 32 points. Boyink was next with four. Dave Horn was high for the Cardinals and Mike Readnour had 14. The book was not quite closed on C. Warren Vander Hill and Ball State. In years to come he would return as professor of history and, at this writing, serves as that university's provost and vice president for academic affairs.

The Dutchmen returned to league play at Alma on Saturday, Jan. 23. Mr. Randall Bosch accompanied the team and would present the most valuable football player award to Jim Northrup at halftime. Ek Buys Jr. did not make the trip but instead went to Grand Rapids where he married Miss Ann Clark of that city. The game was played before 200 fans in the Alma High School Gym. Hope was off to a slow start and led by only three, 40-37, at the half. Alma ace Ferris Saxton was ill and hobbled by a leg injury. He played briefly and scored three points. Warren Vander Hill started the second half by hitting on four straight jump shots, and Hope was on its way to an 87-69 victory. Vanderbilt turned in what Coach De Vette called his best defensive game of the season. Ritsema was high for Hope with 29, Warren Vander Hill was close behind with 27, Jim Vander Hill had 11 and Vanderbilt nine. For the Scots it was a Northrup night, and the versatile athlete led his team with 19. Dave Peters had 17 and Dalton Cantrell 10. The Dutchmen now returned to campus for a week of semester exams.

The Wheaton Crusaders and Coach Lee Pfund were

ready and waiting for Hope on Saturday, Jan. 30. The return game was played before 3,440 fans in Wheaton's Centennial Gym. Still smarting from the Jan. 2 loss, Coach Pfund's charges were off to a 13-point lead with only three minutes gone. Hope caught up and went ahead 20-19 on two free throws by Ritsema, but it would be Hope's only lead. Wheaton led 43-37 at the half, and stretched the margin to 76-53 at the 10-minute mark for the game's largest spread. The final score of 95-80 pleased the large hometown crowd. It was clearly a Wheaton night. Mel Peterson, the UPI All-American, led his team with 37. Rog Johnson got the ball to Peterson often and scored 23 of his own. Center John Dobbert added 17. Ritsema and Warren Vander Hill had 24 and 20 points respectively, Oosterbaan had 11, Jim Vander Hill 10, and Vanderbilt eight.

For the first time in anyone's memory, no one on Hope's starting five was from Michigan. Ray Ritsema was from Momence, Ill., the Vander Hills hailed from Queens Village, N.Y., Bob Reid from Kenmore, N.Y., and Bill Vanderbilt from Adel, Wis. It was not long before someone tagged them "The Outstate Five," and the name stuck. In games and practice, team members earned various monikers. Jim Vander Hill, with spindly legs and innumerable gyrations, became known as "Spider." Diminutive Bob Reid, moving quickly about the floor, was tagged "The Fly." The working together of Spider and Fly pleased the large Civic Center crowds. C. (Charles) Warren Vander Hill's name was perhaps too long. Practical teammates reduced it to the "V."

Four days after the discouraging loss to Wheaton, Hope moved into the second round of MIAA play. It didn't get any easier. The Dutchmen foe at the Civic on Wednesday, Feb. 3, would be their chief challenger, Calvin. The usual full house was on-hand knowing that a championship could be on the line. The Calvin strategy was to gang up on Ritsema with two, sometimes three players. This resulted in a proliferation of fouls, with both teams deadly from the line. Hope led 47-35 at halftime, but went cold after the intermission. Frustration reigned as the Dutchmen failed to score a field goal in the first six minutes. In an eight-minute stretch the Dutchmen went one for 17. But Ralph Honderd did not see action due to an injury, and big Bill Wolterstorff fouled out with 7:07 left in the game. Hope trailed 78-68 with four minutes remaining, and Coach Steen's strategy seemed to be working, at least to some extent. Ritsema had his hands full with the swarming defense, but at this point other team members picked up the slack. Jim Vander Hill stole the ball for a layup, Warren sank a jumper, Reid had a steal and a layup, and Vanderbilt sank two free throws to make it 78-78 with 1:42 left. Warren Vander Hill fouled Len Rhoda who made both pressure free throws putting the Knights in front 80-78 with 56 seconds showing in the clock. Warren Vander Hill first tied the score with a quick field goal, then scored a second jumper to put the Dutchmen up by two with 31 seconds left. A Calvin shot failed, and Vanderbilt was fouled by

LIKE FATHER, LIKE SONS

The Rev. Laverne Vander Hill (center), shows his sons, Jim (left) and Warren, the accounts in the Hope College yearbook of the 1929 basketball team. The elder Vander Hill, who is in Holland this week to conduct chapel services at Hope, was captain of the 1929 Hope team and played basketball under Coach Jack Schouten during the 1927-28-29 seasons. Warren, a senior, is co-captain of this year's Hope team while Jim is a freshman. The Rev. Vander Hill saw his sons play college basketball for the first time Wednesday night in Kalamazoo. He and Mrs. Vander Hill will return to Queens Village, N.Y. on Friday.

Warren Otte. Vanderbilt dropped in both free throws to give Hope the 84-80 victory. Another Hope-Calvin classic was in the books. Free throw shooting by both teams was outstanding. Calvin made 26 of 29, and Hope had 28 of 33. Warren Vander Hill, who seemed to thrive on pressure games, again led the Dutchmen with 33, including 11 of 11 from the line. Bill Vanderbilt was superb with 14 points and eight-of-eight charity tosses. Jim Vander Hill's late game surge netted 12 points, Ritsema managed 11, and Reid had 10. The Knights were led by steady Henry De Mots with 24, and Holland native Warren Otte had 20. Bill Wolterstorff added 13 and Carl De Kuiper 10. The season was far from over, but the "Out-State Five" had demonstrated that they could be more than a two-man show.

The Dutchmen entertained Central State of Ohio on Saturday, Feb. 6. The Marauders were crowd pleasers and the teams again were evenly matched. All of this made for yet another exciting contest. The opening half was played on even terms, with Hope clinging to a 37-35 lead at the intermission. The Dutchmen built what appeared to be a comfortable lead, 61-45, at one point, but with 3:40 remaining Central had narrowed it to 80-70. Coach Waterman now put on a press, which resulted in six field goals while the Dutchmen scored a single free throw. Hope trailed 82-81 with 24 seconds showing on the clock. De Vette signaled for an out-of-bounds play. The ball was handed to Warren Vander Hill who passed in to Ritsema, whose layup was possibly the winning basket, but a confused timer sounded the buzzer midway in the play and the referees ruled that the two points would not count. Subsequently the Marauders missed a free throw and Hope called a timeout with 12 seconds left. The crowd hoped for another Wheaton finish, but this time Warren's jumper rolled off the side of the rim and Central State was the winner, 82-81. Turner Russell led the winners with 18, Stovall had 12, Tony Blaine and Jack May 11 each. Ritsema was high man for Hope with 33, Warren Vander Hill followed with 20, brother Jim had 12, and Vanderbilt 11. The timer's mishap probably cost Hope the win, but Coach DeVette refused to make an issue of it. Central State was a team of good sportsmen and they had made a great comeback. Also, the chagrined timer was a Hope faculty volunteer performing without remuneration.

Guests on the Hope campus in early February were the Reverend Laverne and Mrs. Jeanette Vander Hill of Queens Village, N.Y. The parents of Warren and Jim had never seen their sons perform together in a college game. They would make the trip to Kalamazoo College on Wednesday, Feb. 10, to watch the Dutchmen do battle with the Hornets. The elder Vander Hill had been captain of Hope's 1929 team. There was the usual talk of the "Treadway jinx," and when Kalamazoo scored the first six points there was concern. With his parents in the stands, Jim Vander Hill picked up two quick fouls and made his way to the bench. Sub Boyink came on and Hope scored the next eight points. The score was tied at 8-8 and 10-10, then it was Hope all the way. By halftime it was Hope 46, Kazoo 30, and Boyink had scored 13. A great team effort caused Coach De Vette to call it Hope's "best game of the year." Roger Kramer, a football tackle, and rugged Gordon Rodwan were leaders in Coach Steffen's aggressive style of play. Both fouled out of the game. Oosterbaan, in his hometown, scored a field goal with 2:35 left to make it 82-52, Hope's biggest lead. Ritsema, with 24 points, led his team to the final 83-55 victory and Warren Vander Hill followed with 22. Boyink, in perhaps his best game to date, scored 16. Jim Vander Hill scored seven before fouling out.

Gregg Arbaugh was in town with the Adrian Bulldogs for a game at the Civic on Saturday, Feb. 13. An estimated 2,100 fans were on-hand to see if the Dutchmen could continue unbeaten in the MIAA. Hope's performance in the first half was spotty at best. The scoreboard showed a 16-16 tie at the 10-minute mark, and the Dutchman lead at the half was a single point, 46-45. The second half was a different story, with Hope moving to an 81-59 lead in the next 10 minutes. With 24 seconds left in the game, Boyink's free throw made it 100. He followed with another free throw and a field goal with seven ticks left to give Hope the 103-80 victory. It was again a night of great effort by Ritsema. Such seemed routine for the big left-hander, and the crowd was with him all the way. However, at one point, perhaps in self-disgust, he slammed the ball on the floor. He was rewarded with a technical foul, perhaps his only one ever. An indignant crowd responded with a loud chorus of boos aimed at referees Charlie Stanski and Tony Marfia. This display irked Coach De Vette, who stood with both hands raised to quell the outburst. As far as the fans were concerned, the scorebook was Ritsema's vindication. He ended a great night with 37 points and 27 rebounds. Warren Vander Hill also had a super evening with 29 points, including 11-of-12 free throws. Vanderbilt was also hot from the line with six-of-six, plus three field goals for 12. Jim Vander Hill made five-of-nine from the field and had 11. Jim Neff led the Adrian attack with 25, Bob Howard had 14 and Ray Rolley 13.

The Hope squad traveled to Hillsdale on Wednesday, Feb. 17, to meet John Williams's team in the Dales' Stock Fieldhouse. A meager crowd of 200 saw Ritsema hit his first seven shots enroute to 21 points in the first half. The atmosphere, quite different from that of the Civic Center, did not deter the Dutchmen, who built a 47-36 halftime lead. There was no let-down in the second half with a 19-point advantage being the biggest bulge. Ritsema ended with 32, and "the V" followed with 23. Jim Vander Hill enjoyed his best game to date with 15 points, most coming on long jump shots. Vanderbilt had 10 and Reid eight. Don Bohannon, Hillsdale's splendid forward, led his team with 35, and Dave Simmons added 15. At the final buzzer it was Hope 93, Hillsdale 78.

It was more of the same at Olivet. Only 150 fans from the tiny campus filed into Mc Kay Gymnasium, otherwise known as "the Pit," to witness the contest. Coach Henry Paul had by now abandoned his stall tactics, but the Dutchmen were ready with a pressing defense, just in case. The game was safely in hand by halftime with Hope leading 44-27. Warren Vander Hill hit on 16 of 20 shots for 80 percent and the team overall made 40 of 78 for 51 percent. Warren Vander Hill and Ritsema led the De Vette men to a 94-63 win with 32 and 20 points respectively. Norm Schut sank 10, and cousin "Pooch" Schut had eight. For the Comets it was Dick Groch with 19, Mike Foster with 15, and Paul Bilsing with 10. Hope had clinched a share of the MIAA crown.

At Albion on Wednesday, Feb. 24, the Dutchmen found an aroused group of Britons. Cedric Dempsey had prepared his team well, and they were in the lead 27-17 with seven minutes to go in the half. If the Hope shooters were hot at Olivet, they were equally cold in the Kresge Gym. Albion's halftime lead was 31-25 and Warren Vander Hill, weakened by the flu, had not been effective. In the second half Ritsema picked up his fourth foul with all of 12 minutes remaining. The picture was somewhat dismal when "the Fly," Reid took over the game. His 16-point performance in the second half

VICTORY CELEBRATION

L. to R.: Seniors Roland Schut, Ray Ritsema, Warren Vander Hill, and Daryl Siedentop reflect on four MIAA championships following their final game for Hope College. The photo was taken in the Civic Center locker room after Hope's season ending 74-64 victory over Alma. February 27, 1960.

brought the Dutchmen back. In the eventual 80-68 victory, Reid led his team with 20 points. Ritsema had 17 in limited playing time, and Jim Vander Hill outscored his brother for the first time with 15, but the ailing Warren still managed 14 and Vanderbilt had 10. The Britons' game effort was led by Dale Terrell with 16. Don Barich and Adolph Grundman each notched 12, and Garth Richey had 10. With a game to go, the Dutchmen had clinched their fourth straight MIAA championship.

On Saturday, Feb. 27, the 1943 Hope "Blitz Kids" held a reunion with their ailing coach, Milton "Bud" Hinga. All were in attendance save captain Ets Kleinjans who was in Hawaii, and Robert "Hoots" Rowan. Fond memories were recalled over dinner in Voorhees Hall. The group then proceeded to the Civic Center, where they were guests of honor for Hope's season finale with Alma.

On this night the preliminary game was played between my junior varsity squad and the Aquinas College JV's. I did not realize it at the time, but this would conclude my stint as a basketball coach. Without pressure, it had been pure fun. In retrospect, it was a satisfying send-off. A 55-34 halftime lead blossomed into a 96-75 victory. Captain Jim Hesslink, twin brother of the varsity's Jerry, was the leader with 25 points. He was followed by football end Jon Schoon with 16, Gary Nederveld with 13, and Arlyn Lanting with 11. It was a 9-3 season.

With the championship secure, it was now up to the varsity to play like champions. Alma Coach Wayne Hintz arrived with an eight-man squad. Ace Charlie Saxton was back in action, but Jim Northrup, high scorer in the first game, was mysteriously absent. More than 2,600 fans managed to get into the Civic Center to see Ritz, the "V," Siedentop, and "Pooch" in action for the last time. The Scots' challenge, of course, was to play the role of spoiler. Coach Hintz started with a semi-slowdown game. Ritsema, Vanderbilt, and Warren Vander Hill picked up early fouls, and Hope shifted to a zone defense. The Scots kept pace throughout the entire half, but the Dutchmen finally pulled ahead 41-37 at halftime on field goals by Jim Vander Hill and Oosterbaan. At the 10-minute mark the four-point lead remained, this time at 56-52. The game remained a nail-biter until Coach De Vette inserted Boyink in the lineup. Boyink proceeded to score four field goals and put his team up 74-60 with 1:30 left. Charlie Saxton scored the final four points with two free throws and a field goal to make it Hope 74, Alma 64. At 14-0, Hope was undefeated in league play for the first time since the Blitz Kids did it in 1943. It was somehow appropriate to have the latter team in the stands as the "Outstate Five" completed a most satisfying season. It was also appropriate that Hope's high scorers for the evening were Ritsema and Warren Vander Hill, each with 20 points. Oosterbaan followed with nine and Boyink had eight. Charlie Saxton, bad knee and all, led the Scots with 22. Dalton Cantrell dropped in 17 and Dave Peters had 13.

The All-MIAA team of 1959-60 was made up of Ray Ritsema and Warren Vander Hill of Hope, Don Bohannon of Hillsdale, Bob Howard of Adrian, and Bill Wolterstorff of Calvin. Hope team members selected Vander Hill and Ritsema as the Dutchmen's co-most valuable players. Later, by vote of MIAA players, Ritsema was named the league's most valuable. It marked the first time in conference history that a player had been accorded the honor twice. Warren Vander Hill set a new MIAA scoring record for 14 games with 366 points. Hope's team average of 92.2 points per game was also a new mark. Ritsema and Vander Hill were also named to "Who's Who in Small College Basketball - 1959-60". They joined such notables as Ed Smallwood of national champion Evansville, and Kelly Coleman of runner-up Kentucky Wesleyan. Hope held its post-season banquet on Monday, March 14, with Vice President John Hollenbach as toastmaster. Speaker for the evening was Bob "Gabby" Van Dis of the '43 Blitz Kids. He was intoduced by his former coach, Bud Hinga. Bill Vanderbilt was announced as captain-elect for 1960-61. On March 9, Ray Ritsema had received honorable mention All-American by the UPI, and Warren Vander Hill accepted a fellowship from the University of Denver made possible by the National Defense Education Act.

When a season ends, basketball players experience a definite void in their routine. Late-afternoon practice sessions are over, frozen ground and lingering snowstorms are depressing, and the anticipation of Saturday's game is gone. Ritsema and Warren Vanderhill eased the pain somewhat by playing a few games with the Zeeland Texaco Oilers, a team made up of ex-college stars from around the state of Michigan. In so doing they rejoined Paul Benes, who was a member of the team. The Hope three more than held their own, but crowds were mostly small and it was not the same. No one expected it to be. Hope would field more great teams in the future and crowds would be equally enthusiastic, but with the departure of Schut, Siedentop, Vander Hill, and Ritsema, a very special era had ended.

*   *   *

At Hope College in the spring of 1960, the spotlight was clearly on tennis. Coach Larry Green's young team now had some experience, and the season's results would underscore the improvement. The opening match in Grand Rapids with GRJC was, as usual, exploratory for both teams. The Dutchmen, none-the-less, were impressive and off on the right foot. In singles, Norm Hess (H) defeated Larry Van Spriell 6-0, 6-0. Paul Mack (H) won over Ed Seneyn 6-4, 6-2, Arlyn Lanting (H) defeated Kent De Young 6-0, 6-0, Bob Teall (H) took David Wissink 6-4, 6-4, Stan Vugteveen (H) defeated Herb Freye 6-1, 6-1, and Bruce Laverman (H) was the winner over Wayne Ver Strate 6-4, 6-3. In doubles, it was Hess-Teall over Van Spriell-Seneyn 6-1, 6-1, Mack-Vugteveen defeated De Young-Wissink 6-3, 6-1, and Keith Louwenaar-Neil Paauwe (H) downed Freye-Ver Strate 6-4, 6-4 to complete the 9-0 shutout.

Hope's first MIAA test was at Albion on Saturday, April 23. Hess, a sophomore, was now firmly entrenched at number-one singles. This day he was successful in defeating Larry Elkins 6-1, 3-6, 6-0. Mack defeated Art Smith 6-4, 6-3, Lanting won from John Krafft 6-2, 6-3, Frank Forshew (A) defeated Teall 4-6, 7-5, 6-4, and Don Mc Kersher (A) defeated Vugteveen 4-6, 6-3, 6-1. In doubles, Hess-Teall won from Elkins-Smith 6-4, 6-1, and Mack-Lanting defeated Krafft-Forshew 7-5, 6-4. The 5-2 team victory had not been easy, as witnessed by the three-setters.

Hope's match with Adrian on Monday, April 25, somehow did not reach the newspapers. With details missing, all that is known is that Hope was the victor. On the following Wednesday, April 27, Hope hosted Aquinas and enjoyed an 8-0 shutout. In singles, Hess defeated Travis 6-0, 6-0, Mack took Rutledge 6-2, 6-0, Lanting (H) defeated Lee 6-0, 6-0, Bruce Holmes (H) won from Conrad 6-0, 6-2, and Laverman defeated Kobza (A) 6-1, 6-3. In doubles, Hess-Teall defeated Kobza-Travis 6-0, 6-0, Mack-Vugteveen were winners over Rutledge-Conrad 6-3, 6-0, and Keith Louwenaar-Neal Paauwe defeated Norin-Bochniak 6-3, 6-0.

The Dutchmen were victorious in their second MIAA encounter when Hillsdale came to Holland on Friday, April 29. Coach Green's charges were winners in all the matches except number-two doubles for the 6-1 team victory. In singles, Hess defeated Tom Purvey 6-2, 7-5, Mack won from Phil Smith 6-4, 6-8, 6-2, Lanting defeated Julio Victoria 6-0, 6-0, Teall took John Herring 4-6, 6-4, 6-2, and Vugteveen defeated John Henshel 6-2, 6-1. In doubles, Hess-Teall defeated Purvey-Victoria 6-2, 6-4, and Smith-Herring (HI) defeated Mack-Vugteveen 8-6, 1-6, 6-2.

The competition in Hope's meeting with Calvin seemed similar to that of recent basketball games. The match was played in Holland on Tuesday, May 3, and the teams were evenly matched. In singles, Hess defeated Dave Flietstra 3-6, 6-2, 6-1, and Lanting won from Phil Pommissee 6-1, 6-1, but Calvin's John Musch defeated Mack 6-2, 7-5, Dave Vander Hart defeated Teall 6-3, 6-1, and Ken Oosterhouse took Stan Vugteveen 8-6, 6-3. Trailing 2-3, it was up to the Hope doubles players to pull out the match. The team of Hess-Teall was able to down Flietstra-Vander Hart 6-3, 6-3, but it was tougher for Mack-Lanting, who finally got the best of Pommissee-Musch 8-6, 6-4. Hope's narrow 4-3 team victory kept the team's MIAA victory string intact.

Kalamazoo came to Holland for a match on Wednesday, May 11. The Hornets had won 21 straight MIAA championships, the most recent one under new Coach George Akker. They also sported a record of 145 consecutive dual meet victories, and had no intention of breaking the string. It was soon evident that Kalamazoo, with a rich tradition and superior facilities, played tennis on a different level. In singles, Holland native and future Hope Professor Bill Japinga defeated Hess 6-2, 6-2, Loren Campbell took Lanting 6-4, 6-3, Bob Heider defeated Paul Mack 6-1, 6-4, Jim Van Zandt won over Teall 8-6, 6-3, and Ken Elzinga defeated Vugteveen 6-1, 4-6, 6-3. In doubles, it was Japinga-Campbell over Hess-Teall 6-3, 6-4, and Heider-Barrett over Mack-Lanting 3-6, 8-6, 6-3. The 7-0 shellacking didn't look good on paper, but the Dutchmen and their coach knew they had played pretty well.

Hope was back in the win column at Alma on Saturday, May 14, but it wasn't easy. Mack missed the match and Coach Green elected to give his subs a chance at number-two doubles. Both situations influenced the outcome. In singles, Hess defeated Turner 6-2, 6-0, Lanting was a winner over Johnson 6-3, 6-2, Delevan (A) defeated Vugteveen 6-4, 6-3, Laverman won from Love 4-6, 6-2, 6-3, and De Podesta (A) defeated Bruce Holmes 6-4, 7-5. In doubles, it was Hess-Teall over Turner-Love 6-2, 6-2, and Johnson-Delevan (A) over Louwenaar-Paauwe 6-2, 6-0. Coach Green was thankful to go home with the 4-3 win.

The Dutchmen hosted Olivet in the final dual match of the season, on Monday, May 16. In singles, Hess defeated Bill Pratt 6-3, 8-6, Lanting defeated Dave Mc Kale 6-0, 6-1, Paul Mack took Paul Mc Grath 6-0, 7-5, Bruce Laverman defeated Buchilitz 6-1, 6-0, and Vugteveen was a winner over Phil Smith 6-2, 6-0. In doubles, it was Hess-Teall over Pratt-Mc Kale 6-2, 6-0, and Mack-Lanting over Mc Grath-Smith 6-2, 6-0 to close out the 7-0 team win.

Rain halted the MIAA meet in Kalamazoo on Friday, May 20, with Kalamazoo leading with 28 points to 26 for

LAST TEAM

The 1960 Hope Junior Varsity (9-3) would be my last basketball team. **Seated L. to R.:** Ken Kutzing, Arlen Ten Pas, Captain Jim Hesslink, Dave Bolhuis, Dale Scheerhorn, Jon Schoon. **Standing:** Manager John Blom, Bob Koster, John Fieldhouse, Gary nederveld, Carl Nykamp, Arlyn Lanting, Coach Gordon Brewer.

THE 1959-60 HOPE BASKETBALL TEAM
MIAA CHAMPIONS — 14-0, 17-4 OVERALL

Seated L. to R.: Daryl Siedentop, Bill Vanderbilt, Co-Captain Ray Ritsema, Co-Captain Warren Vander Hill, Jim Vander Hill, Bob Reid. **Standing:** Manager Bob Kreunen, Norm Schut, John Oosterbaan, Rich Bakker, Don Boyink, Ek Buys, Jerry Hesslink, Coach Russ De Vette. Starters Ritsema, Reid, Vanderbilt, and the two Vander Hills were tagged "The Outstate Five.

Hope. The coaches agreed to let the meet stand at that, and Hope finished the season a strong second to the Hornets.

* * *

MARY LOUISE BREID
Miss Breid coached all women's sports at Hope College from 1954-1960.

The Hope women's tennis team kept pace with the men as in posting a 6-0 dual meet record. Victories were two each over Aquinas, Calvin, and Western Michigan University. Through the efforts of Coach Mary Breid, Hope hosted the WMIAA tennis and archery meet on Friday, May 20. Hope finished second in both sports, but the doubles team of Jan Owen and Jean Schregardus took first place, a fitting send-off for their coach. Mary Louise Breid had served as physical education instructor and coach of all women's sports since 1950. She was now accepting a position at the State University of New York (SUNY) at Geneseo, which would enable her to be near and afford some care to her mother. She was often overworked and always conscientious and her services would be greatly missed.

* * *

My fourth season as track coach at Hope began under the capable leadership of two "Jims," co-captains Jim Mohr, a sprinter, and middle distance man Jim Rozeboom. The latter had been sidelined for much of the '59 season but he was back and poised for an outstanding year. As a warm-up, I arranged an "Orange and Blue" intra squad meet on April 16. With the teams evenly divided, the blue team prevailed 62-58 and some of the practice tedium was alleviated.

Once again our opening meet featured Grand Rapids Junior College, this time in Holland on Saturday, April 23. With two events remaining Hope led 59-58, but JC swept the two-mile run and took the mile relay to win by a score of 72 to 59. Hope's seven firsts included a Hope record of 2:01.3 in the 880 by Rozeboom. Other firsts were recorded by Don Gallo in the shot, John Kleinheksel in the broad jump, Roland Schut in the pole vault, Ray Ritsema in the discus, Jon Schoon in the 440, Rich Bakker in the high hurdles, and Bill Vanderbilt, who ended in a three-way tie for first in the high jump at an even 6'. JC's Mike Murray won the javelin with a heave of 190' 11½", very good for the time, and Karl Elliot took both dashes.

Three days later, on Tuesday, April 26, the team traveled to Adrian for a triangular with Adrian and Olivet. On this day Hope's opponents were both undermanned. The Dutchmen had things pretty much their own way as they placed first in 14 of the 15 events. The final score showed Hope with 109 9/10 points to 28 9/10 for Adrian and 23 1/5 for Olivet.

Reality returned on Tuesday, May 3, when Hope hosted Kalamazoo at the Allegan High School track. Clair De Mull (Hope '50) was a coach at the high school at the time, and served as starter for the meet. He also spent considerable time in preparing the track and other facilities for the competition. Coach Warren "Swede" Thomas loved track and field, and brought a fine team to Allegan. From start to finish it was an exciting meet. The Hornets garnered eight firsts to seven for the Dutchmen, and emerged the winner by a score of 70⅓ to 60⅔ — but not without a battle. Hope led by a narrow margin throughout most of the evening, but a Kazoo sweep of the two-mile put them ahead 65⅓ to 60⅔ with one event remaining. A victory in the mile relay would give Hope the meet by one-third of a point! It was not to be, as the Hornet team of Ray Comeau, Atis Grinbergs, Dave Whittingham, and Dennis Fitzgerald edged out Hope's Mohr, Schoon, George Walters, and Rozeboom. Bright spots for the Dutchmen included a lowering by Rozeboom of his mark in the 880 to 2:00.2 and a superb performance by John Kleinheksel in the dashes. Kleinheksel, better known for his prowess in the broad jump, was developing into a fine sprinter, and this night had firsts in both the 100 and 220 with times of 10.0 and 22.5.

Coach Dave Tuuk's Calvin Knights came to Holland for a dual meet on Saturday, May 7. It proved to be a good day for the Dutchmen as they led throughout, notching 10 firsts to four for the Knights. The most exciting race of the day

JIM ROZEBOOM **JIM MOHR**

MARKS OF LEADERSHIP

Rozeboom and Mohr were Co-Captains of the 1960 Hope Track Team. Rozeboom set a new MIAA record in the 880 in the 1960 Conference Meet. He was also the ideal relay anchor man. Dashman Mohr would participate in any event to gain one more point for his team.

was the final event, the mile relay. The Calvin team of Walt Pruiksma, Paul Weener, Al Bierling, and Wayne De Young established an early lead and Hope trailed by 10 yards coming off the last turn, but Hope anchor man Rozeboom caught De Young at the tape and the race was ruled a draw. Calvin swept the two-mile, while Hope did the same in the broad jump and high jump. Hope's 72½-58½ victory seemed convincing, but Coach Tuuk's team would improve steadily and eventually win the league championship at Kalamazoo.

In 1960 it appeared that Hope was finally in a position to challenge Albion in track and field. The Britons of Coach Ike Isaac were in town on Tuesday, May 10, and Hope was off to a good start with sweeps again in the broad jump and high jump. In the former event it was Kleinheksel, Walters, and Mohr, while Vanderbilt, Bakker, and Tom Tornga turned the trick in the latter. Gallo took the shot and Ritsema the discus. Rozeboom was switched to the mile and won with a time of 4:33, a Hope record. When Kleinheksel and Mohr took turns winning the 100 and 220 and Schoon captured the 440, victory seemed imminent. But Albion's Garth Richey took both hurdles and the Britons swept the two-

mile to narrow the margin to 64-62 with but the mile relay remaining. Coach Isaac's team of Carl Clarke, Jim Ferguson, Bruce Berndt, and Jim Kreider prevailed winning the final event to give the Britons the 67-64 victory. Hope's lack of strength in the two-mile had once again proved costly. The Dutch registered eight firsts and tied for a ninth, but Albion's depth paid off.

Hillsdale met Hope at the Allegan track on Friday, May 13. The Dales of Coach Dan Goldsmith had strength in the field events thanks mainly to the efforts of Bart Misyiak. Misyiak would be remembered from the previous fall, when he kicked five consecutive extra points in the football contest at Riverview Park. In this meet he took firsts in the shot and javelin plus a second in the discus behind Ritsema. L.J. Muddy won the broad jump and tied for first in the pole vault with Hope's Tornga. The Dales' other ace was dashman Jim Drake, whose 9.8 in the 100 was outstanding on the cinder track. His 22.4 in the 220 was also good for first place. But Hope had nine first-place finishes to wrap up the meet by a score of 85-45. Hope broke the two-mile jinx when Randy Menken took first and Walters second. Bakker won both hurdle races and tied with Tornga for first in the high jump. Once again, the mile relay was an exciting event. The Hope team of Schoon, Jim Tysse, Vanderbilt, and Rozeboom trailed, and with Jim Drake running anchor prospects were bleak. Drake, however, was not experienced in running the 440. Once again Rozeboom provided a spectacular finish, coming from 10 yards back to beat Drake by two yards at the tape.

In their final dual meet of the season, the Dutchmen traveled to Big Rapids to meet Ferris State College. The Bulldogs of Coach Norm Bennett proved too strong for the Dutchmen as they posted nine firsts and tied for a 10th. Hope's top performance in the 85-45 loss was Ritsema's 136' toss in the discus, a Hope record. Kleinheksel won the broad jump with a leap of 21' 7", his best of the season to that point. Gallo won the shot and Hill the javelin with a surprising throw of 161' 10". The Dutchmen won the mile relay by default as Ferris was disqualified.

As usual, the MIAA conference meet was held at Kalamazoo's Angell Field, this time on Saturday, May 21. The teams were more evenly matched than in previous years, as no school recorded more than three first-place finishes. For Hope it was Kleinheksel winning the broad jump for the third straight year. His distance, short of his own record, was 22' 2". Tornga won the pole vault at 12' 6" as Schut, bothered by a pulled muscle, ended in a three-way tie for second. The performance of the day belonged to co-captain Rozeboom in the 880. Hope drew an outside lane, always a disadvantage, especially when one of the inside runners was Albion's Jim Kreider, who had set a MIAA record in the '59 meet. With a large field of runners in the 880, a race plan is necessary if one's potential is to be realized. Competitors run in lanes around the first curve, then break for the pole trying not to become "boxed in" by the other runners. I felt that if Jim would assume a sprinter's stance and "gun it" for the first 50 or 60 yards he could come out of his lane ahead, would not be likely to cut anyone off, and with his stamina would have things pretty much his own way. An additional reason was the fact that he would not be able to see the other runners. Jim was not comfortable with all of this, but with some reluctance finally agreed. Happily, all went according to plan. Jim established a lead which he never relinquished. He was especially strong in the second lap, widening the gap to 25 yards at the tape. His time of 1:58.9 was a Hope and MIAA record.

Hillsdale's Jim Drake won both dashes, and Alma's Dave Peters took both hurdle races to become the meet's only double winners. Calvin's Stan Koster won the javelin, Jim De Bie took the mile run, and Barry Koops the two-mile. After finishing second, Calvin's mile relay team was disqualified, but the Knights held on to edge Kalamazoo for the championship 51-49. Hope finished third with 37½, Hillsdale had 30, Albion 22⅗, Alma 19⅗, Olivet 10⅗, and Adrian five.

* * *

The Hope golf season of 1960 was not a memorable one, but Coach Bill Hilmert still had his ace, Bob Holt. Others on the team were Wes Nykamp, Tom Klaasen, Bob Klaasen, and Ken Biel. Several of the dual matches were rained out and not re-scheduled, but the Dutchmen opened in Grand Rapids with GRJC on Monday, April 18, as the opponent. Holt tied Dave Rielag 1½-1½, Bill De Pree (JC) defeated Nykamp 2-1, Chuck Heinick (JC) won from Tom Klaasen 2-1, Rom Mooney (JC) defeated Klaasen 2-1, and it was Tom Steketee (JC) over Biel 3-0 to complete the 10½-4½ team victory for the Grand Rapids school.

Hillsdale hosted the Dutchmen on Friday, April 29, and registered a 15-1 victory. The Dales' Ed Swanson was medalist for the day with a 75-86 win over Klaasen. Holt and Nykamp suffered one-stroke defeats. Holt lost to Jack Fauster 81-82, and Nykamp was edged by Del Karnes 89-90. Tim Auseon (HI) defeated Bob Klaasen (H) 81-84, and Jack Salvarino (HI) won over Biel.

It was a better day for Hope at home on Tuesday, May 3. The Olivet Comets were in town for a match at the American Legion Course and caught Hope on the rebound. Holt was back in form and defeated Olivet's Larry Burd 2½-½. Nykamp took Dick Kast 3-0, Tom Klaasen (H) defeated George Drew 2-1, Bob Klaasen won over Ross Brown 2-1, and Biel defeated Paul Bilsing (O) 3-0. The 13½-2½ team victory was a confidence builder going into the May 20 conference meet at Kalamazoo.

In Kalamazoo on Friday, May 20, Holt gave his team something to cheer about, emerging as co-medalist with Del Karnes of Hillsdale. Each had 150 strokes for 36 holes. Hope, however, could do no better than fourth place for the season.

* * *

If there was a "riches to rags" story in 1960, it was that of the Hope baseball team. Coach De Vette's 1959 team had knocked at the championship door until the final day of the season, but the departure of key personnel would head the '60 squad in the wrong direction. Gone were All-MIAA catcher Ron Boeve, shortstop Bob Thomson, and third baseman Gene Van Dongen. Boeve, Thomson, Jerry Boeve, Whitey Beernink, and Wayne Westenbroek were lost via graduation, while Van Dongen would concentrate on studies to insure graduation and a coaching career beyond.

Regulars Gary Bylsma, Tim Vander Mel, and Bob Reid were on-hand, but the remaining gaps would be difficult to fill. The season opened on Saturday, April 16, against Grand Rapids Junior College in that city. On the mound De Vette used Bruce Hoffman, Sharky Vander Woude, and Larry Dykstra, with Ron Vander Molen behind the plate. Hoffman gave up three runs in the first and one in the second. Hope got two back in the eighth, but JC went on to record a 5-2 victory.

One week later, on April 23, Hope opened the MIAA season against Alma. In the first game the Scots combined 13 hits and five Hope errors for a 13-7 win. The Dutchmen made a statement in the sixth, when Gary Bylsma singled, Jim Van Dam doubled, and Tim Vander Mel hit a three-run homer into the left field stands. This narrowed the score to 10-7, but Alma padded its lead with three more in the seventh. In the second game, Hoffman pitched well until the sixth, when the Scots used three hits, three walks, and an error to score five runs enroute to the 7-2 victory. Bylsma relieved Hoffman, and versatile Dykstra was behind the plate.

Hope's first victory would come at Albion on Tuesday, April 26. Vander Woude pitched five innings, but the Dutchmen fell behind and Dykstra came on in relief. The issue was decided in the sixth, when Vander Woude walked, Reid beat out a bunt, and Schut connected for a three-run homer. Bylsma followed with a double and Vander Mel was safe on an error. Jerry Nieusma singled Bylsma home, and Vander Molen cracked the second home run of the inning. The Dutchmen savored the 7-4 victory. It would be one of only two on the season.

The Britons reversed things in the second game, winning 7-3. Hope's three runs came in the sixth inning. Bylsma was safe on an error by the third baseman, and Jim Bultman advanced him to second with a single. Bylsma then drove both men home with a triple. Gary scored the third run on Vander Mel's single.

Hope's doubleheader with Calvin, scheduled for Saturday, April 30, in Grand Rapids, was postponed due to rain. The games were played on Monday, May 2, at Franklin Park, and both went into extra innings. In the first game, Bruce Hoffman gave up just four hits until the ninth inning, when the Knights pushed across the winning run. Jim Kool singled, went to second on Carl De Kuiper's ground out, then came home on a single by Schoon to give Calvin the 3-2 win.

Vander Woude took the mound in the second game after playing first base in the opener. He pitched the entire 13 innings against Calvin's Art Kraai. Vander Woude pitched no-hit ball until the seventh inning, and Kraai was equally effective. The score stood 0-0 after 10 innings, then each team scored two in the 11th. In the 13th, Calvin's Mel De Stigter singled, stole second, then third. He came home with the winning run when the catcher threw wildly to third base. Two 3-2 extra-inning losses in one day comprised a major setback for the Dutchmen and, of course, made sweet music for a deserving Calvin team.

When the Dutchmen traveled to Kalamazoo two days later, they were out of pitchers. Reid, a centerfielder known for his strong arm, was called upon to pitch his first game ever. For most of the game it appeared that Coach De Vette might get away with this move. Hope was off to a good start when Vandenburg singled and Schut doubled. Both came home on Vander Woude's double. Doug Japinga led off the second with a home run to left center. With two out, Vandenburg walked and stole second. Schut was safe on an error, and both scored on Bylsma's single. In the third, Vander Mel was safe on an error and Vander-Woude singled. Bultman sacrificed the runners along and Japinga walked. Reid's single scored two runs and Hope led by a comfortable 9-2 score at the end of three. But the Hornets fought back, and when Reid walked the first man in the seventh, he was relieved by George Heath, who got the next batter on a fly to center. He then gave up a walk and Aftowski singled to load the bases. The veteran John Thompson then collected his fourth hit of the game to drive in two runs and win the game 10-9. Hope had now lost three one-run games in a row.

Conditions did not improve for the Dutchmen in the second game. Bylsma took the mound for Hope, but was unable to keep the Hornets in check. He was relieved by Dykstra, but Kalamazoo went on to win 11-2. The Dutchmen were held to two hits, but scored a run in the third without benefit of a hit. Reid walked and Byslma was safe on an error. Vandenburg and Schut then walked to force in the run. In the sixth, pinch hitter Dave Bonnette singled, but was forced at second on a fielder's choice. Vander Molen walked, and Reid's single to center scored Dykstra. It had been a long afternoon. Hope now stood 1-7 in MIAA play.

Hope hosted Olivet on Saturday, May 14. The games were played at the Zeeland High School field due once again to Tulip time activities at Riverview Park. In the first game, the Comets collected nine hits and eight runs from the offerings of Vander Woude and Pete Bylsma. The Dutch, meanwhile, were held to six hits and two runs. The two came in the fifth on singles by Vandenburg, Schut, and Vander Mel.

Hoffman and Dykstra worked the second game for the Dutchmen with Vander Molen behind the plate. Hope scored four runs in the second without a hit. Two walks, three errors, and a wild pitch netted the scores, and it appeared that the Dutchmen would break their skein of losses. The Comets, however, countered with four runs in the second and added five more in the fifth to take the game 9-4.

Dykstra took the mound at Adrian to close out the season. He gave up but three hits while striking out five. Hope was finally in the win column with the 9-5 victory. Dykstra helped his own cause in the second with a triple which scored Japinga, who had singled. Hope got two more in the third when Vandenburg and Bylsma both walked. Bonnette then came through with a single, scoring Vandenburg. Bylsma crossed the plate as the shortstop bobbled a grounder by Vander Mel. A fourth run came in the fourth inning, when Dykstra was safe on an error, advanced to second on Bultman's single and scored on a single by Vandenburg. Hope put the game away in the fifth with a five-run rally. Walks to Japinga and Dykstra were followed by singles from Niesma, Bultman, Vander Molen, and Bylsma.

In the final game of the campaign, Hope was limited to three hits by the Bulldogs and went down to a 7-3 defeat. Bylsma and Hoffman labored on the mound as Hope ended in last place with a 2-10 record. Such are the fortunes of our national pastime. Many would view it as a dismal season, but for the players each game offered a new challenge, a chance to do better, a chance to win. Several games went down to the final pitch and effort was never lacking. As the 1959-60 school year drew to a close, various awards and achievements were announced. Gary Bylsma was the lone Hope player named to the All-MIAA baseball team. Hess was the recipient of the prestigious Allen B. Stowe Sportsmanship Award in tennis. Tennis ability and leadership are also criteria. Kalamazoo, with a strong showing in spring sports, captured the MIAA All-Sports Trophy with 69 points. Hope was again second, this time with 64 points. At the Hope Honors Convocation, Warren Vander Hill received the Otto Vander Velde All-Campus Athletic Award. Also at the convocation, Al Vanderbush was presented an "H" Club blanket in appreciation of his service as coach of football, tennis, and cross country, and also his leadership as director of athletics since 1954. Vanderbush would now give up his direct involvement in sports to concentrate on Hope's expanding department of political science.

A number of former Hope athletes moved to new positions in the spring of 1960. Arend D. "Don" Lubbers ('53) was named president of Central College in Pella, Iowa. Ron Bos ('53) accepted a position as professor of physical education at Kent State University. He had formerly served as tennis coach at Ithaca College in New York. Football coach Ron Schipper moved from an outstanding tenure at Northville to Jackson High School. He would be joined by Tom Miller ('59), who had just completed an undefeated season at Fennville. Dwayne "Tiger" Teusink ('58) moved up to head basketball and baseball coach at Lee High in Grand Rapids. Paul Wiegerink ('58), late of Harbor Springs High, would become Tiger's assistant in basketball and also handle reserve football at Lee. Daryl Siedentop ('60) was hired by Hope to take over cross country from Al Vanderbush and J.V. basketball from Gordon Brewer. He would also be in charge of the intramural program. Finally, though he didn't visit as a coach, Holland played host to a famous athlete in June. Jesse Owens, of Olympic fame, chose to vacation at the Mooring on the north shore of Lake Macatawa. On June 22 he shot a 77 at the American Legion golf course.

*   *   *

MILTON L. HINGA
1901-1960

Through memory's haze — A curtain call for the legacy of Coach Bud Hinga.

As the 1959-60 school year had unfolded it became apparent that Dean Milton Hinga was not in the best of health. In subsequent weeks his ailment was diagnosed as Hodgkins Lymphoma. Attempts by the medical community to arrest the malady were largely ineffective, but the Hingas hoped for remission and the dean continued to carry out his duties. President Lubbers, business manager Rein Visscher, and treasurer Henry Steffens would each day encourage their longtime friend to join them for the three-block walk to the Wade Drug Store on Eighth Street. At mid-morning Larry Green and I would often make the trek from Carnegie-Schouten Gym to Van Raalte Hall for a coffee break. Along the north side of Van Raalte a first-floor window would fly open and the dean would have a few good natured barbs and other banter for us. But such episodes became less frequent. Our greetings were then extended at his desk. One morning his comment was, "Green, I won't wrestle with you today." His good humor persisted in the face of the often painful debilitation.

Bud Hinga was given a leave of absence for the second semester, but occupied his office whenever possible. As mentioned earlier, a reunion of the coach's 1943 "Blitz

Kids" was held in Voorhees Hall on Feb. 27, and afterward the Coach and players were honored at Hope's season-ending game with Alma. Hinga was quick to congratulate Coach De Vette on his championship, feeling that it was his protege's best coaching performance to date.

The Hingas had moved to an apartment in the west wing of the new Kollen Hall, where they served as house parents. The often spirited men students were asked by resident advisors to "cool it" in the west wing. They complied out of respect for the dean's person as much as for his illness. But time ran out for Bud Hinga. He was moved to Holland Hospital, where he died at 12:30 p.m. on Tuesday, May 31, 1960.

The funeral was held in Dimnent Memorial Chapel at 3 p.m. on Thursday, June 2. President Lubbers, Dr. Harvey Hoffman, and the Rev. Paul Hinkamp conducted the service. The chapel was filled with students, former students, colleagues, townspeople, and friends. Among those in attendance were Dr. John E. Visser, dean of Grand Rapids JC; Charles Forsythe, state director of Michigan high school athletics, and his assistant, Al Busch; also Dale Sprankle and Elkin Isaac of Albion College; and Barney Steen of Calvin College. A closed-coffin decision by family members allowed all to remember him as the affable, outgoing friend and counselor of times past. Pallbearers were six student residents of Kollen Hall: John Tysse, Warren Vander Hill, Bruce Vander Mel, Rowland Van Es, Paul Luidens, and Jim Vander Lind.

Sincere and heartfelt eulogies could hardly do justice to a life that had meant a great deal to me personally. When I was a green freshman in the fall of 1941, he had been my advisor, never too busy to give much-needed counsel. He was also my professor, coach, and even Sunday School teacher. As dean of students, his forte was to solve disciplinary problems firmly but behind the scenes, thereby saving parents and their off-spring needless embarrassment. We were diminished by his death.

*   *   *

The Hope College Class of 1960 graduated on Sunday, June 5 — yet another farewell. Its members had begun college life in September of 1956 even as I began as a college teacher-coach. For four years they had graced the campus, been on my teams and in my classes, made trips, and enjoyed social functions. We learned together, and a certain affinity seemed to result. It was, of course, now time for them to move on, to take their place in a society that needed their kind. They left sport better than they found it. Quite selfishly, I hated to see them go.

HOPE COLLEGE MEN'S TENNIS TEAM — 1960
8-1 in duals — 2nd place MIAA

Kneeling L. to R.: Bruce Laverman, Bob Teall, Paul Mack, Norm Hess. **Standing:** Keith Louwenaar, Arlyn Lanting, Stan Vugteveen, Bruce Holmes, Neil Paauwe, Coach Larry Green.

HOPE COLLEGE WOMEN'S TENNIS TEAM — 1960
6-0 in duals — 2nd place WMIAA

Seated L. to R.: Jean Schregardus, Roberta Russell, Jan Owen. **Standing:** Barb Gray, Kathy Bakker, Ula Oosterbaan, Marilyn Scudder.

CHAPTER 6

COACHING PLUS

During the 1959-60 school year, Hope College Admissions Director Albert Timmer announced that he would retire following commencement in June. A short time later I was approached by members of the administration as to whether or not I would be interested in this 12-month position. While flattered by such consideration, I respectfully declined knowing that it would put an end to any further coaching. Shortly thereafter, Al Vanderbush expressed a desire to devote full-time attention to the expanding Department of Political Science. With administration approval, he asked if I would succeed him as director of athletics. The post would allow me to continue as varsity track coach and assistant football coach. This time the answer was yes. The announcement in April stated that my tenure in the new position would be effective on Sept. 1, 1960.

The new responsibility involved important policy decisions, and as such offered a real challenge. I was aware of the general duties of scheduling, making travel arrangements, preparing a budget, etc., but I soon discovered that there was no written job description. Coach Al was ever helpful in steering me in the right direction, but for some months the phrase "flying by the seat of your pants" took on new meaning.

In many ways, the 1960 football campaign could be characterized as an "almost" season. A 54-man squad reported on Aug. 31 and two-a-day practices followed through Labor Day. The usual losses to graduation were somewhat offset by a solid corps of able returnees. Morale was boosted by the unexpected return of quarterback Jim Fox and halfback Pete Watt. Both had suffered what were thought to be career-ending injuries. Paul Mack returned for his third season as starting quarterback and would enjoy a banner year. Sharkey Vander Woude was the man to inherit the middle linebacker spot vacated by Bill Huibregtse. He would also perform at fullback. Co-captain Mike Blough was shifted back to end, to team with Jon Schoon. Jim Van Dam, without complaint, had made the difficult transition from quarterback to guard and promptly earned a starting berth. Other starters included Rich Bakker and John Hubbard at tackles, Jim Vande Wege at center, and veteran Chuck Truby at guard.

The football squad and most Michiganders took time out on Sept. 10 to watch on TV as Nancy Anne Fleming, Miss Michigan from Montague, was crowned Miss America in Atlantic City. A week later, the team was back in the trenches and ready for the season opener with De Pauw. A good crowd of 4,500 turned out for the Sept. 17 night contest at Riverview Park. The Dutchmen got the first big break when Vander Woude recovered a De Pauw fumble on the second play of the game. Hope took possession on the Tigers' 41 and in four running plays, moved to the 28. On the next play, Mack lofted a pass to end Jon Schoon, who took the ball on the seven and raced into the end zone. Mack's conversion gave Hope the early 7-0 lead with 9:43 gone in the quarter.

Hope's next drive was squelched when John Rubush intercepted a Mack pass on the three-yard line. In the second quarter, the Dutchmen moved to the 15 but didn't score. The Tigers then mounted a 16-play scoring drive with Blunt going in for the TD. A new NCAA rule allowed for a two-point conversion and the Tiger attempt was successful, giving De Pauw an 8-7 halftime advantage. After a punt exchange in the third period, the Dutchmen had the ball on their own 20. John Vandenburg, Steve Slagh, and Vander

Woude moved the ball down field in nine plays, and a Mack-to-Blough pass put the ball on the 16. Hope's linemen then created a huge hole for halfback Ken Visser and he went into the end zone standing up. Mack's kick put Hope back in the lead at 14-8 with 54 seconds left in the period.

In the fourth quarter, Mack intercepted an Ed Meyer pass on the Hope 33 and returned it to the 49. He then found Dale Schoon with a nine-yard pass before Visser and Vander Woude took turns pounding over tackle and guard. Vander Woude went the final four yards to score with 10:42 left in the game. Mack's third conversion made it 21-8. But the Tigers were not finished. A series of completed passes took them to the Hope 15. Two runs and a personal foul penalty put the ball on the six-yard line. At this point, defensive corner back Jim Bultman took charge. On the first play his tackle knocked quarterback Jim Menighan back to the 11. On fourth down it was Bultman again, this time stopping Skeeters on the one to end the threat. The Tigers gained some satisfaction on the next play, when tackle Jim Gladden broke through to tackle Slagh in the end zone for a safety to make the final score Hope 21, De Pauw 10. An opening day victory is always welcome, and several Hope players had come through with good performances. Guards Truby, Van Dam, Den Ouden, and Bishop had been fundamentally sound in carrying out their blocking assignments, making it possible for Visser to rack up 107 yards in 13 carries. Mack was on target with five of 11 passes for 84 yards, and also did the punting and place kicking. The only sour note came from the press box, where De Pauw statisticians complained about the poorly lighted field. They maintained that most Class "C" high schools had a better system. The criticism was probably justified.

Hope's second non-league encounter, also a night game, was played in Ada, Ohio, on Saturday, Sept. 24. Coach Arden Roberson was in his first year at Ohio Northern and was coming of an impressive 41-6 victory over Taylor. Tackle John Hubbard missed the game due to a leg injury. His able replacement was Jan Nienhuis, who had prepped at Holland High. A crowd of 3,500 was on hand at Memorial Stadium as the Dutchmen once again were off to a good start. In the first quarter, following a successful drive, Ken Visser went three yards on a winged T counter play to score, and Paul Mack kicked the point. The Polar Bears responded, also in the first quarter, when quarterback Chumsey Bauman scored on an option keeper play. Joel Spiker's kick was not good, and Hope led 7-6 at halftime.

A Mack punt was blocked in the third period, giving Northern the ball on the Hope eight. The Dutchmen held for three downs before Joel Spiker kicked an 18-yard field goal to put the home team in the lead 9-7. Later, in a similar situation, Spiker attempted a second field goal, but Vander Woude broke through to block it. In the waning minutes of the fourth quarter, freshman halfback John Gray made the game's longest run when he broke free and raced 78 yards

HOPE CO-CAPTAINS — 1960
End Mile Blough
Quarterback Paul Mack

For the first time Hope wore bright orange pants with navy blue helmets.

down the sideline to paydirt. Spiker's kick was wide of the mark, but Ohio Northern had posted its second victory, this time by a score of 15-7. Hope had a slight lead in statistics with 272 total yards and 19 first downs to 271 and 12 for Northern.

More than 3,000 fans turned out for the MIAA opener at Albion's Alumni Field on Saturday, Oct. 1. Hope took the opening kickoff and marched 78 yards to score. Vander-Woude, Visser, and Slagh did most of the work, with Visser going the final four yards. With 7:14 left in the quarter, Mack's extra point attempt sailed wide, leaving Hope with a 6-0 lead. From this point defense prevailed, but late in the half Hope had another scoring opportunity from the Albion 18. Mack's try at a field goal was blocked, however, and the Dutchmen went to the locker room still clinging to the narrow 6-0 advantage.

A momentum swing in the third period saw the Britons mount a 55-yard drive with quarterback Frank Gould going the final yard on a sneak. Phil Willis converted to put Albion up by one at 7-6. The ensuing kickoff was taken by Visser on the Hope 10. Visser broke into the open and a foot race with the lone Albion defender. Blough caught up to the

Briton safety as Visser began to pull away. It was a wild scene along the sideline as the Hope coaches, perceiving the danger of Blough's well intentioned but unnecessary block, shouted "No Mike, no!" as Visser's 90-yard gallop ended in the end zone, the inevitable flag lay on the turf. Blough would shortly redeem himself. A short time later, Albion obliged with a fumble and Hope recovered. Runs by Visser and Vander Woude put the ball on the Briton five. On the next play Mack found Blough in the end zone and the Dutchmen were back in the lead. Mack again had trouble with the point try, leaving the score at 12-7.

With four minutes left in the game, Coach Fraser's charges responded with a 66-yard march. A key play in the drive was a 19-yard pass from Gould to end Ed Brown. Hope defender Kurt Van Genderen got a hand on the ball which flew 10 feet in the air, but Brown was in the right spot to retrieve it on the four. Fullback Gerry Snider went off-tackle for the score and Willis's toe again found the mark. The 14-12 loss would be Hope's biggest disappointment of the season.

Halfback Bob Teall, a shining light on Hope's '59 squad, had secured an appointment to the U.S. Naval Academy. Word was now received that he had made the Plebe team at Annapolis. All in the Hope camp wished him well. Saturday, Oct. 8, brought the Scots of Alma to Riverview for a night game. A crowd of 3,000 turned out to see two evenly matched teams. Alma coach Art Smith, now in his fourth season, relied heavily on quarterback Terry Ebright and halfback Len Fase. With 5:55 left in the first quarter, Mack scored on a 10-yard roll-out around left end. He then kicked the point and Hope was up 7-0. The Scots came back with a surge that included a 41-yard pass from quarterback Terry Ebright to end Jim Greenlees. Ebright then sneaked in from the one and kicked the point to tie up the score at seven apiece. Alma threatened again, moving all the way to the Hope four, but halfback Len Fase fumbled and linebacker Chuck Truby caught the ball in mid air and ran it out to the nine. With six minutes to go in the period, Jim Bultman intercepted a Scot pass on the Hope 23 and carried it to the Dutch 46. A Mack-to-Jon Schoon pass put the ball on the Alma 20. After two running plays, Mack found fullback Sharkey Vander Woude for eight yards and the touchdown. Mack's successful conversion gave Hope a 14-7 lead at the half.

Late in the third quarter, Hope struck again. This time it was Visser breaking off tackle for 24-yards and the TD. Paul Mack's kick was wide of the mark, but an Alma penalty afforded a second chance. This time the kick was true, and Hope's lead increased to 21-7. With three minutes gone in the final period, the Dutchmen were once more on the move, beginning on their own 30. A highlight of the drive was a 57-yard pass play. Mack's toss was gathered in on the Scot 30 by Jon Schoon, who was finally dragged down on the six. Coach De Vette then called for the deceptive winged-T

RICH BAKKER — ALL-MIAA TACKLE 1960
Bakker's outstanding performance was the result of good size, good speed, and good technique.

counter play. From his right wing position, halfback Vandenburg moved across the formation, took a forward hand-off from Mack, followed the post-lead and trap block at left tackle, and went into the endzone for the score. Mack's kick was not good, but the Dutchmen had pushed their lead to 27-7. In the closing minutes the determined Scots pushed the ball to the Hope two, where Ebright fumbled and Hope's Neil Goodrich recovered. Goodrich would thus remember his first appearance in a Hope game. Hope's 27-7 victory featured 97 rushing yards in 11 carries by Vandenburg, and 41 in five attempts by Bultman. Mack had enjoyed perhaps his finest game ever, and Vander Woude had been outstanding at middle linebacker.

In regretful hindsight, Al Vanderbush would blame himself for scheduling Muskingum for Hope's Homecoming game on October 15. A crowd of 4,800 turned out hoping to see the Dutchmen continue their improved play. The Muskies of Coach Ed Sherman stood 3-0 on the season and the coach let it be known that this was the best of all his teams at Muskingum. The small school from New Concord, Ohio, numbered among its graduates the legendary John Glenn, but this season it was fullback Bill "Cannonball" Cooper who made a well-balanced team outstanding. Hope's coaches were aware of Cooper's prowess, but could not know that he would move on to play with the San Francisco 49ers. The Dutchmen were off to a surprisingly good start. Vandenburg took the opening kickoff on the 16 and raced all the way to the Hope 40. He then followed up with 11 more yards to the Muskie 49. On a quick opener, Vander Woude got 14 more to the 35. Next it was Ken Visser on a counter play to the 31, where he fumbled. Phil Wenger recovered for Muskingum, and Hope's offense was done for the day. In a dazzling display on both offense and defense, the Muskies rolled to a 47-0 rout of the Dutchmen. Cooper scored but one touchdown while contributing 153 yards to his team's offensive total of 528 yards. Hope was limited to 51 yards rushing and 54 more on five of 12 passes. All in all, it was a day to forget, and the Dutchmen set about doing just that.

A week later at Kalamazoo they started over. Approximately 1,000 fans turned out on Oct. 22 at the Hornets' Angell Field. Midway in the first period, Hope took a punt on the Kazoo 48 and in 10 plays moved to paydirt. Vander Woude went five yards up the middle for the score, and Mack added the point. In the second quarter, Hope suffered a bad pass from center on a punt and the Hornets recovered on the Dutchman 13. Three plays later, Ed Lauerman scored on a two-yard plunge and Bill Liggett's conversion made it 7-7 at the half.

The Dutchmen mounted a nine-play drive in the third quarter after taking a punt on their own 42. A 30-yard end sweep by Visser proved to be the key play, setting up a two-yard sneak by Mack for the score. John Labahn broke through to block Mack's kick but the Dutchmen had moved ahead 13-7. The kickoff by Hope's Neil Goodrich reached the five, where it was taken by 5' 6" 130-pound Don Le Duc. The diminutive back slipped through to the 46, and in seven plays the Hornets were again on the board. This time it was a 22-yard pass from quarterback Jim Smith to Dan Pell. Liggett's kick put the Hornets back in the lead at 14-13 as the third quarter ended.

With 11:27 remaining in the game, Visser climaxed a 61-yard drive with a two-yard end sweep and Hope was once again in the lead at 19-14 after Mack's kick sailed wide. A determined Kalamazoo team came back strong with a drive to the Hope 10, but Jim Bultman knocked down a Jim Smith pass in the end zone. An offside penalty moved the ball back five yards, and on the next play Smith was sacked by Rich Bakker and Dave Delisle to end the threat. Hope drove to the K 20 with 2:20 left, but lost the ball on downs. The Dutchmen had one more chance. On Kazoo's second down, freshman Roger Van Noord intercepted a Jim Smith pass on the Hornet 20. Vanden Burg went off-tackle to the 12 and Visser circled right end for Hope's final TD. Mack's successful conversion made the final score, Hope 26, Kalamazoo 14. For the players, the Muskingum fiasco was now ancient history.

The Adrian Bulldogs were in town on Saturday, Oct. 29, for a 2 p.m. game at Riverview. A good crowd of 2,500 turned out to see if the Dutchmen could garner yet another MIAA victory. In the first quarter, an Adrian punt was fielded by Bob Bonnette. Excellent coverage nailed Bob on the Hope one-yard line and the Dutchmen were in a deep hole, but halfbacks Vanden Burg and Visser combined for consistent gains on running plays. A 17-yard pass from Mack to Vander Woude put the ball on the Bulldog 12, and Hope was out of the early hole. On the succeeding play, Mack passed to freshman end Ken Quakkelaar for the game's first score. Mack's kick was not good, but the 6-0 lead held up at halftime.

Defense reigned in the second and third quarters as neither team scored, but in the final period Hope put together a 65-yard drive. The series featured a 19-yard pass play from Mack to end Dale Schoon, who was substituting for his injured brother Jon. With the ball on the Adrian four it took four plays before Vander Woude smashed off-tackle for the score. The kick by Goodrich was good to increase the Hope margin to 13-0. Later in the quarter, a Mack punt bounced off the shoulder pads of safety John Fundukian and was recovered by Dick Buckley on the Adrian 39. Jim Fox was now the Hope quarterback. His 13-yard pass to Quakkelaar was followed by a 16-yarder to Dale Schoon, who leaped high to bring the ball down on the 16. Three plays later, Visser went the final four yards on his specialty, a right end sweep. A second conversion by Goodrich increased the Hope lead to 20-0. Hope's kickoff was picked up by John Fundukian on the one-yard line. He managed to break free and it appeared that he would go all the way, but Visser, Hope's last man with a chance, pulled Fundukian down on the Hope 48. Four plays took the Bulldogs to the Hope 15, but a fumble by Bryce Fauble on the next play was recovered by Dale Schoon and Hope's 20-0 shutout was preserved.

Most of Hope's squad would not recall the team's 1958 trek to Hillsdale, but for co-captains Mack and Blough that emotional night remained vivid. Also, fresh in their minds was the 35-7 drubbing suffered at home in 1959. They hoped to do better at the Dales' Stock Field on Nov. 5, 1960. No one could know that it would be the last gridiron clash between the schools in the 20th century.

After dropping its opener to Northern Michigan (29-6), Coach Waters's team had breezed to six straight victories and was on track for another bowl bid. Taking the opening kickoff, the Dales lost little time in driving to the Hope one-foot line, where Dick Mc Donald punched it in for the score. The point try by Jerry Schaffer failed, and the Hillsdale early lead was 6-0. Following the kickoff, the Dutchmen lost a fumble on their own 38. On third down the Dales drove to the six. It appeared that Hope would survive, but on fourth down Chuck Redding, now a junior, threw a strike to end Bob Hankinson for the touchdown. Automatic Bart Misyiak was called upon for the point, and the Dutchmen found themselves down 13-0.

On their next possession, the Dutchmen finally got it

together. In four plays they drove to the Hillsdale 39. A 24-yard pass from Mack to Jon Schoon, plus a penalty, gave Hope a first down on the seven. On second down, Mack hooked up again with Schoon, this time for the TD. A true kick by Goodrich put the De Vette men back in the game, 13-7. Included in Waters's arsenal was MIAA dash champion Jim Drake. On the ensuing kickoff, Drake took the ball on his own two, broke through the first wave, and left the field behind. His 98-yard touchdown streak, beautiful to behold, made it 20-7 after another Misyiak kick. At this point Hope engineered a second comeback. Kurt Van Genderen intercepted a Redding pass, and the Dutch took over on their own 48. In eight plays they were on the Hillsdale six. Included in the drive was a 19-yard aerial, again from Mack to Schoon. Vanden Burg got two yards to the four and Mack threw once again to Schoon, this time in the end zone. The ball was nearly intercepted, but Schoon, with a great effort, managed to hang on for the score. Goodrich made good on the kick to make it 20-14. The momentum swing continued with another Hope drive. With seconds left in the half, the Dutchmen pushed to the Dale one-yard line. A fourth down play failed and Hope's chance to take the lead was gone.

As the teams took the field for the second half, ominous clouds rolled in from the west and the November sky darkened to an unusual degree. The coaches could not recall such gloom in mid-afternoon. In hindsight, it might have been a portent of things to come, not only for that day, but for the future of MIAA football. Dutchman halftime hopes were dashed early in the third quarter, when Hillsdale ace Howard Rogers broke free on a 51-yard touchdown sprint and Bart Misyiak added the point. With the spread now at 27-14, the Dutch were plagued with more bad luck. On the first play following the kickoff, Hope lost the ball on a fumble. With the ball on the Hope 20, halfback Bill Knapp carried for 11, four, and finally five yards for the TD. Misyiak again converted, and the Dutch trailed by a count of 34-14. The Dales' next drive began on their own 40. Their cause was aided by a series of frustrating Hope penalties that moved the ball to the Hope 28. On the next play, sub quarterback Pete Stoner passed to Tom Ridley in the end zone and the kick by C. Roth made it 41-14. Hope's offense now came to life with a 73-yard drive. Steve Slagh went the final two yards, but a Goodrich kick was wide of the mark. With the score at 41-20, Hillsdale subs flooded the field. Their drive stalled and the Dutchmen took over on their own 35. A Mack-to-Bultman pass was complete, and Bultman made it a 50-yard play by racing all the way to the Dale 15. Three plays later, Mack hit Jon Schoon for a six-yard touchdown play and Goodrich added the point With the score at 41-27 and some time remaining, the Dutchmen were suddenly back in the game. Hillsdale regulars quickly returned to the game, most notably Jim Drake. An ill-advised kickoff reached Drake on the 10, and with great acceleration he again left the field behind. Drake's 90-yard sprint, plus a Roth kick, closed out the scoring at 48-27. A superior Hillsdale team was on its way to yet another MIAA championship, but Hope had made it interesting. The Dales' total offense reached 364 yards to 300 for the Dutchmen, including 190 by Paul Mack on 13 of 21 completions. Holland freshman center Steve Egger had played most of the game after an injury to Jim Vande Wege in the first quarter. Hope's inability to punch one in as the half ended, plus the failure to contain Jim Drake, made the difference in the opinion of Coach De Vette.

A Mom and Dad's Day crowd braved the cold on Nov. 12 for a 1:30 game at Riverview Park against Olivet. Hope was a heavy favorite, but Coach De Vette made a few changes, just in case. Borrowing a page from Army's Red Blaik, the Hope mentor installed Dale Schoon as a "lonesome end" opposite his brother Jon. Blough was moved back to tackle to replace the injured John Hubbard. Coach Stu Parsell's Olivet Comets would make giant strides in 1961, but at this juncture were still an undermannned squad. With scarcely four minutes gone, Vander Woude recovered a Bob Ferguson fumble on the Olivet 20. Six plays later, Visser scored on a three-yard off-tackle run. The kick by Goodrich was not good, but this day it would not be crucial. Quarterback Ferguson continued to have problems with the snap. Still in the first quarter, his second fumble was recovered by Hope tackle Jan Nienhuis on the Comet 18. On Hope's second play, Mack's 15-yard pass bounced off Jon Schoon's chest, but with good hands he retrieved the ball before it touched the ground and the Dutchmen had their second TD. This time the kick by Goodrich was good, making it 13-0. In a third sequence, Ferguson finally completed a pass to Bill Smith, but this time Smith fumbled and linebacker Jim Van Dam recovered on the Olivet 34. Vanden Burg went 16-yards off-tackle on the first play, and Visser covered the remaining 16 with a right end sweep. The Goodrich conversion increased the lead to 20-0. With less than a minute left in the first period, Mack completed a 26-yard touchdown pass to lonesome end Dale Schoon, but the play was nullified by a penalty.

In the second quarter, Olivet moved to the Hope eight but a jarring tackle by Quakkelaar threw the Comets back to the 15 and the drive stalled. The next Hope tally was set up by two passes from Mack to Bultman, first for 42 yards, then 15. A third pass to Jon Schoon put the ball on the four, and a Mack toss to Vander Woude in the flat registered the TD. The Goodrich conversion made it 27-0 at the half.

In the first three minutes of the third quarter, Hope marched 64 yards in eight plays. Fullback Vander Woude went over from the one, and a Goodrich kick make it 34-0 for the only scoring of the period. Early in the fourth quarter, Olivet punted to the Hope 46. Coach De Vette was now limiting his offense to interior line rushing plays. Fullback Slagh was given the ball on five straight plays, the last being a three-yard TD plunge over guard. Goodrich again converted, extending the lead to 41-0. Unable to move the ball, the Comets punted to their own 45. Five plays, plus an interference call, put the ball on the Olivet 14. After a yard loss, third-string fullback Paul Hyink went 15 yards up the middle for Hope's seventh touchdown. Bob Bonnette's point try was blocked to keep the score at 47-0. Olivet's nightmare appeared to be over, but, plagued by Murphy's Law the team would suffer yet a final indignity. The last kickoff was somehow mishandled and slithered into the end zone. It was recovered there by Olivet's Tom Nesbitt, preventing a Hope touchdown, but the resulting safety upped the final score to 49-0.

One mark of a competent coach is how well he comports himself in adversity. Parsell passed this test with flying colors. Refusing to blame or berate his players, he exercised great restraint in dealing with a discouraging afternoon. As Hope coaches we could only admire his example.

Hope's season ended at 5-4 overall and 4-2 in the MIAA, the latter good for a second-place tie with Albion. The Dutchmen led the league in total offense with 2,104 yards to 2,092 for Hillsdale. Mack was the league's leading passer with 58 of 107 for 923 yards. His performance made Hope the top passing team in the conference, somewhat of a departure for a team noted for its ground game. Mack, Truby, Vander Woude, and Bakker were named to the All-MIAA team. To no one's surprise, Mack was voted Hope's most valuable player by his teammates. Hillsdale center Duke Davis was selected as the league's MVP and would later receive the Bosch Award.

In their last regular season game, the Dales of Coach Muddy Waters overwhelmed the Kalamazoo Hornets, 68-12. The pasting was not well received by the coaches and administration of Kalamazoo, who felt that they were being used to enhance Hillsdale's opportunity for a post-season bowl bid. There was murmuring elsewhere around the league, and the unrest would reach a climax a month later.

*   *   *

Hope's cross country program in 1960 was directed by 22-year-old Coach Daryl Siedentop, who had graduated from the college three months earlier. Team members included Chuck Holleman, Randy Menken, John Nyboer, Al Osman, Vern Sterk, Glenn Van Wieren, and Bruce Welmers. Siedentop was well received by his runners, but the season would be a tough initiation for the new coach. The Dutchmen recorded wins over Grand Rapids Junior College and Aquinas, but the only MIAA victory would be over the Alma Scots by a 25-34 margin. In the league meet, a superior Calvin team dominated the competition, taking the first four places to win going away. Hope finished seventh, with Glenn Van Wieren the first Dutchman across the finish line in 26th place. In the overall standings it was Alma, Hope,

DRESSED TO THE HILT

Coach Stu Parsell exchanged pleasantries with Hope coaches Russ De Vette (center) and Gord Brewer (right) before the 1960 Olivet game. Under Parsell's direction the Olivet program would experience an impressive turn-around by 1961. In 1960, coaches' game day attire was in the tradition of Tom Landry. Today's more practical garb would come in due season.

and Olivet tied for sixth place. Waiting in the wings, however, was a transfer student from Western Michigan University. Sheridan Shaffer had been a regular on the Western team, but for a variety of reasons had transferred to Hope in September. He had worked out faithfully with the team, and was a co-captain elect for the 1961 season along with Randy Menken.

The fall sports season concluded on Friday, Nov. 19, with the traditional banquet. Al Vanderbush presided and Coach Ron Schipper, Hope '52, was the featured speaker. Vander Woude was named captain of the 1961 team and, as mentioned, Shaffer and Menken would lead the '61 cross country team.

Earlier in the month, Hillsdale College had accepted an invitation to play a post-season football game in the "Mineral Bowl" in Excelsior Springs, Mo. On Saturday, Nov. 26, the Dales gave a good account of themselves in defeating Iowa State Teachers College, 17-6. The problem with all of this was that Hillsdale's participation violated a recently passed MIAA directive disallowing post-season competition on a team basis. The MIAA Board of Governors felt that such an emphasis was not in the best interest of the league and counter to its philosophy. There were and are arguments on both sides of this position, but the action had been taken and subsequently flaunted by Hillsdale. Follow-up action would be taken in a matter of weeks.

*   *   *

While administrators fumed over the Hillsdale situation, the 1960-61 basketball season got underway. Hope opened the campaign at Valparaiso on Thursday, Dec. 1, with a somewhat surprising performance. Hope's starting five included Bob Reid and Jim Vander Hill at the guards, and Gary Nederveld at center. Ekdal Buys Jr. and Captain Bill Vanderbilt manned the forward positions. The game was played on even terms for several minutes, but the Dutchmen pushed ahead and led 34-21 at the half. Hope continued to play strong defense in the second half. A key factor in the contest was the pressure applied by Reid on Valpo guard Fran Clements. Reid's harassment upset the tempo of the Valparaiso offense, and the Crusaders never really got untracked. At the buzzer it was Hope 69, Valparaiso 58. Jim Vander Hill led the Dutch with a game-high 21 points, Bill Vanderbilt had 13, Ek Buys 11, and Bob Reid 10. Fran Clements was high for the losers with 14, and Jim Zweifel had 13.

A crowd of 2,200 turned out at the Civic Center on Saturday, Dec. 3, to witness Hope's home opener against the Muskies of Lakeland, Wis. It was soon apparent that the charges of Coach Robert Spatt would not be a match for the Dutchmen. Hope's halftime lead of 52-22 told the story as Hope cleared the bench for the eventual 88-54 victory. Freshman Glenn Van Wieren led the way for the winners with 17, Bob Reid and Jim Hulst each had 12, Bill Vanderbilt 11, and Jim Vander Hill 10. Captain Roland Schultz and Fred Petzel had 10 apiece for Lakeland.

Hope got a feel for the Lakeland dilemma three days later. On Tuesday morning, Dec. 6, the Hope team left Grand Rapids by plane for Marquette. The Wildcats of Northern Michigan were well prepared by their coach, Stan Albeck. and jumped out to an early 16-8 lead. It was soon 33-13 and at halftime, 44-27. The Wildcats' Wayne Monson opened the second half with five straight field goals, and the spread was soon at 30. Hope narrowed it to 18, but Northern came back for the final 30-point margin, 89-59. Monson and a 6' 3" Chicago freshman named Thomas each had 21 points for the winners. For Hope it was Reid with 13, Van Wieren with 11, and Vander Hill with 10. The plane ride was enjoyable, but not much else.

On Wednesday, Dec 8, the MIAA presidents met in Lansing, Mich., to deal with the Hillsdale situation. Hope was represented by Vice President John Hollenbach. The action taken was to suspend Hillsdale College for a period of two years as a penalty for violation of the MIAA's ruling of no post-season play in team sports. In a bizarre move, the suspension was made retroactive to September of 1960, thus stripping the Dales of their football championship, duly earned and in the books. Albion and Hope had finished second with 4-1 marks, but neither was anxious to claim a title they had not earned. In an attempt to resolve the quandary, league officials eventually declared the championship "vacant."

Hillsdale delayed its response for one week, then on Thursday, Dec. 15, a news conference was called in Detroit. Speaking for the school, President J. Donald Phillips announced that Hillsdale would drop out of the MIAA rather than submit to the suspension, which he termed "hasty, intemperate, unprecedented, and illegal." Phillips maintained that the MIAA Constitution and By-Laws clearly stated that authority in all league matters rested with the faculty and student representatives who made up the Board of Governors. The presidents' "take over," in the eyes of Phillips, was an illegal act. The presidents, with ultimate responsibility for their institutions, felt justified in their action. Hillsdale officials, including the coaches, believed "our only fault was playing good football."

As might be expected, a period of turmoil and ill feeling ensued. De Gay Ernst, MIAA Judge Advocate for 28 years, had not been consulted nor informed. Understandably upset, he threatened to resign. Hope and Calvin decided to honor their contractual commitments to Hillsdale for the remainder of the 1960-61 school year, but other members terminated their competition with the Dales on the spot. Thus ended the league's 72-year relationship with one of its charter members. Thirty-nine years later it remains an unfortunate episode in MIAA history.

MIAA basketball now continued with one less member. Coach Wayne Hintz brought the Alma Scots to the Civic Center for a game on Friday, Dec. 9. An estimated 1,900 fans were on hand to see the Dutchmen move out to a 13-1 lead. A flurry of fouls slowed the game somewhat, but Hope led at halftime, 41-26. Vanderbilt and Buys were effective on the boards, and Van Wieren started for the first time. Reid came on strong in the second half, and led his team to an impressive 85-61 win with 18 points. Vanderbilt notched 14, Vander Hill had 12, Buys 11, and Nederveld nine. Alma's Dave Peters led all scorers with 24, and Ferris Saxton added 14.

Hope traveled to Olivet for a Monday night game with Olivet on Dec. 12. High-scoring Vander Hill was left at home with the flu, and it remained to be seen who would pick up the slack. The Comets, under new coach Gene Anderson, were an improved ball club as the Dutchmen would soon discover. Hope struggled throughout the first half, and trailed at the intermission, 33-28. The Comets continued to play well and led 48-46 at the 10 minute mark, but a 7-0 run put Hope up 53-52 on Norm Schut's field goal. The Dutchmen lead remained precarious at 63-61 with 40 seconds left when Nederveld connected with a sweeping hook shot to make it 65-61. Mike Foster narrowed it to 65-63 with two free throws, but Van Wieren scored with eight seconds left to wrap up the game at 67-63. Van Wieren was the Hope leader with 17 points. Norm Schut, filling in for the ailing Vander Hill, had a stellar performance with 16, Buys had 10, and Nederveld added eight. Olivet's Dick Groch led all scorers with 26, and Mike Foster had 15. In the course of the game, Buys suffered a severe ankle sprain that involved torn ligaments. He would be lost for much of the season.

An estimated 1,700 fans made it to the Civic Center to see Hope take on the Marauders of Central State on Thursday, Dec. 15. Vanderbilt and Vander Hill were weakened by the flu, but took the floor anyway. Coach De Vette was heartened by the return of Boyink for the first time following a foot fracture. Hope played tough against the "leapers," and led at the half, 35-31. The Ohio team however, was not to be denied. With 11:55 remaining, Jim May's basket put his team up 49-48 and it was downhill the rest of the way for the Dutchmen. The final count was Central State, 86-66. Turner Russell led the winners with 25, Jim May followed with 17, and Sam Mc Cloud had 13. It was Mc Cloud's 15 rebounds that spelled doom for the Dutchmen. Boyink, taking over for Ek Buys, was a bright spot for Hope as he scored 23 to lead his team in his first game back. Bob Reid had 12 and Van Wieren 10 in the losing effort.

A slim Saturday night crowd of 1,600 came to the Civic on the last day of the year for the return contest with Valparaiso. The audience would witness one of the most exciting games of the year. Dr. Paul Meadows, the Valpo coach, was still smarting from the season-opening loss to the Dutchmen. After a hard-fought first half, it was Hope 47-39. The Crusaders battled back in the second half and led by a basket with eight ticks left on the clock. At this point, Bob Reid sank a 12-foot jump shot to send the game into overtime. With 1:31 left in the overtime, Jim Zweifel connected on a long shot to put Valpo up 93-92. As the action continued, Vander Hill blocked a shot by Ralph Mollenhoff and Hope gained possession. The ball was moved down court, where De Vette called time out. The inbound pass went to Boyink, who lofted a shot with two seconds remaining. The shot was not good, but Boyink was fouled by Larry Holle. With the game on the line, the Hope senior dropped in both free throws to give Hope the 94-93 victory. Vanderhill was high for Hope with 24, Boyink had 18, Reid 14, and Van Wieren 12. Valpo's Chuck Kriston led all scorers with 31, Bob Schoon had 21, and Jim Zweifel 17.

A second non-league encounter took the Dutchmen to Wheaton, Ill., on Monday, Jan. 2. The Hope-Wheaton series, going back to the 1958 NCAA tournament, had grown in popularity at both schools, and this night a crowd of 3,000 filled the Centennial Gym. Play was even for much of the first half, but a late period spurt gave the Dutchmen a 40-31 halftime advantage. In the second half, Coach Lee Pfund employed a press, but Reid and others repeatedly broke through for high-percentage shots. After five minutes, the Hope lead was 55-43, after 10 it was 64-50. Hope's zone defense gave the Crusaders trouble and resulted in 31 percent shooting by the home team. Hope, meanwhile, was enjoying its best shooting night of the season at 49 percent, especially Vander Hill, who led his team with 29. Vanderbilt had another good night with 18, Reid followed with 16, Van Wieren had 10 and Boyink nine in the 87-72 victory. Bruce Whipple was high for the home team with 17, and Bill Lindberg scored 11. In a period of three days, the Dutchmen had topped two quality teams, both known as the "Crusaders." A post-game meal on the way home seemed to taste better than usual.

Gregg Arbaugh's Adrian team sported a 5-1 record when it came to the Civic Center on Saturday, Jan. 7. Coach De Vette expected a tough game, and it turned out to be just that. Hope pushed ahead 39-31 at the half, but with 3:28 left in the game it was Hope 78, Adrian 74. Vanderbilt was strong in the closing minutes with a field goal and three-of-three free throws. Bob Reid's long jump shot at the buzzer gave Hope its seventh straight point and the 87-76 win. Vander Hill was on fire with 36 points and Reid had 14, while Vanderbilt and Van Wieren each scored 11. Coach Arbaugh got superb performances from Vince Giles and Ron Schult as each scored 25. Jim Neff followed with 11.

Wednesday, Jan. 11, was the date for the Hope-Calvin match-up at the Grand Rapids Civic auditorium. The usual excitement was whetted by the fact that both teams entered the contest with 3-0 league records. Calvin stood 7-0 overall, while Hope was 7-2. Television station WOOD would air the game, and it would be received as far away as Wisconsin. Any fear of TV hurting the gate was dispelled when 5,000 fans streamed through the doors. Coach Barney Steen's team was loaded, and it would be a Calvin night. After the first field goal exchange, the Knights never trailed. The halftime score showed Calvin with an 11-point advantage, 47-36. Coach Steen's charges enjoyed a good shooting night with 48 percent, but the big difference could be traced to rebounds as the Knights took down 56 to 28 for the Dutchmen. Big Bill Wolterstorff led his team to a decisive 98-79 win with 35 points. Ralph Honderd collected 15, Len Rhoda 14, Carl De Kuiper 13, and Hank De Mots 10. Vander Hill did his part for Hope with 30, Bob Reid and Glenn Van Wieren each had 14, and Bill Vanderbilt 11. The Knights were now in the driver's seat and well on their way to a 20-0 season.

Coach John Williams brought the Hillsdale team to the Civic Center on Saturday, Jan. 14. The fact that it was now a non-league contest made little difference once the game was underway. Hope seemed to have recovered from the Calvin loss, took an early lead, and moved to a 56-36 halftime advantage. Between halves, Hillsdale's Duke Davis was presented the diamond-studded gold football, emblematic of the league's most valuable football player. As usual, Mr. Randall Bosch made the presentation. Davis received more than polite applause as Hope fans had witnessed his performances over a four-year period and appreciated the fine athlete that he was.

As the second half proceeded, attention centered on Vander Hill. He had scored 21 first-half points and the crowd sensed that he was in for a big night. De Vette substituted early and often, and the Dales narrowed the margin considerably, largely on the strength of 20 rebounds by Al Durham. Meanwhile, "Spider" Vander Hill continued his torrid scoring pace. He was fouled with 2:11 remaining. Stepping to the line, he dropped in both shots to bring his total to 40 for the evening. This broke Paul Benes's 1958 Hope record of 39. Vander Hill was then removed from the game to a standing ovation. In the eventual 99-90 Hope victory, Vanderbilt scored 11, VanWieren had 10, and Schut and Nederveld each scored 9. Dave Simmons led Hillsdale with 34, and Cliff Turner had 24.

The Hornets of Kalamazoo came to the Civic on Tuesday, Jan. 17. Due to conflicts with high school games, a meager crowd of but 1,500 showed up. Hope employed a pressing man-for-man defense, while Ray Steffen had his team in a zone for most of the evening. The Dutchmen enjoyed a 34-21 lead at the half, but Kalamazoo center Gordon Rodwan had to be reckoned with as he racked up 36 points and took down 22 rebounds. It would not be enough. Off-setting Rodwan's performance it was Jim Vander Hill with 38 points and Van Wieren with a surprising 19 rebounds in addition to his 12 points. Bob Reid scored 13 and Bill Vanderbilt 11 in the 82-68 Hope win. Sub-guard Chuck Wood got 10 for the losers and Jon Lindenberg nine.

Most of the Hope community crowded around television sets on Friday, Jan. 20, to follow the inauguration in Washington of John F. Kennedy as the 35th president of the United States. His ringing challenge to all Americans would be remembered long after his tragic death in 1963. The 60s were now off and running. It would be a memorable decade in world affairs — and in sport.

The Hope team made its way to Albion on Saturday, Jan. 21, for a game in the Kresge Gymnasium. Coach Cedric Dempsey had decided that if the Britons were to win, a four-man zone with a fifth player harassing Vander Hill at every turn would be needed. The "Spider" was fouled frequently and made eight of 13 free throws, but he was held to an uncharacteristic three field goals. The halftime score favored Albion 39-21, and when the Britons outshot Hope 49 percent to 25 percent the issue was decided. Vanderbilt picked up his fourth foul with eight minutes remaining, and fouled out soon after returning to the game. Dennis Groat, with 22 points, led an Albion team effort that produced the eventual 77-59 victory. Jim Papenfus had 16, Bruce Van Draiss 15, and Captain Dale Terrell 14. Vander Hill's 14 led Hope, while Vanderbilt and Schut each had nine. It was a rewarding win for Coach Dempsey, who had been gracious in defeat one year earlier.

Exam week occupied the Dutchmen until Monday, Jan. 30, when the Olivet Comets came to Holland. A crowd of 1,400 watched the De Vette squad come back with a vengeance. Shooting eyes had been sharpened and the Dutch came through with 45 percent. More remarkable was the fact that the Dutchmen committed only eight fouls in the entire game. Hope's 42-25 halftime lead led to a satisfying 93-51 victory, and there was more good news. Vander Hill was back in form to lead his team with 23. Vanderbilt pulled down 15 rebounds and scored 14. Schut also collected 14 and Buys, returning from a severe ankle injury, put in nine second-half points. Reid scored 11, and Boyink matched Buys with nine. Dick Groch was again high for the Comets with 20, and Dave Mc Kale had 11.

Two days later, the Wheaton Crusaders were in town for a return match before a turnout of 2,400. On this mid-week night the hometown crowd would be disappointed. The Dutchmen missed their first 10 shots and trailed at the half 48-35. Lee Pfund's team was well prepared and shot a blistering 53 percent to 34 percent for the Dutch. The Crusaders also out-rebounded Hope 43-34. Frosh guard Dave Winchell led the Crusaders to an impressive 92-71 victory with 18, while veteran Rog Johnson had 17, Glenn Watts 16, and Jon Lindberg 13. Scrappy Bob Reid was at his best in scoring 18 for the losers. Vander Hill had 13, Nederveld 12, Vanderbilt 11, and Venhuizen 10. Van Wieren missed the game due to an ankle injury.

Hope's game at Alma on Saturday, Feb. 4, was played before a crowd of 100 people in the Phillips Gymnasium. The Alma team had been riddled by the loss of four members rendered ineligible at the end of the semester. Coach Wayne Hintz had been forced to call up three intramural players to fill the ranks, and the Dutchmen were caught somewhat off guard. The remaining Scots had no intention of throwing in the towel, and at halftime Hope's lead was a mere three points, 45-42. The contest remained close throughout most of the second half, but the Dutchmen finally wore down the Scots, cashed in on 22-of-29 free throws, and emerged on top, 92-78. Vander Hill was again the Hope high scorer with 35, and Vanderbilt had a strong game with 20. Reid followed with 14, and Venhuizen added eight. Co-captains Tom Mc Phillips and Dave Peters carried the load for Alma with 36 and 20.

The Hope team always looked forward to a trip into the Chicago area, especially when the opponent was Coach Dick Triptow's Lake Forest team. In the Feb. 4 game the teams were evenly matched, but the Foresters managed a three-point lead at 38-35 as the half ended. The Dutchmen pulled ahead in the second half, but saw their lead slip away in the final 3½ minutes. Hope still managed a one-point lead (67-66) with 30 seconds remaining, but Tom Lewis was fouled, and converted both attempts to put the Foresters up

68-67. Vander Hill's final shot bounced on the rim, then slid off. John Sime was immediately fouled and made both free throws to close out the scoring, Lake Forest 70 - Hope 67. Tom Lewis led all scorers with 30, and Phil Sokody added 17 for Coach Triptow's team. Vander Hill was high for Hope with 27, Schut contributed 12, Reid and Buys each had nine, and Vanderbilt eight.

The long journey to Adrian took place on Saturday, Feb. 11, and the Bulldogs were waiting. They had not had a victory over Hope in five years, and a crowd of 1,500 squeezed into Ridge Gymnasium to see if Gregg Arbaugh's team could break the string. The first half was fairly even, but at intermission it was Adrian 36-25. Hope gained ground in the second half, and came within one at 62-61 on Vander Hill's field goal with two minutes left. The officials ruled that Vander Hill had charged on the play. It was his fifth personal, and the Dutchmen were without their big gun the rest of the way. Hope racked up six more field goals than Adrian, but the Dutchman press resulted in numerous fouls. Adrian's last 12 points were on free throws, and the Bulldogs outscored Hope 28-10 at the line. The 1,500 fans were jubilant as the home team pulled away to a 70-64 win to end the long drought. Vince Giles played a superb game with 21 points, and was backed up by Ray Rolley with 15. Vander Hill scored 18 before fouling out, Vanderbilt had 13, and Venhuizen 11. Van Wieren returned to the lineup after an ankle injury and scored four.

The Hope-Calvin game on Wednesday, Feb. 15, was the first ever to be televised from the Holland Civic Center, and WOOD of Grand Rapids did the honors. The Knights came in at 15-0 on the season and 8-0 in league play, while Hope stood at 11-7 and 6-3. The usual capacity crowd saw the game tied six times in the first half, but Calvin moved to a 46-38 lead at the intermission. It was anybody's game for the first four minutes, of the second half as Hope pulled to within one, 51-50, but Boyink sat down with four fouls and patterns changed. Splendid Hank De Mots scored five field goals in the last seven minutes and the Knights won the battle of the boards 50 to 38. Bill Wolterstorff led the way to a decisive 97-77 Calvin victory with 28 points. He was followed by Holland native Warren Otte with 18. Guard Carl De Kuiper put in 16, and Hank De Mots 14. For Hope once again it was Vander Hill, this time with 29. Vanderbilt's effort produced 16, Reid had 12, and Van Wieren 11. Of the many fine teams coached by Barney Steen, the 1960-61 squad was arguably the most outstanding. With a 20-0 season record, one wonders how they might have fared in national competition. The ban on post-season competition, recently imposed by the MIAA, now reduced the matter to speculation.

Hope's final home game of the season was played on Saturday, Feb. 18, against Albion. The Britons had downed the Dutchmen 77-59 on Jan. 21, when Coach Cedric Dempsey had chosen to employ a "box and chaser" defense to stop Vander Hill. Dempsey had little reason to change tactics, and this time Larry Pratt was assigned as the chaser. More than 2,000 fans watched a super ball game unfold. The first half was especially close. In one stretch the game was tied six times in the space of one minute. As the half concluded, a long jumper by Adolph Grundman put Albion up by one, 39-38. Dempsey's defensive strategy was mildly effective on Vander Hill, but Boyink cashed in on the four-man zone with 22 points. With 10:50 remaining, Hope had managed to pull ahead, 57-54. In a super effort, Vanderbilt took down 21 rebounds. This led to numerous fast breaks and at one point, a 10-0 Hope run. Vander Hill was forced to sit for a while with four fouls at the 11:47 mark, but the Dutchmen were not to be denied and continued to a convincing 85-64 victory. With 3:29 remaining, the regulars were removed to a standing ovation. Boyink's high of 22 was followed by 17 from Vander Hill. Vanderbilt's 21, rebound, 14-point performance was a huge factor in the win, and much appreciated by the crowd. Schut had 11 points, Reid 10, and Van Wieren nine. For the Britons it was Larry Pratt with 17, Dennis Groat with 14, and Dale Terrell with 11.

The Albion game might have been a good way to end the season, but two games remained-and one was with Ray Steffen's crew in the unfriendly confines of Kazoo's Treadway Gym. The game on Wednesday, Feb. 22, was played before 1,100 howling fans. The Hornets had added 6' 4", 220-pound Roger Kramer to their lineup, as well as Bob Morgan, who had regained eligibility at the end of the term. Kramer was a pro football prospect and fit nicely into Steffen's aggressive style of play. Vander Hill scored the game's first basket, then the Dutchmen experienced an eight-minute drought and the Hornets moved to a 34-26 halftime lead. Hope had shot a meager 22 percent in the first 20 minutes. Hope improved its shooting somewhat in the second stanza, but with the score at 58-53 Kazoo went on a 10-0 run and Bob Morgan made nine straight free throws in the last four minutes to ice the victory at 76-63. Morgan and John Mason each collected 19 points, Jon Lindenburg had 16, and Gordon Rodwan 14. Rodwan was also a bear on the boards with 19 rebounds. The Dutch effort was led by Vanderbilt's 13, Boyink had 12, Reid 11, Vander Hill 10, and Van Wieren nine. It was an off-night for Hope, but Ray Steffen's team had earned victory with a superb team effort.

The last hurrah with Hillsdale was played on Saturday, Feb. 25, in the Stock Fieldhouse on the Dales' campus. Hope's league season was over and the game was anticlimatic in some respects, but both teams played hard and well in the opening period. The Dales' Cliff Turner was at his best for John Williams's team with 20 at the intermission, but Vander Hill and Schut were hot for Hope and the Dutch led 56-48 at the buzzer. Turner added 10 more in the second half, but it was the Dutchmen's turn for a strong team performance and in the end it was Hope 101-85. Vander Hill's 23 points led the Dutchmen, and Bill Vanderbilt bowed out with 18. Schut and Venhuizen each scored 12, and Buys had 10. Cliff Turner's game-high 30 points topped the losers, while Dave Simmons and Bob Alheit each scored 16. As the Hope bus traveled home through a winter night there was the satisfaction that comes with ending the season on a positive note. No one could envision that the teams would not meet again in the 20th century.

Hope finished the 1960-61 campaign with a 13-9 overall record. The team's four-year reign as MIAA champion was over, the 8-4 league mark good for a third place tie with Kalamazoo. The All-MIAA team was composed of Carl De Kuiper, Ralph Honderd, and Bill Wolterstorff from champion Calvin; Jim Vander Hill from Hope; and Vince Giles from Adrian. Giles was the choice for MIAA most-valuable.

*   *   *

If there was a bright spot in 1961 spring sports, it centered in the performance of the baseball team. Coach Russ De Vette, in his final season as head mentor, brought his team from a last place finish in '60 to a second place tie with Albion in '61. He was ably assisted by Daryl Siedentop, who would take over in '62. Alma, under Coach Bill Carr, would notch yet another championship, but not before the Dutchmen had beaten them in the first game of a twin bill.

Hope opened the season by splitting a pair of games with Ferris Institute at Riverview Park. Taking the first game 13-9, the Dutchmen scored one in the first, then enjoyed a five-run second which featured a three-run homer by Glenn Van Wieren over the right centerfield fence. In the sixth it was Norm Schut with a two-run homer and, later, a triple by centerfielder Bob Reid. Veteran lefthander Bruce Hoffman was the winning pitcher, with relief from Neil Goodrich.

It was a different story in the nightcap, when the Dutchmen could manage only three hits off Ferris hurler Isette and went down 3-0. Hope loaded the bases in the sixth, but could not push a run across the plate. Sharkey Vander Woude and freshman Jim Van Til were the Hope pitchers, with Ron Vander Molen behind the plate.

On Tuesday, April 25, work began on a new sports complex at Fairbanks Avenue and 12th Street. The property, formerly owned by Holland's founder, Albertus C Van Raalte, tended to be swampy. The work was poorly engineered, leaving coaches the task of draining fields after only moderate rainfall, but they would be pleased to have their own diamond and track under almost any circumstances.

Wednesday, April 26, found Adrian at Riverview for the MIAA opener. Hoffman was at his very best as he twirled a one-hitter with Art Kramer behind the plate. At the end of the regulation seven innings, neither team had scored. Hoffman aided his own cause by leading off the eighth with a single. Bruce Roelofs was inserted to run for Hoffman, and was sacrificed to second by Jim Bultman. Roelofs made it to third on Kramer's ground out. Norm Schut then delivered a single to win the game, 1-0.

The Bulldogs came back to take the second game, 4-2. Goodrich gave up three runs in the first and one more in the fourth. Hope scored one in the sixth on a single by Schut, an error, and a single by Ron Venhuizen. Another run came across in the seventh, when Vander Woude scored on Schut's single. Hope had two on in the seventh, but failed to score. Reed and Guisenger formed the winning battery, while Goodrich, Vander Woude, and Kramer worked for Hope. Each team collected eight hits.

Freshman Jim Van Til was given the starting assignment in the first of two non-league encounters at Hillsdale on Saturday, April 29. Hope got five runs in the first inning and for awhile it appeared that Van Til would survive, but the Hillsdale bats were also alive and Goodrich came on in the third. The Dutch got single runs in succeeding innings, but in the end it was Hillsdale 9-7. Bultman and Schut led the Hope attack with a double and single apiece.

Two veteran footballers squared off against each other in the second game. Duke Davis was an all-conference infielder for the Dales, while a determined Sharkey Vander Woude took the mound for Hope. In the top of the second inning Davis tripled, then scored on an infield out. In Hope's half of the second, Vander Woude returned the favor by stroking a triple to score Ron Venhuizen and Reid. And that is how it ended. Vander Woude bore down the rest of the way and emerged with the 2-1 victory. Each team had five hits in the last game between the schools. As the Hope bus returned to Holland, neither coaches nor players were aware of a bit of irony. Three years earlier in Detroit, Duke Davis and his fiancee had been united in marriage by the Reverend George Vander Hill, a tackle on Bud Hinga's 1941 Hope football team.

It was back to MIAA play on Wednesday, May 3, against Kalamazoo at Riverview Park. In the opener, Hope banged out nine hits and took advantage of seven Kazoo errors to notch a 12-4 victory. Venhuizen went four-for-four including a triple, and batted in five runs. Vandenburg had a double and two singles, and Reid slammed a triple producing three RBI's. Hoffman was forced to retire after two innings due to a blistered finger, but Goodrich was effective in relief to preserve the victory.

In the second game, Hope was off to an early 4-0 lead, but Vander Woude injured his arm sliding into third and Goodrich was called upon for the second time in the afternoon. The Hornets came up with seven big runs in the bottom of the fourth, due largely to a grand slam home run by outfielder John Persons. Hope got two in the fifth and three more in the sixth to take the lead, 9-7. Persons made it interesting in the Kalamazoo sixth with his second homer, this one a solo blast, but the Dutchmen hung on to take the 9-8 win and both ends of the important twin bill. Bultman led

Hope with a triple, a single, and two RBI's.

Coach Morley Fraser brought the Albion Britons to Riverview on Tuesday, May 9, and went home with a double victory. The first game was a pitchers' battle, with each team garnering four hits. Hoffman had nine strikeouts, but Gary Ketrow emerged the winner with a masterful 2-0 shutout. Adolph Grundman homered over the right field fence in the fourth for the first Briton run. A walk and two hits produced the other. In the nightcap, Albion got four runs in the second, one in the third, and two in the fourth. The Dutchmen came back with three in the fifth and one in the seventh, but the effort fell short, leaving Albion on top by a 7-4 count. Young Jim Van Til was plagued by wildness and four walks in a row brought on Goodrich.

Hope bounced back on Thursday, May 11, when the Calvin Knights invaded Riverview. In the first contest, Goodrich hooked up in a pitchers' duel with Calvin's Walt Danke. Hope scored one run in the first, third, and sixth to take the 3-1 victory. Calvin scored one in the seventh to spoil the shutout. In the second game, Vander Woude scattered seven hits while his teammates got one run in the first, one in the third, then three in the seventh to edge the Knights, 5-4. Reid had four hits in the two games and five RBI's.

Saturday, May 13, found the Dutchmen at Alma against the league's first-place team. Hoffman took the mound for Hope, and was at his best with a four-hitter. A combination of 10 hits and several stolen bases produced the 6-2 Hope victory. Reid had a double and two singles, and Bultman three singles to lead the Dutchmen attack. In the second game, the hitting was reversed, with the Scots collecting 10 while limiting the Dutchmen to four. Hope got one run in the fifth, then back-to-back homers in the seventh by Reid and Vander Molen, but the rally fell short and the Scots were the winners, 9-3.

De Vette closed out his career as Hope's baseball coach at Olivet on Wednesday, May 17. In the opener, Hoffman again pitched a four-hitter, but the Comets enjoyed a big fifth inning. Four Hope errors plus a wild pitch resulted in five Olivet runs. The Dutch managed two runs in the first, one in the third, and one more in the sixth but went down by a 5-4 count. Bultman had three of Hope's nine hits.

In the final game of the season, Hope got off to an early lead by scoring single runs in the first, third, and fourth, three in the fifth, and one more in the sixth, but the Comets got to Vander Woude in the seventh, with a seven-run rally that put them in the lead 9-7. In the bottom of the seventh Hope benefited from four straight walks and Vander Molen scored the tying run on Bultman's long fly to right field. Goodrich came on in the eighth and shut the door with two strikeouts. In Hope's half of the extra inning Schut singled, then moved all the way to third on a wild pitch. With two out, Vandenburg came through with a single to win the game, 10-9.

Hope's overall 9-7 record was a satisfying improvement over 1960. The team's 7-5 mark in MIAA play produced a second-place tie with Albion. It would be Hope's best finish in spring sports for 1961. The Dutchmen led the MIAA in team batting with a .264 average. Reid batted .405, second best in the league. He joined shortstop Jim Bultman and pitcher Bruce Hoffman on the All-MIAA Team.

* * *

Coach Doc Green had visions of a tennis championship in 1961 following a stellar performance by his charges in 1960. He would have to wait one more year. The first blow came when it was learned that Norm Hess, number one singles in '60, would be unable to compete due to illness. Adding to Green's woes was Paul Mack's decision to join the golf team. The season opened in Holland on Friday, April 14, with the customary match with Grand Rapids Junior College. Arlyn Lanting, now at number-one singles, was successful in defeating Van Spriell 6-0, 6-2. Kosel (GR) defeated Bob Tigelaar (H) 6-8, 8-6, 6-4, Semeyn (GR) took Stan Vugteveen (H) 6-4, 6-2, Swart (GR) downed freshman Harvery "Bud" Hoffman (H) 6-1, 6-1, Kramer (GR) defeated Dick Elzinga (H) 4-6, 6-3, 6-1, and Bruce Laverman (H) outlasted De Young (GR) 6-2, 4-6, 6-0. In doubles it was Lanting-Tigelaar over Van Spriell-Semeyn 6-1, 6-1, Swart-Kramer taking Stan Vugteveen-Rich Shattuck 11-9, 6-0, and Dick Welch-Neil Paauwe (H) downing Kosel-De Young 0-6, 6-2, 6-2. Despite the 5-4 team setback, Coach Green was encouraged.

The team traveled to Grand Rapids on Thursday, April 20, and came home a 7-2 winner over Aquinas. Hope was off to a fast start as Lanting defeated Lee 6-0, 6-0, Vugteveen (H) bested Truax 6-1, 6-3, Hoffman took a three-setter from Reindel 6-2, 2-6, 9-7, Tigelaar defeated Travis 8-6, 9-7, Rutledge (A) won over Elzinga 6-4, 6-2, and Bob Soodsma (H) defeated Kobza 7-5, 7-5. In doubles, Lanting-Tigelaar defeated Lee-Truax 6-0, 6-2, Vugteveen-Rich Shattuck took Rutledge-Travis 8-6, 6-4, and Dobza-Reindell (A) defeated Tom Hoekstra-Laverman (H) 6-4, 7-5.

Calvin was in charge all the way when the Dutchmen traveled to Grand Rapids on Tuesday, May 2. Oosterhouse (C) took Lanting in 3 sets 6-3, 2-6, 6-3, Dave Vander Hart (C) defeated Hoffman 6-2, 6-3, Vugteveen picked up Hope's only win against Musch 6-3, 6-4, Fleitstra (C) defeated Tigelaar 6-3, 7-5, and Vander Borg (C) won over Shattuck 6-1, 6-0. In doubles, it was Oosterhouse-Vander Hart over Lanting-Tigelaar 10-8, 3-6, 9-7, and Musch-Fleitstra over Vugteveen-Shattuck 6-2, 7-5 for the 6-1 Knight team victory.

On the following day, Hope hosted Olivet and got back on the winning track with a 7-0 shutout. Lanting won over Mitchell 6-0, 6-0, Hoffman defeated Mc Kale 6-0, 6-0, Vugteveen defeated Mc Grath 6-1, 6-2, Tigelaar took Black 6-3, 6-2, and Shattuck got the best of Waldron 6-0, 6-2. In doubles, Lanting-Tigelaar won from Mitchell-Black 6-3,

6-1, and Vugteveen-Shattuck defeated Mc Kale-Mc Grath 6-1, 6-2.

The Alma team that came to Holland on Tuesday, May 9, featured the league's best in George De Vries, who would later win the MIAA singles championship as well as the Stowe Sportsmanship Award. In singles this day, De Vries beat Lanting 6-3, 6-3, Hoffman defeated Lowell 7-5. 12-10, Turner (A) took Vugteveen 8-6, 6-2, Tigelaar defeated Sherman (A) 6-3, 4-6, 6-1, and Tom Hoekstra bested Brintnall (A) 6-3, 6-3. In doubles, it was De Vries-Lowell (A) over Lanting-Tigelaar 8-6, 5-7, 6-3, but Vugteveen-Shattuck prevailed over Sherman-Brintnall 6-3, 6-2 to give Hope the narrow 4-3 team victory.

The Dutchmen faced another strong challenge on Saturday, May 13, with the Albion Britons furnishing the opposition. In singles, it was Lanting over Meitzke 6-1, 6-1, Hoffman over Smith (A) 6-2, 6-1, Vugteveen took Barks 7-5, 6-1, Tigelaar got by Hammond 6-4, 7-9, 6-2, and Hoekstra defeated Mc Kersher 6-4, 6-2. The Britons came back strong in the doubles matches, as Smith-Meitzke defeated Lanting-Hoffman 8-6, 7-9, 6-3, and Barks-Hammond won over Vugteveen-Shattuck (H) 3-6, 8-6, 6-4. Hope's 5-2 team victory made it three in-a-row.

The brief winning streak came to an end in Kalamazoo on Tuesday, May 16. It was a familiar story as the Hornets shut out the Dutchmen 7-0. Loren Campbell defeated Lanting 6-2, 6-3, Bob Heider took Hoffman 6-1, 6-2, Phil Rose defeated Vugteveen 3-6, 6-3, 6-0, Jack Hulst won over Tigelaar 6-3, 6-1, and Ken Elzinga defeated Tom Hoekstra 6-3, 6-4. In doubles, it was Campbell-Rose winners over Lanting-Tigelaar 6-2, 6-2, and Jim Harkema-Jack Hulst over Vugteveen-Rich Shattuck (H) 6-0, 6-0. Hope now stood 3-3 at the end of the MIAA dual meet season. Somewhere along the line, the Dutchmen had dropped a postponed match to Adrian, but there is no record of the details.

The MIAA conference meet was held as usual in Kalamazoo on May 19-20. Kalamazoo was again an easy winner with 37 team points. Adrian, with its best team in years, finished second with 21, Calvin had 19, Hope 16, Albion 10, Alma 7, and Olivet 0. Hope points came in first- and second-flight consolation doubles, when Lanting-Tigelaar defeated George De Vries-Dave Turner of Alma, and Vugteveen-Shattuck won from Bob Sherman-Bruce Brintnall, also from Alma. The Dutchmen had hoped for more than their overall fourth place finish, but prospects were bright for 1962.

*   *   *

Hope track in 1961 was not spectacular, but ups and downs made it interesting. The Dutchmen recorded victories over Alma, Muskegon Community College, Adrian, Olivet, and Kalamazoo. Losses were suffered at the hands of Grand Rapids Junior College, Calvin, Hillsdale, and Albion. A bright light throughout the season was the running of Jim Rozeboom. The senior captain remained unbeaten in all meets in his specialty, the 880-yard run. The opening meet took place on Saturday, April 15, on the cinder track at Houseman Field in Grand Rapids. Grand Rapids Junior College was first in eight events to Hope's seven. In addition to Rozeboom, the Dutchmen got firsts from Tom Van Dyke in the pole vault, Bob Mackay and Bakker in the high jump, Rich Bakker in the high hurdles, and freshman Bob Fialko in both dashes. The meet was decided when JC's Bob Tucker won the low hurdles in the next-to-the-last event. Hope made it close by winning the mile relay with the team of Al Haysom, Van Dyke, Jim Tysse, and Rozeboom. The final score was GRJC 67, Hope 64.

The Hope victories over Alma and Muskegon Community College were accomplished in a triangular meet held in Holland on Friday, April 21. Alma grabbed six first-place finishes to five for the Dutchmen and four for MCC, but the final count showed Hope with 72½ points, Alma with 51, and Muskegon with 37½. The Scots' Dave Peters was a triple winner with firsts in the long jump and both hurdles, while Hope's Bob Fialko placed first in both dashes.

The Hope-Calvin track meet on Saturday, April 29, was held on Calvin's new campus, just off the East Beltline in Grand Rapids. The Knollcrest campus was being constructed on a former golf course and boasted but one new classroom structure at the time, but an unusual running track had also been laid out on the choice piece of property. The running surface consisted of very fine rubber tire filings mixed with hot asphalt, which was packed down with a pavement roller. Calvin's was only the second such track in the country, with the University of Kentucky being the pioneer. Hope's track, now under construction would be similar and available in 1962.

Coach Dave Tuuk had the ideal team to go with his new track. The Knights took nine of 15 firsts, and ended the afternoon with an 81⅓ to 49⅔ victory. Barry Koops, Jim De Bie, and Ray Hommes swept the mile and Koops, Hommis, and Tom Boersma did the same with the two-mile. Sandy Leetsma took first in both dashes. Hope's firsts were recorded by John Brunson in the javelin, Bill Drake in the pole vault, Mike Schrier in the long jump, Bakker in the high hurdles, Rozeboom in the 880, and Ron Te Beest in the low hurdles.

The Adrian Bulldogs were in Holland on Tuesday, May 2, and the Dutchmen got back on the winning track by posting a 92½-38½ victory. Brunson won the javelin, Drake the pole vault, Dave Bach the shot, and Schrier the long jump. Bill Vanderbilt led a sweep of the high jump with a mark of 6' even. Bob MacKay was second, and Bakker third. Rozeboom took on the tough double of the mile and 880, and won both events. Hope got sweeps in both dashes, with Terry Terwilliger and Fialko tying for first in the 100 and Fialko taking the 220. Bakker captured the high hurdles, and

Te Beest the lows. Adrian won the discus, two-mile, and mile relay when the Hope team was disqualified.

Olivet, Hillsdale, and Hope met at the Allegan High School track for a triangular on Saturday, May 6. Hillsdale coach Dan Goldsmith had assembled the Dales' best team in several years, and one can only speculate as to how they might have fared in the league meet. This day the Dutchmen were haunted by erstwhile members of Muddy Waters's football team. Bart Misyiak won the javelin and shot put, and placed third in the discus. Jim Drake won both dashes with ease and ran a leg on the winning mile relay team, while Bob Hankinson took first in the discus. All told, the Dales had 12 of 15 firsts to win the meet with 89⅔ points to 45⅚ for Hope, and 26½ for Olivet. Hope's firsts went to Mackay in the high jump, Bakker in the high hurdles, and Rozeboom in the 880. Olivet failed to win an event, but registered five seconds. Twenty-four years would pass before Hope and Hillsdale would meet again in track and field. Finally, on April 3, 1985, the teams got together on the Dales' new blue and white track. This time Hope came away the winner, 96 to 64.

Tuesday, May 9, found the Dutchmen at Kalamazoo's Angell Field for a dual meet with the Hornets of Coach Swede Thomas. It would be a homecoming for Hope freshman Mike Schrier. Mike's father had been active in athletics at Western State Teachers College in the hometown, and was on hand to watch his son perform. Mike responded with a career-best leap of 21' 6½" to win the long jump, then surprised everyone by taking the 220-yard dash in the fine time of 22.7. He also finished third in the 100-yard dash to complete a Hope sweep in that event. The teams were evenly matched, making it an exciting meet from start to finish. Kalamazoo managed eight first-place finishes to seven for the Dutchmen as Coach Thomas pulled out all the stops. Ray Comeau was a triple winner, taking the 440 and both hurdle races. Big Roger Kramer was first in both the shot and discus, and Russ Shelb took both the mile and two-mile. With one event to go, it was Kalamazoo 63, Hope 62. Hope' mile relay team, with a great anchor leg by Rozeboom, prevailed to give the Dutchmen a 67-63 victory and put the cap on Mike Schrier's day in the sun.

One week later, on Tuesday, May 16, the Dutchmen came back to reality at Albion. Coach Ellkin Isaac's strong team dominated from start to finish in winning 10 of the 15 events. The Britons were convincing in racking up 91⅓ points to just 38⅔ for the Dutchmen. I felt that it would not be in the best interests of Rozeboom to lock horns with Albion's Jim Krieder in the 880 prior to the league meet. Accordingly, he was entered in the mile run and emerged the winner with a time of 4:32.4, a new Hope record. Coach Isaac apparently had similar thoughts as Krieder was moved to the 440, which he won in a time of 52.4. Meanwhile, the Britons' Dick Riley took the 880 in the fine time of 2:00.5. Besides Rozeboom, Hope's other winners were Brunson in the javelin and discus, MacKay in the high jump, and Bakker in the high hurdles.

The MIAA meet in Kalamazoo on Saturday, May 20, saw five league records fall. Three belonged to Calvin as Ralph Honderd put the shot 48' 5", and Barry Koops ran the mile in 4:21.7 and the two-mile in 9:42.2. Adrian's Dave Pfister hurled the discus 141' 8½", and Hope's Rozeboom broke his own 880 record of 1:58.9 with a mark of 1:57.8. Calvin finished first in six events, and scored a total of 66⅔ points to take the title. Albion was second with 49⅔, Kalamazoo third with 44⅔, Hope fourth with 27, Alma fifth with 18, Adrian sixth with 15, and Olivet seventh with four. Hope's lack of first-place potential took its toll, as it did for Albion. Each team garnered but a single gold medal. In contrast, Adrian took three firsts, but did not score otherwise.

* * *

Hope's spring sports slide continued throughout the golf season. Bill Oostenink of the biology department took over as coach when Bill Hilmert took on additional administrative duties. It turned out to be a tough road for a new coach. Team members included Jim Wiersma, Wes Nykamp, Paul Mack, Bob Klaasen, Tom Klaasen, and Ken Biel. The Dutchmen won a practice match from Calvin on April 13, but it was pretty much downhill from that point on. Hope dropped matches to Kalamazoo, Albion, Hillsdale, Olivet, and Grand Rapids Junior College.

The league meet was held at the Kalamazoo Country Club on Friday, May 19, and the host Hornets won as expected with a score of 821. Albion followed with 842, Alma was a surprising third with 856, Olivet totaled 860, Adrian was fifth with 868, Calvin sixth with 876, and Hope last with 891. Albion's Dave Krause took medalist honors with a 36-hole total of 157. Hope's Jim Wiersma ended in a three-way tie for second with a total of 159, perhaps the high point of the Hope season.

* * *

While 60-61 was not a banner year for Hope sports, the Dutchmen had their moments. Highwater marks were reached in football and baseball second-place ties, in basketball victories over Valparaiso and Wheaton, and in Rozeboom's new MIAA record in the 880-yard run. Albion edged Kalamazoo for the All-Sports Trophy with 59 points to 58 for the Hornets. With no championships, Hope was not a contender.

As the school year came to a close, De Gay Ernst announced his retirement. As MIAA Judge Advocate he had served the league well for 28 years. Also of note to Hope followers was the appointment on April 18 of Ron Schipper (Hope '52) as head football coach at Central College in Pella, Iowa. His long tenure at Hope's sister institution would include a national championship in 1974.

CHAPTER 7

STRUGGLES AND COMEBACKS

When the 1961 Hope football players reported for practice on Sept. 1, they could not help but notice the glistening new Van Zoeren Library located on Graves Place. It would serve the college well for the next 27 years. In 1988 it would be replaced by the Van Wylen Library, but would then be refurbished to serve a variety of functions as Van Zoeren Hall.

On the sports scene, Roger Maris stroked home run number 53 enroute to capturing Babe Ruth's longtime record, and "Golden Boy" Paul Hornung led the Green Bay Packers in an exhibition win over the Giants. Coach Russ De Vette welcomed 17 returning lettermen, but the ranks were thin in terms of experienced linemen. Center Jim Vande Wege was the lone regular returning except for end Jon Schoon, who would be late in reporting, being laid low by a virus. Ken Quakkelaar would also be tardy, due to an injury suffered during the summer. Due to an infamous "Pine Creek Spring Party," several players were placed on social probation and rendered ineligible for one semester. All in all, expectations were not quite as high as in the past four or five years.

On the bright side were Captain Sherwood "Sharky" Vander Woude, who would see action at five different positions, and a promising group of freshmen linemen that included Jon Norton, John Stam, Bob Schrotenboer, Andy Zwemer, and Joe Kusak. The departure of Hillsdale left an Oct. 21 gap in the Hope schedule that proved impossible to fill at such a late date. The abbreviated seven-game schedule would turn out to be, in some ways, a blessing in disguise. At season's end, Hope would know how it felt to walk in Olivet's shoes.

Hope and Valparaiso met for the first time in football on Saturday, Sept. 23. The game was played in Valpo's Boucher Bowl in a sea of mud. Rain had persisted for two days and continued throughout the contest. Sixteen punts were exchanged as the teams fought for field position. In the second quarter, the home team's John Knight scored on a 19-yard run up the middle. His kick was good and the Crusaders led 7-0 at the half. The teams slogged back and forth throughout the third quarter with no scoring threats. With seven minutes left in the game, John Knight scored again, this time on a six-yard reverse play. The kick was again good, and the lead moved to 14-0. With four minutes remaining, quarterback Vander Woude attempted a pitchout, but the wet ball slipped out of his hands. Somehow it was deflected to halfback Roger Abel, who found an opening and raced 68 yards to the Valpo two. Freshman Cal Poppink tried a quarterback sneak and got to the one before fullback Paul Hyink took it in for the score. Vander Woude attempted a pass for the point but was sacked, leaving the final score at 14-6.

A night of negatives continued for the Dutchmen. It was soon discovered that both locker rooms had been broken into during the game. An assessment revealed that a total of $420 had been taken from the various lockers, $213 belonging to Hope players. Though not at fault himself, Athletics Director Dick Koenig felt the host school was responsible. Within a few days I received a check from Koenig reimbursing the players who had incurred a loss.

Hope's home opener matched the Dutchmen against Wheaton in a 7:30 game on Sept. 30. The night contest would be the first meeting between the schools in football. The Crusaders were coached by Jack Swartz, who had taken over from veteran coach Harvey Chrouser, now devoting full time to the athletic directorship. Prominent in the Wheaton lineup were diminutive quarterback Dave Iha, known as "Hawaiian Eye," and senior co-captain guard George Kraft. Six years later Kraft would join the Hope coaching staff for a long and distinguished tenure.

Wheaton came into the game with a 2-0 record, having downed Northern Illinois 7-2 and Valparaiso 35-13. The hometown crowd of 2,500 got a look at the Dutchmen's new jerseys, with numbers on the shoulders plus numbers on their helmets for the first time. The Crusaders pushed across their first score with 1:26 remaining in the first quarter on a pass from the 5' 7" Iha to end Rodney Johnson. Tom Jarman's kick was wide, and the Wheaton lead was 6-0. Hope's defense held for most of the second period, but things fell apart near the end of the quarter. With 3:36 remaining, fullback Albie Harris climaxed an 82-yard drive with a right end sweep to paydirt. This time Jarman's kick was true, extending the lead to 13-0. Following the kickoff, Don Close intercepted a Hope pass to give the Crusaders another chance in the final seconds. With one second remaining, Albie Harris repeated his right end sweep for the TD and Jarman converted. The 20-0 lead at halftime loomed large for the frustrated Dutchmen.

Hope closed the door in the second half, but the damage had been done. The Dutch regained their toughness on defense, holding the explosive Crusaders scoreless throughout the second half, but Wheaton's defense proved even tougher. Hope's lone offensive threat came in the third quarter, when the team drove to the visitors' one-yard line. Failure to punch in the ball left the Dutchmen victims of a 20-0 shutout.

A crowd of 4,500 filled the stands at Riverview Park on Saturday, Oct. 7, for Hope's homecoming game with Albion. Halftime festivities featured Roy Shaberg's marching band and Homecoming Queen Barbara Ver Meer, a senior from Hudsonville. Albion drew first blood when halfback J. B Elzy skirted left end with one second left in the first quarter. The kick attempt by Paul Willits was not good. In the second quarter, freshman Bob Schrotenboer recovered a Briton fumble on the Albion 15. In an effort to produce more offense, Coach De Vette had moved Vander Woude to left half and inserted Jim Bultman at quarterback. The Dutch now moved in six plays to the Albion two. It was a Bultman pass to end Dale Schoon in the end zone that put Hope back in the ballgame. The kick by Neil Goodrich split the uprights, and Hope had its first lead of the season at 7-6. Later in the period it was again Schrotenboer, combining with Vander Woude to recover a J. B. Elzy fumble on the Albion 47. In seven plays Hope was home with a second TD. The scoring play came on a 15-yard pass from Bultman to Vander Woude with 1:54 left in the half. The conversion by Goodrich gave Hope a 14-6 halftime lead and De Vette's move seemed to be paying off.

Momentum shifted to the Britons in the second half as they mounted a 65-yard drive that culminated in a two-yard

SHERWOOD "SHARKEY" VANDER WOUDE MIAA CO-MOST VALUABLE PLAYER — 1961
Vander Woude saw action at all four backfield positions and was the league's outstanding linebacker. Above (23) he gains ground against Albion.

plunge off-tackle by co-captain Ray Hoag. A run attempt by Frank Gould failed, and Hope still led 14-12 with 9:29 left in the third. A Hope drive in the fourth quarter was halted on the Albion 20, and Coach Fraser's team took over the game. In 17 plays against a tiring Hope defense, the Britons crossed the goal line with J. B. Elzy going the final two yards. Darwin Christianson made the two-point conversion on a pitchout from Gould, and Albion was in the lead 20-14. Hope managed one rushing first down following the kickoff but was forced to punt, giving the Britons possession on their own 20. Vander Woude, who played at middle linebacker on defense, was now on the bench with an injury. It made a difference. Hoag broke loose for a 52-yard run before he was pulled down by Bultman on the Hope 11. Elzy made it to the two, and Hoag went in for the final score of the game. Hope's best effort had fallen short, and the Britons went home with a hard-earned 26-14 victory.

Coach Stu Parsell's recruiting efforts at Olivet had finally paid off, and the Comets would enjoy their best season in many years. Hope's night game at Olivet on Saturday, Oct. 14, was actually played on the field at Charlotte High School in an attempt to encourage greater community support. A crowd of 1,500 responded. After a scoreless first quarter, the Comets took advantage of a short Hope punt and marched 36 yards to score. The touchdown was set up by a six-yard pass from quarterback Dave Cutler to freshman wide receiver Dominic Livedoti. Fullback Chuck Cilibraise went the final two yards, and Olivet was on the board 7-0 following Dan Dinoff's conversion.

Hope freshman Jim Bekkering recovered an Olivet fumble late in the first half, which led to the Dutchmen's only score of the night. With 1:58 remaining, a Bultman-to-Shuck pass put the ball on the Olivet 17. In the scramble, Shuck lost both of his low cut shoes. After a two-yard gain by Bultman, Jon Schoon leaped high to take a Bultman pass

THE 1961 HOPE FOOTBALL SQUAD THE LONGEST SEASON — 0-7, LAST PLACE MIAA

First Row L. to R.: Keith De Zwaan, Fred Van Tatenhove, Jim Bekkering, Gary Teall, Roger Abel, Neil Goodrich, Dick Buckley, Bob Serum, Cal Looman, Paul Hyink, Frank Vanderhoff. **Middle Row:** Jim Shuck, Steve Slagh, Jon Schoon, Bob Stranyak, Kurt Van Genderen, Bill Byrne, Jim Vande Wege, Sherwood "Sharkey" Vander Woude, Ralph Jackson, Ken Quakkelaar, Dale Schoon, Jim Bultman, Jerry Nieusma. **Top Row:** Bill Hill, John Norton, John Stam, Jim Burnett, John Van Dam, Dave Nykerk, Cal Poppink, Andy Zwemer, Doug Diggle, Paul Teusink, Dave Oakley, Joe Kusak, Russ Kleinheksel, Fred Shantholtzer, John Meengs, Roger Van Noord, Pete Van Lierop. **Missing from picture:** Bob Allen, Bob Bonnette, Bob Schrotenboer.

on the two. Steve Slagh bucked to the one, and with 32 seconds remaining Bultman again passed to Schoon, this time for the touchdown. On the two-point try, Schoon took Bultman's pass in the corner of the end zone and Hope went to the locker room with a narrow 8-7 lead.

Cutler was injured early in the game and did not return. This left Coach Parsell with some concern as to whether or not freshman Forest Bone could carry the load. In the third quarter, Charley Brown intercepted a Hope pass on his own 45 and returned it to the Hope 46. Halfback Tom Nesbitt then broke free on a 43-yard run to the Hope three. On a subsequent play, freshman Rog Reinhardt dove off-tackle for one yard and the TD. Dinoff's run for two points failed, but the Comets had regained the lead 13-8. Later in the quarter, pressure on Ken Quakkelaar caused his punt to go straight up in the air. Upon landing it took a reverse bounce to the Hope 38. Thirteen plays later, Nesbitt went the final yard for his second touchdown of the night. Dinoff's kick made it 20-8 with 10:52 remaining. The Olivet defense protected its lead the rest of the way to avenge many lopsided Hope wins in years past. As we congratulated a jubilant Coach Parsell, he could only say, "It really feels good!"

With an open date on Oct. 21, Hope had two weeks to prepare for the Alma game, but four Dutchmen would be out with injuries. Approximately 750 fans turned out at Bahlke Field for the afternoon game on Oct. 28. The Dutchmen's first drive began on their own 45. A series of short runs by Shuck, Slagh, Bill Hill, Bultman, and Paul Hyink resulted in successive first downs. In 13 plays the Dutchmen were at the one, and Shuck went in for the score. The kick by Goodrich made it 7-0 with 5:17 left in the first quarter. In the second quarter, Hope took possession on the Alma 43 and in nine plays moved to the nine. Included were Bultman passes to Hill and Jerry Nieusma plus a 16-yard run by Hill. At this point the Alma defenders chased Vander Woude back to the 26, where he was sacked. Coach De Vette elected to go for the field goal, and Neil Goodrich came through. Once again Hope had a halftime lead, this time at 10-0.

But second half misfortunes continued to haunt the Dutchmen. With 8:54 left in the third quarter, the Dutchmen fumbled on their own 28 and Alma tackle Carroll Ledy recovered. It would take the Scots 14 plays to reach the end zone, but a 13-yard pass from Van Mulligan to end Art Krawczyk helped and Lou Economou dove the final yard for the TD. Terry Ebright's pass for two points failed, and Hope still held a 10-6 lead. It appeared that Hope would make it this time as the clock ticked down, but near the end of the game Hope was forced to punt. The Scots broke through on kicker Quakkelaar, who managed to sidestep the rushers. But instead of kicking the ball, if only for a short distance, Quakkelaar elected to run. He was downed on the Hope 20. Five plays later, with 1:30 remaining in the game, Van Mulligan went two yards over guard for the score. Ebright's pass to Krawczyk was good for the two-point conversion, making the final score Alma 14, Hope 10. Hope's toughest loss to date made for a quiet trip home.

Despite Hope's record, a crowd of 3,000 turned out at Riverview Park for the Mom and Dads Day game on Saturday, Nov. 4. Coach Les Leggett's Adrian Bulldogs were also struggling as the two "have nots" squared off. In the course of the afternoon the Dutchmen would fumble six times, losing four. The Dutchmen fumbled first on their own 13, and Jim Godfrey recovered. Bryce Fauble went one yard for the score, and Dale Bachman kicked the point with 10:53 remaining in the period. Still in the first quarter, Larry Sanholtz intercepted a Hope pass at midfield and returned it to the Dutch 27. A long pass from Jack Wren to John Fundukian was good for a second Bulldog score. Bryce Fauble's run for two points failed, but the Adrian lead was now 13-0 with 7:33 left in the quarter.

It was Hope's turn following the kickoff. The determined Dutchmen marched 70 yards before Vander Woude, on the final carry, fumbled the ball into the end zone, where it was recovered by Jon Schoon for the touchdown. The conversion by Goodrich was good to make it 13-7. That would be the halftime margin.

Another Hope turnover set up Adrian's third TD. With Hope on the move, John Fundukian picked off a Hope pass on the Adrian 10 and returned it to the 41. Bryce Fauble then broke through off-tackle and rambled 59 yards to score. His run for two points again was short, but the Hope deficit now was 19-7. A similar scenario ensued. Another sustained drive took the Dutchmen deep into Bulldog territory, but on the fourth play of the drive Adrian's Sanholtz intercepted a Hope pass on the five. The teams then exchanged fumbles before Bruce Norton hit John Fundukian with a 41-yard pass play all the way to the Hope 34. It was Fauble again, this time off-tackle for 34 yards and his third score of the afternoon. Extra points were another matter, as Fauble failed for the third time to score two. The visitors now enjoyed a 25-7 bulge with 13:16 left in the game.

Freshman Cal Poppink was now inserted at quarterback. Beginning on the Hope 29, Poppink completed four straight passes, the last to end Dale Schoon on the Adrian four. Two plays later, Gary Teall went into the end zone with 8:09 left in the game. A Goodrich conversion narrowed the margin to 25-14. Another drive was not in the books, and as time slipped away the battered Dutchmen were saddled with their sixth straight defeat. The combination of costly turnovers and a great day by Fauble and Fundukian had been too much to overcome.

Hope wound up a dismal season on Armistice Day at Kalamazoo's Angell Field. Vander Woude and Jon Schoon had sustained serious injuries, and did not dress for the game. Bultman's injury also limited his playing time. The Hornets of Rolla Anderson were on their way up with quar-

MIAA MVP

Sherwood "Sharkey" Vander Woude of Randolph, Wisconsin, receives the MIAA Most Valuable Football Player Award from Holland industrialist Randall Bosch. - February 10, 1962.

terback Jim Harkema at he helm. Midway in the first period, Don Le Duc scored on a pitchout from Harkema and Jim Smith kicked the point for the early 7-0 lead. With 1:10 left in the quarter, Harkema hit end John Persons with a five-yard pass for the Hornets' second TD. Smith's conversion made it 14-0.

The Dutchmen, missing several key players, did not throw in the towel. With 9:46 left in the half, Hope got off a drive that culminated in a 29-yard pass from Poppink to Dale Schoon for a touchdown. Goodrich, with an injured leg, attempted the point anyway, but missed, leaving the score at 14-6. In the next exchange, a Kalamazoo punt was fumbled on the Hope 10 and rolled into the end zone. The Hornets' Eglis Lode was there to recover, and with Jim Smith's conversion the score moved to 21-6 at the half.

Kalamazoo's fourth touchdown came on a pass from Harkema to end Dan Pell with 10:53 left in the third quarter. Smith's fourth conversion made it 28-6. The Dutchmen came back to score with a seven-play drive that included runs of 15 yards by Bekkering, 19 by Shuck, and 11 by Poppink. Bultman then entered the game and threw a four-yard TD pass to Dale Schoon. Bultman's pass to Nieusma for two points fell incomplete, but the score moved to 28-12. The Dutch defense was now out of gas and, with 2:44 remaining in the period, Eglis Lodi climaxed another Hornet drive with a two-yard plunge into the end zone. Harkema added insult to injury by passing successfully to Sibilsky for two points to make it 36-12.

Jim Shuck took the kickoff and broke free with a 43-yard run all the way to the Kazoo 21. Hope then fumbled the ball away and the Hornets were on the march once more. Jim Young finished off the 79-yard drive with a five-yard plunge off-tackle. Jim Smith's fifth kick was not good, leaving the final score, 42-12. With a negative end to a negative season, the Dutchmen limped back to Holland. One positive remained. Vander Woude, who saw limited action in two games and missed the finale due to injury, was still named the league's most valuable player along with guard Joe Shurmur of Albion. He was also Hope's lone representative on the All-MIAA team.

* * *

Coach Daryl Siedentop's 1961 cross country team moved up a notch from Hope's 1960 fifth place finish. This was accomplished largely through the efforts of senior captain Sheridan Shaffer, a transfer from Western Michigan University. Other team members were Dirck De Velder, Al Hoffman, Mike Laughlin, Dave Maris, Vern Sterk, Jan Nyboer, Al Osman, and Bruce Welmers. After a tough 28-29 loss to Grand Rapids Junior College, Hope took the measure of Aquinas by a 23-33 score, but dropped a 19-44 decision to a strong Calvin team. In the Calvin meet, the Knights' Ray Hommes edged Shaffer for first place. It would be Shaffer's only loss of the season.

In the Albion meet, Shaffer had some help as Hoffman finished third and De Velder fifth, but the Britons took places six through 10 to win the meet 27-32. Hope was a 21-37 winner at Olivet on Oct. 14, but in a first-time meeting with Valparaiso on Oct. 24 the Dutchmen were beaten 20-40 on Valpo's home course. Two days later at Alma, Hope was an 18-43 winner, and on Nov. 4 in Holland the Dutchmen took Adrian 16-43. On Nov. 11 in Kalamazoo, Coach Swede Thomas's team proved too strong, and despite Shaffer's first place finish the Hornets claimed the victory, 20-42. In the Nov. 14 league meet, also in Kalamazoo, Shaffer was the individual winner, avenging his earlier loss to Calvin's Hommes, who finished second. It was but the third time in the sport's history that a Hope runner had captured the MIAA championship. Joe Esther had been the winner in 1932 and Bob Roos in 1951. Calvin won the team championship in convincing style, while Hope ended its improved season in fourth place.

As the book was closed on fall sports, two Hopeites were in the news. The leadership of Jim Bultman was recognized when he was named captain of the 1962 football team, and Ron Schipper, Hope '52, posted a fine 6-3 record in the first of many outstanding seasons as coach of the Central College football team in Pella, Iowa.

* * *

The 1961-62 Hope basketball season opened without the services of co-captain Bob Reid. During the previous spring, several athletes were involved in off-campus in activity "not in keeping" with established regulations. The resulting disciplinary action rendered them ineligible for a period of one semester. Numbered among the group was the playmaker from Tonawanda, N.Y. His absence would be keenly felt, but Coach De Vette proceeded with a lineup that

MIAA CHAMPION

Holland native Sheridan "Sherri" Shaffer was captain of the 1961 cross country team. He also captured the MIAA individual championship.

included co-captain Ek Buys, Jim Vander Hill, Gary Nederveld, Glenn Van Wieren, and Ron Venhuizen.

The season opened with a two-day trip into the Chicago and Wisconsin area. On Friday, Dec. 1, the team was in River Forest, Ill., to meet the Concordia Cougars of Coach Don Spitz. The teams were probably as evenly matched as two teams could be. The count was 42-42 at halftime, both teams having hot hands at 54 percent. The contest remained a nail-biter throughout the second half, but, with one minute remaining, Concordia had inched ahead 73-70. Two free throws by Nederveld put Hope within one but the Cougars followed with a field goal to go up 75-72. With 30 seconds left, the Dutchmen sank a basket to make it 75-74, but the home team successfully stalled out the remaining seconds and Hope was saddled with the one-point loss. Al Herman led the winners with a game-high 20 points, and Myron Schumacher had 16. Hope got even scoring as Vander Hill led with 19, Venhuizen had 17, Buys 13, and Van Wieren 12.

The Hope team moved on to Waukesha, Wis., for a Saturday night game with Carroll College. The Dutchmen were pleased to find that the official timer for the game would be Howard Becksfort, Hope Class of '41. Howie had been a member of Bud Hinga's 1940 MIAA championship team and was now a math teacher on the Carroll College faculty. For the second consecutive night, Hope would be playing on white, wooden backboards. Budgets were tight, and neither Concordia nor Carroll had as yet converted to the universally accepted glass boards. In another close game, the Dutchmen found themselves trailing 35-30 at halftime. The contest went down to the wire. Hope had managed a 70-69 lead with 32 seconds remaining, but with 20 ticks left Hope committed a foul and the Pioneers' Grant dropped in the free throw to tie the game. The Dutchmen were resigned to an overtime period, but with four seconds remaining Hope was again called for a foul. This time Fuller came through with the charity toss to win the game, 71-70. Grant scored 19 for the winners, Fuller followed with 18, Reichert had 16, and Budde 14 to complete the team effort. For Hope it was Vander Hill leading all scorers with 31, Van Wieren had 13, and Buys 10.

The home opener for Hope was played on Dec. 6 against the Wheaton Crusaders. A small Wednesday night crowd of 1,300 was on hand at the Civic hoping to see the Dutchmen break into the win column. Coach Lee Pfund's team stood 2-0 on the young season with wins over Lake Forest and Macalester. The visitors were strong in the early going and led 42-37 at the half. With seven minutes gone in the second half, Wheaton was still on top, 55-50. At this point Hope went on an 8-0 run and led 58-55 at the 10-minute mark. Fouls and free throws would make the difference in the contest. In a zone defense most of the time, Hope committed but six fouls in the entire game. Meanwhile, the Crusaders were whistled 18 times and the Dutchmen cashed in on 21 of 26 at the line. Each team had 29 field goals, with Hope shooting 42 percent to 35 percent for Wheaton. The Crusaders' last threat came at 4:37 when they narrowed Hope's lead to one point, 64-63. A Dutchmen spurt took them to 75-63 with 11 seconds left, and four more points gave Hope the hard-earned 79-63 victory. Vander Hill and Van Wieren led the way, each with 21 points. Buys followed with 16, Nederveld had 12, and Venhuizen nine. Rog Johnson was the leader for Wheaton with 20, Cal Pederson had 14, and Bill Lindberg 10.

Coach De Vette's 11-man squad opened the MIAA season against Adrian on Saturday, Dec. 9. The team that Coach Gregg Arbaugh brought to the Civic Center had suffered two severe blows. Vince Giles, the league's most valuable player in 1961, had enlisted in the Army, while Jim Neff, another stalwart, had decided not to play. Approximately 1,500 fans watched as the scrappy Bulldogs kept it close throughout the first half and trailed by only five at the intermission, 41-36. The Dutchmen moved out in the second half to leads of 58-48 after six minutes, and 70-54 at the 10-minute mark. As time ran out, it was Hope 93-74. Vander Hill was again high with 31 and Van Wieren had a fine night with 24. Buys followed with 15, and Te Beest scored 10 when Nederveld got into foul trouble. Don Harned led the Bulldogs with 22, while Ron Schult and John Johnson each had 16.

Hope traveled to Olivet on Wednesday, Dec. 13, to meet the Comets in Mc Kay Gymnasium Hope's height advantage would prove too much for the home team to overcome. Nederveld was impressive with 18 rebounds, and captain Buys pulled down 10. Hope's 47-20 lead at halftime left little doubt as to the outcome. Jim Vander Hill scored 27 points, but picked up four fouls and was taken out with 11 minutes left in the game. Following Vander Hill in scoring, it was Nederveld with 16, Buys 13, and Van Wieren 11 in the 81-54 Hope win. Ed Donaldson led the Comets with 14, and high-scoring Dick Groch was held to 13.

The following afternoon, Dec. 14, De Vette's squad traveled to Valparaiso and ran into a meat grinder. The Valpo team was coming off an impressive victory over Western Michigan University, and in no way resembled Hope's opponent of the night before. The 3-0 Crusaders gained a 49-37 lead at halftime and never trailed in the game. At the final buzzer, Valparaiso had established a new scoring record with 106 points to 89 for Hope. Captain Fran Clements led the way with 29 points, and John Lichtenberger was not far behind with 27. Vander Hill was again the leader for Hope with 26 before fouling out with eight minutes remaining. Nederveld scored 20 points, including 12 of 16 free throws, Buys had 12, and Venhuizen 10. The Dutchmen spent the night in Fort Wayne before traveling to Wilberforce, Ohio, for a Friday game with Central State.

The Dutchmen, now playing their third game in three nights, were sluggish in the first half and trailed the Marauders 53-34 at the intermission. In the second half it was a different story as Hope, with the hot hand, outscored Central 51 to 41. The damage, however, had been done and Coach Bill Lucas team pleased the hometown crowd with the eventual 94-85 win. Jerry Cummings was high for the winners with 23, and Bill Hutson completed the one-two punch with 22. Freshman Ted Day added 16. Despite the defeat, Hope could feel good about several performances in the comeback. Vander Hill had another one of his nights with 34 points, including 12-of-12 from the free throw line, Van Wieren was back in form with 19 points, and Nederveld pulled down 18 rebounds to go with his 11 points.

Since most of the players from Coach De Vette's championship teams of 1957, 1958, 1959, and 1960 were still in the general area, it was decided to make a varsity-alumni game one of the regular season contests. Accordingly, fans were informed that they would have one more look at their favorites of the 1950s on Saturday, Dec. 30. JV Coach Daryl Siedentop would be at the helm as player-coach of the alumni team, which struck a note of nostalgia in the large crowd which attended. Included were brothers Ray and Bob Ritsema, Paul Benes, Warren Vander Hill, Wayne Vriesman, Whitey Beernink, Tiger Teusink, Jun Buursma, Roland Schut, and Jack Kempker. Bill Vanderbilt, Don Boyink, and Norm Schut, the most recent graduates, volunteered to join early 50s alums in the pre-lim game against Hope's JV's. The hapless JV's came out on the short end of an 80-57 score, but a good time was had by all. In the varsity contest, one of the attractions for the 1,700 fans was the prospect of brothers Jim and Warren Vander Hill playing against each other. Somewhat surprisingly, the varsity held its own throughout the first half and actually led at the intermission, 45-44. In the end, however, Benes had collected 20 rebounds and Ritsema 15 as of old, and the Alums went on to post an 88-80 victory. It was never a runaway, as the varsity narrowed the gap to 57-55 at one point. Paul Benes, still in great shape, led the winners with 26, Warren Vander Hill had 20, Teusink 12, and Ritsema 11. For the varsity, Vander Hill and Van Wieren were outstanding with 21 each. Buys scored 15 and Nederveld 11. In the course of the game, Nederveld took a knee in the thigh from Paul Benes. The inadvertent contact at first seemed of little consequence, but a hemorrage resulted and Nederveld had to be hospitalized. He would miss several games at a point when he appeared to be on top of his game.

Two days later, on New Year's Day evening, Hope entertained the Taylor Trojans in a non-league game at the Civic. Taylor's Don Odle had coached the Chinese Nationalist basketball team in the 1960 Olympic Games and had convinced one of its stars, Billy Hwang, to enroll at Taylor. In another close contest, the Trojans were able to pull ahead 44-40 at the half despite Vander Hill's 22 points. The game was tied 13 times, the last at 80-80 with 1:24 left. At this point, Ray Durham dropped in two free throws. A field goal and two more charities with three seconds remaining gave Taylor an 86-82 victory. Hwang led Coach Odle's team with 23, and Durham had 22. The big news for the Dutchmen was a new Hope scoring record of 43 points by Vander Hill. Included were 13 of 13 free throws. Buys and Venhuizen each scored 10, and Van Wieren had nine. Te Beest, subbing for the injured Nederveld, played a creditable game on the boards and scored five points.

Hope's next scheduled game was with Albion on Saturday, Jan. 6, but in mid-afternoon of that day I received a phone call from Albion Athletics Director Elkin Isaac. He was calling from a farmhouse six miles outside of Albion with the bad news that the Britons' bus had broken down. Considerable delay would be involved in securing a replacement, which would have to come from Kalamazoo over icy roads. It was finally agreed to postpone the game to Wednesday, Jan. 17.

EKDAL J. BUYS JR.
MIAA Most Valuable Player — 1961-62

The general let-down to all concerned could not be avoided, and, fortunately, was not of long duration. The Scots of Alma arrived more than an hour late on Monday, Jan. 8, after battling snow all the way. With a delayed start, both teams were sluggish in the early going. The Scots never quite recovered and trailed 41-25 at the half. With a score of 59-36 at the 10-minute mark, Hope subs got their chance enroute to a 75-54 Dutchman win. Jim Vander Hill's 27 points included three-of-three free free throws to extend his streak to 28 straight. Ron Venhuizen added 12, while Buys and Van Wieren each had 10. Don Phillippi led the Scots with 15, and Bill Reese had 13. Albion had done Hope a huge favor by upsetting Calvin 84-68 on the previous Thursday, but the season was still young and there would be more bumps along the road.

Wednesday, Jan. 10, would be a down day for the Dutchmen. Smitten with the flu, Coach De Vette spent most of the day in bed. Against the better judgment of wife Doris, he managed to join his team for their trip to the Grand Rapids Civic Auditorium and another go with the Calvin Knights. Gathered were 5,100 howling fans, who were quieted somewhat when Hope moved ahead 36-31 at the half. Van Wieren fouled out with 6:34 remaining, and Te Beest was gone with 3:11 left. The Knights took the lead with

THE 1961-62 HOPE COLLEGE BASKETBALL TEAM
MIAA CO-CHAMPIONS WITH KALAMAZOO

Front Row L. to R.: Ron TeBeest, Ron Venhuizen, Gary Nederveld, Co-Captain Ek Buys, Co-Captain Bob Reid, Glenn Van Wieren, Jim Vander Hill. **Standing:** Manager Bob Kreunen, Art Kramer, Jim Hesslink, Gailerd "Gig" Korver, Curt Haaksma, Dale Scheerhorn, Jerry Hesslink, Coach Russ De Vette.

3:29 remaining on Len Rhoda's jump shot to make it 67-65. The undermanned Dutchmen could not regain the lead, and went down by a final score of 81-70. Hank De Mots led Calvin with 20, Warren Otte had 18 and Carl De Kuiper 15, while Ken Fletcher and Rich Rusthoven helped the Knights to a 57-33 advantage in rebounds. Ron Te Beest had his best game to date in leading his team with 15 points. Jim Vander Hill had 14, Ek Buys 12, and Glenn Van Wieren 11.

Saturday, Jan. 13, found the Dutchmen in Kalamazoo's Treadway Gym. About half of the 1,000 fans were Hope rooters, and their shouts of encouragement echoed off the walls of the ancient structure. Hope's 33-26 halftime lead was gradually diminished as the game wound down. Bob Morgan's long jumper from the corner tied the game at 56 with 4:21 remaining. Kazoo then inched ahead, but with 11:05 left Venhuizen hit a field goal to make it K 61, Hope 58. Two free throws by Vander Hill with 59 seconds left made it 61-60. Kalamazoo was fouled, but missed the free throw. Buys took the rebound and called timeout. Venhuizen fired the last shot with seven seconds remaining, but did not connect. The one-point loss was a discouraging blow, especially on the heels of the recent defeat at the hands of Calvin. Gordon Rodwan was high for Ray Steffen's team with 18, and Holland native Jack Hulst followed with 17. Buys had his best game of the season, combining strong rebounding with 23 points to lead his team. Te Beest scored 13, Vander Hill 12, and Van Wieren 10.

Hope's postponed game with Albion was played in the Civic Center on Wednesday, Jan. 17, and the Dutchmen were back on track. Following an eight-point lead of 49-41 at the intermission, De Vette's team exploded in the second half. The man of the hour again was forward Ek Buys. Strong on both boards, he put down 33 points to lead all scorers in the decisive 92-72 victory. With 1:33 remaining, he was removed to a standing ovation. Vander Hill was back in form with 21, Van Wieren tallied 15, Venhuizen 11, and Te Beest 10. Dennis Groat scored 27 for Albion, and Jim Papenfus had 14.

Hope's troubled first semester was finally over. With semester exams behind them, the Dutchmen took on Lake Forest in the Civic on Saturday, Jan. 27. The game marked the return of Co-Captain Reid and the injured Nederveld.

The Hope team was noticeably rusty after the 10-day layoff, but managed a 39-31 lead at halftime. The margin was increased in the next 10 minutes, and with 9:25 remaining the score stood at a comfortable 65-45. As the Dutchmen "rested on the oars," the Foresters roared back to within two. With one minute left, it was Hope 76-74. Reid then came through with a field goal and Buys made good on two free throws with one second left to wrap up the 80-74 win. Buys continued his fine play with 21 points, Vander Hill had 19, Van Wieren 14, and Venhuizen nine. For the losers it was Jerry Ziegler with 23, and Tom Franke with 15.

With one day's rest, Hope was off to Wheaton for another non-league game on Monday, Jan. 29. A meager crowd of 1,000 was on hand in Centennial Gym, but Coach Lee Pfund had prepared well. Veteran guard Rog Johnson had left the team, but he was ably replaced by the coach's son John. A full-court press gave the Dutchmen trouble. The Crusaders took an early 10-6 lead and never looked back. After trailing 44-36 at the half, the Dutchmen broke the press and came within three at 52-49 on Reid's fastbreak layup, but Hope would get no closer. Vander Hill and Reid fouled out in the closing minutes, and Wheaton went on to record the 89-74 victory. John Pfund led his Dad's team with 23, Cal Pederson had 18, and Captain Bill Lindberg 14. For Hope it was Buys with 16, Vander Hill had 14, Nederveld 12, Reid 11, and Venhuizen nine.

Despite the Wheaton loss, conditions were on the upswing for the Dutchmen. The return of Reid and Nederveld had given the team a much-needed boost, and now the squad was joined by 6' 4" Curt Haaksma, a transfer from Grand Rapid Junior College who would provide additional depth. It was therefore a confident Hope team that traveled to Adrian on Saturday, Feb. 3. Tough defense and strong board work made things difficult for the undermanned Bulldogs. A 41-25 halftime lead increased to 75-49 as the final buzzer sounded. Along the way, the Bulldogs were reduced to a 20 percent shooting average. Buys led the winners with 18, while Nederveld, in his first start since Dec. 30, collected 14 rebounds and scored 15 points. Vander Hill was in single figures for the first time in many moons with nine. He was joined by Van Wieren and Venhuizen, each with eight, but defense was the order of the night and Coach De Vette was pleased with the outcome. Don Harned was high point man for Adrian with 11.

The Olivet Comets were at the Civic Center on Wednesday, Feb. 7, only to catch the Dutchmen on a hot night. After a 50-35 halftime lead, Hope moved on to a 99-79 victory on the strength of 55-percent shooting. Vander Hill's 41 points were the most scored by a Hope player in an MIAA game. Buys notched 15, and newcomer Haaksma had eight, as did Venhuizen and Nederveld. For the Comets it was Dick Groch with 27, Ed Donaldson 18, and Mike Foster 13.

More than 2,500 fans filled the Civic Center on Saturday, Feb. 10, as first-place Kalamazoo came into town. The Dutchmen, still smarting from the one-point loss on Jan. 13, moved out quickly. At the half it was Hope 43-22 as the crowd settled back to view the presentation of the MIAA MVP football award to Hope's Sharky Vander Woude. Hope's lead reached 62-43 at the 10-minute mark before the Hornets narrowed the gap somewhat. The Dutchmen, however, were not to be denied and ended with a 78-67 victory in what De Vette called "our best game of the season." Vander Hill again was high with 25, Buys had 17, Reid and Venhuizen 11 each. For Ray Steffen's crew it was Chuck Wood with 21, Gordon Rodwan with 14, and Jon Lindenberg with nine. Hope was now temporarily in first place with a 7-2 record as compared to 6-2 for Kalamazoo and Calvin.

All remaining games on the schedule would be crucial, but none more so than the Hope-Calvin set-to in Holland on Wednesday, Feb. 14. Exchanges this night would not include valentines, but sportsmanship would continue on the high road, thanks in large measure to the stature of Coaches Steen and De Vette. Would-be interlopers would try every conceivable device to gain entry into the already sold-out Civic Center, but police and ticket takers were alert and ready. As usual, the classic lived up to expectations, with the Knights claiming a 40-37 halftime lead. The Calvin advantage was still at three (61-58) with 7:42 remaining, but Hope moved into a 62-62 tie with six minutes left. Accuracy at the line in the stretch aided the Dutchmen. Buys, Nederveld, Reid, and Van Wieren all made two-for-two. Hope led 75-69 with 1:57 left, but Hank De Mots, always cool under fire, scored twice, making it 75-73 with 20 seconds on the clock. Hope inbounded to Buys, who was fouled with five seconds left. The Hope captain made one of two to give Hope the very satisfying 76-73 win over a worthy opponent. Buys totaled 20 points, Van Wieren followed with 18, Vander Hill had 14, and Nederveld 13. For Calvin it was Rich Rusthoven with 18, Hank De Mots with 17, and Tom Vander Woude with 16.

Hope's game at Albion on Feb. 17 might have been closer had not ace Jim Papenfus fouled out in the first minute of the second half. The Dutchmen were in front with a comfortable 57-38 lead at the intermission, then missed 11 straight shots as the Britons went on a 19-3 run. The lead narrowed to eight points at 72-64 before Hope regained control and went on to a 93-76 victory. Vander Hill had a big night with 34 and Buys had 22, while Nederveld and Van Wieren each got 13. Emil De Grazia was tops for Albion with 25, Dick Groat had 21, and Jerry Chandler 12.

Coach Ray Null brought the Aquinas Tommies to the Civic Center for a non-league game on Wednesday, Feb. 21. In future years the school would change its nickname to "Saints" to better accommodate its women athletes. Once again, the Dutchmen were in charge early and posted a 48-33 halftime lead. As at Albion, De Vette's charges hit a cold streak and got a scare when Aquinas guard Gary Fewless caught fire and poured in 11 baskets. With 1:26 remaining Fewless, a superb dribbler, went "coast to coast" to make it 84-80. The Dutchmen managed to hang on, and with 21 seconds remaining Jim Vander Hill dropped in a free throw to insure Hope' escape with an 87-83 victory. Coaches remain baffled by the phenomenon of momentum loss in the game of basketball.

As the Hope bus departed for Alma on Saturday, Feb. 24, all knew that a victory would be necessary to insure a tie with Kalamazoo for the MIAA title. A home game for the season finale would have been more to their liking. The game was played before 200 fans in the Alma High School Gym. The Hope players were reminded that effort and concentration, not crowds, win ball games. De Vette's charges responded with a 50-32 halftime lead, and were never headed. A bright spot for the Scots was an outstanding performance by freshman Bud Acton. The big center put together halves of 12 and 17 points to lead his team with 29. Don Phillippi was next with nine. Vander Hill closed out the season with one of his hot-night specials. His 37 points included seven-of-seven from the free throw line. Nederveld netted 16, Buys 11, Van Wieren nine, Bob Reid seven, Ron Te Beest five, and the Hesslink twins four each to make the final score 93-70.

Needless to say, the trip home from Alma was a time for reflection by co-captains Buys and Reid as well as Jim and Jerry Hesslink, the other seniors. After early tribulation, all had come together to wind up with a seven-game winning streak and a co-championship with Kalamazoo. Thirty-seven years later, Glenn Van Wieren, as Hope's coach, would experience a similar season when his team would stage an impressive comeback to tie Calvin for the MIAA championship. The 1961-62 All-MIAA team included Ek Buys and Jim Vander Hill of Hope, Gordon Rodwan and Jon Lindenberg of Kalamazoo, and Carl De Kuiper of Calvin. Buys, Hope's co-captain and MVP, was named the league's Most Valuable Player. Ekdal J. Buys, Hope '37, and Mina Becker Buys, Hope '36, could be justly proud.

* * *

In 1962, Hope tennis coach Larry Green believed he had a team whose time had come. Having finished fourth in 1961, the Dutchmen would now be much improved with the return of Norm Hess at number-one singles. Hess had missed the entire 1961 season due to a bout with hepatitis. Green felt strongly that to be in contention for a championship, early season competition was necessary. Accordingly, for the first time since 1941, an ambitious spring trip was arranged. As the team made final preparations, the Holland community was saddened by the passing of Charles E. "Cubby" Drew at age 71. Drew had coached the Holland High School basketball team to a state championship in 1919 with a 14-13 victory over Detroit Northwestern. He

THE HOPE COLLEGE TENNIS TEAM
MIAA CO-CHAMPIONS WITH KALAMAZOO

Standing L. to R.: Dave Zwart, Arlyn Lanting, Harvey "Bud" Hoffman, Coach Lawrence "Doc" Green **Kneeling:** Stan Vugteveen, Norm Hess, Dave Nykerk. **Missing from the picture:** Bob Tigelaar.

was a long-time supporter of Hope teams, and often called Hope coaches with words of encouragement following a discouraging defeat.

The team departed Holland on Saturday, March 31, in private cars, one belonging to Coach Green. The first match was played in Tallahassee, Fla., on Monday, April 2, with the Florida State freshman team furnishing the opposition. The Dutchmen managed a 4-3 victory but found the going tougher the following day, when they took on the Florida State varsity. In the latter match it was Florida State winning 6-3 as Paul Scarpa (FS) defeated Hess 6-2, 6-2, Gordon Smith (FS) won over Arlyn Lanting 6-1, 6-2, Ed Saslana (FS) defeated Stan Vugteveen 6-2, 6-3, Jamie Jamieson (FS) took Dave Zwart 6-1, 6-4, Bud Hoffman (H) defeated Wally Dales 6-2, 6-2, and Dave Nykerk (H) got past Mike Dyer 6-0, 6-2. In doubles, it was Scarpa-Smith over Hess-Lanting 6-0, 6-2, Saslana-Jamieson over Vugteveen-Nykerk 6-4, 6-2, and Zwart-Hoffman over Berry-Dales 11-9, 6-4. Hope's defeat was somewhat easier to take when it was learned that the U.S. Naval Academy had earlier lost to Florida State by the same 6-3 score. Bob Teall, former Hope player, was at number five singles for Navy.

Hope's next stop was in Gainesville to meet the University of Florida team. The Gators were the reigning champions of the Southeastern Conference, and the Dutchmen soon understood why. SEC singles champion Jim Shaffer (F) defeated Hess 9-7, 6-4, Francisco Montana of Chile (F) won over Lanting 6-4, 6-3, Mike Cullinane (F) defeated Vugteveen 6-3, 6-3, Fred Shayal of Israel (F) won from Zwart 6-4, 6-3, Ron Rebhuhn (F) defeated Hoffman 6-3, 6-2, and Jerry Pfeiffer (F) defeated Tigelaar 6-2, 6-2. In doubles, it was Shaffer-Shayal (F) winning from Hess-Lanting 6-3, 6-1, Cullinane-Collins (F) over Vugteveen-Nykerk 6-3, 4-6, 6-0, and Rebhuhn-Pfeiffer (F) over Hoffman-Zwart 6-2, 6-2. While the 9-0 shutout may not have looked good in the papers, Hope had made a respectable showing and now knew what it was like to compete in the "big leagues." Besides, temperatures were in the 70's and prospects for an early suntan were good.

On Thursday, April 5, Hope traveled to Deland, Fla., and recorded a 6-3 victory over Stetson University. The previous day's effort had taken its toll. Coach Green did not think his charges played quite as well, but he would take the win. In singles, Lynn Grate (S) defeated Hess 6-2, 6-2, Dave Mc Ildin (S) took Lanting 6-3, 6-4, Joe Keiper (S) defeated Vugteveen 6-3, 6-4, Zwart won over Don Comelley 6-0, 10-8, Hoffman defeated Don Koker 6-3, 7-5, and Nykerk took Clarence Fause 6-1, 6-2. In doubles, it was Hess-Lanting over Grate-Mc Ildin 6-4, 6-4, Zwart-Nykerk over Keiper-Hunt 6-1, 1-6, 6-3, and Vugteveen-Bob Tigelaar over Reiff-Koker (S) 6-0, 1-6, 6-4.

Friday, April 6, found the Dutchmen in Georgia for a match with Valdosta State College. This day the competition would not be as strong, resulting in a 9-0 Hope shutout. Hess defeated Rick Anderson 7-5, 4-6, 6-4, Lanting won over John Howell 6-2, 6-2, Zwart defeated Jim Nichols 6-1, 6-0, Hoffman took Bill Mc Daniel 7-5, 6-3, Vugteveen won over Walt Altman 6-0, 6-0, and Nykerk defeated Charles Hobby 6-0, 6-0. In doubles, it was Hess-Lanting winning over Anderson-Howell 3-6, 6-4, 6-3, Zwart-Nykerk over Nichols-Mc Daniel 6-2, 6-2, and Vugteveen-Bob Tigelaar over Altman-Benhatt 6-1, 6-1. The final two doubles matches were played in the Valdosta Gym.

Hope's final match in the deep south was played on Saturday, April 7, in Carrollton, Ga. The opponent was West Georgia, and the result was another 9-0 shutout. In singles, Hess defeated Nolan Robinson 6-2, 6-1, Lanting defeated Richard Kennerly 6-3, 6-0, Hoffman defeated Ken Dixon 6-3, 6-4, Zwart took Jim Purcell 6-2, 6-1, Vugteveen defeated Arnold Moore 6-0, 6-1, and Dave Nykerk won from Andy Anderson 6-1, 6-2. Coach Green experimented somewhat in the doubles matches. Hess-Zwart defeated Robinson-Moore 6-0, 6-0, Lanting-Tigelaar took Kennerly-Purcell 6-4, 6-2, and Vugteveen-Nykerk defeated Anderson-Dixon 6-2, 6-1.

As the team journeyed homeward, a stop was made in Muncie, Ind., for a match with Ball State Teachers College on Monday, April 9. Wind and a temperature of 48 degrees did not stop the Dutchmen from taking a 5-2 decision. Hope also won three additional matches tagged as "exhibitions." In singles, Hess defeated Paul Cossell 7-5, 3-6, 8-6, Lanting won over Tom Graham 6-1, 6-0, Zwart defeated Pinkie Bigler 6-0, 6-1, Dick Osting defeated Vugteveen (H) 6-4, 8-6, and Hoffman stopped Dan Tayangamon 6-4, 6-0. In exhibition matches, Nykerk took Mark Thomas 6-3, 6-1, and Tige-

NORM HESS
MIAA SINGLES CHAMPION — 1962

laar defeated Carlton Polk 6-4, 6-3. In doubles, it was Cossell-Bigler over Hess-Zwart 7-5, 7-5, and Lanting-Nykerk over Graham-Osting 6-3, 6-2. In an exhibition match, Tigelaar-Vugteveen defeated Thomas-Tayangamon 6-2, 6-0.

Back in Holland on Saturday, April 14, the Dutchmen continued their competition with larger schools by taking on Miami of Ohio. The first-time meeting between the schools was conducted on the 13th and 22nd Street courts despite cold and windy weather. Enroute to the 6-3 Hope team victory, Hess defeated Stewart Opdycke 4-6, 6-0, 6-3, Pat Gloor stopped Lanting 1-6, 8-6, 6-3, Vugteveen defeated Shelley Alper 6-3, 6-2, Zwart won over Jim Meyer 3-6, 6-1, 6-1, Dave Kolasky defeated Hoffman 8-6, 6-3, and Nykerk stopped Dave Abbott 6-3, 6-3. In doubles, it was Hess-Lanting over Opdycke-Gloor 7-5, 6-2, Tigelaar-Zwart over Alper-Meyer 6-1, 4-6, 6-2, and Kolasky-Fred Bonsack over Vugteveen-Nykerk 6-3, 10-8.

The MIAA season was about to begin, and the Dutchmen would not have long to wait for their biggest challenge. On Tuesday, April 24, the Kalamazoo College team was in town expecting to extend its amazing string of 155 straight dual-meet victories. No one could remember when the Hornets had last been beaten. Actually, it had occurred on May

151

12, 1935, when Albion had prevailed, 5-2. The day did not begin well for Hope. Kalamazoo's Loren Campbell was the victor in number-one singles 6-1, 9-7 when a gallant comeback by Hess fell short. The Hornets' Jack Hulst was also a winner at 6-2, 6-1 over Hoffman. But Lanting defeated Art Walker 6-2, 7-5, Zwart stopped Phil Rose 6-1, 6-2, and Nykerk took quarterback Jim Harkema 6-3, 6-4. Hope entered the doubles competition with a 3-2 team lead, but the Hornets tied it when Hulst-Harkema got the best of Zwart-Nykerk 6-3, 6-3 in number-two doubles. Meanwhile, the number-one doubles match between Campbell-Rose and Hess-Lanting had developed into a grueling three-setter that would last for an hour and a half. Hess and Lanting took the first set 6-4, and Campbell and Rose won the second by the same score. Behind 2-1 in the third set, Hope took the next three to lead 4-2. At this point, "K" made a bid. With Lanting serving and Kazoo leading 0-4, Hope stormed back to deuce, then the fifth-game victory. With momentum on their side, Hess and Lanting captured the sixth game and with it the set 6-4, 4-6, 6-2, and the match 4-3. Overall, the match had taken nearly four hours, finally concluding at 7:15 p.m.

Bad weather forced cancellation of the Calvin dual and postponement of the May 1 meeting with Olivet, but on the weekend of May 4-5 Hope took part in a quadrangular match at Kalamazoo's Stowe Stadium. On Friday, May 4, it was Hope defeating Northern Illinois University 8-1. Hess stopped Keith Robinson 6-4, 6-1, Steve Weiss defeated Hoffman 2-6, 6-0, 6-4, Lanting won over Wayne Bargren 6-2, 6-0, Zwart defeated Jim Pierson 6-4, 6-0, Nykerk took Jack Smith 7-5, 12-10, and Vugteveen defeated Gary Strodtz (NI) 6-1, 6-1. In doubles, it was Hess-Lanting over Robinson-Bargren 6-2, 6-1, Zwart-Nykerk over Pierson-Smith 6-3, 6-1, and Tigelaar-Vugteveen over Strodtz-Weiss 6-0, 4-6, 6-2.

At 10 a.m. the next morning, Hope edged Lake Forest College 5-4 in a match that saw three, four, and five singles plus Hope's number-three doubles team do the honors. Not until Tigelaar and Vugteveen defeated Larry Butler and Jack Reiss 6-4, 6-4, was the issue decided. By afternoon, the Hope team appeared to be out of gas and the Hornets of Coach George Acker moved in for a 6-0 shutout. Kalamazoo's Campbell defeated Hess 6-1, 6-0, Hulst stopped Hoffman (H) 7-5, 6-1, Fischer got by Lanting 6-4, 2-6, 8-6, Walters defeated Zwart 4-6, 6-3, 6-0, Tornga defeated Nykerk 7-5, 6-4, and Harkema took Vugteveen 6-1, 6-4. For reasons unknown, no doubles matches were played. As the Dutchmen returned to Holland, they were thankful that the match was a non-league affair.

The postponed match with Olivet was played in Marshall, Mich., on Monday, May 7. Lanting was unable to make the trip, but Hope's depth overcame his absence and the Dutchman were the victors, 7-0. In singles, Hess defeated Steve Sullivan 6-0, 6-0, Hoffman stopped Fred Meyers 6-1, 6-1, Zwart took Larry Crowley 6-1, 6-0, Nykerk defeated Cronmiller 6-1, 6-0, and Vugteveen defeated Ron Mitchell 6-2, 6-1. In doubles, it was Hess-Vugteveen over Sullivan-Crowley 6-1, 6-1, and Zwart-Nykerk over Meyers-Mitchell 6-0, 6-0.

Hess was unable to make the trip to Alma on Wednesday, May 9, but the singles players moved up a notch and Hope was again a 7-0 winner. Hoffman defeated Bruce Brintnall 6-4, 6-1, Lanting stopped Bryan Hampton 6-1, 6-2, Zwart won over Dave Wright 6-0, 6-0, Nykerk defeated Jim Lynn 6-0, 6-0, and Vugteveen took John Goldener 6-1, 6-0. In doubles, Lanting-Vugteveen downed Brintnall-Hampton 6-1, 6-3, and Zwart-Nykerk defeated Wright-Lynn 6-1, 6-1.

Hope had its full complement of players for the Adrian match in Holland on Tuesday, May 15, and the result was another 7-0 shutout. Hess downed Lavon Wolfe 6-4, 7-5, Hoffman defeated Bill Hazen 6-1, 1-6, 6-0, Lanting stopped Don Douglas 6-0, 6-1, Zwart defeated Dave Mc Kelvey 6-0, 6-0, and Nykerk took Mike Pipton 6-1, 6-1. In doubles, Hess-Lanting defeated Wolfe-Douglas 6-4, 6-2, and Zwart-Nykerk stopped Hazen-Mc Kelvey (A) 6-1, 6-0.

The Dutchmen wound up the dual meet season with a match at Albion on Wednesday, May 16. Hess bested Art Smith 6-3, 6-0, Hoffman defeated Gary Chamberlain 6-1, 6-0, Lanting won from Gil Banks 6-1, 6-3, Zwart defeated Jon Betwee 6-2, 6-0, and Nykerk defeated Tom Dalzell 6-0, 6-0. In doubles, it was Hess-Lanting over Smith-Chamberlain 6-1, 6-2, and Zwart-Nykerk over Mc Farland-Banks 6-1, 6-0 to give Hope its fourth straight 7-0 shutout.

The season concluded with the MIAA meet in Kalamazoo on May 18-19. Host Kalamazoo was still in the driver's seat, but Hope scored points in number-three singles when Lanting defeated Kazoo's Fisher 7-5, 6-4, and also in number-five singles when it was Nykerk over the Hornets' Ed Tornga 2-6, 6-1, 6-4. Kalamazoo countered with victories in number-one and number-two doubles. Campbell-Harkema defeated Hess-Lanting 6-4, 6-3, and Hulst-Tornga stopped Zwart-Nykerk 6-2, 6-4.

One more challenge remained for Hess. In the MIAA singles finals, it was once again Hess versus K's Loren Campbell. The three-set match was played in 90 degree heat and this time Hess prevailed over his longtime nemesis, 4-6, 9-7, 10-8. It was a fitting climax to Hope's premier tennis season. In the overall standings it was Hope and Kalamazoo tied for the MIAA championship with 22 points each. Calvin followed with 16, Albion and Adrian each had eight, Alma six, and Olivet two. At this writing, Kalamazoo College has won every MIAA title outright since that day in May, 1962.

* * *

After serving as an assistant in 1961, Daryl Siedentop was appointed head baseball coach at Hope in 1962. His mentor, Russ De Vette, had produced co-champions in 1953 and 1954, was away at the University of Maine for a year, then returned as head man from 1956 through 1961. Budgetary limitations seemed to rule out a spring trip, but the young coach was not easily deterred. He succeeded in renting an ancient bus from a party in nearby Zeeland, convinced his players to shoulder most of the cost, and headed for Tennessee on April Fool's Day.

On Monday, April 2, Hope squared off against Lambuth College in Jackson, Tenn. With little or no practice, the Dutchmen's play was ragged and seven errors resulted. But Reid and Vander Molen each had three RBI's, and Jim Bultman found himself on base six straight times. The Hope captain was walked four times, was hit by a pitched ball, and rapped out a single. Larry Dykstra and Glenn Van Wieren shared pitching duties, and the overall result was a 10-7 Hope victory for Siedentop in his first outing as a head coach.

Two days later, the team took on tiny Bethel College in Mc Kenzie, Tenn. Lefty Jim Van Til started with Gary Schaap coming on in the sixth. The two combined to register 17 strikeouts, but the Dutchmen again committed seven errors and eventually lost out, 4-3. Hope was limited to six singles.

Back in Jackson the next day, the opponent was Union College. Van Wieren took the mound and went all the way as he struck out two and scattered eight hits for the 5-1 victory. Reid's three-run homer in the third was the big blow for the winners. Union's run also came in the third on Hope's only error of the game.

A Friday, April 6, game with Eastern Illinois was rained out, and the team returned to Holland on Saturday. While not as ambitious as Doc Green's tennis junket, the trip south had paid dividends as the team showed marked improvement. After a week of practice in cold weather, the team traveled to Big Rapids to initiate the regular season with a doubleheader against Ferris Institute. Schaap threw a five-hitter in the first game and had two of Hope's four hits, but offense was lacking and the Bulldogs prevailed 6-2. In the second contest, Glenn Van Wieren gave up just four hits as he retired the side in order in the first, third, fifth, and sixth innings. Hope scored six times in the sixth inning and earned a split for the day with a 7-1 victory.

On Wednesday, April 18, Hope met Wayne State for the first time. The game was played at the 32nd Street diamond because Riverview Park was unavailable. Dykstra pitched a four-hitter, but Wayne pushed across three runs in the third on a double, a triple, and two Hope errors. Hope scored one in the first and one in the fifth, but the visitors hung on to notch the 3-2 victory. Hope had played well, but the next day at Riverview the roof fell in. Grand Rapids Junior College collected 11 hits from the offerings of Van Wieren and Schaap, and Hope made seven errors. The final count was GRJC 14, Hope 3.

Frustration continued in the MIAA opener at Albion on Wednesday, April 25. In the opener Glenn Van Wieren pitched a masterful two-hitter, but a Hope error with the bases loaded gave Albion the two runs needed to win the game. The Dutchmen collected seven hits, but in the end the Britons' Gary Ketrow had a 2-0 shutout. In the second game, Albion got three runs in the second and two more in the fourth on Jerry Chandler's home-run off Dykstra. The Britons picked up a final run in the seventh on two Hope errors and a wild pitch to win, 6-1. Winning pitcher Emil De Grazia gave up but four hits, two by Bultman.

The Hope team ran into more trouble at Alma on Saturday, April 26. Catcher Mike Mulligan was the culprit as he stroked Van Wieren's first pitch for a home-run in both the third and fifth innings. Meanwhile, Osborne, the Scots' pitcher, gave up only two hits in securing the 4-1 victory. A double and single by Bultman was all the offense the Dutchmen could muster. In the second game, the Scots collected 10 hits off the combined offerings of Schaap and Dykstra. The 8-6 Alma win included seven runs on seven singles.

The Dutchmen drought ended in impressive style at Riverview Park on Tuesday, May 1. The Olivet Comets were victims of a one-hit, 8-0 shutout by Dykstra. Meanwhile, Dutchman bats came alive in the first inning. Two walks, combined with singles by Bultman, Kramer, and Venhuizen, produced four runs. Hope added one in the second when Bultman singled, stole second, and came home on a fielder's choice. With one more in the third, Hope closed out the scoring in the sixth with two runs on singles by Kramer, Bill Hill, Vanhuizen, and Ron Vander Molen. The rains came before the second contest could start, and the game would not be replayed.

At Adrian on Saturday, May 5, Dykstra and Schaap gave up nine hits, but the Dutchmen turned 13 hits into a like number of runs and were able to hang on for a 13-10 victory. In the second game, Van Till walked eight but set the Bulldogs down with three hits and seven strikeouts. With the score tied at three in the sixth, Hill singled, then scored all the way from first on Wiegerink's bunt, plus an Adrian error. This proved to be the difference, and gave Hope the 4-3 win to cap a successful afternoon.

Rain moved the Hope games at Kalamazoo from Saturday to Monday, May 14. Dykstra pitched well for the most part in the first game, but a triple by the Hornets' John Persons in the fifth drove in two runs and eventually gave Kalamazoo the 7-6 win. In the nightcap, Van Wieren pitched a six-hit, 4-0 shutout for his first MIAA win. Hope scored single runs in the first, third, fourth, and fifth. Big blows for the Dutchmen were Bultman's double in the third, and a home run by Venhuizen in the fifth.

Hope's season concluded on a positive note against archrival Calvin. The games were played on Tuesday, May 15, at the 32nd Street diamond, as Tulip Time activities preempted use of Riverview Park. Jim Van Til was off to a great start in the first game, striking out the side in the first, sec-

HOPE RUNNERS WORK OUT ON NEW RUBBER-ASPHALT TRACK APRIL 17, 1962

L. to R.: John Nyboer, Dick Bennink, Paul Wackerbarth, Jon Schoon, Tom Van Dyke.

ond, and third innings. After getting the first batter in the fourth for his 10th strikeout, Van Til proceeded to walk nine batters. Van Wieren was called in to stem the tide, but damage had been done. With but three hits, the Knights scored one in the fourth, three in the fifth, and one in the sixth. Hope got five runs on 10 hits, and the game was tied at the end of the regulation seven innings. In the bottom of the ninth, Venhuizen singled and stole second. Van Wieren then came through with a single to win his own game, 6-5.

Schaap started the second game, but was relieved by Dykstra in the fifth with men on first and third. Dykstra got the batter to hit into a double play, then struck out the side in the sixth and seventh innings. Cal Poppink led off Hope's sixth inning with a pinch single, then advanced to second on Dykstra's sacrifice. Kramer's single drove home what proved to be the winning run in Hope's second 6-5 victory of the afternoon. Ron Venhuizen homered in the fifth off loser Jim Kool.

The Dutchmen finished the season with an overall record of 9-10, while their 6-5 MIAA mark was good enough for fourth place. Pitcher Glenn Van Wieren, second baseman Art Kramer, and shortstop Jim Bultman were named to the All-MIAA team. Bultman had batted .333 and was generally considered the best fielding shortstop in the league.

*   *   *

Bill Oostenink, Hope's second-year golf coach, had several goals, but the first one would be to climb out of the MIAA basement. He would be successful in this endeavor. Sophomore Jim Wiersma returned and would again be Hope's number one man. Also on hand were Bill Vandenberg, Ed Van Dam, and freshmen Dave Dalman, Bruce Gibbons, and Dean Overman. The opening match was played at the Kalamazoo Country Club on Tuesday, April 24, with the Hornets outscoring the Dutchmen 12½ to 2½. Wiersma scored one point, Vandenberg one point, and Overman 1/2 point. Kalamazoo's Dave Bellingham was medalist with a 76.

Wiersma led his team to its first victory at Holland's American Legion Memorial Course. Hope outscored Adrian 10-5 as Wiersma took medalist honors with a 78, which also produced three points. Dalman contributed 2½ points, Vandenberg and Gibbons two each, and Overman 1/2 point. Playing best for Adrian were Don De Meritt and Don Hannula, each with an 86.

Hope and Alma braved the rain on Saturday, April 28, with the Scots taking the match 9½ to 5½, and the Dutchmen lost again on Tuesday, May 1. This time it was Olivet inching past the Dutchmen 8-7 in a contest abbreviated by rain. Victory finally came again in a non-league match with Grand Rapids Junior College on Thursday, May 3. Hope's Wiersma and JC's Howard Konwenski shared medalist honors with 71s but the Dutchmen were on top 9½ to 5½ when team points were totaled.

On Tuesday, May 8, the Dutchmen met Calvin at the Hickory Hills course in Grand Rapids. It was a Hope day with the Dutch again gaining a 9½ – 5½ victory. Jim Wiersma scored three points and was medalist with a 76, Dave Dalman and Dean Overman each scored two points, Bill Vandenberg 1½ points, and Ed Van Dam one point.

At the Legion course on Thursday, May 10, Hope lost to Albion in an unusual scenario. Wiersma was medalist with a fine 72 and the Hope team totaled 393 strokes to 401 for the Britons, but individual match-ups gave Albion the 8-7 team victory.

Hope closed out its dual meet season on Tuesday, May 15, at the American Legion course. Visiting Aquinas had too many guns and downed the Dutchmen 13 to 5. No one was able to challenge Aquinas' Kim Kanary, who took medalist honors with a 70. Overman led Hope with an 81 for two points, Dalman's 81 was good for one point, Wiersma had an 82 for one point, and Gibbons also scored one point with an 86.

Hope, Calvin, and Olivet each had 2-4 marks in regular season duals, but the Dutchmen scored higher in the MIAA meet in Kalamazoo on Friday, May 18. Kalamazoo took the Field Day title with a score of 786 and thereby the MIAA championship. Albion scored 870, Alma 872, Hope 887, Calvin 911, Adrian 925, and Olivet 973. Dick Robyn of Kalamazoo was medalist with a 36-hole total of 149. Hope's Jim Wiersma was tied with Robyn with a 75 at the end of 18, but ran into putting trouble and ended with a total of 159. Overman shot 175, Dalman 184, and Van Dam 187. Hope's solid fourth-place finish was a vast improvement over 1961.

* * *

The big news for Hope trackmen in 1962 was the first use of their 440-yard, rubber asphalt track. The new facility included eight 42" lanes, a 200-yard straightaway on the west side, pits and runways for long jump and pole vault, and a high jump area at the south end of the field. Concrete hardstands were in place for the shot and discus. March snow could be plowed from the surface at mid-day, allowing practice by 3:30 p.m. Two sections of portable bleachers were borrowed from the City of Holland and placed opposite the finish line.

The first competition on the new track took place on Saturday, April 21, with another strong team from Grand Rapids Junior College defeating the Dutchmen 89¼ to 41¾. Captain John Brunson led the home team with firsts in the shot and discus, Mike Schrier tied for first in the high jump, Tom Van Dyke ended in a three-way tie for first in the pole vault, and Ron Te Beest won both hurdle races. The Raiders, however, won everything else and had depth in most events.

Hope's first-place potential in 1962 was limited, but on Saturday, April 28, at Olivet, things went well. The Comets' cinder track presented some problems as "clinkers" became lodged between the long spikes used by the Dutchmen on cinders, but Hope captured 10 of 15 firsts and ended with an 81-49 victory. John Brunson was a three-time winner with victories in the javelin, shot, and discus, and Vern Sterk won the mile, Bruce Welmers the two-mile, Rod Sluyter the pole vault, Bob Fialko the 100, Dave Bolhuis the 220, Te Beest the low hurdles, and Te Beest and Gary Nederveld tying for first in the high hurdles.

Hope's first victory on its new track came in a triangular with Alma and Olivet on Tuesday, May 1. This time the Dutchmen had nine firsts in scoring 94 team points to 45 for Olivet, and 20 for Alma. Te Beest was the winner in both hurdle races, while Fialko was also a double winner, taking both the 100, and 220-yard dashes. In one of the best races of the day, Hope's Jon Schoon edged Olivet's Larry Melendy in the 440-dash. Three days earlier, Melendy had won by two-tenths of a second.

On Saturday, May 5, Hope made the long trip to Adrian for a dual meet that was close all the way. The Bulldogs had eight firsts to seven for the Dutchmen. With only the mile relay remaining, the score stood Adrian 65, Hope 61. A victory in this last event would result in a 66-65 Hope victory. It was not to be. The Adrian foursome came through with a strong performance to win the meet, 70-61.

Coach Swede Thomas brought the Kalamazoo Hornets to Holland for a dual meet on Tuesday, May 8. The visitors captured nine firsts and took the contest, 75 to 56. Ray Comeau won both hurdle races and Bill Lynch took both dashes. In the javelin competition, Brunson was beaten by Gordon Rodwan of basketball fame. The margin of victory was one-half inch. Under present NCAA rules, distances over 100 feet are measured to the nearest inch (down). This would have given Brunson a tie. Schrier, a Kalamazoo native, won the long jump and high jump for Hope, and Schoon again took the 440. The Dutchmen won the mile relay with a team of Fialko, Paul Wackerbarth, Mike Laughlin, and Schoon to take some of the sting out of the defeat.

The following day, a strong Valparaiso team came to Holland to test out the new track. Apparently it met with the Crusaders' approval as they cruised to a decisive 93½ – 42½ victory. Cal Poppink tied for first place in the high jump, but Valparaiso won everything else, including an 880-yard relay requested by the visitors. John Knight, who had scored two touchdowns against Hope in September, was the victor in both dashes.

On Tuesday, May 15, the Dutchmen hosted a superior Albion team in the final dual meet of the season. Brunson won the shot put and Van Dyke tied for first in the pole vault, but the Britons had no trouble in racking up a 92-39 victory. Charles Clark was a triple winner, taking first in the high jump and both hurdle races, J.B. Elzy of football fame was first in the 100 and 220 dashes, to add to Albion sweeps in the 440, the mile, and the two-mile. There would be better days and better years for Hope track and field.

The MIAA meet, as usual, was held at Kalamazoo's Angell Field on Saturday, May 19. Calvin, with 10 of 15 first-place finishes, scored 84½ points and ran away with the meet. Kalamazoo finished second with 54½, Albion had 47, and Hope was a distant fourth with 14 points. Adrian was fifth with 13, Olivet had nine, and Alma three. Hope's highest finishes were Brunson's second (170' 6½") in the javelin and Hill's second (20' 10½") in the long jump. Kalamazoo had four firsts and Albion one.

The MIAA's new commissioner was well-known restaurateur Win Schuler, an Albion graduate who had served with distinction as a football official. Schuler promptly donated a new "rotating" trophy for the All-Sports winner. In 1962 it would go to Kalamazoo with a total of 70 points. Albion followed with 60 and Hope moved up to third with 48 points. Calvin had 44, Alma 34, Olivet 20, and Adrian 18.

After a disappointing first semester, Hope had rebounded with co-championships in basketball and tennis plus improved teams in baseball and golf. In sports there is no sweeter word than "comeback." The quest for the MIAA All-Sports trophy would continue.

CHAPTER 8

SPORTS AND "CAMELOT"

As Hope College opened its doors in the fall of 1962, the country was aglow with the performance of its new president, not to mention the attractive and demure first lady. The Bay of Pigs fiasco was largely forgotten, and the Cuban Missile Crisis was yet to be. Jackie's TV tour of the White House and touch football at Hyannis Port were followed eagerly. John F. Kennedy was riding the crest of his popularity. In this "era of good feeling," another popular president was in the news. Hope's Irwin J. Lubbers would begin his final year before retirement.

In this setting, Hope's football staff was under self-imposed pressure to get back on the winning track. Captain Jim Bultman would lead a team sprinkled with sophomores and freshmen, and the road back would not be easy. Practice opened on Saturday, Sept. 1, on a new field located just west of Hope's new running track. A squad of 52 included transfers Joe Kusak from Rutgers, Tom Cousineau from Idaho, and Chuck Veurink from Michigan State. On-hand at quarterback were sophomore Cal Poppink, freshman Harlan Hyink and, waiting in the wings, the ever-loyal senior, Don Mitchell.

Despite Hope's poor showing in 1961, a crowd of 2,000 turned out on Sept. 15 for the opener, a night game at Riverview Park against a new opponent, Ashland of Ohio. The Eagles were guided by Coach Fred Martinelli, now in his fourth year at the Ohio school. The visitors wasted little time in getting on the board, as quarterback Duane Brown passed 26 yards to end Ed Knittle for the game's first score. A true kick was nullified by an offside penalty, and the second attempt failed. With the score at 6-0 in the second quarter, the Dutchmen came back with a 73-yard drive which culminated with a two-yard TD pass from Hyink to his brother Paul. Paul juggled the ball, but finally hung on for the score. The kick attempt by Neil Goodrich was blocked, and the score stood 6-6 at the half.

In the second half, Hope freshman Bill Keur took a punt on his own 14 and, with his shifty running style, returned it to the Ashland 45. Fullback Paul Hyink got free up the middle for seven yards to the 38, but it took four more plays to reach the 23. Poppink then connected with Schoon for an 18-yard gain to the five. Three plays later, it was again Poppink-to-Schoon for the touchdown. Two freshmen combined for the two-point conversion as Harlan Hyink passed to end Roger Kroodsma to make it 14-6 with 5:52 remaining in the third quarter. Still in the third period, Ashland's punter was downed on the Eagles' 39 after a mishandled pass from center. Hope scored again in seven plays, with Harlan Hyink passing 20 yards to Schoon for the TD. This time the conversion by Goodrich was good, and Hope's lead was 21-6. Ashland came back to score in the fourth quarter. The key play was a 47-yard pass from Duane Brown to Ron Lucas that put the ball on the Hope 25. Six plays later, Gary Moose went two yards off-tackle for the score. A Duane Brown keeper was good for the two-point conversion to make the final score, Hope 21, Ashland 14.

The losing streak had finally ended, but Hope's euphoria would last just one week. In another night contest at Riverview, the Dutchmen hosted Valparaiso. Co-Coaches Emory Bauer and Walt Reiner, with the aid of spring practice, had assembled a powerhouse, and Hope would never be in the ball game. The Crusaders were led by co-captains Tyrone Smith at guard, and center Ralph Grant. The visitors could field veterans at every position, including ace quarterback Dave Pohlman. The halftime score stood at 27-0, and

GOOD HANDS
"Good Hands" Jon Schoon scored two touchdowns in Hope's 21-14 victory over Ashland College - September 15, 1962.

by the end of the third quarter it was 34-0. The Dutchmen suffered a final indignity in the closing seconds of the fourth quarter. Hope fumbled a punt on its own 16, and the Crusaders recovered. Dave Pohlman, still in the ball game, passed to Harold Semrock for the touchdown and Mike Sullivan converted to complete the shutout, 48-0. Valpo had racked up 420 total yards to just 91 for the Dutchmen.

The Hope team left Holland at 7:30 a.m. on Sept. 29 for a 2 p.m. game at Wheaton. It was soon obvious that the Dutchmen had not fully recovered from the Valpo thrashing. Captain Bultman was out with a leg injury, and others were not at full strength. Harlan Hyink was given the nod to start at quarterback. A partisan crowd of 5,500 fans at Mc Cully Field watched with glee as their favorites piled up three touchdowns in the first quarter. Hope managed to hold the Crusaders scoreless in the second and fourth quarters, but the charges of Coach Jack Swartz had their offense in high gear to shut out the Dutchmen 31-0. Thus ended a miserable two weeks.

The Dutchmen hoped for better things in the MIAA opener at Kalamazoo on Oct. 6. A crowd of 1,500 at Angell Field watched as Hope got off to a good start by scoring in the first quarter. Ken Quakkelaar intercepted a pass on the Kalamazoo 30 and returned it to the 14. A few plays later, halfback Jim Bekkering went off-tackle for five yards and the score. The kick by Goodrich sailed wide, leaving the score at 6-0. The Hornets responded with an eight-play, 77-yard drive that ended with a 33-yard touchdown pass from quarterback Jim Harkema to Ed Lauerman. Jim Smith's conversion gave the Hornets a 7-6 lead, which they never relinquished. Early in the second quarter, it was the home team with another drive, this one for 64 yards. Eglis Lode scored from one yard out and Jim Smith again converted to make it 14-6 at the half.

Kalamazoo broke the game open in the third period, mainly on the arm of Harkema. Passes of 25 and 53 yards to Tom Vander Molen both resulted in touchdowns. Another Hornet drive of 68 yards ended with a one-yard touchdown plunge by Don Le Duc. Jim Smith made two of three conversions to make it 34-6, but the Dutchmen were not quite finished. Mitchell, until now Hope's third-string quarterback, was inserted to begin the fourth quarter. The patient senior had awaited his turn without complaining. Midway in the period he hit freshman end Bill Hultgren with a 26-yard scoring pass, then followed it with a two-point conversion pass to Schoon, and the score was now a more respectable 34-14. As Kalamazoo drove toward yet another score, Hope's Rog Abel intercepted a Harkema pass on the Hope five. With Mitchell at the helm, Hope sustained a 95-yard march to score. The drive included three Mitchell completions and a one-yard touchdown run by halfback Bill Keur. Mitchell again passed to Schoon for two points to make it 34-22 with 1:21 left in the game. Hope's great comeback effort had fallen short, and was further marred in the closing seconds when Kazoo guard Bob Peters broke through and grabbed the ball as Mitchell was about to pass. Peters rambled 85 yards to score, and with Smith's conversion the Kalamazoo victory margin was 41-22. Coach Rolla Anderson was on his way to an MIAA championship, an undefeated season, and the high point of his coaching career.

A 2 p.m. game with Olivet on Oct. 13 marked Hope's 1962 homecoming. A crowd of 4,500 watched Hope struggle through a closely contested game. Mitchell got a well-earned first start as did Keur at halfback. Hope won the toss and chose to receive. On the second play of the game, from his own 27, Mitchell passed to Schoon, who took the ball on the Olivet 42 and, with 440 speed, outran the defense for the score. The point attempt by Jim Van Dam failed, and Hope led 6-0 with but 1:56 gone in the first quarter. Later in the period, Hope fumbled on the Olivet 45 and the Comets' Irv Sigler recovered. Following 12 plays, Al Burnett rolled out for the final four yards and a TD. The point was not good, leaving the score at 6-6 with 4:12 left in the quarter. Keur took a long kickoff on his own two and returned it to the 26. A personal foul penalty moved the ball to the Hope 41, and eight plays later Bekkering went four yards off-tackle to score. Mitchell's pass attempt for two points failed, and Hope's lead was 12-6 at the half. With 6:51 left in the third quarter, the Dutchmen fumbled on their own nine and Olivet's Len Tyler recovered. On first down, Burnett threw a strike to Dick Smith in the end zone. The two-point try was not good, leaving the score at 12-12 until late in the game. With 2:40 remaining, Hope's Tom De Kuiper intercepted a Burnett pass on the Olivet 30, but on the next play Hope's pass attempt was in turn intercepted by Irv Sigler on the 16. He was finally pulled down on the Olivet 46. The play of the day came with 1:57 remaining. Quarterback Burnett connected with Dominic Livedoti for the game winner, a 54-yard touchdown pass. The kick was good, giving the Comets the hard-fought but much deserved 19-12 victory.

Reeling from four straight losses, the Dutchmen now faced another strong non-league foe on Oct. 20. Eastern Illinois University, with an enrollment of 3,200, seemed an unlikely opponent. Ralph Kohl, the coach at Eastern, had been a tackle on the great Michigan teams of 1948 and 1949. A Muskegon native, he often summered in Saugatuck and was an acquaintance of Coach De Vette. On an earlier trip to Central Michigan, the Eastern team had worked out at Riverview Park. A two-year agreement was subsequently worked out with the first game at Charleston, Ill. Academic commitments prevented Coach Ken Weller from making the trip, adding to the Dutchman woes. A crowd of 5,000 turned out for the 2 p.m. game at Eastern's Lincoln Field. Following a scoreless first quarter, Eastern took over at midfield with an interception and drove for the game's first score. Rod Butler went the final three yards, and the successful conversion made it 7-0. Hope responded with its own drive, and wrapped it up with a five-yard touchdown pass from Mitchell to end Hultgren. Gary Teall ran for two points and, quite surprisingly, Hope found itself leading 8-7. Across the "T" in Hope's backfield were Jim Bultman, Tom De Kuiper, and Jim Bekkering, all from Fremont, Mich. The Dutchmen's good fortune continued as Eastern fumbled the kickoff on the 40 and Hope's Cousineau recovered. On the second play from scrimmage, Mitchell lofted a long pass, which Bill Hultgren took over his shoulder and raced into the end zone. A pass attempt for the two-point conversion was not good, but Hope went to the locker room at halftime with a 14-7 lead.

Mitchell continued his passing attack in the third quarter. Two long aerials to "good hands" Jon Schoon were successful and put the ball on the Eastern one-yard line. Teall then dove in for Hope's third touchdown. The conversion again failed, but the Hope lead was now 20-7. Late in the game, Eastern mounted a drive that moved to the Hope 19, but the Dutchmen held, took over the ball and drove into Eastern territory. With 10 seconds left in the game, it was once again Mitchell-to-Hultgren for another over-the-shoulder catch, this time for 23 yards and Hope's final score. The conversion failed, but nobody cared. The 26-7 Hope victory was, as usual, a team effort, but senior Don Mitchell was clearly the man of the hour. His four years of dedication and plain hard work had paid off in a truly memorable afternoon, one that would go with him the rest of his life.

A strong wind would be a factor in Hope's game at Adrian on Oct. 27. A crowd of 2,000 turned out at Maple Stadium to watch the charges of new coach Charles "Chappy" Marvin. The game was played on even terms throughout, with Hope finally establishing a lead and then fighting to hold on. Adrian was off to a bad start by fumbling the opening kickoff. Kurt Van Genderen recovered for Hope, and three plays later it was Mitchell passing 16 yards to Bill Hultgren for the touchdown. A Mitchell-to-Jon Schoon pass added two points, and the Dutchmen led 8-0. In the second quarter, Hope's Bobby Schantz dropped back to punt. As the protection broke down, Dave Bachman broke through and blocked the kick. Teammate Jim Wilkin picked up the ball and ran 20 yards for the TD. The extra point try was not good, and Hope led 8-6 until late in the quarter. With five seconds left in the half, Adrian's Jim Du Mont kicked a 27-yard field goal to give the Bulldogs a 9-8 lead at the intermission.

With the wind in the third quarter, Mitchell hit Keur with a 16-yard TD pass. Keur then ran successfully for two points and Hope's lead was 16-9. With three seconds left in the quarter, the Mitchell-to-Hultgren combination worked again, this time for 33 yards and Hope's third touchdown.

Mitchell's pass to Jon Schoon for two points was complete, but nullified when the linesman ruled that Mitch had stepped over the scrimmage line before releasing the ball. It would be a fateful decision.

As the fourth quarter opened, the score stood at 22-9 in Hope's favor but the strong wind now favored the Bulldogs. Quarterback Tim Davies proceeded to complete 8-of-13 short passes, four to Dennis Lake. With the ball on the Hope five, Davies ran to the three, then lateralled to Dick Manders who scored. The conversion by Jim Du Mont cut the Dutch lead to 22-16. Hope failed to move the ball, and had trouble punting into the wind. With 5:52 remaining, Tim Davies ran four yards for the tying touchdown. Jim Du Mont's conversion proved to be the winning margin in Adrian's 23-22 comeback victory. Another tough loss for the Dutchmen and a long ride back to Holland.

Nov. 3 was Mom and Dads Day at Hope, and the opponent at Riverview was Alma. The Scots of Coach Art Smith were experiencing a year similar to Hope's 1961 campaign. At the beginning of the school year, Smith announced that he would give up the reins at season's end. It had seemingly been downhill from that point on, and the Scots now stood zero and six compared to Hope's two and five. Despite the records, a crowd of 2,000 was on-hand and parents were given a tribute by the Hope band under the direction of Roy Shaberg. The Dutchmen were the first to score, mounting a 78-yard drive in the first quarter. A 37-yard pass from Mitchell to Schoon was followed by another for 25 yards to the same receiver for the touchdown. The conversion attempt failed, and the scoreboard showed 6-0 with 10:04 left in the quarter. On the second play after the kickoff, Alma fumbled and Hope linebacker Terry Carlson recovered. A 23-yard pass from Mitchell to Hultgren netted Hope's second TD, but the point-after again failed, leaving the score at 12-0. In the second quarter, the Dutchmen again marched to paydirt. The scoring play this time was a 30-yard run by the shifty Keur. When the extra point again failed, the Dutchmen were content to go to the lockerroom with an 18-0 lead.

As the third quarter opened, Keur took the kickoff on the nine and returned it to the 30. A 70-yard Dutchmen drive was aided by passes to Keur and Schoon. Keur crossed the goal line after an 11-yard run to extend the Hope lead to 24-0. Successful conversions would be non-existent on this afternoon. With 12:09 left in the third period, it would be Alma's turn. Returning the kickoff to the 40, the Scots needed nine plays for their 60-yard drive. Van Mulligan went the last two yards for the TD, but Alma also had trouble with the extra point attempt and the score stood at 24-6. With 35 seconds left in the game, Hope put one more on the board. This time it came on a nine-yard pass from Mitchell to Bultman, giving the Dutchmen a 30-6 victory, their third of the season. Mitchell's fine passing had continued, and halfback Bill Keur was impressive with two touchdowns on 124 yards rushing in 13 carries. Fullback Paul Hyink added 91 yards in 18 tries.

Hope closed out the season on Nov. 10 before 2,300 fans at Albion's Alumni Field. The game would be a crowd-pleaser with explosive plays on both sides. The 5-2 Britons of Coach Morley Fraser drew first blood with an old standby. On the first play of the contest, quarterback Frank Gould handed off to halfback Bruce Martens, who faked an end run, drew in the defenders, then passed to end Les Knickerbocker, who galloped 54 yards for the touchdown. The kick by Phil Willis was good, and Albion led 7-0 with just 49 seconds gone. The shocked Dutchmen recovered, and there would be no further scoring in the first quarter. In the second quarter, the Dutchman offense got it together and drove 58 yards to the Briton two-yard line. Sub quarterback Bobby Schantz went in on a sneak to put Hope on the board. A pass for two points was incomplete, and Albion led 7-6 with 13:43 left in the period. Hope' second drive was topped off with a 10-yard touchdown run by the versatile Bultman, now playing halfback. A pass from Mitchell to Schoon was good for two points, and the Dutch took a 14-7 lead.

Two minutes later, running back J. B. Elzy exploded up the middle for 53 yards to give the Britons their second touchdown. Gould's pass for two points failed, but the Hope lead was cut to 14-13. Hope's next possession featured a brilliant pass play from Mitchell to Schoon that covered 56 yards. Schoon leaped high between two defenders, then sprinted 30 yards for the score. The two-point conversion went from Mitchell to Keur, giving the Dutchmen a 22-13 lead with 2:12 remaining. But the half was not over. With 1:26 on the clock, Gould passed to end Jerry Chandler, who broke free and streaked 55 yards to score. Gould's pass for two points failed, and the half finally ended with Hope in front 22 to 19.

Defense prevailed for most of the third quarter, but with 5:38 remaining Elzy would not be denied. This time his 55-yard run put the ball on the Hope one, where Gould scored on a sneak. The kick by Phil Willis put Albion back in the lead, 26-22, with 5:38 left in the third quarter. The Dutchmen were unable to penetrate Albion's fourth quarter defense and the colorful contest ended with Albion a four-point winner, 26 to 22. Elzy, with 176 yards rushing, had made the difference, but Paul Hyink had chalked up 105 yards while Schoon had three receptions for 109 yards and a touchdown.

Rolla Anderson's Kalamazoo Hornets enjoyed a perfect 8-0 season, and captured the MIAA championship with a 5-0 mark. Albion, Olivet, and Adrian tied for the next three places at 3-2, and Hope was fifth at 1-4. Hope's overall record of 3-6 was better than the 0-7 of 1961. Perhaps more could not be said, but the team had been inspired by the leadership of Captain Jim Bultman and quarterback Don Mitchell. End Jon Schoon and center Jim Wiegerink were named the All-MIAA Team. The road back would continue in 1963.

* * *

The loss via graduation of MIAA champion Sherri Shaffer proved too much for Hope's 1962 cross-country team to overcome. Vern Sterk and Bruce Welmers were co-captains of the squad, which included Doug Cook, Dirck De Velder, Al Hoffman, Mike Laughlin, Al Osman, Paul Swets, and Glenn Van Wieren. The Dutchmen of Coach Daryl Siedentop defeated Alma 20-38, Aquinas 25-33, and Olivet 21-36, but came out on the short end, of meets with Adrian, Calvin, Kalamazoo, Wheaton, Loyola, and Albion. The MIAA meet was held on Tuesday, Nov. 13, with Calvin again the winner. At season's end the Dutchmen found themselves in a fifth-place tie with Olivet. A leg injury kept Welmers out of action for most of the season, and the team did well to record three victories.

* * *

Most would agree that the picture was bright as the 1962-63 basketball season unfolded. Defending co-champion Hope would return four starters plus a proven performer in Ron Te Beest, also a starter in several games. Co-captains Jim Vander Hill and Gary Nederveld would be joined by backcourt regulars Glenn Van Wieren and Ron Venhuizen, while freshman Clare Van Wieren from Holland Christian, hoped to break into the starting lineup with brother Glenn. MIAA MVP Ek Buys would be missed, but Vander Hill was the two-time MIAA scoring leader and much respected around the league.

The season opened with a home game on Friday, Nov. 30. The return contest with Carroll College was played in the Zeeland High School gym before a crowd of 1,800. Hope shared the Civic Center with Holland Christian, and Friday night was a high school night. The Maroons would be hosting East Grand Rapids in the Civic while Carroll would play elsewhere on Saturday. Hope was off to a good start and led 42-26 at the half, but the team from Waukesha, Wis., was persistent in the second half and whittled away at the margin. This, combined with 25 percent shooting, resulted in a Hope lead of 65-62 with 1:25 remaining. The Pioneers dropped in a field goal with 36 seconds left to make it 65-64, but the Dutchmen ran out the clock and escaped with the one-point victory. Vander Hill was the Hope leader with 19, Glenn Van Wieren had 14, Gary Nederveld 12, and Clare Van Wieren, in a starting role, had 11. Eric Grant with a game-high 21 points, led the losers.

Hope traveled to Valparaiso the next day and seemed to show the effects of playing the night before. Trailing 47-38 at the half, the Dutchmen narrowed the margin to 66-61 at the 10-minute mark, but Valpo controlled the boards. Three of Hope's starters were saddled with four fouls early in the second half, and the Crusaders moved on to an 85-72 win. For Hope, it was Glenn Van Wieren with a game-high 23 points. Ron Venhuizen followed with 14, Gary Nederveld had 13, and Jim Vander Hill, with an off night, scored 10. Dennis Olson led the winners with 17, and Larry Holle had 15 for Coach Paul Meadows' team.

Approximately 1,600 fans showed up at the Civic Center for Hope's MIAA opener with Kalamazoo on Saturday, Dec. 8. Vander Hill was under the weather but played anyway, being spelled frequently by Dean Overman. The Dutchmen managed a 28-27 lead at the half, then increased the lead to 47-38 at the 10-minute mark, but, with 2:30 remaining, it was Hope 58, Kalamazoo 57. Twelve seconds later, a Clare Van Wieren basket made it 60-57, and with 47 seconds on the clock Venhuizen got free for a layup to give Hope a five-point margin. Kalamazoo's Chuck Wood countered with a field goal to make it 62-59. Nederveld was then fouled and made good on both free throws. Wood scored again with eight ticks left to make the final Hope 64, Kalamazoo 61. Nederveld was high for Hope with 18, Glenn Van Wieren followed closely with 17, Venhuizen netted 13, and Overman came through with eight. Ray Steffen's crew got balanced scoring as Wood led with 16, John Mason had 15, Dale Southworth 13, and Bob Morgan 11.

Vander Hill was in good health and good form at Olivet on Wednesday, Dec. 12. By halftime the rangy forward had knocked down 22 points, and Hope enjoyed an 18-point lead, 48-30. Nederveld took charge of the boards and Hope played its best defense to date. Even with aggressive play, the Dutchmen were whistled for only nine fouls throughout the contest. Substitutes saw considerable playing time in Hope's eventual 84-62 victory. Vander Hill led the way with 31, Nederveld scored 20, Clare Van Wieren 11, and brother Glenn eight. Ed Williamson was high for the Comets with 13, Doug Eveleth had 12, and Mike Boyle 10.

The Dutchmen now embarked on a new venture. For the first time in the school's history, the team would play on the West Coast. A tournament had been organized by the Valley Christian High School Boosters of Bellflower, Calif. In addition to Hope, the participants would be Occidental, Westmont, and the University of Redlands. Games would be played in the Ceritos College Gym in Norwalk, Calif. The Hope squad drove to Chicago's O'Hare Airport in the afternoon of Tuesday, Dec. 18, then boarded a jet at 12:25 a.m. for Los Angeles. Wednesday's activity included seeing the sights and taking in a Lakers game in the evening. Players stayed in homes of Booster Club members.

Thursday's game pitted Hope against Occidental College, and was played before a meager crowd of 700. The Dutchmen held their own in the early going, but the Los Angeles school had a 30-28 lead at the half. Occidental forged ahead in the second half and led by as many as 22 points at one time. The Dutch fought back to within nine but could get no closer. Occidental scored the final field goal to earn the 73-62 victory. Doug Wilsie, the winners' 7' center, led all scorers with 24. Edward followed with 15. For Hope it was Vander Hill with 23, Glenn Van Wieren 12, and Nederveld 10.

161

SPIRITED PLAY

Hope's Glenn Van Wieren (44) played, and later coached, with great intensity. Others in the picture are Ron Venhuizen (32), Ron Te Beest (42), and Kalamazoo's John Mason (53).

Westmont had fallen to Redlands in a close game (72-68) and now faced the Dutchmen in Friday's game. The Warriors appeared to be short handed with a squad numbering only seven players, but all contributed and four ended in double figures. Westmont's 36-34 halftime margin increased to 10 and stood at seven with 3:30 remaining. The Hope attack was hampered when Vander Hill picked up his fourth personal with 13 minutes to go. At the buzzer it was Westmont 86, Hope 74. Skelton paced the winners with 23, Mc Adams had 22, Odell 18, and Davies 16. Nederveld was high for Hope with 24, Vander Hill scored 15, and Overman eight. Clare Van Wieren fouled out early in the second half. The Dutchmen had journeyed a long way to sustain two defeats, but the overall experience had been positive.

In more familiar surroundings, Hope met Valparaiso on Wednesday, Jan. 2. An estimated 1,000 fans at the Civic watched the teams battle to a 40-40 tie at halftime. Te Beest replaced Clare Van Wieren in the starting lineup, but Clare came off the bench to score 12 second-half points, and his jump shot with 5:31 remaining put Hope up 66-65. The lead changed hands six times in the closing minutes. Hope led 72-71 at the 3:15 mark, but with 54 seconds left it was Valpo by one at 75-74. The Crusaders sewed it up with three quick field goals, and went home with an 81-74 victory. Despite the loss, Hope had played well, shooting 45 percent. Rebounds were almost even, with the winners getting 45 to Hope's 44. Knoefel Jones was high for the visitors with 23, and Dennis Olson had 21. Vander Hill led the Dutchmen with 18, Nederveld scored 15, Clare Van Wieren 12, Glenn Van Wieren 11, and Venhuizen 9.

On Saturday, Jan. 5, Hope traveled to Alma to meet a team that stood 6-2 on the season and 3-0 in MIAA play. The Scots of Coach Wayne Hintz had been strengthened by the addition of Ray Moore, a transfer from Alpena Junior College. The Dutchmen were off to a slow start, and trailed 45-35 at the half. Alma's lead was 57-41 with five minutes gone in the second half before Nederveld and Vander Hill took over both boards. Hope caught up with six minutes left, and led 72-71. The lead increased to 83-78 with 1:12 on the clock, and the Scots were forced to foul. Center Bud Acton fouled out, and Hope went on to win the spirited contest, 87-80. Glenn Van Wieren was high-point man for his team with 22 before being ejected, along with John La Rue, for fighting. Vander Hill tallied 18, Venhuizen had one of his better games with 16, and Nederveld scored 12. Ray Moore had a hot night for the Scots with 31, Bud Acton 15, and Bill Pendell eight.

More than 1,600 fans were on hand at the Civic Center for Hope's game with Wheaton on Tuesday, Jan. 8. Rebounding and free throw accuracy would be key factors in what was becoming a favorite non-league rivalry. Hope took a 36-30 lead to the locker room at halftime, then turned up the heat with 51 percent shooting in the second half. The largest margin came with 8:18 left, when Hope's lead was 67-50. The Dutchmen owned a 57-39 advantage in the rebound department and cashed in on 20 of 29 free throws enroute to the 88-73 win. Nederveld topped the Dutchmen with 26 points, while Vander Hill and Glenn Van Wieren each scored 20. Venhuizen had 10 and Clare Van Wieren seven. For Wheaton it was John Pfund with 21 and Chuck Huibregtse with 19.

A trip to Albion on Saturday, Jan. 12, saw the Dutchmen take on the Britons under new coach Dean Dooley. The game in Kresge Gym was uncomfortably close. Hope trailed for most of the game, but caught-up and tied it at 51-51 with 2:30 left. Vander Hill was in trouble with four fouls, but managed to finish out the game and lead his team to the 60-57 win with 23 points. Glenn Van Wieren was next with 13, Clare Van Wieren had eight, and Nederveld 7. Emil De Grazia led the Briton effort with 18, and Jerry Chandler added 17.

Hope met Calvin in the Holland Civic Center on Tuesday, Jan. 15. For the first time in as long as anyone could remember, the game was not a sellout. It was still a good crowd at 2,300, but only about 140 Calvin students made the trip from Grand Rapids. The Dutchmen led at halftime 44-35 thanks to 23 points by Jim Vander Hill, including 10 of 10 from the free throw line. During the intermission, four Hope professors led the crowd in singing the Calvin alma mater. William Vander Lugt, Bastian Kruithof, Henry Ten Hoor, and Bill Oostenink were all Calvin graduates. The novelty served to relieve tension and was generally well received. The Hope lead increased to 83-64 at the 8:17 mark before the Knights narrowed it to 99-89 at the buzzer. Jim Vander Hill was again the Dutch leader with 39, Glenn Van Wieren followed with 20, Nederveld scored 18, and Clare Van Wieren had 14. Tom Vander Woude was high for the Knights with 25, captain Jim Timmer put in 14, and Ken Fletcher added 13. In rebounds it was Hope 54-33.

It was Adrian at the Civic on Saturday, Jan. 19. The Bulldogs of Coach Gregg Arbaugh were victims of a sizzling first half by the Dutchmen, who fired at a 61 percent average. Clare Van Wieren regained his starting spot, and, as if to justify the move, led his team with 20 points, 18 in the first half. Adrian employed a box-and-chaser on Jim Vander Hill, who still managed 12 points before retiring with a leg injury. Hope's halftime bulge was 61-33, and while the Dutchmen cooled off some in the second half they still managed 51 percent for the game. The Dutchmen were again tough on the boards with a 60-44 advantage. The 95-77 victory showed Clare Van Wieren leading Hope with 20 points, brother Glenn with 16, Nederveld with 14, Vander Hill 12, and Venhuizen 11. For Adrian it was John Johnson with 19, Don Harned 17, Don Numbers 15, and Chuck Stille 11.

Hope suffered a mid-season letdown in its next two contests, both non-league. On Saturday, Jan. 26, the Dutchmen met a solid team in Concordia Teachers College of River Forest, Ill. Approximately 1,400 fans watched at the Civic Center as Hope's 42-41 halftime lead slipped away. Hope appeared to be a step slow, and gave up numerous interceptions, which led to an 80-73 victory for the Cougars of Coach Don Spitz. The game was tied seven times in the early going but Concordia pulled away in the final three minutes. The Cougar guards were especially impressive. Myron Schumacher was the leader with 30, and Dick Wegehaupt had 20. Vander Hill scored 25 to lead Hope, while Glenn Van Wieren notched 17 and Clare had 12. Nederveld and Venhuizen each scored eight.

It was more of the same on Tuesday, Jan. 29, when Hope traveled to Upland, Ind. The Trojans of Taylor, under Coach Don Odle, were hot from the start and combined an effective fast break with accurate out-court shooting. The result was a 50-36 halftime lead that ballooned to a 109-90 victory for the 12-5 Trojans. Larry Winterholder was high for the winners with 28, and Lee De Turk had 26. For Hope it was Vander Hill leading with 23, Clare Van Wieren with 21, brother Glenn with 15, Venhuizen 13, and Nederveld 11. The 6' 7" Roy Anker was elevated from the jayvee team when illness forced Curt Haaksma to drop from the squad.

In a return to MIAA play, Hope hosted Albion on Saturday, Feb. 2. Three days of intense practice seemed to pay

JIM VANDER HILL
MIAA MOST VALUABLE PLAYER — 1963

Vander Hill led the league in scoring for three consecutive seasons, 1960-61, 1961-62, and 1962-63.

off, and 1,700 fans were pleased when the Dutchmen took the lead after 12 minutes and moved to a 45-27 score at the half. Hope pressed its advantage following the intermission, and the margin widened to 30 points. Subs got their chance with 11 minutes remaining, and played a part in the eventual 94-66 victory. Hope's domination of the boards at 69-45 was a telling factor. Clare Van Wieren had his second straight 21-point game to lead the winners. Glenn Van Wieren followed with 18, Vander Hill had 16, and Gary Nederveld nine. For Dean Dooley's crew it was Larry Colburn with 12, Downs 11, and Jerry Chandler 10.

The Olivet Comets came to the Civic on Wednesday, Feb. 6, for a game played before 900 fans. An 8-8 tie after six minutes was broken by a Nederveld basket, and the Dutchmen had the lead for good. Hope's 43-22 halftime lead increased to 77-41 with five minutes remaining for the largest margin. Substitutes played effectively for much of

**1962-63 HOPE BASKETBALL TEAM
MIAA CHAMPIONS 12-0**

Kneeling L. to R.: Cal Poppink, Dean Overman, Chris Buys, Chuck Veurink, Art Kramer, Ron Venhuizen, Glenn Van Wieren. **Back Row:** Manager John Blom, Jim Vander Hill, Gailerd "Gig" Korver, Gary Nederveld, Roy Anker, Clare Van Wieren, Ron Te Beest, Coach Russ De Vette.

the second half, which ended with Hope on the long end, 84-53. Vander Hill led all scorers with 23, while Ron Te Beest, in a sub role, had an excellent game with 15. Clare Van Wieren scored 13, Nederveld 10, and Glenn Van Wieren eight. Jim Everett led the Comets with 13, and Tom Alberts and Mike Boyle each had nine.

The game at Kalamazoo on Saturday, Feb. 9, was close throughout the first half, with Hope finally gaining a 32-26 lead at the intermission. The Dutchmen enjoyed an 11-0 run early in the second half and eventually built a 52-32 lead, but Coach Ray Steffen put on a full-court press and the lead dwindled to 10. In the process the Hornets were whistled for numerous fouls, resulting in the departure of John Mason, Bob Morgan, and Jim Harkema. Hope, meanwhile, committed but four fouls in the half, while cashing in on 13-of-20 free throws. Hope's 74-62 victory margin again featured Vander Hill, this time with 21. Glenn Van Wieren scored 17, Clare had 14, and Gary Nederveld 13. Dale Southworth had 13 for Kalamazoo and John Mason 12 before fouling out.

Hope's trouble with non-league opponents continued on Thursday, Feb. 14, at Wheaton. The Dutchmen played well early and built a 49-37 halftime lead, but blew a 10-point lead later when Wheaton put on a press. The Crusaders moved ahead for the first time at 72-70 with 1:50 left in the game. Hope countered with a field goal, but Kerry Otterby scored a lay-up and John Pfund sank two free throws with 24 seconds remaining to seal Wheaton's 76-72 victory. John Pfund was high-point man for his Dad's team with 28. Backing him up were Chuck Huibregtse and Kerry Otterby, each with 15. Jim Vander Hill's 19 points led the way for Hope, Clare Van Wieren followed with 16, Glenn had 12, Nederveld and Venhuizen eight each.

The largest crowd of the season, more than 2,700 fans, packed the Civic Center on Saturday, Feb. 16, to see the Dutchmen take on a strong Alma team. Nederveld was not in uniform due to a leg injury, but De Vette's team closed ranks and managed a 42-38 lead at the half. The Scots pecked away at Hope's second-half lead, and with 1:08 remaining the Dutchmen led 84-81. Vander Hill had played what De Vette called "his best all-round game." He now dropped in two free throws with 58 seconds on the clock, then two more with 38 seconds left to make it 88-81. Alma's Ray Moore tallied the final field goal, but Hope celebrated its hard-fought 88-83 win. Jim Vander Hill's 37 points led the way for the Dutchmen, Clare Van Wieren scored 20, Glenn Van Wieren added 14, and Te Beest 10. For the Scots of Coach Wayne Hintz, it was Ray Moore with 28, Bud Acton with 19, Bill Pendell 14, and Don Philippi 10.

On Wed., Feb. 20, the Dutchmen traveled to Grand Rapids to meet Aquinas in the West Catholic High School Gym. The Saints had played several MIAA teams during the season, and had beaten them all. With Nederveld still sidelined, Coach De Vette brought Chris Buys up from the jayvee team. Approximately 1,100 fans watched as the game was tied 12 times. Hope led 48-45 at the half, but the Dutchmen trailed 90-89 with 2:30 remaining. At this point, a jump shot by Vander Hill put his team ahead to stay. Venhuizen put in two free throws with 1:51 left. Te Beest captured a key rebound and passed quickly to Clare Van Wieren, whose field goal made it 95-90. Venhuizen added a free throw with 28 seconds on the clock, and the Saints scored the final basket as time ran out. With the 96-92 victory, Hope had finally gotten the best of a strong non-league opponent. It was Vander Hill again, this time with 32, Glenn Van Wieren with 22, Clare Van Wieren 13, and Ron Venhuizen 11. Aquinas had outstanding performances from Ralph Coleman and Gary Fewless, each with 25, and from Ray Bauer with 20.

The long trip to Adrian on Saturday, Feb. 23, concerned Coach De Vette, and with good reason. Gregg Arbaugh had the Bulldogs ready to play, and the first half was not easy. Hope had a five-point lead (41-36) at the intermission, but it narrowed to three (69-66) with eight minutes remaining. With eight seconds left, it was anyone's game as Hope led 80-78. Vander Hill sank two free throws to make it 82-78, but the Bulldogs scored once more to make the final Hope 82, Adrian 80. The home team may have deserved a better fate, but the Dutchmen had escaped with a two-point win. Vander Hill's hot shooting continued as he led all scorers with 34. Venhuizen put in 13, Clare Van Wieren 11, Gary Nederveld returned to the lineup to score 10, and Glenn Van Wieren had nine. Dick Seagert and Don Numbers each had 16 for Adrian, and John Johnson scored 14.

It was somehow appropriate that Hope's final game would be against archrival Calvin. The game on Wednesday, Feb. 27, was played at the Grand Rapids Civic Auditorium before a large crowd that had come to see if the much-improved Knights could spoil the Dutchmen's perfect MIAA season. Custodians at the Civic had done an inadequate job of cleaning after an earlier event, and both teams complained about the slippery floor. The first half did not go well for Hope, as Vander Hill was held to an uncharacteristic four points. Meanwhile, Calvin's Jim Van Eerden was on fire with 16, including four-of-four from the free throw stripe. With 50 percent shooting, the Knights' halftime margin was 35-28. The Dutchmen had taken 42 shots and connected on only 12.

**FAMILIAR SIGHT IN 1963 —
Ron Venhuizen on Base**

Hope outfielder Venhuizen was the MIAA batting champion with a .405 average.

The usual Hope-Calvin tension prevailed in the second half. Hope stayed in the game as Vander Hill got untracked, while Van Eerden was limited to three points. Finally, with 3:19 remaining, Venhuizen's two free throws gave Hope a one-point lead at 63-62. Chris Buys was now in the ball game for Hope. Coach De Vette had shown confidence in the freshman by inserting him in a pressure situation that caused veterans to quake. With 1:55 left, Buys was fouled and cashed in on both shots to make it 65-62. With 1:38 remaining, Glenn Van Wieren put in two more from the line to make it 67-62, but Tom Vander Woude completed a three-point play to make it 67-65. Hope then lost the ball, and in the process fouled Vander Woude, who made one of two to make it a one-point game, 67-66. Buys was again fouled and made one of two to give Hope the 68-66 victory. Vander Hill and Van Wieren led the Dutchmen with 15 each, Venhuizen followed with 14, Te Beest had seven, and newcomer Buys came through with five crucial second-half points. For the Knights of Coach Barney Steen, it was Jim Van Eerden leading with 19, Paul Tuls had 10, and Jim Langeland eight. In the stands this night were the Rev. and Mrs. Laverne Vander Hill who had flown out from New York to see their son Jim play his final game for Hope. Also on hand were the ever-faithful Kelly and Billie Van Wieren, parents of Glenn and Clare.

The Dutchmen finished the season with a 15-7 overall record that included a perfect 12-0 mark for the MIAA championship. Named to the All-MIAA team were Jim Vander Hill and Glenn Van Wieren of Hope, Ray Moore and But Acton of Alma, and John Johnson of Adrian. Vander Hill, the league's leading scorer for three consecutive seasons, was a unanimous choice for the MIAA most valuable player award.

*   *   *

Hope's 1963 spring trip in baseball was not a rousing success in terms of a won-lost record, but the chance to play games every day would pay dividends later. The Dutchmen took their lumps from Memphis State 12-2 and 10-1, from Bethel 11-6, and from Union 6-0 and 13-9. Games scheduled with Southwestern on Saturday, April 6, were rained out, and the team headed home.

On Monday, April 8, Hope made a stop in Greencastle, Ind., to take on De Pauw University, and the Dutchmen were finally in the groove with a 4-3 victory. Glenn Van Wieren pitched five innings of no-hit ball. He issued one walk, but the runner was later erased by a double play. Freshman George "Joey" Bosworth gave up three runs in the sixth on three hits, but Hope got one run in the first and three in the fifth to notch the win. Ron Venhuizen led the way with two hits.

The regular season opened in Detroit on Saturday, April 13, against Wayne State. Hope played well until the eighth inning, when the Tartars scored six unearned runs on two hits, five walks, and two errors. The Dutchmen rapped out 15 hits, but lefty Jim Van Til and Van Wieren had trouble holding Wayne batters in check and the home team went on to record a 12-10 victory.

The first games to be played on Hope's new baseball field took place on Thursday, April 18, with Ferris Institute furnishing the opposition. In the first game, Hope's Joey Bosworth served notice that he would be a force to be reckoned with. In limiting the Bulldogs to two hits, the right hander struck out 10 and walked only one. It was 0-0 at the end of seven, but in the ninth Jim Bultman was safe on an error, then advanced to second on Art Kramer's sacrifice. Rog Kroodsma singled and Bultman moved to third. Ron Venhuizen was hit by a pitched ball to load the bases. Glenn Van Wieren then singled home the winning run to give Hope and Bosworth the 1-0 shutout. Hope collected four hits, two by Kroodsma. It was an ideal way to inaugurate a new field.

In the second game, Ferris got one in the fourth, but Hope tied it in the fifth on an Art Kramer single. Jim Van Til gave up only one hit, but had to retire after spraining an ankle rounding third base. Neil Goodrich relieved, but issued three walks and a wild pitch, which produced two more runs and the 3-1 margin of victory.

Hope met Northwood Institute in a home doubleheader on Saturday, April 30. Freshman Pat Price and reliever Goodrich allowed the Northmen seven hits, but the Dutchmen also got seven, including home runs by Kroodsma and Van Wieren, which proved to be enough to give Hope an 8-5 win. In the second game, Kroodsma was off to a shaky start, giving up four hits and three runs in the first inning. But Hope also got three in the first, and Kroodsma took charge in blanking the visitors the rest of the way. Conrad "Skip" Nienhuis was behind the plate as Hope added four more runs to emerge the winner, 7-3.

Coach Morley Fraser and the Albion Britons were in Holland on Wednesday, April 24, for the opening MIAA doubleheader. In the first game, pitcher Glenn Van Wieren was in top form with a four-hitter and had good support as the Dutchmen played without an error. Coach Siedentop's charges collected six hits and five runs off Briton ace Jim Papenfus to help Van Wieren gain the 5-0 shutout. Keith Balcom and Clare Van Wieren each had two safeties. Hope hits were more plentiful in the second game as the Dutchmen totaled nine. Venhuizen led the way with three and Art Kramer and Cal Poppink each had two, while Jim Van Til and Joey Bosworth held the Britons to just four in recording the 6-3 victory. The twin win would loom large at season's end.

Hope's four-game win streak came to an end at Alma on Saturday, April 27, but good baseball was the order of the day. In the first game, Joey Bosworth pitched a three-hitter, struck out seven and walked none, but Alma scored two runs in the second on a two-base throwing error, Hope's only one of the game. The Dutchmen had six hits, but left seven on base as the Scots' Murphy chalked up the 2-0 shutout.

Alma was off to a fast start in the second game, scoring three in the first off Rog Kroodsma, then adding one in the fourth to make it 4-0. Hope came back with one in the fourth, then tied it with three in the fifth as Glenn Van Wieren tripled with Bultman, Kroodsma, and Venhuizen on base. There was no further scoring until the bottom of the 10th, when the Dutchmen again loaded the bases. Freshman Dan Koop then came through with a single to score Glenn Van Wieren and give Hope the much-needed 5-4 victory. In the course of the game, catcher Art Kramer cut down four out of five Scot runners attempting to steal.

The Dutchmen got two more at Olivet on Thursday, May 2. In the opener, Hope had 11 hits while Van Til held the Comets to six as he walked four but struck out nine. The big blow in Hope's 7-3 victory was Venhuizen's three-run homer in the first inning. In the nightcap, Bosworth walked five but struck out 15. The Dutchmen scored two in the first, then added three more in the fifth on Venhuizen's second three-run homer of the afternoon. But the Comets tied it and sent the game beyond the scheduled seven innings. In the eighth inning, Clare Van Wieren singled and then reached second when Balcom was safe on an error. Poppink put down a bunt, but in attempting to field it pitcher Art Greenstone threw wildly to first, allowing Clare Van Wieren to score from second and give the Dutchmen the 6-5 victory.

Hope took the opener in Holland against Adrian on Saturday, May 4. Kroodsma scattered 10 hits and aided his own cause with a home run. The Dutchmen had a total of nine hits in the 8-2 victory. Adrian won the second game with a 13-hit attack off starter Goodrich and Glenn Van Wieren, who came on the third. Jim Hoke was the big man for the winners with two homers and two doubles in the 7-4 win.

Next for the Dutchmen was a non-league encounter on Wednesday, May 8. Hope bats were silenced by Grand Rap-

THE 1963 HOPE COLLEGE BASEBALL TEAM
MIAA CO-CHAMPIONS WITH ALBION

Front Row L. to R.: Roger Kroodsma, Keith Balcom, Art Kramer, Captain Jim Bultman, Ron Venhuizen, Chuck Veurink, Herm Hoeksema. **2nd Row:** Assistant Coach Eldon Greij, Head Coach Daryl Siedentop, John Knapp, George "Joey" Bosworth, Jim Van Til, Bob Wilson, Steve Nordstrom, Jim Vande Poel (Spring Trip Driver). **3rd Row:** Clare Van Wieren, Dan Koop, Cal Poppink, Glenn Van Wieren, Al Edman.

ids Junior College pitcher Larry Harpman, who set the Dutchmen down with two hits. Hope used Van Til, Bosworth, Goodrich, and Clare Van Wieren on the mound. Sloppy play prevailed as JC committed seven errors and Hope four. GRJC was the eventual winner by a score of 6-3.

Kalamazoo was in Holland on Saturday, May 11, and Hornet pitcher John Mason was at his best. In the first game, he shut the Dutchmen down with but one hit, a single by Poppink. Glenn Van Wieren also pitched well, but had trouble in the first inning. Two walks and an error, plus a single by Frank Stuckey, produced the game's only run and gave Kazoo the win. John Mason attempted to play the ironman role by also pitching the second game, but Hope scored two in the second when Bultman singled with the bases loaded. The Dutchmen got two in the third and another pair in the seventh, when Clare Van Wieren singled and Kroodsma followed with a triple. Kroodsma then scored on a wild pitch to give Hope the 6-2 victory and a split for the day. Joey Bosworth pitched a two-hitter, walking five and striking out nine.

Hope tangled with Calvin on the Knollcrest field on Tuesday, May 14. Van Til took the mound in the first game with Kramer behind the plate. At game's end he had given up but two hits while striking out 10. In the fifth inning, Bultman singled, stole second, went to third on a wild pitch, and scored on Glenn Van Wieren's single. No one crossed the plate again until the seventh, when Glenn Van Wieren walked, was sacrificed to second by Kramer, advanced to third on a wild pitch, and scored on Kroodsma's sacrifice fly. Hope collected six hits, half of them by Bultman. The 2-0 shutout was Van Til's best performance of the season.

In the second game, Hope scored twice in the second inning on Chuck Veurink's triple. Calvin got one in the third, and tied the score at two on Ken Fletcher's single in

JAMES ELDON BULTMAN
Hope College — 1963

Chemistry Major, Hope Football Captain, twice Hope Baseball Captain, later Education Department Chairman, Dean of Social Sciences, President of Northwestern College, and finally, the 11th President of Hope College.

the sixth. The contest was finally called at the end of 10 innings due to darkness. Hope had a total of 10 hits, while the Knights got six off the combined offerings of Kroodsma, Bosworth, and Glenn Van Wieren. Clare Van Wieren led Hope with three hits, and Charlie Veurink had two. The 2-2 tie would haunt the Dutchmen as, at the time, ties did not count in the standings.

The Albion Britons had played well following the double loss to Hope, but, like the Dutchmen, they had suffered one tie. The result was an 8-3 MIAA record and a co-championship with Hope, also at 8-3. Hope's overall mark was 13-11. Named to the All-MIAA Team were Captain Jim Bultman at shortstop, pitcher Jim Van Til, and outfielder Ron Venhuizen. Venhuizen was the league-batting champion with a .405 average. As a final accolade, Jim Bultman won the Jack Schouten most valuable player award for the second year in a row.

* * *

Three veteran tennis players returned from Doc Green's 1962 championship team. Norm Hess, Arlyn Lanting, and Bud Hoffman were joined by three talented freshmen: Byron "Butch" Hopma, Lance Stell, and Jeff Jorgenson. Jim Riemersma would also see action in spot situations. By all accounts the 1962 spring trip had been an unqualified success, and there was no reason not to repeat the venture.

Accordingly, the Dutchmen headed south and met Vanderbilt University in Nashville on Saturday, March 30. Hope's 5-4 victory over the Comodores featured Norm Hess (H) getting the best of Charles Will 6-4, 6-2, Bobby Frist defeated Hopma 6-4, 7-5, Ken Chapin took Lanting 3-6, 6-1, 6-2, Stell defeated Lindsey Builder 6-1, 5-7, 6-4, Hoffman won over Lee Tucker 9-7, 6-3, and Henry Dodge defeated Jorgenson 6-2, 6-1. In doubles, it was Hess-Hopma over Will-Builder 1-6, 6-3, 6-0, Chapin-Frist over Lanting-Hoffman 4-6, 7-5, 6-2, and Stell-Jorgenson over Dodge-Tucker 9-7, 7-5.

In Tallahassee on Monday, April 1, Hope defeated the Florida State freshman team 6-3. In singles, Steve Guse defeated Hess 6-3, 6-2, Hopma took Steve Burtt 6-3, 3-6, 9-7, Randy Cameron (FS) defeated Lanting 6-3, 6-2, Stell won from Jack Jenison 7-5, 6-4, Hoffman defeated Mike Baldwin 6-4, 6-2, and Jorgensen took Vephula 6-2, 6-4. In doubles, it was Hess-Hopma over Guse-Burtt 3-6, 6-1, 6-1, Cameron-Jenison over Lanting-Hoffman 6-1, 6-4, and Stell-Jorgensen over Baldwin-Vephula 6-4, 6-2.

The next day Hope met the Florida State varsity with less success. The Seminoles dominated play and ended with an 8-1 team victory. In singles, it was Len Wood over Hess 6-1, 6-2. Wood was the number-one player in South Africa, but now attending Florida State. Jon Paton defeated Hopma 6-1, 6-2, Paul Bennett won over Lanting 6-0, 6-1, Don Monk defeated Stell 6-1, 6-1, Hoffman, Hope's only winner, defeated Dick Fisher 2-6, 6-3, 6-3, and Ken Alcorn defeated Jorgenson 6-4, 6-3. In doubles Wood-Bennett won over Hess-Hopma 6-1, 6-1, Paton-Monk took Lanting-Hoffman 6-2, 6-2, and Alcorn-Fisher defeated Stell-Jorgenson 6-2, 5-7, 6-3.

On Wednesday, April 3, the Dutchmen were in Gainesville to take on the University of Florida. In singles, it was Jerry Pfeiffer over Hess 6-3, 8-6, Fred Scapa defeated Hopma 6-2, 6-2, Ron Rehbuhn bested Lanting 6-4, 6-2, Stell defeated Bud Agnew 0-6, 6-4, 7-5, Don Lasman took Hoffman 6-3, 6-3, and Lee Landsburg defeated Jorgensen 6-2, 6-1. In doubles, it was Hess-Hopma over Schapa-Dodd 6-3, 6-3, Rebuhn-Agnew over Lanting-Hoffman 6-2, 6-2, and Stell-Jorgensen over Seitz-Davids 6-4, 6-4. Coach Green felt his charges had shown well in the 6-3 loss.

Hope met another strong opponent in Winter Park on Thursday, April 4. The Tars of Rollins stood 10-2 on the season, and downed the Dutchmen, 8-1. John Lawrence defeated Hess 6-0, 6-3, Rol Greco won over Hopma 6-1, 6-4, Bob Bolink defeated Lanting 6-1, 6-2, Dave Ackerman took Hoffman 6-1, 6-1, and Bill Law defeated Jorgensen 6-0, 6-4. In doubles, Hope claimed its only victory when Hess-Hopma defeated Lawrence-Bolink 6-1, 6-1. Greco-Law won over Lanting-Stell 6-2, 6-4, and Calvin-Ward defeated Hoffman-Jorgensen 6-1, 6-2.

With the temperature at 85 degrees, Hope met Davidson on Friday, April 5. The match was played at Daytona Beach as Davidson was also on spring break. The teams were evenly matched, but the Dutchmen managed to eke out a 5-4 team victory. In singles, Hess defeated Bob Arstell 6-0, 6-1, Hopma won over Gene Mc Cutchen 6-0, 7-5, Stell took Schutt 6-2, 3-6, 6-2, Lanting defeated Frank Baumgardner 6-0, 6-1, and John Ariel won over Jorgensen 6-4, 6-2. In doubles, it was Hess-Hopma over Arstell-Rick Reed 7-5, 6-1, Mc Cutchen-Schutt over Lanting-Hoffman 3-6, 6-2, 6-4, and Baumgardner-Backlund over Stell-Jorgensen 7-5, 6-1.

In Deland, Fla., on Saturday, April 6, it was Hope 8-1 over Stetson. Hess got the best of Dave Mc Ilvain 6-3, 6-1, Hopma defeated John Carpenter 6-3, 7-5, and Stell won from Denise Wall 6-1, 6-4. Wall was one of very few women playing on men's collegiate teams in 1963. Lanting defeated Rex Coonley 6-0, 6-2, Hoffman took Rick Reiff 6-2, 6-2, and Charles Beasley defeated Jeff Jorgensen 6-3, 6-4. In doubles, it was Hess-Hopma over Mc Ilvain-Carpenter 6-2, 7-5, Lanting-Hoffman over Reiff-Bambini 6-4, 6-0, and Stell-Jorgensen over Beasley-Faust 7-5, 6-4.

On the way home, the Dutchmen made a stop in Bloomington, Ind., to test the caliber of play in the Big Ten Conference. Indiana University had enjoyed its best year ever in 1962 at 19-3. Hess had the satisfaction of winning the number-one singles over Rod Mc Nervey 1-6, 6-3, 6-4, but it was pretty much downhill from that point on as the Hoosiers chalked up an 8-1 victory. Charles Kane defeated Hopma 6-1, 6-2, Alan Graham took Stell 6-1, 6-0, Jim Binkley defeated Lanting 6-1, 6-4, Bill Wham won over Hoffman 6-3, 6-3, and Bob Wham defeated Jorgensen 6-0, 6-2. The doubles team of Mc Nerver-Kane took Hess-Hopma 6-3, 6-4, it was Graham-Wham over Lanting-Hoffman 6-3, 6-1, and Binkley-Fichter over Stell-Jorgensen 6-2, 6-2.

The Dutchmen opened the regular season with a trip to Grand Rapids on Tuesday, April 16. Their recent experience against strong competition was in evidence as they downed Grand Rapids Junior College 9-0. In singles, Hess defeated Ken Wieland 6-3, 6-2, Hopma defeated Jack Newberry 6-0, 6-1, Lanting defeated Jim Slomner 6-3, 6-1, Stell took Ken Yost 6-1, 6-1, Hoffman defeated Duane Wiersma 6-1, 6-0, and Riemersma defeated Jim Vary 6-0, 6-0. In doubles, it was Hess-Hopma over Wieland-Newberry 6-2, 6-1, Lanting-Hoffman over Slomner-Yost 6-0, 6-2, and Stell-Jorgensen over Wiersma-Vary 6-0, 6-3.

Wheaton and Hope met for the first time in the sport of tennis on Saturday, April 20. Despite the homecourt advantage, Hope had its hands full in finally edging the Crusaders 5-4. In singles, Dennis Bennema downed Hess 6-0, 6-1, Hopma defeated Tom Claus 6-0, 6-2, Jay Hakes took Lanting 6-4, 6-3, Stell defeated Sam Mac Aluso 6-3, 5-7, 6-3, Hoffman defeated Ron Webb 6-3, 6-0, and Hal Peterson downed Riemersma 6-2, 6-2. In doubles, it was Bennema-Claus over Hess-Hopma 6-3, 8-6, Lanting-Hoffman over Hakes-Mac Aluso 2-6, 6-2, 6-2, and Stell-Jorgensen over Webb-Peterson 10-8, 8-6.

The MIAA season for Hope was off to an impressive start with successive 7-0 shutout victories over Albion, Alma, Olivet, and Adrian. And then came Kalamazoo. The result was another 7-0 shutout, but this time Hope was on the short end as George Akker's team demonstrated its superiority over the best that the MIAA could produce. In singles, Kalamazoo's Loren Campbell and Hess continued their intense rivalry with a three-setter that went to Campbell 5-7, 6-4, 6-4. Dick Johnson defeated Hopma 6-0, 6-1, Holland's Jack Hulst downed Lanting 6-0, 6-2, Art Walters defeated Stell 6-2, 6-4, and George Smillie took Hoffman 6-1, 6-0. In doubles, it was Campbell-Jim Harkema over Hess-Hopma 6-2, 6-3, and Johnson-Smillie over Lanting-Hoffman 7-5, 7-5. The match was played on Saturday, May 11, a date the Dutchmen would just as soon forget.

The dual meet season concluded in Grand Rapids on Tuesday, May 14. The Calvin Knights at 4-2 made a strong showing before falling to the 5-1 Dutchmen by a 5-2 team score. In singles, Dave Vander Hart defeated Norm Hess 6-4, 8-10, 6-3, Hopma downed Ken Oosterhouse 6-4, 6-3, Lanting defeated Dick Bultman 6-4, 6-3, Stell took Gord Vander Burg (7-5, 6-4, and Jim Langeland defeated Hoffman 7-5, 4-6, 7-5. In doubles, Hess-Hopma defeated Vander Hart-Oosterhouse 6-2, 8-10, 6-3, and Lanting-Hoffman downed Langeland-Vander Burg 7-5, 7-5.

The May 17-18 MIAA meet was held for the first time in Grand Rapids on Calvin's new Knollcrest Campus. The change of scenery did not seem to bother the Hornets of Kalamazoo, who edged Hope 18-15 in team points to take yet another championship. Hope had finalists in every flight, but won only one. Lanting got the best of Kalamazoo's Hulst 6-3, 5-7, 6-4 in the third-flight finals. In the first-flight finals, Calvin's Dave Vander Hart bested Hess 6-3, 5-7, 6-4 in a match that took 2¾ hrs. Hess had beaten K's Campbell in the first round. Campbell won the consolation title. In the second flight, Dick Johnson (K) defeated Hopma 6-2, 10-8, and Art Walters (K) won over Stell (H) 6-2, 6-4 in the fourth-flight finals. A deserving Dave Vander Hart of Calvin was named winner of the Allen B. Stowe Award.

With an 11-5 overall record, the Dutchmen of Coach Doc Green had enjoyed another outstanding season. Finishing second in the MIAA was certainly no disgrace, and would come to be almost like a championship in years to come to all MIAA teams save Kalamazoo.

Meanwhile, Hope's women, under Coach Joan Pyle, were also enjoying a fine season. In duals, the lady Dutch recorded wins over Aquinas, Adrian, Albion, Calvin, and Western Michigan while losing only to Kalamazoo. In the Field Day meet, Hope finished fourth behind Kalamazoo, Calvin, and Albion. Team members included Joanne Visscher, Daughn Schipper, Barb Kouw, Martie Tucker, Joan Vander Veen, Toodie Finlay, Norma French, and Sally Kooistra.

* * *

Coach Bill Oostenink's golf team had endured a couple of tough seasons, but Hope would move up a notch in 1963. Leading the team was veteran Jim Wiersma, who was joined by Jim Thompson, John Woodward, Ed Van Dam, and Dean Overman, the latter from the basketball squad.

On Monday, April 15, the team was off to a good start with a 10½-5½ victory over Alma at the American Legion Country Club course. Wiersma was medalist with a 73 and a 3-0 win over John Perrin of Alma, who shot an 80. Mike Tucker (A) with an 81 defeated Thompson 2½-½. Thompson had an 84. John Peace (A) with a 79 defeated Woodward 2-1. Woodward was close with an 80. Overman with an 81 defeated Bill Brown (A) 2-1. Brown had an 86. Van Dam (84) had Hope's other win at 3-0 over Alma's John Hendershot at 91.

In a triangular meet with Adrian on Friday, April 26, Hope posted victories over Adrian 11½-4½, and over Defiance of Ohio, 9½-6½. John Johnson of Adrian was medalist for the day with a 74 while Wiersma was best for Hope at 76.

Hope's match in Grand Rapids on Wednesday, May 1, was played at the Green Ridge Country Club with Grand Rapids JC furnishing the opposition. In the 8-7 Hope victory, it was Wiersma over Carl Doornbos 3-0, Thompson over Jim Steevy 3-0, Rich Thiebout over Woodward 3-0, Dave Wessell over Overman 2½-½, while Van Dam and Dick Davey ended in a 1½-1½ tie. Thiebout of JC was medalist for the day with a 78.

The Dutchmen were again winners at the Charlotte Country Club on Thursday, May 2, as they downed the Olivet Comets 10-6. It was Dan Mathews over Wiersma 3-0, Chuck Brown over Thompson 3-0, Overman over Dave Banks 3-0, Woodward over Bruce Mc Donald 3-0, and Van Dam over Bill Knight 3-0. Olivet's Dan Mathews was medallist with a 78, but the Dutchmen took team medalist honors for their 10th point.

The Calvin match at the Legion Country Club on Monday, May 6, was reported in the papers as an 8-7 Calvin victory. Paul Tuls defeated Thompson 3-0, Wiersma defeated Ed Fredericks 3-0, Bob Vander Sand took Overman 2-1, Woodward defeated Brad Prints 3-0, and Jim Harem won over Van Dam 3-0. Paul Tuls was medalist with a 76. Coach Oostenink protested the reported 8-7 Calvin victory on grounds that Hope had not been credited with the one point awarded as a result of team medalist honors. The matter was placed in the hands of Commissioner Win Schuler, who eventually ruled in Hope's favor. The match was then officially listed as an 8-8 tie.

The Dutchmen continued to do well on Tuesday, May 7, when they hosted Kalamazoo. It was Van Dam over Tony Janssen 2-1, Wiersma over Norm Young 3-0, Robert Keyser over Overman 3-0, Thompson over Dave Bellingham 2½-½, and John Persons over Woodward 2-1. The final count showed Hope with 8½, to 6½ for Kalamazoo. Van Dam enjoyed his best day of the year with a 76 and medalist honors.

Hope's victory string was halted at the Kent Country Club on Thursday, May 9, when Aquinas defeated the Dutchmen, 14-6. In a slightly different scoring system, Len Bridge Jr. defeated Overman 4-0, Wiersma edged John Kerzynowski 2½-1½, Thompson defeated Tom Gunn 3½-½, Ron Miller defeated Van Dam 4-0, and Frank Berles won by forfeit over Woodward, who was forced to withdraw after nine holes due to a leg injury. Aquinas's Len Bridge Jr. was medalist with a 73.

It remained for the Britons of Albion to saddle the Dutchmen with their first MIAA loss on Tuesday, May 14. On their home course, the Britons were at their best in registering the 11-5 victory. Medalist Bill Valuck shot a fine 71 in downing Overman 3-0. It was Wiersma over Doug Kelbey 3-0, Fred Adams over Thompson 3-0, Ken Curtis over Woodward 2-1, and Bill Rivers over Van Dam 2-1.

For the first time in several years, the MIAA meet would move from Kalamazoo. The Friday, May 17, match was held instead, in Grand Rapids at the Cascade Country Club, with the last nine holes played in the rain. Alma was the surprise winner for the day with a team total of 831 strokes. Kalamazoo was a close second with 834, and Hope took third with 842. Albion followed with 845, Calvin had 883, Olivet 902, and Adrian 1,014. Mike Tucker of Alma won medalist honors with a 36-hole total of 158. Wiersma ended in a three-way tie for second with 160, but by the flip of a coin won the medal from Bob Keyser of Kalamazoo and John Perrin of Alma. In the overall standings, it was Alma and Kalamazoo tied for first with 20 points, Hope third with 17, Albion fourth with 14, Calvin fifth with 9, Olivet sixth with 4, and Adrian sixth with 0. Individually, Overman had carded 166, Van Dam 171, Thomson 172, and Woodward 173. With the third-place finish the Dutchmen were once more competitive in the MIAA.

* * *

Jon Schoon, better known as a premier receiver in football, was captain of the 1963 Hope track team. It was an improved team, but still had trouble competing with the league's top teams. The season opened with a home meet with Grand Rapids Junior College on Saturday, April 20. Hope did well in the field events, but the JC team won all the running events except an 880-yard relay, which was agreed to as a special event. Hope's team of Dave Bolhuis, Mike Schrier, Jon Schoon, and Chris Buys won in a time of 1:34.7. Chris Buys won the pole vault and shot put, Bob Mackay and Bruce Menning went one-two in the high jump, and Jack Buys took the javelin, but the final count was GRJC 78, Hope 58. JC's Bob Carpenter set a record for Hope's track with a 440 time of 49.9

Kalamazoo hosted a triangular meet on Tuesday, April 23, that included Hope and Adrian. Adrian captured seven firsts, Kalamazoo had five, and Hope three, but with one event to go Hope and the Hornets were tied at 48 while Adrian led with 55. The final event was the javelin throw and Adrian's Tom Smith was the winner, but Hope's Jack Buys took second to give Hope 51 points to Kalamazoo's 49. Adrian won the meet with 62 points. Hope's firsts were recorded by Mackay in the high jump, John Simons in the broad jump, and Chris Buys in the pole vault.

The Olivet Comets were in Holland for a dual meet on Saturday, April 27. Coach Stu Parsell had some good performers, but not enough of them to prevent Hope from winning, 82-49. Chris Buys was a triple-winner for the Dutchmen with wins in the pole vault, shot, and discus. With the straddle roll style, Bob Mackay won the high jump with a Hope record of 6 1¼". Hope's mile relay team of Bill Hultgren, Buys, Mackay, and Jon Schoon finished off the afternoon with a victory in that event. The Dutchmen were able to take firsts in 11 of 15 events.

Hope continued to score well as it hosted the Alma Scots on Wednesday, May 1. Alma's Vic Yorick won the two-mile run and Mike Bowers took the javelin throw, but the Dutchmen were first in the remaining 13 events enroute to a 95-35 victory. Buys again won his three events, and ran a leg on the winning mile relay team. Harlan Hyink was second in the pole vault, and Menning was second to Mackay in the high jump. Gary Holvick and Schoon were one-two in the low hurdles while Schoon and Hultgren went one-two in the 440.

It was a different story when the Adrian Bulldogs came to town on Saturday, May 4. Coach Tom Allen's well-balanced team took firsts in 10 of 16 events and downed the Dutchmen, 77-58. Hope's winners were Holvick in the high and low hurdles, Schoon in the 440, Mackay in the high jump, Ron Hilbelink in the broad jump, and Buys in the pole vault. An 880-yard relay was added to the regular 15 events, and Adrian prevailed when Hope was disqualified.

Hope fared no better at Valparaiso on Wednesday, May 9. Schoon won the 440, Mackay the high jump, and Simons the broad jump, but the Crusaders took firsts in the remaining 13 events and cruised to an 85-50 victory. The cinder track was not clearly marked, and a bizarre turn of events occurred in the low hurdle race. From a staggered start in an outer lane, Valpo's Benz ran into Holvick's lane and over his hurdles the rest of the way to victory. There was no disqualification.

Still reeling from the Adrian and Valparaiso setbacks, the Dutchmen traveled to Calvin's Knollcrest campus on Saturday, May 11. Hope was outclassed by the MIAA champion Knights, but managed to win four events. Buys won the pole vault, Mackay the high jump, Schrier the broad jump, and Jack Buys the javelin. Calvin's Ray Hommes set a Calvin record in the mile with a time of 4:20.7, and Nelson Miedema did likewise in the two-mile with a time of 9:35.7.

At Albion on Tuesday, May 14, Hope was somewhat better, but still came out on the short end, 77-53. Schoon took the 440, Holvick the low hurdles, Buys the shot and pole vault, and Simons the broad jump. Dean Dooley had taken over as the Britons' coach from long-time mentor Elkin Isaac, who now devoted full time to teaching and the athletics directorship. This day the latter would serve as starter and referee.

For the first time in several years, the MIAA conference meet was not held in Kalamazoo. Calvin's new Knollcrest Campus provided a fresh look and the host school again prevailed, this time with 77½ points. Albion followed with 51, Kalamazoo 32, Hope 24½, Olivet 18, Adrian 11, and Alma also with 11. Buys was Hope's only gold medal winner, in the pole vault with a height of 12' 6", his best of the season. MacKay took second in the high jump and Menning was fifth, while Schrier and Simons went three-four in the broad jump. Sterk was fourth in the mile, Schoon third in the 440, Holvick fourth in the high hurdles, and Buys fourth in the shot. Hope's mile relay team picked up one point with a fifth in that event. Jack Schouten, Hope's former coach and athletics director, was honorary referee for the day.

* * *

Kalamazoo repeated as the MIAA All-Sports champion with 69 points, but Hope moved up to second with 54. Next in order were Albion 49, Calvin 40, Alma 31, Adrian 30, and Olivet 21.

* * *

On July 1, 1963, Calvin A. Vander Werf became the eighth president of Hope College. An outstanding student of chemistry, Vander Werf had graduated from Hope in 1937. After earning a Ph.D. at the Ohio State University, he joined the faculty at the University of Kansas. He subsequently became chairman of its department of chemistry. Vander Werf had never been an athlete, but he was "gung-ho" on athletics. He had chaired the Kansas Faculty Committee on Athletics, and informed the Hope coaches that he had been instrumental in recruiting Jayhawk superstars Wilt Chamberlain and Gayle Sayers. The new president was given to alliteration in his descriptions, and thus quarterback Harlan Hyink soon became "Hurlin' Harlan" and, at a later time, freshman photographer Tom Renner was tagged "Telephoto Tom." The phrase "on the cutting edge" was often used by Vander Werf, and it was clear that he hoped to have his institution in that position.

Opening football drills in 1963 began on Monday, Sept. 2. Coach Russ De Vette greeted 55 candidates, including 28 freshmen, and it was hoped that the squad would jell quickly enough to put Hope in a winning mode. Defensive end Ken Quakkelaar was the captain.

Hope's opener at Ashland College was unique in that the Dutchmen were truly "Flying" Dutchmen. A guarantee

MAINSTAYS IN HOPE'S 1963 OFFENSE

The passing combination of Harlan Hyink (44) to Bill Hultgren (82) was complimented by the running of halfbacks Chuck Veurink (45) and Bill Keur (23).

Harlan Hyink

Bill Hultgren

Bill Keur

Chuck Veurink

172

from Ashland made it possible for me to charter a Capital Airlines DC-3 out of Grand Rapids, and a Hope football team flew for the first time. The 40-man contingent left the Kent County Airport at 1:30 p.m. on Saturday, Sept. 14, landed in Mansfield, Ohio, then proceeded to Ashland via bus for the 8 p.m. game.

Defenses had the better of it in the first half, but late in the second quarter Ashland's Chawanski booted a 17-yard field goal and the Eagles led 3-0 at the intermission. Hope miscues led to the remaining Ashland scores and the eventual 24-0 shutout. The Dutchmen were hampered by the absence of two key players--Roger Kroodsma and Bill Keur did not make the trip due to injuries--but Hope simply did not play well. Early in the third quarter, a Hope punt was partially blocked. It was picked up by Eagle fullback Gary Moore, who ran 37 yards for the touchdown. The kick by Chawanski was good, and as the quarter ended it was Ashland 10, Hope 0. With seven minutes left in the game, Ashland's Wier intercepted a Hyink pass and raced 55 yards to score. The point was again good, making it 17-0. Following the kickoff, the Dutchmen fumbled deep in their territory and the defenders of Coach Fred Martinelli recovered. Eagle halfback Moose went the final five yards, and Chawrnski converted to give Ashland the 24-0 win. Hope, unable to generate any offense, had lost four of five fumbles and had penetrated beyond the 50-yard line only once. The team was back in Grand Rapids by midnight, hoping for better things in the week ahead.

Hope's second game was also in Ohio, this time a first meeting with Findlay College on Sept. 21. Byron E. Morgan was in his first year as coach of the Oilers, and it was his team that drew first blood. In the first quarter, halfback Lane broke loose on a dive play and went 20 yards to score. The point try was not good, but Findlay enjoyed the early 6-0 lead. Later in the period, Jim Van Dam blocked a Findlay punt but the Dutchmen failed to score. On Hope's next possession, Hyink hit Hultgren with a 20-yard pass to the three-yard line. Halfback Chuck Veurink then went off-tackle for the TD.

The point attempt was blocked, leaving the score at 6-6. Following the kickoff, Findlay marched the length of the field with Odell Barry going the final yards for the score. This time the conversion was good, and the Oilers led 13-6 at the half.

Early in the third period, Findlay put together pass completions of five and 15 yards, plus a 35-yard sprint by halfback Lane, to score a third time. The conversion increased the Oilers' lead to 20-6. Still in the third, a Hyink pass was intercepted and in six plays it was Lane again crossing the goal line. The extra point failed, but the Findlay lead was now 26-6. In the fourth quarter, freshman Randy Meulman blocked a Findlay punt and end Tom Cousineau recovered for the Dutchmen. Quarterback Bobby Schantz made it to the one on a keeper, and halfback Jim Bekkering went in for the score. Hyink then passed to Joe Kusak for two points to make it 26-14. Late in the game, a Findlay defensive end picked off a Hyink pass on the Hope 25 and ran it into the end zone. The successful kick made the final score Findlay 33, Hope 14.

ALL-AROUND PLAYER

Fullback Charlie Langeland (43) excelled as a power runner, blocker, and receiver.

After the season's discouraging start, the Hope coaches were heartened by the return of Kroodsma and Keur, though the latter would be used sparingly for a time. The Wheaton Crusaders of Coach Jack Swartz came to Holland on Sept. 28 for a night game at Riverview Park. On a rainy night, only 200 fans huddled under the covered grandstand. The first quarter was a standoff, but Hope struck early in the second period following a long punt return by Bekkering. Bekkering took the ball on the Hope 46 and was finally pulled down on the Wheaton 24. Seven plays later, Veurink went three yards on a right end sweep for the game's first score. Steve Wessling's kick put Hope ahead 7-0, but midway in the quarter Bob Bates intercepted a Hope pass and seven plays later quarterback Larry Sims was into the end zone with a two-yard sneak. The kick failed, leaving Hope in the lead 7-6. Wheaton was on the march again with a 62-yard, nine-play drive. Albie Harris scored on a 12-yard sweep with 1:36 left in the quarter. The run for two points by Larry Sims failed, but the Crusaders took a 12-7 lead to the locker room at the half.

After two exchanges in the third period, Hope mounted a drive from its own 20. The Dutchmen moved the ball with off-tackle smashes and two long passes. A Hyink-to-Hultgren aerial covered 37 yards and placed the ball on the Wheaton 38. A few plays

later, the same combination went for 26 yards and the touchdown. Hyink then passed to Kusak for two points, and Hope led 15-12 with 5:24 left in the period. The visitors showed their stuff in the fourth quarter with a nine-play march that covered 74 yards and reached paydirt with 10:49 left in the game. Albie Harris went over guard for the score and Tom Jarman kicked the point for a 19-15 lead, which held up the remainder of the game. The Dutchmen had shown some improvement, but a loss was still a loss.

Hope's first MIAA opponent was Kalamazoo, the 1962 league champion. A crowd of 3,000 turned out at Riverview to see the Dutchmen do battle with the Hornets of Coach Rolla Anderson. Hope was in early trouble when the visitors mounted a first quarter drive of 61 yards. Eglis Lode went up the middle for the final three yards, and John Persons kicked the point to give Kazoo a 7-0 lead with 2:05 left in the period. In the second quarter, the Hornets were relentless with an 83-yard march and this time Ron Creager dove through for four yards and the touchdown. Persons's kick made it 14-0 with 6:55 left. Hope aided the Kazoo cause by fumbling the ensuing kickoff, and K's George Lindenberg recovered on the Hope 13. The Dutch could not contain Ed Lauerman on an end sweep, and the Hornets had their third TD. Persons's kick was again in the right place to make it 21-0 with 5:42 left in the half. The Dutchmen wre finally able to move the ball and found themselves on the Kazoo 33 with three minutes remaining. After a holding penalty, the Dutchmen were on the 12. A Hyink-to-Hultgren pass put Hope on the board, but the pass for two points failed and it was 21-6 at the half.

The second half began with another Kalamazoo drive, but linebacker Jim Van Dam stopped the threat with an interception on the Hope 12. A momentum swing was in progress, but the Dutchmen still had problems. A 33-yard pass from Hyink to fullback Charlie Langeland moved the ball to the Kalamazoo 28, but the Hornets held. Later, the Dutchmen posed a real threat as they reached the eight, but a fourth down pass fell incomplete and Kazoo took over. Three plays later, Eglis Lode fumbled and Hope's Van Dam recovered on the Kalamazoo 22. After a two-yard loss, Hyink again found Hultgren in the end zone for Hope's second score. A pass to halfback Keur was good for two points,

CENTERED ON EXCELLENCE
Center Fred Van Tatenhove was Hope's most valuable player in 1963.

and the gap narrowed to 21-14 with 8:56 left in the game. The Hope defense had come to life, and the Dutchmen were on the march again, this time to the Hornets' 30, but an illegal procedure penalty and a last-minute interception ended the threat. The Dutchmen had paid the price for too many first-half miscues.

With back-to-back losing seasons and now an 0-4 start, conditions were grim. No one needed to tell Hope's coaches that "the natives were restless." Taking stock of the situation at the dawn of week five, we found reason to be confident that our team could indeed turn the corner. Two of the losses had been by the margin of one touchdown. There was no shortage of talent, especially on offense. Hyink was a proven passer and had an outstanding target in Hultgren, not to mention Kusak, Keur, Veurink, and Langeland, all sure receivers. The running attack was above average with left half Veurink (fastest man on the baseball team) and shifty Keur at the other half. Perhaps the find of the year had been freshman Charlie Langeland of North Muskegon. Langeland's combination of abilities made him the consummate fullback: speed and power as a runner, good hands as a receiver, and unusual effectiveness as a blocker. The line was solid across the front, with center Fred Van Tatenhove leading the way. The return of Kroodsma at middle linebacker had strengthened a defense that had been a question

November 14, 1963 - "GLORY DAY"

In the first row L. to R.: Glenn Van Wieren, President Vander Werf, cheerleader Mary Finlay, Captain Ken Quakkelaar, Coach Russ De Vette, Gary Holvick, Ken Carpenter.

mark. Could the pieces finally come together for a turn-around? We would find out at Alma on Saturday, Oct. 12.

Jim Van Dam had fractured a bone in his hand during the Kalamazoo game and would be out of action for two games. His replacement at guard for the Alma game was Bob White of Homewood, Ill. Alma, under new coach Bill Carr, stood 1-3 on the season, and coupled with Hope's 0-4 record crowd interest was at a low ebb. Some 500 die-hard fans were scattered throughout the Bahlke Field stadium. In the middle of the first quarter, Langeland intercepted an Alma pass on the Scots' 37. Three plays later, Langeland, now on offense, drove one yard up the middle for the game's first score. Wessling kicked the point, and Hope was off on the right foot at 7-0. With four minutes gone in the second quarter, the Scots came back with a pass from Tom Miller to Van Mulligan that covered 44 yards. Lou Economou completed the drive by diving one yard over guard for the score. Jim Flora was successful on a rollout for two points, which put the Scots up 8-7. The lead held up at halftime after Hope blocked an 18-yard field goal attempt.

With 1:50 left in the third period, Hyink lofted a pass to Hultgren that covered 39 yards and resulted in Hope's second TD. The point try was not good, but Hope had regained the lead at 13-8 as time ran out in the quarter. The combination worked again with 12:12 left in the game and a Hyink-to-Hultgren pass for two points made it 21-8. There was no further scoring and the Dutchmen had finally notched a win. Hultgren finished with six receptions for 145 yards, and Charley Langeland rushed for 73 yards in 14 carries. The Hope secondary chipped in with four interceptions.

Adrian, with a 3-1 league record, was Hope's homecoming opponent on October 19. A crowd of 4,000 filled the stands at Riverview to see if the Dutchmen could manage back-to-back wins. Hope scored first with 5:39 left in the first quarter, when Wessling kicked a 16-yard field goal. The Hope defense held after the kickoff, and on fourth down the Adrian kicker fumbled the snap from center. Hope recovered on the Adrian 13. A Hyink-to-Veurink pass put the ball on the two, and on the next play Veurink hurdled over right tackle for the touchdown. Steve Wessling's kick made it 10-0 at the half. In the third quarter, Hyink again found Veurink with a pass, this time for 17 yards to the Adrian two. Keur then went off left tackle for the score. The kick attempt was not good, but things were going well for the Dutchmen with a 16-0 lead.

A quarter of play remained, and the Bulldogs were not finished. At the 13:29 mark, Jim Dumont intercepted a Hyink pass on the Adrian 35. Eight plays later, Adrian pushed across its first score on a one-yard sneak by quarterback Phil Kench. His run attempt for two points was not good, but the visitors were on the board at 16-6. As the Dutch defense tired in the closing minutes, Adrian put together an 86-yard drive that culminated in an 18-yard touchdown pass from Phil Kench to Dick Goodrich. Kench's second run for two points was again stymied, but the score moved to 16-12. The Hope defense stiffened in the closing minutes thanks to stellar performances by Kroodsma, Van Tatenhove, and Poppink, and Hope had finally won two in row.

Albion was heavily favored in its homecoming game with Hope on Oct. 26. A crowd of 6,000 greeted the Dutchmen at the Britons' Alumni Field. The opening kickoff had to be delayed when the Hope bus blew a tire three miles west of Battle Creek. Fortunately, a school bus from Paw Paw High School happened along and stopped to investigate. Hope players and their gear were hurriedly piled into the school bus, which got them to Albion with a minimum delay. The Greyhound's rear tire was changed and the empty bus made it to Albion at about kickoff time.

Keur received the opening kick, and with a fine return made it to the Hope 40. Eleven running plays by Keur, Veurink, and Langeland took the ball to the Britons' 13. With fourth down and four, Hyink found Hultgren in the end zone for Hope's first score. Wessling's successful conversion made it 7-0 with 9:11 left in the first quarter. In the second quarter, Hope's Paul Bast tackled Bob Parrit on the Albion two after a fumbled punt. Unable to move, the Britons punted to their own 39. Two plays later, end Joe Kusak got behind the Albion secondary and grabbed a 35-yard Hyink pass for Hope's second touchdown. Wessling's point attempt was blocked, but Hope's lead was now 13-0. A subsequent Albion drive took them to the Hope 13 when Poppink was called for pass interference. The Britons moved to the five on the next play, but time ran out in the half with the Dutchmen still leading 13-0.

The determined Britons took the second half kickoff and marched to the Hope 26, but on fourth down Quakkelaar broke through from his end position for a sack of quarterback Dave Neilson on the 33. A seven-play Hope drive saw Veurink sweep right end to the Albion 12. He was then rewarded with a pass from Hyink for the TD. Hyink's pass to Kusak was good for two points and the Dutchman lead was 21-0 with 7:20 remaining in the third quarter. Coach Morley Fraser's team got it together in the fourth period and marched 67 yards to score. Neilson completed five of six passes, and J.B. Elzy went three yards around end for the touchdown. The two-point try failed, leaving the score at 21-6. The Dutchmen held for the remaining three minutes in their best performance of the season. Hyink completed 10 of 18 passes for 114 yards, while Langeland rushed for 80 yards, Keur for 44, and Veurink for 42. The return of guard Jim Van Dam also helped. Elzy's 53 yards led the Briton attack.

When the Dutchmen pulled into Olivet on a cold Nov. 2, the Comets were still smarting from an earlier 10-9 last-minute loss to Albion. Now in Coach Stu Parsell's fifth season, the Comets had again fallen on hard times. Adding to Parsell's woes was the sidelining of ace receiver Dominic Livedoti, who had broken an arm and was out for the season. A Reed Field crowd of 150 braved the elements to see if the Comets could turn it around. It would be a spectator game with plenty of scoring. Hope struck first. With 7:58 left in the first quarter, Veurink scored on a one-yard sweep and Wessling kicked the point. Olivet responded with 1:23 remaining when Irv Sigler passed to Jim Pobursky for a TD, but the two-point try failed, making it 7-6 Hope. Early in the second quarter, fullback Langeland bulled two yards up the middle for the second Dutchman score. This time, Hyink hit end Kusak for two points to make it 15-6. Later in the period Veurink was loose again, this time on a 13-yard sweep to paydirt. The two-point pass went to Langeland, increasing the margin to 23-6. With 46 seconds left in the half, a Hyink-to-Hultgren pass was good for 29 yards and the fourth Hope TD. This time, Hyink faked a pass and ran in for two points to make it 31-6. The Dutchman defense held, and Hope had possession once again with just 11 seconds remaining. Hultgren succeeded in getting beyond the Comet defender, gathered in a Hyink bomb, and raced into the end zone. The play covered 51 yards. A run for two points was stopped, but Hope's lead was 37-6 at the half.

The third quarter belonged to a game Comet team that shut down the Dutchmen and mounted a drive of its own. Quarterback Sigler went the final three yards on a sneak, but the kick sailed wide, making it 37-12. Most of the fourth quarter was scoreless, but with 2:50 left in the game Olivet's Tom Gorman scored on a one-yard plunge and Larry Melendy ran for two points to narrow the margin to 37-20. With 35 seconds remaining, Hyink found halfback Jim Bekkering open, and with good speed Bekkering ran 25 yards to score Hope's sixth touchdown. A run for two points failed, leaving the score at 43-20. In the game's last series, the Comets filled the air with passes. One was taken in by Kroodsma, who raced 40 yards to score as time ran out. Hope's 49-20 win was the fourth in a row and nailed down an MIAA co-championship with Kalamazoo.

An anti-climatic non-league encounter remained. At 2 p.m. on Nov. 9, Hope hosted Eastern Illinois University in the annual Mom and Dads Day game. Approximately 2,800 fans turned out at Riverview Park on a dreary, rainy day. Prof. Bob Cecil provided a 36-piece band to entertain the guests of honor at halftime. The Panthers of Eastern mounted a strong defense, and there was no scoring until late in the first half. With about two minutes remaining, Hyink got off a 43-yard pass to his favorite receiver and Hultgren made it to the nine-yard line. Two plays later, Langeland went three yards to score on a trap play. Wessling kicked the point with 1:17 left, and Hope led 7-0 at the intermission.

HOPE COLLEGE FOOTBALL TEAM — 1963
MIAA CO-CHAMPIONS WITH KALAMAZOO

Front Row L to R: Dave Huesingveld, Ken Postma, Jon Norton, Charlie, Langeland, Harlan Hyink, Joe Kusak, Dave Oakley, Chuck Veurink, Bill Keur, Jim Bekkering, Roger Abel, Manager Dennis Oehm. **2nd Row:** Manager Stu Levey, Ade Slikkers Jr., Cal Poppink, Bruce Menning, Gary Holvick, Bobby Schantz, Max Schipper, John Smith, Jerry Gibbs, Bob White, Paul Bast, Jeff Jorgensen, Glen Gouwens, Jim Kreunen. **3rd Row:** Jim Van Dam, Steve Wessling, Tom Cook, Jerry Saggers, Randy Meulman, Mike Barendse, Lee De Witt, Fred Van Tatenhove (MVP), Ralph Jackson, Tom De Kuiper, Ken Carpenter, Ron Milican. **Back Row:** End Coach Ken Weller, Bill Hultgren, Captain Ken Quakkelaar, Paul Johnson, Fred Smies, Jim Erlich, Carl Dell, Menno Sytsma, Carl Van Wyk, John Meengs, Roger Kroodsma, Tom Cousineau, John Stam, Line Coach Gordon Brewer, Head Coach Russ De Vette.

After a scoreless third period, Eastern came to life in the fourth quarter with a 74-yard, 11-play drive that included four pass completions. Quarterback Jim Lynch went the final three yards for the score. When Lynch attempted a run for the two-point conversion, he was stopped by Kroodsma, De Kuiper, and Cousineau, preserving Hope's 7-6 lead with 2:38 left in the game. Hope's final drive was aided by a pass interference call that placed the ball on the Eastern two-yard line. Another right end sweep by Veurink produced the score and the two-point conversion made it 15-6 as the game ended.

"Comeback" may be the sweetest word in the jargon of sports. It was certainly savored by the Hope team and coaches in 1963. After being written off at 0-4, the Dutchmen had responded with five straight victories, an MIAA co-championship, and a winning season. In recognition of the accomplishment, Thursday, Nov. 14, was declared "Glory Day" with a Carnegie Gym celebration plus an afternoon game of touch football played by Hope co-eds. Harlan Hyink, Bill Hultgren, Joe Kusak, and Fred Van Tatenhove were All-MIAA selections, and Van Tatenhove was named Hope's most valuable player. Kusak and Roger Abel were captains-elect for 1964. The mood was definitely positive on Nov. 16 when Dr. Calvin A. Vander Werf was officially inaugurated as the eighth president of Hope College.

* * *

Senior Vern Sterk was captain of Hope's 1963 cross country team. He was joined by other veteran runners, namely Bruce Welmers, John Nyboer, Glenn Van Wieren, and Dirck De Velder. The latter would miss most of the season due to an early injury, but the addition of freshmen Ron Bowman and Gary Peiper would give Coach Daryl Siedentop the boost needed to move up a notch in the MIAA standings. Bowman displayed a talent that made him the team's number one performer in every meet. Peiper was usually not far behind.

Early season losses were suffered in meets with Muskegon Community, 23-32, Grand Rapids Junior College, 23-32, and Spring Arbor, 17-39. Undaunted, the Dutchmen bounced back with victories over Alma, 18-44,

Kalamazoo, 23-38, Adrian, 22-33, and Olivet, 18-42, before falling to champion Calvin, 15-44, and Albion, 19-42. The dual meet season ended on a positive note with a non-league victory over Aquinas, 23-36. Hope finished 5-5 overall and 4-2 in the MIAA.

Rain and a wind-swept course made conditions miserable for the MIAA meet at Albion on Tuesday, Nov. 12. Albion's captain, Mike Conwell, was the individual winner with a time of 20:30.2 for the four-mile course. Calvin's Ray Hommes was second in 20:59. The Knights' depth was again a factor as Coach Dave Tuuk's team captured its sixth straight championship with 29 points. Following in line were Albion with 41, Hope 96, Adrian 110, Alma 136, Kalamazoo 143, and Olivet 156. Ron Bowman in 12th place was first to finish for the Dutchmen. Hope's solid third place finish overall would loom large when All-Sports points were tallied in the spring.

*   *   *

With fall sports completed, thoughts turned to the approaching basketball campaign. Friday afternoon, Nov. 22, found me in my office at the west end of Carnegie-Schouten Gym. While working on arrangements for the upcoming season, I was interrupted by a student bounding up the stairs and into the office. The student was Bruce Menning, an end on our football team and one of my high jumpers in track. Generally calm, Bruce was visibly affected. His message was that President Kennedy had been shot, perhaps fatally, in Dallas, Texas. A short time later on black and white television, we watched an overwrought Walter Cronkite struggle for control, remove his horn rimmed glasses, then announce that President Kennedy had been declared dead at Parkland Hospital.

The nation's trauma extended to its campuses. Games and other activities were canceled. Gloom prevailed as the country gave vent to its grief. Images remain of a nightmarish weekend: Jackie's bloodstained pink suit, the swearing-in of LBJ aboard Air Force One, *The Tonight Show* preempted by Skitch Henderson's orchestra playing a dirge that seemed not to end, the bizarre confrontation of Jack Ruby and Oswald, Monday's funeral cortege, the riderless horse, John-John's salute, the gray and the cold of Arlington National Cemetery, and, finally, the soldier's off-key rendering to *Taps* when cold lips would not function as desired.

In a later interview, Jacqueline Kennedy likened their White House stay to "Camelot - one brief shining moment," and the nation concurred. A memorial book by presidential aides Kenneth O'Donnell and David Powers took its title from an old Irish folk song, *Johnny, We Hardly Knew Ye*. It seemed to fit.

*   *   *

NEW LOOK DUTCHMEN

Hope had new quarter sleeve jerseys for the '63-'64 season.
L. to R.: Ron Venhuizen, Glenn Van Wieren, Ron Te Beest, Chris Buys, and Clare Van Wieren.

Life, of course, continued. Time heals, and youth on our campus would be served. As some semblance of normalcy returned, Coach De Vette prepared his charges for the 1963-64 basketball season. While not a banner year, it would have moments of superb performance and great excitement. In a search for something novel, Coaches De Vette and Siedentop found it in their choice of home uniforms. In the tradition of Evansville and their legendary coach Arad McCutcheon, the Dutchmen would sport white quarter-sleeve jerseys with "Hope" in navy script to match the navy numbers.

As the season progressed, the Dutchmen would realize how much they missed high-scoring Jim Vander Hill and center Gary Nederveld--not to mention Ron Te Beest, who would spend the first semester in Washington, D.C., as part of his political science major. But there was good news as well. Proven performers returned in the persons of guards Ron Venhuizen and Glenn Van Wieren, with the latter serving as captain. Clare Van Wieren was a returning regular at forward and big Bill Potter was back after a semester. Chris Buys had made a strong showing as the 1962-63 season ended, and a new addition was Al Palmer, who had attended Kellogg Community College.

The season opened with an 86-62 Hope victory at Lake Forest on Saturday, Nov. 30. The Dutchmen lead at halftime was 41-28 as the team enjoyed balanced scoring. Glenn Van Wieren led with 23, Venhuizen had 16, Clare Van Wieren 12, Potter 10, and Palmer eight. Ron Holder was high for Coach Dick Triptow's team with 17, and Bill Steen had 11.

Two days later the team went south again, this time to Valparaiso, where the opposition was considerably stronger. Hope had a cold start and trailed 22-6 after seven minutes. The Crusaders took a 46-32 halftime lead and never trailed. Captain Dennis Olson led his team to a decisive 98-74 win with 21 points. Smith followed with 16, and Eynon added 15. Clare Van Wieren led the Dutchmen with 17, Venhuizen had 14, Buys and Glenn Van Wieren each notched 10, and Palmer again had eight.

Word was received on Dec. 5 that Webb Maris, veteran basketball coach at Grand Rapids Junior College, had been sidelined by a coronary. His replacement would be Warren Vander Hill, Hope class of 1960. All at Hope wished both men well. Meanwhile, the home opener was played against a good Wheaton team on Saturday, Dec. 7. A Civic Center crowd of 1,800 watched the Crusaders build a 44-36 half-time lead, then attempt to stave off a Dutchmen rally. Late in the game, Hope gained an 82-80 lead on two free throws by Glenn Van Wieren, but a field goal by Steve Miller knotted the count at 82. With 27 seconds remaining, John Pfund was fouled and made good on the free throw to make it 83-82. Hope's final attempt was thwarted when Tom Carney picked off a pass and put in a layup. He was fouled and completed the three-point play to give Coach Lee Pfund and his team the 86-82 victory. Pfund led the winners with 29, Steve Miller had 14, Chuck Huibregtse 12, and Tom Carney 11. Potter had an outstanding game for Hope with 28 points, his best performance to date. Glenn Van Wieren had 17, brother Clare 15, Palmer 10, and Overman eight.

The Dutchmen expected trouble at Alma on Wednesday, Dec. 11. The Scots, with three players at 6' 5" and one at 6' 6", were co-favorites with Calvin to take the MIAA title. After trailing 47-41 at halftime, Hope battled back to a 69-69 tie with seven minutes left, but Potter fouled out and Bud Acton's two free throws put the Scots ahead to stay at the 6:25 mark. Hope's shooting went cold, while 5' 6" Tom Miller hit 12 of Alma's final 14 points. Acton led his team to the 89-81 victory with 26. He had good support from Tom Miller with 23, and Bill Pendell with 22. For Hope it was Glenn Van Wieren with 25, Clare put in 14, and Venhuizen 13. Overman, who started for the first time, and Potter each had 10. The Scots were impressive with 23-of-27 free throws.

Westmont College of Santa Barbara, Calif., under new coach Dan Arens, was making a tour of the Midwest and Hope was able to fit into the team's itinerary by playing on Monday, Dec. 16. Christmas season commitments made the Civic Center unavailable and the game was moved to the Holland High Fieldhouse, where a surprising crowd of 1,000 turned out. Hope trailed 46-36 at the half, but fought doggedly to catch up. With six minutes to go, the Dutchmen were within one, 67-66, on some fine play by Potter, Palmer, and Buys. Glenn Van Wieren, who played the entire game, scored six straight free throws near the end and Overman added two more to put Hope up 73-72 with 2:17 remaining. It was Hope's first lead of the game. Two of Glenn's free throws made it 75-72 with 1:02 left, and two more with nine ticks left increased the lead to 77-72. Roland Skelton scored a field goal as time ran out to make the final, 77-74. Glenn Van Wieren led his team to the hard-fought victory with 18 points, Venhuizen followed with 16, Clare Van Wieren had 10, Bill Potter nine, and Al Palmer eight. Westmont's Roland Skelton led all scorers with 33, and teammate Bill Odell added 18.

The Westmont win and Van Wieren's great effort seemed the needed spark to get the Dutchmen going. Hope hosted Albion on Wednesday, Dec. 18, before another crowd of 1,000. A Hope halftime lead of 45-35 had to be protected against the scrappy Britons. With 8:15 left, Albion had moved up to 65-60, but would get no closer. Venhuizen was high for the Dutchmen with 31 in the 89-77 victory. Glenn Van Wieren followed with 23 to give Hope an unusual guard output of 54 points. Al Palmer chipped in with 12. Larry Colburn was high man for the Britons with 17, and Don Genson had 14.

Following the holiday break, Hope teamed with Kalamazoo in a two-night opponent exchange. In the Civic Center on Wednesday, Jan. 2, Kenyon College of Ohio edged Kalamazoo 77-75 while Hope defeated Concordia of River Forest, Ill., 77-66. Venhuizen scored 20 for the winners and Ernie Tiemann had 18 for Concordia.

On Thursday, Jan. 3, the teams moved to Kalamazoo, where the Hornets downed Concordia 82-79 and Hope took Kenyon in a close one, 79-76. Kenyon held a narrow 34-31 lead at the half and the game was tied 12 times. The final tie was 76-76 with 1:58 remaining. Potter sank a free throw with 1:30 left to put the Dutchmen ahead to stay and Overman cashed in on two more with the clock showing seven seconds. The 79-76 Hope victory extended the Dutchman win streak to four. Potter was the leader with 19, and Carl Walters, now up from the jayvee squad, had 14. Overman and Glenn Van Wieren each scored 10. Ken Klug was high for the Kenyon Lords with 22 and Brian Farney had 16. In the second game, Kalamazoo edged Concordia 82-79 in the first meeting between the two schools.

The Hope-Calvin game at the Civic Center was played before a full house on Wednesday, Jan. 8. The first half was closely contested, with the Knights holding a 42-37 lead at the intermission. Calvin pulled away in the second half and pushed its lead to 64-47 for the game's biggest margin. The Dutchmen fought back, but the final showed Calvin the winner, 90-82. Jim Van Eerden had a game-high 23 points, Bill Knoester 18, Ken Fletcher 14, and Jim Fredericks 14 as the Knights shot 46 percent versus 31 percent for the Dutchmen. Clare Van Wieren scored 15, Walters 14, Glenn and Venhuizen 10 each.

In the fall of 1963 through the efforts of Dr. James Harvey, Hope's dean of Students, a soccer team had been organized, partly to accommodate Hope's growing number of international students. Two practice games were arranged with Calvin's junior varsity team, and the plan was to move to a full schedule in 1964. Now plans were announced to further expand the intercollegiate program by starting a swim team. An arrangement with West Ottawa High School provided four hours a week of practice time using the West Ottawa pool and the school's coach, Henry Reest. Twenty-three students indicated interest in the program, which included a practice meet with Albion. Conditions were not ideal, but Hope was getting started with yet another sport.

The basketball season continued with Olivet at the Civic Center on Saturday, Jan. 11. The Comets had come to play, and the hotly contested game saw the Dutchmen scratch for a 34-33 lead at halftime. Jim Everett's field goal as the second half began gave Olivet its only lead, 35-34. Hope pushed to a 54-42 lead at the 10-minute mark, but the Comets cut it to five with a minute left. In the face of a press, Glenn Van Wieren broke through and passed to Venhuizen for a layup to make it 68-63. Jim Everett scored the final basket, and the Dutchmen were thankful for the 68-65 victory. Glenn Van Wieren led his team with 17, Venhuizen scored 12 and Clare Van Wieren 11. Ed Donaldson was high for Olivet with 20, and Jim Everett had 17.

Approximately 600 fans were scattered in Kalamazoo's Treadway Gym on Wednesday, Jan. 15, to see the Dutchmen suffer through a cold first half, shooting at just 25 percent. It was 44-29 Kalamazoo at the half, and the Hornets pushed their lead to 65-43 with 13 minutes remaining. At the 6:50 mark, Hope put on an effective press and outscored Kazoo 26-13 in that period, but it was not enough and Ray Steffen's charges were the victors, 91-84. Jim Peters led "K" with a game-high 24, Dick Johnson followed closely with 22, and freshmen Tom Crawford had 15. For Hope it was Glenn Van Wieren with 22, and Venhuizen 21. Palmer and Walters each scored 12.

It was another discouraging night for the Dutchmen at Adrian on Saturday, Jan. 18. Both teams stood at 2-3 in league play, but the Bulldogs were in charge with a 57-40 halftime bulge. Hope's second-half zone press produced 52 percent shooting and almost did the trick, but the Bulldogs held on for a 97-95 win. Matt Garrett led Gregg Arbaugh's team with 20, Dick Seagert had 19 and Ron Stevens 15, while Jon Hall and Don Numbers each scored 14 to round out the splendid team effort. Venhuizen led Hope with 26, Glenn Van Wieren scored 21, Walters 15, and Clare Van Wieren 11.

Hope bounced back with an 89-71 victory over Lake Forest on Saturday, Jan. 25. A meager Civic Center crowd of 800 watched the Dutchmen again employ their zone press. A 44-29 Hope lead at the half increased to a 23-point spread at one point, and subs got their chance. Walters led Hope with 22 and Clare Van Wieren, playing center for the first time, scored 17. Potter had 14 and Venhuizen 12. The Foresters got 20 points from Ron Holder, 16 from Bob Garner, and 14 from Marv Zagora.

Following the semester break, Te Beest returned from Washington, D.C., and rejoined the team. A trip to Wheaton on Tuesday, Jan. 28, found the Crusaders ready and waiting.

Coach De Vette, now with somewhat different personnel, juggled his lineup. Simons, starting for the first time, joined Venhuizen at guard. Glenn Van Wieren was moved to forward with Te Beest, and Clare Van Wieren started at center. The first half was played on even terms, with Wheaton pulling ahead 44-41 at the intermission. The second half, however, belonged almost completely to the Crusaders as guards John Pfund and Kerry Otterby took charge. Hope managed a 54-47 advantage in rebounds, but Wheaton controlled all other aspects in marching to a 111-71 victory. Pfund led the scoring parade with 23, Otterby followed with 19, and Tom Carney had 13. Bill Province and Marty Koehn each scored 12. For Hope it was Venhuizen with 16, Potter scored 13, Clare Van Wieren 11, and John Simons eight.

After a night at the Oak Park Arms Hotel, the Dutchmen moved on to River Forest for a game with Concordia on Wednesday, Jan. 29. Again there would be lineup changes. This time, Buys was given a shot at the guard position with Venhuizen, the Van Wierens took over the forwards, and Bill Potter was back at center. Leading 38-34 at halftime, the Dutchmen pulled away early in the second half enroute to an impressive 78-59 win. Clare Van Wieren responded to the position shift with 24 points to lead the Hope attack. Potter was also effective with 21. Glenn Van Wieren had a great night on the boards with 16 rebounds to go with his 10 points. Venhuizen added nine. Dan Grotelueschen was best for Don Spitz's team with 16.

Officials Marv Bylsma and Chuck Bult worked the Hope-Alma game at the Civic Center on Saturday, Feb. 8. The rough-and-tumble affair was witnessed by 1,800 fans, who got more than their money's worth. To begin with, both teams were hot from the floor. Hope had 45 of 90 for 50 percent, while Alma countered with 50 of 98 for 51 percent. A determined effort by the Dutchmen produced a 58-50 advantage in rebounds against the taller Scots and helped Hope to a 62-56 halftime lead. Before the evening was out, the Dutchmen would go to the line an amazing 46 times and cash in on 37, while the Scots were making 19 of 29. Aggressive play by both teams took its toll as the game wound down. Alma's Bud Acton fouled out with 4:47 left, while Ray Moore and John La Rue left with three minutes remaining. Hope lost Clare Van Wieren and Bill Potter in the final five minutes. As the score mounted in the closing minutes, Alma took a 115-113 lead, but Glenn Van Wieren was fouled with six seconds left. With the pressure on, Hope's captain dropped in both free throws to send the game into overtime. In the first 90 seconds of the overtime, Buys scored six straight points on two free throws and two field goals. With three minutes remaining, Overman and an Alma player were involved in a scuffle that some described as a wrestling match. Both players were ejected. With 2:22 on the clock, Bill Pendell fouled out, reducing Wayne Hintz's nine-man squad to just four players, who finished the game in a four-man zone. With Hope leading 123-117, Buys

180

added a field goal and Alma sank two free throws to make it 125-119. Hope then stalled for more than a minute before Venhuizen was fouled. His two free throws with 15 seconds left ended the scoring and gave Hope the 127-119 victory. Glenn Van Wieren, back at guard, led the way for Hope with 32, Venhuizen followed with 31, Potter had 24, Chris Buys 21, Clare 14, and Dean Overman five. Bill Pendell collected 34 for the Scots, Ray Moore had 27, Bud Acton 25, and Tom Miller and Kurt Shultz each had 10. Various scribes were delighted to list the various broken records: Hope team scoring, Civic Center scoring, combined scoring, and most scores in losing. It had been a night to remember.

In stark contrast to the Alma game, Hope's performance at Albion four days later was mostly downhill. Shooting at 27 percent for the game, the Dutchmen trailed 50-37 at the half. The Britons, meanwhile, were at the top of their game with strong board work from 6' 8" Bruce Brown and the scoring of sophomore Dave Anspaugh, a transfer from Tri-State of Indiana. Te Beest did not make the trip due to a back injury, and Gailerd Korver was out for the season with an elbow fracture suffered in practice. Hope's zone press was not effective, and the Britons cashed in with numerous easy layups on their way to a 101-87 victory. Anspaugh led the winners with 26, Don Genson had 21, and Moliere 14. Hope's one bright spot was Bill Potter, whose 50 percent shooting netted 31 points, his best performance of the season. Clare Van Wieren followed with 17, brother Glenn had 15, and Ron Venhuizen eight.

Hope hosted the Tommies of Aquinas on Saturday, Feb. 15, before a crowd of 1,400. The game was closely contested most of the way. A Glenn Van Wieren free throw knotted the score at 56-all as time ran out in the half. Hope continued to play well, but with 4:52 remaining Aquinas took the lead on a field goal by Dennis Alexander and the Tommies were ahead to stay. The Dutchmen trailed 109-104 with 44 seconds left and were forced to foul. Gary Fewless scored the final nine points for the visitors, and center Ray Bauer, with a sweeping left hand hook, scored 33 to lead his team to the final 113-108 victory. Dennis Alexander had 29 and Fewless 25. Venhuizen had a big night for Hope with 36, and Clare Van Wieren put in 30. Glenn followed with 16, Potter had 14, and Chris Buys 10.

Despite Hope's up-and-down season, 5,000 fans crowded into the Grand Rapids Civic for the Calvin game on Wednesday, Feb. 19. The floor was again slippery from untold other activities, and the Dutchmen ended the evening with a 27 percent shooting average. The floor bothered the Knights very little as they shot 52 percent, moved to a 44-36 halftime advantage, and increased the margin to 20 points midway in the second half. The Hope performance was marred by many mistakes, including numerous stolen passes. The usual crowd excitement was missing as the Knights recorded an easy 105-71 victory. Jim Van Eerden led the way with 23, Ken Fletcher had 20, Dave Zondervan 15, and Kim Campbell 12. For the disappointed Dutchmen it was Clare Van Wieren leading with 16, followed by Venhuizen with 15, Glenn Van Wieren with 12, and Ron Te Beest with 11.

Hope traveled to Olivet on Saturday, Feb. 22, for a game in McKay Gymnasium, a structure completed in 1927. In the space of three days, the crowd had diminished from 5,000 to 500, but the game would be as dramatic as any, save the Alma contest at Hope. Hope managed a 46-40 lead at the half, but the Comets of Coach Gene Anderson had nearly done the Dutchmen in earlier in Holland and came on strong in the second half. Olivet was on top 86-83 with just eight seconds left, plus the chance to put it away with a free throw. But the free throw was missed. Clare Van Wieren took the rebound and attempted to call time out. Inexplicably, he was fouled with five seconds left. Now the timeout was taken and the coaches calmly explained to Clare that he must make the first free throw, then shoot the second in such a way that it would come off the front of the rim. Those who play know that this is difficult to effect, but Clare nodded as if it were a piece of cake. Potter and the 6' 7" Anker were inserted to replace Simons and Veurink, who had been in for pressing purposes. Stepping to the line, Clare calmly dropped in the first shot. His second-shot execution was perfect. Four men went up for the ball as it rolled off the front of the rim, but Potter, with two fingers, reached the highest and secured the tip-in to send the game into overtime at 86-all.

The Comets gained first possession in the overtime and proceeded to stall for 2½ minutes. Irv Sigler then moved in for a layup but missed. Potter scored the first overtime basket, but Olivet took the lead 89-88 on a three-point play. Hope reclaimed the lead on a second field goal, but the persistent Comets came back with 1:25 remaining and it was Olivet 91, Hope 90. With 49 seconds left, Potter scored again to put Hope up 92-91. Clare Van Wieren was fouled with 49 seconds on the clock. He ended the evening by sinking both free throws to give Hope a most satisfying 94-91 victory. Clare Van Wieren's 35 points led all scorers, and Buys added 18. Venhuizen had 13, and Glenn Van Wieren and Potter each had 11. Ed Donaldson led Coach Anerson's squad with 24, Tony Kruzman had 14, and Dave Gosselein 13.

The Kalamazoo Hornets enjoyed a hot night at the Civic Center on Wednesday, Feb. 26. A crowd of 1,400 watched as Coach Steffen's players made 53 percent of their shots and took a 48-34 halftime lead. The Dutchmen battled back to within four points on two occasions and trailed 93-89 with 1:30 left, but fouls from a pressing defense hurt in the closing minutes. Eight of Kazoo's last 10 points came on free throws. Coach De Vette felt that the Hornets' poise under pressure was a determining factor in their 103-98 victory. It marked the first time in the school's history that a Kalamazoo team had scored over 100 points. Dick Johnson with 22 and Dale Southworth with 21 were high for the winners. Jim Peters had 17 and Tom Nicholai 15. For the Dutchmen, it was Glenn Van Wieren leading the way with 24,

Venhuizen scored 22, Buys had 16, Te Beest 13, and Clare Van Wieren 11.

Hope's season finale was played at the Civic on Saturday, Feb. 29, against Adrian. In first-round play the Bulldogs had shaded Hope 97-95, and they now hoped for a repeat while the Dutchmen were determined to end the campaign on a positive note. More than 1,600 of Hope's faithful turned out to see five seniors play their last game before the hometown crowd. This time it was Hope all the way. The Dutch built a 47-32 halftime lead, and did not let up. With 5:41 remaining and the score at 85-54, Hope's team on the floor was composed of seniors Glenn Van Wieren, Ron Venhuizen, Ron Te Beest, Chuck Veurink, and Art Kramer. At this point the five were removed to a standing ovation. In his swan song, Glenn Van Wieren led his team with 25 points, 21 rebounds, and nine of 10 free throws. Venhuizen also had a good night with 17, Buys and Clare each had 13, and Dean Overman scored eight in Hope's impressive 90-66 victory. Don Numbers was high for the Bulldogs with 19, Ingham scored 16, and Dick Seagert 13.

Hope's 11-11 season ended on a positive note despite a fifth-place finish in the MIAA at 5-7. Glenn Van Wieren was the scoring leader with 372 points, while Venhuizen was just one point behind with 371. Glenn Van Wieren was named to the All-MIAA team along with Bud Acton and Ray Moore of Alma and Calvin's Jim Van Eerden and Ken Fletcher. To no one's surprise, Glenn Van Wieren was selected as Hope's most valuable player. Acton was honored as the MIAA's MVP.

* * *

The objective of Hope's spring trip in baseball was to secure playing time in a warm climate against quality teams. In 1964 this was accomplished. Playing in Tennessee, the Dutchmen split games with North Park, Ill., winning 7-3 and losing 14-3, also taking Southwestern 1-0 before losing 9-8. Hope dropped a 4-2 decision to Memphis State, then tied Union College as rain halted the contest at 3-3. Homeward bound on Monday, April 6, the team met Notre Dame in South Bend in the home opener for the Irish. Many believed this to be the first baseball game between the two schools, but a previous game had been played on April 17, 1926, also in South Bend. In that contest Hope was pummeled 16-1 as Lee Kleis collected Hope's only hit and drove in the lone run. The Dutchmen were better prepared in 1964 and held off the Irish for 12 innings before being edged by a 6-5 score.

With experienced players at nearly every position, Coach Siedentop knew that he could field a strong team. The pitching corps of Joey Bosworth, Jim Van Til, Glenn Van Wieren, Roger Kroodsma, and Gary Schaap was especially impressive. Veteran catcher Art Kramer was backed up by Skip Nienhuis, while starting outfielders included Cal Poppink, Don Troost, and 1963 batting champion Ron Venhuizen. Around the infield it was Clare Van Wieren at first, Chuck Veurink at second, Tom De Kuiper at third, and Rog Kroodsma at short when he was not on the mound. A strong bench would also make a difference as the season got underway.

The MIAA season opened at Riverview Park on Wednesday, April 15, against archrival Calvin. In the first game, Van Til was at his best with a three-hit shutout, walking five and striking out 12. Hope scored four runs each in the second, third, and fifth innings to record the 12-0 victory. Venhuizen led the Hope batters with two doubles. In the second game, it was a different story as big Ken Fletcher set the Dutchmen down with a one-hitter enroute to a 3-0 shutout of his own. Fletcher contributed to his own cause by stroking a two-run homer. The Knights collected six hits off the offerings of Van Wieren and Bosworth.

Bosworth was on the mound for Hope at Albion on Saturday, April 18. The league took notice as he pitched 10 innings of shutout ball, gave up one hit, and walked none. In the first of the 10th, Glenn Van Wieren singled, stole second, and scored on brother Clare's double. Bosworth blanked the Britons in the top of the 10th to gain the hard-earned 1-0 shutout. The second game was rained out.

On Wednesday, April 22, Hope traveled to Big Rapids for a non-league doubleheader with Ferris State. The first game was a wild affair, with Hope getting 19 hits and 12 walks, and scoring 10 runs in a big sixth inning. Glenn Van Wieren was on the mound for Hope, with relief from Schaap as the Dutchmen chalked up a 23-10 victory. In the second game, pitcher Roger Kroodsma helped himself with a home run in Hope's five-run first inning. Hope added two more runs in the second, then held on for the eventual 7-6 win. Three Hope pitchers, Kroodsma, Van Til in the fourth, and Bosworth in the fifth, walked 14 Ferris batters and the game almost slipped away. Buck Gramlech had a two-run homer for the Bulldogs. Nienhuis was behind the plate for the Dutch.

Coach Bill Carr brought the Alma Scots to Riverview on Saturday, April 23. It was all Alma in the first game as the Dutchmen committed six errors. The Scots' big seventh inning produced five runs, including a two-run homer by Murphy. The combination was more than enough to give Alma the 8-1 victory. The Dutchmen turned the tables in the second game behind the four-hit pitching of Bosworth, who walked five, but struck out 14. Hope, meanwhile, had a four-run first inning, had 10 hits, and never trailed in salvaging the split with a 9-4 victory.

Hope had now split games with Calvin and Alma, and was in need of a double win. It came on Saturday, May 2, against Olivet at Riverview. In the first game, Glenn Van Wieren went the distance with Nienhuis behind the plate. He gave the Comets but three hits, walked three, and struck out 10 in the 2-1 victory. Hope's two runs came in the fourth on two walks and a single by Troost. In the second game, it was

THE 1964 HOPE BASEBALL TEAM
MIAA CHAMPIONS

Kneeling L. to R.: Tom Cook, Pete Haverkamp, Wayne Cotts, Phil Pluister, Conrad "Skip" Nienhuis, Chuck Veurink. **2nd Row:** Tom De Kuiper, Roger Kroodsma, Jim Van Til, Steve Nordstrom, George "Joey" Bosworth, Art Kramer. **3rd Row:** Gary Schaap, Cal Poppink, Clare Van Wieren, Don Troost, Ron Venhuizen, Glenn Van Wieren. Missing — Coach Daryl Siedentop.

Joey Bosworth striking out 15 in a five-hit, 3-0 shutout. The Dutchmen got all three runs in the third, when Kramer singled, Bosworth walked, and Haverkamp singled. Glenn Van Wieren then walked to force in a run. Venhuizen and Kroodsma followed with singles to score the other two. Hope had a total of eight hits.

Hope stepped out of league play on Tuesday, May 5, to meet Central Michigan in a novel afternoon-night doubleheader. The Chippewas took the afternoon game by an 11-5 score on the Hope field, then shut out the Dutchmen 5-0 in the nightcap at Riverview. In the opener, Van Til and Kroodsma gave up six hits while Hope could only muster five. The real difference came as the Dutchmen committed four errors. In the night game, the Dutch bats were largely silent, as singles by Nienhuis and Cotts were the only Hope hits. Mid-America Conference baseball, with athletic scholarships, was probably still a notch above that of the MIAA.

The race for the conference championship continued on Saturday, May 9, at Adrian. In the first game, Hope banged out a total of 16 hits, scoring five runs in the third and six more in the fourth. The big blow in the third was a triple by Kramer, while in the fourth a double by Cotts was the telling blow. Bosworth pitched five strong innings before giving way to Schaap in the 15-3 victory. In the second game, the Dutchmen again had a big third inning as five runs crossed the plate. Included were home runs by Glenn Van Wieren and Van Til as well as a triple by Kroodsma. But the Bulldogs came back to tie it in the fifth, and the Dutchmen were hard-pressed to finally gain the eventual one-run victory, 9-8. The winning run came in the sixth with two outs. Kramer doubled and Venhuizen delivered the game-winner with a single. Van Til was relieved by Glenn Van Wieren in the fourth and Bosworth came on to pitch the seventh.

Hope hosted Grand Rapids Junior College in a single game on Thursday, May 14, and the Raiders, with fine athletes, came to play. Joey Bosworth pitched a three-hitter and set 14 down with strikeouts, but the visitors led 2-0 after four. Hope got one back in the fifth, but the game went into

GEORGE "JOEY" BOSWORTH
All-MIAA — 1964 Hope's MVP

With the U.S. Team
Tokyo Olympics — 1964

Tryout with Kansas City, 1965. Bosworth and Jim Kaat, two Hopites talk it over in Minnesota.

the ninth with Grand Rapids leading 2-1. In the last of the ninth, Roger Kroodsma singled, stole second, then scored on Pete Haverkamp's single. Cal Poppink's sacrifice put Haverkamp on third and a wild pitch gave Hope the narrow 3-2 victory.

The Dutchmen closed out a successful season at Kalamazoo on Wednesday, May 20, but not without a struggle. Joey Bosworth gained his fifth league victory against no defeats with another top performance. In the first game, he allowed but two hits and walked one batter, who was thrown out by catcher Kramer. Hope scored one run in the fifth, but the Hornets tied it in their half of the inning. The winning run came in the sixth, when Glenn Van Wieren walked, moved to second on Chuck Veurink's single, made it to third on a passed ball, and scored on an infield error to give Hope and Bosworth the 2-1 victory.

Van Til took the mound in the second game and was relieved by Glenn Van Wieren in the sixth. Kramer was behind the plate in this, the season finale. In the second inning, Kroodsma tripled and Troost walked. Clare Van Wieren then delivered the big blow of the game, a three-run homer. Hope's other run came in the fifth, when Haverkamp walked and advanced to third on Kramer's single. It was somehow appropriate that Glenn Van Wieren would drive home the final run of the season with a single in Hope's 4-1 victory.

With a 9-2 MIAA record, Coach Siedentop and the Dutchmen could now claim Hope's first undisputed championship in the school's history. The Dutchmen were 14-8 overall and led the league in team batting with a .290 mark. Haverkamp led the Dutchmen with at .357, while Alma's Pat Murphy was the MIAA batting champ with a fine .474 average. Clare Van Wieren and Joey Bosworth were named to the All-MIAA team, and the latter also received the Jack Schouten most valuable player award. Bosworth gave up but one earned run in 40 innings of MIAA play for an earned run average of 0.23. He was later selected to be part of a 20-man team that represented the United States in a series of exhibition games at the 1964 Olympic Games in Tokyo, Japan. This in turn, led to a tryout with the Kansas City (later Oakland) Athletics, but an arm injury would end his chance for a career in the majors.

Senior Glenn Van Wieren, a three-sport athlete, ended his fine career as part of a championship. He would know many more, most notably as Hope's basketball coach beginning in 1977.

* * *

The 1964 Hope spring tennis trip was not a booming success, but with Butch Hopma, Dave Zwart, Lance Stell, and Dave Nykerk returning Coach Doc Green knew he had the makings of a fine team. Also in the mix were junior Jack Schrier and freshman Craig Workman. Hope suffered six

HARVEY "BUD" HOFFMAN

MIAA Coaches selected Hoffman to receive the Allen B. Stowe Sportsmanship Award in 1964. A senior, Hoffman hailed from Scarsdale, New York.

straight defeats in the south before salvaging a lone victory as the tour neared its completion. Scores were as follows: Vanderbilt 8½ - Hope ½, Florida State 9 - Hope 0, Davidson 6 - Hope 3, Columbia College 6½ - Hope 3½, Rollins 6 - Hope 3, University of Florida 8 - Hope 1, Hope 7 - Florida Reserves 1, and Indiana University 9 - Hope 0.

The Dutchmen opened the regular season on a positive note with a 7-2 non-league victory at Wheaton. In singles, Dennis Bennema defeated Hopma 6-1, 6-2, Workman defeated Tom Claus 6-4, 6-1, Stell took Jay Hakes 6-4, 4-6, 6-2, Zwart won over Sam Mac Aluso 6-3, 6-4, Hoffman defeated Ron Webb 6-4, 6-1, and Schrier took Russ Enlow 6-3, 6-1. In doubles, it was Hopma Workman over Bennema-Claus 6-4, 6-4, Zwart-Hoffman over Hakes-Enlow 6-2, 3-6, 6-2, and Macaluso-Webb over Schrier-Nykerk 6-4, 8-10, 6-4. The match was played on Friday, April 10, and took on added meaning when it was learned that Wheaton had earlier defeated Iowa State 6-3.

The following day, still at Wheaton, Hope defeated Mac Murray College of Jacksonville, Ill., 9-0. It appeared that Doc Green's team was well prepared for the MIAA.

It was Calvin at Hope on Wednesday, April 15, in the first round of league play. In singles, Hopma defeated Dick

Bultman 6-3, 6-3, Workman defeated Jim Edson 6-2, 6-0, Stell defeated Gord Vander Brugge 6-0, 6-1, Hoffman defeated Bert De Leeuw 6-4, 6-2, and Zwart defeated Peter De Jonge 6-1, 6-4. In doubles, it was Hopma-Workman over Vander Brugge-Edson 6-2, 6-2, and Hoffman-Zwart over Bultman-De Leeuw 4-6, 6-3, 6-3. For the 7-0 team victory an official MIAA match consisted of five singles and two doubles. In exhibition singles play, Schrier defeated Jerry Van Wyke 7-5, 6-1, and the team of Stell-Schrier defeated Prince-De Jonge 6-2, 6-0.

The pattern would continue. On Saturday, April 18, Hope traveled to Albion, and after a three-hour rain delay defeated the Britons 7-0. At home one week later, the Dutchmen downed the Alma Scots, again by a 7-0 count. Saturday, May 2, on the road at Olivet the 7-0 shutout was repeated. Despite the long trip to Adrian on Saturday, May 9, it was more of the same, with Hope coasting to another 7-0 shutout.

Hoping for a stronger test, the Dutchmen hosted Miami of Ohio on Friday, May 15. Competition in the Mid-America Conference was decidedly tougher, but in the end it was Hope winning 5-4. In singles, Hopma defeated Bill Thompson 5-7, 8-6, 6-1, Workman defeated Fred Bonsack 4-6, 6-2, 6-1, Ray Gates defeated Stell 6-2, 6-8, 6-4, Dick Meredith defeated Hoffman 6-3, 6-2, Charles Freiburger defeated Nykerk 6-3, 3-6, 6-3, and Schrier defeated Dan Sebastian 8-6, 9-7. In doubles, it was Hopma-Workman over Thompson-Bonsack 6-2, 9-11, 6-2, Gates-Meredith over Zwart-Stell 6-2, 6-2, and Hoffman-Dave Nykerk over Sebastian-Freiburger 8-6, 6-2. It was a satisfying victory over a class team and the Dutchmen were as ready as they could be for the big one at Kalamazoo.

At Stowe Stadium on Wednesday, May 20, Hope's fine team found out once again just how talented the Hornets were. Dick Johnson, George Smillie, Art Walters, Bill Jones, and John Koch proceeded to win all five singles. Coach George Akker's team completed the 7-0 shutout in doubles as Johnson-Smillie defeated Hopma-Workman 6-3, 6-2, and Jones-Koch took Hoffman-Stell 6-8, 6-1, 6-4 in the day's only three-setter.

The league meet was held at Albion on Friday-Saturday, May 22-23. The flight finals once again pitted Hope against Kalamazoo, with the result a near carbon copy of the dual meet held a few days earlier. Kalamazoo was a deserving champion, while Hope, in second place, was well ahead of the rest of the field. Coach Green and the Hope community were pleased when the league's coaches selected Harvey "Bud" Hoffman as recipient of the prestigious Allen B. Stowe Sportsmanship Award. Barney Steen of Calvin made the presentation to the Scarsdale, N.Y., senior.

* * *

With the departure of Bill Oostenink from the Hope faculty, Bill Hilmert was once again called upon to coach the golf team. Returnees included Jim Wiersma, Dean Overman, and Jim Thompson. Bill Potter of the basketball team and Bryan Dolphin filled out the team. Records are incomplete, but Hope did defeat Calvin 9½-6½ in the opener at the Hickory Hills course in Grand Rapids on Tuesday, April 14. Wiersma shot an 80 for medalist honors. Against Grand Rapids Junior College, it was Potter leading the Dutchmen to an 8½-6½ victory with a 78 and medalist honors. Potter continued to be hot against Alma on Saturday, April 25, with an 80, but the Scots' Denny Nelson shot a 78 and Alma showed its strength with a 12½-3½ win.

Hope entered the MIAA meet on Friday, May 22, with a 3-3 dual meet record, but had to settle for fourth place as Alma took the top spot with a team total of 773 strokes. Albion was second with 788, Kalamazoo third with 801, Hope fourth with 808, Olivet fifth with 852, Calvin sixth with 853, and Adrian seventh with 898. John Perrin of Alma was medalist with a 36-hole total of 148. Wiersma shot 153, Overman 160, Thompson 161, and Potter 170. Dolphin was unable to finish and Gordon Korstange filled in.

* * *

Hope fielded a stronger track team in 1964, but when the Dutchmen dropped their first three meets many were not so sure. Senior Captain Bob Mackay provided strong leadership, and the addition of transfers Dave Lane and Gilbert Ogonji gave Hope the needed punch in the 440 and mile relay. Two new events, the 440-yard relay and the 330-yard intermediate hurdles, were added to MIAA meets beginning with the 1964 season. The long-overdue sprint relay added excitement, while the latter event, run over eight hurdles at a height of 36", was a stepping stone to the longer 400 meter hurdles, an Olympic event.

Saturday, April 11, was opening day for the Dutchmen at Houseman Field in Grand Rapids. The Raiders of Grand Rapids JC had another strong team, took nine of 16 firsts, and won in a close meet, 72-63. Hope had the satisfaction of winning its first ever 440-yard relay as the team of Bob Fialko, Bill Hultgren, Jim Bekkering, and Chris Buys did the trick. Other firsts for the Dutchmen were Gary Peiper in the 880, Mackay in the high jump, Buys in the shot and discus, John Simons in the broad jump and Taibi Kahler in the javelin.

Four days later at Calvin's Knollcrest track, the Dutchmen met the MIAA champions and put up a good battle. The Knights took 11 firsts to five for Hope, but the Dutchmen showed some depth with 11 seconds and six thirds. The final count showed 75½ for Calvin to 60½ for Hope, but the Dutchmen could point to two Hope records. Bob Mackay took the high jump at 6' 1½" and the mile relay team of Hultgren, Ken Carpenter, Ogonji, and Lane won the event with a mark of 3:27.5.

In the first home meet on Saturday, April 18, Hope met the Britons of Coach Dean Dooley. Now in his second year,

Dooley had another fine team that, like Calvin, took 11 firsts from the Dutchmen enroute to an 82-54 win. But as always, there were some bright spots for the home team. Simons won the broad jump with a fine leap of 22' 2"; Fred Shantholtzer and Buys went one-two in the discus; Gary Holvick was a double winner in the hurdle events and set a Hope record in the intermediates with a time of .40.4; and the mile relay team of Hultgren, Carpenter, Ogonji, and Lane was again victorious. Albion's Dave Middlebrook won the high jump over MacKay, but Mackay took a few mental notes on how to proceed in their next meeting. The Britons' Mike Conwell won the mile and two-mile, while J.B. Elzy of football fame was strong in winning both dashes.

One week later, on Saturday, April 25, Hope hosted an outmanned Alma team. Coach Wayne Hintz, primarily a basketball man, was about to resign from the Alma staff and his team may have sensed his lack of enthusiasm. Charles Yurick, Alma's two-miler, won his event and Chris McKee took the 100-yard dash, but Hope won all the rest and had sweeps in the high jump, broad jump, shot, discus, 440, 880, and mile run. The Dutchmen were not in a position to gloat over their 116-19 win, having dropped their first three meets, but the feel of victory was welcome.

Hope hosted Olivet on Saturday, May 2, and again dominated the meet in winning by the score of 100-35. But Coach Stu Parsell had some fine competitors, and there were some interesting match-ups along the way. The 440-yard relay proved to be the most exciting event of the afternoon, as the Olivet team of Bill Teller, Ord Rice, Mike Rabbers, and Todd Weddon edged the Hope team of Fialko, Buys, Holvick, and Hultgren in times of 44.8 to 44.9. Hope's Gary Peiper won the mile, hard-working Sterk took the 880, and John Nyboer, good naturedly referred to as "the idle idol," won the two-mile.

The Hope team evened its season on Saturday, May 9, by hosting Adrian College. Coach Tom Allen had some good performers but not enough of them, and the Dutchmen prevailed, 94-41. Steve Neff of the Bulldog basketball team won the pole vault with a mark of 12', running back John Fundukian won the 220 in 23.4, Mike Koppitsch took the discus, and Sandy Johnstone came in first in the two-mile run. Hope won the other events, and set school records in both relays. In the 440, Fialko, Simons, Holvick, and Hultgren circled the track in 43.7 for the victory, while the mile relay team of Hultgren, Carpenter, Ogonji, and Lane, who were now quite accustomed to each other, ran in the fine time of 3:27.1.

Hope's fifth home meet in a row was held on Monday, May 11, with Valparaiso furnishing the opposition. This would be the Dutchmen's biggest challenge since the Albion meet. The Crusaders wanted to include the triple jump as a seventh field event, and, since it was a non-league meet, I agreed. It was a fateful decision. Going into the final running event Valpo held a 66-64 lead, but Hope's mile relay team of Hultgren, Carpenter, Ogonji, and Lane won the

HIGH JUMP CHAMP

Captain Bob Mackay was the MIAA high jump champion in 1964.

event in a Hope record time of 3:26.3, giving the Dutch a 69-66 team lead. But the triple jump remained. Ogonji was the only Hope team member to have participated in the event, and he had not done it yet at Hope. Valpo's one-two finish in this last event gave them the meet by a 74-70 score. In addition to the relay, Hope's other record performance was turned in by Holvick in the intermediate hurdles with a time of 39.9.

With its relatively new and unique rubber-asphalt track, Hope had little trouble arranging home meets. On Saturday, May 16, the University of Illinois-Chicago team came to Holland for another exciting meet that would go down to the wire. Recent rains left the broad jump pits under water and that event was not contested, but Hope managed to win eight of the remaining events to seven for UIC. With one race left, the score was tied at 61. Once again, the Hope mile relay team of Hultgren, Carpenter, Ogonji, and Lane came through to win the event, by a margin of two seconds over the Chicagoans. This time the Hope record was lowered to 3:26.0, but more importantly it delivered a 66-61 team victory.

In the last week of the season, Coach Swede Thomas brought the Kalamazoo Hornets to Holland for a meet on Tuesday, May 19. Thomas again had some top performers. Sprinter Bill Lynch won the 100 in the fine time of 10.1 and the 220 in 22.7. Distance man Tom Hoopengardner took the mile and two-mile, George Lindenberg won the 880, and Ken Calhoun, using one of the metal poles of the day, soared 12' 7½" to win the vault. But Hope swept three field events and took both relays in posting an 86-50 victory. In the shot, it was Chris Buys, Ken Dulow, and Fred Shantholtzer. In the discus, it was the same three with Shantholtzer winning, followed by Buys and Dulow. Kahler won the javelin throw, with Jeff Powell taking second and Jack Buys third.

For the first time in 18 years, the MIAA Field Day meet was held at Albion College. The May 23 championship meet was the first at Alumni Field since Coach Dale Sprankle's Britons had captured the title in 1946. Sprankle had passed away on Nov. 11, 1963, and thoughts this day were on one whose career as coach and educator was of the highest order.

Competition was keen as the meet progressed. Calvin and Hope each had four gold medals, Albion and Olivet three each, Kalamazoo one, and Adrian one. Hope's Bob Mackay and Albion's Dave Middlebrook renewed their rivalry in the high jump, with the Hope captain turning the tables for the victory. Menning finished third. Shantholtzer surprised the field by winning the discus, and Lane won the 440 for the Dutch. As the meet neared its conclusion, Albion and Calvin battled for the title. Going into the final event, it was Albion 56, Calvin 54. However, first place in the mile relay belonged to the Dutchmen, as Hultgren, Ogonji, Carpenter, and Lane set a new MIAA record of 3:25.4. Calvin finished second to gain four points, but Albion managed to edge out Adrian for third and the crucial three points necessary to take the championship, 59-58. Hope moved up a notch to third place with 42 points, while Kalamazoo squeaked by Adrian for fourth place, 29-28. Olivet took fifth with 24, and Alma failed to score.

RECORD SETTERS
Hope's mile relay team established a new MIAA record in the 1964 league meet at Albion. From the top: Dave Lane, Gilbert Ogonji, Ken Carpenter, Bill Hultgren.

* * *

When tabulations were announced for the MIAA All-Sports Trophy, Hope was the winner for the first time in a decade. The rules stated that the schools would be awarded points for their six best performances in the seven MIAA sports. The Dutchmen were champs in baseball, co-champs in football, second in tennis, third in track, third in cross-country, and fourth in golf for a total of 58 points to 55 for runner-up Albion. Calvin finished third with 53. It was somewhat ironic that Hope would not count its fifth-place finish in basketball. The huge rotating trophy was presented by Commissioner Win Schuler to AD Gordon Brewer, who proudly accepted for the college, its athletes and coaches.

ALL-SPORTS CHAMPS
MIAA Commisioner Win Schuler presents the 1964 MIAA All-Sports Trophy to Hope Athletics Director Gordon Brewer. The presentation followed the league track meet at Albion.

CHAPTER 9

UPS AND DOWNS AND NEW SPORTS

The 1963 football campaign had concluded on a positive note with five straight victories and a co-championship. Throughout the summer, hopes were high for an even better year in 1964. But, as so often happens, a series of circumstances combined to dismantle the backfield and rob the team of much of its talent. The graduation of ace halfback Chuck Veurink was taken in stride, but an early season injury sidelined Bill Keur, and problems with eligibility did the rest. Tackle Menno Sytsma, biggest man on the '63 squad, decided to remain home in California, and quarterback Bobby Schantz also did not return. Holland native John Stam, a tackle with considerable talent, suffered from a shoulder injury and a series of boils that would keep him out of action until the final game of the season. On the plus side, Hope still had the passing combination of Harlan Hyink and end Bill Hultgren, but guards Tom Bast and Ade Slikkers were injured in practice, as was safety man Ken Feit. All three would miss the opener.

In this depleted state, the Dutchmen hosted a strong Findlay team in a night game on Saturday, Sept. 19. The result was predictable. Findlay had defeated Hillsdale 34-12 a week earlier and had little trouble turning a 12-0 halftime lead into a 37-0 rout. Hope's best scoring chance came in the first half on a 12-play drive to the Findlay 17, but a Hyink pass to the end zone was intercepted by Byron Morgan to end the threat.

On Saturday, Sept. 26, the Dutchmen traveled to Chicago for a second non-league contest, this time against Wheaton. The night game was played in the rain and mud at Red Grange field. In first half, Hope lost halfback Bill Keur with a shoulder separation and fullback Tom De Kuiper with torn cartilage in his knee. The Dutchmen fumbled on their own 30 with the game but five minutes old. Wheaton made two first downs before fullback Bob Bennett plunged three yards for what would be the game's only touchdown. The point try failed, but the Crusaders led 6-0 with 9:47 left in the quarter. In the second quarter, Hope recovered a Wheaton fumble on the Hope eight-yard line, but three plays later Harlan Hyink was tackled in the end zone for a safety to make it 8-0 at the half. As the field became a quagmire, neither team could score. Hope suffered its third serious injury of the night when halfback Jim Bekkering sustained a concussion and was taken to the hospital. He would return to Holland on Monday via ambulance. Hope's only bright spot seemed to be the stellar defensive play of Tom Pelon and Vern Plagenhoef.

Seven Hope regulars were out of action as Hope opened MIAA play at Kalamazoo's Angell Field on Saturday, Oct. 3. The Hornets were helped by some fine punting early in the game. One rolled out on the four and a second one on the one-yard line. Unable to move the ball, Hope sent its punt only to its own 22. Five plays later, Eglis Lode broke free for seven yards up the middle and the game's first score. Rick Russell converted to make it 7-0 with 1:48 left in the quarter. In the second quarter, Kazoo's Ron Creager intercepted a Hope pass on the Hornet 32 and a sustained drive was climaxed when Rick Russell plunged five yards for the touchdown. The kick failed, but the lead was now 13-0 with 4:31 left in the half. Hope's offense again sputtered, and the Dutchmen were forced to punt from their own 35. Seven plays later, the Hornets were home again with Lode diving for the final yard. A pass for two points failed, leaving the halftime score at 19-0.

A third quarter Hope punt rolled into the end zone, but

it clearly was not Hope's day. An illegal procedure penalty forced a second punt, and this time Bob Sibilsky took the kick on his own 20, followed his blockers, and raced 80 yards for Kalamazoo's fourth touchdown. Russell passed to Mike Gohl for two points, making it 27-0. Hope's next punt was to the Kazoo 35. The return, plus a pass interference call, put the ball on the Hope 31. Six plays later, Dennis Steele went two yards over guard for another score. The pass for two points failed, but the game was now well out of reach at 33-0. Midway in the fourth quarter, the Dutchmen finally found their offense and drove 58 yards for their first touchdown of the season. In the drive, Hyink completed passes of 28 yards to Hultgren and 18 and 11 yards to Bruce Menning. Halfback Keith Abel went in from the one, but Hyink's run for two points failed, making it 33-6. To add insult to injury, on the last play of the game Mike Saxby intercepted a Hope pass and rambled untouched for 49 yards and the touchdown. A failed dropkick left the final score at 39-6. Hope's running game had been virtually non-existent, but Hyink and Plagenhoef had combined to complete 11 of 33 passes for 140 yards. In total yards from scrimmage it was Hope with 159 to 158 for the winners.

The practice week of Oct. 5-9 consisted of hard work and soul searching by players and coaches alike. There was nowhere to go but up. On Saturday, Oct. 10, Hope hosted Alma, and the Dutchmen were heartened when a crowd of 3,000 turned out at Riverview Park. In the game's first quarter, Hope took an Alma punt and, in a series of plays, moved to the Scots' 31. Included was a 12-yard run by Bekkering. At this point quarterback Hyink connected with end Roger Kroodsma, who went in for the game's first score. Steve Wessling converted, and the Dutch led 7-0 with 4:24 remaining in the period. When Alma failed to move, Hyink was again on-target, this time to Bruce Menning, who was pulled down on the one-yard line, but a penalty followed by a fumble ended the threat. Near the end of the half, Plagenhoef intercepted an Alma pass on the Scot 41 and returned it all the way to the eight. With 48 seconds left in the half, it was again the combination of Hyink to Kroodsma for the TD. Wessling's kick sailed wide, but Hope led 13-0 at halftime.

In the third quarter, the Scots moved to the Hope 23 but failed on fourth down and the Dutchmen took over. Hope sustained a 13-play drive that included a mixture of runs and passes. Hyink went the final yard on a sneak, then passed to Hultgren for two points to up the Dutchman lead to 21-0 with 3:42 left in the quarter. The Scots' offense came to life in the final quarter when quarterback Mike Knowlton passed to Schaitberger, who took the ball on the 50 and rambled all the way for the score. The attempt for two points failed, and the score stood at 21-6 with 13:29 left. Alma's last drive was halted on Hope's two-yard line. As the Dutchmen took over, Alma linemen broke through and spilled Keith Abel in the end zone for a safety to make the final score, 21-8. Defense

ACTION AT ITS BEST

President Vander Werf produced Hope's 1964 Homecoming program, writing most of the copy, selecting the cover photo, and writing the caption: Towering Tom Pelon, Hope freshman end, leaps high for a key interception in the Hope-Alma game on October 10. Senior Roger Abel looks up ready to assist, and Alma end Dave Warren stretches to receive the pass that never came. — Albion won the game 27-6.

had stymied the ground game for both teams. Hope rushed for 72 yards while holding the Scots to just 19, but Hyink had completed 10 of 24 passes for 130 yards and the beleaguered Dutchmen had their much-needed first victory of the season.

Saturday, Oct. 17, found the Hope team in Adrian for a game with the Bulldogs at Maple Stadium. Defense was the order of the day, and at the end of three-quarters the game remained scoreless. In the third quarter, Hope had marched to the Adrian two-yard line, but could gain only one yard in three plays. On fourth down, Hyink's pass was intercepted in the end zone. In the fourth period, Roger Abel broke free for a 22-yard run to the Adrian 18 and additional runs put the ball on the five, but Adrian defenders broke through three times to throw Hope runners for losses. Late in the game, Hope was forced to punt. The pass from center was high and kicker Phil Rauwerdink fell on the ball on the Hope 11. Hope held for three plays, but on fourth down Adrian's Bob Butz kicked a field goal from the 16 for the game's first and only score with just 4:54 remaining. In the

VENERABLE RIVERVIEW
Venerable Riverview Park, a city-owned facility, was home to Hope baseball until 1963 and to Hope football until 1979.

final minutes, Hyink passed to Hultgren for 20 yards, then to Kroodsma for 15 and Hope was on the Adrian 30. The next aerial was a long bomb that slid off the fingertips of Hultgren on the five-yard line. A final pass was intercepted by Adrian on the 20, and the threat was over. After a good performance against Alma, the 3-0 setback was devastating.

League leader Albion provided Hope's homecoming opposition on Saturday, Oct. 24. An interesting sidelight developed when President Vander Werf decided that the game program that we had been providing our patrons was simply not adequate. He vowed to produce the best program Hopeites had ever seen, and with the assistance of "Telephoto Tom" Renner, a sophomore from Riverdale, Ill., took over the project. Considerable time and effort went into the venture, but the finished product was indeed something to behold. Included were individual pictures plus write-ups of all 55 football players, 10 cheerleaders, and the Queen and her court. Nearly every aspect of college life at Hope was covered in the 32-page book, which had 116 photos in all and sold for 25 cents. There were some repercussions. To cover the considerable cost, individuals and local businesses were solicited. Most had recently made a contribution to the college, and there was some displeasure at the resulting "double dip." During the week I received a phone call from Albion Athletics Director Elkin Isaac, who wondered just what was going on. He had been awakened at 6:30 a.m. by President Vander Werf seeking specifics on Albion for use in our program.

Meanwhile, 1-4 Hope prepared to meet 5-0 Albion. A surprising crowd of 4,000 turned out at Riverview Park hoping for an upset. For a time, such appeared to be possible. With 25 seconds left in the first quarter, Hope's Roger Abel took a punt on his own 25, eluded several tacklers, then outran the safeties for a 75-yard touchdown scamper. Wessling's kick was wide, but Hope took a 6-0 lead into the second quarter. The Dutchmen held on for most of the period, but a late Albion drive put the Britons in scoring position. With five seconds remaining, quarterback Dave Neilson threw a five-yard pass into the end zone, which bounced off the chest of the intended receiver and into the hands of halfback Jim Royer. The kick attempt by Doug Mc Donald was not good, making it 6-6 at halftime. The Britons showed championship potential by dominating the second half. After four minutes of play, halfback Paul Danforth scored on a 10-yard off-tackle smash and this time Doug Mc Donald's kick was good, giving Albion a 13-6 lead. The Dutchmen aided the Albion cause by fumbling the kickoff on their own 24. Six plays after the Albion recovery, Wallis went two yards for the Britons' third score to make it 19-6. In the fourth quarter, the Hope punter again was victimized by a bad pass from center and the ball was downed on the Dutch 14. Three plays later, it was Russ Wallis scoring again, this time on a three-yard end run. Wallis then ran for two points, increasing the lead to 27-6. With 2:03 left in the game, frosh quarterback Randy Telman completed a 41-yard pass to Hultgren, who was stopped on the six-inch line. On the next play, Telman fumbled the snap and the Britons recovered to sew up the 27-6 victory. There was more bad news for the Dutchmen when it was learned that end Bruce Menning would be lost for the season with a pinched nerve.

Hope's fortunes would not improve as the college hosted the Olivet Comets on Oct. 31. The Dutchmen were now forced to rely on a long list of substitutes, and the result was a continued succession of misplays. A Riverview crowd of 2,200 groaned when a Hope snap was fumbled midway in the opening quarter and recovered by Olivet linebacker Frank Ignac. Four plays later, the Comets were on the board as Forest Bone scored from the one and a successful conversion made it 7-0. The woes continued in the second quarter, when the Hope safety mishandled a punt and the Comets' Dick Easton recovered on the Hope nine. It took just three plays for quarterback Alan Burnett to move into the end zone and give the visitors a 14-0 halftime lead. There was no scoring in the third period, but early in the fourth quarter Olivet's Dan Fitzpatrick intercepted a Hyink pass on the Hope 40 and returned it to the 19. Two plays later, Irv Sigler swept right end for a 17-yard touchdown run. The conversion upped the lead to 21-0, and the Comets were not finished. Late in the game, Coach Parsell's team mounted another drive. Included was a fine run of 26 yards by Sigler and a 17-yard pass from Al Burnett to Dominic Livedoti. Terry Dawson went the final yard on a plunge over center, and the misery was over for Hope at 28-0. The Dutchmen had fumbled five times, lost four, and had five passes intercepted.

The season was not over, not quite. On Nov. 7, a crowd of 1,900 braved the cold at Riverview for Mom and Dads Day. Hope's opponent was Ohio Northern of Ada, Ohio. The Polar Bears were coached by Arden "Stretch" Roberson and stood 6-2 on the season. Halfback Keith Abel had recovered from an earlier injury, and tackle John Stam, who had stayed with the team, was healthy for the first time all season. Despite the discouraging performance of a week earlier, the Hope team had come to play. In the opening quarter, the Dutchman defense held, and when Northern punter Gary Warner dropped back to punt, end Paul Wassenaar broke through to block the kick. Hope took over on the Northern 16 and scored in five plays. Keith Abel went three yards off-tackle for the TD with 2:54 left in the quarter. Wessling's kick failed, but Hope led 6-0. Late in the half, Northern threatened following a 49-yard pass completion to the Hope 14, but linebacker Terry Carlson intercepted the next pass in the end zone and Hope's narrow 6-0 lead was intact at the intermission.

Late in the third quarter, the Polar Bears made it to the Hope seven, but another jarring tackle by Wassenaar stopped the drive. Still in the third period, another drive was halted when Hope's Paul Bast recovered a fumble on the Dutch 38. After two running plays, Hyink connected with Kroodsma, who took the ball on the 20 and dashed into the end zone. Kroodsma then kicked the point to give the Dutchmen a 13-0 lead with 1:52 left in the third. In the fourth period, Northern moved to the Hope 13 after two face mask penalties and a 16-yard pass play, but a stunting Gary Holvick got through to drop the passer on the 48 and end the drive. As the game wound down, Pelon intercepted a Northern pass on the Polar Bears' 25 and returned it to the 17. With 1:17 remaining, Hope worked the ball to the one and Hyink sneaked in for the score. Kroodsma converted with five seconds left. A Hope team that refused to fold had ended its season with a 20-0 shutout of a very good Ohio Northern team. The Dutchmen had found their running game with the return of Keith Abel, who rushed for 96 yards, and Bekkering added 51, but all agreed that tough defense had made the difference.

As expected, Albion captured the MIAA championship with a 5-0 record. Olivet was second at 4-1 while Hope, Alma, and Adrian tied for the third spot with 1-4 records. Tom Cousineau was elected Hope's most valuable, and Olivet's Irv Sigler was named the league's MVP. Hope's only member of the All-MIAA team was end Gary Holvick.

* * *

Hope's frustrating fall continued with cross country. Coach Daryl Siedentop's charges actually compiled a commendable 4-2 dual meet record, but when it was discovered that Hope had inadvertently used an ineligible runner, all meets were forfeited and the Dutchmen ended in last place.

* * *

On the positive side, Hope's first official soccer team gave a good account of itself. The idea of a Hope soccer team had been promoted a year earlier by Dr. James Harvey, Hope's dean of students, who saw a need to accommodate the school's growing number of international students. A field was laid out on the former football practice field on Fairbanks Avenue, and a few practice games were arranged. Now, in the fall of 1964, an eight-game schedule was arranged and the squad had a full time coach in the person of Dr. Phillip Van Eyl, a professor in the department of psychology. Van Eyl's European background and great enthusiasm for the game made him an ideal choice.

In its opening game, the team surprised everyone by playing to a 1-1 tie with Wheaton College. The Crusaders' program had been in place for several years. No games were scheduled with the Calvin varsity, but Hope played the

HOPE'S FIRST OFFICIAL SOCCER TEAM — 1964
The team compiled a 6-1-1 record.

Front Row L. to R.: Ray Cooper, Robert De Sawal, Neil Sobania, Gibson Dallah, Bennett Ametefe, Walter Bruinsma, Pierre Sende, Danny Bao, Jamie Zeas.
2nd Row: John De Velder, Ben Bao, Jacob Ngwa, Jim Pierpont, John Wang, Coach Phil Van Eyl, Brian Bailey, Gerald Auten, Nicholas Raballa, Al Griswold, David Yntema.

Knights' freshman team twice, winning both games by 5-0 scores. The Dutchmen also played a two-game series with Goshen College, winning by scores of 6-5 and 8-2. Oakland University of Rochester, Mich., was also defeated by scores of 5-1 and 8-2. Hope's only embarrassment was a 12-0 thrashing at the hands of the freshman team from Michigan State University. The season record of 6-1-1 was a credit to the organizational ability and coaching expertise of Coach Van Eyl, not to mention the talents of young men from various parts of the globe. The first-year performance served notice that the sport was here to stay.

*   *   *

Hope's fifth-place finish in the 1963-64 basketball campaign made the Dutchmen an unlikely favorite to take the title in 1964-65, but there were hopes of moving up in the standings. Clare Van Wieren and Dean Overman were co-captains of the team that opened its season with a home game against Valparaiso on Wednesday, Dec. 2. Coach Gene Bartow's team enjoyed a hot first half shooting 50 percent, but the Dutchmen stayed close, moving into a tie five different times. In the waning minutes of the half, 6' 6" center Ken Rakow scored three quick field goals and the Crusaders moved to a 45-37 advantage at the intermission. Hope was guilty of numerous defensive lapses in the second half, and Valpo capitalized with 40 shots to only 26 for the Dutch. The 1,700 fans went home disappointed as the visitors coasted to an 83-64 victory. Ken Rakow led the winners with 27 and had support from Rich Eynon with 22. For Hope it was Overman, the only senior on the team, with 14, Van Wieren with 13, and Floyd Brady with 12.

The new kid on the block was freshman Floyd Brady from Chicago's Harlan High School. Through the efforts of the Rev. Chester Meengs, a friend of his father, he was made aware of Hope and liked what he saw. It was obvious to Coach De Vette from the start that here was a quality ball player. No one on the squad was surprised when he was picked as a starter in the first game. He would soon capture the imagination of the fans and provide them with many exciting moments over the next four years.

Hope traveled to Chicago on Saturday, Dec. 5, to meet

Elmhurst College. The game was played at the York Township High School Gym and was a homecoming of sorts for Brady, whose high school teammate, Don Boughton, was the leading scorer for Elmhurst. A first half press bothered the Dutchmen, and the Bluejays moved to a comfortable 59-38 lead at the intermission as Boughton showed his stuff with 32 points. Van Wieren was assigned to the Wilson Junior College transfer in the second half and Boughton was held to two field goals, but the damage had been done and Elmhurst took the contest 102-93. Boughton's 36 points led the winners, while Dancy had 17 and Don Anderson 16. Van Wieren played a fine game overall for Hope and led his team with 27. Brady did well in his hometown with 14, Bill Potter had 13, Carl Walters 10 and Chris Buys had a like number.

The Dutchmen recorded their first victory of the season in a close game at Adrian on Wednesday, Dec. 9. The score was tied seven times in the first half, but Hope inched ahead 39-38 at the intermission. The Bulldogs rallied in the second half and built a 67-60 lead with nine minutes remaining. A 7-0 run by the Dutchmen tied it at 67 with 5:41 left. Walters then stole the ball for a layup and Hope was ahead to stay. Hope's balanced attack finally produced an 86-76 victory, with Van Wieren and Brady each scoring 22. Walters had a strong game with 16 and Potter added 11. For Adrian it was Mike Garrett leading with 19, Dick Seagert had 13, and Lee Kennedy 12.

The Olivet team came to Holland on Saturday, Dec. 12, with a new coach in the person of Vince Sigren. There was added interest in the game as Sigren and Coach De Vette had been teammates for the Big Reds of Muskegon High School at an earlier time. Hope was off to a strong start, and led 38-21 at the half. Hot shooting continued in the second half, and after seven minutes Hope's lead was 52-27. This was the time to insert substitutes, but the subs could not cope with the Olivet press and were outscored 23-12. With the score at 64-50 the regulars returned and found it hard to get back in the groove. Five straight field goals by the Comets in the final minute narrowed the margin to 80-75, but Walters sank two free throws with three seconds left to give Hope the 82-75 victory. The scrappy Comets had mounted quite a comeback, especially in light of the fact that they were out-rebounded 83 to 44. Freshman Floyd Brady was impressive with 25 points and 22 rebounds, and Van Wieren scored 23 and had 19 boards, while Roy Anker had one of his best games with 12 points and 21 rebounds. Jim Everett was the leader for Olivet with 21 points, and D. Gosselin had 20.

When the Scots of Alma invaded the Civic Center on Dec. 16, they also were guided by a new coach. With the resignation of Wayne Hintz, Alma turned to Dr. Sedley Hall to fill the post and hoped to make a run for the MIAA title. A Wednesday night crowd of 1,200 watched the Dutchmen dominate the boards 50 to 28 in the opening half enroute to a substantial lead. Roy Anker's baseline hook shot with three seconds left made it 50-28 at the intermission. Subs were inserted and played about half of the second half. A layup by Dennis Weener with 1:42 remaining put the Dutchmen over the century mark for the first time in the season, and De Vette's crew moved to 3-2 with the 103-73 victory. Van Wieren was the big gun for the winners with 25, Walters and Potter each had 13, and Buys scored 12. Bill Pendell led the Scots with 23, and Mike Knowlton had 16.

Hope ushered in 1966 with a 90-84 win on Friday, Jan. 1, against a strong Aquinas team in the Civic Center. In notching their fourth straight victory, the Dutchmen again had to cope with veterans Gary Fewless and Dennis Alexander, who engineered a 39-37 lead for the Tommies at halftime. But Van Wieren, Brady, and Buys took over in the second half, and it was Hope moving to victory at the buzzer. Buys and Carl Walters were especially successful in shooting over the Aquinas zone. Van Wieren was the Hope leader with 25, Brady had 21, Buys 18, and Walters 16 in the fine team effort. Dennis Alexander was high for Aquinas with 23, and Gary Fewless had 20.

Hope's modest win streak came to an end the following day, when the team traveled to Wheaton to meet the ever-tough Crusaders. A zone press defense bothered the Dutchmen, who found themselves down 60-45 at the half. Walters and Brady got into foul trouble, and Wheaton pulled away against their replacements. Anker was outstanding in blocked shots and rebounds, and Hope was good at the free throw line with 22-of-28, but it was not enough to stop Coach Lee Pfund's team from chalking up a 104-80 victory. John Pfund led his dad's team with 20 points, Bill Province followed with 16 and Kerry Otterby had 14. Van Wieren was high man for Hope with 22, Buys had 12, and sub John Simons added eight.

At Albion on Wednesday, Jan. 6, the Dutchmen hoped for a comeback, but the aggressive Britons were tough on the boards and took a 39-33 halftime lead. Hope narrowed the margin to three, twice in the second half, but Coach Dean Dooley got good mileage from his bench and staved off the threat when the Dutchmen shaved the lead to 80-77 in the final minute. The Britons' eventual 84-79 victory was the product of very balanced scoring. Bruce Brown, Don Genson, and Dave Anspaugh each scored 14, while Roger Moliere had 13 and Larry Downs 12. For Hope it was Brady back in form with 22, Buys with 18, Walters with 16 and Van Wieren with 15.

Coach Dick Triptow brought his Lake Forest team to the Civic Center on Saturday, Jan. 9, for another close contest. Hope managed a 41-32 halftime advantage, but a zone press by the visitors was effective and 5½ minutes into the second half it was Lake Forest 49, Hope 48. With the score tied at 68-all and four minutes left, Anker scored a field goal and Van Wieren was good on four free throws to put Hope up 74-69. Two field goals by the Foresters in the last 20 sec-

HOPE VS. CALVIN — FEBRUARY 24, 1965

At tip-off time the emotional pitch is mirrored in the starter's faces.
L. to R.: Roy Anker, Carl Walters, Clare Van Wieren, Floyd Brady, and Don Kronemeyer.

onds cut the margin to one, but the Dutchmen held on for the 74-73 victory. Consistent Van Wieren led the winners with 21, and Floyd Brady was a strong force with 14 points and 23 rebounds. Carl Walters scored 10. For Lake Forest it was Fred Broda leading with 26 and Ron Hopkins with 12.

Hope and Calvin squared off in the Grand Rapids Civic Auditorium on Saturday, Jan. 13. More than 3,000 fans watched a game that was close for the first 10 minutes, but the Knights were in charge at halftime with a 35-24 lead. Early in the second half, an 11-0 Calvin run built the lead to 51-30 and the usual Hope-Calvin excitement had not materialized. Coach Barney Steen got solid performances from Ken Fletcher and Ed Douma as each scored 23 in the convincing 87-64 Calvin victory. Jim Fredericks added 11. Brady had 16 for Hope, Van Wieren got 12, and Anker nine in a generally sub-par performance for the Dutchmen. The Hope jayvees also were beaten, but guard Don Kronemeyer scored 33 points and would join the varsity as a starter in the next game.

Putting the Calvin game behind them, the Dutchmen now entertained another tough league opponent. On Saturday, Jan. 16, a crowd of 1,600 waited to see if Hope could bounce back against the Kalamazoo Hornets. The game would be tied 14 times and there would be 10 lead changes. Kalamazoo played well and held a 44-41 halftime lead. With 11:59 to go, a fast break layup by Kronemeyer gave Hope a 65-64 lead, but with 6:02 left the Dutchmen were down 79-74. At this point, a 9-0 run climaxed by Van Wieren's "falling away" layup at 2:08 gave De Vette's team an 83-79 lead. Tom Nicholai scored a field goal for the Hornets with 1:30 remaining, but Walters cashed in on two free throws in the closing seconds to make the final Hope 85-81. Hope's 49-25 margin in rebounds was a factor in the victory. Van Wieren led his team with 23 points, and was followed closely by Brady with 22. Potter had 15 and Kronemeyer, in his first start at guard, scored 11. Tom Nicholai was high for the Hornets with 29, Western Michigan transfer Jack Barkenbus had 13, and Jim Peters and Bob Pursel each had 12.

One week later, again on the home court, Hope met Concordia Teachers College of River Forest, Ill. The absence of Brady, Hope's flashy freshman, was sobering news for coaches and team members as well as the 1,600 who turned out for the game. Brady was confined to the health clinic with a severe case of tonsillitis, and would take in the game via radio. As usual, Coach Tom Faszholz came in with a strong team, and Concordia led 36-34 at halftime. In the second half, Kronemeyer was at the top of his game and Coach De Vette also got help from Bruininks, Poppink, and Buys off the bench. Buys's field goal with 3:30 to go tied the game at 68-all. With 51 seconds remaining, Don Kronemeyer drove for a layup and completed the three-point play to make it 71-68. Two free throws by Buys in the closing seconds gave the Dutchmen the hard-fought 73-70 victory. De Vette pointed to a key block in the closing minutes that gave his team a much-needed possession. Kronemeyer proved that he belonged on the varsity by leading his team with 21 points. Van Wieren followed with 12, Carl Walters had 11 and Dave Bruininks eight. High man for the Cougars was Dave Schrader with 24, followed by 6' 6' Tom Ruppert, who had an outstanding night with 16 points and 20 rebounds.

Hope was back in action following the semester break, and hoped to reverse an earlier nine-point loss to the Elmhurst in Chicago. The Jan. 30 encounter was witnessed by 1,200 Civic Center fans, who were glad to see Brady recovered and back in action. Early in the contest, Hope was successful in breaking the Elmhurst press leading to numerous fast break layups and hot shooting at 51 percent. Hope led 42-36 at the intermission, but the game would be tied three times in the second half. Hope's fifth and sixth points were scored on a "wrong way" basket by Elmhurst's John Dancy. Disoriented after taking the tap on a jump ball, Dancy dribbled to the Hope basket and laid it in. Brady who was nearest to the play, was given credit for the field goal. Brady accepted the gift and continued on to lead the Dutchmen with 23 points in the 92-75 victory. Van Wieren was next with 22, and Kronemeyer had another good night with 16. Anker and Buys each had 10. For Elmhurst it was Don Anderson with 19, Knapp had 18 and Don Boughton 14.

The Dutchmen traveled to River Forest for a return game with Concordia on Wednesday, Feb. 3, and were off to a nightmarish start. The team turned the ball over 14 times before completing a shot and trailed at the half 42-28. Following the intermission, the Dutchmen got it together and outscored the Cougars 33-13 in the first 12 minutes. With eight minutes remaining, Hope had managed a five-point lead at 60-55, but with 1:30 left it was 70-67 Concordia. A free throw upped the margin to 71-67. Brady scored to make it 71-69. Weener was then fouled. The free throw was missed, but Brady leaped high for the rebound and his put-back made it 71-71. The Cougars scored next, and Hope quickly took a timeout. A shot attempt by Buys was off the mark, and the rebound was taken by Concordia. Hope was forced to foul and the game's last point was scored after time had expired, leaving the final at 74-71 Concordia. Dave Schrader led the winners with 17 and Rau added 16 as the Cougars moved to 13-2 on the season. Anker played his best game of the season for Hope with 19 points. He was matched by Brady, also with 19. The Hope guards, Walters and Kronemeyer, each scored 11.

Coach Gregg Arbaugh and his Adrian squad were at the Civic Center on Saturday, Feb. 6, and the 1,800 fans in attendance were in for another nail-biter. It was Hope by three (45-42) at the intermission, but in the second half the Bulldogs gradually built a 10-point lead. The Dutchmen fought back and a Brady basket with 1:07 remaining brought them within one, 86-85. Buys missed two free throw attempts, but fought back to score the go-ahead field goal, making it Hope 87-86. Hope then rebounded a missed Adrian shot and called timeout. With 20 seconds left, the ball was worked to Brady, who scored on a hook shot, giving Hope the all-important three-point margin. Mark Garrett scored an unchallenged field goal at the buzzer, and Hope had squeaked by, 89-88. De Vette had gotten a satisfying mix of scoring from his starters. Van Wieren was the leader with 21, Brady had 19, Walters 18, Kronemeyer 15, and Roy Anker 12. Adrian's superb effort was led by Mark Garrett with 21, Lee Kennedy had 19, Ingham scored 15 and Dick Seagert 14.

At Olivet on Wednesday, Feb. 10, the Comets managed a 35-33 lead with eight minutes left in the first half. At this point Coach Vince Sigren had his team hold the ball, but Hope intercepted a pass, tied the score and went on to a 47-40 lead at halftime. Foul trouble plagued the Dutchmen in the second half as Van Wieren, Brady, and Anker all went to the bench with four. But substitutes came through, and Hope's lead with 3:30 left was 95-70. Kronemeyer was outstanding with 25 points in the 99-82 victory. Van Wieren was next with 21, Brady had 17 and Potter eight. Buzz Luttrell of Allegan, and Gordon Lofts each had 21 for the Comets and Mike Rabbers added 18.

Hope continued its winning ways at Alma on Saturday, Feb. 13. The Dutchmen were up 51-43 at halftime, and when 6' 5" Dave Gray fouled out early in the second half, Hope took control of the boards racking up 64 rebounds for the game. A field goal by Dave Bruininks with 2:10 remaining gave the Dutchmen their 100th point enroute to the 106-81 victory. Walters was the scoring leader for Hope with 26, Brady had 20, Kronemeyer 18, Van Wieren 16, and Potter 11. For the Scots it was Bill Pendell with 21, Mike Knowlton 17, and Dave Gray 14.

Dean Dooley's Albion Britons provided plenty of excitement at the Civic Center on Wednesday, Feb. 17. Both teams entered the contest with 7-2 MIAA records, and 2,000 fans turned out to watch Hope's high-scoring quintet. After a wild first half that saw 11 ties and 11 lead changes, Hope pulled ahead 58-52 at the intermission. In the end it was Hope's 51-percent shooting plus a 56-24 advantage in rebounds that produced the 109-92 victory. Van Wieren was especially effective with 35 points, Walters followed with 21, Potter had 19, and Brady 17. Don Genson was high for the Britons with 26, Larry Downs collected 18, and Dave Anspaugh had 16.

Wheaton College had defeated Hope six straight times when the team arrived at the Civic for a game on Saturday, Feb. 20. A near-capacity crowd of 2,400 hoped that the Dutchmen might break the string and continue to score near the century mark. The Crusaders were fast becoming Hope's number one non-league rival, and once again the competition was intense. Hope led by a single point, 50-49, at the half, but a tip-in by Anker in the first minute of the second half put his team up 53-51 and the Dutchmen never trailed thereafter. Breaking the Wheaton press with a series of long passes, the home team seemed to be in charge, but with 8:30 remaining the Crusaders pulled to within three, 91-88. Potter scored the next two field goals, and the offense continued to roll. Brady and Anker were both in foul trouble midway in the second half, but the team still managed a 105-89 lead with three minutes left, then sewed it up with a final of 115-100. Brady led the Hope parade with 26, Kronemeyer was close behind with 24, Van Wieren had 23, Walters 14, and Potter 12. For Wheaton it was Bill Province with 28, John Pfund with 22, and Kerry Otterby with 11. Following the game, it was learned that Adrian had prevailed over Albion 109-104 in four overtimes! This would be the equivalent of an additional half game.

From a spectator standpoint, Hope's 23-point loss to Calvin on Jan. 13 had been a bummer but, by Wednesday, Feb. 24, excitement had returned and 2,500 jammed the Civic Center to watch the long-time rivals battle for the MIAA championship. The game would be tied 12 times. The Knights pushed to a 50-45 lead at halftime, then scored again in the first 10 seconds of the second half to make it 52-45. This would be the biggest spread of the game. Tension mounted as the minutes ticked away. Anker fouled out with 7:03 left, and the Dutchmen cause suffered as he had just completed four-of-four second half field goals and had taken down seven rebounds. Potter took up the slack with 15 rebounds, but Hope could muster only 16-of-32 free throws while the Knights were making 16-of-25. Hope trailed 83-80 with two minutes left when Walters dropped in a free throw and Potter followed with a field goal to tie it at 83. A free throw by Calvin's Kim Campbell gave his team the lead 84-83, but with nine seconds left Brady's basket seemed to decide the contest at 85-84. However, to the dismay of Coach De Vette, a Hope foul was called with just three seconds remaining. Kim Campbell again stepped to the line and under great pressure, put in the point that would send the game into overtime at 85-85.

HOPE 104 — CALVIN 102
February 24, 1965.

The all round play of Carl Walters (30) was instrumental in Hope's 104-102 victory in double overtime, February 24, 1965. Calvin players are Rick Duistemars (24) and Jim Fredericks (5).

From the line Don Kronemeyer releases the game winner . . .

. . . then reaps his reward.

In overtime it was Floyd Brady with three points, Potter with two and Carl Walters with two. Things were looking good for the Dutchmen with a 92-89 lead, but as time ran out Rick Duistemars scored on a crucial three-point play to knot the count at 92-92. The second overtime period would be as dramatic as any in the history of the country's top small-college rivalry. Calvin took the lead on field goals by Jim Fredericks and Campbell, but Walters countered with a basket and Van Wieren was successful with two free throws to tie it again at 96. Calvin sub Chris Den Ouden then came through with two from the line, and Van Wieren scored an off-balance layup to make it 98-98. This would be the 15th tie of the game and came with 2:43 remaining. Once again the Knights managed a four-point bulge as Fredericks scored on a jumper and Campbell dropped in two free throws, 102-98. Kronemeyer, who had been having a rare off-night, drove the lane for a layup with 1:31 left, and the margin narrowed to 102-100. Walters, who by all accounts was playing the game of his life, drove the lane to score with nine seconds on the clock and the partisan crowd "raised the roof" as the scoreboard showed 102-102. The real drama was yet to come. Calvin fired a final shot that missed the mark with just two ticks left. Kronemeyer took the rebound and attempted to throw a long pass. Inexplicably, he was fouled by Kim Campbell as the buzzer sounded! With no time on the clock, the Hope freshman went to the line for a one-and-one with the game and the MIAA championship in his hands. As his shot parted the net, bedlam ensued. All the world loves a winner, and the crowd surged onto the floor to hoist Kronemeyer on shoulders and bear him to the sideline. With some difficulty and the aid of the officials, he returned to the line to drop in the now-meaningless second shot. It was finally over, Hope 104, Calvin 102.

Coaches De Vette and Steen called it an "even" game. Both agreed that this night the difference had been the play of Walters, who led the Dutchmen with 25. Brady scored 24, Van Wieren 17, Potter 14, and Kronemeyer 10. Calvin's scoring was also evenly divided. Rick Duistemars was the leader with 21, Ken Fletcher had 20, Fredericks 18, Campbell 17, and Ed Douma 16. There was no Hope practice on Thursday.

**THE 1964-65 BASKETBALL TEAM
MIAA CHAMPIONS**

Seated L. to R.: Jim "Dutch" Poppink, Jim Klein, Bill Potter, Roy Anker, Floyd Brady, Jerry Zwart. **Standing:** Manager Bob Kilbourn, Dennis Weener, Chris Buys, Don Kronemeyer, Co-Captain Clare Van Wieren, Co-Captain Dean Overman, Carl Walters, Dave Bruininks, Coach Russ De Vette.

HOPE'S FIRST WRESTLING TEAM — 1964-65

L to R: Dave Lubbers, Dan Howe, Chris Miller, John Wormuth, Harold Huggins, Bernard Brower, Ron Kronemeyer, Mike Vogas, Coach Eldon Greij.

Hope closed out its season at Kalamazoo on Saturday, Feb. 28, in the only afternoon contest of the year. A crowd of 1,000 turned out to see if the champions could withstand an expected let-down. It was soon obvious that the Dutchmen were not about to end the campaign on a negative note. Building on a 48-35 halftime lead, the team moved the score to 68-44 for the game's widest margin. A Potter tip with 2:31 remaining gave the Dutchmen 100 points and put them over the century mark for the fifth straight game. Overman, the lone senior on the squad, closed out his career by making the final basket and giving Hope the 102-91 victory. Hope shot a sizzling 56 percent in the season finale, and Brady was high man with 29. Van Wieren had 23, Walters 16, and Kronemeyer 11. For the Hornets it was Jim Peters with 25, Tom Nicholai 22, Jack Barkenbus 15, and Tom Crawford 13.

Hope concluded the season with seven straight wins, a 10-2 mark in the MIAA, and 16-6 overall. Clare Van Wieren, Hope's MVP, was named to the All-MIAA team along with Ken Fletcher of Calvin, Larry Downs of Albion, Mike Rabbers of Olivet, and Dick Seagert of Adrian. Ken Fletcher was voted the league's most valuable player.

* * *

Hope's newly added sports proved to be a mixed bag. As noted earlier, soccer was off and running with considerable support. The winter sports, however, found the going tougher. Wrestling was introduced when biology professor Eldon Greij volunteered to coach the first team. Those signing up included Dave Lubbers, Dan Howe, Chris Miller, John Wormuth, Harold Huggins, Bernard Brower, Ron Kronemeyer and Mike Vogas. With Carnegie-Schouten Gym reserved largely for basketball practice, the wrestlers were usually relegated to one of the handball courts for their workouts. Despite a game effort by Coach Greij and his charges, lack of experience was much in evidence, and the team ended its first season at 0-7.

At the insistence of President Vander Werf, a men's swim team had been organized during the winter of 1963-64. It was my belief that such a program would be hard-pressed to succeed without our own coach and facility. The arrangement included rental of the pool at West Ottawa High School plus the services of the school's coach, Henry Reest. Reest had proven his ability as a coach with an excellent program at West Ottawa, but his first responsibility was to his own team, and they understandably enjoyed the prime time hours for practice. Hope's early morning treks to the north side in the dead of winter had little appeal and made recruiting a nightmare. As interest lagged, Hope was unable to field a full team and the attempt was finally abandoned. Thirteen years later, with a new facility (Dow Center) and a full time coach in the person of John Patnott, the program would become the envy of the league.

* * *

In the waning days of March of 1965, restless Hope athletes welcomed the chance to travel south and bask in the sun. Doc Green's tennis team departed on Saturday, March 29, and stopped in Muncie, Ind., for a match with Ball State. The action took place indoors, and the Cardinals prevailed 6-4 by winning all but one singles match. The Dutchmen took the three doubles matches. Scheduled competition against Oglethorpe in Atlanta had to be canceled due to illness in the Oglethorpe ranks. The next day, Hope met the University of Florida in Gainesville and suffered an 8-1 setback. The doubles team of Dave Nykerk and Don Kronemeyer produced Hope's only win at 7-5, 6-4. In Winter Park on Wednesday, March 31, the Dutchmen were again on the short end of an 8-1 score, this time at the hands of Davidson, but on Thursday the team put up a good battle before succumbing to Duke University by a 5-4 score. In an afternoon match on the same day, the Dutchmen were downed by Rollins 7-2. In Miami on Friday, April 2, Hope lost another close one, edged by Columbia University 5-4. The team enjoyed lunch with Minnesota pitcher Jim Kaat, and in the evening were guests of the Minnesota ball club for its spring training game with the Houston Astros.

The spring trip concluded on Saturday, April 3, with another loss to Rollins, again by a 7-2 score. Journeying homeward, the team was scheduled to meet Indiana University in Bloomington on Monday, April 5, but rain forced a cancellation. Though the team returned with an 0-7 record, three of the matches had been close and the experience gained would pay off in the regular season. Having watched as the Astros recorded a 10-2 victory over the Twins, Doc Green and his charges took note of the debut of the Houston Astrodome on April 9. Hometown fans cheered as their team downed the New York Yankees 2-1 in 12 innings. Texan LBJ was on hand and watched from one of the gilded boxes.

The Dutchmen opened their regular season on Saturday, April 10, by pinning a 7-2 defeat on Wheaton in Holland. In singles, it was Butch Hopma (H) over Greg Crawford 3-6, 6-1, 6-3, Jay Hakes (W) defeated Lance Stell 6-2, 7-5, Randy Nykamp (H) took Don Coates 6-3, 6-2, Dave Nykerk (H) defeated Roger Bitar 5-7, 6-0, 6-0, Don Kronemeyer (H) won from Sheldon Hurst 6-1, 6-4, and Craig Holleman (H) defeated John Hess 6-3, 6-4. In doubles, it was Hopma-Nykamp over Crawford-Coats 6-3, 6-4, Hakes-Bitar over Nykerk-Kronemeyer 4-6, 7-5, 6-3, and Stell-Carl Walters over Hess-Hurst 6-1, 1-6, 6-3. Hope's basketball guards were now contributing on another kind of court. On this particular day, Hope's accomplishment was somewhat overshadowed by other activity in Holland. The windmill De Zwaan was dedicated on Windmill Island in the presence of Prince Bernhard of the Netherlands and Michigan Governor George Romney.

Hope's first MIAA encounter took place on Calvin's Knollcrest Campus on Wednesday, April 14. The number-two doubles match was halted by rain, but Hope had carried the day by that time and emerged a 5-1 winner. In singles, Hopma defeated Dick Bultman 5-7, 6-1, 6-1, Nykamp defeated Jim Edson 9-7, 6-1, Kronemeyer downed Bert De Leeuw 5-7, 6-4, 6-4, Nykerk defeated Joel De Koning 6-3, 6-2, and Pete De Jonge defeated Holleman 6-3, 4-6, 6-4. In an exhibition match, it was Tom Prins over Walters 6-3, 4-6, 6-1. In doubles, Hopma-Nykamp defeated Bultman-Edson 6-0, 6-1. As mentioned, an interesting number-two doubles match was finally canceled due to rain. At the time in the first set, Kronemeyer and Nykerk were tied at 10-10 with De Leeuw and Stielstra.

On Wednesday, April 21, the Dutchmen had little trouble in downing Grand Rapids Junior College 9-0. This was followed by a trip on April 24 to Alma where the Scots were also blanked, this time by a score of 7-0. The match with Albion in Holland on Wednesday, April 28, was not a shutout, but the Dutchmen were clearly in charge as they registered a 6-1 victory. In singles, it was Albion's Per Schott getting the best of Hopma 6-1, 3-6, 6-2, Stell took Paul Nowakoski 6-2, 6-3, Nykamp defeated Dick Brink 6-2, 6-8, 6-2, Kronemeyer defeated Bill Smith 6-4, 6-4, and Nykerk defeated Joe Mc Culloch 6-2, 3-6, 6-4. In doubles, it was Hopma-Nykamp over Schott-Nowakoski 6-2, 6-3, and Kronemeyer-Stell over Brink-Joe Read 6-2, 7-5. In an exhibition singles match, Craig Holleman defeated Kurt Leighton 1-6, 6-3, 6-3.

The Hope team traveled to Olivet on Saturday, May 1 to register another 7-0 shutout, and did the same a week later when the Adrian Bulldogs made the trip to Holland. The seven-match win streak was halted in Mount Pleasant on Thursday, May 13, when Central Michigan downed the Dutchmen 6-3. In singles, Hopma defeated Tim Mc Cormack 6-4, 6-4, Tom Murphy defeated Stell 6-2, 6-3, Nykamp defeated Tom Johnson 6-3, 1-6, 6-3, Kronemeyer defeated Dennis Elkins 7-5, 6-2, Bill Kooiners defeated Nykerk 6-4, 6-1, and John Allen defeated Holleman 6-4, 6-1. In doubles, it was Mc Cormack-Murphy over Hopma-Nykamp 9-7, 7-5, Elkins-Kooiner over Stell-Kronemeyer 6-3, 7-5, and Johnson-Allen over Nykerk-Holleman 7-5, 6-4.

In a showdown on Wednesday, May 19, Hope hosted George Acker's Kalamazoo team, and once again the Hornets were simply too strong. The Dutchmen managed to avoid a shutout when Hopma and Nykamp defeated Dick Johnson and Bob Engels 6-2, 12-14, 6-2, but Kazoo won everything else in posting a 6-1 victory. Three days later, in the league meet at Kalamazoo, it was more of the same. Johnson repeated as singles champion and was named the league's most valuable player. In doubles, however, Hope's Hopma and Nykamp emerged as MIAA champions by again downing Kazoo's Dick Johnson and Bob Engels 1-6, 6-3, 6-4. In team standings, it was Kalamazoo with 20 points, Hope 13, Albion 8, Calvin 4, Alma 3, Olivet 1, and Adrian 0. Dick Bultman of Calvin was chosen by the coaches as recipient of the Allen B. Stowe Sportsmanship Award.

*   *   *

Hope's 1965 baseball team failed to register a win in a somewhat abbreviated spring trip. The team left on Friday, March 26, but the scheduled game at Indiana Central was canceled due to bad weather. A Monday game was also rained out, but on Tuesday, March 30, the Dutchmen met Southwestern of Memphis in a game that went 12 innings. Four Hope pitchers combined to strike out 15 batters, but Southwestern took the game 1-0 on a double steal in the final inning. The next day, Memphis State took both ends of a doubleheader, downing the Dutchmen, 5-1 and 4-0. On Thursday, April 1, it was Lambuth edging Hope 3-2 in 10 innings, and on Friday the Dutch fell to Union 12-4. A Saturday game was rained out, and the team returned to Holland winless but well prepared to tackle the regular season.

Hope tasted victory for the first time in 1965 at Spring Arbor. In a doubleheader played on Saturday, April 10, the Dutchmen took the first game 5-2 behind the three-hit pitching of Roger Kroodsma and despite four Hope miscues. Steve Piersma was behind the plate. In the second contest, Paul Terpstra and Don Kroodsma combined for a one-hitter, but walks and errors gave the game away. Dan Krueger's sixth-inning single produced the only Hope run, and the Cougars claimed a 2-1 victory.

The MIAA season opened at Calvin on Wednesday, April 14, and Coach Siedentop's team was off to a flying start by taking both ends of the double bill. In the opener, Hope collected 11 hits off four Calvin pitchers and chalked up a 14-0 shutout behind the six-hit pitching of Terpstra. The Dutchmen had six doubles in the contest, two by Pelon. Hope took the second game by a 2-1 score behind a strong performance by Don Kroodsma, who gave but two hits while walking four. The game was called after six innings due to darkness. Skip Nienhuis was behind the plate in the first game, while Piersma was Kroodsma's battery mate.

Tuesday, April 20, found the Hope at Valley Field in Grand Rapids for a non-league game with Grand Rapids Junior College. The Dutchmen used five pitchers and two catchers in recording their third straight win, 7-3. Terpstra led the 10-hit attack with three singles. The JC batters were limited to five safeties as 16 went down via the strikeout route.

Hope's games at Alma on Saturday, April 24, were a study in contrast. The Scots took the first game 1-0 when Lanny Caverly singled in the second, stole second, and scored on Dick Skinner's double. Terpstra and Rog Kroodsma allowed five hits in the losing cause, while Alma's Tim Pete shut the Dutchmen down with three singles. In the nightcap, Don Kroodsma was brilliant with a no-hitter that included 11 strikeouts and four walks. He was aided by two fielding gems, both in the second inning. Don Troost speared a line drive in right field, and Rog Kroodsma made a diving catch in center field to help preserve the no-hitter. Hope collected 10 hits in the eventual 17-0 rout.

The Dutchmen continued to play good baseball as they hosted Albion on Wednesday, April 28. In a tight first game, the score stood 4-4 in the seventh when Terpstra singled, then stole second. Nienhuis walked and Rog Kroodsma was safe on an infield single to load the bases. Veteran Clare Van Wieren then came through with a single to drive in Terpstra with the winning run. Don Kroodsma pitched a one-hitter, but walked six. The victory was made tougher by six Hope errors. Hope breezed to a 15-5 victory in the second game that featured home runs by Cal Poppink and Dan Krueger. Hope garnered 14 hits, while Terpstra and Mark Johnson were effective on the mound.

At Olivet on Saturday, May 1, Don Kroodsma was in similar form, giving up but one hit and walking seven. The Comets got one in the second and two in the seventh to notch the 3-2 win. All three Olivet runs were unearned. Steve Piersma drove in both Hope runs in the second with a single. Hope turned the tables in the second game, winning another close one. With the score tied 1-1 in the eighth inning, pitcher Terpstra won his own game with a triple. He was able to score on Don Troost's fielder's choice when the throw to the plate was not in time.

An estimated 200 fans turned out for a non-league night game at Riverview Park on Friday, May 7. The game with Grand Rapids Junior College turned out to be a wild affair as the Dutchmen collected 10 runs in the sixth inning. Roger Kroodsma went four-for-four with a home run off the grandstand roof, a triple, and two singles. To offset the Dutchman hitting barrage, pitchers Johnson and Ron Matthews managed to walk 16 JC batters! The game was finally called at the end of six innings, giving Hope the 19-16 victory.

Conditions returned to normal the next day, as Hope entertained the Adrian Bulldogs at Van Raalte field. Adrian was a 6-4 winner in the first game by scattering six Hope hits. Wayne Cotts had a double and single. Hope's battery of Don Kroodsma and Pelon in the nightcap was able to produce a 6-3 victory and the much-needed split for the day. In the second inning, Troost walked and Pelon followed with a two-run homer. In the fourth, Van Wieren walked and Nienhuis stroked a homer. The other two runs came in the fifth and sixth innings.

Hope traveled to Mount Pleasant on Wednesday, May 12, and the team divided a twinbill with Central Michigan. The 5-4 Hope victory in the first game was pretty much a one-man show. Rog Kroodsma went all the way scattering 10 hits, then aided his own cause by blasting two two-run homers, one in the fourth and the other in the fifth. Central was the winner in the second game by a score of 7-5 after Hope blew a 5-2 lead.

The 1965 campaign for the Dutchmen ended at home on Wednesday, May 19. The two games with Kalamazoo were crucial to Hope's title chances. A double victory was necessary to earn a tie with Olivet. Going into the sixth inning of the first game, Hope held a 3-0 lead, but the Hornets tied it with three runs on two singles, a double, and a walk. In the top of the ninth, the Hornets nicked Terpstra for three more runs and took the game 6-3. Pelon led the Dutchmen with a single, double, and home run. With title hopes dashed, the Dutchmen buckled down in the second game to end on a positive note. Kazoo took an early 3-0 lead, but Hope came back with two in the second, then won the game with a seven-run outburst in the seventh. The 9-3 victory gave Hope an 8-4 MIAA record and a solid second-place behind Olivet. The overall Dutchman record was 12-10. The Comets finished at 9-3 to win their first MIAA baseball championship in 57 years, having last turned the trick in 1908. Hope placed two men on the All-MIAA team in the persons of second baseman Wayne Cotts and pitcher Don Kroodsma. How Roger Kroodsma was overlooked remains a mystery.

* * *

Hope's 1965 effort in golf would produce a fourth-place finish in the MIAA. Coach Bill Hilmert had lost Jim Wiersma and Jim Thompson through graduation, and Dean Overman decided to pass up the season in his senior year. Despite the presence of veteran Bill Potter, the season was off to a rocky start with three straight losses. On Tuesday, April 20, it was Alma 12½, Hope 3½ at the West Ottawa course. Potter defeated J. Lind 3-0, D. Nelson (A) defeated George Cook 3-0, J. Odell (A) defeated Larry Cain 2½-½, Jerry Knowlton (A) defeated Gordon Korstange 3-0, and Dave Blandon (A) took Bruce Gibbons 3-0. Nelson was medalist with a 76.

On the same course three days later, it was Calvin 11½, Hope 4½. Scores were not impressive, with Potter carding an 82, Korstange 83, Cain 83, Cook 90, and Gibbons 93. On Tuesday, April 27, it was Albion's turn at the Duck Lake course. The Britons' Fred Adams helped his team to an easy 13½-2½ victory with a fine 71 to take medalist honors. Korstange was Hope's only winner as he shaded Bill Rivers 2-1. Potter had an off day with a 91.

The Dutchmen broke into the win column at the American Legion course on Friday, April 30, with a 9-7 victory over Olivet. Mike Snow (O) defeated Cook 2-1, Dave Biggers (O) defeated Cain 2-1, Korstange defeated Ed Peters 3-0, Potter defeated Bob Ferguson 2-1, and Jim Everett defeated Hope's Ken Kolenbrander 2-1. Hope received one point for the lowest team score.

After dropping a 10-5 decision to Grand Rapids Junior College, Hope registered its second win at Adrian on Friday, May 7. The 13½-½ victory saw Potter defeat Steve Dhondt 2½-½, Korstange defeat Mike Boyle (A) 3-0, Cook defeat Bob Fleming 2-1, Cain defeat Larry Drummond 3-0, and Kolenbrander defeat Jerry Smith 3-0. Cook took medalist honors with a 77.

Back home on Tuesday, May 11, the Aquinas Tommies were too much for the Dutchmen and posted an 11½-4½ victory. Cain tied Sharon Wilder 1½-1½, Tom Gunn defeated Potter 2½-½, Degenhorst defeated Korstange 2-1,

Tom Wojdygo defeated Cook 2-1, and Pat Amarine defeated Kolenbrander 2½-½.

In another home match on Thursday, May 13, Hope downed Grand Valley 12½-2½. Potter was at his best with a 73 to defeat Rog Perkins 3-0, Ron Kolvalski defeated Korstange 2½-½, Cook defeated George Bisbee 3-0, Cain defeated Brian Leatherman 3-0, and Kolenbrander defeated Bob Montague 2-1.

Hope traveled to Kalamazoo on Wednesday, May 19, and came home with an 11-5 victory. Potter was again medalist with a 74 to defeat Chuck Hiddema 3-0, Cook defeated Dan Beardsley 3-0, Al Heath defeated Korstange 2-1, Cain defeated Bouwens 2½- ½, and Willhohn defeated Kolenbrander 2½ -½.

The Dutchmen were back in Kalamazoo two days later for the MIAA meet at the Kalamazoo Country Club. In team standings, it was Albion the winner with 795 points, followed by Alma 808, Calvin 811, Hope 840, Olivet 865, Kalamazoo 906, and Adrian 945. Mike Snow of Olivet was medalist with a 36-hole total of 148. Jud Lind of Alma was second with 151, while Hope's Bill Potter and Dave Tuls of Calvin tied for third with 154. The Hope team had shown considerable improvement as the season progressed, but had to settle for the overall fourth place finish in the MIAA.

* * *

In 1964, Calvin track coach Dave Tuuk and Hope coach Gordon Brewer finally convinced the other MIAA coaches that dual meet results should count one half towards the league championship. As the second season under this arrangement began, it was evident that new meaning had been given to the dual encounters, even as it had in cross-country, tennis, and golf. Participants with modest ability were now able to make a significant contribution to their team's quest for a title. Senior 440-man Dave Lane was captain of Hope's 1965 team and his subsequent performance would more than justify the honor.

The Dutchmen opened at home on Wednesday, April 14, against another strong Calvin team. The Knights took firsts in 12 of 16 events in posting an 80-56 victory. Hope's individual victories came in the mile run, when Gary Peiper beat out Jack Bannink; in the broad jump, where John Simons won with a leap of 20' 4¼"; in the high jump, as Ron Borst and Bruce Menning went 1-2; and in the 880, as Steve Reynen ran 2:02.4. Calvin won both relays and Dave Ver Merris set a Calvin record of 49.2 in the 440. He also scored 12½ points for his team.

Saturday, April 24, was not an ideal track day as Hope hosted an undermanned Alma team. With the temperature hovering around 40 degrees, plus a strong crosswind, Hope proceeded to win 15 of 16 events, enroute to a 115-21 victory. Sim Acton's javelin toss of 138' 5" was the only Alma first, and the Scots were glad to get on the bus and head for home. There would be better days.

RECORD SETTER
Ron Borst set a new Hope high jump record in 1965 with a leap of 6'5.

At Albion on Wednesday, April 28, Hope met a team much like the Calvin Knights and the Dutchmen again lost by an 80-56 score. This time Hope won both relays, but Coach Dean Dooley's Britons came through with 11 firsts, including two Albion records. Rex Curry won the 880 with a 1:59.5 mark, and high jump ace Dave Middlebrook took his event with a leap of 6' 5".

Hope's up-and-down season continued one week later with another home meet, this time with the Olivet Comets of Coach Stu Parsell. Hope's 109-27 victory included a Hope record in the 440 by Lane. His 49.6 bettered the previous mark of 50.1 set by Dave Spaan in 1958. Ideal weather conditions contributed as Hope's mile relay team lowered the school record to 3:24.6 in the meet's final event. Team members were Bill Hultgren, Jim Pierpont, Mike Paliatsos, and Lane. Olivet's Jack Rall took the shotput, and Irv Sigler of football fame won the javelin, but the Dutchmen took first in all other events.

Prior to the Olivet meet, Hope had journeyed to Delaware, Ohio, to participate in the first Great Lakes Colleges Association track and field meet. Albion and Kalamazoo also took part in the May 1 meet at Ohio Wesleyan University. Wooster placed first, followed by Denison, Wabash, Albion, Ohio Wesleyan, Oberlin, Hope, Kenyon, and Kalamazoo. The best Dutchman marks in the meet included

Lane's 49.9 in the 440 for second, and Ron Borst's 6' 3" in the high jump, also good for second.

At Adrian on Saturday, May 8, Hope bested the Bulldogs 91-45 by winning 11 of the 16 events. The Dutchmen had sweeps in the high jump with Borst, Menning, and Floyd Brady, and also in the 440 with Paliatsos, Pierpont, and Hultgren. Gary Holvick won both hurdle races, and Lane, switched to the 220, won in the time of 23.0.

Tuesday, May 11, found the Dutchmen at Valparaiso in a triangular that also included Marquette University. The host school dominated the meet with 94 points, Marquette was second with 46, and Hope managed a close third with 41. Borst claimed Hope's only first in the high jump with a mark of 6' 3¼", a Hope record.

Coach Dick Smith of Grand Rapids JC brought another strong team to Holland on Saturday, May 15. The Raiders captured nine of 16 firsts, but the Dutchmen took nine seconds and seven thirds to keep it close. A JC sweep in the pole vault finally spelled defeat for the Dutchmen by the margin of two points, 69-67. Don Crawford edged Lane in the 440, 49.3 to 49.4, but Lane came back to take the 220 and also ran anchor on Hope's winning mile relay team.

Hope bounced back with an 88-48 win at Kalamazoo's Angell Field track on Wednesday, May 19. Coach Swede Thomas's team took six firsts, but the Dutchmen got the other 10 and had sweeps in the shot, discus, high jump, and 440-yard dash. Holvick again won both hurdle races. Kazoo's Bill Lynch was the victor in both dashes with the fine times of 9.9 and 22.9.

After trips to Calvin in 1963 and to Albion in 1964, the MIAA Field Day meet was back in Kalamazoo on Saturday, May 22, 1965. Albion would enjoy one of its best days in MIAA track, with seven gold medals and three-league records enroute to a total of 78 points and yet another MIAA championship. Dave Heth's vault of 13' 1½ " was a new mark, as was Dave Middlebrook's leap of 6' 6" in the high jump and Rex Curry's time of 1:55.9 in the 880. Calvin finished second with 53 points and a new league record of 38.5 by Ben Snoeink in the 330 intermediate hurdles. Hope was five points back in third place with 48 points, winning both relays and the 440-yard dash. In the 440-yard relay, the team of Holvick, Hultgren, Bob Thompson, and Ray Cooper ran the oval in 43.2, a new MIAA and Hope record. Dave Lane won the 440 dashes in 49.4, breaking his own Hope record. The mile relay team of Pierpont, Palliations, Hultgren, and Lane set an MIAA and Hope record with a time of 3:23.1. Ron Borst finished second in the high jump behind Middlebrook, but his jump of 6' 5" was also a Hope record. Kalamazoo finished fourth with 30 points, Olivet was fifth with 16, Adrian finished sixth with eight, and Alma was seventh with seven points. The Dutchmen were pleased with their performance and an overall third-place finish. Dave Lane was named the MIAA's first most valuable trackman. Key performers would return for the 1966 campaign.

MIAA MVP

Hope's Dave Lane received the MIAA's first Most Valuable Trackman award in 1965.

* * *

Hope was forced to surrender the coveted All-Sports trophy to Albion as the Britons totaled 71 points to 54 for the second-place Dutchmen. Calvin had 51 for third, Kalamazoo was fourth with 39, Olivet fifth with 36, Alma sixth with 27, and Adrian seventh with 16. Another year of rewarding sports competition was now in the MIAA record books.

MIAA CHAMPION

Hope's mile relay team set an MIAA record in 1965. **L. to R.:** Jim Pierpont, Mike Paliatsos, Bill Hultgren and Dave Lane.

CHAPTER 10

BIG-TIME SPRINGTIME

Hope's 1965-66 quest for athletic prominence began modestly in the fall, held its own through the winter, then came on strong in the spring. A well-balanced program was ever the goal, and the MIAA All-Sports Trophy continued to be the best reflection of such achievement. The large revolving trophy now rested in Albion's Kresge Gym, and the Dutchmen had fond hopes of bringing it back after a year's absence.

Following a three-year term, MIAA Commissioner Win Schuler resigned, citing the need to devote more time to his burgeoning restaurant business. His replacement, appointed on August 31, was John C. Hoekje. Hoekje had enjoyed an impressive high school coaching career, and had served for a number of years as an MIAA football official. The other big news around the league was the opening of Calvin's new Knollcrest Fieldhouse with a seating capacity of 4,400.

During the summer of '65, I represented Hope at Camp Geneva on the shores of Lake Michigan. One of the student counselors there was Hope senior Bruce Menning. We spoke at some length about the upcoming football season, and I found that Bruce was wavering. With Captain Roger Kroodsma and ace receiver Bill Hultgren firmly implanted at the end positions, his chances for playing time seemed limited. The prospect of two-a-day practices under a hot September sun also had little appeal for a senior sub. I assured him that he was indeed an important cog in our team plans and hoped that he would not pass up this, his last season.

Football practice for the Dutchmen got under way on Monday, Sept. 6, and the coaches were much relieved when Menning entered the gym to draw a uniform. Guard Ken Postma was back after a year at Western Michigan, but linebacker Terry Carlson was lost due to a back injury. It was decided that the returning Joe Kusak would be used at defensive end and offensive tackle. As practice progressed, a rash of injuries made it necessary for several players to be used both ways. As a result, the team was not really prepared for its opener at Ohio Northern on Sept. 18.

A crowd of 3,000 was on-hand for the night game at Lima Stadium. Hope lost the ball five times on fumbles and suffered three interceptions. With eight turnovers, the result was predictable. Late in the first quarter, Northern turned its first interception into a score when Danny Isocheim went seven yards off-tackle to paydirt. The conversion made it 7-0. In the second quarter, quarterback Mike Kobilarcsik scored on a bootleg and another conversion made it 14-0. Later in the period, Harlan Hyink was again intercepted and the Polar Bears made it to the Hope 12. At this point, Paul Levigne kicked a field goal to make it 17-0 at the half.

In the third quarter, a fumbled punt gave Northern the ball on the Hope two. Ray Loiselle went in for the score, and Levigne again converted to make it 24-0. Hope's woes continued later in the period with yet another lost fumble. This time, Yocheim scored his second TD on a seven-yard pass. The kick was not good, but the game was out of reach at 30-0. There was no scoring in the fourth quarter, but Hope's performance had been a coach's nightmare and could only be described as dismal.

A sore throwing arm kept Hyink out of practice for most of the next week, and Gary Frens was the starter in Hope's home opener, an afternoon contest against Wheaton on September 25. While the Dutchmen were taking their lumps in Ohio, Wheaton had downed Albion by a 21-14 score. Hope was a decided underdog, but the community showed its support with a crowd of 2,000 at Riverview. The fans would be rewarded as a different Hope team showed up for this contest. Hyink entered the game in the second quarter, and with four completions took his team to the half-yard line as time ran out in the scoreless first half.

Midway in the third quarter, Hultgren was injured. His replacement was Menning. With 7:35 left in the quarter, quarterback Hyink lofted a long one to Menning, who took the ball on the Wheaton 17 and outran the defense for what would be the game's only score. The play covered 50 yards. As he ran across the green endzone, I thought of Camp Geneva. The kick by Kroodsma was good, making the final score Hope 7, Wheaton 0. The Dutchman defense had limited the Crusaders to 100 yards of total offense, 63 of them rushing. Included were ends Joe Kusak and Paul Wassenaar, tackles Bill Barger and Max Schipper, nose guard Ken Carpenter, and linebackers Kroodsma and Steve Piersma.

Veteran halfback Bill Keur had reported late, but saw action in the Wheaton game and now strengthened Hope's running game. The Dutchmen traveled to Adrian on Oct. 2 to meet the Bulldogs of Coach Charles "Chappy" Marvin. A crowd of 1,000 in Maple Stadium watched as neither team was able to push over a score in the opening quarter. Midway in the second period, Adrian's Terry Richards attempted a field goal from the 26, but the kick sailed wide of the mark. On the next series, the Dutchmen fumbled on their own 31 and Roger Davidson recovered for Adrian. Three runs by Harlis Chavis plus a 17-yard pass completion put the ball on Hope's three-yard line. Chavis then went off-tackle for the score. The conversion by Joe Murphy made it 7-0 Adrian at the half.

There was no scoring in the third quarter, but near the end of the period Hope began to move after Adrian's Perry Foor attempted, for the third time, to run from punt formation. Hope forced a five-yard loss and took over on the Bulldog 41. With 51 seconds gone in the fourth period, Hope scored after a 14-play drive. Keur carried seven times, while the big play was a 13-yard screen pass to fullback Charlie Langeland that put the ball on the seven. Keur finally went in from the two. Hyink, with good protection, passed to Keith Abel near the sideline for the two-point conversion and Hope led 8-7. On their first possession following the score, the Dutchmen engineered a nine-play drive that included a 24-yard pass to Menning and a 14-yard toss to Abel, who was pulled down on the one-yard line. Keur went in for his second TD, and Kroodsma kicked the point to make it 15-7. Adrian threatened in the closing minutes, but Schipper recovered a fourth down fumble and Hope ran out the clock.

Hope's two-game win streak was halted by Olivet in a disappointing home game on Oct. 9. After a scoreless first quarter, the Comets took advantage of a Dutchman turnover to win the game. Late in the second quarter, linebacker Haydon Moorman recovered Hyink's attempted pitchout on the

HOPE 7 — WHEATON 0
September 25, 1965

Hope receiver Bruce Menning (81) sprints away from Wheaton defenders to complete a 50-yard pass play and the game's only score.

Hope 21, and seven plays later fullback Tony Grimaldi plunged one yard for the score and Jim Pobursky converted to make it 7-0 with 1:51 left in the half. That was the ball game. Hope did not get into Olivet territory in the first half, and only twice in the scoreless second half.

Seven turnovers and a poorly played first half spelled defeat for Hope at Albion on October 16. Briton quarterback Dave Neilson was at his best as he threw four touchdown passes in the first half. A Hope fumble on the Dutchman 35 led to the first score as Neilson connected with end John Ellinger. Reed converted to make it 7-0 with 8:37 gone in the first quarter. On their next possession, the Britons climaxed a 40-yard drive with a four-yard TD pass, again Neilson to Ellinger. Reed's kick was true, moving the score to 14-0. Three minutes into the second quarter, it was Albion again on the march. This time the drive covered 62 yards, and yet again it was Neilson to Ellinger for the TD. Joe Reed's third conversion pushed the score to 21-0. Coach Morley Fraser's team kept the pressure on and, with 1:34 left in the half, Neilson passed 17 yards, this time to Lloyd Harper, for the Britons' fourth touchdown. Reed's kick was perfect, and Albion was decidedly in the driver's seat with a 28-0 lead at the half.

Following some halftime adjustments, Albion found the going a little tougher. There was no scoring in the third period. Hope had been held to just four yards rushing in the first half, but got in gear for 113 in the second. With 13:42 left in the game, Keur scored on a 10-yard dive play. Dennis Wilder's run for two points failed, and the score stood 28-6. The Dutchmen mounted one more drive, and, with 1:35 remaining, Dennis Wilder scored on a five-yard run. Hyink's run for two points failed, and the game ended at 28-12.

Clearly, Neilson's first-half performance had been the difference. Hope lost three fumbles and was intercepted four times, but the defense had found itself in the second half.

Alma provided the opposition for Hope's homecoming on Oct. 23. The Scots, under new Coach Denny Stolz, would be impressive in succeeding years, but Stolz had not yet assembled the talent that would bring the coach and his teams three championships over the next five years. A crowd of 2,500 turned out to watch a Hope team rebounding from two league losses. The Dutchmen had learned something of their true abilities in the second half against Albion, and the momentum carried over. Alma appeared to have the early edge after a short Hope punt went only to the Dutchman 34. The Scots drove to the Hope two, then fumbled and Wassenaar recovered. Hope's drive of 98 yards in 13 plays featured a 40-yard run by halfback Tom De Kuiper. Keur went the final yard off-tackle, and Kroodsma kicked the point to make it 7-0 with 5:54 left in the first quarter. Seven seconds into the second quarter, De Kuiper got off another long run, this time for 30 yards. This was followed by a 23-yard touchdown gallop by Keur. Kroodsma's kick was wide of the mark this time, and Hope's lead moved to 13-0. With 9:35 left in the half, Keur climaxed another Hope drive by going eight yards off-tackle for his third TD of the half. Kroodsma's kick was good, and Hope's lead was 20-0.

The Scots failed to move following the kickoff, and the Dutchmen took over. Early in the series, Hyink handed off to Langeland on a trap play up the middle and the big fullback, with deceptive speed, broke free for a 47-yard scoring sprint. The kick was not good, but Hope's lead moved to 26-0. This time the Scots responded with a six-play drive of their own. Fullback John Milks went three yards up the middle for what would be Alma's only score. The conversion failed, leaving the count at 26-6. With time running out in the half, Hyink threw a perfectly timed screen pass to Langeland who, behind excellent blocking, broke away for 68 yards and the touchdown. The scoreboard showed 21 seconds on the clock as Hyink passed to Kroodsma for two points to make it 34-6 at the half.

The Scots' defense stiffened following halftime adjustments and there was no scoring in the third period, but with 41 seconds gone in the fourth quarter Keur took the ball on the deceptive counter-crisscross reverse play from the winged T. With linemen and backs carrying out their assignments, Keur was untouched for 21 yards and the score. The Hyink-to-Kroodsma combination was again successful for two points, and the margin increased to 42-6. Hope's lineup was now made up entirely of substitutes. Third-string quarterback Clint Schilstra found end Jim Holtsclaw open, and the 24-yard completion resulted in Hope's final score of the afternoon. The try for two points failed, leaving the final score, 48-6. The Dutchmen had produced a total of 460 yards of offense, but the defensive effort was especially pleasing to Coach De Vette, who singled out the performance of ends Kusak and Wassenaar, and middle linebacker Kroodsma. Alma Coach Denny Stolz was not happy with Hope, feeling that the coaches had "piled it on" despite wholesale substitutions by the Dutchmen. There would be ample payback in succeeding years.

The Hope community was saddened by the passing of Russ De Vette's mother in late October. The Muskegon funeral took place on Saturday, Oct. 30, and Coach De Vette would understandably not be present for Hope's game at Kalamazoo. Coach Ken Weller stepped into the breach and called an outstanding game. The question now to be answered was whether or not the Alma performance was some sort of a fluke. A crowd of 2,000 at Kalamazoo's Angell Field would soon have the answer. The afternoon game saw an aggressive Kroodsma break through to block a Hornet punt on the Kalamazoo eight. Four plays later, quarterback Frens went in from the one and Kroodsma converted to make it 7-0 with 5:22 remaining in the quarter. Kazoo came back with a drive to the Hope two, where quarterback Rick Russell was stopped on fourth down by Wassenaar and linebacker Steve Piersma. Defense prevailed until late in the second quarter. With one minute left in the half, Pelon intercepted a pass on the Kalamazoo 41. In five plays the Dutchmen were knocking at the door with the ball on the 11. A key play in the drive was a screen pass from Hyink to Langeland that covered 25 yards. On the next play Hyink threw a flat pass to Langeland, who fell into the end zone for the touchdown. Kroodsma's kick made it 14-0 with 37 seconds left in the half.

A third-quarter Hope drive ended when Hyink passed to Keur, who took the ball on the two-yard line and went in for the score. Kroodsma's kick was wide, leaving the count at 20-0. In the fourth quarter, Hope marched 76 yards in six plays with a 34-yard Hyink-to-Hultgren pass the big gainer. De Kuiper went two yards off-tackle for the TD. Hyink's pass to Kroodsma was good for two, increasing the margin to 28-0. Later in the period, Abel returned a Kalamazoo punt 16 yards to the Hornet 48. A pass interference call gave Hope the ball on the Kazoo four-yard line. Halfback Dick Bont took the ball in for the game's final score. Piersma's kick attempt was not good, but Hope's 34-0 shutout was a convincing victory. Coach Rolla Anderson's team had had an off-day, but would end in a two-way tie with Hope for second place in the MIAA.

Hope had opened the season on a negative note against an Ohio team and would close it the same way. Nov. 6 was Parents Day and the opponent was Bluffton College, again from the Buckeye State. A Riverview Park crowd of 2,000 watched a scoreless first quarter on a damp and foggy day. Beaver Coach Ken Mast, now in his fifth year, had his team ready. The Dutchmen, on the other hand, seemed to have lost their intensity after two outstanding league games. A defensive lapse in the final five minutes of the first half cost the home team the contest. Bluffton quarterback Art Tuel opened the scoring with a 24-yard TD pass to end Jim Sommer, and Dave Enz converted for a 7-0 lead. Hope had a good kickoff return to the 44, but failed to make a first down. Five plays later, Tuel passed five yards to Eldon Gerber for the Beavers' second score, and Enz again converted to make it 14-0. This time Hope returned the kickoff to the 35, but a Hyink pass was intercepted by Doug Court and returned to the Hope 20. A Tuel-to-Sommer pass was good for 12 yards, and Gerber's run put the ball on the one. Mike Goings went in for the score, and the kick by Enz gave Bluffton a 21-0 bulge at the half.

The Dutchmen finally got on the board in the third quarter. Wassenaar recovered a Bluffton fumble on the Beavers' four-yard line, and Hyink followed up with a scoring pass to Hultgren. The two-point conversion attempt failed, and the Beaver lead was 21-6 with 8:47 remaining in the third quarter. Hope had three chances to pull the game out in the fourth quarter, but was unable to capitalize. Quarterback Tuel lost the ball on his own four-yard line when gang-tackled by Kroodsma, Wassenaar, Paul Oakes, and Bill Beebe, but Hope gave the ball back on the one when the center snap was fumbled. After a Bluffton punt, Hyink threw a wobbly pass to Abel, who made it to the Beavers' seven, but on the next play the ball was again fumbled away. The defense did its job forcing another Bluffton kick. De Kuiper took the punt on his own 35 and returned it all the way to the visitors' 19, but the Dutchmen could muster only one yard in four plays. In the closing seconds, Bluffton completed a 41-yard pass, then unwisely attempted a lateral which went awry. Hope's Vern Plagenhoef pounced on the ball, but the Hope possession was on the Dutchmen's own six-yard line. On the second play, Hope suffered its final indignity when Frens was tackled in the end zone for a safety, ending the game at 23-6. It was hardly the way to end the year and somewhat overshadowed Hope's resurgence after adversity, which resulted in a 4-4 season and a second-place tie (3-2) in the MIAA with Kalamazoo, which had been soundly beaten.

Halfback Bill Keur scored eight touchdowns to lead the MIAA in scoring, while Roger Kroodsma was named Hope's Most Valuable Player. The two were Hope's representatives on the All-MIAA team, and Charlie Langeland was captain-elect for 1966.

* * *

The 1965 cross-country team compiled a 2-4 record in MIAA dual meets. The Dutchmen lost some close ones, but were in every meet except the Albion run. Hope's losses were to Adrian 27-28, Olivet 25-30, Calvin 22-33, and the Britons 15-50. Victories were recorded over Alma 24-31, and Kalamazoo 25-32. The league meet was held at Calvin on Tuesday, Nov. 9, with a strong Albion team taking the honors. The big surprise of the meet was the fine perfor-

ALL-MIAA
Sophomore Cal Oosterhaven was Hope's top cross country runner in 1965. He finished second in the MIAA meet at Calvin College and was named to the All-MIAA Team.

mance of Hope sophomore Cal Osterhaven, who finished second behind Albion veteran Jim Dow. Dow crossed the line at 21:21, while Osterhaven's time was 21:36. Other contributing team members were Wayne Meerman, Rich Bisson, Clayton Beery, and Dan Howe. In team scoring, it was Albion 27, Adrian 49, Calvin 90, Hope 108, Olivet 135, Alma 143, and Kalamazoo 169. Hope's conference meet performance produced an overall fourth-place tie with Olivet. This would be important in the springtime tally of all-sports points. Cal Osterhaven was further honored by being named to the All-MIAA team.

* * *

Soccer was not yet an MIAA sport, as only Calvin and Hope fielded teams. Seeking some sort of league affiliation, Coach Phil Van Eyl was able to secure membership in the college division of the Midwestern Collegiate Soccer League. Following the early Hope successes would be sorely tested in the tougher competition. Members included Ball State, Calvin, the University of Illinois Chicago, Indiana Tech, Lake Forest, Mac Murray, Maryknoll Seminary, and Wheaton. The Dutchmen were off to a good start with an opening 4-2 win over Calvin on Wednesday, Sept. 22. Hope's Walt Bruinsma broke a 2-2 tie in the second half, and Pierre Sende added the final goal on a pass from Fred Schutmaat.

Three days later at Lake Forest, Hope suffered a 6-2 defeat as the home team scored five times in the second half. In a non-league game at Oakland on Tuesday, Sept. 28, Hope bounced back with a 7-1 victory as Captain Jaime Zeas scored four times. Saturday, Oct. 2, found the Dutchmen in Glen Ellyn, Ill., where they were able to eke out a 2-1 victory over Maryknoll.

On Wednesday, Oct. 6, Hope hosted the University of Illinois, Chicago, and came out on the short end of a 5-3 decision after a 2-2 halftime score. At Calvin on Tuesday, Oct. 19, the Knights had their revenge with a 5-1 victory. Doug Nichols scored Hope's only goal. In a home game on Friday, Oct. 22, Hope hosted Wheaton and played to a 1-1 tie at halftime, but the Crusaders scored the winning goal with 10 minutes remaining to notch the 3-2 victory. The Dutchmen were also beaten 8-0 by Goshen before closing out the season on Nov. 6 with a 5-1 victory over Oakland.

* * *

Clare Van Wieren was captain of the 1965-66 Hope basketball team, which opened a 22-game schedule at home against Concordia of River Forest, Ill. A crowd of 2,200 turned out at the Civic Center on Saturday, Dec. 4, to watch the Dutchmen prevail in a very close contest. Hope managed a 43-42 lead at the intermission, then went on a 9-0 run to open the second half, but the Cougars tied it at 64 and took a 72-69 lead with 7:18 remaining. The Dutchmen came back to take the lead on a jumper by Don Kronemeyer and were ahead to stay in the eventual 91-84 victory. Clare Van Wieren led the way with 25 points, Kronemeyer had 22, Floyd Brady 17, Carl Walters 16, and Roy Anker nine. For Tom Faszholz's Cougars, it was Tom Ruppert with 22, Terry Peiper with 15, and Bob Castons with 14.

The Hope squad was encouraged by its opening performance, but the next two outings would be disappointing. At Valparaiso on Tuesday, Dec. 7, Coach Gene Bartow employed a full-court zone press, which threw the Dutchmen off. After building a 57-41 halftime advantage, the Crusaders breezed to a 104-85 victory. Vern Curtis did most of the damage with 24 points, while Rich Eynon had 16 and Dick Jones 15. Clare Van Wieren led all scorers with 27, Kronemeyer had a strong game with 20 and Brady had 11.

At Wheaton's Centennial Gym on Friday, Dec. 10, the Dutchmen again ran into a full-court press, but this time were better prepared and actually held a 43-38 lead at halftime. But two minutes into the second half, Wheaton took the lead and never trailed again. Hope cut the margin to four with six minutes left, but the Crusaders moved on to a 97-88 victory. Hal Hinds was high for the winners with 22, Noll

MIAA MVP

Clare Van Wieren was voted the MIAA's Most Valuable Player for the 1965-66 season.

followed with 18, and Rog Weavers, a Grand Haven product, had 16. Hope's scoring was evenly divided with Kronemeyer getting 19, Van Wieren 18, Walters 17, and Brady 15.

Coaches De Vette and Siedentop now decided to alter their MO. Instead of separate varsity and JV groups, the two would be combined into one 17-man squad that would practice together. Some of the JV's would see action in both games. Four in this category for the Dec. 15 game at Adrian were freshmen Lloyd Schout, Cal Beltman, Dave Utzinger, and Bruce Van Huis. The game at Ridge Gymnasium would be a nail-biter with hectic final seconds. The Dutchmen led 48-43 at halftime and pushed their lead to 75-62 at the 10-minute mark, but the Bulldogs fought back to shave the lead to 87-84 with two minutes left, then tied it at 90-90 with 57 seconds remaining. At the 1:30 mark, Walters had fouled out and freshman Utzinger got the call. Now with 22 seconds left, Utzinger, in the left corner, dribbled down the baseline with a go-ahead layup, 92-90. The Bulldogs were quickly down the floor with a shot, but it missed and Anker cleared the board. De Vette called time out with 10 ticks on the clock. On the inbounds play, Brady was fouled. His missed free throw was rebounded by Van Wieren, who was immediately fouled. The Hope captain sank both free throws to sew up the hard-fought 94-90 win. Van Wieren led the Hope charge with 22, Brady had 19, Kronemeyer 15, Anker 13, and Walters 10. Adrian's gallant comeback effort was led by Mike Garrett with 29. Ron Stevens and Jim Ingham each contributed 19, and Paul Martini had 12. The long trip home for the Dutchmen was a happy one, and no one enjoyed it more than the freshman Utzinger, whose key basket may have saved the game.

Hope's holiday action would take place in Schenectady, N.Y., beginning on Tuesday, Dec. 28. The occasion was a four-team round robin tournament hosted by Union College. The Reverend J. Dean Dykstra, Hope '40, welcomed the Dutchmen at the airport and was a gracious host throughout the tourney. Hope met Union on the opening night and posted an 87-75 victory. Successful fast breaks led to a 48-31 halftime advantage, and the Dutchmen led throughout. Van Wieren was high with 29, Kronemeyer had 14, and Brady 11. Giancola led Union with 16, Greg Olson had 13, and Urbelis 12. On the second night, Hope took on the prestigious Massachusetts Institute of Technology. Hope managed a 37-33 halftime lead, but the Engineers played a slow-down game and took away some of the Dutchman fast break potential. With three minutes left, it was Hope 61-60, but MIT scored the next basket and held Hope to one point for the remainder of the game, taking the contest 72-61 despite the cheering of 400 members of the Reformed Church Youth Fellowship who had come to support the Hope team. Dave Jansson was high man for the winners with 24, Alex Wilson scored 20, and Ferrera 11. Kronemeyer led the Dutchmen with 20, Brady had 12, and Van Wieren 11. In the final game on Thursday, Dec. 30, Hope's opponent was De Pauw of Greencastle, Ind. The first half was played on even terms, with De Pauw holding a 32-30 edge at the intermission. Hope tied it at 36-36 early in the second half, but De Pauw scored the next field goal and never again trailed in posting a 77-67 win. Stan Bahler led the 47 percent shooting with 37 points, Morgan Everson had 17, and Jack Hogan 11. For Hope it was Brady with 19, Anker 18, Van Wieren 17 and Don Kronemeyer eight. Hope's 1-2 tournament record was not impressive, but the overall experience in the East was positive.

Back in Michigan on Wednesday, Jan. 5, Hope entertained MIAA opponent Olivet before a crowd of 1,700. Turnovers and cold shooting put the Dutchmen behind 46-45 at halftime, and the Comets continued to lead. With 2:08 remaining, it was Olivet, 86-85. A drive by Kronemeyer with what would have been the go-ahead basket missed the mark, and the Comets came back with three free throws to make it 89-85. A jumper by Brady with 40 seconds left made it 89-87, but the visitors put in two free throws with 14 seconds left to sew up the 91-87 victory. Walter "Buzz" Luttrell was high for Coach Sigren's team with 20, while Gordon Lofts and Marty La Porte each garnered 16. Van Wieren led Hope with 23, Kronemeyer had 18, Brady 16, and Potter also had 16. In the midst of defeat, Coach De Vette was encouraged by Potter's fine game.

Hope traveled to Alma on Saturday, Jan. 8, and got back on track with an 88-69 victory over the Scots under new coach Charles Gray. The contest was played at the Alma High School gym, and the Dutchmen were out front 49-31 at halftime. The lead was maintained throughout the second half behind a sizzling 54 percent shooting performance. Walters came through with his best game to date with 18, points and Van Wieren also tallied 18. Anker had 15 and Brady 14. For Alma it was John Toland leading the way with 19, Rick Warmbold had 15, and Jerry Knowlton 14.

At this point, Hope's Don Kronemeyer announced that he would be transferring to Central Michigan University. Reasons for the transfer were not entirely clear, but his departure dealt a blow to the Dutchmen hopes for a championship. The MIAA title race continued with a home game on Wednesday, Jan. 12, against the Albion Britons of Coach Dean Dooley. More than 1,500 fans watched Hope shoot 54 percent and move to a 42-23 advantage at halftime. Hope's domination of the boards, 52-35, was a deciding factor. The Dutchman lead was 72-42 with 7:29 remaining, and with six minutes left all regulars were on the bench. Brady with 22 was the leader in Hope's 89-69 victory. Van Wieren scored 21, Walters 17, and Potter eight. For the Britons, it was Tom Balistiere with 10 and five other players with eight apiece.

The Hope-Calvin contest in the Holland Civic Center on Jan. 15 was simply more of the great rivalry that fans had come to expect: two fine teams playing before a capacity crowd, maximum effort, and spirited competition down to the wire. Calvin was off to an early 14-4 lead, then extended it to 26-11 with 10:26 left in the half. But Brady, now playing guard, scored 17 points in the next 10 minutes. His mid-court steal and driving layup gave the Dutchmen a 46-45 lead at the buzzer. There were two ties to open the second half, one on two free throws by Walters with 16:31 remaining. Hope did not trail again, but the count was tied three more times. Van Wieren had picked up four fouls and spent some time on the bench. He returned with the score at 70-70 and promptly put in a jumper to give Hope the lead for good. A basket and free throw by Walters gave Hope 75 points, and Van Wieren's jumper with 3:55 remaining was the Dutchmen's last field goal. The Knights put on a strong press, but committed 10 fouls in the closing minutes. Hope's final six points were free throws in the 83-78 victory. Anker fouled out attempting to stop Calvin's Bill De Horn, but Jim Klein came in with an impressive defensive effort as the clock wound down. Brady was again tops for the winners, with 24 points. Walters followed with 23, Van Wieren had 16, and Tom Pelon, in his first varsity game, scored six. De Horn was high for Barney Steen's crew with 24, Ed Douma scored 18, Kim Campbell 12, and Jim Fredericks 10. Calvin led in rebounds 54 to 42.

The Dutchmen were involved in a key game in Kalamazoo's Treadway Gym on Wednesday, Jan. 19. A sparse, weeknight crowd of 400 did not dampen the intensity of either team. Hope appeared to be in good shape at halftime with a 39-26 lead, but the Hornets stormed back to take the lead at the 9:16 mark. The Dutchmen's strong defense now helped them regain the lead. Brady's 12-foot jumper at the 3:40 mark brought his team within one, 65-64. His next move was a steal and quick pass to Van Wieren, whose 21-foot shot put Hope ahead 66-65 with 2:16 left. After a Walters steal, a Brady jump shot upped the lead to 68-65, but Tom Crawford countered with a field goal to make it 68-67 with 1:17 remaining. At this point, Brady came through with four straight free throws, and Hope had breathing room at 72-67. Harold Dekker dropped in a jumper with 16 seconds left to make it 72-69, and Van Wieren was fouled to stop the clock. He sank both free throws for the 74-69 final. Anker had picked up his fourth personal early in the second half, but Klein did an admirable job of filling in. Van Wieren again led his team, this time with 22, Floyd Brady had 16 and Carl Walters 12. Tom Crawford was high man for the Hornets with 17, and Harold Dekker added 14.

The MIAA's first round was now in the books, and Hope turned to non-league competition. The Dutchmen hosted a tough Wooster team on Saturday, Jan. 22. Coach Al Van Wie's team came in with a 12-2 record, and played control ball for the most part. Hope's zone defense was effective early, and the Dutchmen managed a 41-39 lead at the half. The Scots' 69-62 lead with five minutes to play was the game's biggest margin. Hope tied it at 72-all with 1:10 remaining for the eighth tie of the game. Wooster's George Baker tipped one in with 36 seconds left, and Buddy Harris added two free throws to give the Scots the 76-72 victory. Harris was the scoring leader for the winners with 24, George Bakler had 16, and Tim Jordan 14. For Hope it was Van Wieren with 25, Brady 15, Anker 12, and Walters nine.

Spring Arbor was a first-time opponent for Hope at the Civic Center on Friday, Jan. 28. The Dutchmen enjoyed a decided height advantage, as the Blue Jays of Coach Hank Burbridge averaged just six feet even. Hope built a 48-38 halftime lead, but the visitors were deadly from out-court and tied the count at 71 with five minutes left. Then, in a four-minute stretch, Van Wieren scored 10 points and Bill Potter six to put the game away with a final score of 93-84. Van Wieren had a game-high of 29 points, Carl Walters put in 19, Roy Anker and sophomore Tom Pelon each had 10, and Floyd Brady, who fouled out with six-and-a-half minutes left, had eight. For Spring Arbor, it was 5' 11" Steve Robbins with 21, Gary Owens with 17, and Kent with 14.

In yet another home contest, Hope entertained Wheaton on Wednesday, Feb. 2, before a crowd of 1,900. Gary Rypma, a transfer from Calvin, was eligible with the new semester. A quality ball player, Rypma arrived just in time. At the 13:32 mark of the first half, mainstay Carl Walters

DR. BARNEY STEEN

Calvin's Coach Steen won six MIAA basketball championships in a 13 year tenure, 1953-1966. His well coached teams were worthy opponents and added luster to the now legendary Hope-Calvin series.

suffered a dislocated knee and would be lost for the season. Meanwhile, Hope with a rebound advantage, moved to a 40-26 halftime lead. The biggest Hope lead was 49-30, but the Crusaders of Coach Lee Pfund pecked away at the lead and narrowed it to 79-74 with 35 seconds remaining. Jim Klein scored the final basket with three ticks left to give Hope the 83-75 victory.

Hope fans remembered the struggle at Kalamazoo's Treadway Gym on Jan. 19, and 2,250 fans turned out to witness what they knew would be a barn-burner at the Civic on Saturday, Feb. 5. None were disappointed. The teams played on even terms throughout an intense first half. Brady's jumper at the buzzer put Hope up by one, 45-44, at the intermission. Fifteen lead changes during the contest added to the excitement. Van Wieren's turn-around jumper at the 10:35 mark made it 61-60, a lead that would not be surrendered. The game continued to be close, but in the closing minute a field goal and free throw by Brady made it 85-79. Kalamazoo scored the last basket with 20 seconds left, but time ran out and the Dutchmen had gotten past a tough MIAA challenge with the 85-81 win. It had been another Brady night, with the talented sophomore notching 31 points. Van Wieren followed with 23, Potter had 11, and Gary Rypma eight. Freshman Cal Beltman also impressed with his speed and leaping ability. For Ray Steffen's Hornets, it was Tom Crawford scoring 21, Jim Peters 20, Gene

211

Nusbaum 17, and Bob Pursel 11.

On Wednesday, Feb. 9, the Dutchmen met the Tommies of Aquinas in the Grand Rapids West Catholic Gym. News of Walters's knee surgery had a sobering effect, but others stepped up to take up the slack. Hope led 48-40 at the half, but the charges of Coach Red Dornbos, quite surprisingly, out-rebounded the Dutchmen 60-41. Hope was able to offset that advantage by shooting at a 50 percent clip. Anker was ill and played only sparingly. The Tommies tied it at 64-64, then moved ahead by one and never trailed thereafter. Dennis Alexander led his team to the 94-91 victory with 27, Tom Steiner collected 22, Bob Topper 17, Phil Saurman 16, and Joe O'Toole 12. Van Wieren was tops for Hope with 28, Brady had 23, and Bill Potter 19.

A Civic Center crowd of 2,300 turned out on Saturday, Feb. 12, to see the Dutchmen return to the win column. A determined Adrian kept the pressure on, and Hope struggled to gain a 36-31 halftime advantage. Midway in the second half, the Dutchmen blew a 12-point lead, then came back to lead 69-67. At this point, Hope put on a 10-0 run and the game was out of reach at 79-67. Van Wieren, now dubbed "Mr. Consistency," led his team with 22, Brady scored 18, and Bill Potter 13, while Anker and Rypma each had 10 in the 82-73 win. Hope was hot with 59 percent shooting in the second half. For Adrian it was Chuck Stille with 24 and Mark Garrett with 14.

Hope invaded Olivet's Mc Kay Gym on Wednesday, Feb. 16, hoping to reverse a four-point loss to the Comets on Jan. 5. By playing a zone in the first half, the Dutchmen avoided foul trouble but trailed 31-28 at intermission. In the closely fought contest, free throws would make the difference. Olivet led in field goals 27 to 23, but the Dutchmen cashed in on 18-of-26 charities while the Comets could muster only five-of-14. Floyd Brady scored the first two field goals of the second half, and the Dutchmen kept the lead though the score was continually close. Jim Everett brought the home team to within two, 57-55, with just 2:29 remaining, and it was 59-57 on Buzz Luttrell's field goal with 53 seconds left. Two free throws by Van Wieren made it 61-57 with 23 seconds remaining, but another Luttrell basket cut it to 61-59 at the 16-second mark. Brady made a single free throw with 11 seconds left, and Van Wieren was fouled at the buzzer, making both shots to give Hope the victory, 64-59. Hope's scoring centered around three starters. Van Wieren and Brady each scored 20, while Anker was close behind with 19. For the Comets it was Buzz Luttrell with 13, Jim Everett, Rex Thwaits, and Marty La Porte with 10 each in what had to be a tough loss for Coach Vince Sigren.

On Saturday, Feb. 19, a Civic Center crowd of 2,300 turned out to see Clare Van Wieren, Roy Anker, and Bill Potter in their final home appearance. The Alma Scots were undermanned, and the game was never close as the Dutchmen fired at a 67 percent clip. Enjoying a 50-27 lead at halftime, all Hope players got into the act as the team cruised to a 109-55 victory. Van Wieren was the leader with 31 points, Roy Anker scored 22, Floyd Brady 17, Bill Potter and Tom Pelon each had eight, and Bruce Van Huis seven. Leaders for the Scots were Rick Warmbold with 16 and Dave Gray with 13.

The Dutchmen could have used some of the Alma victory points at Albion on Wednesday, Feb. 23. The Britons of Coach Dean Dooley jumped out to an 8-0 lead and built it to a 41-37 halftime advantage. Hope's first lead did not come until the 13-minute mark of the second half, when a Rypma field goal made it 48-47. The lead was increased to four points, but later a Larry Patrick jumper tied it up at 55-55. Hope's last lead came on Potter's rebound field goal to make it 59-57 with 5:15 remaining. A Brady lay-up tied it at 63-63 with 1:09 left, but the Britons led 66-63 with seven seconds on the clock. Van Wieren scored at the buzzer, but the Britons had gained a hard-fought 66-65 victory. Captain Larry Downs led the winners with 21, Ed Stephens followed with 18, and Larry Patrick had 12. For Hope it was Brady with 17, Van Wieren had 16, Anker 12, and Potter eight.

Hope wrapped up its season against Calvin on Saturday, Feb. 26, in a 4 p.m. game at the Knollcrest campus. Hope had taken the first game by five points on Jan. 15, but Coach Barney Steen had announced his retirement with this game and the Knights, behind a crowd of 4,200, were determined that he leave with a win. Key to the contest were three quick fouls called on Van Wieren. With Van Wieren on the bench and 14:23 remaining in the half, the Dutchmen struggled, but Jim Klein's jumper at the buzzer tied it up at 35-all.

In typical Hope-Calvin fashion, the game remained close throughout the second half, with the Dutchmen holding a 64-59 lead with 5:56 to play before Wes De Mots tied it at 67-67. The final four minutes proved decisive as Calvin center Bill De Horn scored four lay-ups, a tip-in, and a free throw. The Knights outscored Hope 8-3 in the last two-and-a-half minutes to take the game 79-72, and also the MIAA championship with an 11-1 record. Hope finished second at 9-3. Wes De Mots, in a substitute's role, led his team with 21, Ed Douma had 20, and Bill De Horn 14. Hope's Roy Anker saved his best for the last game of his career. With hooks, jumpers, and great board work, he led the losers with 22 points. Brady followed with 20 and Van Wieren, with limited playing time, had 17. At this writing, Dr. Roy Anker is a member of the Calvin College faculty as a professor of English. Coach Barney Steen bowed out with an MIAA championship, his sixth in a 13-year tenure. As coach and director of athletics, his leadership and sense of fair play were contributing factors in the recognized stability of the MIAA.

The 1965-66 All-MIAA basketball team consisted of Clare Van Wieren and Floyd Brady of Hope, Bill De Horn of Calvin, Olivet's Gordon Lofts, and Jim Peters of Kalamazoo. In subsequent polling, Clare Van Wieren was voted the league's most valuable player. In a post-season team meeting, Hope named Floyd Brady and Carl Walters as captains-elect for the 1966-67 campaign. On March 26 it was announced that Don Vroon, three-time All-MIAA guard at Calvin, would succeed Barney Steen as coach of the Knights. Five days later, Hope announced that 1966-67 Glenn Van Wieren would replace cross country and baseball coach Daryl Siedentop, who would be granted a two-year leave of absence to pursue a doctorate at Indiana University in Bloomington.

* * *

Hope's fledgling wrestling program continued to struggle. Part-time coach Sid Huitema made a gallant effort to mold a team from a small squad, but the cards were stacked against him. Squad members included Larry Bone, Dan Howe, Hal Huggins, Erwin Johnson, Wint Johnson, and Charley Langeland. Forfeitures in several weight classes were necessary, and late-season injuries compounded the problem. The team was eventually reduced to four men and the final meet with Olivet had to be canceled. The season's one bright spot was the 7-2 mark compiled by Langeland, who carried over some of his football expertise.

* * *

Coach Bill Hilmert felt that he had the makings of a good golf team as the 1966 season approached. Bill Potter, Bill Forbes, George Cook, Gord Korstange, and Larry Cain were proven performers, and it showed in Hope's opening 12½-2½ victory over Kalamazoo on Monday, April 18. Bill Potter was medalist with a 77, and the team appeared to be off and running. The Dutchmen continued to be competitive, but dropped close matches to Albion, Calvin, Alma, and Olivet while getting the best of Adrian.

On Wednesday, May 18, Hope met defeat at the hands of Grand Valley by an 11½-3½ score. The match was played on Hope's home course at the American Legion course, and when Bill Forbes came through with a 76 the team had hopes of doing well two days later on the same course. On Friday, May 20, Hope hosted the MIAA meet and enjoyed its best day since the season opener. The day's results showed Albion the winner with a 36-hole total of 785, and, to everyone's surprise, Hope just three strokes behind in second place with 788. Alma followed in third with 796, Calvin had 803, Olivet 820, Adrian 827, and Kalamazoo 844. Alma's Jim Gettleman was medalist with a new Field Day record of 141 (73-68) and was named the MIAA's most valuable player. Hope's Bill Forbes finished second to Gettleman with a 149 (71-78). In the overall seasonal standings, Hope managed to climb up to fourth place, a finish that would be important in computing All-Sports points.

* * *

In late March, Doc Green's tennis squad made its annual trek to warmer climes. Again, the Hope coach did not shy away from tough competition and the team took its lumps. On Thursday, March 31, the Dutchmen met Rollins twice in Winter Park, Fla. Both matches went to Rollins 9-0. The next day, it was Duke 8-1, with Ron Visscher posting Hope's only victory at number-three singles. In the afternoon, it was Columbia 7, Hope 0. On Saturday, April 2, the team had breakfast with Jim Kaat, then in spring training with the Minnesota Twins. Later in the day, Hope was on the short end of an 8-1 tussle with Davidson. Visscher was again the lone Dutchman in the win column. On Monday, April 4, the team learned a few more lessons, this time in a 9-0 setback at the hands of the University of Florida. As the team headed for home, a stop in Carrollton, Ga., produced the trip's only victory. All team members played as Hope rolled to an 11-0 win over West Georgia State on April 7. The trip concluded in Bloomington, Ind., on Saturday, April 9, with the Hoosiers of IU administering yet another 9-0 shutout.

The regular season opened on Monday, April 11, with Hope hosting the Chippewas of Central Michigan University. The well-tanned, but much-pummeled Dutchmen now reaped the rewards of their rigorous week in the south with their own 9-0 shutout. In singles, it was Craig Workman over Bill Kooiman 4-6, 6-3, 6-4, Lance Stell defeated Dennis Elkins 6-1, 6-4, Ron Visscher took Tom Johnson 6-3, 8-6, Jack Schrier defeated Jerry Kennedy 6-3, 7-9, 6-3, Craig Holleman defeated Bill Johnston 6-1, 6-4, and Jeff Jorgenson won over Mike Grove 2-6, 8-6, 6-3. In doubles, it was Workman-Visscher over Kooiman-Kennedy 4-6, 6-3, 6-2, Stell-Holleman over Elkins-Johnson 6-3, 4-6, 6-0, and Schrier-Jeff Green over Johnston-Grove 12-10, 6-1.

Hope went into the "Hornets' nest" at Kalamazoo on Saturday, April 16, and emerged once again on the short end of a 9-0 contest. It was now evident that Coach George Acker's teams were the equal of most of the NCAA University Division schools that Hope had competed against. In singles, George Smillie defeated Workman 6-0, 6-2, Bill Jones defeated Stell 6-1, 6-0, John Koch took Visscher 6-3, 6-2, Bob Engels defeated Jorgenson 6-1, 6-1, and Don Swarthout defeated Schrier 4-6, 6-3, 6-1. In doubles, it was Koch-Jones over Workman-Visscher 6-2, 6-2, Swarthout-Ron Creager over Stell-Chuck Klomparens 6-2, 6-2, and Tindwell-Colvert over Schrier-Jeff Green 8-6, 4-6, 6-3.

The Dutchmen bounced back on Monday, April 25, by shutting out visiting Calvin, 9-0. In singles, competition Workman defeated Bert De Leeuw 7-5, 7-5, Stell defeated Joel De Koning 6-4, 2-6, 6-1, Visscher won over Don Klop 6-1, 6-1, Schrier defeated Phil Stielstra 2-6, 6-2, 6-3, Jorgenson took Tom Prins 6-0, 6-1, and Holleman defeated Phil Ippl 6-0, 6-2. In doubles, Workman-Stell defeated De Leeuw-De Koning 6-1, 6-2, Visscher-Holleman defeated Klop-Prins 6-0, 6-4, and Schrier- Green won over Stielstra-Pott 6-3, 6-2.

On Friday, April 29, the Dutchmen hosted Miami of Ohio and squeezed out a 5-4 victory. In singles, Dave Hill defeated Workman 6-3, 6-1, Jim Mc Cormick took Stell 8-6, 6-3, Visscher defeated Bob Zerbst 7-5, 3-6, 6-1, Bob Phillips took Schrier 6-4, 3-6, 6-2, Jorgenson defeated Allen Lewis 6-4, 6-4, and Holleman defeated Al Rexinger 6-4, 6-4. In doubles, it was Workman-Visscher over Hill-Mc Cormick 7-5, 6-3, Lewis-Zerbst (M) over Jorgenson-Holleman 4-6, 6-2, 6-1, and Schrier-Green defeated Armstrong-Phillips 7-5, 4-6, 6-1 to decide the match.

With the exception of Kalamazoo, Hope continued its domination of MIAA teams with 9-0 victories at home over Alma on Wednesday, May 4, and Olivet on Saturday, May 7. The result was the same at Adrian on Saturday, May 14. There is no record of a dual with Albion, and the match may have been rained out with rescheduling not possible.

The MIAA meet was held once again at Kalamazoo's splendid Stowe Stadium on May 20 and 21. The tournament finals were a virtual repeat of the earlier Hope-Kalamazoo dual match, and with the same result. Kalamazoo won all nine contests, and in each case the vanquished opponent was a Hope Dutchman. In team points it was Kalamazoo with 27, Hope 18, Calvin 8, Albion 5, Alma 3, Adrian 2, and Olivet 0. Again, Hope's solid second contributed 10 points in the All-Sports race. The Hornets'

George Smillie was voted the league's most valuable player, and Calvin's Bert De Leeuw was recipient of the Stowe Sportsmanship Award.

* * *

Hope's 1966 baseball team was 3-5 on its annual spring swing through the south. Three of the five losses were by the margin of one run, and Coach Daryl Siedentop felt his team had performed well in light of the fact that only limited workouts had been possible during the month of March. Hope began the trip with an 8-4 decision over Bethel in Mishawaka, Ind. and concluded the trek with a 5-2 decision over Goshen on April 11. In between, the Dutchmen managed a 6-4 win over Southwestern in Tennessee after dropping a 6-4 contest to the same team. A strong David Lipscomb team edged Hope 8-7, Memphis State was a 6-5 winner, and Union took the Dutchmen twice by scores of 9-6 and 5-4.

The regular season opened with Spring Arbor on Wednesday, April 13. Wet grounds at Van Raalte Field forced a move to Riverview Park, where lefty Paul Terpstra appeared to be in mid-season form in the first game with a one-hitter. Clare Van Wieren's double in the second inning scored two runs, and a homer by Paul Troost in the fifth cleared the right field fence to wrap up the 3-0 shutout. Hope also took the second game by a 6-2 count. Featured were a single, double, and home run by Charlie Langeland, as well as a steal of home by speedy Cal Beltman. The latter would prove a telling weapon in Hope's march toward a title.

CATCHERS AND PITCHERS WITH THEIR COACH

L. to R.: Steve Piersma, Conrad "Skip" Nienhuis, Coach Daryl Siedentop, Don Kroodsma, Roger Kroodsma, Paul Terpstra. This combination helped bring home the MIAA Championship in 1966.

The Dutchmen were temporarily stymied in the MIAA opener at Kalamazoo on Saturday, April 16. In two tight games, Hope came up short by scores of 4-2 and 7-6. In the first contest, Rog Kroodsma pitched well enough to win, but Hope bats were silent. Don Kroodsma pitched the nightcap with help from Gary Frens in the fifth. A three-base infield error plus a squeeze bunt gave Kalamazoo the win. The big blow for Hope was a triple by Troost. The battle would be uphill from this point.

Still at Riverview, Hope hosted Grand Rapids Junior College on Friday, April 22. Mark Johnson went the distance on the mound while his teammates banged out 11 hits, made no errors, and won by an 8-2 score. Skip Nienhuis and Vern Plagenhoef shared duty behind the plate, with the latter driving in four runs. Troost contributed a home run as Hope got back into the win column.

Returning to league play, Hope met Calvin at Van Raalte Field on Monday, April 25. Don Kroodsma took the mound for the Dutch in the first game, but needed help from Frens in the sixth. Hope collected nine hits, including a two-run homer by Plagenhoef in the first inning. The Dutchmen added one run in the fifth and two more in the sixth to wrap up the 5-3 win. Troost and Terpstra each had three hits for the winners. In the second contest, Rog Kroodsma pitched a four-hit, 8-0 shutout. Hope batters were again in form with 10 hits, including a Charlie Langeland home run.

Hope played a non-league night game at Riverview Park on Thursday, April 28. Kalamazoo furnished the opposition, and this time the Dutchmen prevailed by an 8-2 score. Coach Siedentop used five pitchers in the contest, and gave all squad members a chance to play. Hope's Dan Krueger stroked a home run, while Tom Pelon and Clare Van Wieren each had triples. Van Wieren's blow came in a four-run fifth inning.

The Dutchmen would try to continue the roll at Albion on Monday, May 2. Hope was off to a good start in the first game with two runs in the opening inning, but pitcher Don Kroodsma ran into trouble and was relieved by Frens in the second. A big third inning spelled victory for the Dutchmen as they pushed across eight runs. An insurance run was added in the sixth in the eventual 11-7 win. Albion collected seven hits, but committed four errors. Rog Kroodsma was tough on the mound in the second game as he pitched a four-hitter, walked three and struck out seven. He enjoyed fine support as teammates pounded out 11 hits, including a Troost triple and doubles by Dan Krueger and Terpstra.

Hope's modest win streak came to an end when the team hosted Alma on Wednesday, May 4. In the first game, the Scots scored four times on seven hits while ace pitcher Tim Pete set the Dutchmen down with two hits. Hope avoided a shutout in the bottom of the seventh on an error, a walk, and Plagenhoef's double, but time ran out and Alma posted the 4-1 victory. Hope turned the tables in the second game with a 4-3 win. All four runs came in the first frame, and the Dutchmen managed to hang on the rest of the way. Hope used Don Kroodsma, Mark Johnson, and Rog Kroodsma on the mound with the latter helping the cause with a home run. The split kept Hope in title contention. The Olivet Comets were in town on Saturday, May 7, to do battle with the Dutchmen. Rog Kroodsma took the mound in the first game, and came through with a three-hitter, struck out 10 batters, and was helped along by five Olivet errors. Hope had but five hits in the 5-3 victory. Frens went all the way in the second game, allowed five hits and struck out eight. The Dutchmen came up with three runs in the first, added two each in the third and fourth, and a final tally in the seventh to post the 8-1 win. Nienhuis had two of Hope's five hits.

Tuesday, May 10, found the Dutchmen hosting yet another non-league team. This time the opponent was Aquinas of Grand Rapids. In a ragged game, both teams committed six errors, but the Dutchmen came through with 13 hits while the Tommies could manage only one. The issue was never in doubt after Hope's seven-run first inning. Rog Kroodsma and Piersma belted home runs in the 19-4 victory, which was called after the sixth inning.

The Dutchmen wound up the season in a crucial doubleheader at Adrian on Monday, May 16. Hope needed a twin win to capture the MIAA championship. Coach Siedentop called on Rog Kroodsma in the opener and the ace right hander responded with a brilliant three-hitter. He was backed by an 11-hit Hope attack that included Langeland's home run and a triple by Tom Pelon. The 9-2 victory put Hope just a game away from the title. Frens pitched well in the second game, allowing but six hits in six innings, but

LONG JUMP — MIAA MEET, 1966.
Floyd Brady's talents were not limited to basketball.

the Bulldogs led 2-0 going into the seventh and Hope had but one hit to that point. Rog Kroodsma was called in one more time to relieve Frens. He retired the side without a score and set the stage for a dramatic conclusion in Hope's half of the seventh. Wayne Cotts led off with a double and, after a flyout by Pelon, scored on Rog Kroodsma's single. Plagenhoef was a strikeout victim, but Piersma was safe on a costly Adrian error. Skip Nienhuis then came through with a single to score Kroodsma with the tying run. With two out, Langeland walked to load the bases. With the wheels turning, Coach Siedentop now inserted the speedy Beltman to run for Piersma at third. Beltman got the signal to steal and was safe at the plate with the winning run and the MIAA championship. Rog Kroodsma had the distinction of being the winning pitcher in both games. To no one's surprise, Rog Kroodsma was named the MIAA's most valuable player. The Hope pitcher and all-round player also joined teammate Conrad "Skip" Nienhuis as a member of the All-MIAA team. Hope's overall record stood at 17-8, 14-3 not including the spring trip. The Dutchmen's 9-3 MIAA record had produced an undisputed championship and 12 points towards the All-Sports Award.

* * *

The 1966 season loomed as a year of great promise for Hope trackmen. For the first time in league history, Hope would host the MIAA championship meet. Leading up to the big one would be eight dual meets, five at home on Hope's now five-year old rubber-asphalt track. Adding variety to the schedule, the Dutchmen would make an overnight trip to Delaware, Ohio, for the second annual Great Lakes Colleges Association meet at Ohio Wesleyan University.

Hope's captain was Dearborn senior Bill Hultgren. Hultgren had enjoyed an outstanding career as a receiver on Hope's football teams. He might well have rested on those laurels, but instead trained hard for the 440 and took his leadership role very seriously. With team balance and depth in most events, prospects were bright indeed.

Saturday, April 16, found the Dutchmen off to a good start as they hosted Kalamazoo. Placing first in 11 of 16 events, Hope led all the way and ended with an 80-56 victory. Doug Formsma, who had spent his first two years at Grand Rapids Junior College, was the star of the afternoon. The junior distance man not only won the mile and two-mile runs, but set Hope records in both events. His respective times were 4:28.2 and 9:54.7. Dashman Ray Cooper also entered the record books in winning the 100-yard dash. His 9.9 performance tied the 29-year old mark set by Don Martin in 1937. Cooper was also first in the 220, second in the long jump, and anchored both winning relays for an afternoon total of 15½, points while Les Cole, Chris Buys, and Kent Candelora enjoyed a sweep in the shot put.

Hope's second MIAA dual took place on Wednesday, April 20, at Calvin's Knollcrest campus track. In many ways it resembled the Kalamazoo meet. Hope again was the victor in 11 of the 16 events, and Doug Formsma repeated as winner of the mile and two-mile runs. In each case, he broke his own recently established Hope records as the Dutchmen recorded an 84-52 team victory. Hope had sweeps in the mile with Formsma, Wayne Meerman, and Cal Osterhaven, and in the shot put with Chris Buys, Les Cole, and Kent Candelora.

The GLCA meet at Ohio Wesleyan on Saturday, April 30, was marred by an all-day rain, but the overall experience proved positive. Coach Jerry Rushton's Earlham team took first-place honors with 67 points. The Quakers were followed in order by Wabash, Oberlin, Wooster, Hope, Ohio Wesleyan, Albion, Kenyon, and Denison. Hope's 27 points included second-place finishes in the mile run by Formsma, in the high jump by Floyd Brady, and in the 440-yard relay by the team of Walt Reed, Hultgren, Bob Thompson, and Cooper. The Great Lakes Colleges Association, a distinguished midwestern academic consortium, also hoped to extend the relationship to athletics when feasible.

Tuesday, May 3, was a red-letter day for the Dutchmen as they entertained the Albion Britons of Coach Dean Dooley. In the history of the two schools, Hope had never won in the sport of track and field. The '66 meet was closely

MIAA CHAMPION

Steve Reynen's dramatic victory in the 880 yard run was the turning point for Hope in the 1966 MIAA Championship Meet. **Above:** Reynen receives congratulations from Commissioner John C. Hoekje.

contested throughout. Albion won seven events, but Hope took nine including both relays, and at the end of the day the Dutchmen had the long-sought victory by a score of 73-63. Cooper won both dashes and anchored both relays. Buys was a double winner in the unusual combination of shot put and pole vault. Formsma lowered his Hope record in the two-mile with a time of 9:51.1 in beating out the veteran Jim Dow. Brady won the high jump and finished second in the long jump, being edged by two inches in the latter event, and Jim Pierpont was a surprise winner in the 330 hurdles. Jeri Stilles was superb for the Britons in winning the tough double of mile run and 880. His times were 4:28.6 and 1:59.9.

The following afternoon found the Dutchmen at Alma High School's cinder track for a meet with the Alma College Scots. Denny Stolz, Alma's new football coach, was also the track coach. He had not yet had time to assemble an effective group, and Hope dominated, 91-35. The Dutchmen won 12 of the 15 events contested. The 330-yard intermediate hurdle race was canceled when it was discovered that the course had been improperly measured. Hope had sweeps in the mile, javelin, and pole vault.

Hope's third dual meet of the week took place on Saturday, May 7, with the Olivet Comets in town. Coach Stu Parsell had stellar performers in Jack Rall, Karl Wilson, and Gordon Lofts, but lacked the necessary depth to cope with Hope's overall balance. Wilson was a double winner in the long jump and 440, Rall won the shot put, and Lofts the high hurdles, but the Dutchmen took the other 12 events enroute to a 108-28 win. Doug Nichols set a Hope record in the javelin with a heave of 181' 5". This bettered Walter De Velder's 1929 mark of 175' 2". Two other Hope records fell as Pierpont lowered the 330-hurdle record to 39.5 and Formsma bettered his own two-mile mark with a time of 9:42.5.

A strong Valparaiso team was in town on Tuesday, May 10, to take on Hope in a non-league dual. Hope had never beaten the Crusaders in track, but continued the relationship with the larger school, just 110 miles away. Valpo again insisted that 17 events be contested, including the unfamiliar triple jump. The Dutchmen were off to a shaky start when thy dropped the baton in the 440-yard relay, resulting in a gift of five points to the visitors. The Crusaders proceeeded to take nine firsts to eight for the Dutchmen, but this day depth would be a deciding factor. With 12 seconds and eight thirds, Hope tipped the scales in an 84-61 victory. Buys led sweeps in the discus and pole vault, and also had a second in the shot put. Brady was also a double winner, taking the high jump and long jump. Other Hope winners were Sid Disbrow in the 440, Steve Reynen in the 880, Pierpont in the 330 intermediate hurdles, and the mile relay team of Disbrow, Reynen, Hultgren, and Cooper. All in all, it was a satisfying first victory over a worthy opponent.

Coach Jay Flanagan brought the Adrian Bulldogs to Holland on Saturday, May 14, for the final MIAA dual meet of the season. Hope again had troubles with the 440-yard relay, this time being disqualified for passing the baton outside the last exchange zone. But Hope won 13 of the remaining 15 events to win with a 94-42 score. Hope had a sweep in the shot put with Buys, Cole, and Candelora. In the discus, the order was Cole, Buys, and Jim "Dutch" Poppink. Adrian's Doug Moss won the high hurdles in the excellent time of 15.0, but was surprised in the 330 event when Pierpont won with a Hope record of 39.4. Floyd Brady again won the long jump and high jump, while Doug Formsma lowered his Hope record in the mile to 4:23.8.

One last hurdle remained for the Dutchmen in seeking a first undefeated dual meet season. On Tuesday, May 17, the team traveled to Houseman Field in Grand Rapids for a meet with ever-troublesome Grand Rapids Junior College. Coaches Dick Smith and Gordie Hunsberger were adept at getting the most out of team members, even as they did in football, with roles reversed. A steady rain throughout the afternoon held down performances as Hope took nine events and the Raiders seven. The Dutchmen won both relays, Pierpont took both hurdle races, and Formsma was first in the mile and two-mile runs. Dashman Cooper copped the 100 and 220 and anchored both relays, while Nichols, Candelora, and Dave Duitsman swept the javelin event. Don Crawford kept JC in the running with victories in the 440 and long jump, but Hope finally had a victory over its Grand Rapids neighbor by a score of 77½ to 58½.

The big event of spring '66 was Hope's hosting of the MIAA Track and Field Meet on Saturday, May 21. The first-time experience for the Hope community called for consider-

MIAA ALL-SPORTS CHAMPS

The MIAA All-Sports Trophy returned to Hope College in 1966. Commissioner John C. Hoekje holds the rotating trophy. The smaller award held by Gordon Brewer would remain as permanent property of the college.

able planning and attention to detail. Excellent help and cooperation was received from the City of Holland and especially from the Parks Department under Mr. Jacob De Graaf. Portable "Tulip Time" bleachers were delivered to the west side of the track and eventually provided seating for 1,200 spectators, Hope's largest track crowd ever. Grand Rapids television station WOOD was granted permission to tape the Saturday finals and arrived with considerable equipment.

Officials for the meet included Jay Formsma, Livonia – starter and referee; Dr. Kenneth Weller, Hope – clerk of the course; Bill Lambert, Grand Rapids – head finish judge; George Mather, Albion – official scorer; and Leonard Wilkins, Grand Rapids – public address announcer. The day dawned with ideal weather conditions, and, following morning preliminaries, all was in order for an exciting afternoon of MIAA athletic competition.

At the conclusion of the field events, Albion was the leader with 21 points, followed closely by Hope with 19. Adrian with 16 and Olivet with 14 were within striking distance. It will be recalled that the baseball season had concluded in dramatic fashion with Hope speedster Cal Beltman stealing home with the winning run against Adrian. Beltman was now borrowed from Coach Siedentop to run the first leg of the 440-yard relay. The move paid off as Beltman, Hultgren, Thompson, and Cooper were first at the tape in the afternoon's opening event. Albion's Jerri Stiles followed with a 4:24.7 victory in the mile, and Calvin's Dave Ver Merris won the 440 before Cooper took the 100-yard dash in 9.9. Adrian's Doug Moss had established an MIAA mark of 14.9 in the high hurdles in an earlier preliminary. He now won the final in 15.0. The Britons' Bob Turner took second and Pierpont third, giving Albion and Hope 41 points each as team leaders. With five events remaining, the meet's turning point came in the 880-yard run. Briton Jerri Stiles had already won the mile and was the favorite, but Hope's Steve "Spud" Reynen's great effort produced the race of his career. Reynen passed all runners in the second lap in taking the gold in a fine time of 1:57.9. Stiles finished fourth and teammate Dave Erickson fifth, but Hope had inched ahead by two points. In the remaining events, Cooper took the 220 and Briton Bob Turner the 330 hurdles, but Pierpont was a close second. Formsma followed with an MIAA record of 9:47 to take the two-mile. The meet ended with Hope finishing second in the mile relay behind Calvin. With the outcome already decided, Albion did not place in the relay event. Scorer George Mather's final tabulations showed Hope the winner with 66 points, followed by Albion with 57. Others in order were Adrian with 37, Calvin with 32, Olivet had 19, Alma 15, and Kalamazoo 14.

Several team members and their coach remained after the meet to savor Hope's first track championship since 1953. The undefeated dual season coupled with the field day performance was a fitting climax to a rewarding sports year, but there was more to come. Hope had recaptured the MIAA All-Sports Trophy with 62 points. Albion was close behind with 58, Calvin had 48, Kalamazoo 38, Alma 33, Adrian 29, and Olivet 22. Thus concluded a memorable year in Hope athletic history.

The Championship Trophy was not too heavy for Captain Bill Hultgren. — May 21, 1966

THE 1966 HOPE COLLEGE TRACK TEAM
MIAA CHAMPIONS

Front Row L to R: Tim Mayer, Bill Cook, Jim Pierpont, Chris Buys, Bruce Menning, Captain Bill Hultgren, Jim "Dutch" Poppink, Kent Candelora. **Middle Row:** Arlin Ten Klay, Doug Nichols, Ken Schroeder, Dave Duitsman, John Barwis, Floyd Brady, Bob Thompson, Ray Cooper, Sid Disbrow, Walt Reed. Back Row: Manager Doug Honholt, John Tysse, Wayne Meerman, Doug Formsma, Cal Oosterhaven, Jerry Poortinga, Tim Ferrell, Gary Peiper, Steve Reynen, Coach Gordon Brewer. Missing from picture: Rich Bisson.

CHAPTER 11

THE BEST OF BRADY

By the late 60s the so-called "counter culture" was in full swing, and symptoms could be found on Hope's campus. There was no open revolt as at Cal Berkeley and elsewhere, but Hope was not immune to the issues of Vietnam, the racial divide, and the ever-widening generation gap. An atmosphere of unrest found expression in numerous modes, including music of the period. Songs emanating from dorm rooms were perhaps the truest measure of the general discontent. The Beatles' *Yesterday* found its counterpoint in Bob Dylan's *The Times They Are A-Changin*, an angry challenge to the older generation, and *Blowin' In The Wind*, a song of gentle despair. Paul Simon and Art Garfunkle produced the touching *Bridge Over Troubled Water*, and who will ever forget the picture of black protesters gently swaying to the strains of *We Shall Overcome*.

Behind sloppy dress and now-longer hair, Hope students were searching for elusive answers. No real spokesperson seemed to emerge, but many were drawn to Floyd Brady, Hope's top athlete of the time. Brady did not seek notoriety, but a persona of quiet confidence combined with athletic prowess stamped him as a leader, if sometimes a reluctant one. His demeanor, somehow above the fray, resulted in a calming influence on blacks and whites alike.

* * *

Floyd Brady did not play football, but the 1966 team could have used his many talents. The 52-man squad that reported on September first was led by Captain Charlie Langeland, and as usual, hopes were high. Hope opened the season at Riverview Park on Sept. 17 against Augustana College of Rock Island, Ill. It was the first meeting between the schools in football, and developed into a defensive struggle. Hope's only show of offense occurred in the first quarter, when Langeland took a screen pass from Frens and raced 22 yards to the one-yard line. Hope then proceeded to fumble twice, losing the second one, and the threat was over. With 3:47 left in the half, Augustana's Tom Tessitore kicked a 25-yard field goal, which was set up by a Hope fumble. There was no further scoring until late in the third quarter. With 25 seconds remaining in the period, Tessitore got his second field goal, a 32-yarder. Defense prevailed the rest of the way, and the Vikings went home with the 6-0 win. Hope led 16-7 in first downs, gave up 131 yards rushing and none in the air, but an offensive punch would have to be found.

One week later, on Sept. 24, the Dutchmen were at Wheaton's Mc Culley Field for an afternoon game. Hope was without the services of halfback Harry Myers due to a conflict with the Jewish Holiday, Yom Kipppur, and center Ken Carpenter, who had flown to Schenectady to be with his father, who was seriously ill. A good crowd of 4,000 was on-hand for what would be an exciting small-college game. The Hope coaches had spent considerable practice time in setting up a sideline punt return with Walt Reed as the receiver. The device is seldom entirely successful, but with five minutes gone in the opening quarter the Crusaders' Don Griffin boomed a towering, 46-yard kick which Walt took on his own 28, got "behind the wall" of his carefully placed blockers, and raced 72 yards to score. A pass for the two-point conversion was not good, but Hope enjoyed the early 6-0 lead. The home team was not long in responding. Five minutes into the second quarter, halfback Roger Cornelius got free up the middle and streaked 74 yards for the TD.

221

Don Griffin converted to make it 7-6. Fumbles continued to plague the Dutchmen as tackle Larry Neal recovered a miscue on the Hope 31. The Wheaton drive culminated with a 13-yard dash, again up the middle, this time by fullback Bob Bennett. Griffin's second conversion made it 14-6.

The Dutchmen came back with their first sustained drive of the season, a 66-yard march capped by a seven-yard left end rollout by Frens for the TD. The two-point attempt again failed, but Hope had narrowed the gap to 14-12 at the half. There was no scoring in the third period, but the Dutchmen came close when Steve Wessling's field goal attempt missed by inches. In the fourth quarter, Keith Abel returned a punt 16 yards to the Hope 41. Clint Schilstra, now at quarterback, passed 12 yards to slotback Ray Cooper, then connected for 43 yards to Reed to the Wheaton four. Langeland bucked off-tackle twice, going in from the one-foot line on his second try. Hope's third try for extra points failed, but the Dutchmen had moved in front 18-14. Later in the period, Reed recovered a fumble on the Wheaton 45, but the drive stalled on the 37. With one minute left in the game. Hope's center sailed the ball well over the head of punter Ken Feit, resulting in a 25-yard loss. Wheaton moved from the Hope 38 to the 21 on a pass from Dave Carlson to Jerry Webb, then another to Mark Dauber, giving the Crusaders a first down on the Hope 10, but stellar defensive play by Feit and Langeland resulted in four straight incomplete passes and Hope's 18-14 victory was preserved. Schilstra "took a knee" twice and time ran out.

An hour or so into our return trip, Gary Holvick, one of our ends, suffered a delayed reaction to heat and injury. In the midst of a busy freeway, trainer Doc Green stopped the bus, summoned an ambulance, and had the boy in a hospital in record time. It was yet another testament to Larry Green's composure in emergency situations. Holvick was back home and in good shape by the next day.

Hope hosted Adrian on Saturday, Oct. 1, before a crowd of 2,700. The Dutchmen were off to a shaky start when the Bulldogs' Pete Yelorda returned the opening kickoff 76 yards to the Hope 19. Some strong defense prevented a score, but on the first Hope possession the ball was fumbled and Adrian's Barry Conlin recovered on the Hope 27. Two plays later, sub quarterback Greg Howells passed 29 yards to halfback Yelorda for the game's first score. Terry Richards's kick made it 7-0 with little more than three minutes gone in the first quarter. Adrian then returned the favor with a fumble of its own, which was recovered by Holvick on the Adrian 20. Holvick was rewarded with a 20-yard TD pass from Frens. The two-point conversion try was not good, and the Bulldogs led 7-6. Still in the first quarter, the alert Holvick again recovered an Adrian fumble, this time on the 35. A subsequent Hope drive was halted when Walt Reed was stopped inches short of the goal line as the quarter ended. Adrian scored in the second period when Pete Yelorda got his second TD on a one-yard plunge over guard.

HOPE 18 — WHEATON 14
September 24, 1966

Hope safety man Walt Reed got "behind the wall" on this punt return against Wheaton and raced 72 yards for the opening touchdown.

The kick attempt by Terry Richards failed, but the Bulldogs took a 13-6 lead to the locker room at the half.

In the final minute of the third quarter, the Bulldogs took over on their own 26. It was Yelorda again with an eight-yard right end sweep, then a 66-yard breakaway off-tackle for his third score. A Richards kick was wide, but the score mounted to 19-6. The Dutchmen engineered a fourth quarter drive that ended with Frens going over from the one on a sneak. The two-point attempt failed, and the count now stood at 19-12 with four minutes left in the game. Wessling's long kickoff was returned only to the Adrian eight, and the Hope defense dug in. After three tries, the Bulldogs had lost three yards to the five. Earlier, Ken Carpenter had nearly blocked an Adrian punt, and quarterback Eddie Maczko now wisely took a safety, making it 18-14 with 1:55 left. The ensuing free kick went only to the Adrian 44, and Hope still had a chance. A Frens-to-Langeland pass put the ball on the 25, but Frens was sacked for a five-yard loss on the next play. Two incomplete passes were followed by a wild fourth down scramble by Frens, who was downed for a 17-yard loss. The game was over.

Hope's disappointment continued at Olivet on Oct. 8. On a windy afternoon, the Dutch were without the services of Wessling, Ken Carpenter, and Mark Menning due to injuries. The Comets dominated throughout and breezed to an

18-0 victory. Hope's pass and punt protection broke down repeatedly, with disastrous results. In the first quarter, Bill Ash blocked a Frens punt and Barry Jackson went three yards for the game's first score. Bob Jansen's kick made it 7-0 with 2:18 left in the period. Reed took the kickoff, but made it only to the 10. The Dutchmen made it to the 27, but a penalty put them back to the 22 with third and eight. Olivet sophomore Loran Van Beveran then broke through to drop Frens on his own two-yard line. In this grim circumstance, punter Frens had only the strong wind going for him. Somehow the porous line managed protection, and Frens boomed the punt of his life. Olivet's three safeties misjudged the kick, which sailed well over their heads and, with a roll, came to rest on the Comet two-yard line! The punt, which covered 96 yards from scrimmage, remains an NCAA Division III record at this writing. Unfortunately, it would be Hope's only bright spot in a dismal afternoon. Frens would suffer the indignity of two safeties, and the Comets' Barry Jackson would score his second TD from the one to give his team the 18-0 victory. The Dutch had managed only 72 yards of total offense, and dobbers were down.

Hope's homecoming game with Albion on Oct. 15 was a clear case of darkness before the dawn. Coaches know that when things go bad, through the fault of no one, injuries seem to mount. Myers sustained an injury in a P.E. class, Jay Van Hoeven suffered a broken thumb, and John Huisman, Don Kroodsma, and Tom Pelon sustained injuries of one sort or another, with the latter two sidelined for the season. In spite of the gloomy picture, a crowd of 4,500 turned out at Riverview Park, a vote of confidence not to be overlooked. The Britons, undefeated in league play, opened the scoring in the first quarter with a 27-yard field goal by Bill Scheuller, but the Dutchmen responded with a 63-yard drive, which featured a 41-yard touchdown pass from Schilstra to Holvick. A high pass from center foiled the extra point try, but Hope was surprisingly in front, 6-3. The Dutchmen had possession two minutes later, when Doug Falan's punt into the wind went only to the Albion 33. Keith Abel carried three times for 14 yards, and Langeland added nine more. Reed and Harry Rumohr combined for seven to the three. Abel was given the ball on the next play, but fumbled into the end zone, where Hope guard Al Kinney recovered for the touchdown. Steve Wessling's kick was wide, but the Dutchmen took a 12-3 lead to the locker room at the half.

Neither team got into the other's territory in the third period. In the fourth quarter, Hope fumbled and lost possession on the 38. A few plays later, Chuck Scarletta scored from four yards out, but Scheuller's kick was short and Hope was still on top, 12-9. With 6:54 left, the game appeared to be slipping away, but a wild finish ensued. The Dutchmen again fumbled, this time on their own 22. In desperation, the Hope defense held for three downs. On fourth down, the ball was again given to Chuck Scharletta, but this time he was gang tackled by Lee Berens, Bill Beebe, John Oonk, and Feit. Hope took over, but failed to make a first down. Frens's fourth down punt into the wind went only 14 yards, and the Britons were in position to put the game away. Dick Vanderlinde passed 11 yards to Lloyd Harper, putting the ball on the Hope 20. Three incomplete passes followed, and a fourth down screen failed to make it to the first down marker. The Albion defense was equally tough, and Hope was faced with fourth down with 12 seconds remaining. Gary Frens attempted to run into the end zone for a safety, somehow failed and he was tackled. With two seconds left, Clint Schilstra, as in the Wheaton game, ended the contest by taking a knee while the Britons attempted to strip the ball. It would be the Britons' only league loss in their march to the MIAA championship.

Alma's Bahlke Field was the scene of the Scots' homecoming on Oct. 22. The Dutchmen continued to play inspired ball, but this day Dame Fortune kept her distance. At the controls for the Scots was freshman quarterback Tom Jakovac. He would lead Coach Denny Stolz's teams for the next four years and be instrumental in two championships. Early in the first quarter, Alma recovered a Dutchman fumble on the Hope 34. Mike Mitchell gained four and Dennis Bongard three before Jakovac rolled out around left end and went 27 yards for the score. The kick by Jeff Blough was good, and the Scots were ahead to stay with 11:44 remaining in the quarter. Hope managed to get into Alma territory only twice in the first half, and the Scots' 7-0 lead held at the intermission. In the third quarter, with good gains by Abel and Langeland, Hope made it to the Alma 17 only to be halted on fourth down.

In the fourth quarter, a Jakovac-to-end John Wooten pass put the ball on the Hope 10. Jakovac then repeated his left end rollout and went the distance to score. Jeff Blough's kick failed, but the Alma lead was 13-0 with 13:40 left in the game. It was now the Scots' turn to fumble, with Hope's Bill Bauer making the recovery on the Hope 20. When the Dutch running game bogged down, Schilstra passed to Cooper, who took the short pass and, using his dashman's speed, left all behind in a 79-yard sprint for the goal line. In lining up for the extra point, Hope was penalized three times and the two-point try failed, making it 13-6 with 1:11 remaining in the contest. Hope's on-side kick was recovered by Alma lineman Jim Ceceri and the game was over. Hard tackling had been the order of the day. Alma fumbled six times and lost five, while the Dutchmen were forced into five bobbles, losing four. More bad news for the Dutchmen was a knee injury to Reed, which would put him out for the remainder of the season.

Saturday, Oct. 29, was Parents Day at Hope, and a loyal crowd of 4,500 filled Riverview Park. Carpenter was removed from Hope's depleted ranks when his ailing father passed away in Boston and Ken flew to the funeral. Kalamazoo, Hope's opponent for the day, was also plagued by injuries, but saw a chance to up-end the struggling Dutchmen.

The Hornets' first opportunity came on a Hope fumble at midfield. Two plays later, Kalamazoo's Dennis Steele broke away for a 48-yard touchdown run and Rick Russell converted for the early Kazoo lead. But the Dutchmen came back with an 11 play, 77-yard drive climaxed by Abel's five-yard TD plunge. A Frens-to-Cooper pass was good for two points, and Hope inched ahead 8-7. In the second quarter, the Dutchmen mounted an 80-yard drive with Frens scoring on a sneak from the one with 5:46 left in the period. A Wessling kick failed, but Hope led 14-7 at halftime.

In the first series of the third quarter, Hope rounded out a 65-yard drive with a quick opener, resulting in a 25-yard TD run by Abel. Frens's pass to Holvick netted another two and the Dutchmen lead moved to 22-7, but four plays later Dennis Steele broke away for 24 yards to score his second touchdown and a Rick Russell to Dennis Benson pass for two points made it 22-15. Hope scored again in the first minute of the fourth quarter, when Menning picked off a Rick Russell pass on the Kalamazoo 27. Gary Frens went the final three yards to score, but the two-point conversion try again failed. With the score now at 34-15, the injury jinx was catching up to both teams and defense was not the order of the day. Wessling's kickoff was taken by on the 11-yard line by Dennis Steele, who ran untouched for 89 yards and his third score. The extra point was not good, but the count was now 34-21.

The Hornets' next move was an on-side kick, which Hope's Bob Ulrich recovered. Three rushes by Abel were followed by a Frens-to-Langeland screen pass that went for 40 yards. Three plays later, Frens passed four yards to freshman end Tom Thomas for the sixth Hope TD. A Frens pass to Myers was good for two, and the scoreboard showed Hope 42, Kalamazoo 21. The "track meet" continued as Kazoo responded with the well-worn "flea flicker" play. Russell passed 19 yards to Lee Tichenor, who lateralled to Steele, who ran the remaining 60 yards for his fourth touchdown of the afternoon to make it 42-29. The Dutchmen mounted one more drive. With 1:29 on the clock, Abel went three yards for Hope's seventh touchdown. The point try failed, but Hope savored the 48-29 victory. The Dutchmen had pleased the Parents Day crowd with 425 yards of offense, but were nearly matched by the visitors' 407.

The mood was upbeat following the Kalamazoo win, and hopes were high for a break-even season at Bluffton, Ohio, on Nov. 5. It was not to be. A Nov. 4 phone call from Bluffton informed that the field was unplayable due to an accumulation of snow. We felt strongly that Bluffton should carry out the obligations of a signed contract and urged alternatives including postponement, an alternate site, even a guarantee to play the game at Hope. After considerable negotiating, it became evident that Bluffton officials simply did not want to play the game under any circumstances. Thirty-four years have now passed since the incident, and further scheduling has not taken place.

It is difficult to describe the disappointment and empty

MIAA CHAMPION

Hope's Doug Formsma was the MIAA cross country champion in 1966. Doug was undefeated in MIAA competition and was voted the league's most valuable runner.

feeling on the part of the Hope players and coaches. At this low moment, Holland industrialist Bill Beebe stepped into the breach. Beebe, whose son Bill Jr. was a team member, offered to charter a bus and transport the entire Hope squad to Ann Arbor for the Nov. 5 contest between Michigan and Illinois. Mr. Beebe assumed all expenses, including a post-game dinner, and his great generosity took the sting out of the earlier disappointment. Illinois Coach Pete Elliot was able to defeat brother Bump of Michigan 28-21 in an exciting game that saw Mother Elliot change sides in the stands at halftime. The grateful team returned to Holland in good spirits, already looking forward to the 1967 campaign.

Hope's 2-3 MIAA record was good for a fourth-place tie with Kalamazoo. Champion Albion's only loss came at the hands of Hope, and last-place Adrian's only win came at the expense of Hope. Halfback Keith Abel, center Ken Carpenter, and corner back Charlie Langeland were named to the All-MIAA team, while Abel and guard Mark Menning were co-captains-elect for the '67 season.

*   *   *

The new cross-country coach in 1966 was Glenn Van Wieren, who would replace Daryl Siedentop for two years while the latter earned a doctorate at Indiana University. Van Wieren, a former three-sport athlete at Hope, would run the gamut of coaching experiences in a continuing career at Hope. In this season he was fortunate to have the services of Doug Formsma, who joined the team after two years at Grand Rapids Junior College. Formsma joined 1965 All-MIAA runner Cal Osterhaven and other faithful squad members to produce a 4-2 MIAA dual meet record and an eventual second-place tie overall. Albion and Adrian got the best of Hope (26-30 and 19-43), but the Dutchmen took Calvin in a thriller 28-29 as Formsma and Osterhaven finished 1-2. In the Alma meet it was Formsma, Osterhaven, and Wayne Meerman finishing 1-2-3 for the 17-42 win. The Dutchmen defeated Olivet 19-42, then won another close one from Kalamazoo by a 27-29 score. Doug Formsma was an impressive first in all meets, including the league meet at Kalamazoo on Nov. 8. Tom Swihart of Adrian finished second, but the Bulldogs as a team slipped to fourth place behind Hope, thus making possible the tie for second overall. Doug Formsma was a unanimous choice for the MIAA's most valuable runner award. Hope had not captured first place in the league meet since Sheridan Shaffer accomplished the feat in 1961.

*   *   *

Hope continued to compete in the tough Michigan-Indiana-Illinois Soccer Conference, and 1966 would not be a banner year. The Dutchmen were encouraged by their opening performance, a 4-3 overtime victory over Calvin. It was, however, a non-league contest, and the early optimism gradually faded. Hope dropped matches to Lake Forest, Mac Murray, Goshen, Calvin, Maryknoll Seminary, and Earlham. With a 0-5 league record and 1-7 overall, there was little to cheer about. Searching for something positive, Coach Van Eyl's team found the answer in a post-season contest following the final defeat. The November 18 issue of the *Anchor* gave a brief description of the action: "In an expected victory, the fired-up squad marched triumphantly over the Hope Women's Field Hockey Team, 4-1." Team member Al Griswold's last word said it all: "It was a fitting climax to an uninspiring season." The team had not lost its sense of humor, and there would be better days.

*   *   *

Carl Walters and Floyd Brady were co-captains of Coach De Vette's 1966-67 basketball squad, and their presence would be a telling factor down the stretch. The team's prospects were further enhanced by the return of Don Kronemeyer after a brief stint at Central Michigan University, and the transfer to Hope of Jim Schoon from Ohio University. Schoon was a cousin of former Hope football players Jon and Dale. Glenn Van Wieren would begin an illustrious basketball-coaching career at Hope by taking over the jayvee squad.

On Thursday, Dec. 1, the Dutchmen traveled to River Forest, Ill., to open the season against the Concordia Cougars of Coach Tom Faszholz. The Dutch expected a spirited tussle, and were somewhat surprised to be leading 42-32 at halftime. With seven minutes to go, Hope had increased its lead to 70-57, but guard Bob Kasten brought the home team back with five field goals, and the Dutchman lead was narrowed to 73-72 with 1:50 remaining. A fast break basket by Tom Ruppert with 1:20 left gave the Cougars their only lead at 76-75. Brady then scored what would be the winning basket with 45 seconds on the clock. Two Concordia shots missed, but the scrappy Cougars got the rebound and called timeout with nine ticks left. Coach De Vette then put his team in a 1-2-2 zone, and Walters was able to intercept Kasten's inbound pass. A seemingly sure field goal by Brady somehow missed, and Concordia had the ball out of bounds. With four seconds left, Bob Kasten fired from mid-court but missed, and the Dutchmen escaped with the 77-76 win. Brady, playing center for the first time, was superb with 30 points, Gary Rypma followed with 10, while Kronemeyer and Schoon each had nine, and Jim Klein eight. Kaspar was high for Concordia with 17, and center Tom Ruppert was impressive with 13, plus 21 rebounds.

The first home game brought the Crusaders of Valparaiso to the Civic Center on Saturday, Dec. 3. Coach Gene Bartow, sometimes referred to as "Clean Gene," had his team ready, and despite a 37-37 half-time tie pulled away to a 74-62 victory. A 47-34 advantage in rebounds aided the Valpo cause. Dick Jones led the winners with 24, and 6' 6" Ken Rakow contributed 12 points and 21 rebounds. Floyd Brady was high for Hope with 18, and Don Kronemeyer had 14. Bruce Van Huis came off the bench to score nine and Jim Schoon added eight.

Wednesday, Dec. 7, marked one of the earliest dates on record that Hope and Calvin met during their many seasons as basketball competitors. The host Knights, under new Coach Don Vroon would play before a capacity crowd of 4,400 in the Knollcrest Fieldhouse. Hope played well early and held a 38-27 lead at the intermission, then increased it to 54-32 in the first four-and-a-half minutes of the second half. But the Dutchmen suddenly went cold, not scoring another field goal after Rypma's jumper with 9:45 left. A 9-0 Calvin run closed it to 66-64, and Hope was in deep trouble. Rypma was fouled with 1:15 remaining and made one-of-two to make it 67-64 before Calvin sub Ed De Vries made his team's final field goal, narrowing it to one point, 67-66. Jim Kos fouled Rypma with seven seconds left. The free throw was missed, and Calvin called timeout. The ball came in to the Knights' Tom Dykema, who was hounded by Hope sophomore Cal Beltman. Dykema's 35' desperation shot at the buzzer failed, and yet another Hope-Calvin classic was in the books. Dykema had scored 10 points in the first half, but was held scoreless in the second by the hustling Beltman. Coach De Vette cited this as a key factor in the narrow 67-66 victory. Floyd Brady was at his best with 30 points to lead Hope, while Beltman's great night included 16 points. Rypma added 12. For the Knights it was Kim Campbell with 17, Wes De Mots with 16, and Tom Dykema with 10. Hope's Kronemeyer was limited due to illness.

Hope's game with Alma on Saturday, Dec. 10, was played at the Holland High Fieldhouse due to a scheduling conflict at the Civic Center. A surprising crowd of 2,000 turned out to witness a close first half. The Dutchmen were ahead 43-37 at the intermission, but the Scots had stayed in the game thanks to Gordon Hettrick and Ron Sober, both transfers from Soo Tech. But in the first nine minutes of the second half, the Dutchmen shot 51 percent and outscored Alma 23-8. Bruce Van Huis, a first-time starter for Hope, scored nine points, and pulled down 18 rebounds. Kronemeyer was the scoring leader, with 16 in Hope's eventual 90-58 victory. Brady had 13, Carl Walters and Gary Rypma each had 12, and Jim Schoon netted 10. Gordon Hetrick led Coach Charlie Gray's charges with 20, Ron Sober had 11, and John Fuzak nine.

On Wednesday, Dec. 14, the Dutchmen were greeted by a vociferous student crowd of 500 in Albion's Kresge Gym. Dean Dooley's team was small and fast. Employing a pressing defense, the Britons forced Hope into 20 first-half ball-control errors, and led 41-39 at the intermission. They also put in the first two field goals of the second half, but at this point Brady and Van Huis took control of the boards. With less than three minutes left, Hope held a 77-72 lead, but the game went to the wire before the Dutchmen pulled it out, 81-74. Brady was the Hope leader with 21, Van Huis had 15, Rypma 14, Kronemeyer 12, and Walters eight. Freshman Rick Ziem was high for the Britons with 18, Jim Bell notched 12, and Don Genson and Bill Breckenfeld each had eight. Hope was cold in the first half with only 29 percent, while Albion could manage only 21 percent in the second half.

In late December, Hope hosted a "Dutch Classic" Tournament at the Civic. Participating were Central College of Pella, Iowa, Northwestern College of Orange City, Iowa, and Michigan Lutheran of Detroit. On Thursday, Dec. 29, the Lutherans defeated Central 83-81 in overtime, while tiny Northwestern (675 students) was a 93-80 winner over Hope. This first meeting between the schools was of special interest as the Red Raiders' coach Paul Muyskens had been co-captain and most valuable player on Coach De Vette's 1949-50 Hope team. Irv Mellema was the Northwestern leader with 25, while Floyd Brady was high for the Dutchmen with 27. Of note was the appearance of freshman Bruce Mc Creary in the Hope lineup. He followed Brady with 19 points. In the second night's action, Northwestern took home the trophy by defeating Michigan Lutheran 82-75 and Hope won the consolation game 92-89 over Jack Walvoord's Central team. Brady was again high for Hope with 26, Walters had 17, Mc Creary 14, Rypma and Kronemeyer eight each. Jim Stone led Central with 23, center Lyle Kooiker had 19, Dave Witvoet 11, and Dennis Herrema 10.

The Dutchmen ushered in 1967 with a trip to Wheaton on Monday, Jan. 2. A strong first half by both teams produced a 36-36 tie at the intermission, but Brady picked up his fourth foul with 10 minutes remaining. The Crusaders then gained a rebound advantage and moved on to a 95-69 win. Arlyn Westergreen led Lee Pfund's team with 23, John Jauchen contributed 15, and Jeff Jonswald 13. Brady had 16 in Hope's losing cause, while Walters had 12, and Kronemeyer and Rypma nine each.

Wednesday, Jan. 4, marked a return to MIAA play against Kalamazoo at the Civic. The usual dog-fight prevailed in the first half, with Hope holding a slim 35-34 lead as the teams went to the locker room. A 10-0 burst by Hope in the first two-and-a-half minutes of the second half put the Dutchmen in the driver's seat, but the Hornets fought back to make it 64-59 with 6:24 remaining. At this point, Gary Rypma came off the bench to lead a second Hope surge. His four field goals in the last five minutes helped seal the eventual 82-70 victory. Meanwhile, Brady was putting on another classic performance with tips, dunks, jumpers, layups, and hooks, for a game-high 36 points. Don Kronemeyer followed with 15, Walters had 12, and Rypma 10. Bob Trenary was high for Ray Steffen's crew with 28, and Ralph Wellington had 22. Hope won the rebound contest, 59-34.

An estimated 1,800 fans turned out at the Civic on Saturday, Jan. 7, to see Hope do battle with 0-7 Lake Forest. In a lack-luster first half, the Dutchmen shot only 26 percent and could produce only a 33-32 lead at halftime on Lloyd Schout's two free throws. In the first 3:50 of the second half, the Foresters went on a 12-2 run to take a 44-35 lead as they sensed a chance for their first win. Their lead was narrowed to 58-53 with 2:02 remaining. A tip-in by Van Huis and single free throws by Mc Creary and Brady made it 58-57 with 1:20 left. Coach Dick Triptow then ordered a stall. Hope finally fouled Austen Penny with 37 seconds on the clock. The free throw was missed and the Dutchmen moved quickly down court, where four tries at the basket failed and a jump ball was called. Hope got possession on the jump and quickly called timeout. A play was set up with Carl Walters receiving the ball. His 13-foot jump shot, with five seconds remaining, won the game for Hope, 59-58. A Lake

**THE 1966-67 HOPE BASKETBALL TEAM
MIAA CO-CHAMPIONS WITH KALAMAZOO**

Kneeling L. to R.: Co-Captains Floyd Brady and Carl Walters **Standing:** John Leenhouts, Rick Bruggers, Jim Schoon, Bruce Van Huis, Jim Klein, Coach Russ De Vette, Lloyd Schout, Gary Rypma, Dave Utzinger.

Forest shot at the buzzer bounced twice on the rim, then rolled off. It was sickening defeat for Coach Dick Triptow and his charges, who had put up such a valiant fight. Brady came through with 19 points to lead Hope, Van Huis had 10 points and 17 rebounds, Rypma scored eight. For the losers, it was Fred Broda and Austen Penny with 13 each, Mike Hogan with 12, and Doug Dunbar with 11.

The Dutchmen had an easier time on Wednesday, Jan. 11, when Coach Gregg Arbaugh brought the Adrian Bulldogs to the Civic. Hot shooting (45 percent) and a 68-38 advantage in rebounds led to a 100-63 victory. Hope's margin of 53-33 at halftime meant that subs would have considerable playing time. Two free throws by John Leenhouts pushed Hope to the century mark. Frustration led to a rough game, with a total of 52 fouls being called. Brady was again at the top of the scoring list with 29 points. Walters had 12, Don Kronemeyer 10, and Cal Beltman eight. Al Werbish and Jim Ingledue played well for Adrian as each collected 19 points.

Hope ran into trouble at Olivet on Saturday, Jan. 14. A Hope zone defense was effective in the first half and produced a 30-27 lead at the intermission, but a second half press forced the Dutchmen into a game total of 24 turnovers. An 11-1 surge at the end of the contest gave the Comets the 70-64 victory. Jerry Allocco was high for Coach Vince Sigren's team with 17, Gordon Lofts had 14, La Porte 11 and Rex Thwaits 10. Kronemeyer had a good game for Hope with 23, Brady followed with 20, Rypma had nine and Walters eight.

Over the next two-and-a-half weeks, De Vette's team would play three non-league games before taking on Calvin again. It was the Aquinas Tommies in the Civic Center on Saturday, Jan. 21. Coach Red Dornbos's team enjoyed a height advantage, but when the rebound count was taken, the teams stood even at 46. Hope's 36-30 halftime lead increased to 21 points midway in the second period, but an Aquinas press cut the lead to 66-55 with six minutes left.

The Dutchmen managed a 16-13 advantage in the closing minutes to take the contest by an 82-68 margin. Brady again led his team, this time with 25. Klein had one of his better games with 14, Rypma tallied 11 and Van Huis 10. Freshman Pat Ryan came off the bench for Aquinas to lead the losers with 23, Jagels added 15 and Dennis Alexander 12.

One week later, bad weather forced postponement of the scheduled Saturday game. After a 10-day layoff, the Dutchmen were on the road to Wooster, Ohio, on Monday, Jan. 30. After trailing 40-35 at the half, Hope won the rebound battle 54-53, and scored one more field goal than Wooster, but lost the game at the free throw line as the Scots made 20 of 24 while Hope could only muster 13 of 19. Tim Jordan and George Baker led Al Van Wie's team to the 69-65 victory with 19 points each. Larry Hackenberg had 12 and Rich Thompson 11. Brady put in 22 for Hope, Gary Rypma scored 11 and Jim Klein nine.

It was another close one at Lake Forest on Saturday, Feb. 4. After a 35-35 tie at halftime, the Foresters played tough and inched ahead in the closing minutes for the 69-65 win. Hope led in field goal points 56-52, but Coach Triptow's team swished 17 free throws to only nine for Hope. Fred Broda was hot for the home team with 26, Austen Penny had 14, and Doug Dunbar and Mike Hogan each had 12. Brady and Walters divided scoring honors for Hope with 15 each, Van Huis had 13, Rypma nine, and Schout seven.

The Calvin Knights of Coach Don Vroon met Hope at the Civic on Wednesday, Feb. 8, in another showdown in the now-fabled rivalry. Calvin had taken the first round contest on Dec. 7 in a 67-66 thriller and was now strengthened by the return of center Bill De Horn after a semester's absence. De Vette had elevated Tom Dykstra and Bill Bekkering from the jayvee team to fill some varsity vacancies. Vroon chose to go with a zone in the first half, and Hope countered with the hot hand of Walters. The Dutchmen led by 10 several times in the opening period and left the floor at the intermission with a 40-30 bulge.

In spite of a 47-33 lead in rebounds, the Knights could get no closer than five points in the second half, thanks in large part to Hope's 51 percent shooting. The usual full house partisan crowd watched with glee as De Vette's charges moved to the 83-74 victory. Hope's largest lead was 66-51 with 8:26 remaining. The Calvin cause suffered when Kim Campbell and Dean Douma fouled out. Brady was at his dependable best with 29 points, but it was the performance of Hope guards Rypma and Walters that nailed down the victory. Rypma tallied 19 and Walters 18. Van Huis added eight. Bill De Horn was the main man for Calvin with 20 points and 22 rebounds. Dean Douma also scored 20 points.

At Alma on Saturday, Feb. 11, the Dutchmen enjoyed a hot hand in the first half and had the lead 51-40 at the intermission, then almost lost it as the Scots' Gordon Hetrick continued to bomb from all angles. Van Huis sprained an ankle at the 8:22 mark of the second half, and the team's rebounding suffered. Hope's lead narrowed to one point, 76-75, with 4:05 remaining. A Hope stall brought the Scots out of their zone, and Walters was fouled with 3:03 on the clock. His free throw made it 77-75, but John Fuzak sank one of his own, and it was 77-76. Freshman Rick Lorenz missed the front end of a one-and-one with 1:20 left, and Brady was immediately fouled. His free throw was good, and Walters added another with 15 ticks remaining to make it 79-76. Gordon Hettrick closed out an impressive evening with a long jumper at the buzzer, but Hope escaped with the 79-78 victory. Floyd Brady's 26 points led the De Vette men, Walters scored 18, Klein had 14, and Gary Rypma nine. Alma's Gordon Hettrick led all scorers with 32, John Fuzak had 15, Bill Simmons 10, and Rick Lorenz eight.

The trials of Treadway continued when Hope traveled to Kalamazoo on Wednesday, Feb. 15. Coach Ray Steffen employed 1-2-2 and 2-3 zone defenses effectively in the first half, and the Dutchmen could score only seven of 29 field goal attempts. The injured Van Huis did not dress for the game, and Kalamazoo denied Hope second shots by controlling the defensive boards. The Hornets posted a comfortable 39-23 lead at halftime, and the Dutchmen could get no closer than eight points in the second half. The 75-63 Kalamazoo victory featured Bob Trenary with 31 points, while Tom Crawford and Gene Nusbaum each had 15. Brady's 17 points led the losers, Walters scored 12, Rypma 10, and Klein, filling in for Van Huis, had nine.

The Dutchmen came home to host a strong Wheaton team on Saturday, Feb.18. In the usual spirited game between these two teams, Hope committed 14 fouls in the first half and Coach De Vette was forced to turn to his bench. A crowd of 2,000 watched the Crusaders move to a 41-40 halftime advantage. De Vette switched to a zone in the second half, and the visitors' shooting cooled to 23 percent. Wheaton's outside game suffered a blow when guard John Pierucki picked up his fourth personal with 12:43 left in the game. The Dutchmen were a different team in the second half, and came through with an 85-76 victory on the strength of several fine performances. Brady was again the leader with 22, Klein was strong with 18, Walters scored 12, Rypma 11, and Utzinger, in his best game of the season, dropped in 10. For Wheaton it was John Pierucki with 20 and John Jauchen with 17.

At Adrian on Wednesday, Feb. 22, Hope was in charge all the way, building a 42-32 halftime lead, increasing it to 77-54 at one point and going on to an 88-72 victory. Van Huis started for the first time since his injury, and scored nine as Klein moved to forward. Hope's co-captains did the bulk of the scoring, with Brady getting 34 and Walters 17. Klein had 11. A huge factor in the game was Hope's torrid night at the free throw line as the Dutchmen cashed in on 28 of 31. Al Werbish was high for Gregg Arbaugh's crew with 17, while Stewart had 16 and Martini 13.

When Olivet came to the Civic Center on Saturday, Feb. 25, the Dutchmen were aware that one of their two MIAA losses had come at the hands of the Comets. Hope had not taken care of the ball with 24 turnovers resulting in a six-point loss. A near-capacity crowd of 2,400 was on-hand to see their favorites now do an about face. Hope's 56 percent shooting in the first half produced a 48-31 margin at the intermission, but as the game progressed it was Hope's 63-26 domination of the boards that led to the eventual 93-63 victory. In team scoring, it was Brady again with 24, Klein and Van Huis each had 17, Walters 14, and Rypma 11. Gordon Lofts, Olivet's premier center, led all scorers with 25, and Jerry Allocco had 10.

With a share of the title on the line, Hope wound up the season by hosting the Albion Britons on Wednesday, March 1. In contrast to the Olivet game, the Dutchmen were cold at the start, registering but one field goal in their first 12 tries. The team then found its concentration and pulled ahead 38-33 at the half. De Vette's 1-2-2 zone in the second half was effective, and, combined with a sizzling 60 percent shooting average, produced the 87-64 victory and an MIAA co-championship with Kalamazoo. Schoon scored Hope's final basket with four seconds left, and the entire team was given a standing ovation. Rebounds were again a telling factor, with Hope getting 46 to 26 for the Britons. Floyd Brady ended on a high note with 34 points, 23 in the second half. Bruce Van Huis followed with 17, while Jim Klein and Gary Rypma each contributed nine. For the Britons of Coach Dean Dooley, it was guard Ed Stevens leading the way with 20 and Bill Breckenfeld getting 18. Hope ended at 15-7 overall and 10-2 in the MIAA. The title was De Vette's eighth in the last 11 years.

Hope held its winter sports banquet on Monday, March 13. Speaker for the evening was Dr. Barney Steen, recently retired basketball coach from Calvin College. When the All-MIAA team was announced, it included Floyd Brady of Hope, Bob Trenary and Tom Crawford of Kalamazoo, Gordon Lofts of Olivet, and Kim Campbell of Calvin. Carl Walters was named to the second team. Floyd Brady led the MIAA in scoring, rebounding, and field goal percentage, and was a shoo-in as the league's most valuable player. Brady and Gary Rypma were chosen as co-captains for the 1967-68 season.

* * *

Coach Sid Huitema and the Hope wrestlers struggled through a 1-9 season in 1966-67. The lone victory was a narrow 21-19 win over the Calvin Knights, who were also finding it tough to get a program started. A bright spot for the Dutchmen was the performance of freshman Gary Cook, who was undefeated in meets with other MIAA schools. A league meet of sorts was conducted at Kalamazoo on Saturday, Feb. 18. Host Kalamazoo took first-place honors with 64 points, followed by Adrian 62, Olivet 50, and Hope 27. Gary Cook of Hope took first place in the 137-pound weight class. Calvin did not enter a team.

Coach Huitema's part-time status made coaching and recruiting difficult, but he kept the program alive and the department of physical education and athletics was grateful for his efforts. Wrestling would not become an official MIAA sport for another two years and would not count toward the All-Sports Trophy in 1966-67, but a concerted effort was now underway to upgrade the program.

* * *

The spring sports outlook at Hope in 1967 was generally positive. The one exception was golf, where Coach Bill Hilmert conceded that the going would be tough. Some good rounds were played by Captain George Cook, Dennis Bobeldyk, and freshman Fred Muller, but opposing teams were just a bit better. Hope got by Grand Rapids Junior College 8-7 and shut out Olivet 15-0. In the remaining matches, scores were lopsided and not in favor of the Dutchmen. The MIAA league meet was held at Alma's Pine River Country Club with Albion the winner and Alma runner-up. Alma had placed first in dual competition, resulting in an Albion-Alma tie for the championship. Alma's John Beckett was medalist with a 158 for 36 holes, while Bruce Miller of Albion was selected by the coaches as the league's most valuable player. Hope finished in sixth place.

* * *

The 1967 presence of Doug Barrow and Ron Visscher, among others, would aid Coach Doc Green in maintaining a strong hold on second place in MIAA tennis. The annual spring trip found the Dutchmen spending most of their time as participants in the Rollins College Invitational in Winter Park, Fla. As the team traveled south, a stop was made in Carrollton, Ga., to meet and defeat West Georgia, 8-1. The match was played on Saturday, March 25. Two days later, the score was reversed as the Dutchmen took it on the chin from powerful Duke. Visscher, at number-three singles, was Hope's only winner. Following two days of rain, the Dutchmen bowed to Jacksonville University in a close one 5-4, then were beaten 7-2 by Davidson in an afternoon match. On Friday, March 31, it was host Rollins downing the Dutchmen, again by a 7-2 count. On their way home, the team stopped on Saturday, April 1, for a match with the University of the South in Sewanee, Tenn. Hope was a 7-2 winner this time, and moved on to Bloomington, Ind., to take on Big Ten power Indiana University. After absorbing a 9-0 shutout at the hands of the Hoosiers, it was time for the Dutchmen to begin play in their own league.

Unfortunately, in the revolving MIAA schedule, Hope's first opponent would be the Hornets of Kalamazoo. In a home match on Saturday, April 15, the visitors proved to be as strong as ever in tagging the Dutchmen with an 8-1 defeat, as Visscher was the only winner. In singles, it was Bill Jones over Barrow 6-2, 6-1, John Trump over Craig Workman 6-2, 6-1, Visscher defeated George Scott 6-3, 6-4, Burt Bothell defeated Craig Holleman 7-5, 2-6, 7-5, Don Swarthout won over John Schadler 6-1, 6-2, and Phil Vandenberg took Tibor Safar 6-1, 10-8. In doubles, Jones-Dave Tidwell defeated Barrow-Visscher 7-5, 6-2, Trump-Scott defeated Workman-Jeff-Green 7-5, 6-4, and Swarthout-Bothell took Holleman-Schadler 6-2, 6-0.

With the tough matches now behind them, the Dutchmen proceeded to profit from the experience. At Calvin on Monday, May 1, it was Hope 7, Calvin 1. Things were off to a shaky start when Barrow was upset 6-1, 6-4 by the Knights' Burt De Leeuw, but Workman came on to defeat Ben Pekhelder 7-5, 3-6, 7-5, Visscher defeated Don Klop 6-4, 6-3, Holleman took Jim Bolt 2-6, 6-3, 6-3, Schadler defeated Dave Post 6-2, 6-1, and it was Tibor Safar over John De Vries 6-0, 6-1. The doubles match between Barrow-Visscher and De Leeuw-Pekhelder was tied 6-6 when the rains came and as such was not counted, but Visscher-Jeff Green defeated Klop-Bolt 6-4, 6-4, and Holleman-Schadler won over Post-DeVries 6-3, 7-5.

A rainy spring was causing postponements, and coaches found themselves scrambling to fit in make-ups. On the day following the Calvin match, Hope played host to Albion and notched another win. In singles, it was Barrow over Jack Jones 6-3, 6-1, Workman over Kurt Leighton 6-3, 6-3, Visscher over Don Gruhl 6-2, 6-2, Holleman over Bill Smith 6-3, 6-3, Schadler over Bryan Kiehl 6-3, 6-1, and Safar over Lew Collins 6-3, 6-3. In doubles, Barrow-Workman defeated Jones-Leighton 6-4, 6-3, Safar-Tom Thomas defeated Collins-Jim Hall 6-4, 6-2, and Visscher-Green defeated Bill Smith-Joe Reed 7-5, 6-3. The 9-0 win was Hope's first shutout of the season. There would be more.

Hope's third match in three days was played at Alma on Wednesday, May 3. In singles, Barrow defeated Tom Lozen 6-2, 6-3, Workman defeated Mark Sylvester 6-4, 7-5, Visscher defeated Bill Nichols 6-2, 6-1, Holleman took Ron Sexton 6-3, 6-1, Schadler defeated Don Anderson 6-3, 6-1, and Safar defeated Dennis Williams 6-2, 6-2. In doubles, it was Barrow-Workman over Lozen-Sylvester 6-2, 6-0, Visscher-Green over Nichols-Paul Croom 11-13, 6-2, 6-2, and Holleman-Schadler over Williams-Anderson 6-4, 6-4.

At Olivet on Saturday, May 6, Hope was again a 9-0 winner. In singles, Barrow defeated Ted Traye 6-1, 6-0, Workman defeated Tom Kolansa 6-2, 6-2, Visscher defeated Gary Siemers 6-0, 6-0, Holleman defeated Ken Brockway 6-2, 6-0, Schadler defeated Dennis Ferrand 6-0, 6-0, and Safar took Bob Brooks 6-0, 6-0. In doubles, it was Barrow-Workman over Traye-Kolansa 6-0, 6-2, Visscher-Green over Brooks-Ferrand 6-0, 6-0, and Holleman-Schadler over Brooks-John De Puy 6-0, 6-0.

Hope stepped into the Mid-America Conference on Tuesday, May 9, to take on Central Michigan University in Mount Pleasant. The Dutchmen were again on target, and came away with a 7-2 victory. In singles, Barrow defeated Bill Johnson 9-7, 6-0, Workman took Tom Johnson 6-3, 4-6, 6-4, Visscher defeated Dan Troviess 6-2, 6-2, Holleman defeated Chuck Reed 6-4, 3-6, 6-1, Schadler defeated Jerry Kennedy 6-1, 6-3, and Cornell Monte of Central defeated Safar 6-4, 10-12, 7-5. In doubles, it was Barrow-Workman over Johnson-Johnson 6-3, 1-6, 6-2, Troviess-Monte of Central over Visscher-Green 6-0, 4-6, 6-4, and Holleman-Schadler over Kennedy-Reed 8-6, 6-3.

Back home on Saturday, May 13, Coach Green wound up the dual meet season with another 9-0 shutout, this time at the expense of Adrian. In singles, it was Barrow over Hank Mayo 6-1, 6-0, Workman over Chuck Chase 6-2, 6-0, Visscher over Bill Chase 6-0, 6-0, Holleman over Len Hollosy 6-1, 6-0, Schadler over Dick Williams 6-1, 6-0, and Safar over Jerry Miller 6-1, 6-0. In doubles, Barrow-Workman defeated Chase-Chase 6-0, 6-0, Visscher-Green defeated Mayo-Hollosy 6-2, 6-0, and Safar-TomThomas defeated Williams-Miller 6-3, 6-1.

In the league meet at Kalamazoo on May 19-20, to no one's surprise, the host school again walked away with the championship. Team scores showed Kalamazoo with 27 points, while Hope was in second with 17, followed by Calvin third with nine, Albion fourth with eight, and Alma fifth with two. Adrian and Olivet failed to score. Hope had finished a solid second in the league overall, and had done its part in the race for the All-Sports Trophy. Craig Workman was elected Hope's MVP. An All-MIAA team was selected, which in singles included Bill Jones, John Koch, and John Trump of Kalamazoo, Workman and Ron Visscher of Hope, and Bert De Leeuw of Calvin. The doubles selectees were Jones and Koch of Kalamazoo, Craig Workman and Doug Barrow of Hope, and Bert De Leeuw and Ben Pekelder of Calvin. Bill Jones was named the MIAA most valuable player, and Hornet teammate John Koch was recipient of the Stowe Sportsmanship award.

* * *

There is some irony in the fact that Coach Glenn Van Wieren's first MIAA championship was not achieved in the sport of basketball, but in baseball. In 1967 Van Wieren was serving as a two-year substitute for Daryl Siedentop, who was pursuing a doctorate at Indiana University in Bloomington. Don Troost and Wayne Cotts were co-captains of a team that would get off to a slow start, then find itself in posting a 10-1-1 MIAA record, best in Hope history to that point.

The annual spring trip produced a 2-6 record, and while hardly a smashing success did accomplish the purpose of providing playing time in warmer weather. The victories recorded included a 5-3 win over Troy State on March 29 and a 15-5 runaway against the University of the South on

THE 1967 HOPE BASEBALL TEAM
MIAA CHAMPIONS

Front Row L. to R.: Dan Krueger, Boyd Rasmussen, Dave Abel, Harry Rumohr, Denny Farmer. **Middle Row:** J. Pearson, Charlie Langeland, Gary Frens, Greg Gorman, Nels Bergmark, Tom Pelon **Top Row:** Don Kroodsma, Mark Johnson, Don Troost, Bruce Van Huis, Bob Beishuizen, Coach Glenn Van Wieren. **Missing from the picture:** Co-Captain Wayne Cotts.

April 1. Hope was on the short end of contests with West Georgia 3-2, Troy State 1-0, Gannon College 11-10, Troy State 5-1, and the Pensacola Naval Air Station 16-5 and 5-3.

The regular season opened with the Dutchmen traveling to Mount Pleasant for a twin bill with Central Michigan University. Hope suffered a 3-0 shutout as three Chippewa pitchers struck out 20 Hope batters and allowed just one hit, a single by Cotts. The three Central runs were unearned. Hope built a 9-7 lead in the second game, but it was erased in the sixth when Tom Krawczyk stroked a three-run homer with two out to wrap up the eventual 10-9 victory. Along the way, Hope's Tom Pelon had a grand slam homer in the fourth and Gary Frens followed with a two-run round tripper in the fifth.

MIAA competition began on Saturday, April 12, with Hope hosting Kalamazoo. In the opener the Dutchmen built an early 10-2 lead only to see the Hornets tie it up in the first of the sixth. Hope came back to score the winning run in the bottom half of the sixth. Bruce Van Huis walked, then took second on a Harry Rumohr single. As Van Huis rounded second, the Kalamazoo shortstop tried for a pickoff but threw the ball into right field, allowing Bruce to make it all the way home for the narrow 11-10 win. Don Kroodsma and Mark Johnson were on the mound for Hope. In the second game, the Hornets took a 2-0 lead in the first, but the Dutchmen came back with five in the second and added six more in the fifth for an 11-2 victory. Frens went the distance for Hope, scattering five hits.

A scheduled night game with Valparaiso was canceled because of rain, but the Dutchmen were in action again on Monday, April 24, at Calvin in 35-degree weather. In the first game, Calvin's Jim Bode limited the Dutchmen to three hits and enjoyed an early 1-0 lead, but Hope erupted for three runs in the sixth to take the contest by a 3-1 score. Cotts walked, pinch hitter Frens sacrificed him to second and Charlie Langeland walked. Both runners advanced on a passed ball, then came home on Pelon's triple. Pelon scored the third run on a sacrifice fly by Troost. In notching the win, Kroodsma allowed five hits, walked four, and struckout 10.

In the second game, Gary Frens gave up just four hits, walked two, and struck out 11. Only one Calvin runner got beyond first base. The Knights managed one run, but in the fourth Langeland singled. Troost then came through with the game winner, a two-run homer over the right field fence to seal the hard-fought 2-1 victory.

Hope played a single, non-league game at Kalamazoo on Thursday, April 27. The Hornets garnered 10 hits from the offerings of Johnson, Denny Farmer, and Greg Gorman enroute to a 12-5 win. Coach Van Wieren used 17 players in the contest, and Kazoo's John Armstrong was the winning pitcher.

At home against Albion on Monday, May 1, it was Hope a 9-3 winner in the first game, then coming from behind to tie the nightcap at 3-3 before rain halted play in the eighth. Frens started both games, but Mark Johnson came on in the sixth inning of the opener with the score at 8-2. Hope had 11 hits and scored four times in the first inning. Pelon connected for a three-run homer, and Van Huis had a solo shot. In the second game, Hope scored twice in the fourth for a 2-0 lead, but the Britons came back with three runs on four straight singles in the fifth to take a 3-2 lead. Hope tied it in the sixth when Cotts singled and took second on a Kroodsma bunt. Cotts scored on Langeland's double to left center. At this point, the rain came and the game was not replayed.

Hope gained an all-important split at Alma on Wednesday, May 3. The Dutchmen took the opener 6-3 behind the four-hit pitching of Kroodsma, who struck out nine and walked seven. Hope collected six hits and pushed across four runs in the first inning. The Scots scored single runs in the second, third, and fourth. In the second game, Alma's John Terwilliger shut down the Dutchmen with a one-hitter in posting a 3-0 shutout. A single by Van Huis in the fourth was the only offense Hope could muster. Terwilliger struck out 16 Hope batters. Johnson pitched almost as well, giving up but three hits.

Coach Van Wieren's team traveled to Olivet on Saturday, May 6, knowing that a double victory could clinch an MIAA championship. The Dutchmen had little trouble in the first game, as Kroodsma went the distance giving up but four hits. Meanwhile, Hope bats were alive to the tune of 10 hits that led to an 8-2 victory. Kroodsma also started the second contest, but after three innings it was Olivet 3-2. Frens came on in relief in the fourth and his teammates took the lead with two runs in their half of the inning. The Comets tied it at 4-4 with a single run in the top of the sixth. The game was decided in the bottom of the sixth when Rumohr singled and came home as Frens won his own game with a solid double.

The Dutchmen took a break from league play on Tuesday, May 9, as they entertained the Tommies of Aquinas in a single game. A six-run outburst by the Dutchmen in the first inning pretty much decided things as the score moved to 11-0 before Aquinas got on the board. Johnson pitched six innings of three-hit ball before being relieved by Gorman. Johnson struck out 12. Langeland and Troost each had a pair of hits as Hope's team total of 11 produced the 11-2 win.

On Wednesday, May 10, it was announced that Olivet had named a new basketball coach in the person of Gary Morrison. After eight years at Galesburg-Augusta High School, he would replace Vince Sigren, who was promoted to dean of students. Morrison would do well in his long tenure at Olivet. The former Kalamazoo College star, ever a fierce competitor, was sometimes misunderstood by opponents, but possessed a grand sense of humor and often regaled us at meetings of the MIAA athletics directors.

The baseball season was not quite over. The Bulldogs of Adrian were in town on Saturday, May 13. Their intent of course, was to upset the recently crowned MIAA champs. The Dutchmen were just as determined to continue their winning ways. The opener proved to be another classic. Don Kroodsma went the distance and was staked to an early 4-0 lead, but Adrian got two in the fifth, one in the sixth, then one more in the seventh to tie the game at 4-4. In the bottom of the seventh, Pelon reached second base. Krueger then came through with a single to win the game 5-4.

Gary Frens was on the mound for Hope in the second game and scattered six hits. The contest was scoreless until the sixth, when the Dutchmen rallied for four runs. Two more were added in the seventh to wrap up the game and the season with the 6-1 victory. Langeland went 2-3, and Rumohr had two doubles. As mentioned earlier, Hope's 10-1-1 MIAA record was the best in Hope history and was especially impressive because Olivet and Kalamazoo shared second place with 5-5 records. Co-captains Troost and Cotts had played well in leading their team to the title.

Hope was awarded six places on the 10-man All-MIAA team. Named were pitchers Gary Frens and Don Kroodsma, catcher Tom Pelon, shortstop Harry Rumohr, outfielder Don Troost, and third baseman Charlie Langeland. Langeland won the league batting championship with a hefty .459 average. He was also voted the MIAA's most valuable player. All in all, a season to be remembered.

*   *   *

Several members of Hope's championship track team returned for the 1967 season, and hopes were high for a repeat. The Dutchmen journeyed to Kalamazoo's Angell Field track for the opening meet on Saturday, April 15. The Hornets, with a long tradition in track and field, were simply undermanned as this season began. Hope placed first in all 16 events and took the meet, 126-10. It was a good day for Bill Bekkering, whose vault of 12' 9" was a Hope record.

The Knights of Calvin were in Holland on Wednesday, April 19, for another fine meet. Calvin established three school records, but Hope won nine of the 16 events to take the meet, 79-57. Floyd Brady won the long jump with a leap of 22' 2" and the high jump at 6' 4". Two Hope records fell in the meet: Doug Formsma's two-mile time of 9:40.3 broke the Hope record, while Rick Bruggers and Rich Bisson completed a sweep in that event. Formsma also won the mile. Big guns for Calvin were Dave Ver Merris and Rudy Vlaardingerbroek. Ver Merris took the 440 in a Calvin record time of 48.9, then won the 220 in 22.8. He also anchored the winning mile relay team. Big Rudy V. won the shot, discus, and javelin to give his team 15 points. His 139' 10" heave of the discus was a Calvin mark. Calvin's Dave Heth, an Albion transfer, won the pole vault at 12' 10½". Bekkering equaled Heth's mark, but the latter won on fewer misses. The winning height produced records at both schools.

The dual meet at Albion on Wednesday, April 26, was a rewarding one for Hope as the Dutchmen came away with an 84-52 victory after taking first place in 11 of 16 events. A team bus was as yet unavailable for spring sports, and team members were therefore transported in individual automobiles. This, in turn, resulted in a lack of direct supervision in most of the vehicles. On the return from Albion, it was later revealed, a hard-and-fast no smoking rule was violated in one of the cars. When confronted, four team members did not deny the allegation. The resulting disciplinary action caused a serious reduction in the team's point scoring potential for the remainder of the season.

The Great Lakes Colleges Association meet was held in Crawfordsville, Ind., on Saturday, April 29, with Wabash as host. Hope finished fifth in the 10-team field behind Earlham, Wabash, Oberlin, and Ohio Wesleyan, but ahead of Albion, De Pauw, Denison, Wooster, and Kalamazoo. Bekkering was Hope's man of the day as he won the pole vault at 13' 2½". This established a GLCA record and broke his own Hope mark. Doug Formsma was Hope's other first-place winner with a 4:20.1 time in the mile run. This also bettered his own Hope mark.

Coach Denny Stolz brought his Alma team to the Hope track on Wednesday, May 3. The Scots were strong in the sprints and shotput, but the Dutchmen won all but three events in posting an 89-47 win. The Alma 440-yard relay team of Mike Paterson, Tom Jakovac, Jim Ogg and Tiff Mc Kee won that event and Mc Kee took both dashes, but Hope swept the two-mile run and ended the day with a narrow victory in the mile relay. The Hope team of Paul Steketee, Dan Colenbrander, Bill Cook, and Mike Paliatsos edged the Alma team of Ogg, Tom Fegley, John Miller, and Mc Kee by one-10th of a second. All-round athlete and erstwhile quarterback Tom Jakovac placed in the sprint relay, the 100-yard dash, the high jump, and the pole vault.

Hope hosted Olivet on Saturday, May 6, an ideal day for a track meet. Coach Stu Parsell had basketball star Gordon Lofts, who won the high hurdles, and football standout Al Nagy, who took the high jump, but the Comets lacked the necessary depth to be competitive. Hope won 14 events, including sweeps in the mile, pole vault, 880, and javelin in registering the 110-26 victory. The intermediate hurdle victory by Dave Thomas in a time of 39.1 was a Hope record.

HOPE 89 — ALMA 47
May 3, 1967

Mike Paliatsos edges Alma's Tiff Mc Kee in the mile relay. Alma Coach Denny Stolz in center of picture.

A trip to Valparaiso on Tuesday, May 9, found the Dutchmen on the opposite end of the score in a triangular with Valpo and Manchester. Host Valparaiso won the meet with 73 points, Manchester followed with 56, and Hope was forced to eat humble pie with 52. The Dutchmen did come through with four firsts as Norm Klein took the long jump, Doug Nichols the javelin, Mike Paliatsos the 440, and Doug Formsma the two-mile.

The long trip to Adrian came on Saturday, May 13. Coach Paul Mac Donald's team would post some impressive times, but again, not enough to prevent Hope from registering a 98½-37½ victory. The Bulldogs' Doug Moss won both hurdle races, Dick Hilton took the 440 in 50.4, and Walt Chany set an Adrian record in the 880 with the excellent time of 1:55.0. In the two-mile run, Hope's Doug Formsma bettered his own record with a time of 9:32.3.

In a final tune-up for the MIAA league meet, Hope played host to ever-tough Grand Rapids Junior College. But this would again be a Hope day as the Dutchmen captured 12 of the 16 events, enroute to an 83-52 win. High points for the Dutchmen were Bekkering's 13' 6" vault and Reynen's 880-yard run in 1:57.3, both Hope records.

The league meet at Calvin on Saturday, May 20, was both interesting and unusual. Calvin was the leader in gold medals with five, Hope had three, and Albion but two, yet in the end Albion was the team winner with 57½ points over Hope with 57, and Calvin third with 50. Along the way, six MIAA records were broken, three by Calvin, and one each by Adrian, Alma

ONE-TWO FINISH

Captain Doug Formsma and teammate Rick Bruggers finished 1-2 in both the mile and 2 mile runs in the 1967 MIAA Meet, thus aiding in Hope's title quest.

**THE 1967 HOPE COLLEGE TRACK TEAM
MIAA CHAMPIONS**

Front Row L. to R.: Ken Feit Rick Bruggers, Bill Cook, Jeff Kling, Doug Nichols, Rich Frank, Rich Bisson, Steve Reynen. **2nd Row:** Walt Reed, Paul Sloan, Mike Paliatsos, Mike Oonk, Barry Kromer, Ken Schroeder, Bruce Formsma, Dennis Alexander, Dave Duitsman, Dan Colenbrander. **3rd Row:** Bill Bekkering, Taibi Kahler, Terry Childs, Bruce Ming, Captain Doug Formsma, Paul Hartman, Paul Steketee, Les Cole, Coach Gordon Brewer. **Missing from the picture:** Jeff Hollenbach, Dave Thomas, Norm Klein.

and Hope. Calvin's Rudy Vlaardingerbroek put the shot 49' 10½" for a new mark, teammate Dave Heth vaulted 13' 10", and the Knights' mile relay team of Dennis Van Andel, Joel Vander Male, Sandy De Haan, and Dave Ver Merris combined for a time of 3:21.9. Adrian's Doug Moss was superb in the 120-yard high hurdles with a time of 14.6, the new mark in the 100 was 9.7 by Alma's Tiff Mc Kee, and Hope's Doug Formsma lowered the two-mile record to 9:33.5. Formsma and teammate Bruggers were 1-2 in both the mile and two-mile, while Nichols claimed Hope's other first with a javelin toss of 196' 8" to beat out big Rudy Vlaardingerbroek of Calvin. While Nichols' mark was not a league record, it did surpass his own Hope record of the previous year.

Albion had won the meet by scoring one point in the final event of the afternoon, the mile relay. At first glance, the 1/2 point loss seemed of tragic proportions for the hard-pressed Dutchmen, but seasonal point totals told a different story. Hope had finished first in dual meet competition for 12 points plus 10 for its second in the league meet for a total of 22. Albion's third-place finish in duals netted eight points to go accompany 12 for the league meet first place, giving the Britons 20 points, while Calvin's second in duals plus a third place in the league meet totaled 18. This unusual juxta-position of teams had given Hope the 1967 championship by a margin of two points.

Doug Formsma, Rick Bruggers, and Steve Reynen were named to the All-MIAA team, while Albion's Bob Turner received the MIAA's most valuable trackman award. On Saturday, June 3, Doug Formsma became Hope's first participant in post-season NCAA competition. In the College Division NCAA Meet at Ohio Wesleyan, Doug placed second in the three-mile run with a time of 15:07.

* * *

ALL-SPORTS CHAMPIONS

Hope College retained the MIAA All-Sports Trophy in 1967 with a total of 61 points to 49 for runner-up Kalamazoo. **Above L. to R.:** Gordon Brewer, Russ De Vette, MIAA Commissioner John C. Hoekje, Glenn Van Wieren, and Dr. Kenneth Weller.

WILLIAM VANDERBILT   GEORGE KRAFT

Vanderbilt and Kraft joined the Department of Physical Education and Athletics in 1967. Vanderbilt, Hope '61, was Captain of Hope's 1960-61 basketball team while Kraft had been Co-Captain of Wheaton's 1961 football team.

Perhaps most satisfying for the various Hope coaches was retaining the coveted All-Sports Trophy. Championships in basketball, baseball, and track, plus a strong second in tennis along with points in football, cross country, and golf had produced 61 points to 49 for runner-up Kalamazoo. Once again, the sports year had concluded on a positive note.

Hope's expanding program in physical education and athletics now called for additional staff. In the spring of 1967, Dean Morrette Rider announced the hiring of William Vanderbilt, Hope '61, and George Kraft, a Wheaton grad and co-captain of the Crusaders' 1961 football team. Both would add stature to the department and make invaluable contributions in the years ahead.

* * *

With the All-Sports Trophy tucked away for a second consecutive year, Hope sought to continue the run. In 1967-68, the road would not always be smooth, but disappointments in the fall would be offset by success in the winter and spring. Glenn Van Wieren, now in his second season as cross-country coach, was able to field a strong team, but unfortunately the same could be said of most of the other teams in the league. Senior Paul Hartman was captain of the team that now included junior Rick Bruggers who had proven his mettle during the '67 track season.

Hope opened the season by hosting a double-dual, with Wheaton and Spring Arbor on Saturday, Sept. 23. Wheaton prevailed over Hope, 20-39, Hope tied Spring Arbor 28-28, and Wheaton downed Spring Arbor 17-42. In his first-ever cross country run, Rick Bruggers was the individual winner in a time of 21:35 for the four-mile course.

The annual Hope Invitational was held on Tuesday, Sept. 26, with Bruggers again the winner, this time with a course record of 20:27.8. But the Tommies of Aquinas took the next five places to win the meet with 20 points. Grand

Rapids Junior College placed second with 69, followed by Hope 73, Muskegon Community College 97, and Southwestern Community 112.

The Dutchmen opened the MIAA season at Alma on Saturday, Oct. 7, in a real thriller. Bruggers set a new Alma course record of 20:53 in beating Alma ace Don Yehle for first-place honors. The Scots took second third, and fourth, but Hope's Cal Osterhaven finished fifth, Wayne Meerman was sixth, Rich Bisson seventh, and Rudy Howard ninth. The final tally showed Hope the winner by the narrowest of margins, 28-29.

Saturday, Oct. 14, brought the Adrian Bulldogs to Hope, and Bruggers was again first across the finish line but Adrian took the next three places to nail down a 22-39 victory. Tom Swihart finished second for the winners, while Osterhaven was fifth. One week later at Olivet, it was Bruggers and Osterhaven finishing 1-2 while Bisson and Hartman came in fourth and fifth to assure a 20-35 Hope victory.

Hope hosted Kalamazoo and Oakland on Saturday, Oct. 28, and Rick Bruggers tasted defeat for the first time. The Hornets' John Wismer was the first to cross the line, while Bruggers trailed in fourth place. In a good meet, Kalamazoo emerged the winner, 24-31. Hope also lost to Oakland by a 27-31 count.

On Wednesday, Nov. 1, the visiting Knights of Calvin pinned a 23-37 defeat on the Dutchmen, and Hope's dual meet with Albion scheduled for Saturday, Nov. 4, was cancelled when a bizarre storm dropped six to eight inches of wet snow in the Holland area during the morning hours.

The weather had improved enough by Tuesday, Nov. 7, for Hope to host the MIAA meet. Coach Jay Flanagan's Adrian team finished first with 51 points, Calvin was second with 62, followed by Alma 82, Kalamazoo 85, Hope 104, Albion 107, and Olivet 196. Osterhaven was Hope's first finisher, in eighth place. Bruggers had suffered a late-season leg injury, but ran anyway, finishing 19th. In the overall seasonal standings, it was Adrian winning its first championship in 21 years. In an unusual mix of dual standings plus the league meet, Calvin finished second while Albion, Hope, and Kalamazoo ended in a three-way tie for third. Alma came in sixth and Olivet seventh. Those named to the All-MIAA team included Tom Swihart of Adrian, Don Yehle of Alma, Rick Admiraal of Calvin, Rick Bruggers of Hope, and John Wismer of Kalamazoo. Wismer was voted the league's most valuable.

*   *   *

Phil Van Eyl had been Hope's soccer coach since the sport's unofficial first season in the fall of 1963. He had done much for the program, and successfully engineered Hope's membership in the Michigan-Illinois-Indiana (MII) Soccer Conference. This would be his final year at the helm, and he would be assisted by history professor Michael Petrovich.

Competition in the MII was keen, with most teams having long-established programs, but Van Eyl realized that it gave the team an additional challenge while waiting for the MIAA to adopt the sport. Hope opened the season at home on Wednesday, Sept. 20, with a non-league 1-0 victory over Calvin. Kawala Simwanza booted home the game's only score. At Goshen on Tuesday, Sept. 26, Hope scored first, but finished on the short end of a 4-1 count. The Dutchmen hosted Earlham in another league contest on Saturday, Sept. 30. The hard-fought game went into overtime before the Quakers' Kip Monell scored with four minutes gone to give Earlham the 1-0 win. It was a tough loss for the Dutchmen, especially for goalie Lou Lotz, who played an outstanding game against a tough opponent.

In a league game at Calvin on Wednesday, Oct. 4, Hope lost another close one, this time by a 3-2 score, and the hard luck continued on Saturday, Oct. 7, when the Dutchmen played host to Wheaton. The Crusaders scored three in the first half, then held on for the 3-1 victory as Fred Schutmaat scored Hope's only goal. On Friday, Oct. 13, the Dutchmen were able to halt the skid with a 9-0 victory over a hapless Albion team in the Britons' first year of competition. Fred Schutmaat scored four goals and Manuel Cuba had two. Kalamazoo, also in its first year of soccer, visited Hope on Tuesday, Oct. 17, and was turned back 5-1. This time it was Manuel Cuba's turn to score four goals.

With confidence gained from the two victories, Hope traveled to Lake Forest on Friday, Oct. 20. In one of their better efforts of the season, the Dutchmen were able to come away with a 1-1 tie. Five days later, the team was on the road again for a game with Oakland in Rochester, Mich. Hope was impressive again, this time with a 6-0 victory, but it was back to reality on Saturday, Oct. 28, when Van Eyl's team was beaten 2-1 by a strong Mac Murray team in Jacksonville, Ill. The season ended on a positive note on Friday, Nov. 3, as Hope played host to Wabash. Schutmaat was at his best with two goals, while Al Griswold and Art Hudak each added one as the team gave Coach Van Eyl a grateful sendoff with a 4-0 shutout victory. Hope ended with a 4-6-1 record, but had shown steady improvement.

*   *   *

College football seasons come and go with expected similarity, yet each has its own character, its own set of ups and downs. The downs would dominate for Hope in 1967. The first blow had come during exam week of the previous May. Guard Allan Kinney had come to my office to report that he had been diagnosed with cancer in his chest area. He would be undergoing treatment during the summer months and expected to be ready to go on opening day in September. I was unprepared and shaken by this news, yet deeply moved by his courage and resolve.

Friday, Sept. 1, marked the first day of practice, and Coach De Vette greeted a sizeable squad of 52. Twenty-three

Hope's coaches battled frustration in 1967.

L. to R.: Ken Weller, Russ De Vette, Gord Brewer, Trainer Larry "Doc" Green.

of that number were freshmen, with another 10 sophomores. With but eight seniors on the roster, it was clear that Hope would be inexperienced, especially on defense. True to his word, Allan Kinney was on-hand, but with doctor's orders not to participate. Al's request was to serve as one of the managers, and the coaches welcomed the inspiration of his presence.

In the opener at Augustana on Sept. 16, Hope started seven freshmen on defense. Their talent was evident when the halftime score stood at 0-0. The Dutchmen threatened twice in the first half, but were thwarted by two big interceptions, one by Paul Ander on the Vikings' one-yard line and another by Julius Jerdon on the two. With 3:15 left in the third quarter, Augustana climaxed an 80-yard drive when Tom Tessitore kicked a 37-yard field goal to make it 3-0. Then, with 2:43 left in the game, reserve quarterback Doug Morton completed an 11-play 56-yard drive by passing 11 yards to end Ander for the game's only touchdown. The kick was true to wrap up the 10-0 victory for the Vikings.

A Sept. 23 night game was Hope's home opener against Lake Forest College. The two schools had met several times in basketball, but this would be their first meeting in football. The Foresters' Mike Dau was one of the few coaches in the country still using the single wing formation. It presented a look that the Dutchmen had not seen in a while, and defensive adjustments had to be made. In the first quarter, Lake Forest tailback Tom Woodward's fumble was recovered by Hope's freshman linebacker Bill Leismer on the Foresters' 29. Eight plays later, quarterback Gary Frens scored on a one-yard sneak and Paul Sloan kicked the point to give the Dutchmen an early 7-0 lead. Later in the period, Coach Dau utilized the tailback quick-kick, an old single wing weapon. Hope took possession on its own 41, then moved 59 yards in 12 plays with Keith Abel scoring from the one. Paul Sloan's kick was wide, and Hope's lead was now 13-0. The visitors came back to score from their own 45 when halfback Tom Jaax raced 55 yards for the TD. A pass attempt for the two-point conversion was intercepted by Tom Pelon, and the score moved to 13-6. Hope then drove 73 yards to the end zone, but the scoring play was nullified by a 15-yard penalty, leaving the count unchanged at the half.

On their first possession of the second half, the Dutchmen were successful with another 59-yard drive. The set-up play in the drive was a 19-yard pass from Frens to fullback Frank Lundell. Frens then scored on a two-yard keeper play around right end. He then repeated the play for two points and Hope's lead was 21-6. Alertness by Hope's secondary in the fourth quarter eventually led to another TD. Pelon, Dick Holman, Groy Kaper, and Harold Workman each picked off a pass. Runs by Abel and Walt Reed moved the ball to the Lake Forest 30. Carries by Frens and Abel made it to the 18, where Abel broke free and went the distance to score. Paul Sloan's kick was not good, but Hope's 27-6 victory was well received by the crowd of 2,500.

Hope's next two contests would fall into the "not quite" category, and would be more than frustrating for the coaching staff. On Sept. 30, the Dutchmen traveled to Wheaton, Ill., for a night game at Red Grange Field. It was a homecoming of sorts for assistant coach George Kraft. In his first year on the Hope staff, the former Wheaton co-captain now hoped his charges would show well. A minor irritant at the outset was the discovery that the home team had not bothered to secure Hope's roster for the game program. Instead, they had simply lifted the roster from the previous year's program. The incident, of course, would be the least of our concerns. Hope would encounter kicking problems that would be hard to overcome. In the first quarter, Frens, one of the best punters in Hope history, put one out on the Wheaton three but an illegal procedure penalty nullified the play. On a second attempt, the kick was blocked by end Larry Taylor and the Crusaders took over on the Hope 38. Eight plays later, Wheaton was in the end zone on a quarterback sneak by Joel Detwiler. The kick was blocked, leaving the score at 6-0.

Later in the half, Dick Holman intercepted a pass and returned it to the Wheaton 26. The Dutchmen made one first down but were stopped on the 10, and the score remained at 6-0 at the half. There was no scoring in the third quarter, but in the closing minutes of the game a partially blocked Frens punt went only 16 yards and Wheaton took over on the Hope 34. It appeared that the Dutchman defense would hold, but on a fourth down play senior quarterback David Carlson scored on a 13-yard rollout around left end to give Coach Jack Swartz and his team the 12-0 victory. Hope completed just one of seven passes for 15 yards, while Wheaton completed three of eight for a total of 12 yards. The difference was in rushing yards, as the winners had 212 to 115 for Hope.

The MIAA opener for Hope and Alma was an afternoon game at Alma's Bahlke Stadium on Oct. 7. Coach Denny Stolz had assembled a talented squad and would go undefeated enroute to the Scots' first championship in 16 years. They would score four shutouts, but the Dutchmen would provide their stiffest challenge. Alma drew first blood in the opening quarter on a fake field goal. Halfback-holder Roger Frayer passed to end John Fuzak, and the Scots led 6-0 after a missed extra point. On the next series, Hope marched 80 yards with Frank Lundell finally scoring on a one-yard plunge. The kick was not good, and the teams were tied at 6-6. Later in the half, Alma quarterback Gordon Hetrick scored on a six-yard right end sweep. This time Jeff Blough's kick was good, and the Scots led 13-6 at the half.

Neither team could manage a score in the third quarter, but early in the fourth Alma drove 80 yards with Chris Clark breaking loose for the final 10 yards and the TD. Blough's kick again found the mark and the scoreboard showed Alma 20, Hope 6. The Dutchmen were hardly finished. Taking the ball on their own 17, the offense drove 83 yards in nine plays. Frens went over from the one on a sneak, but the two-point try again failed and Hope trailed 20-12 with five minutes remaining. Determined defenders now stopped the Scots, and Hope gained possession on the Alma 38 after Alma's punt traveled only nine yards. Hope drove to the five and a first down. Two passes by Frens fell incomplete, but,

with 20 seconds left, a Frens-to-Abel pass reached paydirt as time expired. Now with the game in the balance, the Scot defense came through with the play of the game, swarming over Frens on a pass-run option well short of the goal. Hope led in all categories save the score, and the 20-18 defeat was a bitter one to swallow.

Hope had lost to the best team in the league by a mere two points, but close counts only in horseshoes and it was time to move on. Adrian would be Hope's homecoming opponent on Oct. 14, before a good crowd of 4,500. Coach Charles "Chappy" Marvin, now in his sixth season, relied heavily on a big defensive line. Adrian was experiencing a season much like Hope's, but this would not be the Bulldogs' day. They fumbled on their first offensive play, and Hope's Ken Feit recovered on the Adrian 10. Seven plays later, Frens passed four yards to Abel for the early score. The point try failed, but the 6-0 lead held up at halftime. Midway in the third period, Holman intercepted an Adrian pass to start a 53-yard Hope drive that ended with Abel going off-tackle from the one-foot line. The point attempt again failed, but Hope felt more comfortable with a 12-0 lead. Adrian's problem would be turnovers, with seven in all. Later in the half, Feit intercepted a Bulldog pass on the Hope 34, which led to Hope's third touchdown after a 13-play drive. This time it was Lundell crossing the goal line, on a one-yard plunge. The Dutchmen finally came through with an extra point when Pelon put one through the uprights to make it 19-0. With two minutes left in the game, Adrian got on the board when defensive end Dave Livingston intercepted a Clint Schilstra flat pass and rambled 35 yards for the touchdown. The kick was good, and the score took some of the sting out of Adrian's otherwise bad day, but Hope had played well and the homecoming crowd went home happy.

On Oct. 21, the Dutchmen ran into a buzz saw at Olivet. Coach Stu Parsell had one of his better teams, and would lose only to champion Alma. The Comets were off to a fast start, and Hope never recovered. Taking the opening kickoff, the home team drove 77 yards with quarterback Al Nagy going the final yard. Robert Jansen's kick was good to make it 7-0. Olivet scored again when Frens's pass was intercepted on the Hope 32. Fullback Bob Harple went in from the one, and Jansen again converted to make it 14-0. On their third possession, the Comets made it 21-0 when Nagy ran nine yards for his second touchdown and Jansen added his third conversion. The Hope offense finally came to life as Frens connected with a TD pass to Rumohr. The kick was good, and Hope was on the board at 21-7. The Comets, however, promptly marched 62 yards to score again, with Karl Wilson crossing the line. Jansen's fourth kick made it 28-7 at the half, and the Dutchmen were in deep trouble.

Midway in the third quarter, speedy Karl Wilson broke free and raced 75 yards to score. To break the monotony, Jansen ran for the two-point conversion, making it 36-7. In the closing minutes of the period, Frens passed to Pelon for

Hope's second score and the kick made it 36-14. In the fourth quarter, Nagy threw a touchdown pass to tight end Bob Devers, and automatic Jansen upped the score to 43-14. Gary Frens ran four yards for a third Hope TD and the conversion made it 43-21. In the closing minutes, Jansen capped his spectacular afternoon with a long field goal to make the final Olivet 46, Hope 21. Hope's defense had taken a beating as Olivet piled up a total of 453 yards. It was an impressive homecoming victory for Coach Parsell and his charges. The only bright spot for the Dutchmen was the performance of Gary Frens, who completed 13 passes for 120 yards and rushed for another 98.

It rained much of the following week, and the condition of much-used Riverview Park deteriorated. Holland High's varsity and reserve teams also rented the field, and by mid-season little if any turf remained between the 20-yard lines. The City of Holland did not wish to incur the expense of sodding the area during the summer months, and the seeding employed was soon torn up. By the time Kalamazoo arrived for the game on Oct. 28, much of the field was little more than a quagmire. Each team knew it would be important to score early, and the Hornets would be the more successful. In the closing minutes of the first quarter, Kalamazoo tackle Mike Wilson intercepted a Hope pass and returned it 54 yards to the Hope four. Two plays later, halfback John Keck scored on a four-yard run and Bob Lockwood kicked the point for the important 7-0 lead. In the second quarter, the Hornets' De Monte Johnson returned a Frens punt from his own 39 to the Hope 32. After a first down, halfback John Keck threw a 21-yard touchdown pass to end Lee Tichenor. With Bob Lockwood's extra point, it was 14-0.

On the next series, Hope drove 74 yards in 15 plays before Frens registered the first Dutchman score on a one-yard quarterback sneak. Pelon added the extra point to make it 14-7, and momentum seemed to have shifted. Hope mounted another drive, only to be stopped on the three-yard line just before the half. Intermittent rain continued in the second half, and the teams were soon slogging back and forth in four inches of mud. The game ceased to resemble football as neither team penetrated beyond the other's 30 for the remainder of the contest. Hope led in first downs 18-2, in rushing yardage 138 to 44, and in passing yards 99 to 28, but new coach Ed Baker was content to take the 14-7 victory back to Kalamazoo along with the traditional wooden shoes.

Hope's final MIAA match-up was scheduled for Riverview against Albion on Nov. 4. The rains abated somewhat during the week, and it was hoped that the game could be played in something approaching normal conditions. How-

KALAMAZOO 14 — HOPE 7
October 28, 1967

Hope's Steve Piersma contemplating his return to the game from a bale of straw. — Hope's white game pants were never the same.

In a game played with mud 4 inches deep, wide receiver Rich Frank (82) and guard Steve Piersma (62) found little sideline relief from the quagmire.

ever, by mid morning of the fourth, with the temperature hovering around freezing, the clouds opened and six inches of wet snow fell on the Riverview mud. After a careful inspection by the coaches and exhausting any other possibilities, it was my decision that the game should not be played. This would result in a cancellation, not a postponement. A recently enacted MIAA rule stated that once a visiting team had left home and completed a trip, the scheduled contest could not be replayed. The apparent purpose of the rule was to eliminate the expense involved in repeating a team trip, but it now worked a hardship on both teams. The game appeared to be playable until well after Coach Fraser's team had left Albion. The Britons arrived at the appointed hour only to be greeted with news of the cancellation. The officials, headed by Dom Tomasi of Flint and others from the Detroit area, who came from across the state were given their checks and sent home. No one was happy, and most of the flak landed on my doorstep. Nature had dealt us a cruel blow with unfortunate timing. I remain convinced that the decision was in the best interests of the players of both teams.

A let-down was unavoidable. The team's chance for redemption with a final league victory was now out the window. All that remained was an anti-climactic, non-league road game against a strong opponent. On Friday, Nov. 10, the team left on a two-day trek to Ashland, Ohio. Arrangements were made to stay at a south side Toledo motel with three players to a room. We would return to the same motel the next evening following the game.

Coach Fred Martinelli was enjoying the most successful season in Ashland College history with a 7-0-1 record. The 2 p.m. kickoff was under a gray November sky with threatening clouds. The Ashland field was in better shape than Riverview Park, but most of the game would be played in a driving rainstorm. Hope managed a scoreless first quarter, and the teams traded possession 10 times before Ashland scored. From that point, it was downhill Dutchmen. Frens's third punt of the game was blocked by Ashland end Lou Stephenson and recovered by Len Pettigrew on the Hope 12. Two plays later, quarterback Mike Healy scored on a seven-yard rollout around right end. The successful conversion made it 7-0. On another drive, the Eagles capped 61 yards with a 13-yard scoring pass from Healy to end Bill Seder to make it 14-0 at the half.

During the intermission, we received a phone call from Hope Chaplain Bill Hillegonds. Former player and now manager Alan Kinney had lost a gallant battle with cancer. Hope's depressed coaches elected not to share the information with the team, thinking especially of end Ray Cooper, who was Alan's roommate. Late in the third quarter, Ashland scored after a 94-yard march that featured two long runs. The scoring play was a 64-yard scamper by Jim Minnich to make it 20-0. Thirty-four seconds later, Frens was sacked and the ball jarred loose. Ashland recovered, and two plays later Healy again found Seder, this time with a

25-yard scoring strike, and the score mounted to 26-0. George Kraft recalls that as a "rookie" coach he had neglected to bring rain gear. He was soon soaked to the bone. In the fourth quarter, the rain changed to snow as the shivering Coach Kraft watched Ashland score its fifth touchdown, this one on a Healy-to-Dave Gray pass. The play covered 44 yards and increased the margin to 32-0. The Dutchmen completed a forgettable afternoon by fumbling on their own three-yard line with three minutes left in the game. Following the Ashland recovery, halfback Cliff Watson plunged one yard into the end zone. The kick was good to make the final score 39-0.

As we walked onto the field to congratulate Coach Martinelli, he had first to descend from the shoulders of his jubilant team members. They had just completed an 8-0-1 season and were justifiably proud. Martinelli was one of the good guys in coaching. I recall that his elation was tempered by visible concern for our well being. He had not tried to "pile it on", though his team enjoyed complete domination. Hope failed to register a first down in the opening half and got only three in the entire ball game. The Dutch were limited to 72 yards rushing, got only 13 in the air, and failed to advance beyond the 50-yard line.

There was more to come. The trip back to Toledo was understandably quiet as team members pondered the day's events and the bewildering issue of an athlete dying young. I found some solace in the character and reputation of our young men. Over time, I had received many compliments on the fine conduct of our teams both on and off the field. This badge of honor sustained us as coaches when scoreboards did not.

When we arrived at the motel in Toledo, I found the manager waiting for me and knew immediately that something was wrong. He escorted me to one of the rooms occupied by three of our players the night before. The room had been thoroughly trashed, broken lamps, furniture, and general chaos. Completely chagrined, I could only promise that full restitution would be made. In such humiliation it was difficult not to overreact. Obviously some "rough-house" had gotten out of hand. The contrite three agreed to pay for all damages, and the incident was closed. Hope's players, and certainly the coaches, had expected a kinder fate than the 1967 season produced, but forces, many beyond our control, had intervened to leave us with a negative ending.

On Friday, Nov. 17, Hope's fall sports teams met in Phelps Hall for the traditional season-ending banquet. Speaker for the evening was Taylor University football coach Bob Davenport. The former UCLA fullback had an inspirational message and was well received. Guard Mark Menning and linebacker Tom Pelon were named to the All-MIAA team. Gary Frens led the MIAA in total yardage, but was somehow overlooked in the balloting. Frens and Walter Reed were co-captains-elect for 1968. The evening's printed program included the following:

IN REMEMBRANCE
ALLAN CHARLES KINNEY

Faithful member of four Hope football teams.

Born: May 2, 1946
Died: Nov. 11, 1967

*   *   *

Basketball prospects were bright in 1967-68 for Hope's reigning co-champions. The principal reason for optimism, of course, was the return of senior co-captain Floyd Brady, the MIAA's most valuable player. Gary Rypma, the other co-captain, had proven to be a solid performer at guard, as had Bruce Van Huis in the front line. Hope's 24-game schedule opened at Valparaiso on Saturday, Dec. 2, and the going would be tough. Coach Gene Bartow had another strong team, and a fine crowd of 3,000 turned out to see the Crusaders perform. Hope had a surprisingly good first half, and led 30-29 at the intermission. Valpo, however, opened the second half with an 8-0 run and did not trail thereafter in registering a 79-61 victory. Bruce Linder was high for the winners with 19, Dick Jones followed with 15, Sheldon Ferguson had 13, and Tyrone Williams 12. However, in the opinion of most, the best player on the floor was Brady, who led Hope with 33 and pulled down 14 rebounds. Rypma scored 10, but the two obviously needed more help.

Hope's second outing took place on Wednesday, Dec. 6, against Aquinas. The free-scoring game was played at the West Catholic Gym in Grand Rapids with the Dutchmen leading 46-34 at halftime. The Tommies, however, made seven of their first eight shots in the second -half to make it 56-52. But in the end it would be a Hope night, with help coming from some unexpected quarters. The Hope leader was Brady with 34 points and 17 rebounds (hardly unexpected), but freshman Barry Schreiber was on fire with 21, Bruce Mc Creary scored 19, and Rypma had 18. Rypma's two free throws with 1:58 remaining put Hope over the century mark in the eventual 109-93 victory. For Red Dornbos's team it was Paul Jagels leading with 24, Denny Patterson scored 22, and John Chronowski had 16. Hope enjoyed a good night at the free throw line with 21 of 26.

The home opener on Saturday, Dec 9, featured Concordia Teachers College of River Forest, Ill. Coach Tom Faszholz brought in a team that sported a 3-0 record in the young season, and the contest would be nip and tuck to the very end. A near-capacity crowd of 2,200 made it to the Civic Center. Most had come to see if Floyd Brady could continue his sizzling start. They would not be disappointed. The Dutchmen gained a 42-38 halftime advantage, but the score would later be tied at 45-45, 47-47, and 57-57. Finally, on a basket by Dave Utzinger, Hope was up to stay at 60-59 with 9:28 remaining. Hope inched ahead and eventually prevailed 83 to 76. Floyd Brady's crowd-pleasing performance included 40 points, 18 rebounds, and 12 of 13 free throws. Rypma fouled out with 1:14 left, but not before scoring 19 points. Van Huis was also effective with 10 points and 17 rebounds. Neal Kaspar led the scrappy Cougars with 17, Kasten collected 16, and Dave Wild had 13.

Coach Russ De Vette registered his 200th win at Albion on Saturday, Dec.16. Hope led 37-31 at halftime, but the Britons battled back to a 53-53 tie with 11:46 left. There would be three more ties before a Rypma free throw put the Dutchmen up to stay, 60-59. Dean Dooley's zone was effective at times and Brady was held to six points in the first half, but he broke loose with 21 in the second half to lead his team with 27 in the 89-75 victory. Mc Creary was hot with 24, Rypma had 18, and Schreiber 10. Briton center Neil Warriner led the Britons with 18, while Ed Stephens had 17 and Mike Wilson 13.

The Dutchmen played host to the Spartans of Manchester on Dec. 18. The rare Monday night game drew a crowd of 2,000 fans, all wondering how Hope might fare against another Indiana team. Manchester enjoyed a hot first half, shooting 57 percent and going to the locker room with a 47-41 lead. In the all-important first five minutes of the second half, Hope went on a 9-0 run and was never headed. The Dutchmen controlled the boards 63 to 38, and enjoyed balanced scoring. This combination produced an impressive 95-76 victory. Brady led the way for Hope with 24 points and 21 rebounds, while Van Huis had his best game to date with 17 points and 16 boards. Rypma and Mc Creary scored 15 each, and Schreiber was close behind with 14. High man for the Spartans was NAIA All-American Dick Harris with 21. Jerry Walther followed with 14, and Phil Weybright had 12.

During the Christmas break, the Hope team flew to Schenectady, N.Y., to participate in the Union College Round Robin Tournament. Other participants were Union, Lehigh University of Bethlehem, Pa., and the Massachusetts Institute of Technology (MIT) of Cambridge, Mass. Both Lehigh and MIT had "Engineers" as their nickname, while the Union team was known as the Dutchmen. The two "Dutchmen" teams met on Thursday, Dec. 28, and Hope encountered little trouble in posting a 70-58 win after leading 37-27 at the half. Hope's 67-44 domination of the boards was a major factor. Brady led Hope with 26, Mc Creary had 15, Rypma 11, and Van Huis 10. Craig Carlson was high for Union with 12, and Fitz Turner had eight.

The next night, Hope ran into a tough Lehigh man-to-man defense and trailed 37-33 at the half. Bob Lowman with 28 and Don Forrester with 22 led the Engineers to the 71-48 victory over Hope, but Bob Mallinson did considerable damage by holding Floyd Brady to 15 points and only two in the second half. Hope went completely cold in the second half, scoring only six field goals and three free throws. Rypma followed Brady in scoring with 10, and Van Huis had eight.

With a bad game out of the their system, the Dutchmen came back with a solid performance on Saturday night against MIT. A close first half saw MIT take a 29-28 lead at the intermission, but the Dutchmen tied it at 32-32, then built a 12-point lead and moved on to a 68-60 victory. The Hope leader was Brady with 21, Mc Creary had 17, Rypma 13, Van Huis nine, and Tom Pelon eight. Dave Jansson led Coach John Barry's club with 26 and was named the tournament's MVP. Bruce Wheeler scored 13, and Lee Kammerdiner had 13. The trip to the East proved a rewarding experience, and two wins out of three was not bad.

Hope's first game in 1968 was played at Lake Forest on Saturday, Jan. 6. After an 11-point halftime lead (39-28) the Dutchmen would put 10 of their players in the scoring column, but the big news in Hope's 93-70 victory was again Brady. Brady's lay-up with 2:51 left gave him 44 points for the evening and broke the single-game scoring mark of 43 set by Jim Vander Hill against Taylor in January of 1962. Just for good measure, Brady also pulled down 22 rebounds. Rypma and Schreiber each had 10 points, and Pelon eight. With a decided height advantage, Hope out-rebounded the Foresters 84 to 55. Fred Broda had a fine game for Coach Dick Triptow with 29 points, while Mike Hogan and Andy Russo each scored 10.

The first-round Hope-Calvin game was played in the Civic Center on Saturday, Jan. 13. A standing-room-only crowd of 2,700 witnessed the usual fare of tension and excitement. The teams left the floor at halftime with the score standing at 43-43. Brady had been limited to 10 points. The Knights, however, were unable to contain Brady in the second half as he broke loose with 33 more counters for a game-high 43. A three-point play by Gary Rypma put the Dutchmen up 56-53 and they would not trail again. A basket by Calvin's Dean Douma narrowed the lead to 82-80, but successive field goals by Brady widened the gap to 92-82 with 2:23 left. The Dutchmen then held on for the final count of 95-90. A huge plus for the Dutchmen was the rebounding of Bruce Van Huis, who pulled down a career-high 28. Hope won the overall rebound battle 58-45. Free throws were about even, with Calvin getting 18-of-21 and Hope 19-of-32. From the floor, it was Calvin shooting 47 percent to Hope's 43 percent. Individual scoring showed Brady with 43, Rypma with 25, and Van Huis with 13. For Don Vroon's Knights, it was Wes De Mots with 20, Mike (Mickey) Phelps with 19, Dean Douma with 15, and Ed Wiers with 13.

The Dutchmen traveled to Alma on Wednesday, Jan. 17, to meet a charged-up team under new coach Bill Klenk. The Hope team suffered a serious blow when it was learned that starting guard Mc Creary had left the team for personal reasons. He would be replaced by Dave Utzinger. Despite scrappy play by the Scots, Hope held a 39-29 advantage at the half. The Alma strategy was to play rough on Brady in an attempt to limit his point potential. As a result, Brady was at the line 24 times and cashed in on 19 charities to break the Hope single-game mark of 14 set by Glenn Van Wieren four years earlier, also against Alma. The Scots edged the Dutchmen in field goals 32-30, but Brady free throws made the difference in Hope's eventual 88-74 victory. Brady led all scorers with 37 points, Rypma had 21, and Van Huis 17. Gordon Hetrick paced Alma with 17, Drake Serges added 14, and John Fuzak had 11.

At Adrian on Saturday, Jan. 20, the Hope coaches were somewhat surprised to learn that 29-year-old Vince Giles would be in the lineup. Giles, the 1961 MIAA MVP, had spent some time in the Army, but now had returned to Adrian. A full house at Ridge Gymnasium was quieted when the Dutchmen took charge of the boards and moved to a 44-29 halftime lead. Hope's 55-40 bulge in rebounds plus the "Brady factor" proved too much for the Bulldogs. The largest Hope lead was 51-31 with 17:18 remaining. Adrian narrowed the margin somewhat, but in the end it was Hope 76-64. Brady enjoyed another productive night to lead the Dutchmen with 40 points. Rypma and Van Huis each scored 10, and Pelon had eight. Vince Giles showed that he had not lost the touch as he led the losers with 22. Al Werbish and Paul Martini each had 10 for Coach Arbaugh.

The College of Wooster visited the Civic Center on Saturday, Jan. 27. Both teams came in with 10-2 records, and a good game was expected. It was 40-38 Wooster at the half, and the contest continued to be nip-and-tuck throughout the remainder of the game. The count was 70-70 with 3:30 left when the Scots came through with three straight field goals and did not surrender the lead. Freshman guard Tom Dinger led Al Van Wie's team to a 79-74 victory with 26 points. He was followed by Tom Beeching with 17, Rich Thompson 16, and, Mike Beitzel with 12. For Hope it was Brady with 29, Rypma scored 18, Van Huis 17, and Pelon 10.

Hope's woes at Kalamazoo's Treadway Gym continued on Wednesday, Jan. 31. Coach Ray Steffen's team built an early 22-10 lead and led 39-26 at halftime, largely on seven-of-eight shooting by Bryan Vossekuil. The Hornets' zone defense was effective in denying Brady shooting opportunities in the opening half. The closest that the Dutchmen could come was 57-51 with 6:43 left. Kalamazoo led in shooting percentage, 46-37 percent, and in rebounds 42-41 enroute to the 77-62 win. Vossekuil was high for Kazoo with 26, Gene Nusbaum had 20, and Bob Trenary 17. Brady with 28 and sub Randy Adolphs with 12 were the only Hope players in double figures.

Lake Forest College paid a return visit to Hope on Saturday, Feb. 3. A crowd of 2,000 turned out for the non-league contest, anticipating that Floyd Brady would break Paul Benes's career-scoring mark of 1,741 established from 1955 through 1959. Coach De Vette was not oblivious to individual records, but was much more concerned with team play and putting a stop to the current two-game losing skid. President Vander Werf was on-hand and informed us that

HOPE 100 — LAKE FOREST 63
Feburary 3, 1968

Right handed Floyd Brady breaks the Hope College 4-year scoring record with this left hand hook shot against Lake Forest.

when the record was broken, he wanted the game halted in order that the game ball might be presented to Brady. Coach De Vette and I argued that in deference to Lake Forest and Coach Triptow, it would be more appropriate to make the presentation at the game's conclusion and thus not interrupt the flow of play. The president, however, was adamant in his position. Rank has its privileges and the officials were informed to stop the game whenever the record-breaker parted the nets. Sports Information Director Tom Renner, camera in hand, stalked the sidelines. He was eminently successful. With 13:14 remaining in the first half, right-handed Floyd Brady lofted a left-handed hook shot to break the record and Renner's photo was perfectly timed. Game action was stopped and players on both teams cooled their heels while the ceremony took place and a somewhat embarrassed Brady accepted the ball.

Lake Forest proceeded to tie the game at 33-33 with 4:46 left in the half, but the Dutchmen regained their composure and built a 49-37 lead at the intermission. A 10-2 Hope run to open the second half made it 59-39, and the regulars were on the bench for the final quarter. With eight seconds left, a corner shot by John Leenhouts made the final, 100-63. Brady, ignoring the hullabaloo, had 32 points

BASKETBALL MILESTONE

Floyd Brady was presented the game ball in recognition of his fete.

and 19 rebounds before retiring to the bench. Van Huis followed with 17 and Rypma scored 14. Adolphs, Ted Zwart, and Bill Bekkering each dropped in eight. Sophomore Mike Maiman led the Foresters with 14, freshman Al Shethar had 11, and Fred Broda 10. Coach Triptow, one of the game's true gentlemen, exercised great restraint in offering his congratulations.

First-year coach Gary Morrison brought the Olivet Comets to the Civic Center on Wednesday, Feb. 7, to play before a mid-week crowd of 1,900. Morrison, the former Kalamazoo College standout, this night opted for slow-down tactics. As a result, neither team could mount more than a two-point lead and the halftime score stood at 20-20. Shortly after the intermission, Floyd Brady stole the ball and threw a long pass to Van Huis alone under the basket. The lay-up made it 26-24, and the Dutchmen managed to stay on top of the rest of the way. Hope's biggest lead was 54-43 with 3:15 remaining. Five Hope players had four fouls before the contest was over, but none fouled out. Brady led his team to a hard-fought 59-54 victory with 27 points, Rypma tallied 19, and Bekkering, starting for the first time, scored six. Center Gordon Lofts, who also starred in football and track, was the Comet leader with 20. Max Lindsay followed with 10, and Benny Benford had eight.

On Saturday, Feb. 10, again at the Civic, Hope had an 11-0 lead before the Albion Britons got untracked, then increased the margin to 46-31 at the half. The Britons shot 44 percent for the evening compared to 36 percent for the Dutchmen, but Hope's 78-32 domination of the boards gave them many more opportunities as they cruised to an 84-68 win. Hope's big three were Brady with 25, Rypma 19, and Van Huis 17. For the Britons it was sophomore Mike Wilson leading the way with 25, Ed Stephens had 16, and Macy added nine.

The Adrian Bulldogs ran into a hot-shooting Hope team in the Civic on Valentine's Day. The Dutch hit 56 percent overall and led 45-37 at the half. There was some concern when Floyd Brady picked up his third foul with 2:39 left in the first half, but the senior stayed out of trouble the rest of the way. Adrian got within four on three different occasions in the second half, but Hope's 54-37 control of the boards and Brady's 36 points made the difference. Adolph's corner jump shot with 1:37 left put Hope over the century mark enroute to the 105-82 victory. Van Huis put on a superb performance with 22 points and 21 rebounds. Rypma also scored 22. For Gregg Arbaugh's crew, it was Kim Rank with 18, John Cosnek and Al Werbish with 16 each, and Vince Giles with 10.

The rematch with Calvin was an afternoon contest at Knollcrest on Saturday, Feb. 17. The Knights had taken a few lumps along the way, but Coach Don Vroon had them ready for Hope plus a crowd of 4,500 to cheer them on. With deadly outcourt shooting, it would be a Calvin afternoon. The Knights took a 47-39 lead to the locker room at halftime and were never headed. Mike Phelps was the Calvin leader with 30 points, mostly from outcourt, and Tom Dykema, starting in place of the injured Dean Douma, had a super game with 23 points. Wes De Mots put in 19, and Jim Kos had 12 in Calvin's 94-79 victory. Captains Brady and Rypma had 27 and 18 points for Hope, while Barry Schreiber added 11 and Bruce Van Huis had 10. Hope had 41 rebounds to 37 for Calvin, but the Knights' accuracy from the floor prevented the Dutchmen from catching up.

Bill Klenk's Alma Scots were at the Civic Center on Wednesday, Feb. 21, only to be caught up in another Brady special. By halftime, Floyd had scored 28 points and the Dutchmen were on top 56-43. Ever the competitor, Coach Klenk employed an effective press in the first minutes of the second half, and narrowed the gap to 62-60 with 15:32 remaining. But Hope's mastery of the boards pushed the Dutchmen again into a sizeable lead and attention focused on Brady. Fans were aware that he was nearing the MIAA four-year scoring mark set by Henry Hughes in 1953-57. With 1:41 left in the game, Brady sank a left-hand hook off the glass to give him 1,117 MIAA points, one above the Hughes total. A standing ovation ensued, and the Dutchmen moved on to a 98-81 victory. Brady's record night netted a total of 40 points and somewhat overshadowed a fine performance by Van Huis, who scored 26. Rypma was also effective with 15. Gordon Hetrick was high for the Scots with 18, Drake Serges had 17 and Al Vander Meer 15.

With an undisputed championship on the line, Hope hosted old nemesis Kalamazoo on Saturday, Feb. 24. The Dutchmen were still smarting from a 77-62 defeat in Treadway Gym on Jan. 31. Hope had not played well, while Ray Steffen had gotten a super performance from his crew. A

HOPE 62 — KALAMAZOO 60 (OT)
February 24, 1968.

Floyd Brady "does the honors" following Hope's wrap-up of the 1967-68 MIAA Championship.

crowd of 2,600 would now aid the hoped-for homecourt advantage. The first half was played on even terms, with Hope clinging to a 30-27 advantage at the intermission. The determined Hornets would not go away, and moved into a 55-51 lead with 2:34 left in the game. Kazoo scored again, but Hope's Utzinger came through with two clutch field goals to keep his team within two at 57-55. On Hope's next possession, Floyd Brady scored a baseline lay-up to tie the game at 57-57, but he was charged with his fifth foul on the play and was out of the game. With 28 seconds showing on the clock, Bob Trenary made the first free throw to put his team up 58-57. Trenary missed the second try and Utzinger took the rebound. Hope worked the ball for 15 seconds, then Schreiber drove for the basket and was fouled. Schreiber swished the first free throw to tie it up at 58-58. The second attempt missed, but in the melee for the rebound Hope's Tom Pelon was fouled. The free throw was missed, and the Hornets had the ball with eight seconds left. Bob Trenary's shot at the buzzer failed, and it was overtime.

Hope never trailed in the overtime, but the contest was not decided until the final seconds. The Dutchmen took a 61-58 lead on a Schreiber free throw plus a field goal by Rypma. With 1:15 remaining, Kazoo made it 61-60 on Ralph Wellington's shot from the corner. An errant Hope pass then gave the Hornets two more shots. Both were missed, and Rypma secured the rebound. He was immediately fouled and made the second to make Hope's lead 62-60. Kalamazoo failed to get off a shot in the final eight seconds against Hope's zone, and the De Vette men were finally undisputed MIAA champions. Brady's 25 points carried his team, but Schreiber, Rypma, and Utzinger with 10, nine, and seven points were tenacious when Brady was no longer on the floor. Bob Trenary and Tim Williams each scored 13 for Coach Steffen, and Gene Nusbaum had 10.

When the Wheaton Crusaders came to the Civic on Wednesday, Feb. 28, there was some indication that the Dutchmen might have left it all on the floor in the Kalamazoo encounter. Coach Lee Pfund's red-hot shooters scored 62 points in the first half alone, while Hope could muster only 44. The count was 84-61 with eight minutes remaining. The Dutchmen mounted a comeback, but it fell short and the Crusaders went back to Chicago with a 99-90 victory. Senior John Jauchen was impressive with 38 points and 24 rebounds. He was followed by Grand Rapids guards Tom Dykstra with 21 and John Pierucki with 17. Brady's 31 points topped the Hope effort, while Rypma scored 22 and Van Huis had 10.

The season finale was played at the Mc Kay Gymnasium in Olivet on Saturday, March 2. The champion Dutchmen were determined to overcome the hardships of playing in "the pit" and end on a positive note. After leading 45-40 at the half, Hope increased the margin to 68-58, then suddenly went cold and failed to score a field goal for the next seven minutes. Finally, with 4:37 left and the score tied at 78-78, a jumper by Randy Adolphs plus a tip-in by Van Huis put the Dutchmen up 82-78. A basket by Bill Dawson narrowed it to 82-80, but field goals by Brady and Rypma made it 86-80 with one minute to play. Hope closed its season with the 89-82 victory. Co-captains Brady and Rypma ended in grand fashion as each scored 28 points to lead the Dutchmen, while Bruce Van Huis was also hot with 18. Brady's 28 gave him a career total of 2,004. For Olivet, it was Gordon Lofts with a super effort including 24 points and 26 rebounds. Also in the losing cause, Jerry Alloco scored 18 and Bill Dawson 15. Olivet's 51-40 edge in rebounds was due largely to the presence of Lofts. Hope's season ended at 17-6 overall and 10-2 in the MIAA.

The 1967-68 All-MIAA team included Floyd Brady of Hope, Vince Giles of Adrian, Gordon Lofts of Olivet, Gordon Hetrick of Alma, and Mike Wilson of Albion. Hope's winter sports banquet was held on Monday, March 11, with Barry Werkman as master of ceremonies. Rev. Walter De Velder offered the invocation. De Velder was one of Hope's top athletes of the 20s and held the javelin record for many years. Speaker for the evening was Larry Glass, varsity basketball coach at Northwestern University. Randall Bosch was on-hand to present the MIAA most valuable player award to Floyd Brady, who had captured the honor for the second year in a row. In a team vote, Bruce Van Huis and John Leenhouts were named co-captains for the 1968-69 season.

* * *

THE 1967-68 HOPE BASKETBALL TEAM MIAA CHAMPIONS
17-6 overall — 10-2 MIAA

Seated L. to R.: Dave Utzinger, Co-Captain Gary Rypma, Co-Captain Floyd Brady, Bruce Van Huis, Barry Schreiber. **Standing:** Manager Tom Hammersma, Assistant Coach Bill Vanderbilt, Randy Adolphs, John Leenhouts, Ted Zwart, Bill Bekkering, Tom Pelon, Head Coach Russ De Vette.

Nine basketball championships in the space of 11 years was no mean feat for Coach De Vette and his players. For some days, the campus basked vicariously in this signal achievement. Then it was time to move on. As teams practiced for spring sports and prepared to head south, a shot rang out in Memphis. On Thursday, April 4, Martin Luther King Jr. was gunned down by an assassin. King's premonition of death in a recent speech had gone largely unnoticed, and the shocked nation found itself in turmoil. Many felt that bigotry had taken its final step, and that racial warfare might ensue. Confusion reigned across Hope's campus as students groped for some meaningful response to the tragedy.

With encouragement from faculty and administration, student leaders eventually decided that pent-up feelings might best be allayed by a silent and solemn march, a practice employed so often by King himself. Accordingly, on the morning of April 5, about 1,000 students assembled on College Avenue in front of Graves Hall. The group proceeded north to Eighth Street, then west to Central Avenue, and south to Centennial Park.

President Vander Werf addressed the assemblage with appropriate remarks, as did Herman Ridder, president of Western Seminary. Then, at the request of Dr. Vander Werf, senior Floyd Brady was introduced. From a mound near the fountain, Brady spoke to the gathering in his deliberate and subdued manner. A text of his message is not available, but his remarks, devoid of rage or rancor, had an overall effect of reassurance. Called upon one more time in a tough situation, he had delivered far more than a basket.

* * *

When Dean William Hilmert was unable to continue as Hope's golf coach in 1968, Dr. Robert Brown of the psychology department stepped into the breach. Team members were captain George Cook, Dennis Bobeldyk, Tim Jalving, Charles Mc Mullin, Fred Muller, and Willie Jackson. Professor Brown was a golf addict of the first order, and soon arranged Hope's first-ever spring trip. Between April 8 and 13, the team participated in various tourneys in the state of Kentucky and scored at least one victory, a 6-0 decision over High Point, N.C.

The going was tough in the regular season, but the Dutchmen managed a 15-0 shutout of Adrian, a 13½ -1½ win over Olivet, a 12½-2½ decision over Bethel, and a 5-4 victory over Eastern Michigan. Hope's 2-4 record in the MIAA landed the Dutchmen in sixth place for the season. Losses came at the hands of Grand Rapids Junior College, Kalamazoo, Albion, Alma, Aquinas, and Calvin, the latter an 8-7 squeaker.

* * *

Glenn Van Wieren's baseball team, reigning champion in the MIAA, was off to a good start with a 5-2 victory at Goshen College on Friday, April 5. Don Kroodsma, Mark Johnson, and Gary Frens shared pitching duties, giving up but four hits while striking out 18. Dan Krueger was the hitting star, with three safeties. The team then proceeded to Panama City, Fla. On Monday, April 8, it was Gulf Coast Junior College 9, Hope 1, but the Dutchmen came back the next day to down the Pensacola Naval Air Station by a 10-7 count as Harry Rumohr collected three hits. A Wednesday game with Bradley University was rained out, but on Thursday, April 11, Hope used the long ball to defeat Troy State of Alabama by an 8-6 score. Don Kroodsma slammed a three-run homer, and Bob Kidd had a solo shot. Frens was the winner in relief. On Saturday, April 13, it was Georgia Southwestern 4, Hope 1, and on Monday, April 15, at Valparaiso the Crusaders held Hope to three hits while collecting 10 to beat the Dutchmen by a 5-1 score.

A 3-3 spring trip record was not bad for a team with limited practice, and Coach Van Wieren hoped to pick up where the team had left off the previous spring. The MIAA season opened at Kalamazoo on Monday, April 22, with two excellent games. Hope scored two runs in the first, then hung on as Kroodsma pitched a masterful two-hit, 2-1 victory. Only two balls were hit out of the infield by the Hornets. In the second game, Frens scattered five hits enroute to a 1-0 shutout. Hope's run came on a Dave Abel triple followed by Nels Bergmark's single.

Hope hosted Central Michigan on Wednesday, April 24, a cold and rainy day. Dennis Keith and Dick Nordstrom shared pitching chores in the opener. Central scored four runs in the sixth, and went on to down the Dutchmen 6-1. Johnson went the route for Hope in the second game, giving up five hits and three walks while striking out nine. Hope also had five hits, including Tom Pelon's solo homer, which gave Hope the 2-1 victory.

Aquinas was at Hope on Friday, April 26, for a single non-league game. Kroodsma, Dennis Keith, and Frens scattered five hits as Hope registered a 4-1 win. Bob Kidd had three runs batted in, and Rumohr stroked a sixth inning home run. The Dutchmen were now 7-4 on the young season and 2-0 in the MIAA. There was every reason to be upbeat, but at this point Hope's fortunes plummeted.

Tough times began when the Calvin Knights visited Hope on Wednesday, May 1. In the first game, Kroodsma gave up six hits and walked two, but his effort was overshadowed by Calvin's Bruce Bode, who gave Hope only three base runners and struck out 10. The Knights got one run in the second, then two more in the third on a wind-aided home run to right field. This was enough for a 3-1 victory. Hope's run came in the fifth, when Kidd tripled and came home on a wild pitch. The second game was a classic pitchers' battle. Paul Milkamp and Frens each allowed but, two hits, but with two outs in the third, Calvin's Jim Kett

**Centennial Park, Holland, Michigan
April 5, 1968**
Floyd Brady (far left) speaks to students and faculty following the assassination of Martin Luther King Jr.

walked, then came home on Jim Tuinstra's double to center field. This was the only run of the game, as Hope left eight men on base. The 1-0 loss was hard to take, but one-run games would continue to be the order of the day.

Hope ran into more hard luck at Adrian on Saturday, May 4. The Dutchmen were off to a strong start when back-to-back doubles by Steve Piersma and Rumohr produced a run, but the Bulldogs came back with single runs in the fourth and sixth to take the 2-1 victory. The Dutch were further frustrated when the rains came in the sixth inning of the second game with the score at 0-0. The game was called and would not be replayed.

It was more of the same when Alma invaded Holland on Thursday, May 9. In the first game, the Scots pushed across single runs in the second, fifth, and seventh innings. Hope narrowed the gap to one run on Rumohr's two-run homer, but pitcher Gordon Hetrick held on for the 3-2 win. The nightcap was an eight-inning heartbreaker for pitcher Frens, who gave three hits, walked two, and struck out 14. Alma scored one run in the first and Hope tied it in the fifth. Jim Tate scored both of Alma's runs, the second on John Fuzak's game-winning single in the eighth. With the 3-2 and 2-1 losses, the Dutchmen were struggling.

Hope ended the skid at home on Saturday, May 11, against Olivet. In the first game, the Comets' Barry Jackson nicked Johnson for a two-run homer in the first, but the lefty would be tough the rest of the way. Johnson would strike out 10 in the 7-2 victory. A big blow for Hope was a two-run double by Kidd in the third. Hope had three runs in the sixth off losing pitcher Jim Fish. Kroodsma and Frens teamed up for a 4-2 victory in the second game. Hope had only four hits off Barry Jackson, but one was a bases-loaded triple by Kidd in the third.

The Dutchmen closed out a frustrating season at Albion on Wednesday, May 15. Coach Morley Fraser nailed down his fourth MIAA championship with an 8-0 shutout in the first game. Kroodsma went the route in the second game, giving up six hits and two runs, but had to settle for a 2-2 tie as the game was called in the fourth inning due to darkness. It seemed to typify Hope's 9-10-2 overall record. The Dutch ended 4-6-2 in the MIAA for a sixth-place finish. Six league games had been decided by one run. Another sore spot was the fact that despite some outstanding performances, no Hope player made the All-MIAA team.

* * *

Doc Green's Hope tennis teams had become perennial second-place finishers in the MIAA. Considering the "Kalamazoo factor," this could be considered tantamount to a championship. They would repeat in 1968, and the veteran mentor would again have the privilege of coaching his son Jeff. The spring trip provided the usual stiff competition, but the Dutchmen were able to emerge with a 4-4 record. On Saturday, April 6, it was Hope 5, Eastern Michigan University 4. As the team moved into the south, it was Hope 6, High Point, N.C. 0 in a rain-abbreviated match. On Tuesday, April 9, North Carolina State took the Dutchmen by a 7-2 score, and the next day it was Duke 7, Hope 2, but in the latter contest Hope's Doug Barrow defeated Duke's Chuck Saacke 5-7, 6-3, 6-4 in number-one singles. The Barrow-Ron Visscher doubles team was also victorious. Later in the day, it was Wake Forest 8, Hope 1 as Barrow and Visscher again did the honors for Hope. Davidson downed the Dutchmen 8-1 on Friday, April 12, with Ron Visscher winning at number-two singles. Hope bounced back with a 6-3 victory over Pfeiffer College on Saturday, April 13, then stopped in Muncie, Ind., on the way home to edge Ball State. The Dutchmen won five of the six singles matches to take the 5-4 match.

In MIAA play, Hope disposed of the "misery" early, then went on to better things. On Monday, April 22, the Dutchmen traveled to Kalamazoo to absorb much of the usual fare. In singles, John Trump defeated Barrow 5-7, 6-3, 6-1, and John Brummet defeated Visscher 6-2, 6-4, but Don Kronemeyer had rejoined Doc Green's squad and took the measure of George Scott 6-2, 6-3. It was Kalamazoo the rest of the way with Bill Struck over Craig Holleman 6-2, 6-0, Rick Watson defeated Jack Van Wieren 6-1, 6-0, and Dave Tidwell defeated Jim Fortney 6-0, 6-2. In doubles, it was Trump-Brummet over Barrow-Visscher 6-4, 10-8, Struck-Bert Bothell over Holleman-Jeff Green 6-2, 6-1, and Watson-Don Swarthout over Kronemeyer-Fortney 6-0, 6-2 for the 8-1 Kalamazoo win.

The keen competition in Hope's home match with Calvin on Wednesday, May 1, resulted in five three-setters. In singles, it was Barrow over Ben Pekelder 6-2, 4-6, 6-4, Visscher defeated Jim Bolt 6-0, 6-3, John Lappenga defeated Kronemeyer 1-6, 6-4, 6-4, Holleman took Don Klop 1-6, 6-4, 6-1, Mark Van Faasen defeated Van Wieren 6-2, 4-6, 6-2, and Dave Post defeated Fortney 7-5, 9-7. In doubles, Barrow-Visscher defeated Pekelder-Van Faasen 6-3, 6-1, Kronemeyer-Safar won over Klop-Bolt 6-8, 6-4, 7-5, and Fortney-Green defeated Lappenga-Post 6-4, 7-5 to give Hope the 6-3 victory.

The Dutchmen were impressive at Adrian with an 8-1 victory on Saturday, May 4. In singles, Barrow defeated Rick Meyer 6-2, 6-0, Visscher defeated Stan Ling 6-0, 6-0, Kronemeyer defeated Chuck Chase 6-1, 6-0, Holleman took Bill Chase 6-1, 6-2, Fortney defeated Steve Tabb 8-6, 6-1, and Safar defeated Paul Swan 6-2, 6-4. In doubles, it was Barrow-Visscher over Meyer-Swan 6-0, 6-2, Kronemeyer-Holleman over C. Chase-B. Chase 6-3, 6-1, and Tabb-Campbell over Fortney-Green 6-2, 1-6, 7-5.

Hope stepped out of MIAA play on Monday, May 6, to host Central Michigan University. Doc Green's crew was again successful, this time by a 7-2 score. In singles play, Barrow defeated Bill Johnston 6-1, 6-0, Visscher defeated Dan Travis 6-3, 6-1, Jerry Kennedy defeated Kronemeyer by forfeit, Holleman defeated Chuck Reed 6-2, 6-2, Safar defeated Wit Tryjo 4-6, 6-1, 6-4, and Fortney defeated Lee O'Bryan 6-2, 6-3. In doubles, Barrow-Visscher defeated Travis-Kennedy 6-2, 6-1, Johnston-Tryjo defeated Fortney-Green 6-3, 6-4, and Holleman-Safar defeated Reed-O'Bryan 6-3, 1-6, 6-1.

The Dutchmen recorded their only shutout of the season when Olivet came to Holland on Saturday, May 11. The 9-0 win included singles victories by Barrow over Dick Gary 6-0, 6-0, Visscher over Tom Kolassa 6-0, 6-1, Kronemeyer over Marty Pierce 6-0, 6-0, Safar over Zame Kolestock 6-0, 6-1, Fortney over Dennis Ferrand 6-0, 6-0, and Travis Kraai over John Westle 6-1. In doubles, it was Barrow-Visscher over Kolassa-Kolestock 6-0, 6-0, Kronemeyer-Safar over Gary-Pierce 6-2, 6-0, and Fortney-Green over Ferrand-Westle 6-2, 6-1.

At Albion on Wednesday, May 15, the Dutchmen suddenly had their hands full. In singles, Barrow defeated Jack Jones 6-1, 7-5, and Visscher defeated Dave Brown 6-1, 6-1, but Albion's Don Gruhl defeated Kronemeyer 1-6, 6-4, 6-3, Bryan Kiehl defeated Safar 3-6, 6-4, 6-1, Ken Hall defeated Fortney 2-6, 7-5, 6-3, and Joe Reed took Kraai 8-6, 6-2. Trailing 4-2 in team points, the Dutchmen were under pressure to do the job in doubles. Barrow and Visscher came through by defeating Jones-Brown 6-2, 6-4, then it was Kronemeyer-Safar over Reed-Ron Isaac (son of AD Elkin Isaac) 6-4, 2-6, 7-5, and Fortney-Green defeated Gruhl-Kiehl 6-2, 8-6 to squeeze out the 5-4 team victory.

The MIAA meet was held at Albion on May 17-18 with Kalamazoo taking first in all nine events. Team points and places were as follows: Kalamazoo 27, Hope 14, Calvin 10, Albion 6, Alma 4, Adrian 2, and Olivet 0. Once again, no team could mount even a mild threat to the Kalamazoo dynasty, but Hope's solid second provided a measure of satisfaction. John Trump of Kalamazoo was recipient of the Allen B. Stowe Sportsmanship Award.

*   *   *

The track team captains for Hope in 1968 were dashmen Ray Cooper and Walt Reed, and half-miler Steve Reynen. The tri-captain approach was a first for Hope College track, and the trio's leadership would make the season a memorable one. In early and mid-March, Hope had token entries in indoor meets at North Central of Illinois and at Western Michigan University. Results were modest, but there were indications that the team would have good balance, plus some outstanding performers. This was confirmed in Hope's first outdoor meet, the Wabash Relays in Crawfordsville, Ind., on Saturday, April 13. Wabash Coach Owen Huntsman had arranged a genuine "fun" meet, where all events were relays and no team scores were kept. Field event teams included three men, while the usual four-man teams competed in the running events. Hope fared well, taking first in the javelin with Nate Bowles, Kent Candelora, and Doug Nichols, and also first in the mile relay with a team of Reed, Ralph Schroeder, Bruce Geelhoed, and Cooper. The Dutchmen also placed second in the 440-yard relay, the sprint medley, and the distance medley. A third in the intermediate hurdle relay left the members of the Hope squad feeling good about their venture into Hoosier land.

On Wednesday, April 17, the team journeyed to Houseman Field in Grand Rapids for a triangular with Grand Rapids Junior College and Olivet. On a cold and rainy afternoon, the Dutchmen won 12 of the 16 events with a team score of 97½-37 against Olivet and 35½ for the usually strong JC team.

Continued bad weather forced postponement of Hope's opening MIAA dual meet from Saturday to Monday, April 22. Kalamazoo football coach Ed Baker was also handling track for the visiting Hornets, and had not yet had time to assemble a representative team. The result was a 118-27 Hope victory, with the Dutchmen sweeping seven events. Rick Bruggers set a Hope record in winning the mile run in a time of 4:18.2. Cooper was a winner in both dashes and both relays, while Floyd Brady won the high jump at 6' 4".

The second of five home track meets for Hope was the hosting of the fourth annual Great Lakes Colleges Association Meet on Saturday, April 27. Competition was tough in the 10-team field, but Hope managed a fourth-place finish with 38 points. Earlham and Ohio Wesleyan battled down to the wire for the championship, with the latter pulling it out by 1/2 point, 52-52½. Dave Thomas captured Hope's only first with a victory in the 440 intermediate hurdles. His time of 55.5 was a Hope record. Wabash was a strong third with 50 points, followed by Oberlin 26, Denison 24, De Pauw 13½, Wooster eight, Albion, and Kenyon 0.

Hope traveled to Calvin on Wednesday, May 1, for the most important dual of the season. The Dutchmen would be without the services of vaulters Ken Feit and Bill Bekkering, and also hurdler Jeff Hollenbach, but the meet would have all the ingredients of a classic dual encounter. The Knights of Coach Dave Tuuk were off to an early lead in the field events as superstar Rudy Vlaardingerbroek took the shot put, javelin, and discus. His javelin throw of 203' 5" was especially impressive. Walt Kooyer, in the absence of Feit and Bekkering, captured the pole vault at 13". Kooyer would later have an impressive tenure as track coach at Holland High School. Brady won the high jump and long jump. His mark of 23' 1" in the latter event was the best since John Kleinheksel's 23' 6½" in 1958. John Tysse kept Hope in the running by winning the triple jump.

Performers on both teams continued with maximum efforts, but Calvin continued to lead. Dashman Cooper was at his best in taking the 100 and 220 in 9.8 and 21.9. Both were Hope records, as was Hope's 43.1 time in winning the 440-yard relay. Victories by Bruggers in the mile and two-mile, plus seconds by Reed in the 100 and 220, got the Dutchmen to within 10 at 75-65, but only the mile relay remained. Calvin's team, anchored by Dave Ver Merris, then finished the meet with an impressive time of 3:19.8 for a

MIAA FIELD DAY MEET
Albion College — May 18, 1968

Ken Feit set a new MIAA record in winning the 1968 pole vault competition. His leap of 14' 9" bettered the existing record by nearly a foot.

Calvin record and an 80-65 team victory over Hope. The loss would haunt the Dutchmen later in the season.

It was Adrian at Hope on Saturday, May 4. Coach Jay Flanagan had outstanding performers in hurdlers Doug Moss and Ron Labadie, 880-man Walt Chany, and distance runner Tom Swihart, but his squad lacked depth. There was concern in the Hope camp as Cooper, a pre-med student, would miss the meet due to MEDCAP exams, but his fellow captain, Walt Reed, stepped up to take the 100 and 220 in the fine times of 10.1 and 22.6. Bruggers was also a double winner as the Dutchmen won 14 of the 17 events, enroute to a 102-43 victory. The day's best race was the 880-yard run with Adrian's Walt Chany winning in the outstanding time of 1:56.8. Hope's Rich Frank followed with 1:58.7, and the Bulldogs' Dean Henderson was third with 1:59.4. MIAA champion Doug Moss won the high hurdles in the excellent time of 14.8, while Hope's Hollenbach edged Adrian's Ron Labadie for second place. Thomas beat Moss by two seconds in the intermediates.

Alma coach Denny Stolz was putting together a track team that included some of his football team. They would be in the driver's seat by 1970. Hope traveled to Alma on Wednesday, May 8, and received a strong challenge from the Scots before coming home with an 82-63 victory. Hope's 440-yard relay team was disqualified, but Cooper

THE HOPE MILE RELAY TEAM — 1968

The team's mark if 3:20.8 was an MIAA record and remains a Hope record as the event has been replaced by the 1600 meter relay. **L. to R.:** Ray Cooper, Bruce Geelhoed, Ralph Schroeder, Walt Reed

was back and a one-two finish by Cooper and Reed in the 100 and 220 helped turn the tide. The Scots had six firsts and shared a seventh. Bruggers was again a double winner for Hope in the distance runs, while Steve List won both hurdle races for Alma.

The home dual meet with Olivet was occasion for four Hope records. Bruggers's new marks in the mile and two-mile were 4:15.5 and 9:32.3. Cooper's 9.8 in the 100-yard dash tied his own record of May 1, and the Dutchman mile relay team of Reed, Schroeder, Geelhoed, and Cooper combined for a clocking of 3:22.3. The Comets' Gordon Lofts won the high hurdles in 15.4 and Kurt Chubner took the pole vault, but Hope was first in the other 15 events to record a 126-19 win. The Dutchmen had sweeps in the mile, 880, long jump, triple jump, and javelin.

When Hope hosted Albion on Tuesday, May 14, Feit was back from an injury and promptly won the pole vault with a Hope mark of 14' ½". Bruggers turned the mile over to Paul Hartman, Dan Colenbrander, and Chris Haile, who swept the event. Bruggers, meanwhile, ran to a Hope mark of 1:56.1 in the 880. He was followed by Frank and Reynen for a sweep in that event. Reed took over the 100 and 220 from Cooper and won both in times of 10.3 and 22.6. Cooper asked for a shot at the 440 and blazed around the oval in a new mark of 48.7. Schroeder and Geelhoed completed the sweep in that event. Floyd Brady won the high jump for the third meet in a row. A bright spot for the Britons was the performance of Craig Cossey, who set an Albion record in the triple jump with a mark of 45' 3". He also won the long jump with a leap of 21' 6". Over the years the Britons had enjoyed numerous lopsided wins over Hope, and the Dutchmen could hardly be blamed this day for savoring 14-of-17 firsts and the 104-41 victory.

Hope team members could sense that they were peaking at the right time, and looked forward to the 77th annual MIAA Field Day Meet at Albion. The team bus left Holland on Friday afternoon, May 17, and the Dutchmen would stay overnight in Albion to be ready for the Saturday morning field events, as well as qualifying rounds in the running events. Accommodations had been made at the Albion Holi-

THE 1968 HOPE COLLEGE TRACK TEAM
MIAA CO-CHAMPIONS WITH CALVIN

Front Row L. to R.: Assistant Coach Doug Formsma, Sid Disbrow, Paul Hartman, Rich Bisson, Herm Kuiper, Walt Reed III, Jim Mattison, Bob Blanton, Dave Thomas, Ken Feit, Doug Nichols, Alan Folkert, Rick Bruggers, Manager Doug Myers. **Back Row:** Assistant Coach Bill Vanderbilt, Barry Schreiber, Steve Van Pelt, Bill Bekkering, Jeff Hollenbach, Mike Brown, Dave Duitsman, Ray Cooper, Floyd Brady, Ralph Schroeder, Bruce Geelhoed, Steve Reynen, Chris Haile, Paul Steketee, Rich Frank, Karl Nadolsky, Coach Gordon Brewer, Ben Van Lierop. **Missing from the picture:** Nate Bowles, Kent Candelora, Dan Colenbrander, Bruce Formsma, Mike Hansen, Mike Oonk, Konrad Raup, G. John Tysse.

day Inn, and as the bus rounded a curve on I-94 we were surprised at words on the motel marquee, "Welcome Hope College Track Team." Other teams housed at the motel were not happy that Hope should be singled out, but the Dutchmen saw it as a good omen and enjoyed the evening.

Saturday, May 18, dawned bright and sunny, a perfect day for track and field. The composition of Albion's red track was a mixture of crushed tile and clay. Thanks to Athletics Director Elkin Isaac, it was in near-perfect condition. As expected, Hope's main competition would come from Calvin. The Knights were in the lead after the field events with 29 points, largely on the strength of first-place finishes in the shot, discus, and javelin by Rudy Vlaardingerbroek. Albion was a surprising second with 28½, while Hope had 27 as Brady took the high jump and a now-healthy Feit set an MIAA record in the pole vault. Using a brown fiberglass pole of questionable quality, Feit had a leap of 14' 9", nearly a foot higher than the existing record held by Dave Heth of Calvin. Nichols, Candelora, and Bowles helped the Dutch cause by taking second, third, and fourth in the javelin.

As the afternoon unfolded, the Dutchmen found themselves in an uphill battle against Calvin. A total of nine MIAA records would fall by the meet's conclusion, and five would belong to Hope College. Calvin would capture two, while Adrian and Albion would each have one. Midway in the running events, Hope inched ahead of Calvin 51-47 as Ray Cooper and Walt Reed finished one-two in the 100-yard dash. Adrian's Walt Chany had a super run in the 880. His record-breaking 1:54.6 somewhat overshadowed Hope's Frank, who took second with a personal best of 1:56.5. Then it was time for Thomas, who ran 54.2 in the intermediate hurdles for an MIAA and Hope record. Bruggers had earlier set a new league mark in the mile with a time of 4:19.3. Cooper's 22.1 in the 220 was Hope's fourth record of the afternoon, and there was more to come. Bruggers's victory in the two-mile run netted his second gold medal, and Hope's mile relay team of Reed, Schroeder, Geelhoed, and Cooper finished the day in style by winning the race in a time of 3:20.8, an MIAA and Hope record. Geelhoed's third leg of 50.1 was his best ever, and Cooper was tops at anchor with 48.5. The Dutchmen took first in eight of the 17 events, and finished with 82 points. Calvin was second with 60, followed by Adrian 43, Alma 35, Albion 33½, Olivet 16, and Kalamazoo 2½. Floyd Brady, Rick Bruggers, Ray Cooper, Ken Feit, and Walt Reed were named to the 15-man All-MIAA team. Cooper, who experienced a disheartening football season and the loss of his roommate, now closed out his career by being voted, for the second time, the league's most valuable trackman. Few would dispute the fact that Saturday, May 18, 1968, was Hope's finest hour in track and field to that point. The earlier dual meet loss meant that the overall championship would be shared with Calvin, but both teams were worthy.

Seven Hope squad members took part in the NCAA College Division Mid-East Regional at Ohio Wesleyan University on June 1. Hope finished fifth in a field of 29 schools, and Calvin was just five points behind in sixth. Nichols placed second in the javelin, and Candelora took fifth. Feit and Terry Lobochefski of Ohio Wesleyan both vaulted 14', but the latter won the gold on fewer misses. Bruggers was second in the mile run in a time of 4:12.9, a Hope record that he would break the following year. Ray Cooper was third in the 100, and Hope's mile relay team of Reed, Geelhoed, Bruggers, and Cooper was also third. Geelhoed had the fastest leg at 50.0. The mile performance by Bruggers qualified him for the NCAA College Division Championships on June 7-8. The meet was held at California State College at Hayward. This was an Olympic year, and all events were in metric measurements. In a qualifying race on June 7, Bruggers finished fourth in the 1,500 meter in the excellent time of 3:53.3. His eighth-place finish in the finals was in 3:56.2.

*　　*　　*

It was commencement time again in late May, and in the procession were many who had worn the orange and blue for Hope. Included, of course, was 6' 3" Floyd Brady, looking stately and reserved in cap and gown. His next stop would be Princeton Theological Seminary for a Master of Divinity degree. He also earned a master's degree in public administration from Rutgers, then served eight years as associate chaplain at Dartmouth College. Several positions in his hometown of Chicago have led him to full-time service in youth work. Today he continues to "give back" to society through his position as president and CEO of the *Dr. H.B. Brady Foundation*, named in honor of his father. At a 30-year Hope class reunion, the delighted buzz across campus was, "Floyd Brady is here!"

CHAPTER 12

WHEN PRIDE STILL MATTERED

The turbulent 60s continued in form with the tragic assassination of Robert Kennedy in California on June 5, 1968. A Hope grad was summoned to the scene when Vice President Hubert Humphrey contacted brain surgeon Jim Poppen, Hope '26, in Boston. Poppen flew immediately to Los Angeles, arriving while the victim was still alive, but little could be done and Kennedy died a few hours later. The decade's third assassination of prominent public servants caused Americans everywhere to question the stability of our society. The unrest was exacerbated by violence in August at the Democratic National Convention in Chicago, and by the behavior of some of our athletes at the Olympic Games in Mexico City. A ray of sunshine piercing such gloom was the Dec. 22 wedding of Julie Nixon and David Eisenhower, both at age 20. The Dutch Reformed ceremony was performed by Dr. Norman Vincent Peale.

Hope fans, accustomed to at least some championships each year, would now find their loyalty severely tested. In the final two years of the decade, the Dutchmen would be hard-pressed to finish on top as other schools took their turns at titles. Often by mid-season it would be evident that a Hope championship was out of reach. This period then, would be a test of character, of loyalty, perseverance, and pride.

* * *

The depressing ending of the 1967 football season was incentive enough for Hope's coaching staff to mount a huge effort to improve in '68. As practice opened on Monday, Sept. 2, the signs were good. The first day turnout of 75 was the largest since the immediate post-war years. There was solid leadership in co-captains Gary Frens and Walt Reed, plus some unexpected additions. Running back Nate Bowles was a talented transfer from Rutgers University, and Fremont junior Bill Bekkering, better known as a pole vaulter, was out for the first time and would soon make his mark as a wide receiver. In a somewhat radical move, Coach De Vette decided to switch veteran Gary Frens's from quarterback to fullback. It was felt that the move would capitalize on Frens' ability as a ball-carrier and blocker. Meanwhile, Hamilton sophomore Groy Kaper had impressed with his passing and seemed ready for the quarterback position. Bowles would join Frens in the running department. For the first time in 20 years, I would not be coaching football. With growing administrative duties in the fall and additional involvement with Division III of the NCAA, it seemed prudent to limit my coaching to track and field in the less-hectic spring. Anyone who has coached football misses it when they stop and I was no exception, but the responsibility of line coach was now in good hands with George Kraft.

Hope opened the season against Franklin of the Hoosier College Conference. The game was played at Franklin's Goodell Field before a crowd of 1,500. Coach Stewart "Red" Faught was now in his 10th season with the Grizzlies, and had annexed the HCC Championship in 1966. In the opening quarter, a Groy Kaper pass was intercepted by Steve Smith. A 58-yard Franklin drive followed, and was climaxed by a 17-yard touchdown pass from quarterback John Buerger to halfback Terry Hoeppner. The kick by Keith Gerbers was good, and the Grizzlies led 7-0 at the end of the first quarter. Hope then drove to the Franklin 24, but failed on fourth down. On the next play, Buerger threw a 76-yard TD pass to Gerbers, who also converted to make it 14-0 with 11:15 left in the half. The Dutchmen responded with a

72-yard drive in nine plays that ended with a 21-yard pass from Kaper to Rich Frank for the touchdown. Bekkering's kick was good and Hope was on the board, but trailed 14-7. A second Dutchman drive took the Hope nearly all the way, but a fumble on the two-yard line ended the threat just before halftime.

Franklin received the second-half kickoff and marched 63 yards to score. The big play in the drive was a 52-yard pass from Buerger to Hoeppner, which set-up a one-yard TD dive by fullback Mike Bailey. Gerber's kick made it 21-7. Hope came back with a drive to the Franklin six, but failed on fourth down by one foot. Frens, now on defense, intercepted a pass on the Franklin 28, but on the second play Hope again fumbled the ball away. A Grizzlie punt was taken on the Hope 33 by freshman Phil Schaap, who broke free and raced to the Franklin eight. Frens gained two to the six before Groy Kaper threw a strike to Bekkering in the end zone. Bekkering's kick was wide, making it 21-13 with 4:10 remaining in the game. The Dutchmen's next drive began on their own 36. With Kaper showing great poise, three complete passes to Bekkering and Harry Rumohr put the ball on the Franklin one-yard line. On a running play, Rumohr, while struggling to free himself from tacklers, fumbled the ball and Franklin's Steve Grey recovered. With three minutes remaining, Buerger engineered a six-play drive through the air which ended with a 16-yard touchdown pass to John Holmes. The successful conversion by Holmes gave Franklin the 28-13 victory. The Dutchmen had squandered numerous opportunities as they turned the ball over on six of eight fumbles. One lesson learned was that Coach Red Faught believed in throwing the ball. He was ahead of his time with his version of the so-called "west coast offense." Groping for something positive, the Hope coaches found it in the performance of halfback Nate Bowles, who rushed for 201 yards in 20 carries.

Hope's second away game was played at Lake Forest on Sept. 21. After a shaky start, things would go better. Forester Coach Mike Dau was of the old school and still employed the single-wing formation with an unbalanced line. The contest was played before a crowd of 1,000 with the temperature hovering around 85 degrees. Midway in the first quarter, the Foresters got off a drive from their own 49 that ended with a 22-yard touchdown pass from tailback Larry Niwa to end Steve Klingman. The conversion by Walt Eschelbach made it 7-0, but the lead would not hold up. The Dutchmen soon solved the secrets of the single-wing, and the Foresters would be limited to a total of 56 yards rushing for the game. With eight minutes left in the half, Hope moved 85 yards in 10 plays. The drive was capped by a 31-scoring pass from Kaper to Bekkering. Bekkering then kicked the point to tie it up at 7-7. In subsequent action, linebacker Karl Nadolsky recovered a Lake Forest fumble on the Hope 40. On the next play, Kaper hit Frank with a pass covering 48 yards and ending on the 12. A six-yard

**HOPE 13 — WHEATON 7
September 28, 1968**

Bill Bekkering's late game interception saved the day for Hope against Wheaton. In the action above Bekkering steps in front of halfback Craig King (20) to pick off the Rick havens pass with 1:18 left in the game.

pass to Bob Haveman put the ball on the six, and Bowles then circled right end for the score. Bill Bekkering's kick was again good, and Hope's halftime lead was 14-7.

After a scoreless third quarter, the Foresters tried a quick kick, but the ball went only to their own 45. Kaper then completed passes of six and 38 yards to Bekkering, putting the ball on the one. Kaper scored on a quarterback sneak, but Bekkering's kick was blocked, leaving the score at 20-7. Late in the quarter, Hope scored again after a 69-yard drive. The scoring play was a repeat of Hope's second TD, with Bowles going in on a five-yard right end sweep. Bekkering's third conversion made it 27-7 with 1:05 remaining. With 37 seconds left, freshman Phil Schaap intercepted a Forester pass and Hope drove to the six-yard line as the game ended. Hope had not beaten a powerhouse, but breaking into the win column was welcome.

Coach Jack Swartz brought the Wheaton Crusaders to Riverview for an afternoon game on Sept. 28. The stands were not full, but a crowd of 2,500 watched the visitors draw first blood with a 48-yard drive in 11 plays. Fullback Bill Scholl went the final five yards off-tackle, and Jim McKean's kick made it 7-0 with 6:01 left in the quarter. The Dutchmen came back with a 59-yard march of their own. The 13-play drive ended with a nine-yard touchdown pass from Kaper to Bekkering. Bekkering's kick was wide, leaving the score at 7-6. Later in the second period, Hope drove to the Wheaton five, largely on four carries by Gary Frens

254

that netted 22 yards, but Wheaton held. The Crusaders then reeled off 75 yards to the Hope 20, where fullback John Beaver fumbled and Haveman recovered for the Dutchmen on the Hope 29. With 1:56 left in the half, Kaper passed to Frens, who scampered down the sideline for 31 yards. On the next play, Kaper hit Frank on a post-pattern that went the distance. This time Bekkering split the uprights, and Hope led 13-7 at the half.

The second half opened with Randy List's 56-yard kick-off return to the Hope 38. Wheaton drove to the four, where a jarring tackle by Bill Leisner caused a fumble and Hope's Ted Rycenga recovered. Hope's cause was aided throughout the game by a 41-yard punting average from Gary Frens, but the second half found the Dutchmen making heroic stands to head off several Crusader threats. At one point it was fourth and two for a Wheaton score when Reed tackled Scholl for a three-yard loss to end the drive. Bowles then gained 23 yards in four carries to get the Dutchmen out of trouble. Later in the fourth quarter, Wheaton was back on the Hope 22 with fourth and three. This time, linebackers Leisner and Haveman stopped Scholl after a one-yard gain. With 1:18 left in the game, Wheaton was on the Hope 11. Quarterback Rick Havens tried a square out pass to halfback Craig King, but Bekkering stepped in front for the interception and Hope ran out the clock. Wheaton had dominated play in the second half, but defensive gems gave Hope the 13-7 victory.

Denny Stolz, Michigan college Coach of the Year in 1967, brought the MIAA champion Alma Scots to Riverview Park on Oct. 5. The Scots were riding a 12-game winning streak and would prove to be too much for the Dutchmen. Hope blew an early opportunity when quarterback Tom Jakovac fumbled on his own 25 and Nadolsky recovered. Three carries by Frens put the ball on the Alma 15, but at this point a Kaper pass was picked off by Robert Zins on the 13 and the Scots were ready to roll. Fourteen plays later, the visitors had marched 87 yards with Jack Prince going in from the one. Jeff Blough converted to give Alma the 7-0 lead with 6:15 left in the quarter. Later in the period Jakovac passed 18 yards to end John Fuzak for a second TD, and with Blough's kick it was 14-0. Hope moved the ball well and drove to the Alma 16 before Kaper's fourth down pass was batted away by Rick Ledy. Following an exchange of punts, Alma went 48 yards in six plays. The scoring play this time was a 24-yard pass from Jacovac to Chad Creevy. Blough's third conversion made it 21-0. The Dutchmen took the kickoff and drove 66 yards to the Alma 14, but Groy Kaper's fourth down pass was again incomplete. With 17 seconds left in the half, Hope's luck changed when Alma's Jack Prince fumbled and Keith Van Tubergen recovered. On Hope's first play, a Kaper-to-Rumohr pass put the Dutchmen on the board. Bill Bekkering's kick sailed wide, leaving the halftime score at 21-6.

The Scots scored again with 4:45 left in the third quarter. Jakovac went in on a one-yard roll out around right end. This time the kick failed, but the lead was now 27-6. With 13:19 left in the game, Alma's Chris Clark dove off-tackle for the game's final score. Blough made it three out of four to give Denny Stolz's team an impressive 34-6 victory. Kaper had been sacked eight times while Jacovac suffered only one.

The Alma contest left Hope with Reed, Van Tubergen, and Jim Roedvoets all on the injured list. They would miss an exciting, see-saw game at Adrian on Oct. 12. Bill Davis was the new coach at Adrian and, along with assistant Tom Heckert, hoped to turn things around for the Bulldogs. Hope was in the hole early by virtue of a fumbled punt which was turned into a touchdown by running back Ron Labadie. Mark Doody converted to give Adrian a 7-0 lead with the game only minutes old. The Dutchmen were quick to recover, and drove 62 yards in 13 plays with Bowles going off-tackle for five yards and the score. Bill Bekkering's kick tied it at 7-7 with 4:57 left in the quarter. The Hope defense did its job, but the fourth down punt was again fumbled by the safety man and Adrian recovered on the Hope 24. Four plays later, quarterback Barry Beck went in on a sneak from the one. Doody again converted, making it 14-7. With 9:30 remaining in the second quarter, the speedy Labadie broke free and raced 66 yards to score. Doody's kick was perfect and the score moved to 21-7. The Dutchmen were now down, but far from out. Bowles's 39-yard kickoff return was followed by a 41-yard drive which included three Groy Kaper completions. The march ended with a one-yard scoring sneak by Kaper. Bekkering's kick narrowed the margin to 21-14. Near the end of the half, Hope was again in possession. Kaper completed a pass to Bekkering for 36 yards, then followed with a 22-yard strike, again to Bekkering and this time for a touchdown. Bekkering's third conversion tied the game at 21-21 with just 44 seconds left in the half.

In the third quarter, Labadie was guilty of a rare fumble which was recovered by Frank on the Adrian 19. The Bulldog defense held for three downs, but on fourth down Frens put a 32-yard field goal through the uprights and, for the first time, Hope had the lead at 24-21. The Hope comeback was soon thwarted, when a Kaper pass was picked off by Steve Rulewicz on the Adrian 48. Quarterback Beck was on target with three of five passes, the last one to Greg Cady for 24 yards. With the ball on the one, fullback Rulewicz plunged in for the score and Doody's fourth conversion gave the lead back to Adrian at 28-24. In the fourth quarter, linebacker Bill Leisner intercepted a Beck pass to give Hope possession on the Adrian 36. Eight plays later, it was again the Kaper-to-Bekkering combination for an eight-yard scoring pass. Bekkering now matched Doody with his fourth straight conversion, and Hope was back in the lead at 31-28 with 9:22 remaining. As the Dutchman defense began to tire, Adrian marched 62 yards to score, with Steve Rulewicz going the final three yards off-tackle. Doody was again perfect to make it 35-31 Adrian. With 6:22 remaining the Hope

255

still had time, but with 5:39 left the Dutchmen fumbled on their own 27 and Larry Merx recovered for the Bulldogs. The costly miscue sealed the Dutchmen's doom. Seven plays later, Labadie scored on a three-yard run and Doody's automatic toe gave Adrian the satisfying 42-31 homecoming victory. Despite the disappointment of defeat, Bill Bekkering had performed brilliantly with seven receptions for 107 yards, three touchdowns, and four conversions.

Hope's own homecoming would take place on Oct. 19 with Olivet furnishing strong opposition. Guests of honor were members of Hope's fabled '58 team of a decade earlier. That, plus a crowd of 4,300, was the proper incentive for a Dutchman comeback, but with 8:30 gone in the opening period Kaper went down with an ankle sprain and the game was left in the hands of freshman Jon Constant. Constant had been well trained by his father, Don Constant, the head football coach at Grand Haven High School. Four plays after entering the game, Constant was in the end zone on a quarterback sneak. Bekkering's kick was not good, and Hope's lead was 6-0. The lead did not last long. The ensuing kickoff was taken by Olivet dashman Karl Wilson, who raced untouched for 85 yards and the touchdown. The kick by Hal Hooks was good, and the Comets moved ahead 7-6. In the second quarter, a Frens punt was misjudged by Glenn Johnson. The ball bounced off Johnson and into the end zone, where it was recovered by Hope guard Ken Otte for a touchdown. Bekkering's kick put Hope back in the lead at 13-7 with 5:27 left in the half.

On the second play following Hope's kickoff, quarterback Eric Witzke was thrown for a seven-yard loss. The tackle forced a fumble, and Keith Van Tubergen recovered for Hope. Six plays later, Constant passed seven yards to end Tom Thomas for the TD. The conversion failed, but Hope led 19-7 at the half. As the second half opened, quarterback Witzke redeemed himself by marching the Comets 80 yards in six plays. Wilson scored his second touchdown on a four-yard end sweep, and Hooks converted to narrow the score to 19-14. Hope controlled the ball for eight plays before Jon Constant completed a 67-yard pass play to Nate Bowles for Hope's fourth score. The two-point conversion attempt failed, but the Dutchman lead was now 25-14. Late in the third quarter, Hope took advantage of a 25-yard Comet punt into the wind. This time the Dutch went 56 yards in just three plays. The big gainer was a 48-yard burst off-tackle by Bowles. Frens then went over from the two. The Dutchmen again elected to go for two points, and halfback Dick Bont was successful on a right end sweep to up the Hope lead to 33-14.

The Comets were far from finished, and responded late in the quarter with 60 yards in the air and another score. It was Karl Wilson again, this time with a four-yard sweep. Hal Hooks made it 33-21, and momentum was with Olivet. With seven minutes remaining in the game, a Frens punt was blocked by Jess Bobo on the Hope 35. Footballs bounce in strange ways and this one came back to Frens, who broke away for 17 yards and a first down. The Dutch did not score, but used up another five minutes. With just over two minutes left, the Comets pushed across the game's final score when Witzke went in on a sneak. Another conversion by Hooks made the final Hope 33, Olivet 28. The much-needed Hope victory had produced a lot of offense, to the delight of the crowd. Constant had completed 12 of 18 passes, rushed for 60 yards, scored a touchdown and passed for two more.

Hope's third homecoming game in-a-row was played at Kalamazoo on Oct. 26, and was decidedly different from the previous two. A key feature for the Dutchmen in the scoreless first half was the 42.2 punting average of Gary Frens. In the second half, after an exchange of punts, Hope moved from its own 30 to the 44 on a Kaper pass to Rumohr, but at this point a Hope fumble was recovered by Kazoo's John Weurding. On the first play Gary Armstrong passed to Lee Tichnor, who broke away but was pulled down from behind by Frank on the Hope eight. Halfback De Monte Johnson ran off-tackle twice. On the second carry, he was hit on the two with a jarring tackle by linebacker Bill Leismer. The resulting fumble was recovered by Rumohr. In five straight carries Nate Bowles moved the ball from the two to the 25-yard line. Staying on the ground, the Dutchmen were finally stopped at the Kalamazoo 40. Frens had been injured in the second quarter and Bob Haveman was now called upon to punt. His kick came to rest on the Hornets' four-yard line. The Dutchman defense now did its job, and John Keck's punt was good for only 12 yards to the Kazoo 21. Bowles carried three times to the 10 before Kaper found Rumohr open in the end zone for the game's only touchdown. Frens came on to kick the point to make it 7-0 with 13:53 left in the game. The charged-up Hornets proceeded to drive from their own 38 to the Hope 18. With fourth and 11 on the Hope 13, Gary Armstrong passed to end Lee Tichenor. Rumohr broke up a sure touchdown by tipping the ball away. The Dutchmen were unable to move the ball and found themselves with fourth and five on their own five. Punter Haveman was then instructed to take a safety in the end zone, making the score 7-2. Haveman's free kick was taken by Tom Simpson at the K 25, where he was swarmed on by Hope tacklers. With 1:20 left, Gary Armstrong completed three passes to the Hope 29, but two passes to the end zone fell incomplete and Hope was the victor, 7-2.

With two straight league victories and an overall 4-3 record, Hope seemed to be a team on the move, but a knee injury to Frens would contribute to stinging defeats in the final two games. In a Dad's Day game at Albion's Alumni Field, the Britons dominated play after the first quarter and trampled the Dutchmen 45 to 0. Though un-announced at the time, this would be the last league game for Albion coach Morley Fraser. After 14 years at the helm, Fraser would turn over the reigns to Tom Taylor, a former Albion star. This day the Briton players would show their appreciation with six touchdowns. Sam Trippett crossed the goal line twice, Craig Cossey once and Bill Scheuller kicked a 41-yard field goal to make it 24-0 at half time. During the course of the afternoon, Schuller would also be perfect with six extra points. After a scoreless third quarter, halfback Jim Bell scored to make it 31-0. At this point in the final quarter Fraser inserted his second string, but it made little difference as quarterback Jim Lear passed to Mike Walters, who rambled 73 yards for another TD. The score mounted to 38-0. With 43 seconds remaining Hope was forced to punt. The kick was fielded by Rick Bensinger, who returned it 47 yards to the Hope six. With one second remaining, there was no thought in the Briton camp of "taking a knee." Instead, Jim Lear passed successfully to Lee Porterfield in the end zone and Scheuller followed with his sixth extra point. Energetic substitutes cannot be blamed for wanting to show their stuff, but it was the kind of play that defeated coaches remember. The Dutchmen were better than 45-0, but not on this particular afternoon. In the course of the debacle, Bill Bekkering caught four passes to bring his season's total to 33. This would break Jon Schoon's record of 31 set in 1962.

The battered Dutchmen had little to look forward to on Nov. 9, when a powerful Ashland team came to town for the annual Parents Day game before a crowd of 3,500. The game's first play was a portent of things to come. Ashland's Dennis Boyd took the kickoff by Dennis Stacey on the 10, got free along the north sideline and raced 90 yards for a touchdown. With 13 seconds gone on the clock, it was Ashland 7, Hope 0. For the first time in two years, the Dutchmen now moved the ball against Ashland. Kaper was brilliant in moving his team 59 yards in four plays. A pass to flanker Frank covered 44 yards. This was followed by a 15-yard aerial to Bekkering, who loped into the end zone. Bekkering's kick tied the game at 7-7, and hopes were high for a possible win. It was not to be. The Eagles, with no restrictions on athletic scholarships, were simply too strong. Additional touchdowns were scored by Mike Healy, Mike Norman, and Dave Gray to make it 28-7 at the half.

Gray scored again the second half on a 19-yard run to make it 35-7. Hope then helped the Eagle cause by fumbling the kickoff. A pass from Ron Lab to Bob Di Franko found paydirt, and the score rose to 41-7. Murphy's Law seemed to be in force for the Dutchmen, and this time it was a bad snap on a punt that gave Ashland the ball on the Hope 20. A 17-yard TD pass from Jeff Williams to Boyd upped the count to 48-7, and the Ohio team was still not finished. With 7:53 remaining, Williams hit Jay Hoover with a pass that covered 32 yards and reached the end zone. The point try failed and the Eagles had to be content with a 54-7 score. With 1:53 left, Kaper connected with Rumohr for 51 yards and the game's final score to make it 54-13. There were no excuses, Hope had simply been overmatched.

Hope's overall record of 4-5 was an improvement over 1967, and a 2-3 MIAA mark was good enough for a third-

RICK BRUGGERS
MIAA CROSS COUNTRY CHAMPION — 1968

Hope's Rick Bruggers was voted the leaague's Most Valuable Runner for the '68 season. Above: Coach Barry Werkman looks on as his prize pupil receives the award from MIAA Commissioner John C. Hoekje.

place tie with Olivet. Gary Frens, Bill Bekkering, and Ted Rycenga were named to the All-MIAA team, and sophomore Groy Kaper completed 84 of 164 passes for 1,203 yards and 11 touchdowns.

* * *

Barry Werkman was Hope's cross country coach in 1968, with assistance from Doug Formsma. Rich Bisson was captain of the team that included Rick Bruggers, Dave Brueggemann, Dan Colenbrander, Gene Haulenbeek, Willie Jackson, Jim Mattison, Pete Raynolds, and Bob Scott. The season opened on Saturday, Sept. 21, with a quadrangular at Spring Arbor. Wheaton took the meet with 20 points, followed by Spring Arbor with 59, Hope 61, and Oakland University 78. Bruggers placed first and would remain undefeated throughout the season.

At the Hope Invitational on Tuesday, Sept. 24, it was Aquinas the winner with 23 points, followed by Grand Rapids JC 50, Hope 59, Trinity Christian 109, and Muskegon Community College 146.

The first MIAA dual took place at Calvin on Saturday, Sept. 28, with the Knights posting a 24-35 win. Bruggers was again the winner, and Rich Bisson finished third. Hope hosted Alma on Oct. 5 and came away the winner by a 21-37 score. Bruggers's winning time of 20:04.4 was a course record. In a good meet at Adrian on Oct. 12, the Bulldogs prevailed, 24-35 score, but Bruggers was again the winner while Bisson placed fourth and Gene Haulenbeek seventh. On Oct. 19, in a home meet, Hope got the best of Olivet 21-40, but a week later it was Kalamazoo 20, Hope 39 on the Hornets' course. The dual meet season concluded at Albion on Nov. 2 with Bruggers continuing undefeated.

THE 1968 HOPE SOCCER TEAM
6-4 Overall

Front Row L. to R.: Doug Duffey, Kwesi Fumey, Tim Tam, Manuel Cuba, Tony Mock, Jim Knott, Fred Schutmaat, Jeff Alperin, Waldon Mertz, Tim De Voogd, D. Wang, Mike Bull **Back Row:** Coach Bill Vanderbilt, Nick Augustine, Dave Clark, Art Hudak, Bob Kuhn, Jerry Vande Werken, Tom Goodfellow, De Gaulle Najourma, Lou Lotz, Ernest Motteram, Chuck Van Engen, Jim Hoekstra, John Debrecini, Evan Griffin.

His team, however, was edged by the narrowest of margins as the Britons pulled it out by a 28-29 score. All teams met at Olivet on Tuesday, Nov. 5, for the MIAA meet. Bruggers's winning time of 20:14 was a course record. In team standings, it was Kalamazoo first, followed by Calvin, Adrian, Albion, Hope, Olivet, and Alma. Coach Werkman could be proud of his star runner as Bruggers was a unanimous choice as the MIAA's most valuable runner. Bruggers's outstanding season ended at Wheaton on Nov. 16, when he finished 18th in a field of 313 in the post-season NCAA College Division meet.

* * *

Dr. Phillip Van Eyl had been the soccer coach since the game's inception at Hope in 1964. Now, with the sport firmly established, he would turn the post over to Bill Vanderbilt, one of the newer members of the Hope P.E. department. Vanderbilt would enjoy a large turnout and guide the team to a rewarding 6-4 overall record, including a 3-3 mark in the tough Michigan-Illinois-Indiana Soccer Conference. The season opener was a 7-2 victory over Oakland. Albion, with only its second year of soccer, had assembled a surprisingly strong team, but the Dutchmen played well and emerged with a 3-2 win. The first defeat came at the hands of perennially strong Earlham, 1-0. The Michigan State University club of Coach Gene Kenny proved too tough for the Dutchmen, and laid one on with a 7-0 score.

Undaunted, Vanderbilt's charges played well in downing the Calvin Knights 5-1. Next in line were the Little Giants of Wabash College, in another MII contest. Hope was again victorious, this time by a 9-1 score. The two-game win streak was snapped by Mac Murray, who shut out the Dutchmen 4-0, but Hope bounced back to defeat Kalamazoo 7-1. Hope's sixth victory came at the expense of a good Lake Forest team, 2-0. In the season finale, Wheaton and Hope battled on even terms throughout the contest. With the score tied 3-3 and 45 seconds left in the game, the Crusaders managed to drive home the game-winner and leave the Dutchmen on the short end of a 4-3 heartbreaker. The team was held in high regard around the league, as evidenced by the selection of Manuel Cuba and Fred Schutmaat to the All-MII first team.

The annual Fall Sports Banquet was held on Thursday, Nov. 14, with WKZO Sports Director Larry Osterman as speaker. Phil Rauwerdink was master of ceremonies for the evening as various announcements were made. Gary Frens was voted Hope's MVP in football, and Tom Thomas was captain-elect for 1969. Rick Bruggers was the season's most valuable runner, with Bruce Geelhoed voted captain-elect for 1969. In soccer, Fred Schutmaat and Jim Knott were named co-MVPs, while Art Hudak and Dave Clark would serve as co-captains in 1969.

* * *

Basketball without Brady would be the challenge for Coach De Vette in 1968-69. Captain Bruce Van Huis, the only returning regular, would lead a team consisting of three freshmen, five sophomores, three juniors, and one senior. This "new team" opened at home on Saturday, Nov. 30, against Lake Forest. Fast break, run-and-gun basketball gave Hope a 45-36 lead at the half, but the Foresters' zone press in the second half spelled trouble for the young Dutchmen. Hope was forced into 10 turnovers in a six-minute span, and the score was tied 58-58 with 9:21 left. Lake Forest led 67-65 with 5:50 remaining, but field goals by Randy Adolphs, Barry Schreiber, and Tom Dykstra plus three by Van Huis gave Hope the game 84-71. Van Huis was off to a great start with 31 points and 19 rebounds, while Schreiber was hot with 20. Freshman Marty Snoap added 10. For Dick Triptow's, team it was Mike Maiman with 25, Al Shethar 15, Andy Russo 13, and Mike Hogan 10.

Next for the Dutchmen at the Civic would be Aquinas on Wednesday, Dec. 4. The Tommies of Coach Bill Braunbeck put together a strong first half, and led 48-46 at the intermission after shooting 61 percent. The score would be tied 13 times, the last one coming at the 11:30 mark. At this point, Hope put it all together for a 24-4 run that would sew up the 104-92 victory. Leading the way for the Dutch were freshmen Snoap and Ken Hendrix, with 21 and 20 points respectively. Van Huis had his usual steady game with 16, and Dan Oegema had 10. Coach De Vette also had high praise for another freshman, Holland's own Dan Shinabarger, who scored nine. For the Tommies, it was Pat Ryan leading the way with 23, Tom Van Portfliet had 20, Dave Page 18, and Cliff Gordon 16. Hope's 65-48 advantage in rebounds was a telling factor in the high-scoring affair.

The Dutchmen were feeling good about their opening wins when they traveled to River Forest, Ill., for an afternoon game on Saturday, Dec. 7. Against Concordia, however, everything seemed to go wrong. The experienced Cougars forced 13 Hope turnovers in the first half and led 41-31 at the intermission. The home team also won the rebound battle by a 69-41 margin for the game. The Dutchman performance at the free throw line was a mediocre 12-23. The result was a convincing 88-68 Concordia victory. Leading the way for the winners was Dave Wild with 26. Dave Mueller and Piper each had 12, and Chuck Bjerregard 11. Hope's high man was Van Huis with 16, Snoap 14 and Dykstra nine.

Hope opened MIAA play at Olivet on Wednesday, Dec. 11. The Comets' center was out with the flu, but Coach Gary Morrison had his team primed and Olivet moved to a 36-34 halftime lead. With steady play, the Comets had increased it to 54-51 with 10 minutes to go, but Shinabarger hit four straight field goals as part of a 12-2 run and the Dutchmen prevailed for a 74-68 victory. Hope was 20-29 from the free throw line, and edged the Comets 46-44 in rebounds. Shinabarger and Dykstra led Hope with 15 each, while Van Huis had 12 and Schreiber 11. Benny Benford was high man for Olivet with 16, Max Lindsay had 15 and Denny nine.

Coach Hank Burbridge brought the Spring Arbor Blue Jays to the Civic Center on Saturday, Dec.. 14. The two schools were meeting for only the second time. The previous game was a 93-84 Hope win in 1965. Experience was lacking on both clubs, as neither team could claim more than one senior. Hope enjoyed a nine-point bulge with a halftime score of 59-48, and continued to add to the margin with 52 percent shooting in the second half. A Shinabarger field goal with 4:23 remaining gave Hope its 100th point. The final count showed Hope winning 111-84. Van Huis led the Dutchmen to their fourth victory with 23 points. Dykstra netted 15, Hendrix 14, Adolphs 12, Snoap 11, and Ted Zwart 10. Jerry Byrd was high for the Blue Jays with 25, Jerry Neigh had 18, Lynn Johnson 15, and Andy Sheridan 14.

When the Dutchmen arrived at Albion's Kresge Gym on Wednesday, Dec. 18, they were aware of a deserted campus. Students had gone home for the holidays, and a sparse crowd of 300 would witness the contest. Despite Hope's 50-46 lead at the half, the Britons had forced 12 Dutchman turnovers while committing only two of their own. Hope's last lead was 83-82 with 5:24 left. An 8-1 Albion run gave the home team a 96-90 lead with one minute left. A Snoap field goal made it 98-96 with 21 seconds remaining, but a free throw by Harry Turney gave Dean Dooley's team the 99-96 victory. Turnovers proved to be the difference, with Hope guilty of 22 to just eight for the Britons. Ed Stephens was high for the winners with 24, Dave Robillard followed with 20, Harry Turney had 19 and So Ziem 15. Snoap led the Dutchmen with 21, Schreiber scored 15, and Hendrix 13, while Van Huis and Tom Dykstra each had 12.

A Hope-hosted holiday tournament at the Civic brought in Ohio Wesleyan, Wabash of Indiana, and Union College of Schenectady, N.Y. In the opening round on Friday, Dec. 27, Wabash got by Ohio Wesleyan 67-65 in a game that was close all the way. Frank Shannon was the Wesleyan coach, while Rusty Nichols guided the Little Giants of Wabash. In the second contest, Hope dominated play in downing Union, 110-82. Hope's Dutchmen led the Union Dutchmen 50-38 at the half. Chris Schmid's team had trouble coping with Hope's run-and-shoot tactics, and also lost out in the battle of the boards. Van Huis led the winners with 24, Hendrix had 18, Shinabarger 17, Dykstra 16, Schreiber 10, and Snoap nine. Bill Neidel was high for Union with 24, Jim Getman scored 16, and Dave Shames 13.

Union came back to win the consolation game on Saturday night by taking the measure of Ohio Wesleyan, 63-59. In the second game, Hope won its own tournament by downing Wabash 100-85. Wabash trailed 55-46 at the half and suffered from a 60-41 deficit in rebounds. Snoap spent some time on the bench with four fouls, but was easily the star of the game. The freshman forward was 14 of 15 from the floor and two-of-two from the line for a total of 30 points. Dan Shinabarger followed with 14, Van Huis 13, Ken Hendrix and Ted Zwart 11 each, and Tom Dykstra nine. For Wabash, it was Dave Moore in a fine performance with 32, Dan Jordan with 18, and Pete Volz with nine.

Hope resumed MIAA action by hosting the Adrian Bulldogs on Wednesday, Jan. 8. The vacation lay-off seemed to have taken a toll, and Hope's starting five did not perform well at the outset. In an unusual move, Coach De Vette benched four of the five starters, leaving only Dykstra to team with Schreiber, Adolphs, Oegema, and Zwart. The subs did the job, and Hope's halftime lead was 51-42. The regulars started the second half and played inspired ball the rest of the way. Seventeen rebounds by Van Huis helped the Dutchmen to a 78-43 advantage in that department and the eventual 114-75 victory. Scoring was evenly divided, with Van Huis getting 16, Dykstra 15, Oegema 14, Zwart 13, Shinabarger and Hendrix 12 each, and Snoap nine. Hope had totaled 63 second-half points. Greg Dorrow with 28 points was the bright spot for Adrian. Burns and Mills added 12 each in an otherwise discouraging night for Coach Gregg Arbaugh.

Hope now stood 7-2 in the young season, had scored 100 or more points in four games, and benefited from three flashy freshmen in the starting lineup. Few could have anticipated the six-game skid that was to follow. The trouble began, as one might expect, at Calvin on Saturday, Jan. 11. Hope took an early 22-16 lead on the strength of some fine shooting by Adolphs, but Calvin's Ed Wiers and Bill De Horn took over the boards as Van Huis was on the bench with three early fouls. The Knights' halftime margin was 49-43, and the Dutchmen could never catch up. Coach Don Vroon got outstanding performances from Ed Wiers, who led the team with 20; Mickey Phelps with 18; Del Willink, whose 17 included six of six from the floor and five of six from the line; and Bill De Horn, whose 12 points and 27 rebounds made the difference in Calvin's 94-88 victory. Shinabarger was high for Hope with 22, Hendrix had 17, Van Huis 14, Dykstra 13, and Snoap 10.

The Alma Scots of Coach Bill Klenk ended Hope's 18-game home winning streak at the Civic Center on Wednesday, Jan. 15. The Dutchmen again found themselves on the short end at halftime, this time by a 48-45 count. The competitive Scots were blessed with more talent than in recent years, but Hope tied it up at 56-56 with 15:15 remaining and trailed by only two at 81-79 late in the game. Alma then broke the game open with an 18-8 run that featured Charles Hudson with numerous layups. On the boards it was Alma 59-48. Hudson with 28 and Drake Serges with 26 led Klenk's charges to a very satisfying 99-87 victory. Jerry Hill added 13 and James Lawson 12. Hope had balanced scoring from Van Huis with 20, Shinabarger 19, Hendrix 18, Adolphs 12, and Snoap 10, but the late Alma surge had been too much.

Hope battled the Kalamazoo Hornets in the Civic on Saturday, Jan. 18, and, after trailing 40-35 at the half, took the game into overtime. With Kalamazoo leading 73-71 and 50 seconds remaining, a shot by Snoap missed, but Van Huis wrestled the ball away from Dick Winkley and fed Ken Hendrix under the basket for the tying field goal. The Hornets never trailed in the overtime, made six-of-nine free throws, and held on for the 81-79 win. Dan Laskoski led the way for the winners with 20, Jim Katona scored 17, Dick Winkley had 13, and Gene Nusbaum 12. Hendrix was high for Hope with 19, Dan Shinabarger and Marty Snoap each scored 17, and Tom Dykstra and Ted Zwart had eight apiece. Van Huis was ill, but dressed for the game anyway. He played briefly, but did not score.

Following the exam period, Hope traveled to Ohio on Saturday, Jan. 25. The game against Wooster was played in the Scots' fine new fieldhouse before a crowd of 2,500. The Dutchmen trailed 45-36 at half-time and had a cold night of shooting at just 30 percent. Hope was held scoreless for a four-minute period early in the second half and this, combined with an 8-0 run by Wooster, sealed the 89-73 Scot victory. Guard Tom Dinger had a game-high 28 points to lead the winners. John Cresap scored 15 and center Tim Baab had 10. Van Huis led Hope with 16, Schreiber came off the bench to score 14, Shinabarger had nine and Snoap eight. It was the fifth consecutive victory by the Scots over Hope in a series begun in 1949.

Van Huis missed Hope's game at Lake Forest due to illness, and his absence was a factor in Hope's 79-73 loss. The contest played on Saturday, Feb. 1, featured a strong first half by the Foresters, who enjoyed a 48-33 margin at the intermission. Lorenza Howard, Steve Warren, and Lon Eriks were brought up from the jayvee squad to fill the Hope ranks, now decimated by illness and ineligibility. Hope managed to stay close in the second half, and trailed 76-71 with 21 seconds left. Shinabarger's field goal with 12 seconds remaining made it 76-73, but Triptow's troops got three more free throws to wrap up the 79-73 victory. Mike Maimen was the Lake Forest leader with 26, Al Shethar had 18 and Andy Russo 16. Hendrix had one of his best games in leading the Dutchmen with 25. Tom Dykstra was back in form with 16 and Dan Shinabarger 12. In rebounds it was Hope 43-37.

Coach De Vette was back in familiar territory when the team traveled to Granville, Ohio, on Wednesday, Feb. 5. As a U.S. Marine in 1943-44, De Vette had led a Denison University team to an 18-2 record and had been named to the All-Ohio team. Now, in the first basketball encounter between the schools, Hope would again be without the services of the ailing Van Huis. In many respects the game resembled the recent Lake Forest contest. Hope was behind 46-34 at the half, then closed the gap in the second half. The Dutchmen came closest at 60-58 with 8:19 to go, then had possession with 1:36 remaining and the score at 77-73, but bad passes led to two Denison field goals making it 81-73. A final basket by Schreiber reduced the margin to 81-75 at the buzzer. Charley Claggett with 26 points and 17 rebounds did most of the Denison damage. Wince added 18 points and Sandusky had 11. For Hope it was Shinabarger with 22, Dykstra with 17, Hendrix 14, and Schreiber eight.

Hope resumed MIAA play in a home game against Olivet on Saturday, Feb. 8, hoping to end a six-game losing streak. A somewhat shaky Van Huis was back in uniform. He would be rested some in the second half, but his presence would make a big difference. From the start a scoring duel developed between Shinabarger and the Comets' splendid forward Mike Macias. The Hope freshman had the best of it in the first half with 17 points to 12 for Macias, and for a change, Hope led 57-39 at the intermission. Macias turned up the heat in the second half with 15 points, but the Dutchmen prevailed to end the long drought with a 93-82 victory. Shinabarger led all scorers with 28, Ken Hendrix had 18, Van Huis came through with 15, Snoap 14 and Dykstra nine. For the moment at least, it seemed like old times. Mike Maciasz carried his team with 27, while Max Lindsay and Ken Williams each dropped in 13.

The Dutchmen could have used another home game on Wednesday, Feb. 12, but instead traveled to Kalamazoo, where Ray Steffen and the Hornets put them back in the loss column. Kazoo took a 42-36 halftime lead and then, with tough defense, held the Dutchmen to only 12 field goals in the second half. The Hornets' 52-39 domination of the boards was part of the problem, as were 19 points by Gene Nussbaum, who led his team to the 89-70 victory. Craig Vossekuil scored 16, Dick Winkley 15, and John Weurding nine to give Coach Steffen more than enough. Shinabarger was hot again for Hope with 19, Hendrix had 18 and Dykstra 12.

The Albion Britons of Coach Dean Dooley were at the Civic on Saturday, Feb. 15. The Dutchmen remembered well the game back in December when 22 Hope turnovers and an 8-1 closing flurry had given the Britons the victory. There was determination in the Hope camp to play hard and take better care of the ball. Schreiber provided the needed spark when he came off the bench to score seven first-half points and take down nine rebounds. Hope's 46-41 lead was extended in the hotly contested second half as a strong effort produced a 67-49 advantage on the boards. In the final tally it was two freshman and a sophomore leading the way to a 99-92 victory. Shinabarger led all scorers with 34, and a fired-up Snoap was the complete ballplayer with 27 points and 17 rebounds. Schreiber continued his fine play in the second half and ended with 16 points. Albion's leader was Mike Wilson with 29, Harry Turney followed with 24, and Dave Robillard had 16.

At Adrian on Wednesday, Feb. 19, the Dutchmen led 43-39 at the half despite 14 turnovers. After 11 ties Hope's lead was 72-63 with 8:05 remaining, but Gregg Arbaugh's team played inspired ball for the remaining minutes, took the lead with three minutes left, and moved to a 99-88 victory. Kim Rank played a strong game for the winners with 27, and was followed closely by Bob Mills with 26. Ingledue had 18 and Jim Rommel 12. A fully recovered Van Huis was high for Hope with 23, Hendrix had 20, Dan Shinagarger 19, and Tom Dykstra 11.

Hope and Calvin met at the Civic Center on Saturday, Feb. 22, in the usual "Standing Room Only" classic. This night the teams had opposite goals. Calvin, at 15-3 overall and 9-0 in the MIAA, could assure at least a tie for the championship with a victory. The Hope squad, at 9-10 overall and 4-6 in league play, would struggle to finish at .500. With little to lose, the pumped-up Dutchmen shot out to an early 16-5 lead. Calvin battled back to a 32-31 lead with 2:10 left in the half, but Dykstra put in two free throws to give the Dutchmen an unexpected 33-32 lead at the intermission. The halftime tension, felt by everyone, was relieved somewhat when the Van Buren County Folk Dancers took the floor for a colorful performance, but it was soon back to nail biting time. De Vette's second half strategy was to employ an uncharacteristic deliberate offense that resulted in the teams trading baskets for the first 10 minutes. The Hope lead was 43-42 at this point. With the slow-down, Hope's starters were able to play the entire game with the exception of a brief appearance by Ric Scott in the second half. As Hope's guards began to hit from the outside, the Hope lead gradually increased, and stood at 57-47 with 3:54 remaining. The Knights cut the margin to six with 1:19 left, but Dykstra and Shinabarger combined for six-straight free throws to insure the 71-61 victory and the biggest upset of the season. Dykstra ended with 21, Shinabarger had 20, Hendrix 12, Van Huis 10, and Snoap eight. Mickey Phelps had 14 for Calvin, Bill De Horn 13, Del Willink 10, and Ed Wiers eight. The *Holland Evening Sentinel* gave top honors to "one who never touched the ball," namely Coach De Vette, whose basketball insight once again paid off. Coach Don Vroon was gracious in defeat, saying that the win "was no fluke."

The up-and-down Dutchmen closed out the season on Wednesday, Feb. 26, in Alma's new gym, which featured a Tartan floor. Hopes were high for a break-even season, but it was not to be. The Scots, who would be second only to Calvin, spotted Hope a 37-31 lead at the half, but moved ahead 47-45 with 14:10 left and led the rest of the way. Hope closed to 74-68 with 2:26 left, but two field goals by Al Vander Meer sewed it up at 78-68 and the season was over. Charles Hudson was high for Bill Klenk's charges with 23, Drake Serges had 18, Al Vander Meer 17, and Jerry Hills 15. Dykstra led the Dutchmen with 19, including seven of

THE 1968-69 HOPE WRESTLING TEAM
3rd IN MIAA — 5-5-1 OVERALL (First year for wrestling as an MIAA sport)

Kneeling L. to R.: Rick Hine, Keith Van Tubergan, Dirk Dinkeloo, Captain Rick Vandenberg, Karl Nadolsky, Tom Vickrey, Mike Dornan. **Standing:** Coach George Kraft, Tim De Voogd, Fred Mueller, Jeff Aldrich, Ken Gralow, Dave Van Pamelen, Mark Weinert.

seven from the line. Van Huis scored 14 in his final game for Hope, Hendrix scored 12, and Snoap and Shinabarger each had 11.

Hope ended at 10-11 for the season and suffered from the sidelining of Captain Van Huis at mid-season. At 5-7 in the MIAA, the Dutchmen finished fourth behind Calvin, Alma, and Kalamazoo. Tom Dykstra made 76 of 87 free throws for 87 percent, a Hope record. He would be Hope's captain for 1969-70.

* * *

Wrestling was an official MIAA sport for the first time in the 1968-69 season. Hope's fourth year with the sport would be its most successful to date. When the Dutchmen traveled to Valparaiso on Wednesday, Dec. 11, they were riding a 15-meet losing streak. At the meet's conclusion it was Hope 18, Valparaiso 17. The victory was the first for Coach George Kraft and only the second ever for Hope. Ken Gralow won by a pin, while Dave Van Pamelen, Jeff Aldrich, and Tom Vickrey won their matches by decision. Karl Nadolsky and Buzz Taves tied at 5-5. Things did not go quite as well on Dec. 14 at Taylor, when the Dutchmen came up short by a 24-11 score, but the team went on Christmas break with a 1-1 record and a new confidence.

Hope hosted Alma on Saturday, Jan. 11, and downed the Scots 39-5 on the strength of six pins. On Wednesday, Jan. 15, it was Muskegon Community College getting the best of the Dutchmen, 21-14, and three days later at Albion it was the Britons 22, Hope 18, but the Dutchmen had been competitive in both meets. Hope posted a 33-6 victory over Southwestern of Dowagiac on Saturday, Feb. 1, but dropped a 22-11 decision to Defiance on Feb. 5. A week later at Olivet, the Dutchmen were back in the win column with a 24-11 shading of the Comets. The Kalamazoo Hornets were in Carnegie-Schouten Gym for a meet on Wednesday, Feb. 12, and the Dutchmen again prevailed, this time by a 24-16 score. Hope found the going rough in the nine-school GLCA meet on Saturday, Feb. 15. Vickrey's fourth place in the 152 weight class was the best the Dutchmen could muster. Coach Paul Mac Donald brought a strong Adrian team to Hope on Wednesday, Feb. 19, and went home with a 28-12 win. In the season's last dual meet at Calvin, the two teams battled to a 21-21 tie.

For a time it appeared that Hope would share third place with Calvin, but in the league meet at Adrian on March 1 it was the Dutchmen an undisputed third, behind Adrian and Albion and just ahead of the Knights. The Hope grapplers were led by Captain Rick Vandenberg, with a 9-2 record, and Dave Van Pamelen, who won 10 while losing only once. In the MIAA meet, Vandenberg, Van Pamelen, Ken Gralow, and Karl Nadolsky all took second place in their respective weight classes. Hope would continue to improve but fail to notch a championship in the sport's 20-year run. The MIAA would drop the sport in 1984, with Olivet continuing to compete as an independent.

*   *   *

The 1969 Hope golf season saw an improved team experience high moments and the frustrations so common to the game. Coach Bob Brown had assembled a talented team, but seemingly so had most of the other league members. Squad members included Dennis Bobeldyk, Bob Essink, Bill Forbes, Rick Hine, Willie Jackson, Chuck Mc Mullin, Captain Fred Muller, Tom Page, and Drake Van Beek. The team got in some early season play in three invitationals, at Miami, Fla., North Central of Illinois, and at Alma. In the latter contest Hope finished eighth, but just one stroke behind host Alma, the MIAA defending champion.

After an opening dual meet loss to Kalamazoo, the Dutchmen hosted Calvin on Tuesday, May 6. Fred Muller led his team to an 11-4 victory with a one-over-par 71 and medalist honors. Bill Forbes carded a 77, Rick Hine 79, Tom Page 80, and Chuck Mc Mullin 82. Leading Calvin was Bob De Nooyer with a 74. Dean Douma had a 77, Jack Kalmink 79, Mike De Kuiper 85, and Ed Wiers 86.

In a double-dual at Adrian on Friday, May 6, it was Hope 11½, Adrian 3½, and Hope 8½, Defiance 6½. Muller was again the Hope leader, this time with a 77. Page followed with an 80, Forbes had an 85, and Hine 87. While the wins over Calvin, Adrian, and non-league Defiance were confidence builders, the season's high point came on Tuesday, May 13, when the Dutchmen hosted champion Alma. When all rounds had been played, it was Hope the winner by the narrow margin of 8½ to 6½. Page enjoyed his best outing of the season by taking medalist honors with a 73. Muller was close behind with a 75, Mc Mullin was at his best with a 77, Forbes had an 81, and Jackson 82. Jim Heriford and Jim Goodrich were best for the Scots, each with a 76. John Becker followed with a 77, Pete.Mc Donough and John Miller each finished at 81.

The MIAA meet was held on Friday, May 16, at the Gull Lake Country Club, with Kalamazoo the surprise winner with a score of 781. Alma followed with 785, Hope finished third with 791, and Albion, undefeated in dual meets, fell to fourth with 796, followed by Olivet 810, Calvin 820, and Adrian 851. Hope had finished third in both dual meets

THE 1969 HOPE GOLF TEAM

Front Row L. to R.: Captain Fred Muller, Coach Dr. Robert Brown, Bill Forbes **Standing:** Willie Jackson, Bob Essink, Tom Page, Dennis Bobeldyke, Chuck Mc Mullin. Missing from picture: Rick Hine, Drake Van Beek. Fred Muller took medalist honors at the 1969 MIAA Meet with a 36 hole total of 145 (74-71).

and in the field day meet, but dropped to fourth place when Albion, Alma, and Kalamazoo finished in an unusual three-way tie for the title. Coach Brown had some satisfaction when his captain, Fred Muller, came through with a 36-hole total of 145 (74-71) to take league medalist honors. It was the first time a Hope player had won the honor since 1960, when Bob Holt was co-medalist with Del Karnes of Hillsdale.

*   *   *

An unprecedented 12 new Hope track records had been established by the 1968 team enroute to the MIAA title, but graduation gaps would make the going tough in '69. Also, the rise to prominence of Alma and the continued strength of Calvin would make for a different season. Co-captains Rick Bruggers and Walt Reed would provide leadership and needed points as Hope sought to remain in contention. The return of vaulter Bill Bekkering, injured through most of the '68 season, was an added plus, as was Dave Thomas, now running both hurdle races.

The Dutchmen opened at home on Wednesday, April 16, against Spring Arbor. While Hope's 122⅔ to 22⅔ victory was misleading, there were some impressive first meet performances. Al Folkert ran 15.8 to win the high hurdles, freshman Carlton Golder was outstanding with a 49.8 victory in the 440, Rich Frank took the 880 in 1:57.9, and Reed had his best clocking in the 100 at 10.0.

In another non-league meet, Hope hosted Grand Rapids Junior College on Saturday, April 19. JC won four of the seven field events plus the 100 and 880, but at the end it was Hope 88-57. The Dutchmen had sweeps in the pole vault with Bekkering, Karl Nadolsky, and Doug Nichols, and in the high hurdles with Thomas, Folkert, and Bruce Ritsema. Rick Bruggers was again the winner in the mile and two-mile.

After an impressive start, the Dutchmen were jarred back to reality at the fifth annual Great Lakes Colleges Association meet on Saturday, April 26. The meet was hosted by Oberlin, and Hope finished seventh in a field of 11. Bruggers took first in the mile run and Nichols did likewise in the javelin throw. Thomas was second in the intermediate hurdles and Bekkering took third in the pole vault.

At Kalamazoo on Saturday, May 3, it was again Hope by a wide margin. Kalamazoo's Emmett Deans was first in the shot and Chris Kosciuk took the 880, but Hope won the remaining 15 events in posting a 118-23 victory. A new name appeared in the result sheets when freshman Cliff Haverdink of Hamilton won the 440 in 50.9 and placed second in the 220. He would be heard from in the months to come.

On Wednesday, May 7, the Calvin Knights were in town for a dual meet showdown. Dave Tuuk's team was led by Rudy Vlaardingerbroek, a super athlete by MIAA standards. Before the afternoon was over, he would not only win the shot put, discus, and javelin, his specialties, but also place first in the high hurdles with the very respectable time of 15.4. His discus throw of 148' 5" would be a Calvin record. High points for the Dutchmen were Bruggers's double victory in the mile and two-mile, and Mike Brown's throw of 46' ½" in the shot put. Brown's heave, though second to Vlaardingerbroek, broke the Hope record of 45' 10" set by Ek Buys Sr. in 1937. Buys, an avid supporter of Hope sports, was on-hand to congratulate Brown. Frank was first in the 880 in 1:57.7, Thomas won the 440 hurdles, and Bekkering topped the pole vaulters at 13' 6", but it was a Calvin day and the Knights went home with three new school records and a 90-55 team victory.

Hope traveled to Adrian on Saturday, May 10, for a meet that was abbreviated by cold, rainy weather. Coach Jay Flanagan had ace hurdlers in Doug Moss and Ron Labadie, who went 1-2 in the highs but were beaten by Dave Thomas in the intermediates. In an attempt to gain more points, Flanagan moved 880 champion Walt Chany to the 440 and 220. Chany won the latter, but was beaten by Haverdink in the 440. Except for Moss's 14.8 in the high hurdles, performances were not good. As the rain persisted it was decided to cancel the pole vault and triple jump to prevent injury. Hope's depth, plus 10 of 15 firsts, produced a 72-55 victory and a trip home without injury to anyone.

The Scots of Coach Denny Stolz had jelled into a well-balanced team that was more than ready when Alma visited Holland on Tuesday, May 13. In a good meet, it was Alma an 83-62 winner at the final tally. The Scots chalked up nine firsts to Hope's eight, and finished in style by winning the mile relay. Bruggers took the mile, but was edged by Don Yehle in the two-mile. Mike Brown won the shot put with a throw of 46' 3" to break his recently established Hope record by 2½ inches.

In 1969 the MIAA Field Day Meet was moved up to accommodate changing calendars at some of the schools. Hope hosted the meet on Saturday, May 17, amidst scattered showers. Calvin took firsts in seven of the 17 events, Alma had 4, Hope 3, Albion 2, and Adrian one. The day belonged to the Knights' Vlaardingerbroek, who would later be named the league's most valuable trackman. Rudy's gold medal marks in the shot, discus, and javelin were 51' 7¾", 149' 3¼", and 230' 4". All were MIAA records. In addition, he placed third in the 120-yard high hurdles. Bruggers's winning mile time of 4:17.3 was a league mark as was Thomas's gold medal performance of 54.1 in the intermediate hurdles. Bekkering took Hope's other first in the pole vault with a height of 13' 6". Alma's Yehle broke the two-mile record with a time of 9:29.4, and Adrian's Doug Moss tied his own record of 14.6 in the high hurdles. In team scoring, it was Calvin 84, Alma 70, Hope 41, Albion 36, Adrian 22, Olivet 11 and Kalamazoo eight.

Following the league meet, the Dutchmen won two anticlimactic dual meets, which did not alter their overall third place finish. On Tuesday, May 20, at Albion it was Hope 88-57. Hope won both relays, and Thomas was the winner in both hurdle races. Albion's Craig Cossey took the long jump, triple jump and 100-yard dash. He also placed second in the 220 to top all scorers with 18 points. Hope closed out the season at home the next day with a 96-49 victory over Olivet. Hope was the winner in 13 of the 17 events. Bruggers was allowed the luxury of concentrating on the two-mile run, and his winning time of 9:30.6 was a Hope record. The Dutchmen had sweeps in the javelin and triple jump, but sprinters were switched to other events, resulting in an Olivet sweep of the 100-yard dash. Except for the two-mile record, there was a general lack of enthusiasm, and both coaches agreed that late season duals after the league meet were not a good idea.

The NCAA College Division finals were held at Ashland on the weekend of June 13-14, with Thomas finishing seventh in a qualifying heat of the intermediate hurdles. Bruggers reached the finals in the mile, and his excellent time of 4:12.2 was good enough for seventh place and a Hope record that remains at this writing. The event was won by Duane Ray of Chico State University with a time of 4:08.2. Bruggers, Thomas, Bekkering, and Nichols were named to the All-MIAA team.

* * *

Hope's 1969 southern tennis trek began on Saturday, March 29, and ended on April 5. The Dutchmen of Coach Larry Green got by Miami of Ohio 5-4, then lost to North Carolina State 8-1 and Davidson 7-2. Hope bounced back to edge Juniata of Pennsylvania 5-4 and defeat Belmont Abbey 8-1, both on the same day. Furman downed the Dutchmen 7-2 before Colgate stopped Hope 9-0, and Duke pinned a 5-0 defeat on Coach Green's squad in a match shortened by rain.

The regular season opened on Saturday, April 12, with Hope hosting Eastern Michigan University. Seniors Doug Barrow of Bayside, N.Y., and Ron Visscher of Kalamazoo would play a huge role in the success of Doc Green's team throughout the campaign. This day Barrow defeated Robin Wideman 6-0, 6-2, Visscher took Dave Fisher 3-6, 7-5, 6-4, Travis Kraai (H) defeated Al Jagutis (E) 6-2, 6-3, Jeff Green (H) defeated Morris Gilbert (E) 6-2, 6-2, Mike Dombrowski (E) won over Russ Kiefer (H) 7-5, 6-2, and Craig Schrotenboer (H) defeated Jim Ryan (E) 6-0, 6-1. In doubles, it was Barrow-Visscher over Fisher-Jagutis 6-1, 6-2, Green-Kiefer over Gelbert-Wideman 6-4, 7-5, and Kraai-Schrotenboer over Ryan-Dombrowski 6-3, 2-6, 6-4 to complete the 8-1 team victory.

Hope's fine play continued against Central Michigan at Mount Pleasant on Tuesday, April 22, with a 6-3 win. In singles, Barrow defeated Ken Cowin 6-2, 6-1, Visscher defeated Ken Tabacsko 6-0, 6-2, Dan Travis defeated Travis Kraai 6-0 6-4, Schrotenboer took Pat Murphy 6-1, 6-2, Green defeated Jerome Lentini 6-2, 6-1, and Wilt Treygo defeated Kiefer (H) 6-4, 6-2. In doubles, it was Barrow-Green over Cowin-Tabacsko 6-3, 6-3, Visscher-Kraai over Travis-Murphy 9-7, 7-5, and Lentini-Chuck Thurlo over Schrotenboer-Kiefer 6-0, 6-3.

The GLCA tournament was held at Ohio Wesleyan University on Friday-Saturday, April 25-26. As usual, the competition was very tough, but Kalamazoo, representing the MIAA, took top honors with 20 points. De Pauw was a close second with 18, Denison, Oberlin, and Ohio Wesleyan each had 12, Hope 11, Earlham nine, Kenyon seven, Albion three, and Wabash one.

The MIAA season opened with the Dutchmen at home against Kalamazoo on Saturday, May 3. The Hornets' 8-1 victory was no surprise, and the Dutchmen refused to be discouraged. There would be greener pastures ahead. In singles, it was John Brummet over Barrow 6-3, 6-3, Visscher over Bill Struck 6-1, 0-6, 6-2, Rick Watson over Kraai 6-3, 6-1, Burt Bothell over Kiefer 6-2, 6-0, Dave Tidwell over Green 6-1, 6-3, and Don Swarthout over Schrotenboer 6-0, 6-1. In doubles, Struck-Bothell defeated Barrow-Visscher 8-6, 6-4, Brummet-Watson defeated Kraai-Kiefer (score not available), and Rod Day-Rick Tubbs defeated Schrotenboer-Green 8-6, 6-2.

Things went better at Calvin on Wednesday, May 7. Both teams performed well, but at the end it was Hope 6-3. In singles, it was Barrow getting the best of Ben Pekelder 6-4, 6-2, Visscher over Mark Van Faasen 6-1, 6-1, Dan Klop defeated Kraai 6-1, 6-1, Green defeated Ray Van Dam 6-1, 6-2, Schrotenboer defeated Rick Bruinooge 10-8, 6-3, and Tom Visser took Kiefer (H) 6-4, 6-3. In doubles, Barrow-Green defeated Van Dam-Pekelder 6-2, 2-6, 6-1, Klop-Van Faasen defeated Visscher-Kiefer 7-5, 6-4, and Schrotenboer-Kraai defeated Visser-Bruinooge 6-3, 7-5.

The Adrian Bulldogs were in town on Saturday, May 10, but didn't match up well with the Dutchmen and went home an 8-1 loser. It was Barrow over Rick Meyer 6-1, 6-0, Visscher over Steve Tabb 6-1, 6-0, Dave Mc Pike over Kraai 6-4, 7-5, Green over Dave Chamberlain 6-2, 6-0, Schrotenboer over Ted Johnson 6-0, 6-0, and Hope freshman Dave Laackman over Phil Tutak 6-1, 6-1. In doubles, Barrow-Visscher defeated Meyer-Mc Pike 6-2, 6-1, Green-Kraai defeated Johnson-Chamberlain 6-1, 6-1, and Schrotenboer-Russ Kiefer defeated Tabb-Tutak 6-0, 6-3.

Hope had its third straight win at Alma on Wednesday, May 14, this time by a 6-3 margin. In singles, Barrow defeated Paul Croom 6-0, 6-1, Visscher defeated Dennis Williams 6-0, 6-1, Rich Smith defeated Kraai 7-5, 6-4, Green defeated Benja Oredein 6-0, 6-4, Schrotenboer defeated Jim Powers 6-4, 6-3, and Jim Tarrant defeated Kiefer 11-9, 6-4. In doubles, it was Barrow-Visscher over Croom-Smith 6-2, 6-1, Green-Kraai over Williams-Tarrant 6-4, 6-4, and Powers-Tim Lutes over Schrotenboer-Kiefer 6-1, 6-4.

Hope hosted the MIAA conference meet on May 14 and 15 with most of the matches being played at the 22nd Street courts. Kalamazoo's expected victory was won with 24 team points to 14 for runner-up Hope. Calvin finished third with 11, Alma fourth with five, Albion fifth with three, Olivet sixth with two, and Adrian seventh with one. The highlight for Hope came with the championship play of Ron Visscher at number-two singles. In the finals, Visscher defeated Kalamazoo's Bill Struck 6-2, 6-2.

The following Monday, May 19, the Dutchmen hosted Albion in a good match, and came away the winner by a 6-3 score. In singles, Barrow defeated Jack Jones 6-2, 6-1, Visscher took Bryan Kiehl 6-2, 6-2, Kraai defeated Ken Hall 6-1, 6-4, Green defeated Val Hirscht 6-4, 6-1, Schrotenboer won over Greg Kilby 6-0, 6-3, and Kiefer defeated Lockwood 6-3, 6-1. After the singles sweep, Coach Green decided to reward some of his lesser-known but loyal squad members. Schrotenboer-Kiefer, usually at number-three doubles, were moved up to number-one, where they were defeated by Jones-Kilby 7-5, 6-1, Kiehl-Lockwood defeated Hope's Mark Van Dokkumburg-Marty Begley 6-4, 8-6, and Hirscht-Russo defeated Hope's Roy Welton-Dale Laackman 6-4, 6-4.

Hope ended the regular season with a 9-0 shutout at Olivet on Wednesday, May 21. In singles, it was Barrow over Ted Traye 6-2, 6-1, Visscher over Tom Kloss 6-0, 6-0,

265

Kraai over Scot Bacon 9-7, 6-0, Green over Unir Yildiz 6-2, 6-1, Schrotenboer over Doug Johnson 6-1, 6-0, and Van Dokkumburg over Zame Kolestock 6-2, 7-5. In doubles, Barrow-Visscher defeated Traye-Klosa 6-3, 6-1, Green-Kraai defeated Bacon-Bruce Callendar 6-2, 6-3, and Schrotenboer-Van Dokkumburg defeated Tom Cox-Kolestock (O) 6-1, 6-1.

Hope finished at 12-5 overall and 5-1 in MIAA duals, good enough again for second behind Kalamazoo. Barrow and Visscher were named to the All-MIAA team for the third consecutive year, and Barrow was voted the league's most valuable player, an honor that would not come again to a Hope player until 1985. Don Klop of Calvin received the Stowe Sportsmanship Award. Barrow and Visscher added post-season luster to the year's efforts by combining for a fourth-place finish in doubles at the NCAA College Division tournament.

* * *

It would remain for baseball Coach Daryl Siedentop and his assistant, Jim Bultman, to produce Hope's final championship of the decade. It did not begin well. Following a 1-7 record in the South, the Dutchmen opened the regular season in Mount Pleasant on Saturday, April 12. Central Michigan was in the driver's seat in the opener with a two-hit, 9-0 shutout hurled by the Chippewas' Jim Lange. Marty Snoap had Hope's only hits, and Gary Frens absorbed the loss. In the nightcap, Chuck Zimmerman was almost as effective in a 12-1 victory which featured a seven-run third inning by the Chips. Freshman Jim Lamer had two of Hope's five hits, and pitcher Terry Stehle took the loss.

There was improvement in the home opener against Valparaiso on Saturday, April 19. In the first game, Frens pitched a three-hitter and deserved a better fate. Hope scored two runs in the third and one in the fourth to take a 3-0 lead, but the Crusaders came back with four in the fifth for the 4-3 victory. Included in Hope's five hits were two bunt singles by Bob Cooper. Valpo collected 12 hits off three Hope pitchers, and humbled the Dutchmen 16-0 in the second contest. Randy Roedy went the distance for the winners and limited Hope to three hits.

Hope played host to Aquinas on Saturday April 26. In the first game, Frens was again in good form, giving up but four hits, but the Tommies got one run in the third and a two-out homer in the fifth for a 2-1 victory. The beleaguered Dutchmen, now at 1-12, broke the string in the second game, but not by much. Dick Nordstrom pitched five strong innings before being relieved by Bill O'Connor. Hope scored three runs in the third, one in the fourth, and one in the seventh. Aquinas scored one in the seventh when O'Connor gave up three walks and a single. Greg Gorman came on in relief, but three more runs crossed the plate before Gorman finally got the side out and preserved the

GARY FRENS — HOPE 1969

much needed 5-4 victory. Cooper had four hits for the Dutchmen, and Lamer smashed a two-run homer.

The team from Spring Arbor traveled to Holland on Tuesday, April 29. Hope again managed a split by taking the first game 6-4, then dropping the second by a 6-2 count. Lamer's three-run homer contributed to the Hope win, as did two hits by Ric Scott. Stehle, with relief from O'Connor, was the winning pitcher. Spring Arbor got four runs in the fifth inning of the second game to break a 2-2 tie, then held off the Dutchmen for the 6-2 win. Nordstrom took the loss.

The worm began to turn as Hope opened MIAA play at home on Saturday, May 3, against Kalamazoo. In the first game, the Dutchmen gave Frens a cushion by scoring five runs off Gary Armstrong in the first inning. With the score at 5-0 in the sixth inning, Coach Siedentop decided to remove Frens for a possible appearance in the second game. In another heady move, Frens remained in the game as the right fielder. In the final inning, reliever O'Connor loaded the bases. At this point Frens was summoned back to the mound. The Hornets scored one run on a fielder's choice and another on a single before Frens put out the fire and garnered the 6-2 victory.

The lead changed hands four times in the second contest before Hope won it 6-5 on a two-out single by Frens in the seventh. Nordstrom was the starting pitcher, but Frens came on in the fourth to become the winning pitcher in both games. Rumohr was three-for-four and Ken Otte stroked a home run in the fifth.

At Calvin on Wednesday, May 7, it was Frens again in the first game, this time with a five-hit shutout. Runs were scarce all afternoon, but one was enough for Hope's 1-0 win. Bob Cooper was safe on an error, made it to second on a fielder's choice by Terry Stehle, and scored on Bob Kidd's RBI single. Frens had two singles in three trips to lead the Hope batters. Bill O'Connor started the second game, and

THE 1969 HOPE BASEBALL TEAM
MIAA CHAMPIONS

Kneeling L. to R.: Assistant Coach Jim Bultman, Captain Gary Frens, Head Coach Daryl Siedentop. **Standing:** Greg Gorman, Steve Berry, Marty Snoap, Terry Stehle, Ken Otte, Dick Nordstrom, Harry Rumohr, Dave Abel, Bob Kidd, Bob Cooper, Bill O'Conner, Ric Scott, Dave Raterink, Jim Lamer, Mike Hinga, Bob Beishuizen

was supported by four runs in the Hope first inning. Nordstrom came on in the fourth with Hope leading 4-3. He allowed no runs and retired the last 11 in a row. Cooper had three for four in Hope's nine-hit attack that produced the eventual 8-3 victory.

A strong Adrian team gave Hope trouble at Van Raalte on Saturday, May 10. In the opener the Dutchmen scored one run in the fourth, but the Bulldogs tied it in the sixth on Al Smith's home-run. Hope was able to load the bases in the seventh and Rumohr's single gave Hope the 2-1 victory, one more in the win column for Frens. In the second game, Adrian led from the start and downed the Dutchmen 7-1. The Bulldogs collected 10 hits off the slants of Stehle and Nordstrom, while winning pitcher Vic Wolven limited the Dutchmen to five scattered singles.

It was a make or break day for the Dutchmen at Alma on Wednesday, May 14. Hope would go with its top pitcher in the first game and hope for the best in the second. Frens was equal to the task with a five-hitter, striking out five and walking only one. The Dutchmen scored one in the second, but Alma tied it in the fourth. A Cooper single in the fifth drove in Frens and Scott to make it 3-1, then added one more in the seventh for the 4-1 victory. The nightcap was indeed a wild affair. Nordstrom started and seemed to have things well in hand going into the seventh with a 9-2 lead, but at that point the roof caved in. Before the inning was over, Alma had sent 13 batters to the plate. With the score at 9-6, O'Connor relieved Nordstrom. O'Connor gave up two more runs before Coach Siedentop once again called on Frens. Frens was nicked for two more runs before finally retiring the red-hot Scots, who now had taken a 10-9 lead. In the bottom of the seventh, Otte walked, then went to third on a double by Rumohr. Frens walked to load the bases. Scott hit a ground ball to third base, where the usually reliable John Fuzak threw wildly to the plate, allowing Otte to score the tying run. Cooper then came through with a single to score Rumohr, giving Hope the 11-10 victory. An earlier big blow for the Dutchmen was a three-run homer by Otte in the third inning. Once again, Frens was the winner in both games.

At Olivet on Saturday, May 17, Frens was impressive in recording his seventh MIAA victory of the season, a league record. Hope's ace lefty gave up a lone single in the third inning, struck out four and walked three. With the score at 0-0 in the seventh, Scott walked and came home with the winning run as Frens won his own game with a double. In the second game, Nordstrom pitched the best game of his career, scattering three hits and allowing no one beyond second base. In the second inning, Otte and Rumohr had successive singles. Frens's sacrifice somehow ended in a collision at first base, allowing two runs to score. That would be enough to give Hope a 2-0 shutout and the MIAA championship.

Hope's final game was a 16-inning marathon at home against Albion. Frens and Gary Horner hooked up in a pitchers' duel, and both went all the way. Hope had 13 hits to five for Albion, but the Britons took the 2-1 victory on three Hope errors in the 16th. The second game was cancelled when the rains came.

The Dutchmen ended the season at 12-13 overall, but a great comeback had netted the MIAA title with a 9-2 record. Shortstop Jim Lamer, second baseman Harry Rumohr, and pitcher Gary Frens were named to the All-MIAA team. In addition, Frens won the batting championship with an average of .385. Gary Frens was a shoo-in as the MIAA's most valuable player.

* * *

On Friday, April 17, 1969 it was announced that Dr. Kenneth J. Weller had been selected as the new president of Central College in Pella, Iowa. His administrative talent had been evident for some time on Hope's campus, and it was simply a matter of time before he would move up the ladder. While we rejoiced at Central's good fortune and Ken's new challenge, there was concern at the gap which now existed in our coaching ranks. Weller's football insight, experience, and enthusiasm could not be easily replaced. The new faculty person would be an instructor in economics and business administration, but not a coach. These circumstances, plus the advanced time of the year, dictated my return to coaching in Russ DeVette's final year as head football coach.

Unlike some of his coaching colleagues, Russ De Vette was not confined to the narrow world of football. His wide variety of interests and activities had a common denominator, service. If some thought this was spreading it too thin, they could rest assured that when it was time for football, his concentration and dedication were complete. Now, in his final months as head man, he would choose a bold course. After a careful assessment of the talent on hand he decided to adopt an offense recently originated at the University of Houston by Coach Bill Yeoman, who referred to it as the "Houston Veer." The system was later refined as the "Wishbone" at the University of Texas by Darrell Royal. The veer formation, much like a pro set, included two set-backs side-by-side, a wide flanker and tight end on one side, and a split end on the other. The running part of the offense was in some ways a throw-back to the Split-T formation used so successfully by Bud Wilkinson and his Oklahoma teams of the 50s. The main man was the quarterback, who would move down the line of scrimmage and either (one) hand off to the fullback, or (two) keep the ball and head up field, or (three) pitch the ball to the halfback four yards deep, thus the term "triple option." Not to be overlooked was a fourth option, when the halfback would fake a run and pass to any one of three receivers.

Hope's 1969 program roster listed 52 names. Included were some returning regulars who seemed to be naturals for the veer's requirements, at least on paper. Running the show would be quarterback Groy Kaper, who by now held most of Hope's passing records. Jon Constant had also shown well in a backup role. Bob Haveman, Hope's leading ground gainer in '68, returned at fullback, and the halfback position was in good hands with Harry Rumohr. An all-conference infielder in baseball, Rumohr had good speed and a strong throwing arm. He had been a high school quarterback and was ideal for the "fourth option" as described above. Bill Bekkering at split end was unmatched in the league as a receiver, and big Jim Lamer left little to be desired at tight end. Flanker Rich Frank, a top 880-man, also had good hands. Across the line, it was Bart Merkle and Gerry Swierenga at tackles, Bill Hondorp and Dave Pruim guards, and Jim De Horn at center. All were experienced and eager to tackle the new system. Pruim would be one of thousands to lose their lives in the World Trade Center on September 11, 2001.

We all knew, of course, that a team on paper is not enough. There remained the question of defense, the guys who give the ball back to the offense for more chances to score. In preparing for the opener, we benefited from consultations with Coach Bill Doolittle at Western Michigan University. The Broncos were also switching to the veer, and we found it helpful to attend one of their scrimmages. In an eight-year stint as a high school coach I had employed the option play, and now a part of my assignment was to work with Kaper and Constant on their maneuvers down the line. We seemed to be making progress, but would soon learn that there was a long way to go.

The Hope team traveled to Defiance, Ohio, for its opener on Saturday, Sept. 13. The 2 p.m. contest began in the Dutchmen's favor, when a James Fitzgerald fumble was recovered by Hope's Howard Ducharme on the Defiance 34. Five plays later, Kaper threw a three-yard scoring pass to freshman end Ted Albrecht, who was substituting for the injured Bekkering. Mike Hinga's conversion made it 7-0 in the early going. It was a different story in the second quarter, as Hope miscues led to three scores by the Yellow Jackets. Quarterback Jerry Griffith scored on a one-yard sneak, and Jim Van Horne's kick made it 7-7. A fumbled Hope pitchout was recovered by Defiance, and halfback Gary Evans scored on a nine-yard end sweep. Van Horne's second kick made it 14-7 with 6:33 left in the period. On Hope's next possession, tackle Tim Predeiri took another mishandled pitchout in midair and rambled 32 yards for the TD. Jim Van Horne's third conversion made it 21-7 at the half.

Hope's defense was not up to the task in the second half, and Defiance scored three more times. In the third period, Jerry Griffith threw a 12-yard scoring pass to Gary Evans and Van Horne's kick made it 28-7. In the fourth quarter, it was sub halfback Duane Laux going over from the two-yard line on a dive play. The kick was not good, leaving the score at 34-7. Sophomore halfback Paul Smith closed out the scoring with a five-yard slant off-tackle to make the final score Defiance 40-7. Bright spots were few and far between for the Dutchmen, but Kaper and Constant had combined to complete 14 of 35 passes for 174 yards.

SIDELINE WOES
HOPE 13 – FRANKLIN 13 — September 20, 1969
Franklin College came on to tie Hope with 1:23 left in the game.

L. to R.: Quarterback Jon Constant (14), Asst. Coach Gordon Brewer, Head Coach Russ De Vette, halfback Peter Grimes (36), Captain Tom Thomas (86), and Asst Coach George Craft. Helmet decals commemorated the 100th year of intercollegiate football.

Of special interest to Holland fans was a game played at Riverview Park on Friday, Sept. 12. The night contest pitted Holland High School against West Ottawa for the very first time. Dave Kempker, Hope '54, was the Holland coach, while Ron Wetherbee, Hope '58, directed the West Ottawa team. In a good game, Holland prevailed, 26-14. A crosstown rivalry would soon develop and be anticipated each season.

The home opener for Hope was a night game on Saturday, Oct. 20, against Franklin of Indiana. The Dutchmen hoped to avenge a 28-13 loss to the Grizzlies in 1968, and were cheered by the return to the lineup of Bekkering and freshman Dana Snoap. The week's practice sessions had emphasized defense for obvious reasons, and the effort would pay off. The game began in a fashion similar to the Defiance contest. Franklin quarterback Don Mullen lost the handle on a pitchout, and Hope's Craig Schrotenboer was there to recover on the 24. A handoff to Haveman was good to the 10, and three plays later it was Haveman again with a two-yard plunge into the end zone. Hinga's kick made it 7-0 with 9:11 left in the first quarter. The Grizzlies returned the favor when the Dutchmen fumbled on their own 27. Don Mullen's 11-yard pass to Keith Gerbers capped a drive to the end zone, and Gerbers's kick made it 7-7 as the quarter ended.

Late in the second quarter, Hope put together an 80-yard drive in 19 plays with fullback Haveman getting his second TD on a five-yard run. Terry Klysz broke through to block Hinga's point try, but the Dutchmen led 13-7 at the half. Each team threatened in the third quarter, but there was no scoring. Jim Leenhouts halted the Franklin drive with a fumble recovery on the Hope 20. The Franklin defense stopped Hope at the Grizzlie 20, and Hinga's field goal attempt sailed wide of the mark. Late in the fourth quarter, the visitors kept a 17-play drive alive when Mullen completed a fourth down pass to Klysz. This was followed by a Hope interference call that put the ball on the 10. Gerbers then scored on a left end sweep with 1:23 left in the game.

Gerbers's kick sailed just wide of the goal post, and the improved Dutchmen were forced to settle for a 13-13 tie.

Hope traveled to Wheaton on Sept. 27 for an 8 p.m. game at Red Grange Field. The Dutchmen would play stellar defense in the second half, but only after considerable damage had been done in the first half. The Crusaders drew first blood with a 70-yard drive. The scoring play was a 31-yard pass from quarterback Joel Detwiler to right end Bill Caraher. Jim Mc Kean's kick was good, and the Dutch were down 7-0 in the first quarter. With 13:37 left in the second quarter, Jim Mc Kean made good on a 27-yard field goal attempt to increase the Wheaton lead to 10-0. At this point the Hope defense asserted itself, and the Crusaders were forced to punt on their own 18. Hope end Dave Gosselar charged in to block the kick, which rolled through the end zone for a safety. The Dutchmen were now on the board at 10-2. Hope received the free kick and marched 55 yards to score in 11 plays. A 21-yard pass from Kaper to Bekkering put the ball on the one, and halfback Peter Grimes took it in for the TD. The try for two points failed, leaving the score at 10-8. Wheaton returned the kickoff 41 yards to the Hope 39, and Don Baker ran 12 yards to the Hope 27. The Hope defense held, but on fourth down the Dutchmen were fooled by a fake field goal as holder Joel Detwiler raced 31 yards around left end for the touchdown. The point try failed, but the Wheaton lead was now 16-8. The Dutchman offense sputtered on the next series, and the Crusaders took over on their own 29. A subsequent 71-yard drive was successful as Detwiler passed 15 yards to Caraher for the latter's second TD. The kick by Mc Kean was good, making it 23-8 at the half.

The Dutchman defense did its part in the second half, holding Wheaton to 22 total yards and no points. The Crusaders were forced to punt six times. The Dutchmen moved into Wheaton four times, but could not punch in a score. Finally, in the closing seconds, Snoap put a jarring tackle on quarterback Jim Stevenson. The ball came loose and, catching it in midair, Snoap raced 49 yards to score as time ran out. The point try was not good, leaving Wheaton's victory margin, 23-14.

The Dutch experience thus far was disappointing, but nothing would compare to the disaster at Kalamazoo on Oct. 4. This was a game that coaches and players alike expected to win. The Hornets of Coach Ed Baker were winless on the season, and faced a grim future when the Dutchmen brightened their prospects with 11 turnovers. The Hornets' first score in the initial quarter came on a 20-yard pass from Gary Armstrong to Frank Gibson. Bob Lockwood's kick made it 7-0, and his field goal early in the second quarter increased the lead to 10-0. On Hope's next possession, Kazoo intercepted a Constant pass to set up another score. Mike Shonefeld went in from the four, and Lockwood converted to make it 17-0 with 57 seconds left in the half. Kaper returned to the game only to have his first pass bounce off the fingertips of Rumohr and into the hands of K's Ed Stehower at the Hope 40. With four seconds left, Gary Armstrong hit Doug Wisnieski with a 35-yard TD pass and Lockwood again converted to put Ed Baker's team in great position with a halftime lead of 24-0.

Kalamazoo's final score came in the third quarter on a keeper-play by quarterback Armstrong. Lockwood closed out a perfect afternoon with his conversion and a 31-0 Kalamazoo victory. The Dutchmen had managed only 24 yards rushing to 123 for the Hornets, and just about everything else had gone wrong. A silent team bus traveled 50 weary miles back to Holland with the prospect of facing MIAA champion Alma just seven days later.

It was a talent-laden Alma team that invaded Riverview Park on Oct. 11. The Scots of Coach Denny Stolz were led by quarterback Tom Jakovac, end John Fuzak, and tailback Chris Clark. Hope mistakes continued as a bad snap on a punt was turned into a score by Clark on a five-yard run. Fuzak's kick made it 7-0 with 8:59 left in the first quarter. Later in the quarter, Jakovac broke free on a keeper and, behind a good block from Chad Creevy, raced 53 yards to score. A Fuzak kick made it 14-0, and the Scots were just getting started. A 73-yard, 12-play march followed, with Clark getting his second TD on a five-yard run. Fuzak's third conversion increased the lead to 21-0 with 3:49 left in the half. The Dutchman defense came alive in the closing minutes of the half and forced an Alma punt. The kick was short, and Hope had the ball on the Alma 44. On a square-out pattern Kaper passed to Bekkering, who faked out safety Jeff Johnson and ran untouched for 69 yards and Hope's first score. The point try failed, but the Dutchmen were on the board at 21-6 as the half ended.

Early in the third quarter, linebacker Bob Zins recovered a Hope fumble and the Scots had possession on the Hope 10. Four plays later, Clark went over from the two and Fuzak's kick made it 28-6. With 4:33 left in the period, Larry Hourtienne scored from the two and "automatic" Fuzak increased the margin to 35-6. To the surprise of most everyone in the stadium, Hope now mounted an 82-yard, nine-play drive to score. Grimes broke away for 15 yards to the Alma 15 and Kaper again passed to sure-handed Bekkering for the touchdown. A two-point try failed, leaving the score at 35-12.

Kaper continued to throw well in the fourth quarter as the Dutchmen scored again. A 60-yard drive included passes of 35 yards to Bekkering and 23 yards to Frank. Rumohr scored on a seven-yard run after a well-executed option pitchout. After a failed kick, the scoreboard showed Alma 35, Hope 18. With three minutes left in the game, the Scots pushed across a final TD. Jakovac passed 14 yards to Rick Manzardo, and Fuzak was good on his sixth straight conversion to give Coach Stolz and his team the 42-18 victory. Hope had found some offense, but a spotty defense still needed work.

Olivet would be Hope's homecoming opponent on Saturday, Oct. 18. The stands were not full, but the 3,000 who turned out would witness an exciting game. A strong wind would be a factor throughout. Hope won the toss and took the wind. Olivet elected to receive Hope's wind-aided kick. Later in the quarter, Hinga was successful with a 40-yard field goal, the longest in Hope history. Early in the second quarter, the Dutchmen added to the 3-0 lead with an 86-yard drive. Hope's backs were gaining confidence in the veer offense and its several options. With the ball on the Olivet 26, Kaper now ran the option play to the left. His pitch to Rumohr came after a good fake, and Rumohr went the distance to score. Kaper passed to Frank for the two-point conversion, and the Dutch lead was 11-0. The Comets were quick to respond when linebacker Bill Ash intercepted a Kaper pass and scampered 54 yards to score. On a fake kick, quarterback Eric Witzke passed to Kurt Chubner for two points and the score narrowed to 11-8.

The Dutchmen would score one more time before the intermission with an 80-yard march. The drive was aided by two 15-yard penalties and an interference call in the end zone. Perhaps the most spectacular play of the series was an option pass from Rumohr to tight end Lamer, who leaped high in the air to pull it down. Kaper went in from the six-inch line, but the ensuing kick was wide, making it 17-8 at the half.

It was the Comets' turn in the third quarter, as fullback Gary Cummings got around right end for 16 yards and the touchdown. The conversion by Hal Hooks made it close again at 17-15. Hope gained possession in the fourth quarter when freshman Dave Johnson intercepted an Witzke pass on the Hope 46. On first down, De Vette called for the option pass. Harry Rumohr's fake run after the pitch drew the defense in, and his strike to Frank allowed the flanker to streak untouched for 64 yards and the score. This time Hinga's kick was good, and Hope had breathing room at 24-15 with 11 minutes left. The seesaw contest continued as Olivet gained possession after blocking a Hinga field goal attempt in the closing minutes. The Comets' drive took them to the one-yard line and Witzke scored on a sneak. Hooks's kick was true, and things were tense with the score at 24-22 and 2:52 remaining. De Vette was careful to insert "good hands" people, and freshman Snoap responded by recovering Olivet's on-side kick. Hope stayed on the ground in gaining an all-important first down. Kaper then ran out the clock, and Hope finally had that illusive first victory. The Dutchmen had 341 yards of offense to Olivet's 201. Workhorse Haveman rushed for 104 yards, and Rumohr completed the halfback pass three times.

Championship hopes had evaporated with two league defeats, but as coaches we believed that our team had matured, turned a corner, and was now coming into its own. However, the Oct. 25 game at Albion's Alumni Field would find the Britons an overwhelming favorite, and with good

HOPE 24 — OLIVET 22
October 18, 1969

A familiar sight during the 1969 season: Quarterback Groy Kaper (11) hands off to fullback Bob Haveman (43) against Olivet.

reason. After 15 impressive years as Albion's head mentor, Morley Fraser had now turned over the reigns to his protégé, Tom Taylor. A Little All-American during his playing days at Albion, Taylor had paid his dues as Fraser's line coach for seven years. Now, with a 5-0 record, his team was the only undefeated team in the State of Michigan. More importantly, his most recent win was a 7-3 decision over reigning champion Alma. During the practice, week several changes were made in Hope's defensive alignment. Across the front, it was now Ted Albrecht and Captain Tom Thomas at ends, Dave Gosselar and Bruce Heustis at tackles and Keith Van Tubergen at middle guard. Linebackers were Karl Nadolsky and Doug Nelson, while Jim Leenhouts and Craig Schrotenboer held down the corner spots. The safety positions were manned by Doug Smith and Carlton Golder.

The changes paid off with a scoreless first period, but early in the second quarter a Dutchman fumble was recovered by Albion's Steve Young on the Hope 26. The Britons were held to three yards in three plays before Bill Schueller made good on a 23-yard field goal. The Hope defense continued to play tough and overcame a second miscue. Another fumble gave Albion the ball on the Hope 30, but a defensive charge led by Nadolsky pushed the Britons back to the 48 and a second Schueller field goal attempt fell short. The Albion defense was equally tough. The Dutchmen failed to mount any offense, but excellent punting by Doug Smith kept the home team in the hole. The 3-0 halftime score was a true measure of the game's intensity.

The third quarter saw six exchanges of punts before Haveman broke free for a 51-yard run to the Albion 15, but another Hope fumble ended the threat. Early in the fourth quarter, quarterback Chris Rundle passed 30 yards to end Jim Mc Millan to set up a 12-yard TD run by fullback Dave

THE 1969 HOPE FOOTBALL TEAM
Russ De Vette's last team as Head Coach.

Front Row L. to R.: Manager Jerry Lauver, Doug Nelson, Tim Snow, Carey Boote, Groy Kaper, Don Stephens, Gary Plooster, Karl Nadolsky, Howard Ducharme, Eugene Tilma, Jeff Winne, Boyd Rasmussen, Ted Albrecht, Carlton Golder. **2nd Row:** Bill Munsell, Rich Jarman, Chuck Cousineau, John Wyns, Ken Weiden, Bob Tiggleman, Jim Grant, Eric Brown, Rich Frank, Harry Rumohr, John Grant, Doug Smith, Dave Johnson, Doug Scott, Bob Haveman, Jim Leenhouts, Peter Grimes, Manager Doug Meyers. **3rd Row:** Assistant Coach Gordon Brewer, Head Coach Russ De Vette, Jim Lamer, Dave Gosselar, Dana Snoap, Bob Smickley, Jon Constant, Merlin Whiteman, Keith Van Tubergen, Gerry Swieringa, Bill Hondorp, Jim De Horn, Jon Burg, Bruce Heustice, Pete Semeyn, Craig Schrotenboer, Bart Merkle, Captain Tom Thomas, Bill Bekkering, Mike Hinga, Dave Pruim, Assistant Coach George Kraft, Assistant Coach Gary Frens.

Egnatuck. Schueller's kick was good, and the lead moved to 10-0 with 13:15 left. The Dutchmen did not fold. Later in the quarter, Hope began a drive that would prove to be the most crucial possession of the game. The big play of the drive was a 50-yard pass play from Kaper to Frank that ended on the Albion eight-yard line. At this point Hope President Vander Werf left his seat in the stands and moved down the sideline to the goal line. The Briton defense stiffened, but Hope inched toward the goal line. On fourth down the ball was given to Haveman, who dove into the line with all he had. It appeared that he had broken the plane of the goal line and we waited for the head linesman's arms to be raised. It did not happen. President Vander Werf returned to his seat reporting to all that Haveman was clearly over the line. His opinion may have been less than objective, but at that point we all wished that he might have been wearing a striped shirt.

In the midst of disappointment, the defenders took the field and forced an Albion punt. This gave Hope the ball on their own 45. A Kaper-to-Frank pass put the ball on the 29. Pass interference was called on the next play, moving the ball to the five. Two plays later, Harry Rumohr went in from the one and no one disputed the call. A Kaper-to-Rumohr pass was good for two, and the score stood at 10-8 with 3:03 remaining. Albion recovered Hope's on-side kick and ran out the clock, and the struggle was over. The two-point win would be the Britons' closest call in their march to an undefeated season and the MIAA championship. With a supreme effort against great odds, the Hope team had come within inches of the upset of the year. Four coaches were very proud.

Hope's final home appearance in 1969 was a Parents Day contest with Adrian on Saturday, Nov. 1. Second-year Adrian Coach Bill Davis relied heavily on the passing combination of Tom Bell to Jim Wallace, and the running of halfback Ron Labadie. The latter had been Hope's undoing in the '68 game. The Bulldogs, however, would have trouble with the various facets of Hope's triple option offense. Of equal concern was the passing of Kaper and Rumohr. The game's first break went to the Dutchmen when Albrecht recovered a Tom Bell fumble on the Adrian 45. On the first play, Rumohr took a pitchout for an 11-yard gain. On the next play, Haveman closed over the Kaper handoff and raced 34 yards to score. Hinga's kick gave Hope the 7-0 lead with 12:39 left in the quarter. Adrian responded with an 80-yard drive that featured a 38-yard pass from Bell to Wallace that put the ball on the Hope 23. Five plays later, Labadie scored on a nine-yard run, but the kick sailed wide and Hope remained in front 7-6.

The second Dutchman drive covered 61 yards in five plays. Behind Bart Merkle's block it was Haveman again, this time going 25 yards to the end zone. On the point try,

A Tribute To Russ De Vette

In His Final Home Game As Head Football Coach

At its regular meeting in the fall of 1968, the Board of Trustees of Hope College created a special Committee on Intercollegiate Athletics for the purpose of examining the total intercollegiate program at the college. At their 1969 spring meeting, the Board of Trustees gave a vote of confidence to this program by suggesting that "the place of intercollegiate athletics in the total college program at Hope as it has been philosophically accepted through the years is sound." The Board accepted the recommendations of the Committee on Intercollegiate Athletics, including the following guideline: "As a basic policy objective, no person should be the head coach for more than one sport."

The 1969 football season, therefore, marks Russ DeVette's final year as head football coach, and this game today marks his final home appearance in that capacity.

Russ DeVette has been associated with Hope College football as a player and coach for almost thirty years with time out taken only for two stints in the Marine Corps, graduate school, and two years as assistant football coach at the University of Maine. Like all coaches whose tenure takes them over a period of time, his teams have had their ups and downs. He has known the disappointment and frustration of the past three years as his Flying Dutchmen compiled a 9-15 record, and he has also known the high moments which accompany a streak such as the 23-4 record his teams put together from 1957-1959.

Throughout it all, however, several traits are noteworthy for their admirability and their consistency. Coach DeVette possesses a keen strategic football mind. His teams have never suffered for lack of imaginative offensive and defensive strategies, be it in a losing season or a winning season. He is totally devoted to the well-being of his players as they pursue their total education at Hope College. Sometimes this devotion to their well-being results in a conflict between the well-being of the individual player and the success of the team. The mark of this man is that his decisions in such cases are easily predictable. He refuses to use a college football player as a means to an end, no matter how desirable that end might seem at the spur of the moment. When conflict occurs, his loyalty is always to the individual player. Finally, and perhaps most admirably, Russ DeVette is a man of his times. In an era when too many football coaches pride themselves in their sole guardianship of 19th century traditions, he continues to be a remarkably contemporary individual. In his educational, social, political, and religious commitments Russ DeVette continues to form the base from which he can speak relevantly to the issues which confront the students and faculty at Hope College.

In this, his last home football game, we pause to pay him tribute and to offer our thanks for a job well done.

- Daryl Siedentop

The above page was included in the HOPE-ADRIAN football program of Nov. 1, 1969.

FINAL SCORE: HOPE 29 — ADRIAN 12

holder Constant fielded a bad snap and ran the ball in for two points to make it 15-6. Later in the second quarter, Adrian suffered another bad break when a Bell-to-Wallace touchdown was called back because of illegal procedure. De Vette quickly inserted freshman Dave Johnson, who promptly intercepted Bell's next pass on the 20. After a short Hope punt, an Adrian field goal try was short and the score remained 15-6 at the half.

In the third quarter, the Dutchmen capitalized on a roughing-the-kicker penalty which gave them the ball on the Bulldog 24. A 14-yard Kaper-to-Bekkering pass put the ball on the 10, and Haveman did the rest for his third TD. Hinga's kick raised the count to 22-6. With 8:28 left in the game, Gosselar recovered an Adrian fumble on the Hope 40. The veer offense was now functioning as diagramed. A 16-yard run by Rumohr was followed by Haveman with 31 more. A 14-yard Kaper-to-Frank pass put the ball on the Adrian 25, and sub halfback Grimes took it the rest of the way. Hinga's kick was good, and the Hope lead increased to 29-6.

Coach De Vette now made sure that as many substitutes as possible got onto the field. Parents had come to see their sons play, and each had made a contribution through the season. Adrian scored late in the game on a three-yard plunge by fullback Steve Rulewicz. The two-point try failed as the score moved to 29-12. Constant moved Hope into Adrian territory as the game ended. Coach De Vette was taken aback when jubilant Hope players hoisted him on their shoulders. There are times when championships take a back seat. Bob Haveman finished the day with 135 yards in 17 carries, and Harry Rumohr 118 yards in 22 carries. Haveman was named MIAA player of the week.

Hope's final football game of 1969 was played on a gray November day in Upland, Ind. Hope and Taylor had enjoyed a basketball relationship, but this Nov. 8 encounter would be their first on the gridiron. A non-league game away from home, Hope's fourth place finish in the MIAA, and cold weather combined to limit our following to a mere handful. The coaches were especially pleased, however, to spot Norm and Shirley Japinga and their friends Cal and Betty Fleser huddled in the stands. Japinga and Fleser had officiated a high school game the previous night in Niles, Mich., then took lodging in Plymouth, Ind., and joined us the next day. Such loyalty meant a great deal to us on this particular day. Its non-league status notwithstanding, the game would be charged with emotion for Hope players and coaches alike.

The teams had played a common opponent in Franklin. Taylor defeated Franklin 20-6, while Hope's game ended in a 13-13 tie. With increased confidence in their defense, the Dutchmen kicked off, held, and took over on the Hope 29. A 71-yard drive followed, with Rumohr going over from the one. A Hinga kick was not good, but the Dutchmen were out front 6-0 with 7:30 left in the first quarter. Late in the quarter, Taylor fumbled a Hope punt and De Horn recovered on the Taylor five. As Haveman gained one yard, Coach De Vette noted that split end Bekkering was not well covered by the defense. For the first time all season, his call was an option pass to the left with Haveman doing the passing. It may have been the only pass of his career, but running to the left, right-handed Haveman took the pitchout, made the difficult pivot to his right and threw a wobbly pass into the end zone, where it was gathered in by Bekkering for the score, two Fremont boys teaming up for a touchdown. Hinga's kick made it 13-0.

With about five minutes left in the half, the Trojans began a drive of their own. On one play, a wide receiver ran a crossing pattern, took the pass and was tackled by Hope cornerback Craig Schrotenboer. The receiver did not get up. With trainer and doctor on the field, and after some delay, it was determined that the player had suffered a fractured leg. As the player was removed by stretcher, Schrotenboer's concern mounted. To do bodily harm to an opponent was farthest from his mind, and his empathy was genuine. Shaken and distraught, Schrotenboer came to the sidelines and could not bring himself to return to the game. As coaches we were deeply moved by his concern for a fellow player. Hard, tough football and compassion need not be strange bedfellows. Craig played for the right reasons, and we were immensely proud.

The Taylor drive continued as quarterback Dave Ticknor completed an 18-yard pass to flanker Chuck Malone for the Trojans' first score. The conversion by senior Joe Romine made it 13-7 at the half. In the third quarter, Kaper moved the Dutchmen 76 yards in 12 plays. Included were passes of 13 yards to Frank, 21 to Lamer, and 23 to Bekkering. Rumohr went in from the one for his second TD, and Hinga's kick increased the lead to 20-7. Later in the quarter, Kaper was trapped in his own end zone for a safety, making it 20-9. Taylor returned Hope's free kick to the Dutch 43, and on the second play Ticknor completed a 41-yard pass play to Dick Van Yteren who was finally pulled down on the one-yard line. Ticknor went in on a sneak and Romine's kick cut Hope's lead to 20-16.

Momentum was on the Taylor side in the fourth quarter. Early in the game, Hope safety John Wyns had made some defensive mistakes. The Shelby freshman now huddled under a parka on the bench. With but a four-point spread, the Trojans were again on the march. At a crucial point, insight and intuition told De Vette that the next play would be an aerial to the wide receiver. Without hesitation, he grabbed Wyns and sent him in for one-on-one coverage. With specific instruction, good speed, and a chance to redeem himself, Wyns was ready. The pass came as expected and Wyns's interception turned the game around. In subsequent action, Snoap recovered a Taylor fumble on the Trojan 20. Four plays later, Kaper's 10-yard pass found Bekkering in the end zone. The kick failed, but the Dutchmen had persevered against another quality team. As Hope savored the 26-16 victory, the November day somehow seemed warmer.

The season ended in marked contrast to the Ashland finale of 1968. As mentioned earlier, "comeback" may be the sweetest word in sport. The MIAA coaches did not see fit to name a single Hope player to the All-MIAA team, but we knew that in this season we had experienced something special. Now, as our Greyhound journeyed northward on U.S. 31, even the weather seemed to relent. A late ray of sun pierced dark blue clouds and the overall effect was, what else - orange and blue! Another chapter in the grand pageantry of college football.

* * *

Hope teams in cross country and soccer fell on hard times in the fall of 1969. Hope was fortunate in securing the services Doug Formsma to coach the harriers. He had been the league's most valuable runner himself in 1966, but despite his efforts it would turn out to be a long season. Tuesday, Sept. 23, was the date for the annual Hope Invitational, and when the Dutchmen finished fourth out of four the handwriting was on the wall. A strong Calvin team finished first with 39 points, Spring Arbor followed with 46, Aquinas 48, and Hope 80.

At Kalamazoo on Saturday, Sept. 27, Coach Formsma and Captain Bruce Geelhoed tasted victory for the first time. Hornet ace John Wismer finished first, but Hope runners took third, fourth, fifth, sixth, and seventh to take the meet by a score of 25 to 32. Unfortunately, Hope's next opponent was Calvin. The powerful Knights came to Holland on Wednesday, Oct. 1, took the first six places, and journeyed home with a 15-48 victory.

The Dutchmen finished eighth out of nine at the GLCA meet on Saturday, Oct. 4, before hosting Alma one week later. The Scots, led by Don Yehle, were riding the crest in cross country and track, and took the Dutchmen by a score of 15 to 49. Hope improved in hosting Olivet on Oct. 18, but lost a heartbreaker when the Comets' Mike Cronan and John Martin finished 1-2 to win a squeaker, 27-28.

At Albion on Oct. 25, the Britons were in charge all the way as Keith Wattles led his team to a 15-46 victory. Hope's Brian Claxton returned from a knee injury and finished sixth. In a similar meet, Hope hosted Adrian on November 1. Coach Jay Flanagan had an interesting duo in Neal and Roger Kingsbury. The twins finished in a tie for first as the Bulldogs beat the Dutchmen by a 15-45 score.

The MIAA meet was held at Adrian on Friday, Nov. 7, with Calvin the winner as expected. In an unusual finish, it was Calvin at 42 and Alma and Albion tied in second with 59, followed by Adrian, Kalamazoo, Hope, and Olivet. Hope closed out the season by participating in the NCAA College Division meet at Wheaton on Saturday, Nov. 15. The team was greeted by frigid temperatures, strong winds, and two inches of snow. Eastern Illinois University took the meet, with Eastern Michigan University finishing second. Ron Stonitsch of C.W. Post College was the individual winner. Hope finished 47th in a field of 51, then suffered the problem of a bus breakdown on the way home.

* * *

With soccer scheduled to become an MIAA sport in 1970, Coach Bill Vanderbilt prepared his team for what would be its last season in the tough Michigan-Illinois-Indiana Soccer Conference. Hope had enjoyed a solid season in 1969, but now the ranks were riddled by graduation. Especially felt was the loss of several with scoring potential. The season opened on Saturday, Sept. 20, at Maryknoll Seminary in Glen Ellyn, Ill. The Dutchmen were off to a good start with a 1-0 victory, but were not as fortunate the following Tuesday in East Lansing. Michigan State was simply too much and downed the Dutchmen by 6-0, but any time the Spartans could be kept in single digits it was somewhat of a moral victory.

Earlham proved to be even tougher. In a home game on Saturday, Sept. 27, it was the Quakers 8, Hope 0. The Dutchmen bounced back one week later to edge Wabash 2-1 in perhaps their best performance of the season. At Albion on Wednesday, Oct. 8, it was the Britons 4, Hope 1 and three days later in Jacksonville, Ill., the Highlanders of Mac Murray took Hope, again by a 4-1 score. At home on Oct. 17, Hope was in the game all the way as Wheaton finally prevailed with a 2-0 shutout. Co-captains Art Hudak and Dave Clark rallied their team for an all-out effort at Calvin on Wednesday, Oct. 21. The archrivals battled through two overtimes before Calvin put in the winner to notch the 2-1 victory. At Van Raalte Field three days later, a similar effort paid off as Hope shut-out Kalamazoo 1-0 for the third Dutchmen win. The season ended at Lake Forest on the last day of October. The Foresters played extremely well, and the Dutchmen were forced to go home on the short end of a 4-0 count. The season of strong competition would be instrumental in producing seven victories in 1970 with the opening of MIAA play.

* * *

Senior Tom Dykstra was captain of Coach De Vette's 1969-70 basketball squad, a little man with a big responsibility. Gone by graduation was center Bruce Van Huis. When illness sidelined him in the 1968-69 campaign, the team had struggled and his team value was apparent to all. Board work would now be in the hands of sophomore Ken Hendrix and freshmen Dave Gosselar and Tom Wolters. Gosselar and Jon Constant were adjusting from the football squad, as was Dana Snoap. The season opener pitted Hope against Aquinas in Grand Rapids. The Dec. 3 game would be played in the Tommies' new fieldhouse, and Coach Phil Kahler's team was well prepared as NAIA rules permitted an earlier start. The Tommies liked their new quarters, shot 50 percent, and led 39-27 at the half. An Aquinas zone was effective, but Hope narrowed the gap to 69-66 with 3:30 remaining. At this point, Marty Snoap suffered an ankle sprain and an 18-4 Aquinas run put the game away. Mark Simons led the home team to the 87-70 win. He was followed by Tom Van Portfleet with 19, Pat Ryan had 16, Bob Pratt 15, and George Kopko 12. Shinabarger was the Hope leader with 16, Marty Snoap had 14, Hendrix 11, and Dykstra nine.

The home opener on Saturday, Dec. 6, brought Concordia of Illinois to the Civic Center. A crowd of 1,900 was pleased to see the Dutchmen put it all together. The Cougars of Coach Tom Faszholz were at a height disadvantage, and would lose the rebound battle 94-55. Four of the five Concordia starters were in early foul trouble, and Hope took a 55-47 halftime lead. Hope's control of the boards led to numerous fast breaks and the eventual 117-70 victory. Fans were surprised when Hope's scoring leader turned out to be freshman Dana Snoap, younger brother of Marty. Dana's 19 points and 14 rebounds were the evening's highlights. Shinabarger and Hendrix each scored 18, Marty Snoap had 17, and Dave Harmelink 11. Woody Kraemer with 12 was the Concordia leader, Dave Heiden had 11 and Terry Morrison nine.

The season's third game was played in the Civic on Wednesday, Dec. 10, against Calvin. Neither school was especially happy with such an early season meeting, but the MIAA schedule rotation made it necessary. Earlier in the day, we learned that Russ De Vette was in bed with a bad case of the flu and for the first time in memory would be unable to coach his team. Assistants Bill Vanderbilt and Daryl Siedentop would do a fine job of filling in. Calvin was the halftime leader at 42-38 but the Dutchmen battled back, largely on an outstanding performance by Gosselar. A field goal by Marty Snoap with 1:11 remaining gave Hope the lead at 80-79, but a free throw by Mike Phelps sent the game into overtime. Two field goals by Marty Snoap made it 84-80 in OT, but Calvin center Ed Wiers came through with eight points, and two clutch free throws by Phelps with six seconds left made it 91-87. A driving layup by Dan Shinabarger was not enough, and Calvin was the winner, 91-89. Ed Wiers had a great night with 31 for the Knights, Phelps followed with 21, and Doug Taatjes had 14. In Hope's tough loss, Hendrix scored 22, Shinabarger had 21, Gosselar 20, and Marty Snoap 14. Calvin had a narrow edge in rebounds at 65-62.

Hope traveled to Spring Arbor on Saturday, Dec. 13 and was unable to match its intensity of the two previous games. The Cougars pushed a 52-45 halftime lead to an eventual 97-81 victory. Hope had the boards at 76-73, but 29 percent shooting was the culprit in the defeat. Jerry Byrd led the winners with 31, Bob Tomkins had 16, while Jeff Trautman and Lynn Johnson each scored 10. Marty Snoap led Hope with 13, and Dave Gosselar had 10.

The Holiday Tournament at Quantico, Va., was a homecoming of sorts for Coach De Vette. Called back to active duty in the Marine Corps, he had served several months at the Quantico base during the Korean conflict. In a first round game on Thursday, Dec. 18, Hope lost to the New York Institute of Technology, 71-65. The Dutchmen held a 35-32 halftime lead, were down 49-39 in the second half, then tied it at 63-63 with 4:43 to play. New York controlled the remainder of the game to take the six-point victory. Rich Brown led the winners with 19, and Mike Harris and Jim Dalton each had 16. Ken Hendrix was high for Hope with 21, and Shinabarger scored 19.

Things went better the following night as Hope downed Ohio Dominican 82-71. The lead changed hands 11 times in the first half as the Lakers moved into a 33-31 lead at the intermission. It was 60-58 Hope with 6:33 remaining, but the Dutchmen pulled away to the 11-point win. Gosselar played his best game to date with 20 points, Shinabarger had 17 and Dana Snoap 13. Bud Underwood was high for the losers with 22, and Bill Maurer scored 18. Hope took the consolation game with a 93-70 victory over the Quantico Marine Corps team. Ken Hendrix was high for Hope with 20 and Tom Dykstra had 13. No record was available of Marine Corps scorers. Mount Saint Mary's of Maryland won the tourney, defeating New York Tech 95-78. Jim Phelan, St. Mary's coach, was a long-time friend of Russ De Vette.

Back home on Saturday, Jan. 3, the Dutchmen hosted St. Josephs of Rensselaer, Ind. The Pumas of Coach Jim Holstein came in with a 6-1 record, and had just beaten De Paul University of Chicago in an 86-85 thriller. St. Joseph's was outrebounded by the Dutchmen 64-52, but the Pumas were hot with 46 percent shooting and led 34-32 at the half. Hope stayed close in the third quarter, but, with the score at 54-50 and 10:53 remaining, Ted Hillary scored three straight field goals for St. Joseph's and the Dutchmen did not challenge again. Bill Gladieux was high for the visitors with 18, and was followed closely by Ted Hillary with 17 in the 80-72 victory. Roger Morgan added 15 and George Brun had 12. Following graduation, Hillary would become an MIAA official and work numerous Hope games. In subsequent years he moved up to NCAA Division I competition, working many of the nation's top contests. On this particular night, Hope was held to 33 percent shooting. Gosselar was the Dutch leader with 12, Marty Snoap had 11 and Hendrix nine.

At Kalamazoo on Wednesday, Jan. 7, Hope matched the Hornets in the first half and it was 35-35 at the intermission, but "the trials of Treadway" took over in the second half. Aggressive play by Ray Steffen's crew resulted in 29 percent shooting by the Dutchmen, who were then outscored 44-24. Adding to Hope troubles was a discouraging nine-of-20 from the free throw line. John Weurding led Kalamazoo to an impressive 79-59 victory. Dick Wenkley had 12, while David Lee and Dan Laskoski each scored 10. For Hope it was Dan

Shinabarger with 16, and Tom Dykstra with 10.

Hope's second-half collapse at Kalamazoo did not discourage hometown fans, and the Civic was full for the Hope-Albion game on Saturday, Jan. 10. The faithful were rewarded with perhaps the most exciting game of the season. Le Roy Millis was the new Albion coach, and his charges took a 46-42 halftime lead. The Dutchmen fought back, and with 2:39 remaining it was 90-89 Albion. With the score at 96-94 and just four seconds remaining, Hendrix was fouled. His clutch free throws sent the game into overtime at 96-96. By this time, three Albion regulars had fouled out. Taking advantage of the situation, Hope outscored the Britons 16 to 11 to take the 112-107 victory. Shinabarger had a hot night with 37, Dykstra put in 22, Marty Snoap scored 15, Gosselar had 14, and Hendrix 13. For Albion it was Mike Wilson leading the way with 25, Jay Brown followed with 19, Rick Ziem had 15, and Harry Turney 14. Hope won the rebound war 69-55.

The game at Adrian on Wednesday, Jan. 14, was characterized by excellent shooting in the first half. Both teams shot 50 percent, but Hope scored four more field goals and two more free throws to lead 49-39 at the intermission. Free throws would make the difference in the final outcome. The determined Bulldogs would have the best of it in field goals, 34-33, but the Dutchmen were best at the line with 32 to Adrian's 20 in the 98-88 Hope victory. For the Dutchmen, it was Shinabarger again, this time with 26 points. Dykstra scored 17, Marty Snoap 16, Hendrix 12, Gosselar and Tom Wolters eight each. Gary Rank led Gregg Arbaugh's team with 24, Steve Balyo added 17, and Gary Barcus 15.

At Alma on Saturday, Jan. 17, Hope lost the rebound contest 58-40 and eventually the game, 76-62. Hope was still in the game at halftime, trailing 37-31, but Coach Bill Klenk had talent at every position, with Captain Charles Hudson especially effective. Hudson led the Scots with 27, Al Vander Meer had 14 and Jerry Hill 13. Ike Neitring and John Fuzak each contributed eight. Hendrix led the Dutch with 12, but Dan Shinabarger was held to nine. Marty Snoap and Scott each had nine to match Shinabarger. The Dutch cause suffered when Gosselar went down with a knee injury two minutes into the game.

As Hope prepared to host Lake Forest on Saturday, Jan. 24, Coach De Vette received some bad news. Hendrix was sidelined with a severe case of influenza traceable to a virus. He would miss the next five games. His replacement in the starting lineup would be Scott. Things evened out a bit when it was learned that Lake Forest would be without the services of 6' 5" center Rick Wolff. Hope's fast break was working early in a fashion not seen in several games. The easy layups resulted in 65 percent shooting in the first half and a comfortable 59-35 lead at the intermission. With 4:33 left in the game, a field goal by Hope's Dan Edwards made it 101-64, and the final tally was Hope, 111-71. Shinabarger's 24 points led the way, while a great effort by Scott netted 22. Edwards followed with 16, Dykstra had 10 and Wolters eight. Al Shethar was high for the losers with 26, Frank Hogan scored 19 and Mike Maiman 14. Hope dominated the boards, 74-40.

PURE SHOOTER
"Shin" presented problems for any defender.

Gary Morrison's well-coached Olivet team would not be denied at the Civic on Thursday, Jan. 29. Hope trailed 40-36 at the half, but fought back after the intermission. A three-point play by Dykstra gave Hope a 53-50 lead at one point, but a 10-0 run by Olivet with 4:30 left broke open the game, and the Comets went on to win by a score of 96-84. Mike Maciasz and Benny Benford did most of the damage with 28 and 26 points respectively. Max Lindsay and Bill Newhouse each had 12. Dykstra was the leader for Hope with 18, Dana Snoap had 15, Gosselar 14, Shinabarger 11 and Ric Scott 10.

The Dutchmen hosted Adrian on the last day of January, and were in trouble most of the way. The Bulldogs took a 38-33 halftime lead and built it to 76-68 with 4:06 left in the game. Frosh forward Gary Barcus scored a field goal to make it 78-71, but fouled out with 2:34 remaining. Two other Adrian starters also fouled out in the closing minutes. The Dutchmen continued to peck away at the lead. Three free throws plus a steal and lay-up by Shinabarger gave Hope its first lead at 81-80. Two more from the free throw line by Gosselar made it 83-80 before Adrian's John Okenka scored to make the final Hope, 83-82. Scott had another fine game to lead the Dutchmen with 19. Guards Dykstra and Shinabarger each scored 18, and Gosselar had 14. Gary Barcus almost did it for the Bulldogs with 30 points before fouling out. Center Dave Shulerk had 13, John Okenka 12, Gary Rank 10, and Kim Rank 8. In the absence of Hendrix, Adrian won the rebound contest 55 to 47.

In the opening days of February, Hope would play two non-league contests. A trip to Lake Forest on Wednesday, Feb. 4, found the Dutchmen with a hot hand in the first half, resulting in a 41-33 lead at the intermission. Fifty-six percent shooting overall, while limiting the Foresters to 31 percent, was the main factor in the 83-74 victory, while a 60-53 edge in rebounds also helped. Hope's balanced scoring included Dana Snoap with 17, Shinabarger 16, Scott 14, Marty Snoap 12, and Dykstra 10. Frank Hogan was high for Dick Triptow's team with 30, Al Shethar had 12 and John Hermann nine.

In a return game on Saturday, Feb. 7, it was Denison at the Civic. For a time it appeared that the Dutchmen might extend their win streak to three. Hope was sharp in the first half, shot 56 percent, and took a 41-36 lead to the locker room at the intermission. Coach Rich Scott rallied his team in an evenly played second half, and it was 62-62 with 4:47 remaining. At this point, Mike Selee came off the Denison bench to score six straight points. With 1:06 remaining, Denison had taken a 69-64 lead and Hope was forced to foul. Marty Snoap put in two free throws to make it 69-66, but Denison free throws and a final field goal by guard Larry Claggett gave the Big Reds the 10-point victory, 76-66. John Sloan registered 24 for the winners, Andy Wieland scored 16, and Phil Wince 14. For Hope it was Dana Snoap leading with 20, brother Marty followed with 14, and Shinabarger and Dykstra each had 11. The game was decided at the free throw line as Denison made 20 of 26, while Hope could garner but 10 of 20.

The second round of MIAA play began on Wednesday, Feb. 11, with Hope at Calvin. Hendrix returned to the Hope lineup after missing five games, but was used sparingly. Despite Hope's 8-10 record, a crowd of 4,400 turned out to see the Knights take a 37-29 lead at the half. Coach Don Vroon was now using a 1-4 offense effectively as the team shot 53 percent to Hope's 30 percent. It was not a Hope night as the Knights dominated the boards 51-28 and held Dan Shinabarger to four points. Mike Phelps led Calvin to a convincing 82-63 victory with 25 points, Del Willink added 19, Doug Taatjes had 14, and Ed Wiers 10. Dykstra with 15 was the only Hope player in double figures. Dana Snoap and Hendrix each had seven, and Dave Gosselar eight.

Hope traveled to Olivet on Saturday, Feb. 14, and the slide continued in the first half. The Comets, behind Mike Maciasz with 14 and Ben Benford with 12, racked up 50 points to 38 for the Dutchmen at intermission time. In the locker room, Coach DeVette assigned Hendrix and Lorenza Howard to stop Maciasz and Benford. The responsibility

HOPE 125 — ALBION 104
February 21, 1970

Dan Shinabarger set a new Hope scoring record with 51 points at Albion in 1970.

was accepted. Hendrix was all over Maciasz, and the big center was shut down with just three points. Benford was limited to seven. Meanwhile, the Comets were having trouble containing Shinabarger, who returned to form with 32 points, 25 in the second half. Included were 12-of-13 free throws. The Dutchmen may have been out of the title race, but pride still mattered as their second half comeback produced a satisfying 95-88 victory. In addition to his defensive gem, Hendrix dropped in 15 points. Dana Snoap and Edwards each scored 14. For Olivet it was Max Lindsay and Ben Benford with 19 each and Mike Maciasz with 17. The Comets won the boards 47-40, but, this night, not the game.

Ray Steffen was in town on Wednesday, Feb. 18, with the troublesome Hornets. With nothing to lose, Coach De Vette decided to shake up the lineup a bit. Starters for Hope would be Dana Snoap and Edwards at forwards, Hendrix at center, and Shinabarger and Howard at the guards. The game was a hard-fought, even match for 20 minutes, and the teams left the floor with the score tied at 37-37. The contest continued to be close throughout the second half, but near the end the Hope defense lost some of its intensity. The Hornets scored seven straight points to take a 74-67 lead with 1:17 remaining. Marty Snoap scored the final field goal with three ticks left, but it was too little too late, and Kalamazoo was the winner 77-73. Hope's effort produced a 53-51 edge in rebounds, but Kazoo's late rally had sealed the game. John Weurding led the winners with 22, Bryan Vossekuil had 16, Dan Laskoski 13 and Jim Katona 11. Shinabarger was high for Hope with 19 and Howard, in his first starting role, scored 17. Dana Snoap and Edwards each scored eight.

Hope's game at Albion on Saturday, Feb. 21, soon developed into a scoring marathon. In the Jan. 10 game the Britons had trouble stopping Dan Shinabarger, who dropped in 37 points in the Dutchmen's 112-107 overtime win. De Vette hoped to capitalize on the Holland sophomore's great ability to stop on a dime and go straight up for a jump shot. Teammates were unselfish and cooperative in carrying out this objective. The 54-54 halftime score was the most by two teams in MIAA history. Shinabarger had scored 18 by intermission time and was just getting started. The De Vette plan continued to be successful as Dan put in 33 more in Hope's eventual 125-104 victory. The Dutch total of 125 points was the most ever by a Hope team in a regulation game, and Shinabarger's 51-point performance remains a Hope record 32 years later. Snoap and Hendrix each added 11 points, and Dykstra had 10. Dave Robillard had a fine game in leading Albion with 28, Mike Wilson and Rick Ziem each scored 19, Harry Turney had 13, and Jay Brown 12.

In the final week of the season, Hope hosted the University of Wisconsin-Parkside. The Rangers of Coach Steve Stephens were fielding their first varsity team, but were not without some veteran talent. The lineup included 6' 8" center Mike Madsen and guard Jim Hogan, a junior college All-American at Rockford, (Ill). JC. Parkside entered the game with a 10-9 mark. However, Shinabarger continued to be hot and Hope led 46-40 at the half. The Dutchmen were also able to take down 63 rebounds to 47 for the visitors. The Rangers proved to be a worthy opponent, and the issue was not decided until the closing minutes when the Dutchmen were able to hang on for the 87-83 victory. Shinabarger led all scorers with 38, Scott scored 20, Gosselar 10, and Hendrix 8. Marty Snoap missed the game with a bad case of the flu. Jim Hogan lived up to his reputation by scoring 33 for Parkside and Mike Madsen put in 12, while Steve Hagenow and Nick Perrine each had 11.

On Saturday, Feb. 28, Hope closed out the season at the Civic against second-place Alma. A win would give the Dutchmen a third place tie, but it was not to be. With the score tied 43-43 at halftime, Hope had held its own and continued to play well for the first seven minutes of the second half. At that point the defense weakened, turnovers were numerous, and Alma went on a 13-4 run. Ike Neitring, from nearby Grand Haven, led the Scots to the 84-72 victory with 19 points, Charles Hudson scored 16, and Al Vander Meer 14. Shinabarger closed out an impressive season by leading the Dutch with 26. Hendrix and Howard each scored 12, and Dana Snoap had seven. The defeat was costly for the Dutchmen, as it dropped Hope from third to fifth place with a 5-7 MIAA record. Overall, the team ended at 11 and 12. Illness had again hampered the effort at crucial junctures. If the team lacked consistency, it had also known high moments when good performances came from unexpected quarters.

The All-MIAA team included seniors Mickey Phelps and Ed Wiers of Calvin, junior Charles Hudson of Alma, sophomore Dan Shinabarger of Hope, and sophomore Mike Maciasz of Olivet. Phelps was named the league's most valuable. Captain Tom Dykstra was the lone senior on Hope's squad, and De Vette hoped to field a strong team in 1970-71.

* * *

Wrestling was an official MIAA sport for the first time in the 1969-70 season, and Coach George Kraft's charges would finish fourth. There were some good performances along the way, and Hope's improving team would tie Olivet for third place in the MIAA's season-ending league meet. Squad members included Jim De Horn, Tim De Voogd, Mike Dornan, Rick Hine, Kevin Holleman, Rocky Ingalls, Jerry Lauver, Karl Nadolsky, and Rick Vander Linde.

In the season opener at Calvin on Friday, Dec. 4, the Dutchmen ended in an unusual 21-21 tie with the Knights. At Valparaiso four days later, Hope lost to the Crusaders with a 23-17 score, but Vander Linde, Hine, Nadolsky, and Ingalls all posted wins. The Dutchmen hosted Grand Rapids Junior College in Carnegie-Schouten Gym on Dec. 13 in a match they would rather forget. JC dominated in all categories and won by a 42-0 score. Following the Christmas break, the Dutch came close against Southwestern Community College, but still came out on the short end of a 19-16 score.

The season's first victories came against Kalamazoo, 23-13, and Grand Valley, 38-8. Later it was Muskegon Community College 34, Hope 10, and Olivet 23, Hope 20 in a close one. The Dutchmen took Calvin a second time by a 29-13 score, and made it two over Kalamazoo in their strongest showing of the year with a 35-12 win. Albion downed the Dutch 32-13, and Adrian was even stronger with a 37-10 victory. Coach Kraft had hoped for better than the 4-7-1 record, but three of his squad members had impressive individual records. Karl Nadolsky at 12-3-3 was named to the All-MIAA team, Rick Vander Linde at 14-5-1 was named the team's most valuable wrestler, and Rick Hine was the top winner at 16-4-2. The three would nail down all-conference honors the next year.

* * *

Spring sports for Hope in 1970 were not spectacular. There were no championships but, as usual, there were some outstanding performances: a 6-0, 6-0 win in tennis, a new record in track, a clutch hit in baseball, or just a solid round of golf.

When it was learned that Dr. Robert Brown would not be able to continue as golf coach, we were fortunate to secure the services of Bob Klaasen, Hope '61. Bob was a former Hope golfer who would guide the Dutchmen through a sometimes-trying season. The team would be comprised of Rick Hine, Tim Jalving, Charles Lieder, Tom Page, and Drake Van Beek. Freshmen Bob Lucking and Dave Oosting would fill out the squad. After tuning up in North Carolina during spring break, the team participated in the GLCA meet at Wooster on Saturday, April 25. Denison was the winner, while Hope finished a discouraging 11th out of 11. Results of earlier matches with Kalamazoo and Grand Valley were not available, but on Wednesday, April 29, Hope was a 10-5 winner at Calvin. The Knights' Larry Bodema was medalist with a 76. Page came close with a 77. At home on Friday, May 1, Hope played host to Albion and fell by an 11-4 score. A bright spot was Jalving's 79, which took medalist honors.

On Monday, May 4, the Dutchmen took part in the North Central Invitational at Naperville, Ill. Hope finished 14th in a field of 27, and Coach Klaasen could see some improvement, but at Alma on May 6 it was the Scots 11½ - Hope 3½. Hope got its second win at Olivet on Saturday, May 9. The Comets' Jim Byrne was medalist with a 75, but Page countered with a 76 and Hope took the match 9½-5½. Jalving shot 79, Chuck Lieder 80, Drake van Beek 80, and Rick Hine 85.

Hope's May 12 match with Adrian and Aquinas was not reported. The league meet was held at the Kalamazoo Country Club on Friday, May 15. The Hornets finished first with a team total of 784, Albion came in second with 787, Alma was third with 802, Adrian fourth with 809, Hope fifth with 817, Calvin sixth with 839, and Olivet seventh with 872. Calvin's Lloyd Dozeman took medalist honors with a 36-hole total of 150, while Page was not far behind with 153. Hope's overall fifth-place finish was not what Coach Klaasen had hoped for, but some of the sting was taken away when Page was named to the All-MIAA team. Overall, it was Albion and Kalamazoo in a tie for the championship. Albion's Bill Schueller was selected as the MIAA's most valuable.

* * *

For the first time since 1963, Hope's tennis team would fail to finish in the number-two spot. After a shaky start in the Carolinas during spring break, Doc Green's young squad eked out a 5-4 decision over Aquinas on the home courts, but a series of reverses would now be hard on a team that was used to winning. The Dutchmen knew there was trouble ahead when Central Michigan posted an 8-1 win in Holland and Kalamazoo shut the door with a 9-0 shutout at Stowe Stadium.

When the Dutchmen played at Knollcrest on Tuesday, April 28, they were beaten by Calvin for the first time in 10 years. The Knights' 7-2 victory included all but two singles matches. Ben Pekelder defeated Travis Kraai 6-3, 6-4, Mark Van Faasen defeated Gary Teall 6-3, 6-0, Chuck Luyendyk (H) defeated Jim Bolt 6-2, 1-6, 7-5, Rick Smith (H) took Eric Schering 0-6, 8-6, 8-6, Tom Visser (C) defeated Marty Begley 6-2, 6-2, and John Lappenga (C) defeated Russ Kiefer 7-5, 6-2. In doubles, Pekelder-Bolt took Craig Schrotenboer-Smith 6-4, 4-6, 6-1, Visser-Schering defeated Luyendyk-Begley 7-5, 6-3, and Van Faasen-Lappenga defeated Kraai-Teall 8-6, 6-1.

At Albion on Tuesday, May 5, the Britons produced a 6-3 victory over the Dutchmen, their first in 13 years. In singles, Dave Brown defeated Kraai 6-2, 2-6, 6-3, Val Hirscht won over Teall 3-6, 7-5, 10-8, Jack Jones defeated Schrotenboer 6-2, 6-2, Kiefer defeated Bill Hammond 5-7, 8-6, 6-4, Luyendyk defeated Dave Lomas 7-5, 6-8, 6-1, and Smith defeated Dale Lockwood 6-4, 6-3. In doubles, it was Jones-Bill Kilby over Kraai-Teall 6-3, 6-2, Hirscht-Brown over Schrotenboer-Smith 7-5, 0-6, 6-3, and Lomas-Lockwood over Luyendyk-Kiefer 6-1, 4-6, 6-2..

A day later in a tough match at Alma, Hope had its first MIAA win, albeit a close one at 5-4. In singles, Benja Oredein defeated Kraai 6-3, 6-0, Teall defeated Dennis Williams 6-2, 6-3, Rich Smith of Alma (not to be confused with Hope's Rick Smith) defeated Schrotenboer 6-4, 1-6, 6-3, Ark Alaman won over Kiefer 6-1, 6-0, Luyendyk defeated Tim Tarrent 8-6, 6-0, and Hope's Rick Smith defeated Tim Lutes 7-5, 6-0. In doubles, it was Kraai-Teall over Oredein-Smith 3-6, 6-4, 6-2, Schrotenboer-Smith over Alaman-Tarrent 6-5, 4-6, 6-4, and Lutes-Jim Powers over Kiefer-Luyendyk 4-6, 6-3, 6-2.

The Dutchmen won handily on Saturday, May 9, as they hosted the Olivet Comets. In posting the 8-1 victory, the Dutchmen swept the six singles matches and were beaten only at number-two doubles. In singles, Kraai defeated Umur Yildiz 6-1, 6-1, Teall won over Zame Kolestock 6-4, 6-3, Schrotenboer defeated Bob Moon 2-6, 6-4, 6-3, Kiefer defeated Steve White 2-6, 6-1, 6-1, Smith defeated Joe Chittick 6-0, 6-0, and Chuck Luyendyk won over Dick Gary 6-8, 7-5, 7-5. In doubles, it was Kiefer-Luyendyk over Yildiz-Chittick 7-5, 6-0, Moon-Kolstock (O) over Marty Begley-Jim Ticknor 6-3, 6-4, and Bob Zilinsky-Gordy Mc Donald (H) over Gary-White 8-6, 6-4.

Hope made it three-in-a row at Adrian on Thursday, May 14, by downing the Bulldogs 5-2 in an abbreviated match. In singles, Kraai defeated Dick Meyer 6-4, 6-1, Steve Tebb defeated Schrotenboer 6-2, 6-4, Kiefer won over Dave Mc Pike 3-6, 6-2, 10-8, Luyendyk defeated Dave Chamberlain 6-0, 3-6, 6-2, Rick Smith defeated Ted Johnson 7-5, 3-6, 7-5, and Jim Campbell took Hope's Gordy Mc Donald 6-1, 6-1. Only one doubles match was played. Schrotenboer-Smith won by forfeit over Tebb-Campbell.

The MIAA meet was held at Kalamazoo's Stowe Stadium on Friday and Saturday, May 15 and 16. While the Hope players were involved in preliminary matches on Friday, Dr. Kenneth Weller, a former Hope tennis coach, was inaugurated as president of Central College in Pella, Iowa. His tenure would be long and distinguished.

George Acker's Kalamazoo team, strong as usual, swept all singles and doubles in posting 27 points. Calvin and Hope tied for the second spot with 12 points each, followed by Albion 9, Alma fifth, Adrian and Olivet, 2 each. Kalamazoo's Bill Struck won the Stowe Sportsmanship Award and the Hornets' Burt Bothell was named the MIAA's most valuable player. In the overall standings Hope was nosed out by Calvin for second place, but the Dutchmen's late-season comeback ended the campaign on a positive note.

*   *   *

The Hope baseball team won the MIAA championship in 1969 on the strong arm and big bat of senior Gary Frens. With his departure, Coach Siedentop knew that things would be different. The team took its lumps on the southern trip, but took two out of three from Georgia Southwestern and edged Berry, 4-3. Back home on Tuesday, April 14, Hope split a twinbill with Aquinas on the Tommies' home field. In the opener, Brian Mc Knight got the best of Hope's Lon Eriks on the mound and Aquinas came out on top with a 4-2 score. Dick Nordstrom scattered seven Aquinas hits in the nightcap, and Hope was the winner, 6-2. Outfielder Bob Cooper paced the winners with four-for-four, and Nordstrom helped his own cause with two hits.

At Spring Arbor on Saturday, April 18, the Dutchmen won both games. Nordstrom was a 6-2 winner in the first game, as he registered seven strikeouts and walked but one. It was Harry Rumohr's turn to go four-for-four, Bob Kidd and Cooper had two hits apiece, and the game's big blow was a three-run homer by Jim Lamer. Eriks pitched a five-hitter in the second game, and Marty Snoap came through with a pair of two-run singles to aid Hope's cause in the 6-3 victory.

Wednesday, April 22, brought Ferris State to Van Raalte Field, and the Bulldog pitchers were in top form. Morrel hurled a two-hitter in the opener, and Hope went down 4-0 after committing four errors. Eriks was on the short end of a 3-1 decision in the second game as Hope was again victimized by four misplays. Hope's only run came on a double by John Pink and singles by Dave Macias and Rumohr.

The Dutchmen tightened up the defense the next day in time to take a doubleheader from Grand Valley, again at Van Raalte Field. Don Remo was the winning pitcher as Hope took the first game, 4-1. The Dutchmen scored two in the first and one each in the third and sixth. Bill O'Connor was on the mound for Hope in the second game and was effective with a five-hitter. Hope collected 12 hits that produced an 11-3 victory. Ric Scott, Rumohr, Cooper, and O'Connor took hitting honors with two each.

The MIAA opener brought archrival Calvin to Van Raalte Field on Tuesday, April 28. Nordstrom was in control all the way in the opener with a four-hit performance that produced a 2-1 victory. Hope got both runs in the first on singles by Cooper, Snoap, and Doug Smith, plus an error. It was Calvin's turn in the nightcap as Paul Milkamp pitched a 4-0 shutout. Doug Taatjes aided the Knights' cause with a two-run homer.

Details of Hope's doubleheader at Albion were not reported, but Rumohr remembered that the afternoon ended in another split. Hope took the first game by a 5-2 score, but suffered a 2-0 shutout in the nightcap. In yet another home doubleheader on Wednesday, May 6, Hope divided a pair with Alma. Rumohr set the tone for the first game with a two-run home run in the first inning. Hope scored its other two in the fourth on two hits. The Scots got two in the top of the third and one in the sixth, but winning pitcher Nordstrom bore down in the seventh to preserve the 4-3 win. Alma turned the tables in the second contest, with Mike Thurman the winning pitcher. The Scots got two runs in the fourth and added two more in the fifth to sew up the 4-2 victory. Alma's big blow was a two-run homer in the third by Pete Schmidt, who would later enjoy an impressive tenure as Albion's football coach. Remo, O'Connor, and Eriks shared mound duty for Hope.

In a jumbled MIAA season, Hope was still in the hunt, but a blow would be suffered on Saturday, May 9, with the Olivet Comets in town. The Dutchmen took an early 3-1 lead in the first game when John Womack stroked a bases-loaded triple. His second hit, a single in the fourth, drove in another run and Hope scored another in the last of the seventh, but the Comets had already scored eight and held on for the 8-5 win. In the second game, Olivet got three runs off starter Lon Eriks in five innings. Relief pitchers Remo and O'Connor closed the door, but the damage had been done. Hope tallied one in the fourth and another in the seventh, but fell short, 3-2. The double loss to a team that would finish sixth was hard to take.

The Dutchmen met Adrian on Thursday, May 14, on the Bulldogs' field and hoped for a better fate, but Adrian pitcher Rick Johns was tough with a four-hitter and the Bulldogs took the first one by a 2-0 count. Nordstrom pitched well in defeat. The second game was another close one. In the second inning, Hope's Womack made it to second on a two-base error, then scored on a clutch single by Macias. That was the ball game. Bill O'Connor was the winner in the 1-0 shutout.

There were two more nail-biters at Kalamazoo on Saturday, May 16. Hope's 3-2 victory in the first game did not come easily. Remo pitched 4 2/3 innings before being relieved by Nordstrom, the eventual winner. Lamer had three doubles, and scored the winning run on a single by Kidd in the top of the sixth. Hope's second 3-2 victory of the afternoon was decided in the fifth inning. A sacrifice fly by Macias tied the game at 2-2. Then, with Rumohr on third base, Snoap laid down a perfect squeeze bunt and Rumohr scored the winning run. Nordstrom was again the winner in relief.

In the course of the campaign, the Calvin-Kalamazoo contests were rained out and could not be rescheduled. The result was a 7-3 record and the MIAA championship for Marv Zuidema's Calvin team. On a percentage basis, Alma's 8-4 record landed them in second place. Hope was third at 6-6, followed by Albion, Adrian, and Olivet, all with 5-7 records. Kalamazoo finished seventh at 4-6. Outfielder Bob Cooper represented Hope on the All-MIAA team, and Calvin shortstop Mike (Mickey) Phelps was named the league's most valuable. It will be recalled that Phelps was also the MIAA's most valuable basketball player.

In his final season as Hope's head coach, Daryl Siedentop's team ended at 11-9 in the regular season, 6-6 in MIAA play, and 14-15 overall. His teams won five championships in the course of his impressive tenure, including the one in 1967 coached by Glenn Van Wieren while Siedentop was on leave. His new post would be as a member of the Physical Education Department at the Ohio State University in Columbus. His successor would be former captain and assistant coach Jim Bultman.

*   *   *

MIAA track in 1970 belonged to Alma. Coach Denny Stolz had assembled a team of outstanding athletes, and as the season got underway all agreed that the Scots were an overwhelming favorite to nab the title. The race for second place then became the point of interest, with several teams of near-equal ability. The Dutchmen warmed up with three indoor meets during the month of March. Denison hosted the GLCA Indoor Meet on March 7, and the highlight for Hope was Cliff Haverdink's first place in the 300-yard dash. His time of 32.9 tied the GLCA record set in 1969 by Denison's Tom Jefferson. Hope ran into tough competition at North Central's Midwest meet on March 14, but got a workout which bad weather had prevented to that point. On March 21, Eastern Michigan hosted an MIAA section in the EMU Relays at Bowen Field House. Alma dominated as expected, but Haverdink lowered his mark in the 300-yard dash with a time of 31.9 and Steve Van Pelt won the triple jump.

Co-captains Bruce Geelhoed and Dave Thomas would provide excellent leadership for a team with outstanding performers in some events and glaring gaps in others. The opening meet of the outdoor season was the always-enjoyable Wabash Relays in Crawfordsville, Ind., on April 11. The Dutchmen came home with first-place trophies in the 440-yard relay and sprint medley, and also placed third in both the 880 and mile relays.

Saturday, April 18, opened the MIAA season, with Hope hosting Kalamazoo. Coach Hank Harper had a strong performer in Trond Bjornard, who won both the discus and javelin, but the Hornets lacked depth. Hope took 13 of the 17 events, and ended with a 111-29 victory. The meet at Spring Arbor on Tuesday, April 21, was more competitive.

The Cougars won seven events, including the 440-yard relay when the Dutchmen were disqualified. Jim De Horn led a Hope sweep in the javelin with a throw of 147' ½". He was followed by George Bennett and Van Pelt. Haverdink, Chris Gouyd, and Hudson Wilson swept the 220, with Haverdink clocked in 22.7. Ralph Schroeder took the 440 in 52.5, and Dave Thomas the 440 hurdles in 56.0. Performances generally were not outstanding, but Hope was able to go home with a 90-55 victory.

The GLCA Meet was held at De Pauw University on Saturday, April 25, with nine teams participating. Wabash was the winner with 102 points. Next in line were De Pauw with 95, Wooster 91, Ohio Wesleyan 53, Hope 52, Denison 47, Albion 29, and Earlham 27. Tuesday, April 28, took the Dutchmen to Grand Rapids for the annual dual with Calvin. Performances now were improving for both teams. The Knights of Coach Dave Tuuk had seven firsts but Hope took the other 10, including both relays, to emerge the winner, 81-64. Thomas won both hurdle races, and Haverdink took both dashes. The two also ran legs in both relays. Geelhoed's 880 victory in 1:59.5 was one of the better times, as was Joel Vander Male's 50.9 win for the Knights in the 440.

Coach Dean Dooley brought the Albion Britons to Holland on Friday, May 1, for what would be a crucial encounter for both teams. Hope again had victories in both relays, but this time it was not enough. A good Briton team took nine firsts to Hope's eight, and wrapped up the 74-70 victory with Keith Wattles's win in the two-mile run. The javelin went to Albion in a sweep, including winner Tom Morse, Bill Spenser, and Dave Egnatuck. The latter would one day be Albion's coach. The Dutchmen countered with a sweep in the 440. Dashman Bob Luyendyk was the winner in 51.5, Schroeder was second and Dave Raterink third. Haverdink was again a four-time winner, while Bill Bekkering and Karl Nadolsky finished 1-2 in the pole vault.

Hope ran into the expected buzz saw at Alma on Wednesday, May 6. The Scots were at their best and strong in most every event. Ace distance man Don Yehle set Alma records in the mile and two-mile, while Ike Neitring and Steve List did the same in the triple jump and intermediate hurdles. List's mark of 53.9 in the hurdles was especially impressive. Bekkering and Nadolsky went one-two in the pole vault, and the Hope team of Hud Wilson, Thomas, Haverdink, and Luyendyk took the 440-yard relay in 43.2. Haverdink had his best times to date in winning the 100 in 9.9 and the 220 in 21.7, the latter a Hope record. In the end, however, it was Alma 100 and Hope 45.

The Dutchmen bounced back at Olivet on Saturday, May 9. Coach Stu Parsell had received word of the Hope's loss at Alma, and felt that the Comets had a good chance in a home meet. Things seemed to be going his way when the Hope team was again disqualified in the 440-yard relay, but Hope won 12 of 17 events enroute to an 89-52 victory. The Dutchmen enjoyed a rare sweep in the two-mile run with

Brian Claxton, Bob Scott, and Jim Mattison. Haverdink and Thomas were again double winners in the dashes and hurdles.

The season's last dual meet was held on Tuesday, May 19, as Hope hosted Adrian. Coach Jay Flanagan had put together the best Adrian team in several years, and the contest would be close throughout. Hope led 70-66 after winning the mile relay, but the pole vault competition had taken longer than usual and was not yet complete. When the event was finally finished, Bekkering had prevailed with a personal best of 14'-even. Nadolsky tied Bruce Haynes for second at 12', giving Hope the 77-68 team victory. Adrian's Ron Labadie pushed Thomas to a Hope record in the high hurdles at 14.9. This day Cliff Haverdink was assigned the 440 instead of the 100-yard dash. His response was to win the event in a Hope record of 48.3. Meanwhile, Hope was able to sweep the 100 without him. Chris Gouyd was the winner, followed by Wilson and Luyendyk.

The MIAA meet was held at Kalamazoo on Friday and Saturday, May 15-16. The cinder track at Angell Field had fallen into disrepair, but Athletics Director Rolla Anderson was a good friend of Joe Hoy, the AD at Western Michigan University. Anderson was able to arrange the meet on Western's rubber-asphalt track in Waldo Stadium. The track was later removed to accommodate the larger crowds necessary in NCAA Division I football. In the trials on Friday, two MIAA records were established. Adrian's Labadie ran 14.5 in the high hurdles, and Hope's Haverdink had a mark of 21.7 in the 220. Alma was in the driver's seat from the beginning, and interest shifted to Hope and Albion, both of whom entered the meet with 4-2 records in dual competition.

The ever-exciting 440-yard relay was the opening event on Saturday afternoon. Mention must be made at this point of Hope's popular and ever-faithful manager, Doug Myers of Arlington, Va. As the relay members took their positions around the track, Myers shouted encouragement from the stands to Thomas, positioned at the first turn across the track. Thomas heard and acknowledged with a wave of his hand. Wilson was off to a good start and had a good pass to Thomas. Haverdink, in the third spot, ran the longest leg around the curve, and steady Luyendyk brought home the bacon. Hope's winning time of 43.0 was a school record. This was taken as a good omen, and hopes were high for the rest of the meet.

It was a windy day, and some controversy arose over results in the 100-and 220-yard dashes. Cliff Haverdink ran a sizzling 9.6 in the 100, and followed it with a 21.5 in the 220. No one disputed the winner, but starter and referee Jim Kerwin refused to allow the marks as MIAA records due to the wind. I argued strenuously that they should be allowed as there was not, and never had been, a wind gauge at an MIAA meet. No one knew the wind velocity in previous records. I lost the argument, but exercised my prerogative as coach by making sure that they would be counted as Hope records.

RELAY CHAMPIONS

Hope won the 440 yard relay in the 1970 MIAA meet. The time of 43.0 was a new Hope record. **L. to R.:** Hudson Wilson, Dave Thomas, Bob Luyendyk, Cliff Haverdink

The meet proceeded with the Scots nearly doubling the score on their nearest opponent. As the teams prepared for the final event, the mile relay, Hope trailed Albion 44-40. A first place in the relay would be necessary to nail down second place. It would also be necessary for Albion to finish no higher than fifth. This would be a tall order. On May 6, the Alma team of Cal Kerr, Steve List, John Skinner, and Jeff Arbour had beaten Hope by a full four seconds. But with much at stake, the Hope team of Raterink, Thomas, Geelhoed, and Haverdink ran an inspired race. The first three runners kept it close. Anchor man Haverdink caught and passed Alma's Jeff Arbour, then battled to the finish line and victory in 48.4. Olivet edged Albion for fourth place in the relay, giving Hope second place in the team standings with 46 points to 45 for Albion. Alma won the MIAA championship with 91 points, Calvin was fourth with 38, Adrian fifth with 32, Olivet sixth with 12, and Kalamazoo seventh with eight. The Alma Scots claimed six firsts, but quite surprisingly Hope matched them with six. Albion took two gold medals, and Calvin, Adrian, and Kalamazoo each had one. Bekkering won the pole vault at 13', while Thomas captured the intermediate hurdles in 54.3. The Dutchmen were a long ways from first place, but the mood on the bus ride home reflected the satisfaction that comes with maximum effort.

Bekkering, Haverdink, and Thomas were named to the All-MIAA team, and Albion's Craig Cossey was selected as the league's most valuable. In a season post script, Cliff Haverdink qualified for the NCAA College Division Meet at Macalaster College in St. Paul, Minn., where he reached the semi-finals in the 220-yard dash.

* * *

MIAA MILE RELAY
WALDO STADIUM-WMU
Kalamazoo, Michigan-May 16, 1970

Hope's Dave Raterink (445) hands off to Dave Thomas . . .

Geelhoed to Cliff Haverdink for the final leg . . .

Dave Thomas (451) to Bruce Geelhoed . .

In his 6th race of the meet – Haverdink to victory. Anchor leg – 48.4.

MOVING ON....

Hope sports had now passed through the tranquil 50s and the turbulent 60s, and into the 70s. A new era was at hand, and it would be triggered by a fortuitous find. The search for a new football coach was underway at the conclusion of the 1969 season, and there were numerous applicants. The Hope coaching staff had enjoyed strong support from James J. Malcolm, professor of theater on the Hope faculty. Aware of our search, he had a suggestion. At a Young Life camp in Colorado he had become acquainted with one Raymond E. Smith, then the head football coach at Antelope Valley College in Lancaster, Calif. Smith, a UCLA graduate, let it be known that he hoped to move to a four-year college with a Christian orientation. Malcolm was favorably impressed, and felt that the fit at Hope would be a good one for both parties.

Contact was made, and Smith expressed an interest. Our next step was to arrange an interview with Dr. Donald G. Mulder, Hope '48, now a heart surgeon-instructor on the staff of the UCLA Medical School. Dr. Mulder, a former MIAA most valuable basketball player, was happy to oblige. Following the interview, "Duke" Mulder forwarded an enthusiastic recommendation.

As the details unfolded, we were aware that the man's credentials were almost incredible in terms of the qualities we sought. As a senior fullback at UCLA, he had received the ultimate accolade when he was chosen by teammates as captain, outstanding senior, and most valuable player. After leading the Bruins to the Pacific Eight title, he saw action in the East-West Shrine game and the Hula Bowl. He climaxed his career by being named UCLA's Athlete of the Year, and was one of 20 seniors to receive an Outstanding Graduate Award for academic accomplishment.

A three-year pro stint with the Saskatchewan Rough Riders did not prevent him from doing graduate work at the University of Redlands and securing an M.A. degree in administration from Pasadena College. He had coached with success in both football and baseball at Antelope Valley, but the clincher was probably his deep spiritual commitment and service to young people through the Young Life movement.

Needless to say, Smith was offered the position without a dissenting voice. There was, however, little real hope that he would accept. Ray and Sue Smith visited the Hope campus in the dead of a Michigan winter. Coming from sunny California, the shock was considerable. As campus guests they were put up in the Hotel Warm Friend, a venerable structure on Eighth Street but not exactly bursting with warmth. There were other negatives. Hope faculty salaries at

CHANGING OF THE GUARD

Ray Smith was named Hope's head football coach in January, 1970. He would serve in that capacity for the next 25 years and become the MIAA's winningest coach with 91 victories.

the time kept the wolf from the door but did little more. The new coach would have to accept the present assistant coaches, since budget considerations prevented the hiring of additional personnel. Finally, Smith was asked if he could see his way clear to include former head coach Russ De Vette as one of his assistants.

As the Smiths returned to the West Coast we despaired of landing one with such stature and experience. But wonder of wonders, the Friday, Jan. 30, 1970 issue of *The Holland Evening Sentinel* announced that Ray Smith had accepted Hope's offer and would take over in September. Somehow, the positives had outweighed the negatives. There was joy in Mudville!

The account of Ray Smith's tenure will be told by another, but Hope's football fortunes would be in good hands for the next 25 years.

Gordon M. Brewer
July, 2002

Summary of Hope's MIAA Championships
Appendix I

1933-34
Men's Basketball (*)
Golf

1934-35
Football (*)

1936-37 (All-Sports Champs)
Men's Basketball

1938-39
Women's Tennis

1939-40
Men's Basketball

1942-43
Men's Basketball

1945-46
Men's Basketball (*)

1946-47 (All-Sports Champs)
Men's Basketball
Men's Golf

1947-48
Women's Tennis

1948-49
Women's Tennis (*)

1950-51
Women's Tennis

1951-52
Men's Basketball
Women's Tennis
Football (*)
Men's Track

1952-53 (All-Sports Champs)
Baseball (*)
Men's Basketball
Men's Track

1953-54 (All-Sports Champs)
Baseball (*)
Men's Cross Country (*)
Football

1954-55
Women's Tennis

1956-57
Men's Basketball (*)

1957-58
Men's Basketball

1958-59
Men's Basketball
Football (*)

1959-60
Men's Basketball

1961-62
Men's Basketball (*)
Men's Tennis (*)

1962-63
Baseball (*)
Men's Basketball

1963-64 (All-Sports Champs)
Baseball
Football (*)

1964-65
Men's Basketball

1965-66 (All-Sports Champs)
Baseball
Men's Track

1966-67 (All-Sports Champs)
Baseball
Men's Basketball*
Men's Track

1967-68
Men's Basketball
Men's Track (*)

1968-69
Baseball

1970-71
Men's Soccer (*)

1971-72
Men's Cross Country
Men's Track

1972-73
Men's Soccer

1973-74
Men's Cross Country
Football

1974-75
Men's Cross Country

1975-76
Men's Cross Country
Field Hockey
Football
Volleyball

1976-77
Baseball
Men's Cross Country

1977-78
Men's Cross Country (*)
Men's Soccer

1978-79
Men's Cross Country
Football

1979-80 (All-Sports Champs)
Men's Cross Country (*)
Football
Women's Swimming
Women's Tennis

1980-81 (All-Sports Champs)
Men's Basketball (*)
Men's Cross Country (*)
Men's Soccer
Women's Swimming
Women's Track

1981-82 (All-Sports Champs)
Men's Basketball
Men's Cross Country (*)
Football
Women's Swimming
Women's Tennis (*)
Women's Track

1982-83 (All-Sports Champs)
Men's Basketball
Field Hockey
Football
Women's Swimming

1983-84 (All-Sports Champs)
Men's Basketball
Men's Cross Country
Men's Soccer
Women's Swimming
Women's Tennis

1984-85 (All-Sports Champs)
Baseball
Men's Basketball
Men's Cross Country (*)
Football
Women's Swimming
Men's Track

1985-86 (All-Sports Champs)
Baseball
Men's Cross Country
Women's Cross Country
Men's Swimming
Women's Swimming
Men's Track

1986-87 (All-Sports Champs)
Men's Basketball
Men's Cross Country
Women's Cross Country
Football
Golf
Men's Swimming
Women's Swimming
Women's Tennis

1987-88 (All-Sports Champs)
Men's Basketball
Women's Cross Country
Football
Golf
Women's Swimming
Women's Tennis (*)
Women's Track (*)
Volleyball

1988-89
Golf
Women's Swimming
Women's Tennis

1989-90
Baseball
Women's Basketball
Women's Cross Country (*)
Golf
Women's Swimming
Women's Tennis (*)

1990-91
Baseball
Men's Basketball
Men's Swimming

1991-92 (All-Sports Champs)
Women's Golf
Men's Swimming
Women's Swimming
Baseball
Softball

1992-93
Women's Golf
Men's Soccer
Men's Swimming
Women's Swimming

1993-94 (All-Sports Champs)
Women's Golf
Men's Swimming
Women's Swimming

1994-95 (All-Sports Champs)
Men's Soccer
Men's Basketball
Women's Basketball
Men's Swimming
Women's Swimming
Softball

1995-96
Men's Soccer
Men's Basketball
Women's Swimming
Softball
Women's Tennis (*)

1996-97 (All-Sports Champs)
Men's Soccer
Women's Golf
Volleyball
Men's Basketball
Women's Swimming
Baseball
Women's Tennis

1997-98 (All-Sports Champs)
Football
Volleyball
Men's Basketball
Women's Swimming
Baseball
Women's Tennis

1998-99 (All-Sports Champs)
Baseball (*)
Men's Basketball (*)
Women's Golf
Women's Swimming
Women's Tennis
Volleyball

1999-2000
Football (*)
Men's Golf
Women's Basketball
Women's Swimming
Women's Tennis

2000-2001 (All-Sports Champs)
Football
Men's Golf
Volleyball
Women's Basketball
Baseball

2001-2002 (All-Sports Champs)
Women's Golf
Men's Golf
Volleyball
Women's Basketball

MIAA Co-Champions

Hope Coaches of MIAA Championship Teams
Appendix II

Afman, Gregg, MS080, MS083

Breid, Mary, WTE55

Brewer, Gordon, MTR66, MTR67, MTR68, MTR72, WTR81, MTR85, MTR86

Brown, Gene, MS070, MS072

Bultman, Jim, BSB77, BSB85

Dahl, Andrea, WTE87

DeVette, Russ, BSB53, BSB54, MBB57, MBB58, FB58, MBB59, MBB60, MBB62, MBB63, FB63, MBB65, MBB67, MBB68, WTR82, WTR88

Dickinson, Donald, WTE80

Dunn, Maureen, VB97, VB98, VB00, VB01

Eaton, Donna, VB87, WG98

Ebels, Bob, MGO99, MGO00, MGO01

Fritz, Stuart, BSB94, BSB97, BSB98, BSB99, BSB01

Green, Lawrence, MTR52, MCC53, MTR53, MTE62

Grondin, Mary, A78

Gugino, Tod, WBB95

Hinga, Milton, FB34, MBB34, MGO34, MBB37, MBB40, MBB43, MBB46, MBB47

Holman, Jane, WG91, WG92, WG93, WG96

Johnston, Bob, BSB86

Kreps, Dean, FB97, FB99, FB00

Landis, Michael, WSW83

Morehouse, Brian, WBB00, WBB01, WBB02

Mulder, Jed, MG88, MG89

Northuis, Mark, MCC89

Page, Karen, WTE98, WTE99, WTE00

Parker, Sandra, VB75

Patnott, John, Hope, WSW80, WSW81, WSW82, WSW85, MSW86, WSW86, MSW87, WSW87, WSW88, WSW89, MSW91, MSW92, WSW92, MSW93, WSW93, MSW94, WSW94, MSW95, WSW95, WSW96, WSW97, WSW98, WSW99, WSW00

Peterson, Doug, Hope, MG86, MG87

Shire, Tanya, WTE82, WTE84

Siedentop, Daryl, BSB63, BSB64, BSB66, BSB69

Smith, Ray, Hope, FB73, FB75, FB78, FB79, FB81, FB82, FB84, FB86, FB87

Smith, Steve, MSO92, MSO94, MSO95, MSO96

Smith, Tom, WGO01

Snyder, Marj, FH82

Swertfager, Leslie, FH75

Timmer, Albert, MG47

Vanderbilt, Bill, Hope, MCC71, MCC73, MCC74, MCC75, MCC76, MCC77, MCC78, MCC79, MCC80, MCC81, MCC83, MCC84, MCC85, WCC85, MCC86, WCC86, WCC87

Vanderbush, Al, FB51, FB53

VanDommelen, Louise, WTE48, WTE49, WTE51, WTE52

VanTubbergen, Kathy, Hope, WTE88, WTE89, WTE90, WTE96, WTE97

Van Wieren, Glenn, Hope, BSB67, S77, MBB81, MBB82, MBB83, MBB84, MBB85, MBB87, MBB88, MBB91, MBB95, MBB96, MBB97, MBB98, MBB99

Wamsley, Sherry, WSW84

Wise, Sue, WBB90

Key: FB-Football, VB-Volleyball, MCC-Men's Cross Country, WCC-Women's Cross Country, MSO-Men's Soccer, WSO-Women's Soccer, MGO-Men's Golf, WGO-Women's Golf, FH-Field Hockey, MBB-Men's Basketball, WBB-Women's Basketball, MTR-Men's Track, WTR-Women's Track, BSB-Baseball, SB-Softball, MTE-Men's Tennis, WTE-Women's Tennis

Hope's All-Time MIAA Most Valuable Players
Appendix III

Baseball
1966 Roger Kroodsma
1967 Chuck Langeland
1969 Gary Frens
1977 Bill Fobare
1985 Tom Bylsma
1986 John Klunder
1990 Vic Breithaupt
1991 Vic Breithaupt
1998 Michael Meeuwsen
1999 Ryan Tanis

Men's Basketball
1947 Russ DeVette
1948 Don Mulder
1953 Ron Bos
1958 Ray Ritsema
1959 Paul Benes
1960 Ray Ritsema
1962 Ekdal Buys
1963 Jim VanderHill
1966 Clare Van Wieren
1967 Floyd Brady
1968 Floyd Brady
1982 Matt Neil
1984 Chip Henry
1985 Dan Gustad
1987 Matt Strong
1988 Matt Strong
1990 Eric Elliott
1991 Eric Elliott
1995 Duane Bosma
1996 Duane Bosma
1997 Joel Holstege
1998 Joel Holstege

Women's Basketball
1990 Dina Disney Hackert
1995 Kristin Carlson
2000 Lisa Hoekstra
2001 Amanda Kerkstra

Men's Cross Country
1966 Doug Formsma
1968 Rick Bruggers
1971 Greg Daniels
1973 Phil Ceeley
1974 Stu Scholl
1975 Stu Scholl
1976 Lou Hoekstra
1981 Steve Underwood
1983 Steve Underwood
1984 Lindsey Dood
1985 Lindsey Dood
1986 Lindsey Dood

Women's Cross Country
1987 Tauna Jecmen
1988 Tauna Jecmen
1991 Katy Conlen
1992 Marcia Vandersall Bannink

Football
1939 Bob Powers
1949 Nick Yonker
1950 Tom Van Wingen
1958 Larry TerMolen
1961 Sherwood VanderWoude
1971 Ted Rycenga
1973 Ed Sanders
1975 Tim Van Heest
1978 Tim Lont
1982 Todd Holstege
1984* Greg Heeres (offense)
1985 Dirk VerMeulen (defense)
1986 Chris Mendels (offense)
1987 Todd Ackermann (offense)
     Bill Vanderbilt (offense)
     Don Dahlquist (defense)
1993 Chad Ackermann (offense)
1997 Brandon Graham (offense)
1999 J.D. Graves (offense)
2000 J.D. Graves (offense)
2001 Brian Adloff (offense)

Men's Golf
1971 Tom Page
1986 Brian Westveer
1989 Magnus Lundblad
1992 Mike Peddie
1998 Eric Wohlfield
1999 Eric Wohlfield
2000 Aaron VandenBerg
2001 Eric Wohlfield

Women's Golf
1991 Lisa Stover
1992 Lisa Stover
1993 Lisa Stover
1996 Ellen Colenbrander
1998 Ellen Colenbrander
1999 Ellen Colenbrander
2000 Lacey Wicksall

Men's Soccer
1974 Glenn Swier
1975 Glenn Swier
1980 Paul Fowler
1984 Kevin Benham
1985 Kevin Benham
1992 Jeff Utzinger
1995 John Conlon

Women's Soccer
1996 Tina Gill DeKam

Softball
1991 Lisa Walters Jackman
1992 Johanna Pscodna
2001 Carrie Scott
2002 Andrea Adams

Beginning in 1984, a most valuable player was selected on offense and defense.

Men's Swimming
1985 Peter Tilden
1986 Peter Tilden
1987 Rob Peel
1991 Jeff Bannink
1994 Kirk Assink
1995 Dan Knapp
2000 Josh Boss
2001 Josh Boss
2002 Josh Boss

Women's Swimming
1986 Jennifer Straley Larson
1987 Shelly Russell Schafer
1988 Shelly Russell Schafer
1989 Shelly Russell Schafer
1990 Lori Gano Overway
1991 Sarah DeWitt Darby
1992 Dawn Hoving Noorman
1993 Dawn Hoving Noorman
1994 Dawn Hoving Noorman
1995 Kristen Hoving Assink
1996 Kristen Hoving Assink
1997 Lindy Chelf
1998 Laural Horton
1999 Betsy VandenBerg
2000 Erinn VanAuken
2001 Betsy VandenBerg

Men's Tennis
1969 Doug Barrow
1985 Randy Smith
2000 Paul Lillie

Women's Tennis
1986 Colleen Sandro Boyden
1987 Kim Baxter Beckman
1989 Colleen Sandro Boyden
1990 Dani Zurchauer Burke
1995 Audrey Coates Akland
1996 Audrey Coates Akland
1997 Audrey Coates Akland
1998 Lindsay Etheridge
2000 Jennifer Smith
2001 Kristin Kooyer

Men's Track
1965 Dave Lane
1966 Ray Cooper
1968 Ray Cooper
1971 Cliff Haverdink
1984 Rob Appell
1985 Rob Appell
1986 Rob Appell
2001 Joe Kattelus (field performer)

Women's Track
1986 Paula Smith
1988 Mary Busscher
1989 Mary Busscher
1993 Marcia Vandersall Bannink

Volleyball
1983 Linda Percy
1987 DeeAnn Knoll Amos
1997 Becky Schmidt
1998 Becky Schmidt
2001 Amy Brower

All-time Hope College All-MIAA Honorees
Appendix IV

Abel, Keith, FB66
Achterhof, Kristy, WSW88, WSW89, WSW92
Ackermann, Chad, FB92, FB93*
Ackermann, Todd, FB86, FB87*
Adams, Andrea, SB02*
Adams, John, FB53, FB54, FB55
Adloff, Brian, FB98, FB99, FB00, FB01*
Albrecht, Ted, FB71, FB72
Allen, Jeff, MTR84, FB84, MTR85
Allers, Dawn, WTR02
Allison, Rob, MSO98, MSO99
Ames, Randy, FB94, FB96
Anderson, Craig, MSW81
Andree, Katie, WSW84, WSW85
Andrusiak, Mike, FB82
Angeli, Aaron, MSO95
Appell, Rob, MTR84*, MTR85*, MTR86*
Appledorn, Ron, FB50, FB52
Arnold, Audrey, WSW01, WSW02
Assink, Kurt, MSW92, MSW93, MSW94*, MSW95
Avery, Kurt, MS73
Avrit, Tammy, FH83, FH84
Backus, Chris, SBS94
Baker, Rob, BSB82, BSB83
Bakker, Emily, VB96
Bakker, Rich, FB60
Balkema, Mike, FB90
Bannink, Dan, MTR96, MCC96, MTR97
Bannink, Jeff, MSW91*, MSW92, MSW93
Bannink, Jilanne, WCC87, WCC88, WSW89, WCC89, WSW90, WCC90, WSW91
Barckholtz, Todd, G87
Barkes, Tom, W74, W75, FB76
Barrow, Doug, MTE67, MTE68, MTE69*
Barsness, Dana, WCC85, WCC86
Bateman, Sean, BSB99
Bauman, Ken, FB51, FB52
Baxter, Kim, WTE84, WTE85, WTE86, WTE87*
Beal, Dayna, MS82, MS83
Becker, Elizabeth, WSW89, WSW90
Beckman, David, MBB85
Beckwith, Scott, BSB90
Beekman, Lloyd, FB50, FB51, FB52
Behrenwald, Jim, FB82, FB83, FB84
Bekius, Greg, FB78, FB79, FB80
Bekius, Ron, FB58
Bekken, Martin, FB41
Bekkering, Bill, FB68, MTR69, MTR70
Berke, Paul, MTR99
Benes, Paul, MBB57, MBB58, MBB59*
Benham, Kevin, MS83, MS84*, MS85*
Bennett, Darren, MS91, MS92
Benson, Scott, MBB80, MBB81, MBB82
Berghorst, Kate, WSO98
Bergsma, Clayton, MSO99
Bernecker, Mark, FB90
Birch, Nancy, WS90
Blackport, Kyle, BSB01, BSB02
Blacquiere, Bill, FB75, FB77
Bloemers, Lisa, WTR89
Boerman, Kevin, W72
Boeve, Ron, BSB55*, BSB59
Bogard, Jeremy, MCC96, MTR98
Bolhuis, Dave, FB86

Bollone, Brian, MSW91, MSW92
Bombara, Mark, MS76
Bonette, Gerald, FB34
Bongers, Amy, WSW90, WSW91
Bonnell, Mark, MTR92, MTR93
Boodt, Bryan, FB97
Bopf, Dave, MS83
Bos, Amy, WSW97
Bos, Paul, FB52
Bos, Ron, MBB52, MBB53*
Bosma, Duane, MBB93, MBB94, MBB95*, MBB96*
Boss, Joshua, MSW99, MSW00*, MSW01*, MSW02*
Bosworth, Joe, BSB64
Bouchard, Kai, MTE01
Boughton, Diane, WCC82
Bowhuis, Bernie, FB82
Boyce, Mark, FB77
Brady, Floyd, MBB66, MBB67*, MBB68*, MTR68
Brandsma, Lee, MBB73
Brannock, Lee, MBB39, MBB40
Braschler, Doug, FB81
Bratschie, Steve, FB79
Breithaupt, Vic, BSB89, BSB90*, BSB91*
Bride, Matt, FB00
Brinks, Kurt, FB81, FB82
Brintnell, Kevin, MBB96
Brooks, Chuck, FB73, FB74
Brothers, Randy, MSO90
Brower, Amy, VB00, VB01*
Brown, Bruce, MSW88, MSW89
Brown, Dianne, SB86, SB87, SB88, SB89
Brown, Doug, MSW89
Brown, Holly, VB89
Brown, Jeff, FB90
Brown, Mike, MS84
Brown, Stacy, WCC97
Bruggers, Rick, MTR67, MCC67, MTR68, MCC68*, MTR69
Bruininks, Aaron, MCC91, MCC92, MCC93
Bruwer, Josh, FB96
Buchanan, Rhonda, SB85, SB87, SB88
Buikema, Sue, WTR86
Bullard, Monica, WSW92, WSW93
Bultman, Jim, BSB61, BSB62, BSB63
Bunker, Angie, SB02
Burchett, Doug, MCC91
Burgess, Jeff, MSW98
Burgess, Sarah, WTR99, WTR00, WTR02
Bursma, Jim, MS86
Busscher, Mary, WTR87, WTR88*, WTR89*
Buter, Herk, MBB49
Buth, Travis, FB94, FB95, FB96
Buys, Ekdal, Sr., FB36
Buys, Ekdal, Jr., MBB62*
Buys, Matt, MTR89, MTR90, MTR91, MTR92
Byington, Laurie, SB93, SB94, SB95, SB96
Bylsma, Gary, BSB60
Bylsma, Tom, BSB85*
Cain, Ed, FB81
Cameron, Steve, FB79

Camp, Martha, WSW86, WSW87
Campbell, Chad, FB87
Candey, Mark, FB81
Carlson, Chad, MBB02
Carlson, Colly, MBB92
Carigon, Heidi, FH89*
Carlson, Bob, FB82
Carlson, Janet, WSW87
Carlson, Kristin, WBB94, WBB95*
Carpenter, Erik, MTR94, MTR95, MCC95, MTR96
Carpenter, Ken, FB66
Ceeley, Phil, MCC71, MCC72, MCC73*, MCC74, MTR75
Chapman, Elizabeth, WTR99
Chase, Tim, FB86
Cheetham, Teresa, WCC85
Chelf, Lindy, WSW95, WSW96, WSW97
Childs, Garett, MTR00, MCC00, MTR01
Clark, Kelly, FB92
Cline, Kristen, WG94
Clough, John, MS77
Coates, Audrey, WTE94, WTE95*, WTE96*, WTE97*
Cole, Kevin, MCC85, MTR86, MCC86, MTR87
Cole, Thurland, FB82, FB83, FB84
Colenbrander, Ellen, WGO96*, WGO97, WGO98*, WGO99*
Collins, Robert, FB49
Conlen, Katy, WCC91*
Conlon, John, MSO94, MSO95, MSO96
Conrad, Nick, FB00, FB01
Cook, Amy, WTR96
Cooper, Bob, BSB70
Cooper, Doug, FB86
Cooper, Ray, MTR66*, MTR68*
Cotts, Wayne, BSB65
Crandall, Gerrit, FB73
Crane, Bill, FB00
Cratty, Phil, MTR90, MTR91, MTR92, MTR93
Crothers, Al, MS80, MS81, MS82, MS83
Cuba, Manuel, MS70
Currie, Jason, MSO95
Cutler, Randy, BSB83, BSB84, BSB85
Czanko, Lou, MG77, MG79
Dahl, Matt, MSW90, MSW91
Dahlquist, Don, FB86, FB87*
Dalman, George, MBB42
Damon, Paul, FB79, FB80
Damson, Edward, FB33
Dang, Duy, FB87, FB89
Daniels, Greg, MTR71, MCC71*, MTR72, MTR73
Dargene, Mark, G73
Darling, Julie, WTR87, WCC87
Dattels, Chris, MSW98, MSW99, MSW00
Davis, Rog, BSB85
Dawson, Jeff, FB86
DeBoer, Dawn, WSW95, WSW96
DeBoer, Paul, G84
Deckard, Marge, WTR83
DeFouw, Don, FB41
de Haan, Elizabeth, VB97
DeHaan, Tim, MSW01, MSW02
DeJulio, Jim, MS76, MS77, MS79

DeMull, Claire, FB47, FB48, FB49
den Braber, Mike, FB93
Dennison, Bob, BSB51
DeSanctis, Sue, WCC84, WCC85
DeVette, Russ, MBB43, MBB47*
DeVisser, Nate, BSB01
DeVries, Keith, W84
DeVries, Mary, WSW83
DeWitt, Sarah, WSW91*, WSW92, WSW94
DeZwaan, Dave, FB75, FB76
Dick, Leonard, FB47
Dieterle, Steve, BSB90
Dirkse, Emilie, WSO98, WSO99
Disney, Dina, WBB90*
Dood, Lindsey, MCC84*, MTR85, MCC85*, MTR86, MCC86*, MTR87
Dood, Yvonne, WCC86, WCC87
Dornbos, Liz, WSO00
Doyle, Colleen, WSW99
Dressler, Andrew, MSO96, MSO97, MSO98
Drew, Jamie, G79, G80
Droppers, Kurt, FB78
Dugan, Kevney, MTE02
Duistermars, Brad, MBB95
Durante, Llena, WSW97, WSW98, WSW99, WSW00
Dykema, Tim, MSW83, MSW84, MSW85
Earl, Monica, WTE89, WTE92
Eding, Christe, VB96
Edwards, Jerry, MBB48
Elliott, Eric, MBB89, MBB90*, MBB91*
Elmore-Mendenhall, Alicia, WCC92, WCC93, WTR94*
Ernst, Jennifer, WTR98, WTR99, WCC99
Esteves, Dean, BSB97, BSB98, BSB99
Etheridge, Kelly, WTR95
Etheridge, Lindsay, WTR98*
Etterbeek, Jon, MTE86
Evers, Chet, MTR72
Evers, Jill, FH88
Faber, Ken, FB57
Fairfield, Daren, BSB88
Fangmeier, Michelle, WSW98, WSW99
Fazio, Len, FB75
Fead, Dan, MS85
Feit, Ken, MTR68
Fellows, Ben, BSB98
Ficke, Joshua, MSW99
Fletter, Bruce, MCC87, MCC88, MCC89
Flowerday, Craig, MTR89
Fobare, Bill, BSB77*
Formsma, Doug, MCC66*, MTR67
Fowler, Paul, MS79, MS80*, MS81
Fox, Cathy, WTR83, WTR84
Fredericks, Elizabeth, WSW02
Freil, Ron, FB96
Freng, Kevin, MGO97
Frens, Gary, BSB67, FB68, BSB69*
Frens, Rick, FB97
Friedriechsen, Kurt, FB88, FB89
Gaffney, Mary, FH82, FH83
Gaffney, Patti, FH83, FH85
Gallegos, Malachi, FB93, FB94
Gano, Lori, WSW88, WSW89, WSW90*, WSW91

Gantos, Richard, FB56
Gauntt, Frank, MG92, MG93, MG94
Gauntt, Kristie, SB92
Genson, Brad, MSW91, MSW94
Getzinger, Jeff, FB87
Geurink, Ross, MSW01
Gill, Tina, WSO96*
Gillesby, Jon, MTR96
Gingras-Hoekstra, Karen, WBB84, WBB85, WTR85, WBB86, WTR87
Glass, Casey, BSB01
Gonzales, Ryan, FB99
Goryl, Aaron, MSW91
Gouyd, Chris, MTR71, MTR72, MTR73
Graham, Brandon, FB95, FB96, FB97*
Gras, Barb, SB86, SB88
Graves, J.D., FB99*, FB00*
Gray, Sara, WSW00
Greeneisen, Geoff, MSW88, MSW89
Griffith, Ann, WCC84
Grinzinger, Nick, BSB01
Groendyk, Craig, FB77, FB78, FB79
Grotenhuis, Kim, SB99, VB99, SB00, VB00, SB01
Grundvig, Tom, MS71, MS72
Gugino, Wade, MBB90, MBB91, MBB92
Gustad, Dan, MBB85*
Hadden, Mayo, FB37
Hahnfeld, Laura, VB00
Hamilton, John, FB51
Hamstra, Chris, MSW02
Handzo, Matt, FB98
Hansen, Erica, WSW91, WSW92, WSW93
Hansen, Tim, FB84, FB85
Harburn, Todd, FB77
Harrold, Dave, FB85
Hartman, John, FB78
Harvey, James, BSB51
Haven, Neddie, WSW83
Haverdink, Cliff, MTR70, MTR71*, MTR72
Heeres, Greg, FB82, BSB83, FB83, FB84*, BSB85
Heeringa, George, MBB36
Helmbrecht, Spencer, MTE89
Hendrickson, Anne, VB84, SB85
Hendrickson, Bob, MBB53, MBB54, MBB55
Henry, Chip, MBB83, MBB84*, MBB85
Herin, Becky, WTR85, WTR86
Herin, Mary, WTR89
Hescott, Jon, MSW91, MSW92, MSW93
Hester, Matt, MBB86
Hetfield, John, FB91, FB92, FB93
Heydenburg, Deb, WCC82, WTR83, WCC83, WTR84
Heydon, Amanda, WTR97
Heydorn, Bill, FB53, FB54
Higgs, Dick, FB42
Hill, Amanda, WTR96
Hine, Rick, W71
Hoeksema, Renze, MS77
Hoekstra, Lisa, WBB98, WBB99, WBB00*
Hoekstra, Lou, MCC75, MCC76*, MTR77, MCC77, MTR78
Hoezee, Beth, VB94, VB95
Hoffman, Bruce, BSB59, BSB61

Hollebeek, Matt, MSW95
Holstege, Joel, MBB96, MBB97*, MBB98*
Holstege, Todd, FB81, FB82*
Holvick, Gary, FB64
Holwerda, Jim, FB77
Holwerda, Julie, WTR96
Holwerda, William, FB49
Honholt, Josh, MTE02
Honholt, Kenneth, MBB40
Hoogewind, Tim, MTR00
Steve, MSW92, MSW93, MSW94
Horner, Dana, WSW94, WSW95, WSW96
Hornsby Todd, FB97
Horton, Laural, WSW98*
Hosford, Tara, WBB99
Houting, Jane, WSW85, WSW86
Houting, John, MSW88
Hoving, Dawn, WSW91, WSW92*, WSW93*, WSW94*
Hoving, Kristen, WSW93, WSW94, WSW95*, WSW96*
Howard, Mark, MTR80
Hudak, Art, MS70
Huebner, Ed, MSO00
Huibregtse, Bill, FB59
Hulst, Steve, MTR77, MTR78, MTR79, MTR80
Hultgren, Bill, FB63
Hunter, Megan, WSW94, WSW95, WSW96, WSW97
Hutchins, Gary, MS77, MS78, MS79
Hyink, Harlan, FB63
Ireland, Mary Lou, FH82*
Jackson, Kari, WSW96, WSW99, WSW00
Jacobson, Jerry, MBB51
Jansen, Kraig, MTR83, MTR84, MTR85
Japinga, Fred, FB35, FB36
Japinga, Louis, FB31, FB32, FB33
Jecmen, Scott, FB83, FB84
Jecmen, Tauna, WCC85, WCC87*, WTR88, WCC88*, WTR89
Johnson, Amy, FH87, FH88*
Johnson, Charlotte, WSW84
Johnson, Dave, MS76
Johnson, Mark, MTE82
Johnson, Randy, MCC84, MCC85, MCC86, MTR87, MCC87, MTR88
Johnson, Tim, FB78
Jones, Scott, FB90, FB91
Jonker, Zach, MSO98
Kaat, Jim, BSB57
Kamstra, Todd, MS80, MS81, MS82
Kattelus, Joe, MTR00
Keeler, Tim, MSO01
Keller, Andy, FB01
Kempema, Brent, BSB90
Kench, Daren, MG94
Kennedy, Nancy, WG93, WG94, WGO96
Kerkstra, Amanda, WBB00, WBB*
Kerstetter, Ryan, FB00
Keur, Bill, FB65
Kibbey, Bob, FB73
King, Wally, BSB88
Kingma, Craig, MTR86
Kingma, Lynn, WTR88
Kinser, Shawn, MSW93, MSW95, MSW96

Kirkland, Teresa, WSW93, WSW94, WSW95, WSW96
Klein, Art, FB82
Klein, Matt, BSB98
Kleinjans, Everett, MBB42
Klingler, Ryan, MBB99, MBB00, MBB01
Klomparens, Verne, FB34
Klunder, Jim, BSB87, BSB88
Klunder, John, BSB86
Knapp, Dan, MSW92, MSW93, MSW94, MSW95*
Knoll, DeeAnn, VB86, WBB87, VB87*, WBB88
Knott, Steve, G87, G88
Kobes, Ian, MSW01, MSW02
Koelling, Karl, MTR90, MTR91
Koenigsknecht, Kristin, WBB98
Koop, Harvey, FB42
Koops, Karla, WSW86, WSW87, WSW88
Kooyer, Kristin, WTE01*
Kooyers, Warren, FB81, FB82
Korstange, Gordon, FB34
Koss, Kelli, FH90, WS92
Kraai, Travis, MTE71
Kramer, Art, BSB62
Kramer, Connie, WSW83, WSW84, WSW85, WSW86
Kriekard, Glenna, WTR87
Kroodsma, Don, BSB65, BSB66*, BSB67
Kroodsma, Roger, FB65, BSB66*
Kucinski, Jon, MSO01
Kuiper, Mark, BSB93, BSB94, BSB95
Kuipers, Brad, BSB82
Kusak, Joe, FB63
Kuyers, Dave, FB54, FB56
Labbe, Adam, BSB97, BSB98
Lake, Sandra, WCC86, WTR87, WCC87
Lamer, Bob, FB72, BSB73, FB73, BSB74
Lamer, Jim, BSB69, FB70, BSB71, BSB72
Lamie, Tim, FB88, FB89
Lamb, Jim, FB00
Land, Kathy, WTE89, WTE90
Lane, Dave, MTR65
Langeland, Chuck, FB66, BSB67*
Larzelere, Lisa, SB96, SB97, SB98
Leatherman, Amy, WCC92, WTR93, WCC93
Lees, Bob, FB73, FB74, FB75
Leonard, Everett, MGO00
LePage, Jason, MG91
Lillie, Paul, MTE98, MTE99, MTE00*
Lippert, Jarod, MSW98, MSW99
Little, Jay, MSW82
Lock, Terry, BSB76, BSB77, BSB78
Looman, Sara, WSW94
Looman, Susan, WSW94
Lone, Scott, G89
Lont, Tim, FB78*
Lopez, Rich, MS70, MS71, MS72
Loudermilk, Henry, FB78, FB79
Lucas, Becky, WTE94, WTE95, WTE96, WTE97
Luidens, Bob, MS74
Lundblad, Magnus, G88, G89*
Lunderberg, Jon, MTR80, MTR81, MTR82
Maas, B.J., BSB01

MacDoniels, Jeff, MTE96, MTE97, MTE98
Mack, Paul, FB60
Magers, Adam, FB00
Malkewitz, Eileen, SB89, FH89, FH90*
Mann, Dan, MTE00, MTE01, MTE02
Mannes, Nicki, SB93, WBB94, SB94, WBB95, SB95
Marcus, Robert, MBB38, FB38, MBB39
Margaron, Matt, MSO00
Masghati, Mahmood, MS74, MS75
Masselink, Denice, WSW93, WSW94, WSW95, WSW96
Massey, Lynn, WSW90
Matchett, Marie, WCC94, WCC95, WCC96
Mauren, Bill, MTR81, MTR82
McLeod, Kevin, FB92
McLouth, Rick, FB74, FB75
McQuillan, Amy, WTR86
Meeuwsen, Mike, BSB98*
Mendels, Chris, FB86*
Menning, Mark, FB67
Merkle, Bart, FB70
Merritt, Kris, MBB97, MBB98
Methric, Jack, MSW94, MSW95
Meyers, Amy, WTR95, WTR96
Milobinski, Jens, MSW96
Mitchell, Jim, MSW88, MSW90
Moerland, Abe, FB48, FB49
Moffat, Mindy, WSW96
Moger, George, MCC75, MCC77
Mohr, Jim, FB59
Mojzak, Michelle, WSW93
Molnar, Brent, BSB92
Montgomery, Bob, FB40, MBB41
Moore, Wendy, SB95, SB96
Moored, Dave, MSW79
Morren, Dave, FB83
Morscheck, Melody, WSO97
Muelenberg, David, MBB97
Mulder, Don, MBB43, MBB46, MBB47, MBB48*
Muller, Fred, G69
Munson, Lindsay, WG91
Murphy, Christa, SB99
Murray, Julie, WTE99, WTE00
Nadolsky, Karl, W70, W71
Neel, Michelle, WCC93, WCC95
Neil, Matt, MBB81, MBB82*
Nelis, Pat, MSW80, MSW81
Nelson, Keith, FB81
Neudeck, Jeff, BSB88
Newhouse, Blaine, FB84, FB85
Newton, John, FB52
Nicholie, Eric, MTR95
Nichols, Doug, MTR69
Nienhuis, Conrad, BSB66
Nienhuis, Lissa, WBB91
Nolan, Kim, WS93, WS95
Noorman, Jennifer, WSW92, WSW93
Northuis, Dick, MCC76, MCC77, MTR78, MCC78, MCC79
Northuis, Mark, MTR79, MCC79, MTR80, MCC80, MCC81
Nummikoski, Dave, BSB82, BSB84
Nyanor, Jerry, MS85, MS86

Nyboer, Brandon, MSW97, MSW98
Nyenhuis, Gene, FB50, FB51
Nykamp, Keith, MSW93, MSW94, MSW95, MSW96
Nykamp, Ross, FB79
Nykerk, Gerald, MBB34
Oatis, Stefanie, WTR95
Odell, Lindsay, WSO99
Ojert, Magnus, MS84
Olds, Suzi, WTE83
Olenik, Kris, WS89, WS91
O'Keefe, Kevin, MTE90
Ongley, Mark, MCC78
Oosterhaven, Cal, MCC65
Oosterhouse, Brian, FB84
Osmun, Adam, FB97
Osterhouse, J.D., BSB93
Otis, Aaron, FB97
Overbeek, Don, MBB02
Ozinga, Heather, SB97
Paarlberg, Adam, FB98
Paarlberg, Don, FB58
Paganelli, Perry, BSB80
Page, Tom, G70, G71*
Park, Tom, MS82
Parker, Kelly, WSW01, WSW02
Parker, Seth, BSB89
Peddie, Mike, MG90, MG92*
Peel, Rob, MSW84, MSW85, MSW86, MSW87*
Peelen, George, FB59
Pellerito, Gina, WGO95, WGO96, WGO98
Pelon, Tom, BSB67, FB67
Percy, Linda, VB82, VB83*
Percy, Mike, MTR86
Perez, Ed, MTR00, MTR01, MTR02
Petkus, Tony, FB97, FB99
Phillips, Dave, MS72
Piersma, Don, FB51, BSB52, FB52, BSB53
Piersma, Mark, MGO98
Poppema, Laura, WBB01, WBB02
Poppink, William, MBB37
Post, Beth, WTE88
Posthuma, Ron, FB73
Powers, Glenn, MCC73, MCC74
Powers, Robert, FB38, FB39*
Prediger, Steve, FB78
Price, Jennifer, WTR01, WTR02
Pscodna, Johanna, SB91, SB92*
Putnam, Matt, FB98
Rabuck, Steve, MTR00, MTR01
Rahimi, Saum, MTE97
Ramirez, Juan, MS77, MS78
Rapson, Hannah, WSW01
Rebham, Kevin, MS83
Reed, Walt, MTR68
Reed, Bob, BSB61
Reisterer, Amy, WTR84
Reynen, Steve, MTR67
Richards, Blair, MSO96, MSO97
Richards, Blake, MSO92, MSO93, MSO94
Richards, Tom, FB74
Richardson, Kim, WTR99
Rink, Pete, BSB81
Rink, Willie, BSB53, BSB54, BSB55
Ritsema, Ray, MBB58*, MBB59, MBB60*

Roberts, Bill, MCC90
Rodocker, Geoff, MS95
Roe, Paul, MS84, MS86
Roecker, Chris, MSW00, MSW01
Roelofs, Keri, SB95
Romano, Rex, MSW83, MSW84, MSW85
Rose, Todd, MTR88
Rosenbrook, Paul, MS94, MS95
Roy, Heather, SB00
Ruby, Chad, BSB97, BSB98
Rumohr, Harry, BSB67, BSB69
Rumpsa, Josh, FB00
Russell, Shelly, WSW86, WSW87*,
    WSW88*, WSW89*
Rycenga, Ted, FB68, FB70, FB71*
Sanders, Ed, FB73*
Sandro, Colleen, WTE86*, WTE87,
    WTE88, WTE89*
Savage, Scott, MS81
Schaubel, Howard, FB36, FB37
Scheffler, Vince, FB00
Scher, Simone, WSW95
Schlaff, Paul, BSB92
Schlitz, Emily, WTR02
Schmidt, Becky, VB97*, VB98*
Schmidt, Emily, WSW96
Scholl, Stu, MCC72, MTR73, MCC73,
    MTR74, MCC74*, MTR75, MCC75*, MTR76
Scholten, Sherrie, SB90
Schoon, Gretchen, WSO97
Schoon, Jon, FB62
Schoon, J.R., MTR89, MTR90
Schopp, Lee, MS92, MS93
Schopp, Lynn, WS89, WS90, WS91
Scott, Carrie, SB99, SB00, SB01*
Schriemer, Don, FB46
Schuiling, Todd, MBB83, MBB84
Schultz, Ellen, WCC94, WCC95, WTR97,
    WCC97, WTR98, WCC98
Semeyn, Pete, FB72
Sexton, Tom, FB79
Shedd, Ryan, MGO01
Sheehan, Meg, SB02
Sheldon, Josh, MSO96
Shelley, Dan, MSW98
Shinabarger, Dan, MBB70, MBB71,
    MBB72
Shoemaker, Kevin, MCC86
Simonson, Mark, BSB00, BSB01
Skelton, Mike, FB76
Slager, Art, MBB46
Slagh, Brian, MSW00, MSW01, MSW02
Slikkers, Adrian, MBB40
Smith, Doug, FB70, FB71, FB72
Smith, Jennifer, WTE98, WTE99, WTE00*
Smith, Jim, FB95
Smith, Laura, WSW99, WSW00, WSW02
Smith, Michelle, WSW01, WSW02
Smith, Paula, WTR83, WTR85, WTR86
Smith, Quinn, G86
Smith, Randy, FB82, MTE83, MTE84,
    MTE85*
Smith, Sarah, WSW02
Solmen, Susan, WSW84, WSW85
Sotok, Phil, MSW90, MSW91
Sowers, Emily, WTR98, WTR99, WTR00,
    WTR01

Southwell, Mark, MTR80, MTR81,
    MTR82, MCC82, MTR83
Spencer, Mark, FB78
Spoelstra, Watson, MBB31, MBB32
Spring, Sue, FH89
Stawski, Eric, MTE89
Stegeman, Pat, MBB99
Stevens, Craig, G82
Stewart, Mike, FB84
Stewart, Todd, FB85, MTE87
Stover, Lisa, WG91*, WG92*, WG93*
Straley, Jennifer, WSW85, WSW86*,
    WSW87, WSW88
Strong, Matt, MBB87*, MBB88*
Stubbs, Monica, WSW96, WSW98
Stuckey, Jayson, FH89
Stuk, Tim, MSW83
Sturm, Mike, FB84
Suchecki, Kent, FB78
Suminski, Pete, BSB93
Sutton, Becky, WBB02
Sutton, Mike, W79
Swier, Glenn, MS73, MS74*, MS75*
Switzer, Rick, G74
Swope, Kristen, SB95
Talarico, Frank, FB53
Tamminga, Polly, FH82
Tanis, Ryan, BSB99*
Tappen, Bill, FB41
Taylor, Brian, MCC82, MCC83
Teater, Dave, FB73, FB76
TenHave, Lewis, FB76
TerMolen, Larry, FB57, FB58*
Terracciano, Tony, BSB74, BSB77
Tester, Todd, FB99
Thiel, Melissa, WSW94, WSW95,
    WSW96, WSW97
Thomas, Dave, MTR69, MTR70
Thompson, Dewey, FB75, FB76
Thompson, Jannah, WTR96
Thomson, Dana, WTR92, WTR94
Thomson, Bob, BSB58, BSB59
Tilden, Peter, MSW85*, MSW86*
Timmer, Lisa, WBB97, SB97
Timmer, Rebecca, WCC96, WTR97,
    WCC97, WCC98, WTR99
Timmerman, Rolfe, G88
Toohey, Darren, MSO96
Toohey, Sean, MSO96
Torgerson, Erica, WTR00
Troost, Don, BSB67
Truby, Chuck, FB60
Tull, Dave, G89
Updegraaf, Jay, MTE80
Underwood, Stephen, MCC80, MCC81*,
    MTR82, MCC82, MTR83, MCC83*,
    MTR84
Utzinger, Jeff, MS91, MSO92
Van Appledorn, Todd, MSW87, MSW89
Van Assen, Craig, BSB76
Van Assen, Kara, WTR02
VanAuken, Erinn, WSW97, WSW98,
    WSW99, WSW00*
VanBeek, Mike, BSB01, BSB02
VanBlois, Brent, MS87
Vandenberg, Aaron, MGO99, MGO00*
VandenBerg, Betsy, WSW98, WSW99*,
    WSW00, WSW01*

VandenBerg, Erin, WSW00, WSW01,
    WSW02
VandenBerg, Holly, VB86, SB87, VB87,
    VB88, WBB89, VB89, WBB90
Vanderbilt, Bill, Jr., FB86, FB87*
Vander Heide, Derek, MSW95, MSW96,
    MSW97
Vander Hill, Jim, MBB61, MBB62,
    MBB63*
Vander Hill, Warren, MBB57, MBB59,
    MBB60
VanderKamp, Kara, WS93, WS94
VanderKlay, Tom, FB85
Vanderlind, Mert, FB57
Vanderlind, Rick, W71, W72, W73
VanderMaas, Jack, BSB81
VanDerMeulen, Scot, FB79, FB80, MTR81
Vandersall, Marcia, WCC89, WTR90,
    WTR91, WTR92, WCC92*, MTR93*
VanderVelde, Jack, FB50, FB51
VanderWoude, Sherwood, FB60, FB61*
VandeVorde, Scott, MCC83, MCC84
VanDeWege, Ed, MBB48, MBB49,
    MBB50
Van Dis, Bob, MBB46
VanDongen, Gene, BSB59, FB59
VanDuyne, Abby, WTR89, FH90, WTR91
Van Dyke, Tim, FB81
Van Engen, Annette, FH84, SB85
VanHeest, Tim, FB75*
VanHeest, Tom, FB84
VanHoeven, Dan, FB54
VanHoeven, Jim, FB51, FB53
Van Noord, Dave, FB83
Van Overen, Kirsten, WSW87, WSW88,
    WSW90
Van Overen, Kirt, MSW86, MSW87,
    MSW88
Van Putten, Dirk, MSW86, MSW87
VanTatenhove, Fred, FB63
VanTil, Jim, BSB63
Van Tubbergen, Marie, WTE93
Van Tuinen, Craig, FB73, FB74, FB75
VanVoorst, Mark, MS72
Van Wieren, Clare, BSB64, MBB65,
    MBB66*
Van Wieren, Glenn, BSB62, MBB63,
    MBB64
Van Wingen, Tom, FB50*
VanZyl, Shanna, WTR02
Vashaw, Deb, SB91, SB93
Vaughan, Greg, FB98
Veldman, Joe, MCC98, MCC99, MCC00,
    MTR01
Velting, Heather, VB96, VB97, VB98,
    VB99
Venhuizen, Ron, BSB63
VerMeulen, Dirk, FB85
VerMeulen, Tim, FB91
Ver Plank, Mike, MSW82
Victor, John, MCC79
Visscher, Ron, MTE67, MTE68, MTE69
Visser, Bob, MBB52
VonIns, Chris, MSW90, MSW91
Vos, Diane, WSW88, WSW89
Voss, Greg, FB70, FB71
Voss, Marcus, MSO00, MSO01

Vredevoogd, Matt, FB87
Vriesenga, Matt, BSB97
Vriesman, Brian, MBB74
Vroeindewey, Scott, MSW00, MSW01
Vruggink, MSW99
Wade, Dylan, MCC98, MCC99, MCC00, MCC01
Wager, Robert, MGO95
Waite, Melanie, FH73
Walter, Susan, FH87
Walters, Lisa, SB91*, SB92
Wang, Irene, WSW83, WSW84
Ward, Nick, MTR95, MTR96
Waterstone, Jeff, BSB76, BSB77
Watkin, Christy, WTR01, WTR02
Webb, Walter, FB79
Wegner, Dan, FB98
Werkman, Michelle, VB93, VB94, VB95
Westveer, Brian, G86*, G87
Whitehouse, Bobbie, FH86
Whitmore, Bryan, MCC89
Whittemore, Janine, VB90
Wicksall, Lacey, WGO00*, WGO01
Wiegerink, Jim, FB62
Wildgen, Jim, MTR74, MTR75, MTR76
Williams, Travis, FB97
Williams, Tyler, MS95
Winkler, Todd, MS87
Winne, Jeff, FB71
Wohlfield, Eric, MGO98*, MGO99*,
  MGO00, MGO01*
Wojda, Mike, BSB78
Wolffis, Todd, FB80, FB81
Woodcock, Dave, BSB57
Work, Cathy, WTE83, WTE84
Workman, Craig, MTE67, MTE68
Yeiter, Dave, FB73, FB74
Yonker, Nick, FB46, FB47, FB48, FB49*,
  MBB50
Yonkman, Fred, FB51
York, Angie, WTR93
York, Don, BSB52, BSB53, BSB54
Youngs, Mark, MTR98
Zanin, Gina, SB98, SB99
Zeldenrust, Steve, FB83
Zessin, David, FB77
Zeuner, James, FB32
Zimmer, Rachel, SB93
Zupancic, Joe, MSW96, MSW98
Zurchauer, Dani, WTE87, WTE88,
  WTE89, WTE90*

Key: FB-Football, VB-Volleyball, MCC-Men's Cross Country, WCC-Women's Cross Country, MSO-Men's Soccer, WSO-Women's Soccer, MGO-Men's Golf, WGO-Women's Golf, FH-Field Hockey, MBB-Men's Basketball, WBB-Women's Basketball, MTR-Men's Track, WTR-Women's Track, BSB-Baseball, SB-Softball, MTE-Men's Tennis, WTE-Women's Tennis

REFERENCES

BOOKS

De Vette, Russell B. and William R. Vanderbilt. *Coaching Basketball: The Complete Book From Beginning to Championship Play.* Boston: American Press, 1986.

Gray, Charles A. and Todd E. Harburn. *A Tradition of Excellence – 100 Years of Alma College Football.* 1994.

Harburn, Todd E. and Gerald E. Harburn. *MIAA Football.* Chelsea, Michigan: Book Crafters, Inc. 1986.

Kraft, George C. *The Fundamentals of Coaching Football – second ed.* Dubuque: William C. Brown, Publishers, 1992.

Maraniss, David. *When Pride Still Mattered.* New York: Simon and Schuster, 1999.

Matthews, Anne. *Bright College Years.* New York: Simon and Schuster, 1997.

The Milestone – Hope College annual, 1956-1970.

Brewer, Gordon M. *". . . But How You Played the Game!".* Holland: Hope College Publisher, 1992.

Newspapers

The Grand Rapids Press
The Hillsdale Daily News
The Holland Evening Sentinel
The Hope College *Anchor*
The Kalamazoo Gazette

Other Sources

NCAA Basketball Scorebooks – 1956-1970.
Hope College *Alumni Magazine* – 1956 and 1966.
Hope College Basketball, Football, and Track contest programs – selected.
Official Hope Track & Field Results, 1957-1970.
Hope Sports Banquet Programs – Fall, Winter, Spring – selected.

INDEX

A

Abbott, Dave, 151
Abel, Dave, 231, 246, 267
Abel, Keith, 190, 192, 206, 207, 208, 222, 223, 224, 225, 237, 238
Abel, Roger, 141, 143, 158, 177, 190, 191
Acker, George, 118, 152, 169, 186, 200, 213, 281
Ackerman, Dave, 168
Acton, Bud, 150, 162, 165, 179, 180, 181, 192
Acton, Sim, 202
Adams, Fred, 170, 201
Adams, Johnny, 16, 18, 19, 20, 22, 23, 24, 25, 28, 29
Admiraal, Rick, 236
Adolphs, Randy, 242, 243, 244, 245, 259, 260
Aftowski, Jerry, 100
Agnew, Bud, 168
Ahlering, Hugh, 97
Alaman, Ark, 280
Albeck, Stan, 46, 112, 133
Alberts, Tom, 164
Albrecht, Ted, 268, 271, 272
Alcorn, Ken, 168
Aldrich, Jeff, 262
Alexander, Dennis, 181, 194, 212, 228, 234
Alheit, Bob, 137
Allen, Bob, 38, 143
Allen, Jim, 16
Allen, John, 200
Allen, Tom, 171, 187
Allinder, Bill, 19, 40, 41
Allocco, Jerry, 227, 229, 245
Almasy, George, 108
Alper, Shelley, 151
Alperin, Jeff, 258
Altena, Dave, 101
Altman, Walt, 151
Amarine, Pat, 202
American University, 97
Ander, Paul, 237
Anderson, Andy, 151
Anderson, Bruce, 109
Anderson, Don, 69, 93, 113, 194, 195, 230
Anderson, Gene, 133, 181
Anderson, Rick, 151
Anderson, Rolla, 18, 22, 39, 59, 80, 108, 144, 159, 160, 174, 207, 283
Andreason, Harry, 31
Andree, Bob, 28, 51, 53, 54, 57, 73, 74, 75
Andree, Don, 74, 98
Anglin, Dan, 45
Anker, Roy, 163, 164, 181, 194, 195, 196, 209, 210, 211, 212
Annis, Phil, 86
Anspaugh, Dave, 181, 194, 196
Arbaugh, Gregg, 65, 67, 88, 91, 103, 116, 134, 136, 146, 163, 165, 180, 196, 227, 228, 242, 244, 260, 261, 277
Arbour, Jeff, 283
Arens, Dan, 179
Ariel, John, 169
Armstrong, Bob, 90
Armstrong, Gary, 256, 266, 270
Armstrong, John, 232
Arnold, Marv, 45
Arrick, George, 63, 66
Arstell, Bob, 169
Ash, Bill, 223, 271

Augustine, Nick, 258
Auseon, Tim, 122
Ayling, Dick, 21, 22, 25, 55, 58, 70

B

Baab, Tim, 260
Bach, Dave, 139
Bachman, Dale, 144
Bachman, Dave, 159
Bacon, Scott, 266
Badgley, Fernen, 90
Bahler, Stan, 210
Bahlman, Dave, 103
Bailey, Mike, 254
Baker, Don, 270
Baker, Ed, 239, 249, 270
Baker, George, 211, 228
Bakker, Kathy, 120
Bakker, Rich, 71, 72, 73, 86, 95, 101, 102, 120, 121, 130, 132, 139, 140
Balcom, Keith, 166
Baldwin Wallace College, 47
Baldwin, Mike, 168
Balistiere, Tom, 210
Balyo, Steve, 277
Banks, Dave, 170
Banks, Gil, 152
Bannink, Jack, 202
Barcus, Gary, 277, 278
Barendse, Mike, 177
Barger, Bill, 206
Bargren, Wayne, 152
Barich, Don, 114, 117
Barkenbus, Jack, 195, 199
Barr, Fred, 25
Barrow, Doug, 229, 230, 248, 265
Barry, John, 242
Barry, Odell, 173
Barton, Don, 75
Bartow, Gene, 193, 209, 225, 241
Barwis, John, 219
Bast, Paul, 176, 177, 192
Bast, Tom, 189
Bates, Bob, 173
Baty, John, 28
Bauer, Bill, 223
Bauer, Emory, 157
Bauer, Ray, 165, 181
Bauman, Chumsey, 128
Baumgardner, Frank, 169
Bazany, Rick, 76
Bean, Milo, 66
Bean, Ron, 39
Beard, Eugene, 64, 65
Beardsley, Dan, 202
Beasley, Charles, 169
Beatles, 221
Beaver, John, 255
Beck, Barry, 255
Becker, John, 263
Beckering, Ray, 54
Beckett, John, 229
Becksfort, Howard, 146
Beebe, Bill, 208, 223, 224
Beebe, Bill Jr., 224
Beeching, Tom, 242
Beede, Alan, 72
Beernink, Darrell, Whitey, 57, 63, 65, 66, 69, 73, 87, 88, 89, 90, 91, 92, 93, 94, 95, 97, 98, 100, 103, 111, 113, 122, 147
Beery, Clayton, 208
Begley, Marty, 265, 280
Beishuizen, Bob, 231, 267
Beitzel, Mike, 242
Bekius, Greg, 80
Bekius, Ron, 52, 53, 54, 58, 61, 63, 77, 78, 79, 80, 84, 85, 86, 87, 105
Bekkering, Bill, 228, 232, 233, 234, 243, 245, 249, 251, 253, 254, 255, 256, 257, 263, 264, 268, 269, 270, 282, 283
Bekkering, Jim, 142, 143, 144, 158, 159, 173, 176, 186, 189, 190, 274
Bell, Bob, 54
Bell, Jim, 226, 257
Bell, Tom, 272, 274
Bellingham, Dave, 154, 170
Beloit College, 51, 63, 85
Beltman, Cal, 209, 211, 214, 215, 217, 218, 226, 227
Benes, Louis, 87
Benes, Paul, 22, 23, 24, 25, 26, 27, 43, 45, 46, 48, 49, 63, 64, 65, 66, 67, 68, 69, 87, 88, 89, 91, 92, 93, 94, 95, 97, 103, 111, 113, 118, 147, 242
Benford, Ben, 243, 259, 277, 278
Bennema, Dennis, 169, 185
Bennett, Bob, 189, 222
Bennett, George, 282
Bennett, Norm, 102, 122
Bennett, Paul, 168
Bennink, Carroll, 22, 31, 43, 50, 63, 87
Bennink, Dick, 154
Bensinger, Rick, 257
Benson, Dennis, 224
Berens, Lee, 223
Bergmark, Nels, 231, 246
Berkius, Ron, 57
Berles, Dave, 30, 55
Berles, Frank, 170
Berndt, Bruce, 121
Bernhard, Prince, 199
Bernoudy, Ben, 65, 68
Berra, Yogi, 39
Berry, Steve, 267
Berwanger, Jay, 64
Betten, Ron, 55, 75
Betwee, Jon, 152
Biel, Ken, 122, 140
Bierling, Al, 121
Biggers, Dave, 201
Bigler, Pinkie, 151
Bilsing, Paul, 116, 122
Binkley, Jim, 169
Bisbee, George, 202
Bishop, Mike, 128
Bishop, Tom, 110
Bisson, Rich, 208, 219, 233, 234, 236, 251, 257
Bitner, George, 54
Bjerregard, Chuck, 259
Bjornard, Trond, 282
Blaik, Earl Red, 131
Blaine, Tony, 89, 113, 116
Blakeman, Gordie, 106
Blandon, Dave, 201
Blanton, Bob, 251
Blitz Kids, 89
Bloemendaal, John, 102
Blom, John, 164
Blough, Jeff, 223, 238, 255

Blough, Mike, 60, 62, 77, 78, 79, 82, 85, 86, 105, 111 127, 128, 129, 131
Bobeldyk, Dennis, 229, 246, 263
Bobo, Jess, 256
Bode, Bruce, 246
Bode, Jim, 231
Bodema, Larry, 280
Boer, Roger, 30
Boersma, Phil, 30, 55
Boersma, Tom, 139
Boeve, Arnie, 28, 29, 52
Boeve, Jerry, 28, 52, 53, 73, 74, 98, 111, 122
Boeve, Ron, 77, 86, 98, 100, 101, 105, 108, 122
Bohannon, Don, 65, 66, 90, 92, 114, 116, 117
Bohn, Gene, 42
Bolhuis, Dave, 155, 170
Bolink, Bob, 168
Bolt, Jim, 248, 280
Bomer, Charles, 54
Bone, Forest, 143, 192
Bone, Larry, 213
Bongard, Dennis, 223
Bonnema, Lois, 76
Bonnette, Bob, 80, 85, 86, 110, 130, 132, 143
Bonnette, Dave, 123
Bonsack, Fred, 151, 186
Bont, Dick, 207, 256
Boote, Carey, 272
Borgne, Ken, 19
Borr, Warren, 56
Borst, Ron, 202, 203
Bos, Ron, 66, 124
Bos, Tom, 86, 110
Bosch, Randall, 67, 92, 114, 135, 144, 245
Bosworth, George, Joey, 166, 167, 168, 182, 183, 185
Bothell, Burt, 230, 265, 281
Boughton, Don, 194, 195
Bowerman, Charley, 93, 97
Bowers, Mike, 171
Bowles, Nate, 248, 250, 251, 253, 254, 255, 256
Bowman, Ron, 177, 178
Bowser, Larry, 80, 85
Boyd, Dennis, 257
Boyd, Harold, 89
Boyink, Don, 87, 90, 95, 112, 114, 116, 117, 134, 135, 136, 147
Boyle, Chuck, 74
Boyle, Mike, 161, 164, 201
Brady, Floyd, 193, 194, 195, 196, 197, 199, 203, 209, 210, 211, 212, 213, 215, 216, 217, 219, 221, 225, 226, 227, 228, 229, 232, 241, 242, 243, 244, 245, 246, 249, 250, 251, 259
Brady, Pat, 43, 58
Brand, Harry, 103
Braunschweig, Glenn, 17
Breckenfeld, Bill, 226, 229
Bredeweg, Ed, 73, 74, 75
Breid, Mary Louise, 31, 36, 56, 76, 120
Brewer, Daniel Richard, 77
Brewer, Gordon, 77, 84
Brewer, Lorraine, 35
Brice, Bob, 65, 67, 88, 103
Bridge, Len Jr., 170
Brink, Dick, 200
Brintnall, Bruce, 139, 152
Brockmeier, Dick, 22
Brockway, Ken, 230
Broda, Fred, 195, 227, 228, 242, 243
Brodeur, Bill, 59
Bronson, Ron, 50, 51, 58, 59, 60, 71, 77, 78, 80, 82, 84, 85, 105, 107, 108
Brooks, Bob, 230
Brookstra, Bill, 42, 59, 84
Brower, Bernard, 199
Brown, Bill, 170
Brown, Bob, 263
Brown, Bruce, 181, 194
Brown, Charley, 143, 170
Brown, Dave, 248, 280
Brown, Duane, 157
Brown, Ed, 129
Brown, Eric, 272
Brown, Jay, 277, 179
Brown, Mike, 251
Brown, Rich, 276
Brown, Robert, 246, 280
Brown, Ross, 122
Brubaker, Dale, 31, 55, 76, 103
Brueggemann, Dave, 257
Bruggers, Rick, 227, 233, 234, 235, 236, 249, 250, 257, 258, 263, 264
Bruininks, Dave, 195, 196, 198
Bruinooge, Rick, 265
Bruins, Cal, 63, 72
Bruinsma, Walt, 209
Brummet, John, 248, 265
Brun, George, 276
Brunson, John, 139, 155
Brunson, Ron, 140, 156
Buckley, Dick, 82, 84, 86, 110, 130, 143
Buerger, John, 253
Builder, Lindsey, 168
Bull, Mike, 258
Bult, Chuck, 66, 180
Bultman, Dick, 169, 185, 200
Bultman, Jim, 107, 110, 123, 124, 128, 129, 130, 131, 137, 138, 142, 143, 144, 145, 153, 154, 157, 158, 159, 160, 166, 167, 168, 266, 267, 282
Burbridge, Hank, 211, 259
Burd, Larry, 122
Burg, Jon, 272
Burnett, Alan, 159, 192
Burnett, Jim, 143
Burton, Bob, 55
Burtt, Steve, 168
Burwitz, Bob, 29, 30 54, 101
Busch, Al, 125
Butler, Larry, 152
Butler, Rod, 159
Butts, Paul, 23, 25
Butz, Bob, 190
Buursma, Al, 94
Buursma, Albert, Jun, 22, 25, 26, 27, 43, 87, 44, 46, 48, 63, 64, 65, 66, 67, 68, 69, 88, 89, 90, 91, 92, 93, 94, 95, 103, 111, 113, 147
Buys, Chris, 164, 165, 170, 171, 178, 179, 180, 181, 182, 186, 187, 188, 194, 195, 196, 198, 216, 217, 219
Buys Jr., Ek, 112, 145, 146, 148, 149, 150, 161
Buys, Ekdal Jr., 111, 133, 134, 135, 136
Buys, Ekdal Sr., 35, 111, 264
Buys, Jack, 170, 188
Bylenga, Pete, 32
Bylsma, Gary, 73, 74, 75, 98, 100, 122, 123, 124
Bylsma, Marv, 66, 180
Bylsma, Pete, 123, 124
Byrd, Gerald, 259, 276
Byrne, Bill, 110, 143
Byrne, Jim, 280

C

Cady, Greg, 255
Cain, Dick, 70
Cain, Larry, 201, 213
Calhoun, Ken, 188
Cameron, Randy, 168
Camp Geneva, 105
Camp Manitoqua, 105
Camp, Dennis, 70, 101
Campbell, Jim, 280
Campbell, Kim, 181, 196, 197, 210, 226, 228, 229
Campbell, Loren, 118, 139, 152, 169
Candelora, Kent, 216, 217, 219, 248, 250, 251
Cantrell, Dalton, 75, 91, 102, 114, 117
Caraher, Bill, 270
Carey, Tom, 16
Carlson, Craig, 241
Carlson, Dave, 222, 238
Carlson, Norm, 18
Carlson, Terry, 160, 192, 205
Carnegie-Schouten Gymnasium, 16, 36, 37, 49
Carnes, Del, 70
Carney, Tom, 179, 180
Carpenter, Bob, 170
Carpenter, John, 169
Carpenter, Ken, 175, 177, 186, 187, 206, 221, 222, 223, 225
Carr, Bill, 75, 137, 175, 182
Carter, George, 24, 25, 26, 45, 47, 63, 66
Carver, Bud, 23
Castons, Bob, 209
Caverly, Lanny, 200
Cecceri, Jim, 223
Cecil, Bob, 176
Central College in Pella, Iowa, 44
Central State of Wilberforce, Ohio, 45
Centre College of Danville, Ky., 23
Chamberlain, Dave, 265, 280
Chamberlain, Gary, 152
Chamberlain, Wilt, 171
Chandler, Jerry, 149, 153, 160, 162, 163
Chany, Walt, 233, 249, 250, 264
Chapin, Ken, 168
Chase, Bill, 230, 248
Chase, Chuck, 230, 248
Chavis, Harlis, 206
Childs, Terry, 234
Chittick, Joe, 280
Christianson, Darwin, 142
Chronowski, John, 241
Chrouser, Harvey, 68, 92, 141
Chubner, Kurt, 250, 271
Churchill, Winston, 15
Cilibraise, Chuck, 109, 142
Claggett, Charley, 261
Claggett, Larry, 278
Clark, Casey, 72, 73, 102
Clark, Charles, 156
Clark, Chris, 238, 255, 270
Clark, Dave, 67, 258, 259, 275
Clark, Nate, 19, 40, 41
Clarke, Carl, 121
Claus, Tom, 169, 185
Claxton, Brian, 275, 283
Clements, Fran, 133, 146
Clevenger, John, 66
Close, Don, 142
Clute, Monte, 106
Coates, Carl, 32
Coates, Don, 199
Coddington, Mike, 70
Colburn, Larry, 163, 179
Cole, Dick, 113
Cole, Les, 216, 217, 234
Coleman, Kelly, 117
Coleman, Ralph, 165
Colenbrander, Dan, 233, 234, 250, 251, 257
College Division of the NCAA, 68
Collins, Lew, 230
Collison, Bill, 26
Columbus, Burton, 30
Colvin, Fred, 111
Comeau, Ray, 108, 120, 140, 155
Combs, Jim, 72
Comelley, Don, 151

297

Conlin, Barry, 222
Constant, Don, 256
Constant, Jon, 256, 268, 270, 272, 274, 275
Conwell, Mike, 178, 187
Conyers, Jack, 65
Cook, Bill, 219, 233, 234
Cook, Doug, 161
Cook, Gary, 229
Cook, George, 201, 213, 229, 246
Cook, Loren, 29
Cook, Tom, 177, 183
Coonley, Rex, 169
Cooper, Bill, Cannonball, 129, 130
Cooper, Bob, 266, 267, 281, 282
Cooper, Jim, 22
Cooper, Ray, 203, 216, 217, 218, 219, 222, 223, 224, 240, 248, 249, 250, 251
Cornelius, Roger, 221
Cosnek, John, 244
Cossell, Paul, 151
Cossey, Craig, 250, 257, 264, 283
Cotton, Joe, 97
Cotts, Wayne, 183, 201, 215, 230, 231, 232
Coulson, Charles, 62, 77, 86, 105, 107
Court, Doug, 208
Cousineau, Chuck, 272
Cousineau, Tom, 157, 159, 173, 177, 192
Cowin, Ken, 265
Craft, Harold, 103
Crawford, Don, 203, 217
Crawford, Greg, 199
Crawford, Tom, 180, 199, 211, 228, 229
Creager, Ron, 174, 189
Creevy, Chad, 255, 270
Cresap, John, 260
Crickmore, Chuck, 68
Crisler, Coach Fritz, 36
Crocker, Ray, 66
Cronan, Mike, 275
Cronkite, Walter, 178
Crook, Phil, 16
Croom, Paul, 265
Crowley, Larry, 152
Cuba, Manuel, 236, 258
Cullinane, Mike, 150
Cummings, Gary, 271
Cummings, Jerry, 146
Cuprey, Peter, 54
Curry, Rex, 202, 203
Curtis, Ken, 170
Curtis, Vern, 209
Cutler, Dave, 142

D

D' Arres, Paul, 79
Dales, Wally, 150
Dalman, Dave, 154, 155
Dalton, Jim, 276
Dalzell, Tom, 152
Damhof, Gale, 72, 101, 102
Dancy, John, 195
Danforth, Bob, 31
Danforth, Paul, 191
Danke, Walt, 138
Darbee, Bob, 31
Dau, Mike, 237, 254
Dauber, Mark, 222
Daugherty, Hugh, Duffy, 18
Davenport, Bob, 240
Davey, Dick, 170
Davidson, Roger, 206
Davies, Tim, 160
Davis, Bill, 255, 272
Davis, Duke, 109, 132, 135, 137
Davis, Leroy, 52
Davis, Wilbur, 89

Davoob, Dick, 39
Dawson, Bill, 245
Dawson, Terry, 192
Day, Rod, 265
Day, Ted, 146
Dean of Students, 27
Dean, Bud, 54
Dean, Cliff, 75
Dean, James, 15
Deans, Emmett, 264
De Bie, Jim, 71, 101, 111, 122, 139
Debrecini, John, 258
Dechko, Burt, 23
De Does, Ray, 29, 30, 54, 70
De Fouw, John, 62
De Freese, Dick, 31
De Graff, Jacob, 217
De Graw, Ron, 16, 20, 21
De Grazia, Emil, 149, 153, 162
De Haan, Sandy, 235
De Horn, Bill, 210, 212, 228, 260, 261
De Horn, Jim, 268, 272, 274, 279, 282
De Jong, Tim, 110
De Jonge, Carl, 87
De Jonge, Peter, 185, 200
Dekker, Harold, 211
De Koning, Joel, 200, 213
De Kuiper, Carl, 91, 112, 115, 123, 134, 136, 137, 148, 150
De Kuiper, Mike, 263
De Kuiper, Tom, 159, 177, 182, 183, 189, 207, 208
Delavan, Jim, 102
De Leeuw, Bert, 185, 200, 213, 214, 230
Delisle, Dave, 110, 130
Dell, Carl, 177
De May, John, 53
De Meritt, Don, 154
Demidovich, Bill, 17
De Mots, Hank, 88, 112, 134, 136, 148, 149
De Mots, Wes, 212, 226, 242, 244
Dempsey, Cedric, 114, 116, 135, 136
De Mull, Clair, 32, 120
Den Hart, Rodney, 102
De Nooyer, Bob, 263
Den Ouden, Chris, 197
Den Ouden, Dave, 86, 128
Den Uyl, Ron, 22, 32, 43
De Pree, Bill, 122
De Ryke, Dick, 75
De Stigter, Mel, 123
De Turk, Lee, 163
Detwiler, Joel, 238, 270
De Velder, Dirck, 145, 161, 177
De Velder, Walter, 217, 245
Devers, Bob, 239
De Vette, Doris, 15, 35
De Vette, Russ, 15, 16, 19, 27, 29, 34, 36, 38, 41, 43, 49, 51, 54, 58, 59, 65, 73, 80, 82, 84, 90, 94, 95, 112, 116, 122, 137, 138, 141, 149, 164, 171, 175, 178, 193, 194, 197, 209, 225, 227, 235, 236, 241, 243, 245, 246, 259, 260, 261, 268, 276, 285,
De Voogd, Tim, 258, 262, 279
De Vree, Carl, 29, 53
De Vries, Ed, 226
De Vries, George, 75, 102, 139
De Vries, John, 31, 32, 49, 50
Dewey, Tom, 85
De Witt, Howard, 28
De Witt, Jim, Tiger, 62, 84
De Witt, Lee, 177
De Young, Bob, 19, 20, 22
De Young, Don, 62
De Young, Kent, 118
De Young, Wayne, 121

De Zwaan, Keith, 143
Dhondt, Steve, 201
Diaz, Joe, 61
Diaz, Lu, 84
Diekema, Tony, 25, 26
Diephuis, Mary Kay, 31, 56, 76
Di Franko, Bob, 257
Diggle, Doug, 143
Dilbone, Bill, 40
Dilbone, Jim, 82
Dillman, Les, 106
Dilworth, Cal, 38
Dinger, Tom, 242, 260
Dinkeloo, Dirk, 262
Dinoff, Dan, 142
Disbrow, Sid, 217, 219, 251
Dixon, Ken, 151
Dobbert, John, 69, 93, 113
Dodge, Henry, 168
Dodson, Les, 31, 72, 75
Doele, Hank, 62
Dolphin, Bryan, 186
Dombrowski, Mike, 265
Dommisse, Phil, 103
Donaldson, Ed, 146, 149, 180, 181
Doody, Mark, 255
Dooley, Dean, 162, 163, 171, 186, 194, 196, 202, 210, 212, 216, 226, 229, 241, 259, 261, 282
Doolittle, Bill, 268
Doornbos, Carl, 170
Dorn, Stu, 62
Dornan, Mike, 262, 279
Dornbos, Red, 212, 227, 241
Dorrow, Greg, 260
Douglas, Don, 152
Douma, Ed, 195, 197, 210, 212
Douma, Dean, 228, 242, 244, 263
Dow, Dave, 38
Dow, Jim, 208, 216
Dowd, Vince, 92
Dowler, Boyd, 87
Downs, Larry, 194, 196, 199, 212
Dozema, Bill, 56, 75
Dozeman, Lloyd, 280
Drake, Bill, 72, 139
Drake, Jim, 101, 102, 121, 122, 131, 140
Drew, Charles E., Cubby, 150
Drew, George, 122
Driscoll, Bob, 75
Drummond, Larry, 201
Du Mont, Jim, 159, 160
Ducharme, Howard, 268, 272
Duffey, Doug, 258
Duistemars, Rick, 197
Duitsman, Dave, 217, 219, 234, 251
Dulow, Ken, 188
Dumont, Jim, 175
Dunbar, Doug, 227, 228
Duncan, Bob, 29, 45, 68
Dunn, Brian, 78
Durham, Al, 135
Durham, Ray, 147
Durocher, Leo, The Lip, 15
Dyer, Mike, 150
Dykema, Paul, 30
Dykema, Tom, 226, 244
Dykstra, Larry, 98, 122, 123, 124, 153, 154
Dykstra, J. Dean, 210
Dykstra, Tom, 228, 245, 259, 260, 261, 262, 275, 276, 277, 278, 279
Dylan, Bob, 221

E

Earlham College, 22, 44
Easton, Dick, 192

298

Eaton, Llyod, 21
Ebright, Terry, 129, 143, 144
Economou, Lou, 143, 175
Eddy, Clare, 63
Edman, Al, 167
Edman, V. Raymond, 97
Edson, Jim, 185, 200
Edwards, Dan, 277, 278
Eerdmans, William B., 16
Egger, Steve, 131
Egnatuck, Dave, 272, 282
Ehrle, Dick, 32
Eisenhower, David, 253
Eisenhower, Dwight, 15
Elkins, Dennis, 200, 213
Elkins, Larry, 76, 103, 188
Ellinger, John, 206
Elliot, Bump, 224
Elliot, Karl, 120
Elliot, Pete, 224
Ellis, Bob, 46
Elmhurst Relays, 51
Elzinga, Bill, 50, 63, 101
Elzinga, Dick, 138
Elzinga, Ken, 118, 139
Elzinga, Marshall, 75, 102
Elzy, J.B., 142, 156, 160, 176, 187
Emery, Wendell, 19
Engbers, Jim, 55, 56
Engels, Bob, 200, 213
Enlow, Russ, 185
Enz, Dave, 208
Erickson, Dave, 218
Eriks, Lon, 260, 281
Erlich, Jim, 177
Ernst, De Gay, 133, 140
Eschelbach, Walt, 254
Essenberg, Vern, 73, 74, 98, 110
Essenmacher, Larry, 50
Essink, Bob, 263
Esther, Joe, 145
Eugenio, Don, 29, 61, 82
Evans, Gary, 268
Evansville, 97
Eveleth, Doug, 161
Everett, Jim, 164, 180, 194, 201, 212
Everling, Gary, 109
Everson, Morgan, 210
Evert, Janice, 31, 56
Evertse, Carole Lee, 29
Eynon, Rich, 193, 209

F

Faber, Jack, 17, 28, 38, 41, 52, 53, 58, 59, 60, 73, 77, 78, 80, 84, 85, 87, 103, 105
Faber, Ken, Mick, 16, 19, 21, 22, 58, 60, 63
Falan, Doug, 223
Farmer, Denny, 231, 232
Farney, Brian, 179
Fase, Len, 58, 129
Faszholz, Tom, 195, 209, 225, 241, 276
Fauble, Bryce, 130, 144
Faught, Stewart, Red, 253, 254
Faulkenberg, Diane, 76
Fause, Clarence, 151
Fauster, Jack, 122
Feenstra, Harvey, 87
Fegley, Tom, 233
Feit, Ken, 189, 222, 223, 234, 238, 249, 250, 251
Felix, Andre, 43
Fendt, Jack, 17
Ferguson, Bob, 131, 201
Ferguson, Jim, 121
Ferguson, Sheldon, 241
Ferrand, Dennis, 230, 248

Ferrell, Tim, 219
Ferris Institute, 28, 166
Ferzacca, Frosty, 58, 59, 79
Fewless, Gary, 149, 165, 181, 194
Fialko, Bob, 139, 155, 186, 187
Finlay, Mary Toodie, 169, 175
Fish, Jim, 247
Fisher, Dave, 265
Fisher, Dick, 168
Fitzgerald, Dennis, 120
Fitzgerald, James, 268
Fitzpatrick, Dan, 192
Flanagan, Jay, 217, 236, 249, 264, 275, 283
Fleming, Bob, 201
Fleming, Nancy Ann, 127
Fleser, Betty, 274
Fleser, Cal, 274
Fletcher, Bob, 30, 46, 65, 67, 70, 89, 91
Fletcher, Ken, 148, 163, 167, 179, 181, 182, 195, 197, 199
Flietstra, Dave, 103, 118
Flora, Jim, 175
Folkert, Alan, 251, 263, 264
Folkert, Jay, 16
Foor, Perry, 206
Forbes, Bill, 213, 263
Formsma, Bruce, 234, 251
Formsma, Doug, 216, 217, 219, 224, 25, 232, 233, 234, 235, 251, 257, 275
Formsma, Jay, 19, 41, 217, 218
Formsma, Russell, Rud, 35
Forrester, Don, 241
Forshew, Frank, 118
Forsythe, Charles, 125
Fortney, Jim, 248
Foster, Mike, 116, 134, 149
Foulke, Bruce, 73
Foultz, Doyle, 111
Fowler, Joe, 18
Fowster, Jack, 92
Fox, Bill, 64
Fox, Jim, 61, 77, 78, 80, 84, 86, 106, 127, 130
Frank, Rich, 234, 250, 251, 254, 255, 256, 257, 263, 264, 268, 270, 271, 272, 274
Franke, Tom, 149
Frasco, Jack, 92, 96
Fraser, Morley, 20, 28, 42, 61, 74, 85, 106, 129, 138, 142, 160, 166, 176, 206, 240, 247, 256, 257, 271
Frayer, Roger, 238
Frazier, Garland, 38, 107
Fredericks, Ed, 170
Fredericks, Jim, 179, 195, 197, 210
Freiburger, Charles, 186
French, Norma, 169
Frens, Gary, 205, 207, 208, 214, 215, 221, 222, 223, 224, 231, 232, 237, 238, 239, 240, 246, 253, 254, 255, 256, 258, 266, 267, 268, 272, 281,
Freye, Herb, 118
Friberg, Bill, 85, 106
Frist, Bobby, 168
Fry, Bob, 35
Fumey, Kwesi, 258
Fundukian, John, 130, 144, 187
Fuzak, John, 226, 228, 238, 242, 247, 255, 267, 270, 277

G

Gabbert, Bill, 38
Gallo, Don, 72, 102, 120, 121, 122
Gamble, Bob, 20, 42, 61, 62
Gantos, Dick, 16, 20, 21, 39, 43, 59, 60
Gardner, Bill, 70
Garfunkle, Art, 221
Garner, Bob, 180

Garrett, Mark, 196
Garrett, Matt, 180
Garrett, Mike, 194, 210, 212
Gary, Dick, 248, 280
Gates, Ray, 186
Gatsden, Don, 54
Gazan, Harold, 50, 71
Gazmararian, George, 102
Geelhoed, Bruce, 248, 250, 251, 258, 275, 282, 283
Genson, Don, 179, 181, 194, 196, 226
Gerber, Eldon, 208
Gerbers, Keith, 253, 269, 270
Gerig, Bill, 69, 93, 95, 97, 113
Getman, Jim, 259
Gettleman, Jim, 213
Giamatti, A. Bartlett, 27
Gibbons, Bruce, 154, 1155, 201
Gibbs, E.C., Gibby, 45, 64, 65, 89, 112
Gibbs, Jerry, 177
Gibson, Frank, 270
Gilbert, Jerry, 46
Gilbert, Morris, 265
Gilder, Jim, 42
Giles, Vince, 65, 134, 136, 137, 146, 242, 244, 245
Gillis, Bob, 39, 40, 80, 108
Gilmore, John, 110
Gladden, Jim, 128
Gladieux, Bill, 276
Glass, Larry, 245
Glenbard High School, 92
Glenn, John, 129
Gliha, Dick, 52
Gloor, Pat, 151
Glory Day, 49
Glupker, Howard, 108, 110, 111
Gobin, Bob, 110
Godfrey, Jim, 144
Gohl, Mike, 190
Goings, Mike, 208
Goldener, John, 152
Golder, Carlton, 263, 271, 272
Goldsmith, Dan, 50, 71, 101, 121, 140
Goodfellow, Tom, 258
Goodrich, Jim, 263
Goodrich, Neil, 129, 130, 131, 137, 138, 142, 143, 144, 157, 166, 167, 176
Gordon, Cliff, 259
Gorman, Greg, 231, 232, 266, 267
Gorman, Tom, 176
Gosselar, Dave, 270, 271, 272, 275, 276, 277, 278, 279
Gosselein, Dave, 181
Gould, Frank, 128, 129, 142, 160
Gouwens, Glen, 177
Gouyd, Chris, 282, 283
Grabic, Ken, 17
Graffa, Brian, 18
Graham, Alan, 169
Graham, Dave, 75
Graham, Tom, 151
Gralow, Ken, 262, 263
Gramlech, Buck, 182
Grand Rapids Junior College, 28, 50
Grant, Eric, 161
Grant, Jim, 272
Grant, John, 272
Grant, Ralph, 157
Grate, Lynn, 151
Gray, Barb, 120
Gray, Charles, 210, 226
Gray, Dave, 196, 212, 240, 257
Gray, John, 128
Grayam, Mort, 39
Greco, Rol, 168

Green, Jeff, 213, 222, 229, 230, 247, 248, 265, 266
Green, Larry, Doc, 16, 22, 31, 32, 34, 36, 43, 48, 49, 63, 84, 86, 87, 95, 102, 103, 118, 120, 124, 138, 150, 151, 168, 169, 185, 186, 199, 213, 230, 265, 280
Green, Ruth, 16
Greenless, Jim, 129
Greenstone, Art, 166
Greij, Eldon, 167, 199
Grey, Steve, 254
Grieg, Bill, 30
Griffin, Don, 221, 222
Griffin, Evan, 258
Griffith, Jerry, 268
Grimaldi, Tony, 206
Grimes, Peter, 270, 272, 274
Grinbergs, Atis, 65, 66, 89, 112, 120
Grissen, Del, 18, 22, 39, 42
Griswold, Al, 225, 236
Groat, Dennis, 135, 136, 148
Groat, Dick, 149
Groch, Dick, 90, 92, 114, 116, 134, 135, 146, 149
Groman, Bill, 38
Grotelueschen, Dan, 180
Groters, Jarold, 105
Grove, Mike, 213
Gruhl, Don, 230, 248
Grunden, Jim, 38
Grundman, Adolph, 117, 136, 138
Gunn, Tom, 170
Guse, Steve, 168

H

Haaksma, Curt, 149, 163
Hackenberg, Larry, 228
Hader, Bob, 103
Hagenow, Steve, 279
Haile, Chris, 250, 251
Hakes, Jay, 169, 185, 199
Hall, Jim, 230
Hall, Jon, 180
Hall, Ken, 248, 265
Hall, Sedley, 194
Hall, Virgil, 44, 46, 63, 68
Hamilton, Bill, 80
Hamilton, Bob, 54
Hammersma, Tom, 245
Hammond, Bill, 280
Hampton, Bryan, 152
Hankinson, Bob, 109, 130, 140
Hankinson, Tom, 38
Hannett, John, 26, 44, 46, 49
Hannula, Don, 154
Hansen, Mike, 251
Hardenberg, Donna, 31, 56, 76
Harem, Jim, 170
Harkema, Jim, 139, 144, 152, 158, 164
Harkness, Rex, 106
Harmelink, Dave, 276
Harmon, Tom, 16
Harned, Don, 146, 149, 163
Harper, Hank, 282
Harper, Leon, 18, 26, 27, 40, 46, 48, 59, 60, 65, 67
Harper, Lloyd, 206, 223
Harple, Bob, 238
Harpman, Larry, 167
Harris, Albie, 142, 174
Harris, Buddy, 211
Harris, Dick, 241
Harris, John, 90
Harris, Mike, 276
Harris, Tom, 40
Hartman, Paul, 234, 235, 236, 250, 251

Harvey, James, 179, 192
Haulenbeek, Gene, 257
Haveman, Bob, 254, 255, 256, 268, 269, 271, 272
Havens, Rick, 255
Haverdink, Cliff, 264, 282, 283
Haverkamp, Pete, 183, 185
Hayes, Talmage, 73
Haynes, Bruce, 283
Haysom, Al, 139
Haywood, Jim, 16
Hazen, Bill, 152
Healy, Mike, 240, 257
Heath, Al, 202
Heath, George, 123
Heckert, Tom, 255
Heidelberg College, 17, 38
Heidelberg Reverse, 107, 109, 111
Heiden, Dave, 276
Heider, Bob, 118, 139
Heinick, Chuck, 122
Hendershot, John, 170
Henderson, Dean, 250
Henderson, John, 54
Henderson, Skitch, 178
Hendrickson, Jerry, 18, 22, 23, 38, 40, 41, 42, 44, 58, 60, 61, 62, 105, 106, 107, 108, 111
Hendrix, Ken, 259, 260, 261, 262, 275, 276, 277, 279
Henshel, John, 118
Heriford, Jim, 263
Hering, Jon, 103
Herman, Al, 145
Hermann, John, 278
Hero, Jack, 79
Herp, Jerry, 60, 61, 77, 78 82, 84, 86
Herrema, Dennis, 226
Herring, John, 118
Hertel, Rich, 50
Hess, John, 199
Hess, Norm, 102, 103, 118, 120, 124, 138, 150, 168
Hesslink, Jerry, 111, 114, 150
Hesslink, Jim, 117, 150
Heth, Dave, 203, 233, 235, 250
Hetrick, Gordon, 226, 228, 238, 242, 244, 245, 247
Heustis, Bruce, 271, 272
Hiddema, Chuck, 202
Higgs, Dick, 32, 77
Hilbelink, Bob, 71, 72, 73
Hilbelink, Ron, 171
Hill, Bill, 143, 153
Hill, Bob, 42
Hill, Dave, 214
Hill, Jerry, 72, 102, 122, 260, 260, 277
Hill, Leo, 97
Hillary, Ted, 276
Hillegonds, Bill, 240
Hilmert, Jim, 20, 21, 22, 23, 24, 25, 31, 32, 34, 35, 39, 49, 50, 51, 58, 70, 71, 73
Hilmert, William, 70, 101, 122, 140, 186, 201, 213, 229, 246
Hilton, Dick, 233
Hilton, Jerry, 27
Himelink, Bill, 66
Hinds, Hal, 209
Hine, Rick, 262, 263, 279, 280
Hines, Don, 31, 55, 76, 103
Hinga, Jim, 89, 114
Hinga, Mike, 267, 268, 269, 271, 274
Hinga, Milton L., Bud, 18, 27, 29, 44, 89, 101, 111, 117, 124, 125, 137
Hinkamp, Paul, 125
Hintz, Wayne, 63, 66, 88, 117, 133, 135, 162, 165, 180, 187, 194

Hirscht, Val, 265, 280
Hoag, Ray, 142
Hobart, Fred, 18, 59, 60
Hobby, Charles, 151
Hodge, Tom, 18
Hoekje, John C., 19, 205, 217, 235, 257
Hoeksema, Herm, 167
Hoeksema, Jim, 58, 59, 62, 63
Hoekstra, Jim, 258
Hoekstra, Tom, 138, 139
Hoeppner, Terry, 253
Hoerneman, Paul, 17, 38
Hoffman, Al, 145, 161
Hoffman, Bruce, 73, 74, 75, 98, 100, 101, 122, 123, 124, 137, 138
Hoffman, Don, 30
Hoffman, Doug, 110
Hoffman, Harvey, Bud, 125, 138, 150, 168, 185, 186
Hogan, Frank, 277, 278
Hogan, Jack, 210
Hogan, Jim, 279
Hogan, Mike, 227, 228, 242, 259
Hoke, Jim, 166
Holder, Ron, 178, 180
Hollander, John, 16, 20, 21
Holle, Larry, 134, 161
Holleman, Chuck, 132
Holleman, Craig, 199, 200, 213, 214, 230, 248
Holleman, Kevin, 279
Hollenbach, Jeff, 249, 250, 251
Hollenbach, John, 16, 117, 133
Hollosy, Len, 230
Holloway, Sam, 78
Holman, Dick, 237, 238
Holmes, Bruce, 118, 120
Holmes, John, 254
Holmes, Spencer, 103
Holmlund, John, 16, 19, 20, 22, 37
Holstein, Jim, 276
Holt, Bill, 29
Holt, Bob, 54, 70, 101, 122, 263
Holtsclaw, Jim, 207
Holvick, Gary, 171, 175, 177, 187, 192, 203, 222, 223, 224
Hommes, Ray, 139, 145, 171, 178
Honderd, Ralph, 88, 91, 97, 112, 115, 134, 137
Hondorp, Bill, 268, 272
Honholt, Doug, 219
Hood, John, 44, 40, 67, 87
Hoogendoorn, Bob, 87
Hoogendoorn, Jack, 43, 102
Hooks, Hal, 256, 271
Hoopengardner, Tom, 187
Hoover, Jay, 257
Hopkins, Ron, 195
Hopma, Byron, Butch, 168, 185, 186, 199, 200
Horn, Dave, 114
Horner, Gary, 267
Hornung, Paul, 141
Hourtienne, Larry, 270
Houseman Field, 34, 35, 50
Houston Veer, 268
Howard, Bob, 91, 112, 116, 117
Howard, Lorenza, 260, 278, 279
Howard, Rudy, 236
Howe, Dan, 199, 208, 213
Howell, Greg, 222
Howell, John, 151
Hoy, Joe, 283
Hubbard, John, 86, 127, 128, 131
Hudak, Art, 236, 258, 259, 275
Hudson, Charles, 260, 261, 277, 279
Huesingveld, Dave, 177
Huggins, Harold, 199, 213

300

Hughes, Henry, 26, 27, 48, 49, 51, 244
Hughes, Ron, 55, 56
Huibregtse, Bill, 50, 57, 58, 59, 60, 61, 71, 77, 78, 79, 80, 82, 84, 86, 87, 105, 106, 108, 110, 111, 127
Huibregtse, Chuck, 162, 164, 179
Huisman, John, 223
Huitema, Sid, 213, 229
Hulst, Jack, 139, 148, 152, 169
Hulst, Jim, 111, 133
Hultgren, Bill, 158, 159, 160, 171, 173, 174, 175, 176, 186, 187, 189, 190, 192, 202, 203, 205, 206, 207, 208, 216, 217, 218, 219
Humphrey, Hubert, 253
Hunnes, Frank, 35
Hunsberger, Gordon, 106, 217
Huntsman, Owen, 248
Hurd, Jim, 20, 42
Hursh, Anita Marie, 97
Hurst, Sheldon, 199
Hutchins, Robert, 64
Hutson, Bill, 146
Hwang, Billy, 147
Hyink, Harlan, 157, 158, 171, 173, 174, 175, 176, 189, 190, 192, 205, 206, 207, 208
Hyink, Paul, 110, 132, 141, 143, 160

I

Iauch, Joe, 20, 49, 61, 65
Ignac, Frank, 192
Iha, Dave, 142
Ingalls, Rocky, 279
Ingham, Jim, 210
Ingledue, Jim, 227
Ippl, Phil, 213
Ireland, Fred, 64
Irwin, Dick, 31
Isaac, Elkin, 32, 44, 46, 49, 50, 68, 72, 92, 114, 125, 140, 147, 171, 191, 248, 250,
Isaac, Ike, 121
Isaac, Ron, 248
Israel, Jack, 97
Iverson, Brad, 76
Ivocheim, Danny, 205

J

Jaax, Tom, 237
Jackson, Barry, 223, 247
Jackson, Ralph, 110, 143, 177
Jackson, Tom, 55
Jackson, Willie, 246, 257, 263
Jacobson, Bud, 75
Jacoby, Marvin, 29
Jagels, Paul, 241
Jagutis, Al, 265
Jakovac, Tom, 223, 233, 255, 270
Jalving, Tim, 246, 280
Jansen, Bob, 223
Jansen, Howard, 86, 105
Jansen, Robert, 238
Jansen, Tony, 170
Jansson, Dave, 210, 242
Japinga, Bill, 75, 103, 118
Japinga, Doug, 74, 123, 124
Japinga, Norm, 274
Japinga, Shirley, 274
Jarman, Rich, 272
Jarman, Tom, 142, 174
Jauchen, John, 226, 245
Jefferson, Tom, 282
Jekel, Gene, 16
Jellema, Dirk, 56
Jeltes, John, 22, 30, 55, 75
Jenison, Jack, 168
Jerdon, Julius, 237

Jerome, Larry, 76
John Bos Relays, 34, 35
John, Bill, 55
Johns, Barry, 54
Johns, Rick, 281
Johnson, Bill, 31, 230
Johnson, Dave, 271, 272, 274
Johnson, De Monte, 239, 256
Johnson, Dick, 102, 169, 180, 181, 186, 200
Johnson, Doug, 102, 266
Johnson, Erwin, 213
Johnson, Glenn, 256
Johnson, Howard, 75
Johnson, Jeff, 270
Johnson, John, 163, 165
Johnson, Lynn, 259, 276
Johnson, Mark, 201, 214, 215, 231, 232, 246, 247
Johnson, Max, 41
Johnson, Paul, 177
Johnson, Randy, 142
Johnson, Richard, 75
Johnson, Rog, 113, 135, 146, 149
Johnson, Ron, 76
Johnson, Ted, 265, 280
Johnson, Tom, 42, 200, 213, 230
Johnson, Wint, 213
Johnston, Bill, 213, 248
Johnston, Sandy, 187
Jolley, Walt, 55
Jones, Bill, 55, 186, 213, 230
Jones, Dick, 209, 225, 241
Jones, Jack, 230, 248, 265, 280
Jones, Knoefel, 162
Jones, Lee, 19, 41, 45, 48
Jonswald, Jeff, 226
Jordan, Dan, 260
Jordan, Tim, 211, 228
Jorgenson, Jeff, 168, 177, 213, 214
Junewjck, Arnie, 29

K

Kaat, Jim, 15, 48, 51, 52, 54, 90, 105, 199, 213
Kahler, Phil, 276
Kahler, Taibi, 186, 188, 234
Kalmink, Jack, 263
Kammerdiner, Lee, 242
Kamp, Jim, 55
Kanary, Kim, 155
Kane, Charles, 169
Kaper, Groy, 237, 253, 254, 255, 256, 257, 268, 270, 271, 272, 274
Karnes, Del, 122, 263
Kaspar, Neal, 241
Kast, Dick, 122
Kasten, Bob, 225
Katona, Jim, 260, 279
Keating, Kerry, 16
Keck, John, 239, 256
Keiper, Joe, 151
Keith, Dennis, 246
Keizer, Winona, 76
Kelbey, Doug, 170
Keller, Lou, 88
Kellogsville Public Schools, 35
Kempker, Dave, 54, 269
Kempker, Jack, 28, 29, 43, 44, 46, 48, 51, 52, 53, 66, 68, 69, 73, 74, 75, 147
Kench, Phil, 176
Kennedy, Jacqueline, 178
Kennedy, Jerry, 213, 230, 248
Kennedy, John F., 135, 157, 178
Kennedy, Lee, 194, 196
Kennedy, Robert, 253
Kennerly, Richard, 151
Kenny, Gene, 258

Kerr, Cal, 283
Kerwin, Jim, 283
Kerzynowski, John, 170
Ketrow, Gary, 138, 153
Kett, Jim, 246
Keur, Bill, 157, 159, 160, 173, 174, 175, 176, 189, 206, 207, 208
Keyser, Mike, 170
Keyser, Robert, 170
Kidd, Bob, 246, 247, 266, 267, 281
Kiefer, Russ, 265, 280
Kiehl, Bryan, 230, 248, 265
Kilbourn, Bob, 198
Kilby, Greg, 265
Kincannon, Andy, 19, 41
King, Bob, 54
King, Craig, 255
King, Martin Luther Jr., 246
King, Roy, 17
Kinney, Allan, 223, 236, 237, 240
Kinsey, Jay, 97
Kirchoff, Gerald, 63
Kirtley, Rich, 87
Klaasen, Bob, 122, 140, 280
Klaasen, Tom, 70, 101, 122, 140
Klein, Jim, 198, 210, 211, 212, 225, 227, 228, 229
Klein, Norm, 233
Kleinheksel, John, 63, 67, 69, 71, 72, 73, 87, 95, 102, 120, 121, 122, 249
Kleinheksel, Russ, 143
Kleinjans, Everett Ets, 66, 89, 117
Kleis, Lee, 41, 77
Klenk, Bill, 42, 43, 78, 88, 242, 244, 260, 261, 277
Kling, Jeff, 234
Klingman, Steve, 254
Klingsbury, Neal, 275
Klingsbury, Roger, 275
Klomparens, Tom, 86
Klop, Don, 213, 248, 265, 266
Kloss, Tom, 265
Klug, Ken, 179
Klysz, Terry, 269
Knapp, Bill, 131
Knapp, John, 167
Knecht, George, 59
Knickerbocker, Les, 160
Knight, Bill, 170
Knight, John, 141, 156
Knittle, Ed, 157
Knoester, Bill, 179
Knott, Jim, 258, 259
Knowlton, Jerry, 201, 210
Knowlton, Mike, 190, 194, 196
Kober, Al, 48, 51, 52, 53
Kobilarcsik, Mike, 205
Koch, John, 186, 213, 230
Koehn, Marty, 180
Koenig, Dick, 141
Kohl, Ralph, 159
Kok, Jim, 25, 26, 30
Koker, Don, 151
Kolansa, Tom, 230, 248
Kolenbrander, Ken, 201
Kolestock, Zame, 248, 266, 280
Kollen Hall, 18
Kollen, Gerrit J., 16
Kolvalski, Ron, 202
Konwenski, Howard, 155
Kooiker, Lyle, 226
Kooiman, Bill, 213
Kooiners, Bill, 200
Kooistra, Sally, 169
Kooistra, William, 30
Kool, Jim, 123, 154

Koop, Dan, 166, 167
Koopman, Don, 64, 88, 111
Koops, Barry, 71, 111, 122, 139, 140
Kooyer, Walt, 249
Kopko, George, 276
Koppitsch, Mike, 187
Korstange, Gordon, 186, 201, 213
Korver, Gailerd, Gig, 164, 181
Kos, Jim, 226, 244
Kosciuk, Chris, 264
Koster, Stan, 71, 73, 122
Kouw, Barb, 169
Kraai, Art, 91, 100, 123
Kraai, Travis, 248, 265, 266, 280
Krachunas, Al, 65
Kraemer, Woody, 276
Krafft, John, 55, 103, 118
Kraft, George, 142, 235, 237, 240, 253, 262, 272, 279
Kramer, Art, 137, 153, 154, 164, 166, 167, 182, 183, 185
Kramer, Bill, 29, 30
Kramer, Roger, 116, 136, 140
Krantz, Gus, 79
Krause, Dave, 140
Krawczyk, Art, 143, 144
Krawczyk, Tom, 231
Kreider, Jim, 85, 102, 121, 122, 140
Kreilick, Tom, 70
Kresge Gym, 26, 44
Kreunen, Jim, 177
Kriston, Chuck, 134
Kromer, Barry, 234
Kronemeyer, Don, 195, 196, 197, 199, 200, 209, 210, 225, 226, 227, 248
Kronemeyer, Ron, 199
Kroodsma, Don, 200, 201, 214, 215, 223, 231, 246, 247
Kroodsma, Rog, 157, 166, 167, 168, 173, 174, 176, 177, 182, 183, 185, 190, 192, 200, 201, 205, 206, 207, 208, 214, 215
Krueger, Dan, 200, 201, 215, 231, 232, 246
Kruisenga, Marv, 101
Kruithof, Bastian, 163
Kruzman, Tony, 181
Kubiak, John, 78
Kudiack, Jim, 29
Kuhn, Bob, 258
Kuiper, Herm, 251
Kusak, Joe, 141, 143, 157, 173, 174, 176, 205, 206, 207
Kuyers, Dave, 16, 20, 21, 22, 31, 37, 38, 39, 42, 43
Kuyper, Bill, 70, 106

L

Laackman, Dale, 265
Lab, Ron, 257
Labadie, Ron, 249, 250, 255, 256, 264, 272, 283
Labahn, John, 130
Lake, Dennis, 160
Lambert, Bill, 217
Lamer, Jim, 266, 267, 268, 271, 272, 281
Landeryou, Vic, 18, 39
Landsburg, Lee, 168
Lane, Dave, 186, 187, 188, 202, 203
Lange, Jim, 266
Langeland, Charlie, 173, 174, 175, 176, 206, 207, 208, 213, 214, 221, 222, 223, 224, 225, 231, 232
Langeland, Jim, 165, 169
Langsford, Roy, 79
Lanting, Arlyn, 117, 118, 120, 138, 150, 152, 168
Lapenga, John, 280
La Porte, Marty, 210, 212

Lappenga, John, 248
Larkin, Jim, 82, 109
Larsen, Don, 39
Larson, Dick, 62, 106
La Rue, John, 162, 180
Laskoski, Dan, 260, 276, 279
Lasman, Don, 168
Lauerman, Ed, 130, 158, 174
Laughlin, Mike, 145, 155, 161
Lautenbach, Don, 62
Lauver, Jerry, 272, 279
Laux, Duane, 268
Laverman, Bruce, 102, 118, 120, 138
Lawrence Tech, 24
Lawrence, Frank, 42
Lawrence, John, 168
Lawson, James, 260
LBJ, 178, 199
Leak, Lanny, 85
Lear, Jim, 257
Leaske, Fred, 24, 32
Leatherman, Brian, 202
Le Duc, Don, 130, 158
Ledy, Carroll, 143
Ledy, Rick, 255
Lee, David, 276
Leenhouts, Jim, 269, 271, 272
Leenhouts, John, 227, 243, 245
Leetsma, Sandy, 139
Leggett, Les, 108, 144
Leighley, Joyce, 31, 56, 76
Leighton, Kurt, 200, 230
Leismer, Bill, 237, 255, 256
Lentini, Jerome, 265
Leonard, Rich, 62
Lepard, Keith, 72, 73
Leppi, John, 21, 32, 34, 50, 51
Levey, Stu, 177
Levigne, Paul, 205
Lewis, Jerry, 89
Lewis, Tom, 135, 136
Lichtenberger, John, 146
Lieder, Charles, 280
Liggett, Bill, 79, 130
Lind, Jim, 55, 75
Lind, Jud, 202
Lindberg, Bill, 134, 146, 149
Lindberg, Jon, 135
Lindenberg, George, 174, 187
Lindenberg, Jon, 135, 136, 149, 150
Linder, Bruce, 241
Lindsay, Max, 243, 249, 261, 277, 278
Ling, Stan, 248
List, Randy, 255
List, Steve, 250, 282, 283
Livedoti, Dominic, 142, 159, 176, 192
Livingston, Dave, 238
Livingston, Walt, 17, 38
Lobochefski, Terry, 251
Lockwood, Bob, 239, 270
Lockwood, Dave, 280
Lode, Eglis, 144, 158, 174, 189
Lodovisi, Vic, 38, 39
Lofts, Gordon, 196, 210, 212, 216, 227, 229, 243, 245, 250
Loiselle, Ray, 205
Lomas, Dave, 280
Lombardi, Vince, 87
Looman, Cal, 143
Loras College, 92
Lorenz, Rick, 228
Los Angeles State University, 97
Losey, Bill, 89, 92, 114
Lotz, Lou, 236, 258
Louwenaar, Keith, 118, 120
Low, Ron, 18, 28

Lowman, Bob, 241
Lozen, Tom, 230
Lubbers, Arend D., Don, 124
Lubbers, Dave, 199
Lubbers, Irwin J., 15, 27, 35, 77, 86, 124, 125, 157
Lucas, Bill, 146
Lucas, Ron, 157
Lucking, Bob, 280
Lude, Ron, 26
Luidens, Paul, 125
Lundell, Frank, 237, 238
Luttrell, Walter, Buzz, 196, 210, 212
Luyendyk, Bob, 282, 283
Luyendyk, Chuck, 280
Lynch, Bill, 155, 187, 203
Lynch, Jim, 177
Lynn, Jim, 152

M

Maat, Ron, 111
Maatman, Herb, 112
Mac Aluso, Sam, 169, 185
Mac Donald, Paul, 233, 262
Mace, Dick, 106
Machiele, Rich, 86
Macias, Dave, 281
Maciasz, Mike, 261, 277, 278, 279
Mack, Paul, 77, 78, 80, 82, 84, 85, 86, 102, 103, 105, 106, 107, 108, 109, 111, 118, 120, 127, 128, 129, 130, 131, 138, 140
Mac Kay Gymnasium, 23
Mackay, Bob, 139, 140, 170, 171, 186, 188, 222, 279
Maczko, Eddie, 222
Madsen, Mike, 279
Maiman, Mike, 243, 259, 260, 277
Maison, Doug, 60, 61, 63, 67
Malcolm, James J., 285
Mallinson, Bob, 241
Malone, Chuck, 274
Malton, Don, 31
Manchester of Indiana, 25
Manders, Dick, 160
Manzardo, Rick, 270
Maris, Dave, 111, 145
Maris, Roger, 141
Maris, Webb, 179
Marshall, George C., 108
Martens, Bruce, 160
Martin, Don, 32, 34, 216
Martin, Joe, 29, 30, 54
Martin, John, 275
Martinelli, Fred, 157, 173, 240
Martini, Paul, 210, 242
Marvin, Charles Chappy, 159, 206, 238
Marx, Skip, 30, 55
Maser, Walt, 26, 65, 67, 88
Mason, John, 136, 161, 164, 167
Mast, Ken, 207
Masteller, Jerry, 74, 100
Masters, Dave, 109
Mather, George, 217, 218
Mathews, Dan, 170
Matthews, Dan, 78
Matthews, Eddie, 97
Matthews, Ron, 201
Mattison, Jim, 251, 257, 283
Maurer, Bill, 276
Mawby, Leroy, 16
May, Jack, 116
May, James, 112, 113, 134
Mayer, Tim, 219
Mayo, Hank, 230
Mc Cloud, Sam, 134
Mc Conkie, Bob, 100

Mc Cormack, Tim, 200
Mc Cormick, Jim, 214
Mc Cormick, Mickey, 17
Mc Creary, Bruce, 226, 241, 242
Mc Culloch, Joe, 200
Mc Cullough, Bob, 16
Mc Cutchan, Arad, 97
Mc Cutchen, Gene, 169
McCutcheon, Arad, 178
Mc Daniel, Bill, 151
Mc Donald, Bruce, 170
Mc Donald, Dick, 130
McDonald, Doug, 191
Mc Donald, Gordy, 280
Mc Donough, Pete, 263
Mc Grath, Paul, 118
Mc Henry, Jack, 108
Mc Ildin, Dave, 151
Mc Ilvain, Dave, 169
Mc Kale, Dave, 118, 135
Mc Kean, Jim, 254, 270
McKee, Chris, 187
Mc Kee, Tiff, 233, 235
Mc Kelvey, Dave, 152
Mc Kersher, Don, 118
Mc Knight, Brian, 281
Mc Leod, George, 108
McLeod, Rod, 110
Mc Millan, Jim, 271
Mc Mullin, Charles, 246, 263
Mc Nally, Bill, 41
Mc Neese State, 23
Mc Nervey, Rod, 169
Mc Phillips, Tom, 135
Mc Pike, Dave, 265, 280
Meadows, Paul, 87, 134, 161
Meengs, Chester, 193
Meengs, John, 143, 177
Meerman, Wayne, 208, 216, 219, 225, 236
Melendy, Larry, 155, 176
Mellema, Irv, 226
Melin, Gene, 70, 80
Menighan, Jim, 128
Menken, Randy, 111, 121, 132
Menning, Bruce, 170, 177, 178, 188, 190, 192, 202, 203, 205, 206, 219
Menning, Curt, 31, 32, 34, 42, 58, 61, 171
Menning, Mark, 222, 224, 225, 240
Menzer, Jim, 41, 50, 51
Meredith, Dick, 186
Merkle, Bart, 268, 272
Mertz, Waldon, 258
Merx, Larry, 256
Meulman, Randy, 173, 177
Meyer, Dave, 86
Meyer, Dick, 280
Meyer, Ed, 128
Meyer, Rick, 248, 265
Meyering, Ed, Whitey, 56, 66, 88, 103
Meyers, Doug, 272
Meyers, Fred, 152
Middlebrook, Dave, 187, 188, 202, 203
Miedema, Nelson, 111, 171
Milican, Ron, 177
Milkamp, Paul, 246, 281
Milks, John, 207
Miller, Bruce, 229
Miller, Chris, 199
Miller, Herb, 70
Miller, Jerry, 230
Miller, John, 233, 263
Miller, Ron, 170
Miller, Steve, 179
Miller, Tom, 57, 58, 77, 84, 103, 105, 124, 175, 179, 181
Millis, Le Roy, 277

Mills, Bob, 261
Ming, Bruce, 234
Minnich, Jim, 240
Miracle, Roger, 75
Misyiak, Bart, 109, 121, 130, 131, 140
Mitchell, Don, 110, 157, 158, 159, 160
Mitchell, Mike, 223
Mitchell, Ron, 152
Mock, Tony, 258
Moerland, Abe, 77
Moffat, John, 19, 40, 41
Mohr, Jim, 50, 62, 71, 73, 77, 78, 80, 82, 85, 86, 101, 102, 106, 107, 108, 120, 121
Mokray, Bill, 97
Molenaar, Hal, 22, 23, 24, 25, 26, 27
Moliere, Roger, 194
Mollenhoff, Ralph, 134
Monchan, Mike, 38, 39
Monell, Kip, 236
Monk, Don, 168
Monson, Wayne, 112, 133
Mont, Tommy, 106
Montague, Bob, 202
Montana, Francisco, 150
Monte, Cornell, 230
Moon, Bob, 280
Mooney, Rom, 122
Moore, Arnold, 151
Moore, Dave, 260
Moore, Gary, 173
Moore, Ray, 162, 165, 180, 181, 182
Moore, Tom, 106, 110
Moorman, Haydon, 206
Moose, Gary, 157
Moran, Dave, 26
Moran, Joe, 26, 76
Morgan, Bill, 47, 48, 64
Morgan, Bob, 148, 161, 164
Morgan, Byron, 189
Morgan, Byron E., 173
Morgan, Dick, 53, 73, 74
Morgan, Roger, 276
Morrison, Gary, 25, 26, 46, 48, 49, 232, 243, 259, 277
Morrison, Terry, 276
Morse, Tom, 282
Morton, Doug, 237
Moss, Doug, 217, 218, 133, 135, 149, 150, 164
Mossier, Ken, 39
Motteram, Ernest, 258
Muddy, L.J., 121
Mueller, Dave, 259
Mueller, Fred, 262
Mulder, Donald G., 285
Mullen, Don, 269
Muller, Fred, 229, 246, 263
Mulligan, Mike, 153
Mulligan, Van, 143, 160, 175
Munisch, John, 103
Munn, Clarence Biggie, 18
Munsell, Bill, 272
Murdoch, John, 111
Murphy, Joe, 206
Murphy, Pat, 185, 265
Murphy, Tom, 200
Murray, Mike, 120
Musch, John, 118
Musial, Stan, 15
Muskingum, 129
Muyskens, Paul, 226
Myers, Doug, 251, 283
Myers, Harry, 221, 223, 224

N

Nadolsky, Karl, 251, 254, 255, 262, 263, 264, 271, 279, 282, 283
Nagurski Jr., Bronco, 87
Nagy, Al, 233, 238
Naismith, James, 65
Najourma, De Gaulle, 258
Nameth, Dan, 19
National Association of Intercollegiate Athletics (NAIA), 27, 49
Naughton, Bob, 93
Neal, Larry, 222
Neale, Earl, Greasy, 58
Nederveld, Gary, 117, 133, 134, 135, 145, 146, 148, 149, 150, 155, 161, 162, 163, 164, 165, 178
Nederveld, Gordon, 110
Needham, Dave, 87, 111
Needham, John, 43, 50, 63, 87
Neff, Jim, 112, 116, 134, 146
Neff, Steve, 187
Neidel, Bill, 259
Neigh, Jerry, 259
Neilson, Dave, 176, 191, 206
Neitring, Ike, 277, 279, 282
Nelson, Carl, Pill, 63, 86
Nelson, Dave, 36
Nelson, Denny, 186
Nelson, Doug, 271, 272
Nesbitt, Tom, 132, 143
Nettleson, John, 110
Newberry, Jack, 169
Newell, Pete, 25
Newhof, Tom, 25, 26, 46, 48, 64, 66
Newhouse, Bill, 277
Nicholai, Tom, 181, 195, 199
Nichols, Bill, 230
Nichols, Bob, 63
Nichols, Dale, 58
Nichols, Doug, 209, 216, 217, 219, 233, 234, 235, 248, 250, 251, 264
Nichols, Jim, 151
Nichols, Rusty, 259
Nienhouse, Ev, 22
Nienhuis, Conrad, Skip, 166, 182, 183, 200, 201, 214, 115
Nienhuis, Jan, 110, 128, 131
Nieusma, Jerry, 84, 86, 108, 110, 123, 124, 143, 144
Niwa, Larry, 254
Nixon, Julie, 253
Nordstrom, Dick, 246, 266, 267, 281
Nordstrom, Steve, 167, 183
Norman, Mike, 257
North Carolina A & T (Agricultural & Technical), 97
Northern Illinois University, 68
Northern Michigan College, 58
Northup, Jim, 66, 75, 88, 91, 100, 106, 111, 114, 117
Norton, Jon, 141, 144, 177
Notre Dame, 182
Nowakoski, Paul, 200
Noyd, Bill, 111
Null, Ray, 149
Numbers, Dick, 165
Numbers, Don, 163, 180, 182
Nusbaum, Gene, 212, 228, 260, 212, 228, 242, 245, 260, 261
Nyboer, Jan, 145
Nyboer, John, 132, 154, 177, 187
Nyhuis, Jay, 72, 95
Nykamp, Paula, 76
Nykamp, Randy, 199, 200
Nykamp, Wes, 101, 122, 140
Nykerk, Dave, 143, 150, 151, 152, 185, 186, 199

O

Oak Park Arms Hotel, 92
Oakes, Paul, 208
Oakley, Dave, 143, 177
O'Bryan, Lee, 248
Ochsner, Tom, 30
O'Connor, Bill, 266, 267, 281
Odell, Bill, 179
Odle, Don, 147, 163
O'Donnell, Kenneth, 178
Oegema, Dan, 259, 260
Oehm, Dennis, 177
Ogg, Jim, 233
Ogonji, Gilbert, 186, 187
Ohio Northern University, 110
Ohrman, Bob, 26, 46, 48
Okenka, John, 277, 278
Olson, Arthur, Swede, 28, 29, 52, 54, 73, 74, 84
Olson, Dennis, 161, 162, 178
Olson, Greg, 210
Oonk, John, 223
Oonk, Mike, 234, 251
Oostenink, Bill, 140, 154, 163, 170, 186
Oosterbaan, John, 111, 112, 114, 116, 117
Oosterbaan, Ula, 120
Oosterhaven, Cal, 208, 216, 219, 225, 236
Oosterhouse, Ken, 118, 169
Oosting, Dave, 280
Opdycke, Stewart, 151
Oredein, Benja, 265, 280
Orhman, Bob, 40
Ortquist, Dick, 28, 29
O'Shaughnessy, Wayne, 19, 60
Osman, Al, 132, 145, 161
Osterman, Larry, 258
Ostermeyer, Larry, 98
Osting, Dick, 151
Otis, Ken, 41
O'Toole, Joe, 212
Otte, Ken, 256, 266, 267
Otte, Warren, 91, 112, 115, 136, 148
Otterby, Kerry, 164, 180, 194, 196
Ousterling, Dave, 54
Overkamp, Fred, 111
Overman, Dean, 154, 155, 161, 162, 164, 170, 179, 180, 181, 182, 186, 193, 198, 199, 201
Overway, Les, 75, 103
Owen, Janet, 56, 76, 120, 120
Owens, Jesse, 124
Owens, Gary, 211

P

Paalman, Russ, 101
Paarlberg, Don Punch, 37, 40, 57, 61, 77, 78, 82, 84, 85, 87, 103, 105
Paauwe, Neal, 118, 120
Page, Tom, 263, 280
Paliatsos, Mike, 202, 203, 233, 234
Palmer, Al, 178, 179, 180
Papenfus, Jim, 135, 148, 149, 166
Pappadikis, Nick, 23, 25
Parks, Dave, 23, 25
Parrit, Bob, 176
Parsell, Stu, 109, 131, 132, 142, 143, 171, 176, 187, 192, 202, 216, 233, 238, 239, 282
Paterson, Mike, 233
Patnott, John, 199
Paton, Jon, 168
Patrick, Larry, 212
Patterson, Denny, 241
Paul, Henry, 41, 44, 61, 65, 68, 84, 92, 114, 116
Payne, Phil, 45
Peace, John, 170
Peale, Dr. Norman Vincent, 253
Peddie, Norm, 72
Pederson, Cal, 146, 149
Peelen, George, 59, 77, 80, 82, 105, 107, 108
Peelen, Matt, 39
Peiper, Gary, 177, 186, 187, 202, 219
Peiper, Terry, 209
Pekelder, Ben, 230, 248, 264, 280
Pell, Dan, 130, 144
Pelon, Tom, 189, 192, 200, 201, 207, 210, 211, 212, 215, 223, 231, 232, 237, 238, 239, 240, 242, 244, 245, 246,
Pendell, Bill, 162, 165, 179, 180, 181, 194, 196
Penny, Austen, 226, 227, 228
Perkins, Rog, 202
Peron, Juan, 15
Perrin, John, 170, 186
Perrine, Nick, 279
Perry, Doug, 79
Persons, John, 137, 144, 153, 170, 174
Pete, Tim, 200, 215
Peterman, Jim, 86
Peters, Bob, 159
Peters, Dave, 107, 114, 117, 122, 133, 135, 139
Peters, Ed, 201
Peters, Jim, 180, 181, 199, 211, 212
Peterson, Hal, 169
Peterson, Mel, 69, 93, 95, 97, 113
Pethers, Clayton, 90
Petrovich, Michael, 236
Pettigrew, Len, 240
Petzel, Fred, 133
Pfeiffer, Jerry, 150, 168
Pfister, Dave, 140
Pfund, John, 149, 162, 164, 179, 180, 194, 196
Pfund, Lee, 69, 93, 95, 113, 114, 135, 146, 149, 194, 211, 226, 245
Phail, Elmer, 86, 100
Phelan, Jim, 276
Phelps, Mike, Mickey, 242, 244, 260, 261, 276, 278, 279, 282
Phillippi, Don, 147, 150, 165
Phillips, J. Donald, 133
Pierce, Marty, 248
Pierpont, Jim, 202, 203, 216, 217, 218, 219
Piersma, Steve, 200, 201, 206, 207, 214, 215, 239, 247
Pierucki, John, 228, 245
Pinechaff, Dean, 31
Pink, John, 281
Pipton, Mike, 152
Pixley, Bob, 70
Pixley, Phil, 103
Plagenhoef, Vern, 189, 190, 208, 214, 215
Pleune, John, 72
Pleune, Peter, 22
Plooster, Gary, 272
Pluister, Phil, 183
Pobursky, Jim, 176, 206
Poe, Walt, 40, 60
Pohlman, Dave, 157, 158
Polen, Bob, 110
Polizotto, Scott, 108
Polk, Carlton, 151
Pollard, Henry, 90
Pommissee, Phil, 118
Poortinga, Jerry, 219
Poppen, Jim, 253
Poppink, Cal, 141, 143, 144, 154, 155, 157, 164, 166, 167, 176, 177, 182, 183, 185, 195, 201
Poppink, Jim, Dutch, 198, 217, 219
Porterfield, Lee, 257
Post, Dave, 248
Post, Ernie, 105
Post, Lynn, 16, 18, 21, 23
Post, Stu, 59, 86
Postma, Bob, 45, 55
Postma, Ken, 177, 205
Potter, Bill, 178, 179, 180, 181, 186, 194, 195, 196, 197, 199, 201, 202, 210, 211, 212
Powell, Jeff, 188
Powers, Bryan, 38
Powers, David, 178
Powers, Jim, 265, 280
Pratt, Bill, 118
Pratt, Bob, 276
Pratt, Larry, 136
Predeiri, Tim, 268
Preston, Jim, 39
Preston, Wally, 70
Previte, Jim, 38
Prewitt, Willie, 102
Price, Pat, 166
Priebe, Jerry, 70
Prince, Jack, 255
Prins, Tom, 200, 213
Prints, Brad, 170
Province, Bill, 180, 194, 196
Pruiksma, Walt, 121
Pruim, Dave, 268, 272
Purcell, Jim, 151
Purdy, Tom, 76, 103
Pursel, Bob, 212
Purvey, Tom, 118
Pyle, Joan, 169

Q

Quakkelaar, Ken, 130, 131, 141, 143, 158, 171, 175, 176, 177

R

Raab, Marv, Marvelous, 21, 22
Rabbers, Mike, 187, 196, 199
Rainey, Harold, 44
Rakow, Ken, 193, 225
Rall, Jack, 202, 216
Ramsey, Merle, 45, 66
Randall C. Bosch Award, 27
Rank, Gary, 277, 278
Rank, Kim, 244, 261, 278
Rasmussen, Boyd, 231, 272
Raterink, Dave, 267, 282, 283
Raup, Konrad, 251
Rauwerdink, Phil, 190
Ray, Duane, 264
Raynolds, Pete, 257
Readnour, Mike, 114
Rebhuhn, Ron, 150
Redding, Chuck, 82, 109, 130
Reed, Chuck, 230, 248
Reed, Joe, 206, 230, 248
Reed, Mel, 34
Reed, Rick, 169
Reed, Walter III, 216, 219, 221, 222, 223, 234, 237, 240, 248, 249, 250, 251, 253, 255, 263
Reese, Bill, 147
Reest, Henry, 180, 199
Regan, Phil, 23
Rehbuhn, Ron, 168
Reid, Bob, 87, 89, 91, 95, 98, 111, 112, 113, 115, 117, 122, 123, 133, 134, 135, 136, 137, 138, 148, 149, 150, 153
Reiff, Rick, 169
Reiner, Walt, 157
Reinhardt, Rog, 143
Reiss, Jack, 152
Remmelts, Jim, 30
Remo, Don, 281
Renner, Tom, 171, 191, 243
Rexinger, Al, 214

Reynen, Steve, Spud, 202, 217, 218, 219, 233, 234, 235, 248, 250, 251
Reynolds, Jim, Jellybean, 45, 48, 51, 59, 61, 65, 66, 67, 71, 82, 90, 109
Rhoda, Len, 115, 134
Rhomberg, Bill, 92, 93
Rice, Ord, 187
Richards, Terry, 206, 222
Richendollar, Jim, 109
Richey, Garth, 61, 85, 89, 92, 102, 114, 117, 121
Ridder, Herman, 246
Rider, Morrette, 16, 29, 84, 235
Ridley, Tom, 109, 131
Riegel, Bill, 23
Rielag, Dave, 122
Riemersma, Dwight, 22, 23, 24, 25, 26, 27
Riemersma, Jim, 168, 169
Riley, Dick, 140
Riley, Gary, 31, 55
Ritsema, Bob, 22, 25, 26, 27, 43, 44, 45, 47, 48, 49, 147
Ritsema, Bruce, 264
Ritsema, Ray, 44, 45, 48, 50, 51, 63, 64, 65, 66, 68, 69, 72, 73, 87, 88, 89, 90, 91, 92, 93, 94, 95, 97, 101, 102, 111, 112, 113, 114, 116, 117, 118, 120, 121, 122, 147
Ritt, Elvin, 28
Ritt, Erv, 20
Rivers, Bill, 170, 201
Riverview Park, 28, 191
Robbert, Jan, 50, 51
Robbins, Steve, 211
Roberson, Arden, Stretch, 128, 192
Roberts Memorial Stadium, 97
Robillard, Dave, 259, 279
Robinson, Keith, 152
Robinson, Nolan, 151
Robyn, Dick, 155
Rock, Matt, 17
Rodwan, Gordon, 116, 135, 136, 148, 149, 150, 155
Roe, Bruce, 111
Roedvoets, Jim, 255
Roedy, Randy, 266
Roelofs, Bruce, 137
Roger, Norm, 70
Rogers, Howard, 41, 109, 131
Rolley, Ray, 88, 91, 116, 136
Roman, Albie, 53
Romine, Joe, 274
Rommel, Jim, 261
Romney, George, 199
Roos, Bob, 145
Rose, Phil, 139, 152
Roseley, Jay, 70
Rosenboom, Pat, 55
Rosetti, Jack, 19
Rothi, Gene, 77, 111
Rotman, Arnie, 26
Rottschafer, Dyke, 42, 86
Rowan, Robert, Hoots, 117
Royal, Darrell, 268
Royer, Jim, 191
Rozeboom, Jim, 63, 71, 73, 101, 120, 121, 122, 139, 140, 127
Rubush, John, 127
Ruby, Jack, 178
Ruiter, Allen, 110
Rulewicz, Steve, 255, 274
Rumohr, Frank, 238
Rumohr, Harry, 223, 231, 232, 246, 247, 254, 255, 256, 257, 266, 267, 268, 270, 271, 272, 274, 281
Rundle, Chris, 271
Rupp, Tyrone, 41, 61, 63, 105, 106, 108, 111

Ruppert, Tom, 195, 209, 216
Rushton, Jerry, 216
Russell, Dale, 97
Russell, Rick, 189, 190, 207, 224
Russell, Roberta, 120
Russell, Turner, 90, 116, 134
Russo, Andy, 242, 259, 260
Rusthoven, Rich, 148, 149
Ryan, Jim, 265
Ryan, Pat, 228, 259, 276
Rycenga, Ted, 255
Rynbrandt, Cal, 62, 86
Rypma, Gary, 211, 212, 225, 226, 227, 228, 229, 241, 242, 244, 245

S

Saacke, Chuck, 248
Saddler, Jim, 54
Sadler, Ed, 40
Safar, Tibor, 230, 248
Saggers, Jerry, 177
Saint Michael's College, 97
Salathiel, Lyndon, 107
Salvarino, Jack, 122
Sandahl, Bill, 29
Sanholtz, Larry, 144
Saslana, Ed, 150
Saunders, Bob, 30
Saurman, Phil, 212
Saxby, Mike, 190
Saxton, Charlie, 117
Saxton, Ferris, 88, 91, 97, 114, 133
Sayers, Gayle, 171
Scapa, Fred, 168
Scarletta, Chuck, 223
Scarpa, Paul, 150
Schaap, Gary, 153, 154, 182, 183
Schaap, Phil, 254
Schadler, John, 230
Schaffer, Jerry, 68, 130
Schantz, Bobby, 159, 160, 173, 177, 189
Scheid, Chuck, 38
Schering, Eric, 280
Schilstra, Clint, 207, 222, 223, 238
Schipper, Daughn, 169
Schipper, Max, 206
Schipper, Ron, 17, 90, 105, 124, 132, 140, 145
Schmid, Chris, 259
Schmidt, Pete, 281
Scholl, Bill, 254
Scholten, Carolyn, 56, 76
Scholten, Harvey, 101
Schoon, Bob, 134
Schoon, Dale, 22, 128, 130, 131, 142, 143, 144
Schoon, Jim, 225, 226, 227, 229
Schoon, Jon, 106, 110, 111, 117, 120, 121, 122, 127, 129, 131, 141, 142, 143, 144, 154, 155, 157, 158, 159, 160, 170, 257
Schott, Per, 200
Schout, Lloyd, 209, 226, 227, 228
Schouten, Jack, 16, 23, 171
Schrader, Dave, 195, 196
Schram, Ben, 70
Schregardus, Jean, 120, 120
Schreiber, Barry, 241, 242, 244, 245, 251, 159, 160, 161
Schrier, Jack, 185, 186, 213
Schrier, Mike, 139, 140, 155, 170
Schroeder, Ken, 219, 234
Schroeder, Ralph, 248, 250, 282
Schroer, Dick, 88
Schrotenboer, Bob, 141, 142, 143
Schrotenboer, Craig, 265, 266, 269, 271, 272, 274, 280
Schubel, Jerry, 31
Schuler, Win, 49, 84, 156, 170, 188, 205

Schuller, Bill, 223, 257, 271, 280
Schult, Ron, 112, 134, 146
Schultz, Norm, 44, 68
Schultz, Roland, 133
Schulz, Dick, 21
Schumacher, Myron, 146, 163
Schuman, Ken, 41
Schurr, Wayne, 74
Schut, Norm, 72, 73, 87, 90, 95, 100, 116, 118, 122, 123, 133, 134, 135, 136, 137, 138, 147
Schut, Roland, Pooch, 44, 48, 50, 63, 67, 69, 70, 72, 87, 95, 97, 101, 102, 111, 113, 116, 120, 147
Schutmaat, Fred, 209, 236, 258, 259
Schwalback, Tom, 58, 59, 79
Scipper, Max, 177
Scott, Bob, 257, 283
Scott, Doug, 272
Scott, George, 230, 248
Scott, Ric, 261
Scott, Rich, 278
Scripter, Dick, 76, 103
Scudder, Marilyn, 120
Seagert, Dick, 165, 180, 182, 194, 196, 199
Sebastian, Dan, 186
Seder, Bill, 240
Selee, Mike, 278
Semeyn, Pete, 272
Semrock, Harold, 158
Sende, Pierre, 209
Seneyn, Ed, 118
Sennet, Jim, 30
Serges, Drake, 242, 244, 260, 261
Serum, Bob, 143
Sexton, Ron, 230
Shaberg, Roy, 106, 110, 142, 160
Shade, Bill, 20
Shaffer, Jim, 150
Shaffer, Sheridan, 132, 145, 225
Shames, Dave, 259
Shannon, Frank, 259
Shantholtzer, Fred, 143, 187, 188
Sharda, Rich, 30, 56
Shattuck, Rich, 138, 139
Shayal, Fred, 150
Shelb, Russ, 140
Shercliff, Mickey, 89
Sheridan, Andy, 259
Sherman, Bob, 139
Sherman, Ed, 129
Shethar, Al, 243, 259, 260, 277, 278
Shinabarger, Dan, 259, 260, 261, 262, 276, 277, 278, 279
Shonefeld, Mike, 270
Shonta, Chuck, 78
Shuck, Jim, 107, 108, 110, 111, 142, 144
Shulerk, Dave, 278
Shultz, Kurt, 181
Shurmur, Fritz, 85
Shurmur, Joe, 145
Sibilsky, Bob, 190
Siebling, Ron, 38, 39
Siedentop, Daryl, 44, 47, 52, 53, 54, 64, 68, 69, 73, 87, 88, 89, 90, 92, 94, 95, 112, 113, 114, 118, 124, 132, 137, 145, 147, 152, 153, 161, 166, 167, 177, 178, 182, 185, 192, 200, 209, 213, 214, 215, 218, 225, 230, 266, 267, 276, 281, 282
Siemers, Gary, 230
Sigler, Irv, 159, 176, 181, 192, 202
Sigren, Vince, 194, 196, 210, 212, 227, 232
Simala, Dave, 84, 86
Sime, John, 136
Simmons, Bill, 228
Simmons, Dave, 116, 135, 137
Simon, Paul, 221

305

Simons, John, 171, 180, 181, 186, 194, 202
Simons, Mark, 276
Simpson, Ken, 110
Simpson, Tom, 256
Sims, Larry, 174
Simwanza, Kawala, 236
single wing, 36
Sippel, Ken, 68
Skala, Jim, 23, 25, 44, 45
Skala, Mike, 68
Skestone, Frank, 29, 30
Skinner, Charlie, 29, 53, 75
Skinner, Dick, 200
Skinner, John, 283
Slagh, Steve, 80, 84, 86, 106, 107, 108, 127, 128, 131, 143
Sliede, Juris, 31
Slikkers, Ade Jr., 177, 189
Smith, Jack, 152
Sloan, John, 278
Sloan, Paul, 234, 237
Slommer, Jim, 169
Sluyter, Rod, 155
Smallwood, Ed, 117
Smickley, Bob, 272
Smies, Fred, 177
Smillie, George, 169, 186, 213, 214
Smith, Al, 267
Smith, Art, 42, 58, 78, 106, 118, 129, 152, 160
Smith, Bill, 131, 200, 230
Smith, Chuck, 46
Smith, Dick, 19, 159, 203, 217
Smith, Doug, 271, 281
Smith, Gordon, 150
Smith, Jerry, 201
Smith, Jim, 18, 39, 108, 130, 144, 158
Smith, John, 177
Smith, Paul, 268
Smith, Phil, 118
Smith, Raymond E., 285
Smith, Rich, 265
Smith, Rick, 280
Smith, Steve, 253
Smith, Sue, 285
Smith, Tom, 171
Smith, Tyrone, 157
Smits, Charlie, 50, 62, 72
Snider, Gerry, 129
Snoap, Dana, 269, 270, 271, 272, 274, 275, 276, 277, 278, 279
Snoap, Marty, 259, 260, 261, 262, 266, 267, 276, 277, 278, 279, 281
Snoeink, Ben, 203
Snow, Mike, 201, 202
Snow, Tim, 272
Snyder, Gord, 55
Snyder, Jerry, 109
Sober, Ron, 226
Soeter, John, 22
Sokody, Phil, 136
Sommer, Jim, 208
Soodsma, Bob, 138
South Dakota State University, 97
Southwest Missouri State University, 97
Southworth, Dale, 161, 164, 181
Spaan, Dave, 31, 32, 34, 35, 49, 50, 51, 70, 72, 73, 101, 202
Spaeth, Ron, 31
Spatt, Robert, 133
Spenser, Bill, 282
Spiker, Joel, 128
Spitz, Don, 145, 163, 180
Spragg, Warren, 41
Sprankle, Dale, 49, 92, 125, 188
St. Norbert College, 68
Stacey, Dennis, 257

Stafford, Maynard, 26, 49
Stagg, Amos Alonzo, 64, 65
Stam, John, 141, 177, 189, 192
Stampf, Joe, 64, 65
Starr, Bart, 87
Start, Ed, 25, 26, 46, 48, 64, 66
Stauffer, Gary, 45, 47
Steele, Dennis, 190, 224
Steele, Ray, 226
Steen, Barney, 25, 26, 45, 64, 66, 88, 91, 111, 125, 134, 149, 165, 178, 186, 195, 197, 211, 212, 213, 229
Steen, Bill, 178
Steen, Pete, 50
Steevy, Jim, 170
Steffen, Ray, 25, 46, 48, 65, 66, 88, 91, 112, 135, 136, 148, 149, 161, 164, 180, 181, 211, 228, 242, 244, 261, 276, 278
Steffens, Henry, 48, 124
Stehle, Terry, 266, 267
Stehower, Ed, 270
Steiner, Tom, 212
Steketee, Paul, 233, 234, 251
Steketee, Tom, 122
Stell, Lance, 168, 185, 186, 199, 213
Stephans, Bill, 23
Stephans, Bruce, 26, 67, 88
Stephens, Don, 272
Stephens, Ed, 212, 241, 244, 259
Stephens, Steve, 279
Stephenson, Lou, 240
Sterk, Vern, 132, 145, 161, 171, 177, 187
Stevens, Ed, 229
Stevens, Ron, 180, 210
Stevenson, Jim, 270
Steward, Bob, 39
Steward, Doug, 25, 26, 48
Stielstra, Phil, 213
Stiles, Jerri, 216, 218
Stille, Chuck, 163, 212
Stoel, Tom, 62
Stolz, Denny, 100, 207, 216, 223, 233, 238, 250, 264, 270, 282
Stolz, Stan, 47
Stone, Jim, 226
Stone, Mike, 85
Stoner, Pete, 131
Stonitsch, Ron, 275
Stork, Ron, 45
Stout, Jim, 18, 19, 20, 28
Stover, Conrad, 63, 68
Stowe, Dr. Allen B., 31
Stranyak, Bob, 143
Strayer, Herb, 111
Strodtz, Gary, 152
Struck, Bill, 248, 265, 281
Stuckey, Frank, 167
Stulberg, Hal, 52
Sullivan, Jim, 89
Sullivan, Mike, 158
Sullivan, Steve, 152
Swan, Paul, 248
Swanson, Ed, 70, 122
Swarthout, Don, 213, 230, 248, 265
Swartz, Jack, 141, 158, 173, 238, 254
Swets, Paul, 161
Swieringa, Gerry, 268, 272
Swihart, Tom, 225, 236, 250
Sylvester, Mark, 230
Sylvester, Stan, 24
Sytsma, Menno, 177, 189

T

Taatjes, Doug, 276, 278, 281
Tabacsko, Ken, 265
Tabb, Steve, 248, 265

Taber, Tom, 78
Tallman, Ed, 74
Tam, Tim, 258
Tanja, John, 75
Tarrent, Tim, 265, 280
Tate, Jim, 247
Tate, Tom, 45
Taup, Jim, 32, 72
Taves, Buzz, 262
Tayangamon, Dan, 151
Taylor, Jerry, 109
Taylor, Larry, 238
Taylor, Tom, 42, 61, 62, 85, 87, 92, 256, 271
Te Beest, Ron, 139, 140, 146, 147, 148, 150, 155, 161, 162, 164, 165, 178, 180, 181, 182
Teall, Bob, 107, 108, 109, 110, 118, 120, 129, 150
Teall, Gary, 143, 144, 159, 280
Tebb, Steve, 280
Telfer, Lee, 65
Telgenhof, Charlie, 57
Teller, Bill, 187
Telman, Randy, 192
Ten Hoor, Henry, 163
Ten Klay, Arlin, 219
Ten Pas, John, 63
Ter Molen, Larry, 31, 32, 34, 35, 42, 50, 57, 58, 59, 60, 61, 63, 71, 73, 77, 82, 84, 85, 86, 87, 92, 102, 103, 105
Terpstra, Paul, 200, 201, 214, 215
Terrell, Dale, 117, 135, 136
Terwilliger, John, 232
Terwilliger, Terry, 139
Tessitore, Tom, 221, 237
Tetzlaff, Jim, 46
Teusink, Alan, 87
Teusink, Dwayne, Tiger, 22, 25, 30, 43, 45, 46, 47, 48, 55, 63, 64, 65, 66, 68, 69, 75, 124, 147
Teusink, Paul, 143
Thiebout, Rich, 170
Thomas, Dave, 233, 249, 250, 251, 263, 264, 282, 283
Thomas, Mark, 151
Thomas, Neil, 109
Thomas, Tom, 224, 230, 256, 258, 264, 271, 272
Thomas, Warren, Swede, 20, 41, 102, 120, 140, 145, 155, 187, 203
Thompson, Bill, 186
Thompson, Bob, 203, 216, 218, 219
Thompson, Jim, 170, 186, 201
Thompson, John, 65, 67, 91, 123
Thompson, Rich, 228, 242
Thomson, Bob, 22, 26, 28, 29, 44, 64, 69, 73, 74, 75, 98, 100, 101, 122
Thorpe, Tom, 107
Thurman, Mike, 281
Thwaits, Rex, 212, 227
Tichenor, Lee, 224, 239
Ticknor, Dave, 274
Tidwell, Dave, 248, 265
Tiemann, Ernie, 179
Tigelaar, Bob, 138, 151, 152
Tiggleman, Bob, 272
Tilma, Eugene, 272
Timmer, Albert, 29, 54, 55, 70, 127
Timmer, Ben, 101
Timmer, Blaine, 17, 32, 37
Timmer, Jim, 163
Toland, John, 210
Tolodziecki, Gordon, 31
Tomasi, Dom, 240
Tomilson, Sam, 111
Tomkins, Bob, 276
Tomkins, Bud, 79

306

Top, Bob, 75
Tornga, Ed, 152
Tornga, Tom, 101, 102, 121, 122
Trautman, Jeff, 276
Travis, Dan, 248, 265
Travola, Harold, 39
Traye, Ted, 230, 265
Treadway Gym, 26
Trenary, Bob, 226, 228, 229, 242, 244, 245
Treygo, Wilt, 265
Triggs, Byrel, 30
Trippett, Dick, 135
Triptow, Dick, 178, 194, 226, 227, 228, 242, 243, 259, 260
Triptow, Sam, 257
Troesch, Frank, 20
Troesch, Mike, 49
Troost, Don, 182, 183, 185, 200, 201, 230, 231, 232
Troost, Paul, 214, 215
Trosko, Fred, 16, 78
Troup, Mike, 28
Troviess, Dan, 230
Truby, Chuck, 102, 105, 106, 108, 127, 129, 132
Trump, John, 230, 248
Tryjo, Wit, 248
Tubbs, Rick, 265
Tucker, Bob, 139
Tucker, Chuck, 26
Tucker, Lee, 168
Tucker, Marty, 169
Tucker, Mike, 170
Tuel, Art, 207
Tuls, Art, 48
Tuls, Dave, 202
Tuls, Paul, 165, 170
Turner, Bob, 218, 235
Turner, Cliff, 135, 136, 137
Turner, Dave, 102
Turner, Fitz, 241
Turney, Harry, 259, 277, 279
Tutak, Phil, 265
Tuuk, Dave, 31, 71, 111, 120, 139, 178, 202, 249, 264, 282
Tyler, Len, 159
Tysse, G. John, 251
Tysse, Jim, 122, 139
Tysse, John, 125, 219, 249

U

Ulrich, Bob, 224
Underwood, Bud, 276
University of Dubuque, Iowa, 32
Urshalitz, Bob, 18, 30, 39, 55, 59
Utzinger, Dave, 209, 210, 227, 228, 241, 242, 245

V

Valuck, Bill, 170
Van Andel, Dennis, 235
Van Ark, Harm, 66
Van Beek, Drake, 263, 280
Van Beveran, Loran, 223
Van Dahm, Tom, 16
Van Dam, Ed, 154, 155, 170
Van Dam, Jim, 107, 110, 123, 127, 131, 159, 173, 174, 175, 177
VanDam, John, 50
Van Dam, John, 143
Van Dam, Ray, 265
Vande Griend, Orville, 50
Vandenberg, Bill, 110, 154, 155
Vandenberg, Bob, 84
Vandenberg, Harold, 78
Vanden Berg, Ron, 103

Vandenburg, John, 61, 86, 101, 102, 105, 106, 110, 123, 127, 129, 130, 131, 137, 138
Vandenburg, Phil, 230
Vandenburg, Rick, 262, 263
Vande Poel, Jim, 167
Vanderbilt, Bill, 71, 72, 73, 87, 89, 91, 95, 102, 111, 112, 113, 114, 115, 116, 117, 120, 121, 122, 133, 135, 136, 139, 147, 235, 245, 251, 258, 275, 276
Vander Brugge, Gord, 185
Vander Burg, Gord, 169
Vanderbush, Al, 15, 16, 35, 37, 45, 49, 58, 61, 64, 75, 87, 89, 92, 105, 106, 109, 111, 114, 124, 127, 132
Vander Hart, Dave, 118, 138, 169
Vander Hey, Doug, 22
Vander Hill, Dave, 46, 48
Vander Hill, Jim, 111, 112, 113, 114, 115, 116, 117, 133, 135, 136, 137, 145, 146, 147, 148, 149, 150, 161, 162, 163, 164, 165, 178, 242
Vander Hill, Jeannette, 116, 165
Vander Hill, George, 137
Vander Hill, Laverne, 44, 115, 116, 165
Vander Hill, Warren, 44, 45, 46, 49, 57, 63, 64, 65, 66, 67, 68, 69, 87, 88, 89, 90, 91, 92, 93, 94, 95, 97, 111, 112, 113, 114, 116, 118, 124, 125, 147, 179
Vanderhoff, Frank, 143
Vander Laan, Roger, 46
Vander Lind, Jim, 71, 73, 125
Vander Lind, Mert, 18, 20, 22, 26, 28, 29, 38, 39, 40, 41, 42, 43, 51, 52, 53, 54, 58, 59, 61, 63, 73, 74, 75
Vanderlinde, Dick, 223
Vander Linde, Rick, 279
Vander Lugt, William, 163
Vander Male, Joel, 235, 282
Vander Meer, Al, 244, 261, 277, 279
Vander Mel, Bruce Tim, 52, 53, 98, 100, 122, 123, 125
Vander Molen, Ron, 122, 123, 124, 137, 138, 153
Vander Molen, Tom, 158
Vander Sand, Bob, 170
Vander Veen, Joan, 169
Vander Werf, Calvin A., 171, 175, 177, 191, 199, 242, 246, 272
Vander Woude, Sherwood, Sharkey, 79, 80, 86, 87, 98, 100, 102, 106, 107, 108, 110, 122, 123, 127, 128, 129, 130, 131, 132, 137, 138, 141, 142, 143, 144, 145, 149
Vander Woude, Tom, 149, 163, 165
Vande Wege, Jim, 86, 110, 127, 131, 141, 143
Vande Werken, Jerry, 258
Van Dis, Bob, Gabby, 117
Van Dokkumburg, Mark, 265, 266
Van Dongen, Gene, 38, 39, 40, 59, 62, 77, 78, 82, 84, 97, 101, 105, 106, 107, 108, 111, 122, 123
Van Dyke, John, 70
Van Dyke, Tom, 139, 154, 155, 156
Van Eenenaam, Dave, 49
Van Eenenaam, Isla, 18
Van Eenenaam, Ron, 102
Van Eerden, Jim, 165, 179, 181, 182
Van Engen, Chuck, 258
Van Engen, Dutch, 17
Van Es, Rowland, 55, 75, 86, 87, 102, 110, 111, 125
Van Eyl, Phillip, 192, 193, 208, 225, 236, 258
Van Farowe, Harvey, 50
Van Fassen, Mark, 248, 265, 280
Van Genderen, Kurt, 110, 129, 131, 143, 159
Van Gilder, Don, 74, 85
Van Hoeven, Donald, Doc, 16, 18, 19, 20, 21
Van Hoeven, Jay, 223

Van Horne, Jim, 268
Van Huis, Bruce, 209, 212, 225, 226, 227, 228, 229, 231, 232, 241, 242, 244, 259, 260, 261, 262, 275
Van Ingen, John, 16, 30
Van Leuwen, Bruce, 86, 110
Van Liere, Clairie, 15
Van Lierop, Ben, 251
Van Lierop, Pete, 143
Van Noord, Roger, 130, 143
Van Pamelen, Dave, 262, 263
Van Pelt, Steve, 251, 282
Van Portfleet, Tom, 276
Van Raalte, Albertus C., 137
Van Slyke, Bob, 73
Van Spriell, Larry, 118
Van Tatenhove, Fred, 143, 174, 176
Van Til, Jim, 137, 138, 153, 154, 166, 167, 168, 182, 183
Van Tubergan, Keith, 255, 256, 262, 271, 272
Van Verst, George, 57, 59
Van Wie, Al, 211, 228, 232
Van Wieren, Billie, 165
Van Wieren, Clare, 161, 162, 163, 164, 165, 167, 168, 178, 179, 180, 181, 182, 183, 185, 193, 194, 195, 197, 199, 201, 209, 210, 211, 212, 214, 215
Van Wieren, Glenn, 111, 132, 133, 134, 135, 136, 137, 145, 146, 147, 148, 149, 150, 153, 154, 161, 162, 163, 164, 165, 166, 167, 168, 175, 177, 178, 179, 180, 181, 182, 183, 185, 213, 225, 230, 231, 232, 235, 242, 246, 282
Van Wieren, Jack, 248
Van Wieren, Kelly, 165
Van Wingen, Tom, 106
Van Wyk, Carl, 177
Van Wyke, Jerry, 186
Van Yteren, Dick, 274
Van Zanden, Ted, 62
Van Zandt, Jim, 103, 118
Vary, Jim, 169
Venhuizen, Ron, 135, 137, 145, 146, 147, 148, 149, 153, 154, 161, 162, 164, 165, 166, 168, 178, 179, 180, 181, 182, 183
Venus, Dick, 103
Ver Beek, Carl, 62
Ver Meer, Barbara, 142
Ver Merris, Dave, 202, 218, 233, 235
Vermeulen, Carl, 72
Ver Steeg, Jack, 22
Ver Strate, Wayne, 118
Veurink, Chuck, 157, 164, 167, 168, 173, 175, 176, 177, 181, 182, 183, 185, 189
Vickrey, Tom, 262
Victoria, Julio, 118
Viel, Dave, 111
Vild, Lou, 80
Vincent, Murray, 66
Visscher, Joanne, 169
Visscher, Rein, 124
Visscher, Ron, 213, 229, 230, 248, 265
Visser, John, 22, 23, 24, 26, 27, 43, 49, 125
Visser, Ken, 128, 129, 130, 131
Visser, Tom, 265, 280
Vivlamore, George, 26, 44, 46, 49
Vlaardingerbroek, Rudy, 233, 235, 249, 250, 264
Vogas, Mike, 199
Volz, Pete, 260
Voskuil, Duane, 57, 58, 59, 60, 71, 77, 78, 79, 80, 84, 86, 105, 107, 108, 111
Voss, Harry, 17, 19, 20, 21, 30, 38
Vossekuil, Bryan, 242, 279
Vossekuil, Craig, 261
Vriesman, Wayne, 57, 63, 64, 65, 66, 67, 68, 87, 88, 90, 91, 92, 93, 94, 103, 111, 113, 147

Vroon, Don, 25, 26, 27, 213, 225, 228, 242, 244, 260, 261, 278
Vugteveen, Stan, 102, 118, 120, 138

W

Waanders, Dave, 111
Wabash College, 38
Wackerbarth, Paul, 154, 155
Waddell, Bob, 75
Wagner, Honus, 23
Wagner, Sam, 64, 90, 112, 113
Wahl, Roland, 20, 41
Walchenbach, Jack, 22, 32
Waldo Stadium, 283
Walker, Art, 152
Walker, Clyde, 55
Wall, Denise, 169
Wallace, Dick, 31
Wallace, Jim, 43, 272, 274
Wallis, Russ, 192
Walters, Art, 169, 186
Walters, Carl, 179, 180, 194, 195, 196, 197, 199, 200, 209, 210, 211, 213, 225, 226, 227, 228, 229
Walters, George, 120, 121
Walters, Mike, 257
Walther, Jerry, 241
Walvoord, Jack, 226
Wang, D., 258
Warmbold, Rick, 210, 212
Warner, Gary, 192
Warner, Mike, 16
Warren, Alice, 31, 56, 76
Warren, Steve, 260
Warriner, Neil, 241
Wassenaar, Paul, 192, 206, 207, 208
Waterman, Bob, 20
Waterman, Coach, 116
Waters, Frank, Muddy, 18, 19, 22, 40, 41, 60, 80, 82, 84, 85, 108, 109, 132
Watson, Cliff, 240
Watson, Rick, 248, 265
Watt, Paul, Pete, 19, 20, 38, 39, 42, 77, 78, 79, 80, 82, 84, 85, 86, 105, 127
Wattles, Keith, 275, 282
Watts, Bill, 54
Watts, Glenn, 135
Wayne State University, 22, 43
Weavers, Rog, 209
Webb, Jerry, 222
Webb, Ron, 169, 185
Weddon, Todd, 187
Wedge, Jerry, 58
Weener, Dennis, 194, 195, 198
Weener, Paul, 121
Weersing, Spence, 32
Wegehaupt, Dick, 163
Weiden, Ken, 272
Weinert, Mark, 262
Weiss, Steve, 152
Welch, Dick, 138
Weller, Arie, 36
Weller, Kenneth J., 16, 19, 30, 36, 37, 77, 82, 86, 110, 159, 177, 207, 217, 235, 268, 280
Welling, Earl, 38
Wellington, Ralph, 226, 244
Welmers, Bruce, 132, 145, 155, 161, 177
Welton, Roy, 265
Wenger, Phil, 130
Wenkley, Dick, 276
Werbish, Al, 227, 228, 242, 244
Werkman, Barry, 245, 257
Wesner, Frank, 27, 48
Wessell, Dave, 170
Wessling, Steve, 173, 175, 176, 177, 190, 191, 192, 222, 223, 224

Westenbroek, Wayne, 28, 29, 98, 100, 122
Westergreen, Arlyn, 226
Westerman, Harold, 15
Western, Bill, 55, 101
Western Michigan College, 24
Westle, John, 248
Westover, Herb, 75
Wetherbee, Ron, 17, 20, 40, 41, 42, 53, 54, 59, 269
Weurding, John, 256, 261, 276, 279
Weybright, Phil, 241
Wham, Bill, 169
Wham, Bob, 169
Wheeler, Bruce, 242
Whipple, Bruce, 134
Whipple, Hal, 72
White, Bob, 175, 177
White, Dave, 48, 50, 111
White, Dick, 108
White, Keith, 62, 86
White, Steve, 280
Whitehead, Bob, 69, 93, 113
Whiteman, Merlin, 272
Whitkoph, Owen, 65
Whittingham, Dave, 120
Wickens, Coach Dick, 27
Wideman, Robin, 265
Widmer, Herb, 22, 31, 34, 43
Wiegerink, Paul, 16, 18, 20, 21, 22, 31, 32, 34, 35, 39, 40, 49, 50, 51, 58, 59, 70, 71, 72 73, 101, 124, 153
Wiegerink, Ron, 75, 102
Wieland, Andy, 278
Wieland, Ken, 169
Wiers, Ed, 242, 260, 261, 263, 276, 278, 279
Wiersma, Dennis, 75
Wiersma, Jim, 140, 154, 155, 170, 186, 201
Wild, Dave, 259
Wilder, Dennis, 206
Wilder, Sharon, 202
Wilkin, Jim, 159
Wilkins, Doug, 16
Wilkins, Leonard, 217
Wilkinson, Bud, 268
Will, Charles, 168
Williams, Dennis, 230, 265, 280
Williams, Dick, 230
Williams, Glenn, 22
Williams, Jeff, 257
Williams, John, 45, 48, 66, 89, 92, 113, 116, 134, 136
Williams, Ken, 261
Williams, Tim, 245
Williams, Tyrone, 241
Williamson, Ed, 161
Willink, Del, 260, 261, 278
Willis, Frank, 128
Willis, Phil, 160
Willits, Paul, 142
Wilsie, Doug, 161
Wilson, Alex, 210
Wilson, Bob, 167
Wilson, Hudson, 282, 283
Wilson, Jim, 63
Wilson, Karl, 216, 238, 256
Wilson, Mike, 239, 241, 243, 245, 261, 279
Wince, Phil, 278
Winchill, Dave, 135
Winged-T system, 36
Winkley, Dick, 260, 261
Winne, Jeff, 272
Winterhalter, Dan, 30, 55
Winterholder, Larry, 163
Wismer, John, 236, 275
Wisnieski, Doug, 270
Wissink, David, 118

Witvoet, Dave, 226
Witzke, Eric, 256, 271
Woelfer, Topper, 88
Wojdygo, Tom, 202
Wolchina, Rudy, 18, 39
Wolfe, Bruce, 103
Wolfe, Lavon, 103, 152
Wolff, Rick, 277
Wolters, Tom, 275, 277
Wolterstorff, Bill, 91, 112, 115, 117, 134, 136, 137
Wolven, Vic, 267
Womack, John, 281
Wondra, Jerry, 72, 87
WOOD television station, 109, 217
Wood, Chuck, 135, 149, 161
Wood, John, 23
Wood, Len, 168
Wood, Natalie, 15
Woodby, Fred, 103
Woodcock, Dave, 17, 19, 20, 21, 22, 25, 26, 28, 29, 37, 44, 45, 46, 47, 52, 53, 54
Woodcock, Larry, 75
Woods, John, 27
Woodward, John, 170
Woodward, Tom, 237
Wooten, John, 223
Workman, Craig, 185, 186, 213, 230
Workman, Harold, 237
Wormuth, John, 199
Wren, Jack, 144
Wright, Dave, 152
Wristers, Harry, 43, 50, 111
Wyllie, Larry, 68, 69
Wyns, John, 272, 274

Y

Yehle, Don, 236, 264, 275, 282
Yelorda, Pete, 222
Yeoman, Bill, 268
Yildiz, Unir, 266
Yildiz, Umur, 280
Yorick, Vic, 171
York, Bill, 75
Yost, Ken, 169
Young, Jim, 144
Young, Norm, 108, 170
Young, Peter, 54
Young, Steve, 271
Yuell, Bob, 55, 75
Yurick, Charles, 187

Z

Zagora, Marv, 180
Zeas, Jaime, 209
Zerbst, Bob, 214
Zieglar, Jerry, 149
Ziem, Rick, 226, 277, 279
Ziem, So, 259
Zimmerman, Chuck, 266
Zins, Robert, 255
Zondervan, Dave, 181
Zuidema, Marv, 282
Zupko, John, 18, 40
Zuverink, George, 15
Zuverink, Vern, 52
Zwart, Dave, 110, 150, 152, 185, 198
Zwart, Ted, 243, 245, 259, 260
Zweifel, Jim, 133, 134
Zwemer, Andy, 141, 143
Zwemer, Marian, 57
Zwemer, Tom, 57